RALPH L. WOODS

THE MODERN HANDBOOK OF HUMOR

More than 6,000 Anecdotes, Jokes, Legends, Definitions, Parables, Quips, Comebacks, Bon Mots, and Aphorisms on Hundreds of Subjects Relevant to Modern Lives and Interests. Compiled, Arranged, Cross-referenced, and Indexed for Quick and Easy Use, as Well as for Reading Enjoyment

New York San Francisco Toronto London Sydney

THE MODERN HANDBOOK OF HUMOR

 Library of Congress Catalog Card Number 67–19907

71737

7890 KPKP 7987

Grateful acknowledgment is made to Evan Esar for passages from The Humor of Humor, *1952; to Mrs. Kin Hubbard for passages from Kin Hubbard's books* Back Country Folks, Abe Martin's Wise Cracks and Skunk Ridge Papers, *and* Short Furrows; *all published by The Bobbs-Merrill Co., Indianapolis. Acknowledgment is also made for passages from* Abe Martin's Town Pump *by Kin Hubbard, copyright 1929 by The Bobbs-Merrill Co., renewed 1956 by Mrs. Kin Hubbard, reprinted by permission of the publisher.*

THE MODERN HANDBOOK OF HUMOR

For Speakers, Writers,
Business and Professional Men
and for All Who Enjoy
Sharing Humor with Others

McGRAW–HILL BOOK COMPANY

To Paul Robert Huot,
my twelve-year-old grandson,
who will enjoy some of this book now
and the balance of it as he advances
in years and wisdom—
and in risibility.

INTRODUCTION

Ideally, the introduction to a book of humor should be both informative and rib-tickling. But the ideal is an elusive and sometimes an impossible goal. And reaching for risibility might distract from and thus dilute the usefulness of these few serious comments. I will therefore confine myself to a strictly informative prefatory note, confident that the reader will find a superabundance of amusement in the pages immediately following.

My purpose has not been to put together just another big book of jokes and quips and let it go at that. Rather, I have harvested this humor from all the fields where research may have discovered it: anecdotes from the great and famous of present and past; amusing legends, both modern and classic; occasional fables that make a point entertainingly and effectively; aphorisms of wit and wisdom; definitions much too amusing to gain admittance to ponderous dictionaries; quips that scold and deflate; parables of an ingenuity that cause one to both ponder and smile.

My quest of material for this volume was made both less burdensome and more rewarding because of huge files of material I had gathered for various book and article projects already completed and others yet to be accomplished. In particular, wonderful riches were taken from a large collection of wit—as distinguished from humor—that I have been collecting for some years. I even found some sparkling gems of wit in a file of religious quotations that I have long been compiling.

Confronted and challenged by the mass of material harvested for this book, I found that the next and most important task was to select from it the anecdotes, legends, jokes, fables, definitions, and aphorisms that would be most useful to speakers, writers, and business and professional men and for social use by everyone who likes to have at tongue tip the timely quip or illustrative anecdote.

It was a pleasure and a relief to discover how beautifully the gathered material meshed with the objective of usefulness to the speaker and writer and of relevance to those engaged in business and the professions.

To illustrate: Part One, with fifty-three categories or subject headings on as many aspects of business, industry, money, finance, sales, and service, has a total of 1,126 anecdotes and other items.

Part Two, on politics and government, does not cover a large number of professions but touches upon topics closely related to business and certainly to activities which occupy much of the businessman's thinking. Here one finds 629 more anecdotes, etc., under thirty-four subject headings.

And so it goes with all the professions covered in the book, including lawyers, judges, physicians, teachers, scientists, psychiatrists, clergymen, economists, engineers, astronauts, nurses, diplomats, politicians, orators, athletes, gamblers, actors, authors, critics, newspapermen—and even "professional" drinkers, tourists, philanderers, scandal mongers, flirts, snobs, fashion plates. The material in each of these and other categories is of specific value to those involved in them and quite often of interest and use to business and professional people engaged in different activities.

A book designed for maximum usefulness to speakers and writers and with emphasis on business and the professions must first and chiefly be concerned with those fields of endeavor. But people engaged in such callings have a wide range of interests and activities extending well beyond their special provinces. It was therefore immediately recognized that a book such as this should also provide these men and women with entertaining material they can effectively use when dealing with or engaged in other areas and activities.

For example, it is easy to understand that any one of us—as speaker, writer, or casual conversationalist—might quickly want something amusingly relevant on one or another of the subjects already mentioned, or on housing, middle age, animals, the social whirl, *faux pas*, the military, Ireland, dating and marriage, puns, Heaven and Hell, Texas, ancestors, tipping, calories, or the many other subjects covered in this volume and easily located by using the Index.

It is interesting and gratifying to find that this book, although prepared with the business and professional man in mind, has an appeal and usefulness of much broader scope. As already suggested, this is because business and the professions touch all other areas of life. But it is also because all of us—no matter what our occupation—at some point and to varying degrees become involved in or are affected by business and the professions. This is another way of saying that modern life is an intricate complex of interrelationships, most facets of which yield their goodly quota of wit and humor for the entertainment of us all.

Consequently, although the volume is pointed directly toward the speaker and writer and although its emphasis remains on business and the professions, it, nevertheless, does not attempt to limit either its value or its users to the shop or the office. Our lives, activities, and interests are broader than that—and so, fortunately, are the riches of wit and humor.

Because this volume is designed for both use *and* pleasure, it may be worthwhile to mention a few of the guidelines established for it. There is no "blue" or "black" humor in it, and it has very little "sick" material. On the other hand, there is *some* vulgar and mildly risqué material, but only when it was deemed genuinely entertaining and potentially usable. Certainly there is no smut in these pages and no material likely to offend races or religions. In fact, I recall only one joke in dialect—the retention of which was necessary to the story's point.

There is not—praise be!—a single joke about traveling salesmen and farmers' daughters, though there are plenty of other traveling-salesmen yarns. On the other hand, I must confess that herein are fourteen stories about mothers-in-law, but in several of them the mother-in-law gets the best of it. Anyway, those fourteen mother-in-law stories comprise a mere one-half of 1 percent of the book's total content.

The volume, of course, has it quota of the kind of jokes, gags, and quips heard frequently on television and radio, but it has much else that is richer, more substantial, and surely of greater usefulness because of being more illustrative.

Incidentally, as previously suggested, the book has a great deal more genuine wit than is found in earlier volumes of this nature. Obviously people today are much quicker than of yore to recognize and react to the subtle thrust and to the somewhat more cerebral laugh provokers. We still like the yarn spinner and folklorist in the manner of Lincoln (who, by the way, is represented herein with sixty-three stories), but we increasingly delight in acerbic wit and the lethal riposte. Both types are here in amusing abundance.

But there is not a line in this book about the state of contemporary American humor. I am cheerfully leaving that to the super-serious brow-wrinklers, who might be cured of their concern by a good dose of real humor—of which there is much in these pages.

At first blush it might be supposed that the entertainment value of a volume of humor would be diluted by designing it for use—for practical application and easy reference. Actually, two separate processes are involved, neither of which impinge upon the other. That is to say, first one gathers together all the humorous material he can find for the book and sifts and screens down to the cream of the crop. At this point, and not before, the harvest is broken down into the overall classifications to which the individual items relate, and then the material in each broad classification is subdivided into specific categories or subjects.

Thus, the best material has simply been arranged in the most logical order for pleasant reading, and even for critical judgment if one's bent is in that direction, as well as for quick consultation either under the broad classifications or the specific categories. The extensive Table of Contents provides instant directions to both broad classifications and precise categories, whichever is of immediate interest to the reader. For many this broad and specific guidance to the volume's content will prove sufficient.

However, the reader has not been abandoned to even such ample signposts. The categories are numbered consecutively in the order of their appearance. And each item within each category is again numbered. Thus the first section of Part One (on business and industry) is titled Office Humor, and the first category under Office Humor is Late for Work, which is numbered 1. There are thirteen jokes under Late for Work; consequently they are numbered 1.1 to 1.13. The next category, The Coffee Break, is numbered 2, and the jokes under it are numbered 2.1 to 2.7, and so on throughout the book.

The special value of this system of numbering categories and jokes, etc., is quickly appreciated when one encounters and uses the extensive system of cross-references. At the end of each category, except for a few with no cross-reference, one finds the words "See also," followed by a series of numbers which refer to the category and the joke number within that category. For example, a cross-reference to 22.6 refers to category 22 on economists and statisticians and to joke 6 under that subject heading.

The massive Index refers to the same category and joke numbers but is more probing since it refers to every element and name in every item in the volume and, in addition, tries to anticipate every probable key word and thought likely to come to the mind of the questing user of the book.

In view of the volume's logical arrangement, complete Table of Contents, extensive cross-references, and exhaustive Index, one should quickly and easily locate what it contains for one's use or entertainment.

I am deeply grateful to Herbert B. Greenhouse for his creative contribution to and generous interest in this book's successful maturation and particularly for the imagination and skill he brought to the presentation, arrangement, and captioning of categories. Nor was he at all reluctant to render frequent and often acute editorial judgments. I am equally grateful to my wife, Lillias Watt Woods, for her many arduous labors at various stages of the work and particularly for her uncounted hours of work on the Index.

Finally, it is a pleasure to acknowledge the confidence that my editors at the McGraw-Hill Book Company had in my ability to do this book.

Ralph L. Woods

CONTENTS

Part Two POLITICS, GOVERNMENT, AND THE LAW'S DEFENDERS AND FLOUTERS

Part Eleven THE ANIMAL KINGDOM

Part Twelve CAPSULE WIT AND WISDOM

Part Thirteen SPECIAL SITUATIONS

Part One

BUSINESS AND INDUSTRY

OFFICE HUMOR

1. Late for Work

Anecdotes

1.1

The new stenographer arrived late for work, and her fuming boss said, "You should have been here at nine!"

"Why?" she asked. "What happened?"

1.2

Employer: "Here you are, twenty minutes late again. Don't you know what time we start to work at this place?"

New Employee: "No sir, they're always at it when I get here."

1.3

"What's the idea of coming in here late every morning?" asked the boss.

"It's your fault," said the young man. "You have trained me so thoroughly not to watch the clock in the office, now I'm in the habit of not looking at it at home."

1.4

"Are you doing anything Sunday evening, Miss Lane?" asked the junior partner late on a Friday afternoon.

"No, not a thing," replied Miss Lane hopefully.

"Then," said the junior partner, "please try to be at the office earlier on Monday morning."

1.5

At the East India House the head of the office once reproved Charles Lamb for the excessive irregularity of his attendance.

"Really, Mr. Lamb, you come very late!" observed the official.

"Y-yes," replied Lamb, with his habitual stammer, "b-but consi-sider how ear-early I go!"

1.6

A country bumpkin came to the city and got a job with a construction company, but although a good worker he was always late.

Reluctant to lose so good a man, the foreman told him that if he didn't buy an alarm clock, he would have to let him go.

The first few mornings after that the new man arrived on time, benefit of the alarm clock he had purchased.

But one morning he awoke late; the alarm clock had failed to go off.

Determined to find out the trouble, the earnest clodhopper removed the back of the clock and found a dead cockroach among the works.

"No wonder," he muttered, "the thing didn't go off. The engineer is dead!"

1.7

He was an earnest, unlettered fellow from the backwoods who had come to New York and obtained a clerical job with a large company on Wall Street.

One day he was late returning from lunch. The boss asked him why.

"I was coming down Liberty Street," he explained in his drawl, "and just as I was turning into the building I saw a large crowd of people down the block. I went down to see what had happened. Finally I edged through the crowd, and there was a woman lying prostitute on the sidewalk!"

Definitions

1.8

Punctuality is the thief of time.

—*Oscar Wilde*

1.9

Boss: The man at the office who is early when you're late and late when you're early.

—*Take it or Leave It*

Aphorisms

1.10

There's a close connection between getting up in the world and getting up in the morning.

1.11

Many are called but few get up.

—*Oliver Herford*

1.12

I am a believer in punctuality though it makes me very lonely.

—*E. V. Lucas*

1.13

To do each day two things one dislikes is a precept I have followed scrupulously: every day I have got up and I have gone to bed.

—*Somerset Maugham*

(*See also 10.17, 86.3, 111.34*)

2. The Coffee Break

Anecdotes

2.1

An executive in a large company phoned another department and asked the girl who answered the phone, "Do you have a Sexauer over there?"

"I should say not," snapped the girl. "We don't even have ten minutes for a coffee break."

2.2

At coffee-break time one hot summer day in a New York office, a wistful young man said to the young woman next to him, "I sure wish I was lounging by the lake up in the mountains, fishing or drinking beer or counting my money, or maybe doing nothing but keeping cool."

"And," said the young woman coyly, "if you had all that, wouldn't you invite me to come up there and help you be lazy?"

"I wouldn't promise to do so—no I wouldn't," said the dreamer firmly.

"But," persisted the miss, "if you had lots of beer, wouldn't you have me up to help you drink it?"

"I'm still not promising," said the young man.

"Well," pursued the not-to-be-denied lass, "with that lake of yours—couldn't I come up and swim in it?"

"Now look here," said the owner of imaginary wealth, "if you're too lazy to do your own wishing, just go ahead and sit here and sizzle."

2.3

A stenographer went to her boss and told him she was resigning.

"That's too bad," said the boss. "After all, I did cut down your work load."

"Oh, I've gotten to like the work," said the young woman firmly. "That's the trouble—it's being interrupted by too many coffee breaks."

2.4

"You realize, Miss Twinkleyes, that you are late?" asked the boss.

"Oh, no," said the secretary. "I took my coffee break before coming in."

2.5

The *New Yorker* magazine reports that a Rhode Island factory has a sign reading: PLEASE DO NOT GO HOME ON YOUR COFFEE BREAK.

2.6

An electronic plant in Tokyo has "yawn breaks" every half hour for its 2,000 employees. These last ninety seconds; the workers are urged over a loudspeaker to yawn and stretch to their hearts' content.

Aphorism

2.7

A four-hour day would bring many changes in our lives. For example, we'd have to reschedule the coffee breaks.

—*Skweek*, Granite City, Ill.

(*See also 10.16*)

3. The Typewriter Crew

Anecdotes

3.1

A philosophical New Yorker, who gave up all hope of getting perfect letters from his office typist, now sends the letters out as they come from her mill—spelling errors, erasures, and all. He evens matters with a rubber stamp that he had specially made. It marks in the lower left-hand corner: "She can't type—but she's beautiful."

—*Meyer Berger*, the New York Times

3.2

The boss called his assistant into his office, waved a letter at him, and said, "I thought I told you to hire this new girl on the basis of her grammar?"

"Grammar?" said the office manager. "I thought you said glamour."

3.3

"Miss Glam," said the boss to his secretary, "you are the finest looking girl I have ever employed. You dress well, your manners are perfect, people like you, you respect the confidential nature of your work, and your behavior is exemplary."

The young woman smiled with pleasure and thanked the boss.

"And now that we have taken care of the compliments," concluded the boss, "we are going to discuss your spelling, typing, shorthand, and punctuation."

3.4

Two secretaries were comparing bosses, and one said that her boss was all right except that he was bigoted.

"Bigoted? How come?"

"Well, he thinks words can be spelled in only one way."

3.5

The president of a firm asked a psychologist to judge several applicants for the position of secretary. The choice narrowed down to three girls. Each girl was asked: "What do 2 and 2 make?"

"Four," replied the first girl.

"It might be 22," said the second girl.

"It could be either 22 or 4," said the third girl.

The psychologist reported to the president that the first girl gave the obvious answer, the second girl gave a cautious answer, and the third girl played it both ways. And he told the president that the final choice was up to him, based on the psychological findings.

"I'll take the second girl," said the president, "that lovely blond with the blue eyes."

3.6

"I hear the boss gave his secretary a new fur coat."

"To keep her warm?"

"Oh, no; to keep her quiet."

3.7

The executive called his secretary in and said to her: "Whoopsie, just because I make an occasional pass at you, where did you get the idea that you could do as you damn please around the office?"

"From my attorney," said the secretary.

3.8

One afternoon the boss's wife met him at the office. As they were going down in the elevator it stopped, and a luscious blond secretary got on, poked the boss in the ribs, and said, "Hello, cutie pie!" The wife, without blinking, leaned over and said, "I'm Mrs. Pie."

3.9

"I'm Mr. Smith's wife," said the fortyish woman to a young blond at a cocktail party.

"I'm his secretary," said the good-looking blond.

"Oh," said the older woman, "were you?"

3.10

A wealthy executive honeymooning with his beautiful secretary was discussing her replacement.

"I've been thinking of that, too," said the ex-secretary and new wife. "My cousin would be just right for the job."

"What's her name?"

"Joseph David Smith," replied the bride.

3.11

The office manager asked the girl applicant if she had any unusual talents.

She said she won several prizes in crossword-puzzle contests and in slogan-writing contests.

"Sounds good," said the employer, "but we want somebody who will be smart during office hours."

"Oh," said the girl, "that was during office hours."

3.12

An executive was quite upset at lunch one day with some friends and said, "My secretary has an unusual brain."

"Unusual brain? How do you mean?" asked one of his companions.

"This girl's brain begins working the moment she awakens in the morning, and it keeps on working until she gets to the office—then it quits for the day."

3.13

"How is that new girl doing?" asked the boss.

"Pretty fair," said the chief clerk. "But I think she is a rather nervous person. I notice that as soon as she arrives in the morning she goes immediately to her desk and plunges right into work."

Definition

3.14

Stenographer: A girl you pay to learn how to spell while she's looking for a husband.

—*Franklin P. Jones*

Aphorisms

3.15

There is a pretty secretary who can't add but can sure distract.

3.16

A man spent three months looking for a suitable secretary because he knew it pays to have a good head on your shoulder.

3.17

He was known in the office as most ungrammatical—whenever he dictated to his glamorous secretary he ended his sentences with a proposition.

3.18

If wives knew what stenographers think of their husbands, they would cease to worry.

3.19

A man is about half-way between what his wife thinks he is and what his secretary knows he is.

—*M. W. Terrell*

3.20

The surest way to get a job done is to give it to the busiest man you know—he'll have his secretary do it.

—*H. G. Norman,* Collier's

3.21

Somewhere in the land there must be a secretary named Miss Speller.

(*See also 1.1, 35.1, 35.2, 111.34, 113.5, 161.5, 169.3, 272.23, 276.7*)

4. The Boss and the Bossed

Anecdotes

4.1

"Mr. Smith cannot see you," said the secretary. "He has a strained back."

"Look, miss," said the caller, "I didn't come here to wrestle with him. I just want to talk to him."

4.2

Big George, a fellow who made a good living as a jack-of-all-trades around town, was hired by a man to paint his house at an agreed wage of $2.50 per hour. The home owner returned late in the afternoon and found Big George sprawled out under a tree watching another man doing the painting.

"What's the idea, George."

"Oh, I sublet the job to that fellow on the ladder for $3 an hour."

"But how can you do that? I'm only paying you $2.50, so you're losing 50 cents an hour."

"Yeah, I know that," said Big George. "But it's wuth it to be the boss just once in my life."

4.3

The department head was retiring, and one of the men was taking up a subscription for a dinner and gift for the old guy. One worker refused to chip in. The collector argued and pleaded and said there would be a good dinner and a prize.

"Prize? Why all I'd like to do is to give him a good boot in the backside."

"Say," said the collector, "you must be psychic. That's the first prize."

4.4

The irate boss called the office boy into his office and demanded to know why certain papers had not been delivered to a customer.

"I did the best I could, sir," replied the office boy.

"The best you could, eh?" said the boss. "If I had known I was sending a donkey to do the job, I would have gone myself."

4.5

"If it's all the same with you," said the timid clerk to his boss, who had just returned from a month in the mountains, "I'd like to take my two weeks' vacation now."

"Vacation!" exclaimed the boss. "I've been away for a month; that's enough for both of us."

4.6

An executive wanted a vacation and went to his boss and asked for an extra two weeks, saying, "You know how hard I work and how I concentrate on my work."

"That's just it—two weeks would be enough for you. With your ability to concentrate, you should be able to cram more recreation into two weeks than other people get into four weeks."

4.7

A longtime and faithful employee was complaining to a friend that he had been passed up by his boss for an important promotion. The employee said that he knew the business thoroughly, could handle the job he didn't get, had a fine attendance record, and there were no blemishes on his conduct or performance.

"What, then," asked his friend, "do you think is the reason?"

"It's just that I'm too slow," said the employee.

"Too slow? That doesn't seem to me very important for that job. Anyway, lots of good men are rather slow."

"Oh, I'm not a slow worker—I'm just too slow to laugh at the boss's jokes."

4.8

When Stuyvesant Fish was president of the Illinois Central Railroad, the door of his office opened suddenly and in walked an Irishman with his hat on his head and a pipe in his mouth. "I want a pass to St. Louis," said the visitor.

"Who are you?"

"I'm Tim O'Rourke, a switchman."

"Tim," said Fish, "I am not going to say your request will be refused, but there are certain courtesies a man must observe when he asks for a favor. He should knock at the door before entering; he should remove his hat and take his pipe from his mouth. When he comes in he should say, 'President Fish, I am Tim O'Rourke, one of your switchmen.' Then I would say, 'What can I do for you?' and then you would tell me, and the matter would be settled. Now step outside, come in again, and see if you can't do it better."

So Tim left the room, closing the door. Presently there was a knock on the door. "Come in," Fish called out. In came Tim, hat off and pipe in hand.

"Good morning, President Fish. I am Tim O'Rourke, one of your switchmen."

"How do you do, Mr. O'Rourke. What can I do for you?"

"You can go to hell," said Tim O'Rourke. "I can get a job and a pass on the Wabash."

4.9

"My boss," said a fellow with a lack of warmth, "is a guy you've got to like. If you don't he'll fire you."

4.10

The boss said he had so many worries that if a new one arose, he wouldn't have time to worry about it for at least three weeks.

Aphorisms

4.11

By working faithfully eight hours a day, you may eventually get to be a boss and work twelve hours a day.

—*Robert Frost*

4.12

A report on occupational health published recently says that dislike of the boss is the reason why many employees take a day off. It says nothing about the employer who stays away because he can't stand the sight of his staff.

—*Rotary Bulletin,* Napanee, Ont., Canada

(*See also 1.1–1.17, 2.3–3.4, 3.6–3.9, 3.12, 3.13, 5.1, 5.3, 5.6–5.8, 7.1, 7.12, 7.14, 7.16–7.18, 7.20–7.23, 10.1, 10.2, 10.4, 10.7, 10.8, 10.26, 16.3, 18.1, 20.3, 43.13, 44.1, 44.3, 44.4, 44.6, 136.14, 154.13–154.17, 154.23, 205.5, 205.7, 212.1, 214.3, 268.10, 277.4*)

5. Wages and Raises

Anecdotes

5.1

"One final word, Miss Prim," said the employer to his newest employee. "It must be strictly understood that your salary is not to be revealed to anyone."

"Don't worry yourself about that," said the young woman. "I am as ashamed of it as you should be."

5.2

"You are asking for pretty high wages for one who has so little experience," said the employer to an applicant.

"True," said the applicant, "but it is much harder work for me simply because I know so little about it."

5.3

"I told you to do this two months ago, and now you tell me you forgot. What would you do if I forgot to pay you?"

"Well," said the employee, "I would remind you immediately. I wouldn't wait two months and then make a big stink about it."

5.4

An employee was handed a pay envelope which accidentally contained only a blank check. "Just what I thought would happen," moaned the worker. "My deductions have finally caught up with my salary."

5.5

A man pushed a gun at the paymaster and said, "Let the boys have their pay. Just hand over the withholding taxes, pension funds, hospitalization payments, group-insurance premiums, and welfare funds."

5.6

The tyrannical boss called in his chief clerk and said, "Wilkins, I understand that you have taken to praying for a raise. Now I want you to understand once and for all that I will not tolerate your going over my head."

5.7

When the firm's top buyer, a woman, asked the boss for a raise, he said: "Your salary is already higher than that of any other male buyer here, and they all have families with two or three kids."

"Look," she countered, "I thought we got paid for our production here, not what we produce on our own time at home."

5.8

"So you want a raise? Why, my boy, I worked three years for $15 a month in this store, and now I'm the owner of it."

"Yes, but see what happened to your boss? No man who treats his help that way can hang on to his business."

Definitions

5.9

The definition of a living wage depends upon whether you are getting it or giving it.

5.10

An old-timer is one who remembers when a man did his own withholding from his take-home pay.

—*Rotary Spoke,* Toledo, Ohio

5.11

Promotion cometh neither from the east nor the west, but from the cemetery.

—*Edward S. Martin*

5.12

Nothing can move a man who is paid by the hour; how sweet the flight of time seems to his calm mind.

—*Charles Dudley Warner*

(*See also 7.12, 7.23, 10.13, 16.3, 16.6, 179.13, 229.51, 239.18, 239.19, 240.1, 270.15*)

6. Committees and Conferences

Definitions

6.1

A committee is a group of the unfit, appointed by the unwilling, to do the unnecessary.

6.2

A committee is a body that keeps minutes and wastes hours.

6.3

A committee should consist of three men, two of whom are absent.

—*Beerbohm Tree*

6.4

A committee of five consists of one man who does the work, three others who pat him on the back, and one who brings in a minority report.

6.5

A conference is a place where conversation is substituted for the dreariness of labor and the loneliness of thought.

6.6

A conference is a meeting at which people talk about what they should already be doing.

Aphorisms

6.7

If Moses had been a Committee, the Israelites would still be in Egypt.

—*J. B. Hughes*

6.8

Someone said that if the average American found himself on an airliner about to crash he would move to appoint a landing committee.

6.9

If you want to kill any idea in the world today, get a committee working on it.

—*C. F. Kettering*

(*See also 64.1–64.5, 82.1, 88.1*)

MANAGEMENT AND LABOR

7. Hiring and Firing

Anecdotes

7.1

"What's the idea," asked the boss of his new employee, "of telling me you had five years' experience, when I now find you never had a job before?"

"Well," said the young man, "didn't you advertise for a man with imagination?"

—*The Marion Rotascope,* Marion, Ill.

7.2

Applicants for a job on a Kentucky dam had to take a written examination, the first question of which was, "What does hydrodynamics mean?" One fellow looked at this, then wrote against it: "It means I don't get the job."

—*Joe Creason,* Louisville Courier-Journal Magazine

7.3

Bennett Cerf in his *The Life of the Party* reprints the following from the classified ad columns of a San Antonio, Texas, paper: "Wanted, a big executive, from twenty-two to eighty. To sit with feet on his desk from ten to four-thirty and watch other people work. Must be willing to play golf every other afternoon.

Salary to start: $500 a week. We don't have this job open, you understand. We just thought we'd like to see in print what everybody is applying for."

7.4

"We want a responsible man for this job," said the employer to the applicant.

"Well I guess I'm just your man," said the young fellow. "No matter where I worked, whenever anything went wrong, they told me I was responsible."

7.5

During the war a young fellow, who had been rejected for military service in the draft, applied to a munitions plant for employment. After the preliminary questioning, the employment man took a form, wrote down the man's name and address, age, and other details and then said, "Since this is pretty dangerous work you better tell me where you want the remains sent in case anything happens."

"Well, if you don't mind, mister, I'll just take the remains along with me now." And out the door he walked—or ran.

7.6

"Mr. Pollard," said the secretary, "there is a man outside looking for a job. He said he used to make his living by sticking his arm in a lion's mouth at the circus."

"Interesting. What's his name."

"He said they call him 'Lefty.' "

7.7

A Harvard graduate went to a Midwestern town to live and applied for a job with a department store. The personnel man wrote to one of the employee's references in Boston for information and shortly after received a letter outlining in detail the man's fine social connections and ancestry. The personnel man wrote back to the Boston reference and said, "I believe you have misunderstood my request for information. We want the young man for working purposes, not for breeding."

7.8

A clever young fellow applied for a job in answer to an ad but was told by the manager, "You're much too late. I already have more than a thousand applications here on my desk."

"Well, then," said the young man, "Why not employ me to go through them and classify them for you?"

7.9

A man applying for a job was told by the manager that the firm was overstaffed. "Sure you could start me," said the applicant. "The little bit of work I'd do wouldn't be noticed."

7.10

The story is sufficiently known of two servants, whereof the one told his master, "he would do everything." The other (which was Aesop himself) said "he could do nothing," rendering this reason "because his former fellow servant would leave him nothing to do."

—*Thomas Fuller*

7.11

Mark Twain said that when he was young he was impressed by the story of a young man who landed a job when the employer saw him pick up several pins from the sidewalk outside the firm's office.

So Twain went to the street alongside the office windows of a firm he wanted to work for and began almost ostentatiously to pick up pins he had earlier placed on the sidewalk. After a good number of pins had been picked up, a clerk came out and said, "The boss asked me to tell you to move along. Your idiotic behavior is distracting the people working in the office."

7.12

The nagging wife told her husband that he had not been sufficiently explicit with the boss when he asked for a raise.

"Tell him," said the wife, "that you have seven children, that you have a sick mother you have to sit up with many nights, and that you have to wash the dishes because you can't afford a maid."

Several days later the husband came home and announced he had been fired.

"The boss," he explained, "said I have too many outside activities."

7.13

The boss was asked to write a reference for a man he was dismissing after only one week's work. He would not lie, and he did not want to hurt the man unnecessarily. So he wrote this: "To Whom It May Concern: John Jones worked for us one week, and we're satisfied."

7.14

P. G. Wodehouse tells about the theater manager who found out that his box-office treasurer had for years been dipping his hand into the till. He called the thief into his office. "What is your salary?"

"Sixty a week," said the box-office man.

"It's raised to a hundred. No, we'll make it two hundred."

"Thank you," chortled the treasurer. "I'm overcome."

"One thing more," said the manager. "You're fired!"

Asked later why he had first raised the man's pay before firing him, the manager said, "I wanted to fire the crook from a really good job."

7.15

A shopman with the Santa Fe Railroad was drawn for jury service but asked the judge to excuse him. "We are very busy at the shops," he explained, "and I should be there."

"Oh," said the judge, "you're one of those fellows who think the railroad can't operate without you."

"No, Your Honor," replied the workman, "the point is that I know they can do very nicely without me, but I don't want them to find it out."

"Excused," said the judge.

7.16

"I can lick any man working under me!" declared the arrogant foreman.

"Here's a guy you can't lick," asserted a big, brawny young man.

The foreman looked the man over carefully then said, "You're fired!"

7.17

Henny Youngman said that his brother-in-law gave up his job because of illness. His boss got sick of him.

7.18

"Who are you going to get to fill my vacancy?" asked the just-fired clerk of his boss.

"Vacancy?" said the boss. "My boy, you're not leaving any vacancy."

7.19

Police arrested a man in Sydney, Australia, who got four successive jobs and lost them all after he made anonymous calls informing his employers that their new man was an untrustworthy ex-convict. He had collected the dismissal pay required by law from each of them.

7.20

Two young men of college years began training courses at General Electric Company. After some time, one of them went to the G.E. recruiting agent who had snared him when he was in college and told him he was resigning to enter a seminary.

A few weeks later the other young man went to the same recruiting agent and told him he too was resigning. When asked what he was going to do, he told him he, too, was entering the seminary.

The recruiting agent's boss happened to be there at the time and sneeringly said, "My, you are certainly doing a fine recruiting job for G.E.!"

"Well," said the recruiting agent, "at least they aren't going to Westinghouse."

7.21

Myron Cohen tells about the owner of a large chain of restaurants who went over his books and discovered that his most trusted employee had stolen over a million dollars from the firm.

"I want no scandal," said the owner to the crook. "I'll just fire you and forget about the entire matter."

"Why fire me?" asked the employee. "I now have a yacht, a country mansion, a town house, jewelry, and every luxury you can think of. I don't need a thing, so you can trust me. Why hire somebody else and have to start with him from scratch?"

7.22

"Why did the foreman fire you?" asked the prospective employer.

"You know what a foreman does—stands around all day and watches the other fellows work. Well, my foreman got jealous of me. Seems some of the men thought I was the foreman."

7.23

There was once a bright young man who made himself valuable to his employer. He was clever, sharp, and industrious, and he rose quickly to a position of some importance in the firm. One day a friend convinced the young man that he was not being paid enough considering how valuable he was to his employer. The youth demanded a raise and got it.

After several months the youth decided he should have another raise. The boss gave it to him, though reluctantly.

A little later on the young fellow made a third demand for more money. The boss demurred.

"I know all about your business," the youth declared. "Either you'll pay me what I'm worth, or I'll leave. You know you can't get along without me."

"Oh," said the boss, "That's a rather extravagant statement. What do you suppose I'd do if you died? Do you think we'd have to shut down."

"Well," stammered the young man, "in that case I suppose you'd get along all right."

"Then, in that case," concluded the boss, "We'll just consider you dead. You're fired!"

7.24

The chief executive of a large corporation, who was a stickler for efficiency, made an inspection tour of one of the company's manufacturing units. As he led his aides from department to department, he glowed with satisfaction as machines hummed and men worked swiftly and capably.

Suddenly the ears of the chief executive were tormented by the sound of whistling from behind a partition. He quickly confronted the whistler, a young man sprawled lazily on a chair.

"What's your salary?" demanded the chief executive.

"Who, me?" asked the whistler.

"Yes, you."

"Thirty-five bucks a week," replied the young man before he resumed whistling.

Wheeling on his retinue, the chief executive snapped, "Give this boy $70 and get him out of here at once."

"But, C. E. . . ." began a particularly courageous assistant.

"You heard me—$70 and out," interrupted the chief executive as he strode away.

Later that day an accounting-department officer brought up the subject of the whistler.

"What account shall we charge that $70 to, C. E.?"

"Payroll, naturally," was the official answer.

"But, C. E., that boy didn't work for us. He was a messenger waiting for a delivery receipt."

7.25

Two timid students on their way home for their first vacation from school stopped at an inn overnight. The place was crowded, and the proprietor said the only way he could put them up would be for one to sleep on a warm shelf over the kitchen stove and the other on a bench in the kitchen.

Later in the evening some soldiers carousing at the bar burst into the kitchen, found the two sleeping students, and gave the one on the bench a painful thrashing.

When they left the kitchen the boy on the shelf over the stove thought he should take the other fellow's place on the bench. If the soldiers returned, he reasoned, they would not beat the same boy twice.

The soldiers did return after another hour, and this time decided that since the boy on the bench had already been beaten, it was only fair to administer equal pain and injury to the boy on the shelf, which they proceeded to do, the same lad thus getting two beatings. Which proves that a change of place does not always improve one's circumstances. One can even encounter worse luck.

Definitions

7.26

Experience: What you've got when you're too old to get a job.

—*Leon Abramson*

7.27

A modern employer is one who is looking for men and women between the ages of twenty-one and thirty, with forty years of experience.

Aphorisms

7.28

To *Implement a Program* means: Hire more people and expand the office.

—*Steel,* June, 1951

7.29

When you hire people who are smarter than you are, you prove you are smarter than they are.

—*R. H. Grant*

7.30

One searching for an abundance of perfection will find it in applications for employment.

(*See also 3.5, 3.10, 3.11, 5.1, 5.2, 10.10, 10.13, 10.14, 28.17, 38.16, 41.3, 42.14, 70.6, 70.7, 70.25, 70.28, 70.29, 73.4, 104.8, 122.4, 122.25, 135.3, 135.51, 139.1, 139.7, 141.8, 154.12–154.16, 154.23, 221.9*)

8. Unions and Fringe Benefits

Anecdotes

8.1

Some years ago Walter Reuther, head of the Auto Workers' Union, was being taken through one of the newly mechanized auto plants by a company executive. Pointing to some of the massive automatic processes, he said, "Walter, how are you going to get them in your union?"

"How are you going to get them to buy new cars?" asked Reuther.

8.2

There was a coachman who would always flick his whip as he drove along the road—splitting a horsefly in two or tearing a bumblebee to shreds. But when asked why he would not touch a hornets' nest hanging by the roadside, he said, "No, sir, they're organized."

8.3

Back in 1937 Leonard Lyons reported that one of the early sit-down strikes at an Indiana factory was settled quickly.

The head of the small company told the strikers they might as well be comfortable, so he provided them with blankets and cases of brandy. When the brandy was half-consumed, the boss sent in ten young women to entertain the sit-downers. Then he brought over the strikers' wives so that they could see how comfortable their husbands were. That ended the sit-down strike.

8.4

At least one sit-down strike in a public building was ended rather quickly. The official in charge of the building simply locked all the toilets.

8.5

Australian dock workers once demanded what they called "temptation money," extra pay when they loaded anything they would be tempted to steal, such as tobacco, whiskey, wine, perfume.

—*"Brutus,"* The Recorder, London

8.6

Customer: "What! $300 for that 1,000-year-old table? Last week you quoted me $200."

Dealer: "Yes, that's true. But the unions have pushed up the costs of labor and materials since then."

8.7

Years ago the workers for the Swansea Harbor Improvement Trust, of England, went on strike to protest the management's order that all workmen wear the employer's initials on their working caps.

8.8

The labor leader called at a matrimonial bureau, explained he was in search of a wife, and was given a list of prospects. He quickly picked out a luscious doll of twenty-six years. This, he told the head of the bureau, was the girl he wanted.

"Sorry," said the bureau head, "but you can't have her. You'll have to take this gracious and lovely lady of age forty-nine, on page 28."

"Whassa idea?" shouted the labor leader. "I got the dough, and I want that young thing with the good looks."

"Sorry, sir," insisted the bureau man, "but you will have to take the somewhat elderly woman. She has seniority."

8.9

A labor leader was detailing to one of his associates the troubles he was having with his wife. When the whole account had been given, the associate said, "It may surprise you, but I'd have to agree with your wife."

"Oh, a fink!" exclaimed the labor leader. "I never thought you'd go over to management."

8.10

The Glasgow shopkeeper called his clerk aside, told him profits had been very good during the year, and gave the man a check for $100 as a Christmas present. When the clerk thanked him, the proprietor added that if business continued to be good during the next six months, he would sign the check.

Aphorisms

8.11

Capital and labor both realize time is money, but they can't agree on how much.

—*Maurice Seitter*

8.12

The money the other fellow has is capital. Getting it away from him is labor.

8.13

There's one advantage our company has: Not only do we have a good pension plan, but working here ages you more quickly.

8.14

Capital pats Labor on the back—with an ax.

—*Finley Peter Dunne*

(*See also 135.37, 136.21, 155.6, 191.4, 215.9, 235.29*)

9. Efficiency and Other Experts

Anecdotes

9.1

An important and complicated machine in a factory mysteriously stopped working. Machinists and engineers strived desperately to locate the trouble and correct it, but all failed. Meanwhile production in the plant had to be suspended until an expert could be called to fix the all-important piece of equipment. The expert arrived, tinkered with the machine briefly, tapped here and there with a hammer, and the machine resumed operation.

When the expert submitted his bill for $250, the plant manager was aghast and said to him: "All you did was tap the machine a few times. Please itemize your bill."

The expert took the bill and wrote at the bottom of it the following:

Tapping machine with hammer	$ 1.00
Knowing where to tap	$249.00

9.2

A New England ice and coal business for years enjoyed consistently profitable operations, until a depression struck. Then the owners of the corporation decided to replace their veteran manager with a bright young man from the city. The veteran manager was retained in a relatively minor capacity. A few months after the bright young man had taken charge, he appeared before the owners with his recommendations. As he addressed them he referred to an imposing array of charts and graphs mounted on an easel.

The bright young man climaxed his performance with a chart showing the annual progress of the firm's coal business—high in the winter months, reaching its low point in the summer, and rising rapidly from September to the end of the calendar year. The owners were impressed with the clarity and scope of the presentation.

The veteran manager sat watching his successor's triumph. As it ended he rose to his feet and said, "Yessir, that's a pretty good picture the young fellow's given us of the coal business. And, you know," he added, as he turned the chart upside down, "it's just as good a picture of the ice business when you look at it this way."

The next day the veteran manager was back running the business, and the bright young man returned to the city where scientific management is appreciated.

9.3

Robert Moses told a group of New York hotel executives: "I get around to your hostelries only with architects, engineers and other professional advisers. It reminds me of the handsome tomcat who was taken to the vet and returned home somewhat subdued. His owner explained that he now went out only two or three nights a week as a consultant."

—*Francis Sugrue,* in New York Herald Tribune

9.4

An executive with more ideas and enthusiasm than experience installed a new and elaborate system in his company and then went abroad confident that things would pretty much run themselves.

Upon his return from his two months' vacation he asked how the system was working. "Splendid" replied the manager.

"And how is business?" asked the executive.

"We had to give that up in order to keep the system going," said the manager.

9.5

The efficiency expert was being carried to his final resting place by six pallbearers, when suddenly the coffin lid popped open, the deceased sat up and said, "You bunglers! If this thing had been put on wheels you'd be able to fire four of these men."

9.6

"My husband is employed by a large corporation as an efficiency expert," said the young woman.

"Just what does an efficiency expert do?" asked a neighbor.

"Well," said the first woman, "when we wives do it they call it nagging."

9.7

An efficiency expert, called into a company to find out why they were losing money, stopped one man and asked him what he did. "Nothing," said the employee. The expert turned to another man standing nearby and asked him what he did. "Nothing," was the reply.

"Oh," said the efficiency expert, "too much duplication."

9.8

The already highly efficient organization asked an efficiency expert to make a study to determine if any improvement could be made. The expert reported that everything was functioning perfectly and that the only suggestion he could make was that the turns to the time clock be banked.

9.9

A group at the engineers club were discussing with considerable heat the increasing tendency for men in various occupations to call themselves "engineers" when they have no degrees in any kind of engineering and often no special talents or skills that would justify the term.

"Did you ever hear of an 'aquatic engineer'?" one of the group asked.

"No, unless you mean hydraulic engineer."

"Not the same thing," replied the questioner. "This aquatic engineer is nothing more than a dishwasher."

Harry Golden reminds us that janitors are now often called "maintenance engineers"; salesmen, "sales engineers"; high school guidance counselors, "guidance engineers"; and some theatrical agents call themselves "talent engineers."

Definitions

9.10

An efficiency expert is one who is smart enough to tell you how to run your business and too smart to start one of his own.

—*Anonymous*

9.11

Efficiency consists in getting someone to do the work you don't like to do.

9.12

An expert is a person who avoids the small errors as he sweeps on to the grand fallacy.

—*Benjamin Stolberg*

9.13

An expert is one who knows more and more about less and less.

—*Nicholas Murray Butler*

9.14

An expert is an ordinary guy 50 miles from home.

9.15

An expert is a man who creates confusion out of simplicity.

9.16

An expert is one who is never in doubt, but often in error.

9.17

A coordinator is the guy who has a desk between two expediters.

—*Steel,* June, 1951

9.18

A coordinator is a man who brings organized chaos out of regimented confusion.

Aphorisms

9.19

Be careful about calling yourself an "expert." An "ex" is a "has-been," and a "spurt" is a drip under pressure.

—*Jacob M. Braude*

9.20

No good sensible bee listens to the advice of a bedbug on the subject of business.

—*Elbert Hubbard*

10. Idlers and Eager Beavers

Anecdotes

10.1

Maurice Neill, fuel-oil tycoon of Bernardsville, New Jersey, tells about one of his workers who claimed he had a bad case of bursitis. One morning young Neill queried the man, who lifted his arm only a few inches and complained: "This bursitis is very bad today; I can only get my arm up this far. But yesterday," continued the worker, stretching his arm high above his head, "I could reach way up here."

10.2

An itinerant farm laborer stopped at a farmhouse one hot day and asked for some work. The farmer put him to work in the field, and the man labored with extraordinary vigor in the burning heat. That afternoon the farmer, to make things a bit easier for the man, sent him to the cellar where there was a large pile of apples he wanted sorted into three groups: best apples, good apples, and bad apples.

After several hours the farmer looked in to see how the apple sorter was making out and found that the man had sorted only a few apples. "How come," he asked, "you've done so little work? I felt sorry for you working so hard out in the sun and wanted to give you a break for a few hours."

"Please, mister," pleaded the laborer, "put me back in the field, even if it is hot. I can't stand making decisions."

10.3

After much spirited bargaining, a farmer finally bought a mule from his neighbor, and the two of them walked with the animal to the new owner's pasture. But on the way the buyer noticed that what was represented to him as a sound and healthy beast made slow progress, bumped into a tree, and nearly fell into a perfectly obvious ditch. The buyer turned to his neighbor and said, "You sold me this critter as healthy, but it appears to me to be stone blind."

"You got me wrong," protested the seller. "That mule can see as well as you and I. But it just doesn't give a damn."

10.4

He was an earnest, eager, but terribly slow young lad, working for a pet shop. It took him hours to clean out a few canary cages and another hour to feed the goldfish. Then he asked the boss what he should do next.

"Well," said the boss, "I think you might take the tortoise out for a run."

10.5

"As I understand it," said the heathen, "you propose to civilize me."

"Exactly."

"You want to get me out of the habit of idleness and teach me to work."

"That is the idea."

"And then lead me to simplify my methods and invent things to make my work lighter."

"Yes."

"And after that I'll become ambitious to get rich so that I won't have to work at all."

"Naturally."

"Well, what's the use of going through all that? I don't have to work now."

10.6

Scientific management experts visited a British factory and noticed all the men pushing wheelbarrows except one man. After continued observation they asked the supervisor why this one fellow was not pushing a wheelbarrow. Well, said the supervisor, " 'E 'ates the sight of the bloomin' thing."

10.7

"How long has that office boy worked for you?" inquired a caller.

"About four hours," said the boss.

"Four hours!" exclaimed the visitor. "Why I thought he had been here quite a long while."

"Oh, yes," said the boss, "he's been here, all right; but you asked how long he's worked for me!"

10.8

An employer came upon his foreman, asleep.

"Good heavens," said the foreman to the boss, "can't a man close his eyes for a few minutes of prayer?"

10.9

Some workers remind one of the story of the Rabbi who wanted to be driven to Minsk and made a bargain with a coachman, who warned that the road was rough and his horse Rifke would be treated with every consideration. "I'm very fond of this horse," said the coachman.

Before long they came to a hill. "I can't ask Rifke to carry both of us up it," said the coachman. "You'll have to walk while I drive." The Rabbi agreed without complaint. When they came to another hill, the coachman got out and walked. This kept on all the way to Minsk—every time there was a hill one or the other got out and walked up the hill to spare old Rifke. At the last few hills both men got out and walked because Rifke was getting too tired.

Finally they reached Minsk, half of the distance having been covered on foot. The Rabbi paid the coachman and said, "I have come to Minsk for my congregation. You come to Minsk to make some money. But tell me, why did we bring Rifke?"

10.10

A recruiter for labor approached a young man and asked him if he would like some nice steady work.

"Not if I can do anything else," said the young fellow with refreshing honesty.

10.11

Miranda postively refused to ride on the merry-go-round at the country fair. To her protesting friends she said, "No, indeed; I don't travel on that thing. The other night my husband got on it and rode and rode until I got dizzy watching him. When he got off, I said to him: 'Now that you spent all that money, where have you been?' " And so it often is with eager beavers and their expenditure of energy.

10.12

"Why do you work so hard?"

"It's only because I haven't the nerve to steal."

10.13

A farmer, looking for an extra hand at haying time, offered a job to Tom Watson, who was considered a bit on the foolish side.

"What'll you pay?" he asked.

"I'll pay you what you're worth," said the farmer.

Tom thought for a few seconds, shook his

head, and said, "I'll be durned if I'll work for so little!"

10.14

"Are you looking for work, young man?"

"Not necessarily; but I would like a job."

10.15

"Sam, how do you do your work so well and so fast?"

"Well, Boss, I stick the match of enthusiasm to the fuse of energy, and I just naturally explode."

10.16

A waggish executive at Northrup Aircraft posted the following notice on the bulletin board:

TO ALL EMPLOYEES: Because of increased competition and a keen desire to remain in business, we find it necessary to institute a new policy. Effective immediately, we are asking that somewhere between starting and quitting time, without infringing too much on the time devoted to lunch period, coffee breaks, rest periods, story telling, ticket selling, golfing, auto racing, vacation planning, and rehashing of yesterday's TV programs, that each employee try to find some time that can be set aside and be known as *The Work Break.*

(*See also 2.1 to 2.7*)

10.17

Colonel Stoopnagle, a famous radio comedian, said that "a clock is something they have in an office so you can tell how late you wish you weren't in the morning, what time you go to lunch before and come back after, and how long before you can start stopping work and begin to end the day's work by stalling along until."

(*See also 1.1 to 1.13*)

Definitions

10.18

Work: The worst thing you can do for your health.

—*Howard Brubaker*

10.19

Work is a form of nervousness.

—*Don Herold*

10.20

Idleness: A model farm where the devil experiments with seeds of new sins and promotes the growth of staple vices.

—*Ambrose Bierce*

10.21

Plumber: A fellow who gets paid for sleeping under other people's sinks.

10.22

Occupation: The principal thing one engages in to avoid thinking.

10.23

The schoolboy defined the four principal occupations as addition, subtraction, multiplication, and division.

Aphorisms

10.24

The reason worry kills more people than work is that more people worry than work.

10.25

It is not enough to be industrious; so are the ants. What are you industrious about?

—*Henry David Thoreau*

10.26

The only time people work like a horse is when the boss rides them.

10.27

Every horse thinks his own pack the heaviest.

10.28

I go on working for the same reason that a hen goes on laying eggs.

—*H. L. Mencken*

10.29

I do most of my work sitting down; that is where I shine.

—*Robert Benchley*

10.30

Work is the curse of the drinking classes.

—*Oscar Wilde*

10.31

It is always with the best intentions that the worst work is done.

—*Oscar Wilde*

10.32

It may be true that hard work is respectable, but that doesn't make it popular.

—The Providence *Rotarian,* R.I.

10.33

If you are too busy to laugh, you are too busy.

10.34

Anyone can do any amount of work provided it isn't work he is supposed to be doing at that moment.

—*Robert Benchley*

10.35

A bee is never as busy as it seems; it's just that it can't buzz any slower.

—*Kin Hubbard*

10.36

As busy as a Swiss admiral.

10.37

The eager beaver works twice as hard but doesn't know why.

10.38

It's all in a day's work, as the huntsman said when the lion ate him.

—*Charles Kingsley*

10.39

Work is the greatest thing in the world, so we should always save some of it for tomorrow.

—*Don Herold*

10.40

The world is full of willing people: those willing to work and those willing to let them.

10.41

You can tell some fellows aren't afraid of work by the way they fight it.

10.42

He is such a steady worker that he is really motionless.

10.43

There are but few men who have character enough to lead a life of idleness.

—*Josh Billings*

10.44

He had insomnia so bad that he couldn't sleep when he was working.

—*Arthur "Bugs" Baer*

10.45

Every lazybones deserves a kick in his can'ts.

10.46

Slogan in reverse: Somebody said it couldn't be done—so the hell with it.

10.47

I like work; it fascinates me; I can sit and look at it for hours.

—*Jerome K. Jerome*

10.48

It is impossible to enjoy idling thoroughly unless one has plenty of work to do.

—*Jerome K. Jerome*

10.49

They taught me that happiness could be simply attained. I could either do my duty in that station of life to which it has pleased God to call me; or I could take evening classes in bookkeeping and go one better than He intended.

—*Aubrey Mennen*

10.50

A tramp is a man who won't work. If he won't work he is a politician. If he's a politician, he gives away cigars. If he gives away cigars, he will light them for you. If he lights them for you he is a cigar lighter. If he is a cigar lighter, he won't work. If he won't work, he's a tramp.

—*Evan Esar,* The Humor of Humor

(*See also 7.10, 7.22, 9.7, 64.1, 70.6, 79.29, 112.20, 150.15, 157.16, 170.12, 174.18, 191.4, 205.6, 210.25, 210.26, 211.1, 211.35, 211.36, 212.1, 212.2, 213.5, 213.10, 213.17, 217.2, 217.11, 217.16, 217.17, 235.43*)

CORPORATIONS, INDIVIDUALISTS, ASSORTED SPECIALISTS, GAINERS, AND LOSERS

11. Business, Large and Small

Definitions

11.1

Business: The art of extracting money from another man's pocket without resorting to violence.

—*Max Amsterdam*

11.2

Business is a combination of war and sport.

—*Andre Maurois*

11.3

Big Business: A polite form of larceny, founded on the faith of the stockholders that they, too, will get theirs.

11.4

A small business man is one who is willing to sell his products without hiring a researcher to find out why you want it.

—*Harold Coffin,* the Wall Street Journal

Aphorisms

11.5

The fortunate businessman is one with a business so small he does not have to bribe government officials to let him alone.

11.6

A business is too big when it takes a week for gossip to go from one end of the office to the other.

11.7

Business is like riding a bicycle: either you keep moving or you fall down.

—*John David Wright*

11.8

No man knows where his business ends and his neighbor's begins.

—*E. W. Howe*

11.9

The fact that you cannot serve God and Mammon doesn't seem to hurt business.

11.10

On an examination paper a student wrote: "When several businesses merge it is called a concubine."

11.11

A shady business never yields a sunny life.

—*B. C. Forbes*

11.12

Take the humbug out of this world, and you haven't much left to do business with.

—*Josh Billings*

(*See also 12.1–12.9, 13.1–13.6, 15.1*)

12. Corporations and Capitalists

Anecdotes

12.1

"Why do you call that mule 'Corporation'?" a neighbor asked the farmer.

"Because," said the farmer, "this mule gets more blame and abuse than anything else around here, but he still goes ahead and does just what he damn pleases."

12.2

A man charged with embezzling a large sum of money from a huge corporation was the subject of discussion. "I wonder how a man could loot such a big outfit as that for so long a time without being found out?"

"You must remember," said another man, "that the corporation was pretty busy itself."

12.3

A Russian economist, returned home after an extended visit to the United States, was asked by a friend what he had been doing abroad.

"I went over there to study the death of capitalism," said the economist.

"What are your conclusions?" asked the friend.

"What a wonderful way to die!" whispered the economist.

12.4

The Communist, seeing the rich man in his fine home, says: "No man should have so much." The Capitalist, seeing the same thing, says: "All men should have as much."

—*Phelps Adams*

12.5

A reformer was inquiring into the treatment the law renders to big businessmen who become entangled with the law. One legislator he queried said that he was in favor of confining the punishment to extraordinarily heavy fines.

"Why no jail terms?" asked the reformer.

"Because the record shows," said the legislators, "that the last time some of these capitalists were sent to prison, they had the place in an uproar within three weeks. They had organized all the prisoners and the entire prison staff into the Consolidated Penalty Company, issued thousands of dollars in bonds paying 5 percent, paid the fines of all prisoners, mortgaged the jail and the courthouse, and when they were released had their pockets full of surplus funds of the company."

Definitions

12.6

Corporation: An ingenious device for obtaining individual profit without individual responsibility.

—*Ambrose Bierce*

12.7

A corporation is an artificial person created by law to prey upon the real things.

—*Henry Waldorf Francis*

12.8

Capitalism: The belief that heaven will protect the working girl.

12.9

According to a youth's examination paper: "*Laissez faire* are lazy French women."

(*See also 8.11, 8.12, 8.14, 11.1–11.12, 13.1–13.6, 61.8, 93.38, 142.18, 150.10*)

13. Partners and Entrepreneurs

Anecdotes

13.1

The two partners closed the business early one Friday afternoon and went off together for a long weekend in the country. Seated playing canasta under the shade of trees, one of the partners looked up with a start and said, "Good Lord, Joe, we forgot to lock the safe."

"So what," replied Joe. "There's nothing to worry about. We're both here."

13.2

Two partners went to the cemetery to visit the grave of a deceased partner. They couldn't find the grave. "Maybe he put it in his wife's name," said one.

13.3

"What!" said the boss. "You want a raise in salary, and yet you know darned well what the concern has been through and that it isn't getting any business. You be satisfied with what you are getting—or we'll make you a partner."

13.4

"Well, I'm in for it now," sighed the husband as he sank into a chair at home after he arrived from work.

"What is wrong, dear? Don't tell me you're fired!"

"Oh, no," said the husband despondently. "It's worse than that. The boss is retiring and is giving me the business."

13.5

A New York garment manufacturer complained to his partner that he had been unable to sleep for nights and asked if he had any suggestions for getting to sleep.

"Try counting sheep when you get to bed. The thing gets so monotonous that you'll fall off to sleep in boredom," urged the partner.

The next day the insomniac arrived at the office in a more distraught state than before. "You and your damn sheep," he said to his partner. "I began to count them, and I got up to 25,000. I sheared all those sheep, and before long I had made up 20,000 fine overcoats—beautiful garments of finest quality and tailoring. But then I had a problem: Where am I going to get good lining for 20,000 overcoats? I kept worrying about it the rest of the night, and by morning I was almost out of my mind."

13.6

A man was telling a friend that he was starting a business in partnership with another fellow.

"How much capital are you putting in it?" the friend asked.

"None. The other man is putting up the capital, and I'm putting in the experience."

"So, it's a fifty-fifty agreement."

"Yes, that's the way we're starting out. But I figure in about five years I'll have the capital and he'll have the experience."

13.7

"Dad, what is ethics?" asked the youngster.

The father, a prosperous merchant, pondered for a few moments and said, "Well, son, you know that your uncle and I are in business together. Suppose a customer comes in and buys something worth $10 but by mistake gives me a $20 bill and leaves without waiting for his change. If I split the extra $10 with your uncle—well, that's ethics."

13.8

"Captain Columbus," said a worried sailor on the *Santa Maria* after many days on the Atlantic, "everyone says the world is flat, but you say . . ."

"Quiet yourself, and cease worrying," said Christopher sternly. "I know what I'm talking about when I say the world is not flat."

"But, sir," insisted the seaman, "how do you know this?"

"If the world was flat," said the Admiral of the Ocean Sea, "how could I have gotten the money to make this expedition?"

13.9

"How's business, Sam?"

"Man, it's sure good. I got me a horse for $10, traded it for a bicycle, swapped the bike for two automobile tires, changed them for a bed, and then sold the bed for $10."

"But you made nothing on all that turnover."

"Mebbe not, but then look at the business I done!"

Definitions

13.10

American Enterprise: Making toeless shoes a fashion instead of a calamity.

13.11

Piracy: Commerce without manners.

13.12

Ideas: Funny little things that won't work unless you do.

—*Columbia Record*

Aphorisms

13.13

When two men in a business always agree, one of them is unnecessary.

—*William Wrigley, Jr.*

13.14

No bird is actually on the wing. Wings are on the bird.

13.15

A practical man is one whose judgment is not distracted by the power of seeing above him.

—*Anne Evans*

13.16

Beware of all enterprises that require new clothes.

—*Henry David Thoreau*

(*See also 15.1, 28.11, 61.8, 79.1, 135.49, 243.17*)

14. Togetherness and Teamwork

Anecdotes

14.1

A farmer, plowing with one mule, kept calling out, "Giddap, Bruno! Giddap, Laddy! Giddap, Oscar! Giddap, Joe!"

A stranger asked, "What's his name?"

"Name's Pete," replied the farmer.

"What's the idea, then, of all the other names."

"Oh," said the farmer, "he don't know his own strength; so I put blinders on him and yell a lot of names, and he thinks a lot of other mules are helping 'im."

14.2

When a man was urged to cooperate, he said that the word cooperate suggested to him that he would be expected to *coo* while the other fellow *operated.*

14.3

When the rabbit was being chased by the dog the bystanders called to him to run harder and escape. The rabbit got far enough ahead to stop and call to them, "Thanks for the encouragement, but for goodness' sake shoot the dog."

14.4

Oliver Wendell Holmes used to tell about the time all the people of the world decided to shout "Boo!" at the same time, so that the great shout could be heard on the moon. But when the time came for the great world shout there was nothing but spectacular silence. Everyone was so anxious to hear the great sound that everyone remained quiet.

14.5

The parishioners in a village in a wine-growing region of California decided to honor the fiftieth year in the priesthood of their beloved pastor. Times were bad, and cash was scarce, so they decided that each person would bring a gallon of wine and put it into the padre's almost-empty wine barrel.

When the appointed Sunday came each parishioner arrived with a gallon jug and poured the contents into the pastor's wine barrel. After Mass a delegation of parishioners called on the good father and told him what they had done. The old man was delighted and insisted that they all repair to the wine barrel and drink a glass in honor of the occasion.

But when the wine was drawn it was found to be water. Each thrifty parishioner, thinking that no one else would have the same idea or notice the difference, had brought a gallon of water instead of the promised gallon of wine.

Definitions

14.6

Cooperation: Doing with a smile what you are forced to do.

14.7

A compromise is an agreement whereby both parties get what neither of them wanted.

Aphorisms

14.8

The best way to get on in the world is to make people believe it's to their advantage to help you.

—*Jean de La Bruyere*

14.9

"Note" and *"Initial"* means: Let's spread the responsibility for this.

—*Steel,* June, 1951

14.10

The man who is looking for a helping hand can always find one—attached to his arm.

14.11

And so we plough along, as the fly said to the ox.

—*H. W. Longfellow*

14.12

Mankind should take a lesson from the snowflake. No two of them are alike, yet observe how well they cooperate on major projects—such as tying up traffic.

—*Norva News,* Norfolk, Va.

14.13

One hand cannot applaud.

—*Arabian Proverb*

14.14

Remember the banana: When it left the bunch it got skinned.

(*See also 139.26*)

15. Self-reliance and Self-made Men

Anecdotes

15.1

A certain private in the United States Army during World War II could do nothing by army standards—he was out of step, sloppy, careless about discipline, apparently lazy, hopeless as a soldier. He went overseas with a combat unit. His captain, worried about having such a poor soldier in his company, dreaded to give him a mission with other men, for fear he would let them all down and ruin the whole operation. So the captain sent him out on a solitary patrol, half hoping he would not come back.

When the GI had not returned by daylight the captain had written him off as a casualty, but just when he was getting ready to report the man as missing, the GI showed up with a big batch of prisoners. The astonished officer congratulated him and then asked him, "How come?"

The GI smiled and said, "I know what you think, Captain, but it's just that I like to be in business for myself."

15.2

A small Negro boy stood watching a man at a county fair release small balloons. He saw a red one, then a yellow one, and then a green one each upon release soar into the air.

Finally the Negro boy asked the balloon man, "What would happen if you let go of that black balloon?"

"Sonny," he said, "it isn't the color—it's the stuff inside that makes it soar."

15.3

"Don't talk to me about college!" boasted the self-made man. "Look at me! Do you think for a minute that I'd been any more successful than I am now had I gone to college?"

"Perhaps not," said the professor. "But you would probably have been less inclined to brag about it."

15.4

After talking interminably about himself and his accomplishments, the loud and insufferable bore said, "I'm a self-made man, that's what I am!"

"You knocked off work too soon," said a listener quietly.

Definition

15.5

Self-made Man: A bad example of unskilled labor.

Aphorisms

15.6

No self-made man ever did such a good job that some woman didn't want to make a few alterations.

—*Kin Hubbard*

15.7

Self-made men are very apt to usurp the prerogative of the Almighty and overwork themselves.

—*Edgar Wilson Nye*

15.8

You kin allus tell a self-made man if you'll keep your ears open.

—*Kin Hubbard*

15.9

Self-made men are most always apt to be a little too proud of the job.

—*Josh Billings*

15.10

Consider the postage stamp: its usefulness consists in the ability to stick to one thing till it gets there.

—*Josh Billings*

(*See also 272.4*)

16. Executives and Directors

Anecdotes

16.1

A man who had just been promoted to vice-president boasted of it so much to his wife that she finally retorted: "Vice presidents are a dime a dozen. Why, in the supermarket they even have a vice president in charge of prunes."

Furious, the husband phoned the supermarket in the expectation of refuting his wife. He asked to speak to the vice president in charge of prunes.

"Which one?" was the reply. "Packaged or bulk prunes?"

—*News Wheel,* Kenora, Ont., Canada

16.2

"Gentlemen," said the chairman of the board of a large corporation, "I have before me a report of the greatest significance. Some months ago we appropriated $200,000 for a nationwide survey to find out through hundreds of personal interviews the reply to the question we must have answered if we are to survive and prosper both as individuals and as a free enterprise.

"The question we wanted answered—the question we paid heavily to have solved—is: What makes America tick?

"This question has now been answered by the experts we hired. The answer is on this single sheet of paper. It consists of one powerful word.

"The answer—and I warn you never to forget it—is: PEOPLE."

16.3

"How come you keep a bowl of goldfish on your desk all the time?" a caller asked the executive.

"Because," replied the businessman, "it is relaxing to have something here that doesn't open its mouth to complain or to ask for a raise."

16.4

The big executive stormed out of his office and yelled, "Something's got to be done about those six phones on my desk. For the past five minutes I've been talking to myself."

16.5

The president of the oil company arose at the directors meeting and said: "Gentlemen, you are all familiar with our national campaign to beautify the highways of America. After completing a tour of the nation's roads I am happy to report to you that our efforts have helped in the elimination of those repulsive road signs and in their replacement by beautiful and modern service stations."

16.6

After three months of work the young fellow was called to the office of the president, who said to him, "You have been working here now for three months. Have you been getting any attention?"

The young fellow said honestly, "No, sir—not even one little promotion or increase in pay."

"Well," said the president, "I am going to make you a vice-president and increase your salary $20,000 a year."

"Gee, thanks," said the young fellow.

"Is that all you can say?" asked the president.

"Oh, no," was the reply. "Gee, thanks, Dad."

16.7

A myopic lady without glasses approached a clerk in a grocery store, pointed in puzzlement to a round object which to her seemed to be on a distant counter, and asked: "Is that the head cheese?"

"No, madam, that is his assistant."

16.8

It had taken Ezra all morning to tow the tourist's car in to town behind his team of mules, and when he got back his wife asked him what he charged.

"Fifty cents," said Ezra. "Guess it wasn't too much. Leastwise, he didn't kick up any fuss."

"Fifty cents? Ezra, sometimes I wish you'd do the pullin' and let those mules handle the executive end of the business."

16.9

"My husband has at least 5,000 men under him," she said.

"What does he do?"

"He mows lawns in cemeteries."

16.10

Two young boys, in an adventuresome mood, thought they would each chip in a nickel and buy a cigar. The larger boy lighted the cigar and puffed away at it with apparent contentment, until the smaller boy said, "Come on, now; it's my turn, and I paid half."

"You shut up," snapped the older boy. "I'm the chairman of this company; you're only a stockholder. You do the spitting."

16.11

Chairman Irving S. Olds of the U.S. Steel Corporation was presiding over a stockholders meeting when a woman arose and asked him, "Exactly what are the duties of a chairman; what do you do?"

Mr. Olds, without batting an eye, said, "Madam, the chairman of the board is roughly equivalent to the parsley on a platter of fish."

16.12

During World War I Will Rogers had a suggestion for getting rid of the German submarine menace: "All we have to do is to heat the Atlantic up to 212°F. Then the subs will have to surface, and we can pick them off one by one. Now, somebody's going to want to know how to warm up that ocean. Well, I'm not going to worry about that. It is a matter of detail, and I'm a policy maker."

16.13

The bylaws of a large corporation provided that a substantial sum of money be set aside and divided equally among all the directors who attended the meetings of directors. Since all the directors were wealthy and busy, it was unusual for more than the necessary quorum to be present at any one meeting.

But at one particular meeting all fifty directors showed up during a raging blizzard. Each director, believing the weather would discourage the other directors, went to the meeting in order to get a larger share of the money to be divided among those present.

16.14

The president of one of the big automobile companies opened his directors meeting by announcing: "All those who are opposed to the plan I am about to propose will reply by saying, 'I resign.' "

16.15

The head of a highly successful industry was advised to combine a vacation with a business trip to Europe. The man had become so utterly absorbed in his work that he had only the vaguest notion of what was going on in the world outside his office. He agreed it would be beneficial to take passage on a small and slow-moving vessel.

When the ship encountered a heavy storm in the North Atlantic the executive donned heavy clothing and went on deck to watch the angry terror of the sea. The vessel pitched and tossed, and the man clung tenaciously to the ship's railing, soaked but fascinated by the combat.

Suddenly he heard above the wind the cry, "Man overboard! Man overboard!" And, as he was miraculously able to relate afterwards, "By golly, I looked around and discovered it was me! I was the 'man overboard.' "

16.16

A lightning bug who had fallen into the error of supposing that he was the whole thing, suspended his light for a moment while he engaged in conversation with a pincher-bug that was passing by. At that moment there was some hitch in the works at the electric-light plant, and the whole city was suddenly in darkness. And the lightning bug, thinking that it all came about because he shut off his glow, pompously remarked: "Excuse my mentioning it, but you observe, I suppose, what shape this town would be in if I were to move out of it."

Moral—There is a vast difference between the real value of many people and the estimate they place on themselves.

—*T. A. McNeal*

Definitions

16.17

An executive is a big gun that hasn't yet been fired.

16.18

An executive is a man who talks to the visitors while others are doing the work.

16.19

An executive is a good man who goes around with a worried look—on his assistant's face.

16.20

A big gun is often a man of small caliber and immense bore.

16.21

The big shots are only the little shots who keep shooting.

—*Christopher Morley*

16.22

The big shots are only little shots who have made the most noise.

16.23

Career: A job that starts after 10 A.M.

—*Franklin P. Jones*

16.24

Censure is the tax a man pays to the public for being eminent.

—*Jonathan Swift*

Aphorisms

16.25

The shepherd always tries to persuade the sheep that their interests and his own are the same.

—*Stendhal*

16.26

It is the practice of the multitude to bark at eminent men, as little dogs do at strangers.

16.27

There's nothing that you and I make so many blunders about, and the world so few, as the actual amount of our importance.

—*Josh Billings*

16.28

He who comes up to his own idea of greatness must always have had a very low standard of it in his mind.

—*William Hazlitt*

16.29

Some men never feel small, but these are the few men who are.

—*G. K. Chesterton*

16.30

The superiority of some men is merely local. They are great because their associates are little.

—*Samuel Johnson*

16.31

He who gets too big for his breeches will be exposed in the end.

16.32

After a feller gits famous it don't take long fer some one t' bob up that used t' set by him at school.

—*Kin Hubbard*

16.33

Take a walk through the cemetery. Those guys were big shots, too.

16.34

The modern executive talks golf all morning in the office, and business all afternoon on the links.

16.35

He didn't carve his career—he chiseled it.

—*Walter Winchell*

16.36

Many people reach the heights by putting up a big bluff.

16.37

What men prize most is a privilege, even if it be that of chief mourner at a funeral.

—*James Russell Lowell*

16.38

I have found some of the best reasons I ever had for remaining at the bottom simply by looking at the men on top.

—*Frank Moore Colby*

16.39

Blessed are they who run around in circles, for they shall be known as big wheels.

16.40

If you are not afraid to face the music, you may get to lead the band some day.

—*Edwin H. Stuart*

16.41

Anyone can hold the helm when the sea is calm.

—*Publius*

(*See also 4.1–4.12, 7.3, 7.23, 7.24, 9.4, 19.2, 19.7, 24.4, 28.16, 33.3, 67.1, 136.15, 141.10, 141.11, 235.9, 252.3, 253.2, 267.9, 270.17, 271.41, 272.21, 272.25, 273.9*)

17. The Competitive Spirit

Anecdotes

17.1

Two merchants met on a train just as it was leaving the station. "Where are you going?" asked the first merchant.

"To Minsk," replied the other.

"Aha! You tell me Minsk so I'll think you're going to Lemberg. Now I happen to know that you are going to Minsk. Why be such a liar?"

17.2

The successful businessman was arguing with a competitor and burst forth with: "I'll tell you one thing; there are lots of ways of making money, but there is only one honest way."

"What way is that?" asked his competitor.

"Just as I suspected," snorted the first man. "You don't know!"

17.3

Young Schmidt and oldster Krause ran competing grocery stores in the same neighborhood and frequently engaged in price wars on eggs. Whenever Schmidt lowered the prices of eggs several cents per dozen, Krause promptly met the challenge, whereupon Schmidt would drop his prices still lower, and again Krause would drop his price to meet Schmidt's.

On one occasion the price competition got so

completely out of hand that Schmidt went to Krause and said, "We have got to do something about this. After all, we're both losing money hand over fist."

"I'm not losing any money," replied Krause.

"If I'm losing you must be losing, too," said Schmidt.

"Oh, no," said Krause, "because I've been buying the eggs I sell at cut-rate prices from you."

17.4

Ying and Yang set up competing Chinese restaurants next to one another, and each managed to do quite well. Nevertheless, each proprietor was distressed by the amount of business he was losing to the other.

Finally they sat down to discuss a solution of their mutual problem. They agreed they did not want to merge; they simply wanted to operate their respective establishments prosperously and with peace of mind.

So they decided that each man would manage the other's restaurant. Consequently each manager was perfectly content to see customers enter the restaurant next door.

17.5

In the course of a dispute between two garment manufacturers, one said to the other: "You are so crooked that the wool you're pulling over my eyes is 50 percent cotton."

17.6

The schoolboy had inadvertently kicked a football into the barnyard, near the rooster. "Girls," called the rooster, "come out here and see what is being done these days in other barnyards."

17.7

A golfer kept aiming his ball, but every time he hit an anthill. After this had happened several times, one of the ants said, "If we want to be saved we had better get on the ball."

Definition

17.8

Incentive: The possibility of getting more money than you can earn.

Aphorisms

17.9

Men hustling to do better than competitors have done more for the world than the great souls who dream of universal love.

—*E. W. Howe*

17.10

A rolling stone gathers no moss, but it gains a certain polish.

—*Oliver Herford*

17.11

Anybody can win unless there happens to be a second entry.

—*George Ade*

17.12

There is no glory in outstripping donkeys.

—*Martial*

(*See also 24.8, 36.8, 36.18, 41.4, 41.7, 45.9, 55.10*)

18. Dreamers and Doers

Anecdotes

18.1

The head of a small industrial concern posted DO IT NOW signs all around his office and plant in the hope of getting better results from his workers. Some weeks later, when asked why he was removing the slogan, he said: "It worked too well; the bookkeeper skipped with $2,000; the chief clerk eloped with the best secretary I ever had; three clerks asked for raises; the workers in the factory joined the union and are out on strike; and the office boy threatened to beat me up."

18.2

"Why do you always wish for something you haven't got?"

"What else could one wish for?"

18.3

After the Battle of Austerlitz, Napoleon Bonaparte called representatives of various nationalities among his troops before him and told them he wanted to reward their valor by granting whatever wish they might desire.

A Pole cried out, "Restore Poland!" and a Slovak called out that he wanted a farm. A German soldier asked for a brewery. To each of them Napoleon said grandly, "Your wish shall be granted." Then he asked a Jewish soldier what he wished for, and the Jew said he'd settle for a schmaltz herring. And Napoleon ordered that it be obtained and given to the Jewish soldier immediately.

Later his fellow soldiers twitted the Jew for his absurd request, when he could have asked for a reward of great price and consequence. "We shall see who is the foolish one," said the Jew. "See if Poland is freed or if the one man gets his farm and the other a brewery. In the meantime I'm enjoying my herring."

18.4

Once upon a time I, Chuang Tzu, dreamt I was a butterfly, fluttering hither and thither, to all intents and purposes a butterfly. I was conscious only of following my fancies as a butterfly, and I was unconscious of my individuality as a man. Suddenly, I awaked and there I lay, myself again. Now I do not know whether I was a man dreaming I was a butterfly, or whether I am now a butterfly dreaming I am a man.

—Translated from the Chinese by
Lionel Giles

18.5

In a certain town lived a Brahman named Seedy, who got some barley meal by begging, ate a portion, and filled a jar with the remainder. This jar he hung on a peg one night, placed his cot beneath it, and fixing his gaze on the jar, fell into a hypnotic reverie.

"Well, here is a jar full of barley meal," he thought. "Now if famine comes, a hundred rupees will come out of it. With that sum I will get two she-goats. Every six months they will bear two more she-goats. After goats, cows. When the cows calve, I will sell the calves. After cows, buffaloes; after buffaloes, mares. From the mares I shall get plenty of horses. The sales of these will mean plenty of gold. The gold will buy a great house with an inner court. Then someone will come to my house and offer his lovely daughter with a dowry. She will bear a son, whom I shall call Moon-Lord. When he is old enough to ride on my knee, I will take a book, sit on the stable roof, and think. Just then Moon-Lord will see me, will jump from his mother's lap in his eagerness to ride on my knee, and will go too near the horses. Then I shall get angry and tell my wife to take the boy. But she will be too busy with her chores and will not pay attention to what I say. Then I will get up and kick her."

Being sunk in his hypnotic dream, he let fly such a kick that he smashed the jar. And the barley-meal it contained turned him white all over.

—*The Panchatantra*

Definitions

18.6

A procrastinator is one who puts off until tomorrow the things he's already put off until today.

18.7

Duty: That which sternly impels us in the direction of profit, along the line of desire.

—*Ambrose Bierce*

18.8

Planning: The art of putting off until tomorrow what you have no intention of doing today.

18.9

Prudence is a rich, ugly, old maid courted by Incapacity.

—*William Blake*

18.10

The *difficult* is that which can be done immediately; the *impossible* is that which takes a little longer.

—*George Santayana*

Aphorisms

18.11

The world is moving so fast these days that the man who says it can't be done is generally interrupted by someone doing it.

—*Elbert Hubbard*

18.12

The man who gets to the bottom of things often lands on the top.

18.13

Confucius say ostrich who keep head in sand too long during hot part of day gets burned in end.

18.14

It takes less time to do a thing right than to explain why you did it wrong.

—*H. W. Longfellow*

18.15

The man with vision always gets ahead of the man with visions.

18.16

Sign in office: THE EASIEST WAY TO MAKE ENDS MEET IS TO GET OFF YOUR OWN.

18.17

Always behave like a duck—keep calm and unruffled on the surface but paddle like the devil underneath.

—London *Daily Express*

18.18

Even when you're on the right track, you'll get run over if you just sit there.

18.19

The best way to make your dreams come true is to wake up.

18.20

Depend on the rabbit's foot if you will, but remember it didn't work for the rabbit!

—*R. E. Shay*

18.21

If you think you can win, consider the worm. The early worm gets caught by the bird, and the lazy, carousing worm that always sleeps late is caught night crawling by a fisherman with a flashlight.

18.22

He is as careful as a nudist climbing over a barbed-wire fence.

18.23

Many of those who call themselves dreamers are merely sleepers.

18.24

There are mortgages on every castle in the air.

18.25

When the meek inherit the earth it's going to be lots of fun watching the unmeek take it away from them.

18.26

Little boats should keep near the shore.

—*Benjamin Franklin*

(*See also* 2.2, 4.2)

19. Success and Failure

Anecdotes

19.1

A good-natured woman, because of the location of her house, was often asked for food by tramps. She finally decided to refuse them; it was becoming too burdensome. But shortly after she made her resolution, a good-looking and neat young man stopped and asked her for a little piece of thread. She noticed that his pants were badly ripped, that he had a needle, and she realized he could not get work with his pants in their present condition, so she gave him the thread. The fellow took the thread, went down the road, and sat under a tree for a few minutes, then came back to the house. He told the woman he could not repair the pants unless he had a piece of cloth for a patch. She gave him a small piece of material.

About an hour later the young fellow came again to the house and said, "Madam, these pants are beyond repair. It would be very good of you if you could give me a pair of your husband's old pants." "You're pretty clever," smiled the woman. "You know I'd a-set the dogs on you if you had asked for pants right off." So she gave him a pair of old pants that belonged to her husband.

The young man went behind the barn and changed into the pants given him. Then he returned to the house and told the woman that the pants were sort of big around the waist, but if she would give him some food he was sure they would fit perfectly.

This time the woman burst out laughing. "You're just about the smartest man that's been around these parts in a long time." So she gave him a big dinner. All because he took one step at a time.

19.2

A group of business executives, after deploring the youth of today, turned to their own struggles. After several of the men had given harrowing accounts of their early days in business, one man, younger than the others, said: "I had a pretty rough time of it for a while. But when I saw what the score was going to be, I simply worked harder and longer—and got another hundred thousand bucks from my old man."

19.3

A testimonial dinner was given the town's leading citizen. When he arose to speak he recalled, "When I arrived in this then-little village twenty-five years ago, I had only one, dusty, beaten-up suit, a pair of well-worn shoes, a limited education, and all my earthly possessions in a knapsack. But I worked my way up for the town, and I believe my bank has been good for it, as well as my other contributions—such as our chief industry and a number of our business buildings."

After the dinner one of the young men present, anxious to learn all about the road to success, asked the speaker what he had had in the knapsack. "Well, son," he replied, "there was in it a razor, $20,000 in stocks and bonds, and $25,000 in cash."

19.4

A retired chain-store magnate said to his grandson, "Why don't you go out and get a job? When I was your age I was working for $3 a week. Within five years I owned the store."

"Yes, but, Grandfather, they have cash registers now."

19.5

A millionaire, asked the reason for his success, said, "I never hesitate to give full credit to my wife."

"And how did she help?"

"Frankly," said the millionaire, "I was curious to see if there was any income she couldn't live beyond."

19.6

"I have found the road to success no easy matter," said the businessman. "I started at the bottom. I worked twelve hours a day. I sweated. I fought. I took abuse. I did things I did not approve of. But I kept right on climbing the ladder."

"And now, of course, you are a success?" prompted the interviewer.

"No, I wouldn't say that," replied the businessman with a laugh. "Just quote me as saying that I have become expert at climbing ladders."

19.7

"My boy," said the business executive, "there are two things that are vitally necessary if you are to succeed in business."

"What are they, Dad?"

"Honesty and sagacity."

"What is honesty?"

"Always—no matter what happens nor how adversely it may effect you—always keep your word once you have given it."

"And sagacity?"

"Never give your word."

19.8

Einstein, asked for the secret of his success, said, "If A is success in life, I should say that the formula for success is A equals X plus Y plus Z, with X standing for work and Y for play. But what is Z? That is keeping your mouth shut."

19.9

Jean Cocteau, asked if he believed in luck, replied, "Certainly; how else do you explain the success of those you don't like?"

19.10

When Dr. Allan Gregg was about to retire from his position as vice-president of the Rockefeller Foundation some of his colleagues were discussing how awful it would be after he was gone. Finally Dr. Gregg spoke up. "Relax, gentlemen," he said. "Nothing succeeds like successors."

—*The Pleasures of Publishing*

19.11

A pretentious man had achieved a modest success in the business world and on a visit to his old home town asked a friend, "I suppose the folks around here have heard of my great success?"

"Yes, they know of it."

"And what do they say?"

"They say nothing at all," replied the friend. "Sometimes they laugh."

19.12

"I owe much of my success to a 220-pound bully who kicked sand in my face at the beach when I was a mere 100-pound kid."

"What did you do? Build yourself up and then lick the guy?"

"Oh, no," replied the successful man. "I determined to work hard, save my money, invest it wisely—and now I have my own private beach."

19.13

Henry Labouchere once said: "I don't mind his having all the aces up his sleeve, but I object to his acting as if God had put them there."

19.14

The difficulties of modern life are emphasized by Herbert V. Prochnow, who says a person has to keep his back to the wall, his ear to the ground, his shoulder to the wheel, his nose to the grindstone, a level head, and both feet on the ground. And at the same time he has to have his head in the clouds so that he can look for the silver lining.

19.15

Two broken-down old men sat on a park bench. One said, "I'm here because I never took advice from anybody."

"Shake," said the other man, "I'm here because I took everybody's advice."

19.16

A man opened a fish store and put up a sign reading FRESH FISH SOLD HERE. One of his first customers said he ought to drop the word "fresh." "Obviously, you wouldn't sell fish that was not fresh," he added. So the merchant painted out the word "fresh."

A day or so later another customer argued that the "here" was superfluous since the man had only this one store and wasn't selling fish at any other place. So the easily persuaded merchant crossed out the word "here," the sign then reading FISH FOR SALE.

But still another customer told him he ought to drop the words "for sale." "After all," said this critic, "No one expects you to give the fish away. It's not necessary to remind people you are selling the fish." So with a sigh the man painted out the words "for sale" and was left with a sign reading only FISH.

However, not even this escaped criticism. Another man came in and told the merchant there was no need for the word "fish." "Why, people can smell the fish a block away. Their noses will direct them here if they want to buy fish."

The merchant took down the sign with its one remaining word. But all his customers went to a store across the street with the sign FRESH FISH SOLD HERE.

19.17

A fellow inherited 4 million dollars, but the will provided he had to accept it either in Chile or Brazil. He chose Brazil. In Brazil he had to choose between receiving his inheritance in coffee or nuts. He chose nuts. But then the bottom fell out of the nut market, while coffee went up to 80 cents a pound. He lost everything.

He sold his watch for money to fly back to the United States. He had enough money for a ticket to either Los Angeles or New York. He chose Los Angeles. Just before he took off, the New York plane came out on the runway—it was a brand-new super jet; the Los Angeles plane was a 1928 Ford trimotor with a sway back and took half a day to get off the ground. It was filled with crying children and tethered goats. Over the Andes one engine fell off. Our man crawled up to the cockpit and said, "Let me out if you want to save your lives. Give me a parachute."

"The pilot agreed but added, "On this airline, anybody who bails out must wear two chutes."

He jumped from the plane and as he fell tried to make up his mind which rip cord to pull. Finally he chose the one on the left. It was rusty, and the wire pulled loose. He pulled the other handle. The chute opened, but its shroud lines snapped. In desperation the poor fellow cried out, "St. Francis save me!"

Suddenly a great hand reached down from Heaven, seized the poor man's wrist and let him dangle in midair. Then a gentle voice asked, "St. Francis Xavier or St. Francis of Assisi?"

Definitions

19.18

Success: A matter either of getting around you better men than yourself or getting around better men than yourself.

—*Banking*

19.19

Success: Making more money so you can pay off the taxes you wouldn't have to pay if you didn't have so much money already.

19.20

Successful Man: One who makes more money than his son at college can spend.

19.21

Success is the good fortune that comes from aspiration, desperation, perspiration, and inspiration.

19.22

A failure is a man who has blundered but is not able to cash in on the experience.

—*Elbert Hubbard*

Aphorisms

19.23

The penalty of success is to be bored by the attentions of people who formerly snubbed you.

—*Mary Wilson Little*

19.24

Everything bows to success, even grammar.

—*Victor Hugo*

19.25

The reason why men who mind their own business succeed is because they have so little competition.

19.26

The successful people are the ones who can think up things for the rest of the world to keep busy at.

—*Don Marquis*

19.27

Success is relative. The more success the more relatives.

19.28

Even the woodpecker owes his success to the fact that he uses his head and keeps pecking away until he finishes the job he starts.

—*Coleman Cox*

19.29

You won't skid if you stay in a rut.

—*Kin Hubbard*

19.30

When you get through changing—you're through.

—*Bruce Barton*

19.31

Don't worry when you stumble; remember a worm is the only thing that can't fall down.

19.32

The road to success is filled with women pushing their husbands along.

—*Thomas Robert Dewar*

19.33

Envy provides the mud that failure throws at success.

19.34

Success covers a multitude of blunders.

—*George Bernard Shaw*

19.35

The gent who wakes up and finds himself a success hasn't been asleep.

—*Wilson Mizner*

19.36

Success may go to one's head but the stomach is where it gets in its worst work.

—*Kin Hubbard*

19.37

All you need in this life is ignorance and confidence, and then success is sure.

—*Mark Twain*

19.38

Let us be thankful for the fools. But for them the rest of us could not succeed.

—*Mark Twain*

19.39

Confucius say: Success give man big head, also big belly.

19.40

When success turns a person's head, he is facing failure.

—Milwaukee Newman Club *Bulletin*

19.41

Every man has a right to be conceited until he is successful.

—*Benjamin Disraeli*

19.42

Nothing is so impudent as success.

19.43

Nothing recedes like success.

19.44

Nothing succeeds like excess.

—*Oscar Wilde*

19.45

Success comes in cans, failure in can'ts.

19.46

The worst jolt most of us ever get is when we fall back on our own resources.

—*Kin Hubbard*

19.47

We all have something to fall back on, and I never knew a phony who didn't land on it eventually.

—*Wilson Mizner*

19.48

Perched on the loftiest throne in the world, man is still sitting on his own behind.

—*Michel de Montaigne*

19.49

When you're average, you're as close to the bottom as to the top.

19.50

No bird soars too high if he soars with his own wings.

—*William Blake*

19.51

May bad fortune follow you all your days
And never catch up with you.

19.52

Be nice to people on your way up because you'll meet them on your way down.

—*Wilson Mizner*

19.53

No one is satisfied with his fortune or dissatisfied with his intellect.

19.54

Life is short, but it is long enough to ruin any man who wants to be ruined.

—*Josh Billings*

19.55

The road to ruin is always kept in good repair, and the travelers pay the expense of it.

—*Josh Billings*

19.56

There are only two ways of getting on in the world: by one's own industry, or by the stupidity of others.

—*Jean de La Bruyere*

19.57

If you do big things they print your face, and if you do little things they only print your thumbs.

—*Arthur "Bugs" Baer*

19.58

"Failure has gone to his head," said Wilson Mizner of a guy who strutted through bankruptcy.

19.59

Nothing succeeds like—failure.

—*Oliver Herford*

19.60

Ambition is the last refuge of the failure.

—*Oscar Wilde*

19.61

Failure is the path of least persistence.

19.62

A man may fall many times but he won't be a failure until he says that someone has pushed him.

—*Elmer G. Letterman*

19.63

If at first you don't succeed, try, try again. Then quit. There's no use making a fool of yourself.

—*W. C. Fields*

19.64

If a fellow gets to going down hill, it seems as if everything were greased for the occasion.

—*Josh Billings*

19.65

The only difference between a rut and a grave is their dimensions.

—*Ellen Glasgow*

19.66

Success is not always a sure sign of merit, but it is a first-rate way to succeed.

—*Josh Billings*

19.67

When we are flat on our backs there is no way to look but up.

—*Roger W. Babson*

19.68

The successful people are the ones who can think up things for the rest of the world to keep busy at.

—*Don Marquis*

19.69

Success don't consist in never making blunders, but in never making the same one a second time.

—*H. W. Shaw*

19.70

There's always something about your success that displeases even your best friends.

—*Mark Twain*

(*See also 15.3–15.9, 16.6, 16.16–16.22, 16.31, 16.34–16.36, 16.39–16.41, 18.12, 18.21, 20.5, 20.8, 20.10, 24.26, 93.34, 93.46, 100.15, 135.50, 156.20, 189.4, 193.16, 235.36, 240.3, 242.16, 242.17, 269.32, 269.103, 269.159, 272.25, 278.1*)

20. Production and Profit

Anecdotes

20.1

The executive was asked what part his company had played in the war effort.

"See that big plane over there? Well, we make the clips that hold the blueprints together."

20.2

A sheepherder whose flock became lost in a storm went to his boss and asked him if he wanted him to continue in his employment.

"Certainly," said the boss. "I've no complaints."

"Well, then, you better get me a new flock of sheep," said the herder.

20.3

A young mother looked in the nursery one evening and saw her husband standing silently by the crib, looking down thoughtfully. In his face she could read his wonder and admiration, and she went to him softly and took his hand in hers and said, "A penny for your thoughts."

He looked at her and said, "I can't understand it. How on earth can the manufacturer make a crib like this for $5.95?"

20.4

A watchmaker in England determined that he would do work that was more exquisitely delicate even than that of his Swiss competitors. Finally, he perfected a strand of wire he was confident could not be duplicated by any other watchmaker—it was, he assured himself, the thinnest man could make. He placed this wire in a velvet-lined box and sent it to a Swiss watch manufacturer with a note explaining that it was a sample of the kind of work he was doing in England.

Several weeks later the man in England received a small package from Switzerland. It, too, was a velvet-lined jewel box, and it contained the tiny wire sent from England. Alongside it was a jeweler's lens. Puzzled, the man put the lens to his eye and looked at the hair-like strand of wire. He then discovered that the Swiss watchmaker had drilled a neat hole through the center of the delicate wire.

20.5

During the French Revolution a man from Paris stopped at a village and was asked by a friend what was happening. "They are cutting off heads by the thousands," said the visitor.

"How terrible!" cried the villager. "That could ruin my hat business!"

20.6

When asked, "What was the cause of the Industrial Revolution?" a student replied, "People stopped reproducing by hand and began reproducing by machinery."

20.7

William S. Knudsen, questioned by a House committee about the progress being made in defense production during World War II, finally said, "Gentlemen, it's like this. Despite our modern hospitals, anesthetics, obstetricians, psychiatrists, and gynecologists—despite all the advances in research, medicine, and science—it still takes nine months."

20.8

Talk about hard luck! I bought a gold mine, and we actually bring up some gold, but then they drill deeper, and now the whole thing is loused up because it's gushing oil.

20.9

Jacobs bought a beautiful diamond ring for his wife and at lunch showed it to his friend Levinson, who offered to buy it at a profit to Jacobs. Jacobs later regretted the sale and bought it back from Levinson at a still higher price, but Levinson again bought it back at a price once again higher. Finally Levinson sold the ring to a person unknown to Jacobs. When the latter heard of this final transaction he protested. "How could you do such a stupid thing," he said, "when we were both making such a good living just from that ring."

20.10

Two graduates of the Harvard School of Business decided to start their own business and put into practice what they had learned in their studies. But they soon went into bankruptcy, and an unlettered old fellow took over the business. The two educated men felt sorry for him and taught him what they knew about economic theory.

Some time later the two former proprietors called on their successor when they heard he was doing a booming business. "What is the secret of your success?" they asked him.

"'Taint really no secret," said the old man. "As you know, schooling and theory is not in my line. I just buy an article for $1 and sell it for $2. One percent profit is enough for me."

20.11

One man to another: "We're a nonprofit organization. We didn't mean to be, but we are."

Definitions

20.12

Profiteering: The fortunes of war.

20.13

Sinking Fund: A place where they hide the profits from the stockholders.

—Boston *Transcript*

Aphorisms

20.14

It is a socialist idea that making profits is a vice; I consider the real vice is making losses.

—*Winston Churchill*

20.15

Iron was discovered before someone smelt it.

20.16

A mine is a hole in the ground owned by a liar.

—*Mark Twain*

(*See also 8.1, 9.2, 12.6, 13.5, 18.7, 46.12, 70.12, 229.3, 232.7, 235.9*)

21. Mechanical Brains

Anecdotes

21.1

Gerald L. Phillippe, president of the General Electric Company, said that his research staff asked one of their computers, "Could a computer ever be President?" and after a few brief whirs and spins the machine replied, "I am not now and do not intend to become a candidate for any office; but in the event of a genuine draft I will serve to the best of my ability."

21.2

S. David Pursglove, in *Popular Mechanics,* relates that a computer, given an impossible job, whirred and clicked and clacked all night long and finally collapsed entirely with a blowing of tubes and fuses. The machine had been trying to divide by zero. Mr. Pursglove tells about another computer that responded gently to spoken numbers but would go into amorous hysteria when it heard the seductive click of a spring in a movie camera.

21.3

A computer was being tested for its ability to relate past events. They picked a boy from the audience, got all the data about him from his widowed mother and himself, and fed it into the machine.

"Now, my boy," said the demonstrator, "just ask questions to which you already know the answers. You'll be amazed how accurate the machine replies."

"Where is my father?"

"Your father is fishing in Alaska."

"Wrong," said the mother. "The father is dead."

The demonstrator checked his data and pushed buttons and so on; the machine repeated: "His father is fishing in Alaska."

"What was your husband's name, Madam?" asked the demonstrator.

"Hiram Smithson," she said.

The demonstrator fed the facts into the machine, and the machine replied: "Mr. Smithson is dead, he died the year after the boy was born."

"That's right," said the mother.

"But," the machine went on, "the boy's father is fishing in Alaska."

21.4

An electronic computer, if given the name Mathematical Analyzer, Numerical Integrator and Calculator, would be titled MANIAC.

21.5

Dr. A. D. Booth recently referred to an incident in which a Soviet electronic computer designed to translate English into Russian dealt with the phrase "out of sight, out of mind." As it happened, an American computer geared to translate Russian into English picked up the Russian translation and rendered it back again as "invisible lunatic."

—*Magnus Pyke,* The Science Myth, 1962

21.6

A bored traveler walked up and down the platform waiting for his train, when he spotted a weighing machine. He inserted a penny and waited for the card to drop into the slot at the bottom. It read 169 pounds. On the other side was this warning: "You should avoid traveling this month; keep your insurance paid up and keep close to home. You are in an unlucky phase."

"Bunk!" said the man as he tore up the card and resumed his pacing. But when he again passed the machine he put in another penny and got exactly the same weight and advice. "Rubbish!" snorted the man and discarded the message.

But something drew him back to the machine, and for the third time he inserted a penny. His weight was still 169 pounds, but this time the card read: "Lay off, man. We're not kidding you."

21.7

A large insurance company's billing department was bedeviled by a modern info-machine that persisted in turning out premium notices with the figure $9,000 on them. Technicians were called in and went over the machine tube by tube, part by part, but could not find the source of the trouble.

"I know what the trouble is," said the office boy to the chief technician. "It's that girl over there with the swell figure, the one who works the machine's keyboard."

"We're not interested in that sort of nonsense," said the technician sternly.

"All right, but just watch her, anyway. See how she leans over the keys when she punches 'e.' Now watch her. . . ."

And so the chief technician discovered that a part of the girl's abundant torso was pressed against the keyboard, establishing a delicate point of contact.

"Works every time," grinned the office boy. "It's the right place to hit the 9,000 button."

(*See also 117.4, 190.1*)

22. Economists and Statisticians

Anecdotes

22.1

The friends of a noted American economist arranged a banquet to celebrate his many years of private and public contributions to the nation's thinking. When the festivities ended a group of newspaper reporters asked the guest of honor if he had a message for the people—perhaps some great economic truth distilled from his years of study and thought.

"Well," said the economist, "there are a number of economic truths, but they are rather complex and difficult to express in terms most people would understand. However, they all boil down to one simple fact that history has time and time again proved: *There is no such thing as a free lunch.*"

22.2

A speaker warning against the pitfalls of statistics, pointed out that the families of Princeton graduates average 1.8 children, whereas for Smith graduates the figure was 1.4. He added, "A faulty conclusion would be drawn from these figures—that men have more children than women."

—*The Atlantic Bulletin*

22.3

A successful businessman went back to the campus for a class reunion and, while there, stopped in to visit with his old economics professor. During the visit the businessman idly picked up some final-examination papers on the professor's desk and looked at them. "This is surprising," he said to the professor. "Many of the questions on this paper are the same ones I had in my final examination years ago. I would have thought they'd be different today."

"No," said the professor, "the questions change very little over the years. It's the answers that change."

Definitions

22.4

Economist: A man who states the obvious in terms of the incomprehensible.

—*Alfred A. Knopf*

22.5

An economist is a man who knows more about money than people who have it.

22.6

An economist is a man who wears a watch chain with a Phi Beta Kappa key at one end and no watch at the other.

22.7

Statistician: A liar who can figure.

22.8

Statistician: A man who draws a mathematically precise line from an unwarranted assumption to a foregone conclusion.

Aphorisms

22.9

Economists now say we move in cycles instead of running around in circles. It sounds better, but it means the same.

22.10

If all economists were laid end to end, they would not reach a conclusion.

—*George Bernard Shaw*

22.11

If all the economists were laid end to end, they'd still point in all directions.

22.12

He uses statistics as a drunken man uses lampposts—for support rather than for illumination.

—*Andrew Lang*

22.13

Economists are almost invariably engaged in defeating the last slump.

—*Stuart Chase*

22.14

I have hardly ever known a mathematician who was capable of reasoning.

—*Plato*

(*See also 9.2, 12.3, 33.2, 180.3, 185,3, 264.4, 269.85, 269.128, 270.17*)

23. The Insurance Game

Anecdotes

23.1

The insurance salesman had his prospect on the hook and was about ready to move in for the kill. "Now that amounts," he concluded, "to premiums of $6.90 per month on a straight life. That's what you want, isn't it?"

"Well," said the customer wistfully, "I would like to fool around once in a while on Saturday night."

—*Pure Oil News*

23.2

To illustrate how swiftly life-insurance claims are paid, one salesman said that his company's offices were on the tenth floor of a sixty-floor skyscraper and that one day a man fell off the roof and was handed his check as he passed their floor.

23.3

A young life-insurance salesman walked into the office of an executive and said to him, "I am selling life insurance, but I don't suppose you would be interested."

The executive—sales manager for a thriving corporation—looked at the insurance man in disgust and belligerently said that he certainly did not want any more life insurance.

"In that case," said the salesman, "I'll try somebody else." And he started to leave.

"Wait a minute," said the sales manager. "I employ and train salesman, and I've seen some beauts, but you are the worst I have ever met. You'll starve to death if you continue to talk people out of your product instead of talking them into buying it." Whereupon the sales manager gave the young man a rapid-fire course in the technique of selling insurance. He got so interested in the whole problem that he ended up by signing for a $5,000 life policy on himself.

"Let this be a lesson to you," said the sales manager. "Work out a sales pitch for each individual situation you are likely to encounter and use it to the hilt."

"That's what I've been doing," smiled the young salesman. "You see, I had you figured out before I came in here. I have just used on you my specially prepared pitch for aggressive sales managers."

23.4

An insurance agent, writing a policy for a cowpuncher, asked him if he had ever had any accidents.

"No," said the cowboy, "except once a bronc kicked me, and another time a rattlesnake bit me."

"Don't you call those accidents?" asked the insurance agent.

"No," replied the cowboy, "they done it a purpose."

23.5

The insurance salesman had his man on the hook, ready to sign up for a $50,000 life-insurance policy, but suddenly the prospect put down the pen with which he was going to sign his name and said, "I think I'll wait until April before signing up for this. Come back then."

The insurance salesman packed up his brief-case, stood up, started to leave, then stopped and asked the man, "Whom shall I ask for if you're not here in April?"

That did it. The man signed up for the insurance.

23.6

An overworked and almost overage executive decided to take out some more life insurance while there was still time. He signed the application, took the required physical examination, but then did not hear from his insurance agent. Finally, after weeks had elapsed, he phoned the agent and asked him what was causing the delay. The agent hemmed and hawed. Finally he said that the company doctor had made a chart of the physical examination and that when something wasn't right on it he punched a hole at that point. The chart puzzled the agent so much that he took it home and tried it out on his player piano.

"And," concluded the agent, "I am sorry to tell you that the piano played "Nearer, My God to Thee."

23.7

Jack Kenna, Long Island insurance broker and Republican bigwig, insists it is true that the same day a merchant took out fire insurance his store and all its contents were burned to the ground. When the storekeeper filed an insurance claim, the company, suspecting arson but unable to prove it, wrote the man as follows:

"Dear Sir: You insured your store and its contents against fire at 10:30 A.M. The official report indicates that the fire did not break out until 4 P.M. the same day. Will you be good enough to explain the delay?"

23.8

A farmer whose barn burned down was told by the insurance company that his policy provided that the company build a new barn, rather than paying him the cash value of it. The farmer was incensed by this. "If that is the way you fellows operate," he said, "then cancel the insurance I have on my wife's life."

23.9

A life-insurance salesman sought to have a frequently married man take out life insurance. "Nothing doing," said the much-married man. "I'm none too safe at home now the way things are going."

23.10

"I want to take out a $5,000 fire-insurance policy on my husband," said the lady to the insurance agent.

"On your husband?" said the agent. "You must mean life insurance."

"No, I mean fire insurance. He wants to be cremated when he dies."

Definitions

23.11

Insurance: Paying for catastrophe on the installment plan.

23.12

Life insurance is a contract that keeps you poor so you can die rich.

(*See also 43.14, 93.40, 160.35, 244.19, 263.31*)

24. Good Times and Bad

Anecdotes

24.1

A story about Moses that is certainly not in the Bible relates that the patriarch told the Lord that his people were sorrowing, many unclothed, some hungry, and he asked that they be made happy and contented.

The Lord promised to correct conditions, and of course, did so. But soon thereafter Moses was again in woe, and again was asked by the Lord what He could do for him.

"Lord," cried the prophet, "my house is falling apart and I can get no one to repair it; everyone is too busy enjoying himself."

"But what shall I do?" asked the Lord.

"Lord, make my people as they were before!"

24.2

Two men were discussing their status in life. One said, "I started out on the theory that the world had an opening for me."

"And you found it?"

"Well, sort of," said the first man. "I'm in the hole now."

24.3

Farmer Perkins was sitting on his porch sorrowfully counting the costs of a cloud burst. A neighbor pulled up in a wagon. "Say, Perk," he yelled, "your hogs got washed up down the creek, and they're all dead."

"How about O'Brien's hogs?" asked the farmer.

"They're gone, too."

"And Johnson's?"

"All gone away."

"Well!" exclaimed Perkins more cheerfully. "Guess it warn't as bad as I thought."

24.4

An executive was in habit of pausing every morning as he passed a state institution on his way to work. In the yard one of the inmates went through the motions of winding up and pitching an imaginary ball. Finally, a friend asked the executive why he always stopped to watch this performance.

"Well," he said, "if things keep on going the way they are, I'll be there some day catching for that guy, and I want to get on to his curves."

24.5

A certain sharp attorney was said to be in bad circumstances. A friend of the unfortunate lawyer met Douglas Jerrold, the English wit, and said, "Have you heard about poor R? His business is going to the devil."

"That's all right—then he is sure to get it back again," said Jerrold.

24.6

"How's business?" one man asked another.

"Well, you know how it is," replied the other. "Business is like sex. When it's good, it's wonderful. When it's bad—it's pretty good."

24.7

Two garment manufacturers were complaining about business. One said, "You should see my showroom. It's like a haunted house."

"Don't complain," said the other, "You're lucky to have ghosts."

24.8

The tailoring business was in a deplorable condition for Gittlesohn and his partner. "Only the Messiah could help us," wailed Gittlesohn.

"How could the Messiah help us?" asked the partner.

"Why," said Gittlesohn, "he'd bring back the dead, and then they'd all need new clothes."

"But," protested the partner, "some of the dead are tailors, and we'd have more competition."

"So what?" replied Gittlesohn. "They couldn't compete with us. They wouldn't know anything about this year's styles."

24.9

Two clothing merchants were glumly riding home together on the subway at the height of the Depression. After a long quiet, one of them gave vent to a long, drawn-out sigh. The other turned to him and said: "You're telling *me.*"

24.10

A man was asked to talk to a group of businessmen about the Depression. He tacked up on the wall a large sheet of perfectly white paper. He made a black spot in the paper with a pencil. Then he asked each man to say what he saw. Each man replied a black spot. The speaker then said, "Yes, there is a little black spot. But not one of you saw the big expanse of white paper. That's the point of my speech."

24.11

The interviewer asked the head of the local chamber of commerce if the Depression had had very serious consequences in his town.

"Depression?" replied the local booster. "No, sir, Depression never hit us here. But I must confess that recently we have been going through the worst boom I ever remember."

24.12

During the Depression the story went around about a young man who had a nervous breakdown. His parents brought him to the doctor, who told them to put him somewhere where he would not be disturbed. So they put him in business.

24.13

"I know how to settle this unemployment problem. Put all the women on one island, and all the men on the other. That will solve it."

"How?"

"All of them will get busy building boats."

24.14

A fellow out of work and desperate agreed to take a job with a small-town circus. He was togged out in a tiger skin and told to walk a tightrope much as a real tiger might be supposed to do. During his first performance in this role, he lost his nerve and fell into a cage below where a lion was prowling about. The lion came at him with a terrible roar, and the "tiger" howled back in most human fashion. The lion came up to him with a rush and in a whisper said, "Don't be such a coward! You're not the only guy out of work."

24.15

The workmen stood watching with awe and with apprehension while a huge steam shovel scooped tons of earth and dumped them into waiting trucks to be hauled away. "Look at that damned machinery knocking hundreds of us out of work!" exclaimed one of the men.

"Yeah," said another. "But if we didn't have shovels we'd probably be working with spoons."

24.16

"Poor Joe, since he's lost all his money, half of his friends have dropped him."

"Well, he's still got the other half of his friends."

"Yeah, but they don't know yet that he's lost it."

Definitions

24.17

Good Times: When people who used to go around barefoot start complaining about the price of shoes.

—*Maurice Seitter*

24.18

Depression is a period during which we have to get along without the things our grandparents never dreamed about.

24.19

A depression is a period when you can't spend money you don't have.

24.20

A *recession* is a period in which you tighten your belt. In a *depression* you have no belt to tighten, and when you have no pants to hold up, it's a *panic.*

—*Farm Implement News*

24.21

Status quo is Latin for the mess we're in.

24.22

Unemployment: A breakdown of the economic system in which there is no money to pay workers because the workers have no money to buy goods, because there is no money to pay workers, because they have no money to buy goods, etc., etc.

24.23

Adversity is the state in which a man most easily becomes acquainted with himself, being especially free from admirers then.

—*Samuel Johnson*

Aphorisms

24.24

Business is so bad that even the people who never pay have stopped buying.

24.25

Depressions may bring people closer to the church—but so do funerals.

—*Clarence Darrow*

24.26

"Recessions and depressions don't worry me. I was a failure during the boom," said the businessman.

24.27

I know a fellow who's as broke as the Ten Commandments.

—*John Marquand*

24.28

He is as broke and as frustrated as a pickpocket in a nudist colony.

24.29

He was subject to a kind of disease which at that time they called lack of money.

—*Rabelais*

24.30

Adversity is the only diet that will reduce a fathead.

24.31

By trying we can learn to endure adversity—another man's, I mean.

—*Mark Twain*

24.32

I'll say this for adversity: people seem to be able to stand it, and that's more than I can say for prosperity.

—*Kin Hubbard*

24.33

Sweet are the uses of adversity to the party it doesn't happen to.

24.34

When down in the mouth, remember Jonah: he came out all right.

—*Thomas Alva Edison*

(*See also 22.13, 80.2, 240.13, 234.7*)

MONEY AND MONEY-MAKERS

GIVERS AND TAKERS

25. Borrowers and Lenders

Anecdotes

25.1

A Nebraska newspaper declares the following collection letter produces excellent results: "Dear Sir: A glance at the date of our original invoice will soon prove we've done more for you than even your own mother—we've carried you for twelve months."

25.2

"There is a man outside who wants to see you about a bill you owe," said the secretary to her boss.

"What's he look like?"

"Frankly, Mr. Jones, he looks like you better pay him."

25.3

A man put up a sign outside his store which read QUITTING THE CREDIT BUSINESS UNTIL I GETS MY OUTS IN.

25.4

A sad state of affairs: When you try to pay cash for a purchase, and the clerk looks at you as if to say, "There's a guy whose credit rating must not be any good!"

—*The Rotary Wheel,* Scottsbluff, Nebr.

25.5

The young doctor stood gravely at the bedside, looking down at the sick man, and said to him: "I am sorry to tell you, but you have scarlet fever. This is an extremely contagious disease."

The patient turned to his wife, and said, "My dear, if any of my creditors call, tell them I am at last in a position to give them something."

25.6

"How often," said an annoyed creditor, "must I climb three flights of stairs before you pay this small amount of money you owe me?"

"Do you think I am going to move to the first floor," replied the debtor, "just to make it easier for you to collect from me?"

25.7

When a man came to Nasr-ed-Din, fifteenth-century Turkish sage, for the loan of a rope, the request was refused with the excuse that it was Nasr's only piece and had been used to tie up flour.

"But it is impossible to tie up flour with a rope," protested the borrower.

"I can tie up anything with a rope when I do not wish to lend it," said Nasr-ed-Din.

25.8

When a man wanted to borrow Nasr-ed-Din's ass, Nasr replied that he had already loaned the animal. Thereupon the creature brayed from the stable. "But the ass is there," cried the visitor indignantly. "I hear it."

"What!" cried Nasr-ed-Din. "Would you take the word of an ass instead of mine?"

25.9

Mark Twain was an inveterate book borrower. One day he asked a neighbor for the loan of a certain book. The neighbor said "Yes. But it is my rule that any volume taken from my library must be read on the premises."

Several weeks later the same neighbor wanted to borrow the Twain lawn mower. "Certainly you may use it," said Twain. "But I have made a rule that any lawn mower of mine that is borrowed must be used only on my own lawn."

25.10

Somebody once asked R. B. Sheridan how it was that there was no O attached to his name, since his family was Irish and no doubt was an illustrious one.

"No family," said Sheridan, "has a better right to an O than our family. We owe everybody."

25.11

Two Russian merchants on their way to Minsk were traveling in a carriage and chatting about their social and economic interests. Suddenly a band of armed bandits appeared and ordered them to halt.

"Your money or your life," boomed the leader of the bandits.

"Just a moment please," said one of the merchants. "I owe my friend here 500 rubles, and I would like to pay him first. Yosel," said the debtor, "here is your debt. Remember, we are square now."

25.12

Charles Lamb, meeting an acquaintance, asked for the loan of 5s.; but the friend had only half a crown, which he handed to Lamb.

Some time later, the friend meeting Lamb said, "Ah, by-the-by, you owe me half a crown."

"Not at all," replied Lamb. "You owe me; I asked you for a crown, and you only gave me half. You still owe me the other half."

25.13

"Joe, how about lending me $50?"

"Sorry, I can only let you have $25."

"But why not the entire $50, Joe?"

"No, $25 only; that way it's even—each one of us loses $25."

25.14

A tailor called on James McNeill Whistler, the famous artist, to press for payment of an overdue bill from the customarily delinquent painter. Whistler offered him a glass of champagne. "How can you drink champagne, when you can't pay your bills?" asked the tailor.

"My dear man," replied Whistler, "I assure you that the champagne hasn't been paid for either."

25.15

Wallach borrowed $100 from his friend Barnett, and much to the latter's astonishment the amount was paid back on schedule.

A week later Wallach again needed funds, again borrowed $100, and once more paid it back within a week.

A third time Wallach asked Barnett to lend him $100. This time Barnett said, "Nothing doing. Enough is enough. You've fooled me twice. Three times is too much to expect."

25.16

In asking Dr. Oliver Wendell Holmes for a loan of $10, a woman said to him, "If I don't get the loan I will be ruined."

"Madam," replied the clever doctor, "if a woman can be ruined for $10, then she isn't worth saving."

25.17

Two men who had known each other slightly in Europe met one day in New York. "How are things with you?" asked one of them.

"Pretty fair," said the other. "I've been doing quite well in this country."

"How about lending me $10, then?"

"Why I hardly know you, and you're asking me to lend you $10!"

"I can't understand it," said the prospective borrower. "In the old country people would not lend me money because they knew me, and here I can't get a loan because they don't know me."

25.18

Senator Bourke Hickenlooper tells of the time back in Iowa when his father sent him to the drugstore for 5 cents' worth of asafetida, to be charged to his father.

"What's your father's name?"

"Hickenlooper."

"Here," said the druggist, "take the asafetida for nothing. I'm damned if I'm going to spell asafetida and Hickenlooper both for 5 cents."

25.19

The blacksheep of the family had applied to his wealthy brothers for a loan, which they agreed to grant him at an interest rate of 9 percent.

The ne'er-do-well complained about the interest rate. "What will our poor father say when he looks down from his eternal home and sees two of his sons charging another son 9 percent on a loan?"

"From where he is," said one of the brothers, "it'll look like 6 percent."

25.20

A dentist spotted a deadbeat patient while dining at his country club one evening. He called the patient aside, reminded him that he owed $250 for work done more than two years earlier, and insisted the man pay up. To the dentist's astonishment, the patient pulled a checkbook from his pocket and wrote a check to the dentist for the full amount.

Skeptical about the man's good faith, the dentist went directly to the bank the next morning and presented the check for payment. The teller handed back the check with the explanation that the patient's account was $25 short of the amount of the check. The dentist smiled, went to the customer's desk for a few minutes, came back to the teller, deposited $35 to the account of his former patient, and then again presented the $250 check and walked out with a net gain of $215.

Definitions

25.21

A borrower is one who exchanges hot air for cold cash.

25.22

Credit is like chastity: both of them can stand temptation better than they can suspicion.
—*Josh Billings*

25.23

Pawnbroker: One who lives off the flat of the land.
—*Lionel Shelly*

Aphorisms

25.24

Creditors have better memories than debtors.
—*Benjamin Franklin*

25.25

Here's to our creditors—may they be endowed with the three virtues, Faith, Hope, and Charity.

25.26

Credit is the capital of a younger son.
—*Oscar Wilde*

25.27

It is not only a man's sins but his creditors that will find him out.

25.28

Running into debt doesn't bother me; it's running into my creditors that's upsetting.
—*Gus Edson,* New York Daily News

25.29

A debtor is one who owes another money; a creditor is one who thinks he is going to get back what is owed to him.

25.30

A habit of debt is very injurious to the memory.
—*Austin O'Malley*

25.31

Debt is a trap which a man sets and baits himself, and then deliberately gets into.
—*Josh Billings*

25.32

In the midst of life we are in debt.
—*Ethel Watts Mumford*

25.33

Some people use only half their ingenuity to get into debt, and the other half to avoid paying it.
—*George D. Prentice*

25.34

It is better to give than to lend, and it costs about the same.
—*Sir Philip Gibbs*

25.35

Be careful about lending money to a friend. It may damage his memory.
—*The Gear,* Seymour, Ind.

25.36

The fellow you won't lend money to gets all the sympathy.

25.37

The man who won't loan money isn't going to have many friends—or need them.
—*Wilson Mizner*

25.38

If you would lose a troublesome visitor, lend him money.
—*Benjamin Franklin*

25.39

On a San Francisco Moneylender

Here lies old 35 percent;
The more he made, the more he lent;
The more he got, the more he craved;
The more he made, the more he shaved.
Great God! Can such a soul be saved!

25.40

It was said of one that remembered everything that he lent, but nothing that he borrowed, that "he had lost half of his memory."

25.41

Let us all be happy and live within our means, even if we have to borrer the money to do it with.

—*Artemus Ward*

25.42

The human species is composed of two distinct races: the men who borrow, and the men who lend.

—*Charles Lamb*

25.43

A person who can't pay, gets another person who can't pay, to guarantee that he can pay.

—*Charles Dickens*

25.44

'Tis against some men's principle to pay interest, and seems against others' interest to pay the principal.

—*Benjamin Franklin*

25.45

Nowadays when you lay your cards on the table you can buy practically anything.

—*Changing Times*

25.46

If you want the time to pass quickly, just give your note for ninety days.

—*R. B. Thomas,* Farmer's Almanac, 1897

25.47

Men are able to trust one another, knowing the exact degree of dishonesty they are entitled to expect.

—*Stephen Leacock*

25.48

The quickest way to lose your shirt is to put too much on the cuff.

25.49

When men cease to have faith in each other, they have to start living within their means.

—*Anonymous*

25.50

It saves a lot of trouble if, instead of having to earn money and save it, you can just go and borrow it.

—*Winston Churchill*

25.51

If I owe Smith ten dollars, and God forgives me, that doesn't pay Smith.

—*R. G. Ingersoll*

25.52

As William James said of the boarder: It is much more important for the landlady to know his philosophy than his income.

—*Harry Scherman*

25.53

It takes man to make a devil; and the fittest man for such a purpose is a snarling, waspish, red-hot fiery creditor.

—*Henry Ward Beecher*

(*See also 24.19, 26.23, 26.34, 27.18, 28.1–28.7, 28.9, 28.10, 28.24, 28.25, 31.4, 31.21, 31.35, 32.22, 40.16, 47.1–47.7, 55.2, 94.10, 97.4, 135.50, 136.16, 154.28, 191.30, 193.13, 196.1, 196.4, 196.17–196.19, 198.14, 210.15, 218.11, 240.21, 243.17*)

26. Beggars and Their Benefactors

Anecdotes

26.1

A tramp knocked at a farmer's door and asked for some food. "Are you a Christian?" asked the farmer.

"Why, can't you tell?" asked the beggar. "Look at the knees of my pants. Don't they prove it?" The farmer and his wife noticed the holes in the knees and promptly gave the man some food.

As the tramp turned to go the farmer asked, "By the way, what made those holes in the seat of your pants?"

"Backsliding," said the tramp.

26.2

A tramp with a large and purple-veined nose solicited alms of a housewife. She stared at him accusingly then asked bluntly, "What makes your nose so red?"

"This nose of mine, ma'm," replied the tramp with sudden dignity, "is blushing with pride because it refrains from stickin' itself into other people's business."

26.3

"I'll give you dinner if you'll chop up that pile of wood," said the housewife to the beggar.

"Let's see the menu, first," replied the mendicant.

26.4

"Here, my poor man, is a nickel," said the lady to the beggar. "How did you get into such a miserable state?"

"Lady, I was too much like you are—always givin' big sums to the poor."

26.5

"You ought to be ashamed of yourself, begging for a nickel when you've got two good arms," said the indignant woman to the beggar.

"Do you expect me to cut off an arm for your lousy nickel?" inquired the beggar.

26.6

"Young man," said the nice old lady to the beggar, "I am going to give you a quarter not because you deserve it, but only because it pleases me to do so."

"Thanks," said the mendicant. "But why not make it a dollar so you can really enjoy yourself?"

26.7

"My poor fellow," said the kind old lady, "it must be dreadful to be lame, but just think how much worse it would be if you were blind."

"You're right, lady," agreed the beggar. "When I was blind I was always getting counterfeit money."

26.8

"Would you be willing to donate $2 to improve and beautify your town?" asked an unusually shabby man of a suburban home owner who was manicuring his lawn.

"What's the idea?" asked the suspicious suburbanite.

"Well, for two bucks," grinned the tramp, "I'll move on to the next town."

26.9

The beggar stopped at the tavern named George and the Dragon, but when he asked the landlady for a bit of bread, she was having no part of him. "Get along with ye."

The tramp straggled along the road, stopped, and turned back. "What do you want now?" demanded the landlady.

"I was wonderin'," said the beggar, "if I might have a word with George?"

26.10

A beggar on the street looked enviously at a richly dressed man whom he was asking for help.

"Why," said the rich man, "you have no reason to envy me. I, too, have troubles."

"True," said the beggar, "but I have nothing else but."

26.11

A beggar stopped a man on the street and said, "How about a quarter, pal?"

"Why a quarter? Coffee is only a dime."

"Yeah, but I got a mistress."

26.12

Charles Lamb was stopped by a poor beggar in London on a wet, dreary day. She said, "Please, sir, help me; I've seen better days."

"So have I," said Lamb. "It's a miserable day, even for London." But he gave her a shilling.

26.13

A stout, able-bodied beggar in old New York was noted for his reversible signs. One side read I AM DEAF AND DUMB, and on the other side was I AM PARALYZED. He was a heavy drinker, and when he began to feel his liquor too much he simply turned the sign around.

26.14

It was Christmas time. Shabbily dressed, his face drawn and his eyes dull, he stopped a man and said, "Please, sir, will you not give me some money for my wife and children?"

The stranger, his mind on other things, said not unkindly: "Oh no, my dear man. I would not take advantage of your situation. You keep your wife and children; I do not want them."

26.15

A panhandler asked $100 for a cup of coffee. When asked what was the idea of begging for so large an amount, he said, "Look at these clothes. You can't expect me to go into a restaurant looking like this."

26.16

A man stopped by a beggar on the street said, "I never give money to anyone on the street."

Said the bum, "What do you want me to do? Open an office?"

26.17

"You had better ask for manners than money," said a finely dressed gentleman to a beggar who asked for alms.

"I asked for what I thought you had *the most* of," was the cutting reply.

26.18

Go into the street and give one man a lecture on morality and another a shilling, and see which will respect you the most.

—*Samuel Johnson*

26.19

A wealthy man moved by a beggar's plea gave him a dollar. Later he found the beggar gorging himself on lox and bagel in a nearby restaurant.

"You've got some nerve," he said to the beggar. "Do you think I gave you a dollar for bagel and lox?"

"Look," said the beggar, "I didn't have a dollar and couldn't afford lox and bagel. Now that God has helped me and you've given me a dollar, you complain because I eat bagel and lox. Tell me, wise guy, when can I eat bagel and lox?"

26.20

The clever beggar was broke and hungry, but, undeterred by the circumstances, he went into a restaurant and asked the waitress for two sugar buns. When they were placed before him he looked at them and said he had changed his mind—he would rather have two rolls.

After quickly eating the rolls, the beggar got up to leave, whereupon the waitress came up and said, "Where's the money for your food? You haven't paid for those rolls?"

"What are you talking about, lady? Didn't I give you those two sugar buns for the two rolls—and the price is the same for both."

"Yes, but you didn't pay for the sugar buns."

"Of course I didn't—I didn't eat the sugar buns."

26.21

A bum asks for 20 cents for a cup of coffee.

"But coffee is only 10 cents a cup."

"I know. But I thought you might join me."

26.22

A wandering beggar received so warm a welcome from the town miser that he was astonished and touched.

"Your welcome warms the heart of one who is often rebuffed," said the beggar. "But how did you know that I come from another town?"

"Just the fact that you came to me," said the miser, "proves you are from another town. Here everyone knows better than to call on me."

26.23

A beggar called on a man and gave him a moving story of his troubles. The listener was touched and told the beggar to come back the next day, when he would have some money.

'Impossible. I can't come tomorrow," said the beggar.

"Why not?"

"Sir, I would have you understand that I have already lost too much money by extending credit."

26.24

Two beggars worked as a team, developing a routine that went like this:

They would present themselves to a wealthy man of the town, and one of them would point to his fellow beggar and say with great dignity: "My friend here is descended from saints and scholars, and yet he is destitute."

Upon this the wealthy man would usually give the scion of saints and scholars a generous amount of money.

"A small contribution for my trouble," the other beggar would say.

"Your trouble?"

"Yes, my trouble," replied the beggar. "Didn't I put you into contact with this illustrious man. Didn't I bring him to your house?"

26.25

"What sort of person is he?"

"Well, after a beggar has touched him for a dime, he'll tell you he gave a little dinner to an acquaintance of his."

26.26

A nobleman, extremely rich but a miser, stopped in Ireland to change horses at the town of Athlone. The carriage was surrounded by paupers, imploring alms, but he turned a deaf ear to them and drew up the glass. A ragged old woman, going round to the other side of the carriage, bawled out, in the old peer's hearing, "Please you, my lord, just chuck one tinpenny out of your coach, and I'll answer it will treat all your friends in Athlone."

26.27

A man called on Rothschild, the great banker, and said, "All my life I've been having bad luck, and now I've even lost my job as a musician with the Philharmonic and can't get any work."

"What instrument do you play?" asked the banker.

"The bassoon."

"That's wonderful," said Rothschild enthusiastically. "I love good music, and that is my favorite instrument. In fact I have a bassoon. You must step into the music room here and play something for me."

"It's just as I was saying," wailed the visitor. "Always I have nothing but bad luck. Of all the instruments I might have named, I have to go and say bassoon."

26.28

A professional beggar attempted to see Rothschild but was rebuffed. Thereupon the beggar set up a commotion in the lobby of Rothschild's establishment, shrieking at the top of his voice, "My family is starving and the Baron refuses to see me."

Rothschild, driven to distraction by the commotion, came out. "Very well," he said, "I'm defeated. Here are 10 thalers. If you hadn't made so much noise, you'd have gotten 20."

"Sir," said the beggar, "you are a banker. Do I tell you how to run your bank? I'm a beggar; don't give me begging advice."

26.29

Among the many patrons of the Rothschilds were two brothers who called every month and were given 100 marks each. After a while one of the brothers died, but the remaining brother continued to call on the Rothschilds every month. On his first call after the brother's death, the dispenser of Rothschild's funds gave him his usual 100 marks.

"I should get 200 marks," wailed the beggar. "One hundred for myself and the other hundred for my brother."

"No," said the treasurer. "Your brother is dead. Here is your hundred."

"I refuse to be swindled like this," shouted the beggar. "Am I my brother's heir, or is Rothschild?"

26.30

The Rothschilds' reputation for generosity to oppressed Jews from Poland and Russia was deservedly widespread, and consequently hundreds of paupers made the long trip to Paris and London to beg them for help. One particularly brassy beggar, who received a yearly stipend from Edmund Rothschild told the financier that the annual payment should be increased because the beggar had to marry off his daughter. Rothschild gave the man an extra 500 rubles as a dowry for the daughter but shortly afterward learned that he had been deceived—that the beggar had no daughter since she had died years before.

The next time the beggar called on Rothschild, the banker rebuked him for his deception. The beggar became furious. "True, my daughter is dead and was dead when I mentioned her to you," said the beggar. "But I am her father, and I am certainly entitled to the dowry you gave for her because I am her heir. Are you trying to deprive me of being my own daughter's heir?"

26.31

"You are the prince of beggars," said one of the Rothschilds to Chief Rabbi Adler.

"Rather, I am a beggar of princes," replied the rabbi.

Aphorisms

26.32

The man who first invented the art of supporting beggars made many wretched.

—*Menander*

26.33

He who receives a benefit with gratitude, repays the first instalment on his debt.

—*Seneca*

(*See also 27.1–27.25, 104.2, 165.4, 179.8, 226.9, 226.17, 226.18*)

27. Charity and Contributions

Anecdotes

27.1

A painter in a Connecticut village was asked to contribute to a drive being conducted by the village church. "I'm broke," he explained, "but I'll contribute a $200 picture."

When the drive was completed, the minister explained that it was still $100 short of the goal. "OK," said the artist. "I'll increase the price of my picture to $300."

27.2

A man had asked a Venetian-blind repairman to stop by at his home and pick up a broken blind. The next morning while the family was at breakfast the door bell rang, and the man's wife went to answer. The man at the door said, "I'm here for the Venetian blind." The wife reached for her purse and handed the man a dollar bill. "Another collector," she said to her husband as she resumed her place at the table.

27.3

A collector for a local charity was well primed with information when he called on one of the tougher but well-heeled men of the community. When the prospect looked upon the solicitor with his customary coldness, the caller dispensed with the preliminaries and said, "Our report on your circumstances show that you are now earning in excess of $40,000 a year and that you have made no contributions to local charities."

"Does your financial report also show that my wife, from whom I am separated, is in a mental institution," replied the prospect, "and that my mother is dying of cancer, that my father is paralyzed from a stroke, that one of my brothers is broke and in the last stages of cirrhosis of the liver, that one of my children flunked out of college and is looking for work, that my daughter's husband has been jailed for embezzlement and left her to provide for the four kids? Does your financial report show these things?"

"No, it does not," said the now-embarrassed caller. "In fact, no one in the town knows these things. We would not, of course, have called upon you had we known these distressing circumstances."

"I thought you would understand when it was explained to you," said the supposedly tough but wealthy man. "Since I'm not giving any money to all these people in trouble, you will agree it would be inconsistent for me to contribute to your cause."

27.4

A committee called on John Jacob Astor for a donation to some worthy charity. The old man took the subscription list, looked it over, and wrote out a check for $50. They had expected much more, and one of them ventured to say: "We did hope for more, Mr. Astor. Your son gave us $100."

"Ah," replied the old man, "William has a rich father. Mine was poor."

27.5

The speaker at a fund-raising rally said, "Will all those who wish to contribute $100 please stand up"—then in an aside to the band leader he said, "Quick, play 'The Star Spangled Banner'!"

27.6

Harry Lauder, according to one of the many legends about him, was stopped one day by a collector for a charity and urged to "give till it hurts." Lauder shook his head and said, "Why the verra idea hurts."

27.7

A bear, noticing a sleeping hermit annoyed by a fly, hurled a stone at it, but the stone hit the hermit, a friend of the bear. The bear's intentions were altruistic, but the consequences of the altruism for the hermit were not good.

27.8

A prosperous Wall Street man one day met an old college chum and immediately saw that his friend looked both worried and down-at-the-heels. "Apparently you're not doing too well, George. Can I help you?"

"Yes," said the friend. "My family and I are in considerable difficulty. I need money."

So the prosperous man gave his friend $100 and told him to call him again if he needed help. Six months later the unfortunate fellow again needed some assistance, and the Wall Streeter this time gave him $200. And several months later the same thing happened again, and again later on.

Finally, poor George accosted his wealthy benfactor with another tale of woe, but this time was given only $50, whereupon he said, "It looks as though you're up against it, too. You've never given me anything so small as $50 before."

"Yes," replied the well-heeled fellow, "I've cut down a bit here and there. My children are reaching school age and that is costing me more money."

"Oh, I see," said sponging George. "You're educating your children at the expense of my children."

27.9

Much of the small town had been swept by a disastrous fire, and the victims drew heavily upon the communal funds to rehabilitate themselves. But when one man showed up for aid they questioned him, because his house was untouched by the flames.

"What kind of a fraud are you trying to pull on us?" they asked him. "How did you suffer from the fire?"

"Did I suffer?" he replied. "I tell you that fire nearly scared me to death."

Definitions

27.10

A philanthropist is one who gives away what he should give back.

27.11

Philanthropy is the refuge of people who wish to annoy their fellow-creatures.

—*Oscar Wilde*

27.12

Charity: A thing that begins at home, and usually stays there.

—*Elbert Hubbard*

27.13

Gratitude is merely a secret hope of greater favors.

—*La Rochefoucauld*

Aphorisms

27.14

He is one of those wise philanthropists who, in a time of famine, would vote for nothing but a supply of toothpicks.

—*Douglas Jerrold*

27.15

To enjoy a good reputation, give publicly and steal privately.

—*Josh Billings*

27.16

Not only is it more blessed to give than to receive—it is also deductible.

27.17

It may be more blessed to give than to receive, but it is also more expensive.

27.18

Organized charity, scrimped and iced,
In the name of a cautious, statistical Christ.

—*John Boyle O'Reilly*

27.19

Benevolence is a natural instinct of the human mind; when A sees B in distress, his conscience always urges him to entreat C to help him.

—*Sydney Smith*

27.20

It is not so dangerous to do evil to the generality of men as to do them much good.

—*La Rochefoucauld*

27.21

When a man has nothing in the world to lose, he is then in the best condition to sacrifice for the public good everything that is his.

27.22

If you pick up a starving dog and make him prosperous, he will not bite you; that is the principal difference between a dog and a man.

—*Mark Twain*

Parasite: *27.23*

Great fleas have little fleas upon their backs to bite 'em,
And little fleas have lesser fleas, and so on ad infinitum.

—*Jonathan Swift*

And the great fleas themselves in turn have greater fleas to grow on,
While these again have greater still and greater still and so on.

—*Augustus De Morgan*

27.24

If you help a man who is in trouble, he'll never forget you—especially the next time he gets into trouble.

27.25

I owe much, I have nothing, I give the rest to the poor.

—Last will of *Rabelais*

(*See also 26.1–26.33, 30.36, 30.43, 72.5, 239.1–239.22, 243.18, 243.20, 265.2, 267.2, 272.15*)

THE HAVES AND HAVE-NOTS

28. Bankers and Depositors

Anecdotes

28.1

"You're in a bad state," warned the doctor when the banker came in for a checkup. "Your nerves are shot, you have an ulcer, your heart is palpitating too much, and your blood pressure is too high. Give up banking, get out in the air, and if you must work do something that won't get you too involved in other people's affairs."

So the banker bought out a service station and worked at it. One of his first customers was a stranger who asked for 10 gallons of gas. The banker started to fill the tank and while doing so asked, "Where you heading for?"

"I'm going down to Atlanta and back."

The banker stopped pumping the gas and said, "You can do that on 6 gallons; why not get along on that?"

28.2

The banker summoned to his office the owner of a large local cannery. "About that loan of $50,000," began the banker.

The cannery owner raised a hand and said, "Mr. Banker, what do you know about the cannery business?"

"Nothing at all," said the banker.

"Well, you'd better learn fast because you're in it!"

28.3

A man protested vigorously when the banker curtly refused to extend him a loan, so vigorously, in fact, that the banker became nettled and said, "I'll tell you what I'll do. Few people know that I have a glass eye. It's a perfect piece of work. If you can tell me which eye is the glass one, I'll reconsider my rejection of your loan application."

The customer looked at the banker and promptly said, "Your left eye is glass."

The banker was surprised and asked the customer how he could tell.

"Easy," said the customer. "The glass eye has a touch of human warmth in it."

28.4

A businessman asked his banker for a loan of $50,000. "That's a great deal of money," said the banker. "I will have to have a statement from you."

"Well, sir," said the applicant, "you may quote me as saying that I am very optimistic."

28.5

A banker, newly arrived in Texas and unfamiliar with cattlemen and their problems, pressed a cattleman to pay up a loan. He was indifferent to the borrower's explanation that his cattle were in bad shape and would draw no bids, but that they would be fattened up by the fall and then would be sold.

The banker wrote the cattleman: "Unless I receive payment of the loan by return mail, I will institute suit and take judgment against you for the full amount."

By return mail the banker received this answer: "If you ain't better prepared to meet your Maker than I am to pay this loan, you shore are going to hell."

28.6

The shrewdest and wealthiest man in town asked the bank for a loan of $10 at 5 percent, for which he would put up $50,000 in government bonds as security.

The banker thought it was strange but decided not to argue with so rich and eccentric a customer, although he did say that no security was required. The rich man insisted upon posting the $50,000 in bonds as security.

At the end of the year, when the $10 loan and interest were paid off, the bonds were returned. "The whole transaction still seems an odd one to me," said the banker.

"Tell me," asked the rich man, "is there any other way I could have had those bonds put into a safe-deposit box for a mere 50 cents?"

28.7

Marc Connelly tells about a time when Robert Benchley applied to his bank for a loan and to his surprise was granted it immediately. However, the next day he went to the bank and withdrew all the money he had on deposit there. He explained that he did not trust a bank that would lend money to such a poor risk.

28.8

One banker, with a predominantly socialite clientele, has a delicate way of informing depositors they are overdrawn. He writes them in this manner: "As of August 1 may we inform you, you are no longer banking with us; we are banking with you."

28.9

The banker looked carefully over the files in front of him, then at the mild-mannered man sitting opposite. "I must say," said the banker, "that your affairs are in a helluva mess. Your accounts are overdrawn, your personal-loan payments are well behind schedule, your credit rating has dropped, and it says here that your wife is a big spender. Why don't you get after her and insist that she cut down on her spending?"

"Perhaps I should," replied the applicant for more credit. "But to tell you the truth, I'd much rather argue with you than with her."

28.10

When Chicago newspaper-owner Herman H. Kohlsaat was gravely ill, his wife burst into tears and said, "Oh, Herman, what would I do if anything happened to you?" Kohlsaat, who had his financial difficulties, said, "For pallbearers you could get six bankers. They have carried me all my life."

28.11

An old banker in a small pioneer Western town was being interviewed. He was asked, "How did you get started in banking?"

"It was simple. I put out a sign reading BANK. A man came in and gave me $100. Another came in and deposited $200. By this time my confidence was such that I put in $50 of my own money."

28.12

A young man, asked his father's occupation, said, "He cleans out the bank."

"Janitor or president?" was the next question.

28.13

A janitor in a bank was mopping up the floor one night when the phone rang. He picked up the receiver and said, "Hello." The voice on the other phone said, "Tell me, please, what the Federal Reserve discount rate is, the rate of prime paper, and to what extent foreign travel upsets our balance of payments."

"Mister," said the janitor, "When I said 'Hello' I was telling you all I know about the banking business."

—*The Rotarian,* September, 1963

28.14

A big-city banker was visiting a farm. "I suppose," he said, nodding toward a figure at work in the farmyard, "that is the hired man?"

"No, that is the first vice-president in charge of manure."

28.15

Once each month the old farmer went into town to cash his Social Security check, a veteran's pension check, and a service disability check—all adding up to a neat sum. After this had gone on for several years, the bank president asked the farmer why he didn't put some of the money either in a savings account or on deposit.

The farmer looked at the banker critically and said, "Nope, I don't believe I will. Every time I come in here you're all dressed up in collar and tie and new suit. I allus think you're gettin' ready to go off on a long trip."

28.16

A stranger in New York asked a young man the direction to the Chase National Bank. "I'll take you there for a dollar," replied the young fellow, sensing his questioner was both wealthy and in a hurry.

When the stranger found that his guide had walked all of two blocks for $1 he paid it but said, "That was an easy dollar for you."

"Yes," said the young man, "but you must remember that bank directors get big fees."

28.17

A young fellow just out of college applied to a bank for a job. Asked what kind of work he had in mind, he said something in the executive line. "But we already have twelve vice-presidents."

"Oh, that's all right," said the collegian, "I'm not superstitious."

28.18

A woman who wanted to arrange for the disposal of a $1,000 bond phoned her bank. The clerk asked, "Madam, is the bond for redemption or conversion?"

After a long pause, the woman said, "Well, am I talking to the First National Bank or the First Baptist Church?"

28.19

"Young man, I want to know how much money my husband drew out of his account yesterday," demanded the woman of the teller in a bank.

"I cannot give you that information," said the teller firmly.

"But aren't you the paying teller?" asked the woman.

"Yes, that is correct," replied the young man. "But I'm not the telling teller."

28.20

"Who is he?" said a passerby to a policeman who was trying to pull up a drunk who had fallen into a gutter.

"Can't say, sir," replied the policeman; "he can't give an account of himself."

"Of course not," replied the other. "How are you to expect an account from a man who has lost his balance."

28.21

A Salt Lake City merchant got a customer's check back from the bank stamped NO ACCOUNT. He looked at the signature and noticed it read "U. R. Stung."

28.22

Tristan Bernard, Parisian playwright and *boulevardier,* went to the Banque of France and withdrew his entire account to settle up mounting debts. As Bernard walked out of the bank with his bundle of cash, he turned to the armed guard at the door and said "Thank you, my friend. You may go home now."

Definitions

28.23

Banker: A pawnbroker with a manicure.

—*Jackson Parks*

28.24

A banker is a fellow who lends you his umbrella when the sun is shining and wants it back the minute it begins to rain.

—*Mark Twain*

28.25

A bank is an institution where you can borrow money if you present sufficient evidence to show that you don't need it.

28.26

A financier is a pawnbroker with imagination.

—*Arthur Wing Pinero*

28.27

Finance: The art of passing money from one hand to another until it finally disappears.

(*See also 31.4, 38.13, 88.3, 100.3–100.5, 135.8, 148.8, 179.12, 181.10, 182.1, 194.6, 210.10, 215.4, 217.13, 218.11, 221.9, 243.17*)

29. Solvency and Bankruptcy

Anecdotes

29.1

"For heaven's sake, stop your perpetual worrying," said one businessman to his distraught friend. "Do as I have done—consolidate all worries into three: creditors, business deficits, and simple insolvency."

29.2

"It's strange and interesting to recall how one's ambitions change as one grows older," observed the middle-aged man.

"That's right," said the other man. "When I was young I was determined to become rich."

"But I don't suppose you ever made it?"

"No. By the time I reached thirty, circumstances persuaded me it was easier to change my ambition than it was to make a million dollars. Once I wanted to be a big-league pitcher, then a top comedian—anything for fame. Now I'm glad to settle for solvency and an old-age pension."

29.3

Tristan Bernard, Parisian playwright and *boulevardier,* when told that he was in danger of going bankrupt and would have to practice rigid economy, replied, "Oh, no! I have enough annoyances already without taking on privations!"

Definitions

29.4

Solvent: When you don't bother to smooth down your hair before entering your bank.

29.5

Bankruptcy is a legal proceeding in which you put your money in your pants pocket and give your coat to your creditors.

Aphorisms

29.6

When a man sits down to wait for his ship to come in, it usually turns out to be a receivership.

—*Jacob M. Brande*

29.7

Sign on a bankrupt store: OPENED BY MISTAKE.

29.8

A receiver is appointed by the court to take what's left.

29.9

When you are at the end of your rope, it's a good idea to keep your feet on the ground.

—*D. O. Flynn*

29.10

He is so unlucky that he runs into accidents which started out to happen to somebody else.

—*Don Marquis*

29.11

I never knew any man in my life who could not bear another's misfortune perfectly like a Christian.

—*Jonathan Swift*

(*See also 19.58, 28.2, 28.9, 37.28*)

30. Rich and Poor

Anecdotes

30.1

The millionaire was tired, weary, bored. He called for his Lincoln Continental limousine, got in, and said to the chauffeur: "James, drive full speed over the cliff. I've decided to commit suicide."

30.2

A millionaire is a man who leaves his air-conditioned home, enters his air-conditioned car to be driven to his air-conditioned office, where he works until he leaves for lunch in an air-conditioned restaurant, and then at the end of the day rides in his air-conditioned car to his air-conditioned club, where he goes into the steam room for an hour to sweat.

30.3

When Rubenstein, the famous millionaire, came to a small town in the Ukraine, the people poured out to greet him. He was led by the town officials with all ceremony to the local inn, where he ordered two eggs for breakfast. When he was finished, the inn's proprietor said the charge was 20 rubles.

Rubenstein was both astonished and angered. "Never" said he, "have I been charged so much for two eggs. Are eggs such a rarity around here?"

"No," said the innkeeper, "but millionaires are."

30.4

Early in his career William Jennings Bryan told an interviewer that no man could make a million dollars honestly. Years later, the same reporter, now a well-known editor, again met Bryan, who had by then acquired a substantial fortune, and asked him if he remembered what he had once said about rich men. "Of course I do," said Bryan. "I said a man simply can't make 2 million dollars honestly."

30.5

In the course of an interview with a journalist of advanced economic views who had been critical of him, Andrew Carnegie rebuked his interviewer for his "equal distribution of wealth" theories. The journalist replied with vigor, reminding Carnegie of his own hoarded millions in the midst of great poverty and suffering. The Scotch steel magnate listened for a few minutes and then asked his secretary to bring from the file a statement of the Carnegie total wealth. The millionaire showed the statement to the journalist, did some quick figuring on a scratch pad, reached into his pocket and handed the interviewer 13 cents: "Here, sir, is your share of my wealth."

30.6

"I'm glad to find that your great wealth hasn't changed you," said an old friend to another, after an absence of many years.

"But the wealth has made some changes in me," laughed the wealthy one. "Whereas I used to be considered impolite, now I'm just eccentric, and whereas I used to be thought rude, now they say I'm witty."

30.7

The son stood quietly at the bedside of his dying and wealthy father. "Please, my boy," whispered the old man, "always remember that wealth does not bring happiness."

"Yes, Father," said the son, "I realize that. But at least it will allow me to choose the kind of misery I find most agreeable."

Definitions

30.8

Rich Man: One who isn't afraid to ask the clerk to show him something cheaper.

—*Ladies' Home Journal*

30.9

Distress: A disease incurred by exposure to the prosperity of a friend.

—*Ambrose Bierce*

Aphorisms

30.10

Wealth won't make a man virtuous, but there ain't anybody who wants to be poor just for the purpose of being good.

—*Josh Billings*

30.11

A man once said that his greatest ambition was to get his indigent friends rich, so that he could drop them.

—*Kyle Crichton,* Total Recoil

30.12

If Heaven had looked upon riches to be a valuable thing, it would not have given them to such a scoundrel.

—*Jonathan Swift*

30.13

Many speak the truth when they say that they despise riches, but they mean the riches possessed by other men.

—*Charles Caleb Colton*

30.14

If your riches are yours, why don't you take them with you to the other world?

—*Benjamin Franklin*

30.15

Rich men without convictions are more dangerous in modern society than poor women without chastity.

—*George Bernard Shaw*

30.16

When a man tells you he got rich through hard work, ask him: "Whose?"

—*Don Marquis*

30.17

It must be great to be rich and let the other fellow keep up appearances.

—*Kin Hubbard*

30.18

Many a man would have been worse if his estate had been better.

—*Benjamin Franklin*

30.19

Some people think they are worth a lot of money because they have it.

30.20

Fortune is painted blind that she may not blush to behold the fools who belong to her.

30.21

When Fortune smiles she never shows her teeth.

30.22

Greater qualities are necessary to bear good fortune than bad.

—*La Rochefoucauld*

30.23

Here's to Miss Fortune—may we always miss her.
Here's to Dame Fortune—may we meet and kiss her.

—*J. E. McCann*

30.24

The prosperous man is never sure that he is loved for himself.

30.25

Everything in the world may be endured except continual prosperity.

—*J. W. Goethe*

30.26

When you go up the hill of Prosperity
May you never meet any friend coming down.

30.27

It requires a strong constitution to withstand repeated attacks of prosperity.

—*J. L. Basford*

30.28

Everything that guy touches turns to gold. Everything I touch they make me put back.

30.29

There are few sorrows, however poignant, in which a good income is of no avail.

—*Logan Pearsall Smith*

30.30

If you want to find out a man's income, ask him what incomes should be exempt from taxation.

30.31

There is only one class in the community that thinks more about money than the rich, and that is the poor.

—*Oscar Wilde*

30.32

The poor are the only consistent altruists; they sell all that they have and give to the rich.

—*Holbrook Jackson*

30.33

The poor are rightfully the property of the rich, because the rich made them.

30.34

The real tragedy of the poor is that they can afford nothing but self-denial.

—*Oscar Wilde*

30.35

The poor ye have with ye always—but they are not invited.

—*Addison Mizner*

30.36

Remember the poor— it costs nothing.

—*Josh Billings*

30.37

Another nice thing about being poor; your kids in old age don't break your heart by asking a court to declare you incompetent.

—*C. T. Crawford, Jr.*

30.38

Poverty is so loyal that it sticks with a fellow even when all his friends desert him.

30.39

Poverty is no disgrace to a man, but it is confoundedly inconvenient.

—*Sydney Smith*

30.40

The most inconvenient feature about poverty is that one is apt to get used to it.

30.41

Here's to poverty, that makes us so hard up we can afford but few of the things we'd be better off without.

—*Anonymous*

30.42

He is so seedy that he trembles every time he passes a canary.

—*Evan Esar*

30.43

The middle class are people not poor enough to qualify for charity and not wealthy enough to make any donations.

30.44

A man's soul may be buried under a pile of money.

—*Nathaniel Hawthorne*

30.45

It is not the man who has too little, but the man who craves more, that is poor.

—*Seneca*

30.46

Prosperity makes friends, adversity tries them.

—*Publius*

30.47

Under the influence either of poverty or of wealth, workmen and their work are equally liable to degenerate.

—*Plato*

30.48

Wealth is the parent of luxury and indolence, and poverty of meanness and viciousness, and both of discontent.

—*Plato*

30.49

Poverty is the parent of revolution and crime.

—*Aristotle*

30.50

A prosperous fool is a grievous burden.

—*Aeschylus*

30.51

The covetous man is ever in want.

—*Horace*

30.52

Honesty is the rarest wealth anyone can possess, and yet all the honesty in the world ain't lawful tender for a loaf of bread.

—*Josh Billings*

30.53

If the poor cannot always get meat, the rich man cannot always digest it.

—*Henry Giles*

(*See also 12.4, 19.2–19.5, 23.12, 26.1–26.33, 29.2, 31.17, 31.19, 31.30, 31.43, 31.44, 32.1, 32.5, 32.12, 32.15, 32.28, 35.13, 54.23, 55.9, 61.3, 67.1, 67.21, 102.17, 134.14, 135.13, 135.22, 148.4, 151.1–151.4, 154.48, 154.49, 159.6, 165.8, 165.9, 170.19, 174.18, 177.1–177.14, 177.19, 177.24, 177.26, 179.1–179.16, 181.7, 181.9, 181.10, 181.15, 186.18, 190.10, 191.1, 192.8, 193.19, 194.4, 196.3, 207.35, 210.4, 210.23, 210.29, 211.3, 215.3–215.5, 215.8, 218.20, 219.10, 224.4, 235.30, 235.32, 237.8, 243.12, 265.8, 269.20, 272.15, 273.3, 273.4*)

31. Talk about Money

Anecdotes

31.1

"I've been in this racket six months and have yet to meet a millionaire," lamented the chorus girl.

"What's the point of looking only for millionaires?" asked a friend. "You can't buy happiness with money."

"True," replied the chorine. "But money can put some fun into misery."

31.2

"My friends," said the noted comic jurist, "money is not all. It is not money that will mend broken hearts or reassemble the fragments of a dream. Money cannot brighten the hearth nor repair the portals of a shattered home." He paused and then added, "I refer, of course, to Confederate money."

31.3

"The only difference money makes," said the old-timer, "is that it gives you a chance to gossip on the front porch, instead of over the back fence."

31.4

Two not very expert men were arguing the financial condition of the nation. One man asserted there was a money shortage. The other fellow scoffed at this statement. "There's no shortage of money. Go to the bank and ask them to show you all the money they have stored away in vaults—money by the millions, and in every bank, too. But ask them to lend you some of it, and they ask you what collateral you have. Now that's where the trouble is: collateral. There's plenty of money, but there's a serious shortage of collateral."

31.5

A Senator has made public the rule by which he can tell whether a man is a monetary expert:

"If he talks about money and makes you listen, and when he is through you ask yourself, What is he talking about?, then you know that man understands the money situation."

31.6

If a man runs after money, he's money mad; if he keeps it he's a capitalist; if he spends it, he's a playboy; if he doesn't get it, he's a ne'er-do-well; if he doesn't try to get it, he lacks ambition. If he gets it without working, he's a parasite; and if he accumulates it after a lifetime of hard work, people call him a fool who never got anything out of life.

—*Vic Oliver,* Daily Sketch

31.7

"The principal export of the United States is money," wrote the clever young boy in reply to an examination question.

31.8

One of the old philosophers said, "If you will give me Aristotle's system of logic, I will force my enemy to a conclusion; give me the syllogism, and that is all I ask."

Another philosopher replied, "If you will give me the Socratic system of interrogatory, I will run my adversary into a corner."

A third philosopher standing by said "My brethren, if you will give me a little ready cash, I will always gain my point. I will always drive my adversary to a conclusion, because a little ready cash is a wonderful clearer of the intellect."

Definitions

31.9

Money: A blessing that is of no advantage to us excepting when we part with it.

—*Ambrose Bierce*

31.10

Gold: A metal men dig out of holes for dentists and governments to put back in.

—*Wall Street Journal*

Aphorisms

31.11

Money isn't everything, and don't let anyone tell you different. There are other things, such as stocks, bonds, letters of credit, traveler's checks, checks, drafts.

31.12

Money isn't everything—sometimes it isn't even enough.

31.13

While money isn't everything, it does keep you in touch with your children.

—*Changing Times,* the Kiplinger Magazine

31.14

A fool and his money can go places.

31.15

Money brings everything to you, even your daughters.

—*Honoré de Balzac*

31.16

When a fellow says, "It ain't the money but the principle of the thing," it's the money.

—*Kin Hubbard*

31.17

Money doesn't always bring happiness. A man with 10 million dollars isn't any happier than a man with 9 million dollars.

31.18

There are better things than money in this life, but it takes money to buy them.

31.19

When a man says money can't do anything, that settles it: he hasn't any.

—*E. W. Howe*

31.20

When I was young I used to think that money was the most important thing in life; now that I am old, I know it is.

—*Oscar Wilde*

31.21

If you would know the value of money, go and try to borrow some.

—*Benjamin Franklin*

31.22

Money is called jack because it lifts a load off a fellow's back.

31.23

Money is tender when you have it, and tough when you haven't.

31.24

Money can't buy love, but it can put you in a strong bargaining position.

31.25

No man will take counsel, but every man will take money; therefore, money is better than counsel.

—*Jonathan Swift*

31.26

I don't like money actually, but it quiets my nerves.

—*Joe Louis*

31.27

Money never made a fool of anybody; it only shows 'em up.

—*Kin Hubbard*

31.28

There was a time when a fool and his money were soon parted. Now it happens to everybody.

—*The Rotary Blade,* Bladensburg, Md.

31.29

We know that a fool and his money are very soon parted, but what would be interesting to learn is how they ever got together in the first place.

31.30

A fool and his money are soon invited places.

31.31

A fool with money to burn soon meets his match.

31.32

A young man may have more money than brains—but not for long!

31.33

The safest way to double your money is to fold it over once and put it in your pocket.

—*Kin Hubbard*

31.34

Men get their pictures on money but women get their hands on it.

—*Ruth Sherrill*

31.35

No man's credit is as good as his money.

—*E. W. Howe*

31.36

When it is a question of money, everybody is of the same religion.

—*Voltaire*

31.37

His money is twice tainted: 'taint yours and 'taint mine.

—*Mark Twain*

31.38

There is nothing so comfortable as a small bankroll—a big one is always in danger.

—*Wilson Mizner*

31.39

It's called cold cash because we don't keep it long enough to get it warm.

—*Louis Wolfson*

31.40

A dime is a dollar after the taxes have been taken out.

31.41

One reason you can't take it with you is that it goes before you do.

31.42

There has been much argument in recent years about a fitting motto for the coin of the realm. We suggest "Abide with Me."

31.43

If you want to know what God thinks of money, look at the people he gives it to.

31.44

He that is without money might as well be buried in rice with his mouth sewed up.

—*Chinese Proverb*

31.45

How little you know the age you live in if you fancy that honey is sweeter than cash in hand.

—*Ovid*

31.46

Money alone sets the world in motion.

—*Publius*

(*See also 8.11, 8.12, 11.1, 13.6, 16.13, 17.2, 17.8, 19.2, 19.3, 19.19, 19.20, 22.5, 24.16, 24.19, 24.22, 24.29, 25.1–25.53, 26.4–26.8, 26.11, 26.12, 26.19, 26.21, 26.23–26.25, 26.28–26.30, 26.32, 27.1–27.5, 27.8, 27.10, 27.15–27.18, 28.1–28.11, 28.19, 28.22, 28.25, 28.27, 29.2, 29.5, 30.3–30.7, 30.10–30.14, 30.19, 30.28–30.31, 30.44, 30.45, 30.47, 30.48, 32.2, 32.5, 32.7, 32.11, 32.13, 32.14, 32.19, 32.20, 32.22, 32.24, 32.27, 33.5, 33.8, 33.12, 33.14, 33.15, 34.2, 34.10, 34.13, 35.6–35.8, 35.15, 35.25, 37.22, 79.31, 82.5, 129.5, 159.20, 162.26, 162.31, 162.45, 163.23, 165.5–165.8, 165.79, 165.80, 165.100, 166.9, 170.18–170.22, 174.18, 177.19, 181.7, 195.6, 196.20, 211.33, 239.1–239.22, 269.201, 271.32, 275.2*)

32. Thrift and Spendthrift

Anecdotes

32.1

A mean-tempered, nasty old tightwad of considerable wealth wasn't loved by his relatives. One particular nephew made no effort to disguise his dislike. In fact he was awaiting the day the old guy would be dead and he would inherit a substantial part of the fortune.

One day a member of the family approached the old man and said the young nephew was getting married and wouldn't the old buzzard give the fellow something on such an occasion to make him happy.

"Tell you what," said the old miser, "I'll pretend to be dangerously ill."

32.2

A child's comment on piggy banks: They teach children to become misers, and parents to become bank robbers.

—*Wall Street Journal*

32.3

The covetous man never has money; the prodigal will have none shortly.

—*Ben Jonson*

32.4

Skinflint's wife was going to a shower for a bride, so he suggested she bring the soap.

32.5

A reporter called on a rich man to learn how

he became so wealthy. "It's a long story," said the rich man. "While I'm telling, I'll save the candle." He thereupon blew out the candle.

"You need not go on," said the reporter. "I understand."

32.6

A spendthrift, who had wasted nearly all his patrimony, seeing an acquaintance in a coat not of the newest cut, told him that he thought it had been his great-grandfather's coat. "So it was," said the gentleman, "and I have also my great-grandfather's *lands*, which is more than you can say."

32.7

When a sailor was asked what happened to his money he said, "Part went for liquor, part for women, and the rest of it I spent foolishly."

32.8

The little old lady who was a string collector had one box of string marked: "Too short to be of use."

Definitions

32.9

Thrift: A moss-grown obsession of those primitive men whose only accomplishment was to create the United States of America.

32.10

Economy is going without something you do want, in case you should someday want something which you probably won't want.

—*Anthony Hope*

32.11

Economy: The art of spending money without getting any fun out of it.

32.12

Economy: The wealth of the poor and the wisdom of the rich.

—*Alexandre Dumas*

32.13

Savings: Money that sleeps while you work.

Aphorisms

32.14

In the old days, the man who saved money was a miser; nowadays he's a wonder.

—*Sunshine Magazine*

32.15

To recommend thrift to the poor is both grotesque and insulting. It is advising a man who is starving to eat less.

—*Oscar Wilde*

32.16

Thrift is a wonderful virtue—especially in ancestors.

—*The Sign*

32.17

There is no economy in going to bed to save candles if the result is twins.

32.18

In this free-spending age, the man who preaches economy might as well start by saving his breath.

32.19

If you hide your money in the mattress, you'll have something to fall back on.

32.20

Any young man with good health and a poor appetite can save up money.

—*James Montgomery Baily*

32.21

Life is a matter of ups and downs—keeping appearances up and expenses down.

32.22

He who really wants to save should begin with his mouth.

—*Danish Proverb*

32.23

An income is something you can't live within or without.

32.24

When your outgo exceeds your income, your upkeep is your downfall.

32.25

I'm living so far beyond my income that we may almost be said to be living apart.

—*Hector Hugh Munro*

32.26

All progress is based upon a universal, innate desire on the part of every organism to live beyond its income.

—*Samuel Butler*

32.27

Some folks get credit for having horse sense that hain't ever had enough money to make fools of themselves.

—*Kin Hubbard*

32.28

Extravagance is the luxury of the poor, penury the luxury of the rich.

—*Oscar Wilde*

32.29

The miser and the glutton are two facetious

buzzards: one hides his store and the other stores his hide.

—*Josh Billings*

(*See also* 28.6, 31.33, 46.4, 149.31, 190.7, 190.12, 191.3, 205.16, 265.2, 267.2, 273.3)

33. Inflation and Deflation

Anecdotes

33.1

A man, complaining to his congressman, said, "We have got to put an end to inflation. And we have got to stop deflation."

Puzzled, the congressman asked what it was that he wanted done.

"Well, I think we just ought to have some simple, old-fashioned flation."

33.2

The author of a famous book on economics received a phone call from a stranger, who questioned the author's statistics on the high cost of living. "My wife and I," said the voice over the phone, "eat everything we desire, and it costs exactly 49 cents per week."

"Forty-nine cents a week!" exclaimed the economist. "It's unbelievable. Tell me how you do that, please, and to be sure I understand you correctly, won't you talk a little louder?"

"I can't speak louder," said the voice from the other end. "I'm a goldfish."

33.3

For weeks the executive dropped a dime in the box of the pencil peddler outside of the building every time he passed him. But the executive never took a pencil—just dropped a dime in the box because he felt sorry for the fellow who was up against it. One day when he dropped the usual dime in the box, the peddler said, "I beg your pardon, sir, but as you know prices are going up. My pencils now are 15 cents."

Definitions

33.4

Inflation: When you never had it so good or parted with it so fast.

—*Max Hess*

33.5

Inflation is a condition where nobody has enough money because everybody has so much.

33.6

Cost-of-living Index: A list of numbers which prove that high prices are not expensive.

—*Richard M. Weiss*

33.7

Prices: Materials, wages, taxes, profits added up and divided by customers.

33.8

A dollar is something that can never fall so low as the means people adopt to get it.

—*Bill Nye*

Aphorisms

33.9

A little inflation is like a little bit of pregnancy. It keeps on growing.

33.10

The cost of living is the difference between your net income and your gross habits.

33.11

The worst thing about history is that every time it repeats itself the price goes up.

—*Pillar*

33.12

What this country needs is a good five-cent nickel.

—*Franklin Pierce Adams*

33.13

The reason it is so difficult to make both ends meet is that just when you are about to do so some fools come along and move the ends.

33.14

Be sure to save your money; you never know when it might be worth something again.

33.15

Among the things money can't buy are the things it used to.

34. Budgets and Bills

Anecdotes

34.1

A husband going over the household bills looked up and said to his wife, "In case you don't realize it, my dear, you will not have to worry any longer about keeping up with the Joneses; we've now passed them."

34.2

"I can't make ends meet," complained Jinks.

"How do you spend your income?" asked Jenks.

"It breaks down like this," said Jinks: "About 40 percent for food, 30 percent for shelter, 20 percent for clothing, 10 percent for liquor, and 20 percent for amusement and miscellaneous."

"But that adds up to 120 percent," observed Jenks.

"That's just it," said Jinks.

Definitions

34.3

A budget is an orderly system of living beyond your means.

34.4

Budget: A schedule for going into debt systematically.

34.5

A budget is an attempt to live below your yearnings.

34.6

Budget: A method of worrying before you spend, as well as afterward.

—*Papyrus*

34.7

Deficit as defined by a small boy: "That's what you've got when you haven't as much as if you had just nothing."

34.8

Deficit: The amount you didn't expect to lose.

Aphorisms

34.9

Many of our ambitions are nipped in the budget.

34.10

Yes, there are bigger things in life than money—bills, for instance.

—*Rotary Realist,* LaSalle, Ill.

34.11

The trouble with the average family is it has too much month left over at the end of the money.

—*Bill Vaughan*

34.12

Estimates ought to include an estimate of how much more it will cost than the estimate.

34.13

Research shows that tall men are just as short at the end of a month as anybody else.

(*See also 31.22, 31.34, 31.41, 32.21–32.26, 32.28, 33.2, 33.6, 33.10, 33.11, 33.13, 33.15*)

35. Bulls and Bears

Anecdotes

35.1

The elderly stockbroker denied that he was trying to corner the market.

"I'm having enough trouble," he added, "trying to corner my beautiful secretary."

35.2

The boss said to his secretary, "Miss Jones, please get my broker on the phone."

"Yes, sir. Which one, stock or pawn?"

35.3

A prosperous young Wall Street broker met, fell in love with, and was frequently seen about town escorting a rising actress of gentility and dignity. He wanted to marry her, but being a cautious man he decided that before proposing matrimony, he should have a private investigating agency check her background and present activities. After all, he reminded himself, he had both a growing fortune and a Wall Street reputation to protect.

The Wall Streeter requested that under no circumstances was the agency to reveal to the investigator the identity of the client requesting a report on the actress.

In due time the investigator's report was sent to the broker. It said the actress had an unblemished past, a spotless reputation, friends and associates of the best repute. "The only shadow," added the report, "is that currently she is often seen around town in the company of a young broker of dubious business principles and practices."

35.4

A shady stockbroker persuaded a sucker to buy 5,000 shares of a phony uranium stock and a week later phoned his victim, "You're lucky! The stock doubled in price."

"Buy me another 5,000 shares," said the customer.

Several days later the broker phoned again and said the stock had just hit $3 per share.

"That's high enough for me," said the customer. "Sell all I've got."

"Sell?" asked the broker. "Sell to whom?"

35.5

"Don't you think I've got a chance of making a fortune out of these uranium stocks I have purchased?" asked a man of his Wall Street friend.

"Out of it, yes," replied the Wall Streeter. "But in it, no."

35.6

A charming rascal swindled a woman of $5,000 for stock in a mythical uranium mine and, of course, skipped. When the woman complained to the Better Business Bureau they scolded her for not asking them before passing over the money; they knew about the swindler. "But," said the woman, "I was afraid you would tell me not to give him the money."

35.7

Two Wall Street operators caught a junior clerk dipping his hand in the till to a total of a few hundred dollars. One of the partners wanted to fire the culprit instantly. But the other man urged a more understanding attitude. "After all," he said, "we should remember that we started out on a small scale ourselves."

35.8

A Wall Street operator was set upon by two holdup men one evening. He fought back like a tiger but, after a brutal struggle, was finally subdued.

When the robbers found only a single dime on the man, they asked him why he put up such a terrific fight over one lousy dime.

"It isn't the amount," replied the Wall Streeter. "I simply objected to having my financial condition exposed to total strangers."

35.9

Two Wall Street operators were discussing the stock market. One of them said, "I picked up an interesting item during the winter. It stood at 28 when I bought it, and just yesterday it reached 78."

"Boy, what a buy that was!" exclaimed his friend. "What is it?"

"A thermometer," said the first man.

35.10

In the late 1920s a wealthy Wall Street man so consistently made the wrong moves in the stock market that his friends did just the opposite and consequently prospered greatly. When stocks reached their peak in October, 1929, the man who was never right suddenly sold all his stocks. His friends, as was their custom, therefore did the reverse—they bought all the stocks they could. Shortly thereafter the market collapsed.

When his friends asked the man why he had made the wise decision to sell all his stocks, he said: "When I studied my data and charts it seemed to me a time to buy. But then I realized I had been consistently wrong for two years and that maybe I would be better off if I went contrary to my own judgment. So I sold all my stocks."

35.11

"They say you lost quite a lot in the stock-market crash. Were you a bull or a bear?"

"No, just a jackass," said the speculator.

35.12

A young fellow, gambling like mad in the market and ruining his business, arrived home one evening distraught and desperate.

His wife, who knew nothing about his affairs and their precarious condition, said to him, "Will it be all right, dear, if I go out this evening? This is my bridge night."

"If you wait a minute," said the husband, "I'll go with you, and we'll jump together."

35.13

A subscriber to an investment advisory service of dubious value and integrity wrote to them that he had followed their counsel exactly and now found himself cleaned out. "You have constantly told me," continued the letter, "to communicate with you if I got into trouble so that you could advise me how to act. Now that I am broke, how do I act? Please wire."

Two days later the man received a wire from the service. It read ACT BROKE.

35.14

Wall Street tells about the trader who made a killing in the market. He shot the manager of a Grand Union store.

Definitions

35.15

A stockbroker is a man who can take a bankroll and run it into a shoestring.

35.16

Speculation is a word that sometimes begins with its second letter.

—*Horace Smith,* The Tin Trumpet

35.17

Dividend: A certain per centum, per annum, perhaps.

—*The Dotted Line*

Aphorisms

35.18

I do not regard a broker as a member of the human race.

—*Honoré de Balzac*

35.19

With an evening coat and a white tie, anybody, even a stockbroker, can gain a reputation for being civilized.

—*Oscar Wilde*

35.20

October: This is one of the peculiarly dangerous months in which to speculate in stocks. The others are July, January, September, April, November, May, March, June, December, August, and February.

—*Mark Twain*

35.21

There are two times in a man's life when he should not speculate: when he can't afford it, and when he can.

—*Mark Twain*

35.22

The fellow who jumped to his death from the twentieth floor was a man who was always getting in on the ground floor.

35.23

A market analyst tells you what is going to happen within six months and then after that tells you why it didn't.

35.24

Many a man is burned in the stock market by following a hot tip that is sure fire.

35.25

In investing money the amount of interest you want should depend on whether you want to eat well or sleep well.

—*J. Kenfield Morley*

35.26

A financier says suckers have not deserted the stock market permanently. They are just waiting until prices get too high again.

35.27

He who sells what isn't his'n, must buy it back or go to prison.

—*Daniel Drew*

35.28

Put all your eggs in one basket, and—watch the basket.

—*Mark Twain*

(*See also 16.10, 16.11, 20.13, 43.6, 78.6, 126.22, 142.8*)

ADMEN AND PROMOTERS

36. Wheelers and Dealers

Anecdotes

36.1

Bishop Clement Francis Kelly tells about one Marcus Pollasky who was on the witness stand. The lawyer asked him his business. Pollasky said he was a promoter.

"What is your definition of a promoter, Mr. Pollasky?"

"A promoter is a man who has nothing to sell and who sells it to a man who doesn't want to buy it," replied Pollasky.

36.2

When P. T. Barnum had his museum on lower Broadway in New York, he once hired a man, instructing him: "Go lay a brick on the sidewalk at the corner of Broadway and Ann; another close by the museum; a third diagonally across the way at the corner of Broadway and Vesey, by the Astor House; then with the fifth brick in hand, take up a rapid march from one point to the other, making the circuit, exchanging your brick at every point, and saying nothing to anyone." Barnum refused to tell the man the object of these maneuvers but warned him at all times to be silent and serious. Finally at the end of every hour the man was to "show this ticket at the museum door, enter, walk solemnly through every hall in the building, pass out, and resume your work."

Wily Barnum knew what would happen: Within half an hour 500 people were watching the man with the bricks, who had assumed a military bearing and kept absolute silence. At the end of the first hour the crowd had swelled even more, and every time the man went into the museum on the hour a number of watchers in the crowd followed him in. This went on for several days, until the police asked Barnum to end it as the crowds were obstructing the sidewalks.

36.3

To promote his museum on lower Broadway in New York, P. T. Barnum advertised "free music for the millions." He then hired a band and posted it on a balcony at the front of the building; but Barnum himself admitted it was the worst band he could find, because he knew the discordant notes would drive listeners into the museum to escape the ungodly din.

36.4

In order to relieve the pressure of people inside his museum, P. T. Barnum had a large sign made reading THIS WAY TO THE EGRESS. As a consequence the crowd pushed on their way to see the "egress" and presently found themselves out on the sidewalk, while the hundreds waiting at the front entrance to get in began their move toward the "egress."

36.5

What is called "deaconing" apples was once a fairly common practice—the business of topping off a barrel of apples with the very best specimens. It is said that when one customer complained about the inferior quality of apples found in a just-purchased barrel, the dealer told him that he had opened the wrong end of the barrel. Some apple growers took no chances—they "deaconed" both ends of the barrel.

36.6

An entrepreneur who confined his activities to what Wall Street calls "special situations" heard of a salmon cannery that was up for sale at a bargain price. After his customary careful investigation, the man bought the company. However, sales following the purchase dropped alarmingly. The new owner was soon on the edge of bankruptcy. It developed that the plant's entire pack consisted of white rather than the usual pink salmon.

In desperation the owner called in a public relations man in the hope he might come up with a solution. Within a few days a simple order by the publicity man turned the tide, and the white salmon began to enjoy an unprecedented popularity among consumers.

But rival canneries went to court and succeeded in having the publicity man's order rescinded. The court ruled it was unfair for the cannery to print this simple sentence on each can it sold: THE SALMON IN THIS CAN IS GUARANTEED NOT TO TURN PINK.

36.7

Montague Glass, a famous comedian of other days, used to tell about a merchant stuck with a heavy inventory of fur coats that had gone out of style. He decided to bill fifteen of his best accounts for a dozen coats each and then ship them thirteen coats, depending upon human cupidity to make the deals stick. However, every one of the accounts returned twelve coats for credit.

36.8

Blumberg did such a fine business in his variety store that two rivals—Weinstein and Blintzburg—opened up establishments on either side. Moreover, the two new stores both erected massive signs offering extraordinary bargains. Blumberg thought it over for a few days and then simply put a still larger sign over his store. It read only ENTRANCE.

36.9

A retailer was overstocked with television sets at a time when new models were coming on the market. How to sell these suddenly outdated sets was a serious question.

Finally, the retailer hired a salesman and equipped him with a hearing aid. Then the boss moved his desk to a balcony overlooking the salesroom.

When a customer came in to look at television sets, the salesman would fiddle with his hearing aid and call up to the boss on the balcony: "How much is this set?"

The boss would lean over the railing and call down: "It's just been reduced; it's $340!"

The clerk would look a little uncertain, nod to the customer, fool with the hearing aid, and then say: "It's $240; I think that's what he said."

Before long all the old-model television sets were sold.

"Remember," said the boss to the salesman, "you cannot cheat an honest man."

36.10

During the acute shortage of new automobiles right after the close of World War II, a Broadway character went to a midtown car dealer and asked for a car for immediate delivery. "Not a chance," said the dealer. "All we can do is put you on the list and you'll have to wait six months." As the customer walked out, he tossed a big bundle of bills into the wastebasket, making certain the dealer saw him. That afternoon the dealer phoned the customer that the new car he wanted was ready for delivery. The customer went around and drove away with his new car.

Two days later the dealer phoned the man.

"Say, wise guy," he said, "you're in real trouble. That dough you tossed into the wastebasket is all counterfeit."

"Of course it is," said the customer. "That's why I threw it away."

36.11

One of the legends of the antique business concerns a Madison Avenue, New York, dealer who was visited by a knowledgeable woman. She strolled around the shop casually, but ever sharp-eyed, finally stopping to look at a black cat lapping milk from an old saucer. "I don't see anything today that I particularly want," she told the proprietor. "But that's a pretty cat. Would you sell him to me?"

"She's a nice cat," said the shopkeeper, "but my little boy is very fond of her, and I wouldn't want to sell her."

"What about $25?" said the customer. "You could buy your boy several cats for that."

"Oh well, since you're a good customer, I'll let you have it for that," said the antique dealer with a sigh.

"I might as well take the saucer, too," said the customer as she picked up the cat.

"I'm sorry," said the dealer. "That saucer is a very valuable antique. It is worth a lot of money. Besides, because of that saucer I sell an awful lot of cats to people who know antiques as well as you do."

36.12

One horse trader said bitterly to the other: "That horse you sold me is blind."

"Well, I said he was a fine horse but he didn't look good."

36.13

A New Englander horse trader sold a pair of horses which he guaranteed were willing horses. Shortly afterwards the buyer complained that the horses were very poor workers. "You told me that these horses were willing."

"So I did," said the seller. "And they are willing. One is willing to stop, and the other is willing to let him."

36.14

A poor fellow wandered one day into a small European town, looking for work. When he found nothing, he hit upon a way to raise some funds. He plastered the town with notices that at a certain hour on a certain day he would walk on a rope from one side of the river to the other, a dangerous stunt over a deep and fast-flowing river.

The whole town turned out to witness the performance, each paying a small sum for the privilege of witnessing the spectacle. A rope was stretched across the river, and the acrobat appeared, properly costumed for the act. He tested the rope, peered intently at the river, and turned to face his audience.

"My friends," he said, "I appreciate your presence here. But I must tell you frankly I am not a tightrope walker, nor an acrobat. If I attempt this stunt I will surely drown. I do not believe you would want to witness so certain a death. But if you insist upon being a party to the death of a poor man I will go on. Otherwise, I am grateful to you for your contribution and will retire."

36.15

A gentleman arrived in a small town and hired the local theater for a night several weeks hence. He then put up a large sign across Main Street. It read: HE IS COMING! A week later he put up another sign reading: HE IS COMING TO THE BIJOUR THEATER ON MAY 1! The day before May 1 a new sign read: HE WILL APPEAR AT THE BIJOUR THEATER TONIGHT AT 8 P.M.

That night the man sat in the theater box office and collected $1 from each person until the theater was jammed. He then appeared on the stage, bowed to the audience, thanked them for their appearance and told them he had engineered the whole business on a wager and to demonstrate that people are much too gullible. He refunded the admission money as the people left the theater. On their way out they noticed a large sign reading: HE IS GONE!

36.16

Legend has it that one day Otto H. Kahn, New York banker and patron of the arts, was driving through New York's East Side when he saw a sign: JACOB CAHN, COUSIN OF OTTO H. KAHN.

The next day Kahn's attorney called on Jacob Cahn and told him that if he did not immediately remove the sign he would be sued. A week or so later Otto H. Kahn ordered his chauffeur to drive him past the store. This time Mr. Kahn saw the merchant's new sign: JACOB CAHN, FORMERLY COUSIN OF OTTO H. KAHN.

36.17

Douglas Jerrold plucked a buttercup by the roadside and said, "If it cost a shilling a root, how beautiful it would be!"

Definition

36.18

Promoter: A man who will furnish the ocean if you furnish the ship.

(*See also 37.19, 208.5, 226.2, 239.3, 244.13, 264.3, 269.26, 277.1–277.9*)

37. Advertisers and Publicizers

Anecdotes

37.1

"Do you find advertising pays?"

"Yes, indeed. Why only the other day we advertised for a night watchman and that very night the safe was robbed."

37.2

A merchant, defending his heavy expenditures for advertising, pointed out that a codfish lays about 10,000 eggs a day, but it does so in silence. On the other hand, a chicken lays only one egg a day, but loudly cackles over it. "And," concluded the merchant, "nobody eats codfish eggs, but almost everyone eats chicken eggs."

37.3

The sales manager picked up the roster of his sales force and said to the advertising manager, "This is what gives our company business year after year. I'd like you to show me a single order that advertising ever put on our books."

"I'll answer that question when you show me a single load of hay the sun ever put into the barn," responded the advertising man coldly.

37.4

A salesman of advertising space called on a merchant who said, "Nothing doing. I've been established for forty years and never advertised."

As he turned to leave the salesman asked, "What is that building on the hill?"

"Oh, that is the village church."

"Been there long?"

"A hundred years or so."

"Well, they still ring the bell," said the salesman.

37.5

The editor of a local paper was unable to get advertising from a businessman who said that he never read ads and doubted that anyone else read them.

"If I convince you that people read ads, will you advertise in our paper?" asked the publisher.

"If you can show me, yes," said the businessman.

In the next issue of the paper there was, in small type in an obscure corner of the paper, the following advertisement: WHAT IS JENKINS GOING TO DO ABOUT IT?

Jenkins, the businessman in question, hastened to the editor the next day and said that people were beginning to pester the life out of him with their queries as to what he was up to, what he was going to do. So Jenkins promptly placed an ad in the paper reading: JENKINS IS GOING TO ADVERTISE.

37.6

When Mark Twain was editor of a small-town paper, he received a letter from an old subscriber, complaining that he had found a spider in his paper and asking whether this was a sign of good or bad luck. Mark Twain replied:

"Dear Old Subscriber: Finding a spider in your paper was neither good luck nor bad luck for you. The spider was merely looking over our paper to see which merchant is not advertising, so that he can go to that store, spin his web across the door, and lead a life of undisturbed peace ever afterward."

37.7

The advance man for a circus called on the editor of a small-town paper in Arkansas and asked the charge for a full-page advertisement.

"One hundred dollars," replied the editor.

"How about a half-page ad?"

"One hundred dollars," was the reply.

"And a quarter-page ad?"

"That also would be $100," said the editor firmly.

"How do you figure it? There's no flexibility in your rates."

"It's this way," said the editor. "We've got a note for $100 due on July 1. Your circus opens here on June 30. This is the only paper in town. You have to advertise in our paper, and we have to meet that note. It's as simple as that."

37.8

An elephant met a lion in the jungle and asked, "Why do you make such a fool of yourself by roaring so much?"

"Oh, there's a good reason for it," replied the lion jovially. "They call me the king of the beasts because I advertise."

A rabbit, hiding in the brush, overheard this conversation and was deeply impressed. He thought he would try the lion's strategy and when he encountered a fox tried to roar like the lion—but it came out a tiny squeak. The unimpressed fox had himself a meal in the woods, reminding himself in the process that it does not pay to advertise unless you have the goods.

37.9

The patriots of a small New England town decided to celebrate the placing of a plaque on a public building in memory of the men from the town who had been killed in the war. A traveling salesman for a whiskey company observed with more-than-ordinary interest the preparations.

When the crowd assembled the next day, and the local high school band had played its scheduled airs, the town orator arose and spoke with fervor. He concluded by pointing to the flag-covered plaque and saying, "When the Stars and Stripes are removed we shall see names that will be forever honored and sacred in this community."

When the flag was lifted from the plaque there was a large card reading:

GOODERMAN AND WORTS WHISKEY.

37.10

A manufacturer of contraceptives, although doing a highly profitable business, was convinced he could increase his sales if only he could get his advertising accepted by the mass-circulation magazines. Advertising experts were called in, conferences were held, sample ad campaigns mapped out, but no one was able to come up with copy that would overcome the strict taboos of the magazines and at the same time even hint at the nature and purpose of the product.

Then the owner of the business had what he thought was a brilliant idea, one that the magazines would accept and that would still indicate the kind of merchandise he was offering for sale. It consisted simply of an advertisement reading as follows:

IF YOU WANT CHILDREN THAT'S YOUR BUSINESS.

BUT, IF YOU DON'T WANT CHILDREN, WELL—THAT'S MY BUSINESS.

37.11

A company offered a prize for the best slogan advertising its line of soaps.

One submission was: IF YOU DON'T USE OUR SOAP, FOR HEAVEN'S SAKE USE OUR PERFUMES.

37.12

Arpege once advertised its perfume, in a plastic container, as follows:

NO BOTTLES TO BREAK—JUST HEARTS.

37.13

The gentleman who kicked the lady at the show last evening seeks forgiveness. He was too dumbfounded to offer an apology at the time. Be assured, Madame, that he is not in the habit of kicking women—especially when his wife is present.

—*Advertisement in an Iowa paper*

37.14

Advertisement for dilly beans:

IF YOUR FRIENDLY GROCER DOESN'T HAVE A JAR—KNOCK SOMETHING OFF THE SHELF ON YOUR WAY OUT.

37.15

Advertisement for Seagram's gin:

DRYEST GIN IN TOWN—ASK ANY MARTINI.

37.16

Advertisement for Mexican beer:

THE BEER THAT MADE MILWAUKEE JEALOUS.

37.17

Advertisement in a New York restaurant:

PIES LIKE MOTHER USED TO MAKE BEFORE SHE TOOK TO BRIDGE AND CIGARETTES.

37.18

One advertising man encountered a friend on Madison Avenue and stopped to tell him that a mutual friend in the same business had died. "Oh, how terrible!" exclaimed the second ad man. "What did he have?"

"Not much, really," replied the first ad man. "A small cosmetic account and a whiskey client that wasn't billing very much."

37.19

A congregation in England wanted new hymn books, but they were very poor and could not afford to buy them at the ordinary price. They understood that an advertising agency would arrange to provide the hymn books for a few cents if they were allowed to include a few advertisements. The hymn books were duly delivered on December 24, and the parson called out for the congregation to sing Christmas carol No. 16. And so they arose and sang:

"Hark! the herald angels sing,
Beecham's pills are just the thing.
Peace on earth and mercy mild,
Two for man and one for child."

37.20

Kay Cobelle, of Dallas, reports that a new and not-quite-hep public relations client was unimpressed when wire services picked up a story and picture and gave it nationwide coverage. "What good is it?" snapped the client. "All the pictures are the same!"

Definitions

37.21

Advertising: Something which makes one think he's longed all his life for a thing he never even heard of before.

37.22

Advertising may be described as the science of arresting the human intelligence long enough to get money from it.

—*Stephen Leacock*

37.23

Public Relations Counselor: A press agent with a manicure.

—*Alan Gordon*

37.24

Press Agent: One who takes in lying for a living.

37.25

Propaganda: Baloney disguised as food for thought.

—Cincinnati *Inquirer*

37.26

Propaganda: The other side's case put so convincingly that it annoys you.

Aphorisms

37.27

If you think advertising doesn't pay, bear in mind that there are twenty-five mountains in Colorado higher than Pike's Peak which few people could name.

37.28

Advertise, or the chances are the sheriff will do it for you.

—*P. T. Barnum*

37.29

Before he retired to become a country squire, Henry F. Woods used to say: "Sure, I'm in advertising; I contact, react, and confer."

37.30

Doing business without advertising is like winking at a girl in the dark. You know what you are doing, but nobody else does.

—*Steuart Henderson Britt,* 1956

37.31

Samson had the right idea about advertising. He took two columns and brought down the house.

37.32

Advertisements contain the only truths to be relied on in a newspaper.

—*Thomas Jefferson*

37.33

Faith will never die so long as colored seed catalogs are printed.

37.34

George Martin said hair-restorer ads were "a lot of balderdash."

37.35

All press agents belong to a club of which Ananias is the honorary president.

—*John Kendrick Bangs*

37.36

If you can't convince them—confuse them.

37.37

Fairfax Cone has often said that advertising is the only business in the world in which the inventory goes down the elevator every night.

(*See also 36.2, 36.3, 36.6, 36.14, 36.15, 38.1–38.24, 39.1, 39.2, 43.3, 115.5, 141.12, 162.8, 205.18, 213.14, 214.13, 236.14, 237.9, 265.14, 266.30, 269.163, 277.7*)

38. Ad Boners

38.1

Caterer's Ad:

ARE YOU GETTING MARRIED, OR HAVING AN AFFAIR?

38.2

Sign outside a small hotel:

HAVE YOUR NEXT AFFAIR HERE.

38.3

Advertisement:

EXPERIENCED YOUNG GERMAN GIRL ABLE TO DO FANCY COOING.

38.4

George M——, son of Professor and Mrs. E. S. M——, is now connected with the ——— funeral home, where he will be pleased to see his friends.

—*Louisiana paper*

38.5

We are offering a special on goldfish for the holidays. Six goldfish and large owl, $1.00.

—*Advertisement in Indiana paper*

38.6

Sign in St. Paul laundry:

WE DO NOT TEAR YOUR LAUNDRY WITH MACHINERY. WE DO IT BY HAND.

38.7

There is not a store in the Carolinas with so many imported and exclusive fools as you find at ———.

—*Ad in Charlotte, N.C., paper*

38.8

Wanted: A folding table by a lady with detachable legs.

38.9

Sheer stockings—designed for dressy wear, but so serviceable that lots of women wear nothing else.

—*Ad in New York paper*

38.10

For Sale: Large crystal vase by lady slightly cracked.

—*Long Island paper*

38.11

A North Carolina state booklet says: "Famous mid-south resorts, including Pinehurst and Southern Pines, have . . . more golf curses per mile than anywhere else in the world."

38.12

ETHICAL SPIRITUALIST TEMPLE, 902 S. W. Fourth Avenue

Immorality Demonstrated

Sunday at 2.45 P.M.

—*Florida paper*

38.13

Save regularly in our bank. You'll never reget it.

—Ad in Clifton Forge, Va., *Daily Review*

38.14

300 Acres–partly cut-over part of old farm. No buildings. Side road. Hunting. Absolutely worthless. Price $600.

—*Ad in Maine paper*

38.15

Front room, suitable for two ladies, use of kitchen or two gentlemen.

—*Ad in Connecticut paper*

38.16

GIRLS to sew on men's pants.

—*Want ad in Maryland paper*

38.17

SALE!—25 MEN'S WOOL SUITS—$35.00—THEY WON'T LAST AN HOUR.

38.18

MOTHER'S DAY SPECIAL: DON'T KILL YOUR WIFE. LET OUR WASHING MACHINE DO THE DIRTY WORK.

38.19

What have you to offer in exchange for beautiful wire-haired female?

—*Ad in Texas paper*

38.20

For Sale—A full-blooded cow, giving three gallons milk, 2 tons hay, a lot of chickens and a cookstove.

—*Ad in Washington paper*

38.21

Wanted: A strong horse to do the work of a country minister.

—*Ad in Connecticut paper*

38.22

Toaster $3.50. A gift that every member of the family will appreciate. Automatically burns toast.

—*Ad in California paper*

38.23

Piano Moving. If you have a piano to move, take advantage of our expert service and careful handling. Kindling wood for sale.

—Ad in Rome N.Y., *Daily Sentinel*

38.24

Visit our clothing department. We can outwit the whole family.

—*Ad in New Jersey paper*

(*See also 37.1–37.36*)

39. Madison Avenue Shoptalk

39.1

John Crosby reported the following jargon used by Madison Avenue advertising men:

Well, the oars are in the water, and we're headed upstream.

Let's up periscope and look around.

Let's drop this down a well and see how big a splash it makes.

Let me take a temperature reading of this, and I'll get it back to you.

Mind you, I'm only giving a side-saddle opinion.

Let's guinea-pig that for size.

Don't low-bridge me.

Let's roll some rocks and see what crawls out.
Let's incubate this and see what hatches.
Let's run it up a flagpole and see if anyone salutes.

Crosby also reports that the Hollywood advertising agencies have been known to use such jargon as:

We were blown out of the tub (i.e. lost an account).
Get a boy to carry the grips (that is, get a junior executive to handle detail work).
Keep your pores open on this one.

39.2

Add the following Madison Avenue advertising jargon:

Let's send it uptown as a local and see if it comes downtown as an express.
Let's smear it on the cat and see if she can lick it off.
Let's take it to the lab and see if it's a mushroom or a toadstool.
Let's drive it into the parking lot and see if it dents any fenders.
Let's get down on all fours and have a look at the problem from the client's point of view.
Those men who job-hop from agency to agency have recently been characterized along Madison Avenue as suffering from the Pogo-stick syndrome.

40. Signs of the Times

40.1

A California merchant put a sign over a peephole in a window displaying merchandise for women: FOR MEN ONLY.

40.2

On a display of girdles: LINE TAMERS.

40.3

Sign in brassiere shop: WE FIX FLATS.

40.4

A reducing-salon sign: HAVE YOU ANYTHING TO LOSE?

40.5

Sign in a reducing-salon window: WE CAN TAKE YOUR BREADTH AWAY.

40.6

Sign in a shop window: OUR COSTUMES NOT ONLY MAKE GIRLS LOOK SLIM, THEY ALSO MAKE MEN LOOK ROUND.

40.7

Sign outside a farm: FRESH EGGS BEING LAID NOW.

40.8

Sign: IF OUR EGGS WERE ANY FRESHER, THEY'D BE IMPUDENT.

40.9

A grocery-store sign read: IMPERTINENT EGGS. Asked the meaning of it, the proprietor explained that it meant extra fresh eggs.

40.10

Sidewalk-vendor sign on tomatoes: DON'T SQUEEZE ME UNTIL I'M YOURS.

40.11

A restaurant sign: IT'S TOUGH TO PAY TWO DOLLARS FOR A STEAK. BUT IT'S TOUGHER WHEN YOU PAY ONE DOLLAR.

40.12

Sign in Miami restaurant: IF YOU ARE OVER 80 AND ACCOMPANIED BY YOUR PARENTS, WE WILL CASH YOUR CHECK.

40.13

Two local dairies engaged in an advertising war. One hired a daredevil driver to drive a car around town with a large placard reading: THIS DAREDEVIL DRINKS OUR MILK.

The rival company came out with a larger sign reading: YOU DON'T HAVE TO BE A DAREDEVIL TO DRINK OUR MILK.

40.14

A merchandiser of birdhouses had a rush of orders when he put a sign on them: THIS HOUSE FOR SALE—FOR A SONG.

40.15

A sign outside a Chicago print shop: MARRIAGES ARE MADE IN HEAVEN. BUT WE PRINT THE INVITATIONS.

40.16

Pawnshop sign: PLEASE SEE ME AT YOUR EARLIEST INCONVENIENCE.

40.17

Note left on the door of a music store: JOHANN TO LUNCH. BACH AT ONE. OFFENBACH SOONER.

40.18

A Laundry: WE SOAK THE CLOTHES, NOT THE CUSTOMERS.

40.19

Sign in bar: STAY A WHILE LONGER. YOUR WIFE CAN ONLY GET SO MAD.

40.20

Rest-room signs in a tavern: POINTERS; SETTERS.

40.21

In a cocktail lounge: PLEASE DO NOT STAND WHEN THE ROOM IS IN MOTION.

40.22

Sign in optometrist's window: IF YOU DON'T SEE WHAT YOU WANT, YOU'VE COME TO THE RIGHT PLACE.

40.23

A prankster stole a sign from a nursery reading: LET US DO YOUR PLANTING FOR YOU and put it outside an undertaking establishment.

40.24

Sign outside a Garfield, New Jersey, service station, located on a corner that has traffic-signal lights: LAST GAS STOP BEFORE LIGHTS.

40.25

Service-station sign: FILL YOUR TANK AND DRAIN YOUR FAMILY.

40.26

Road sign: DRIVE CAREFULLY; DON'T INSIST UPON YOUR RITES.

40.27

Sign in an undertaker's window: DRIVE CAREFULLY—WE CAN WAIT.

40.28

Road Sign in Connecticut: DRIVE LIKE HELL, AND YOU'LL GET THERE.

40.29

Sign on a Connecticut road: IF YOU MUST RUN DOWN PEOPLE, DO SO IN CONVERSATION IN YOUR LIVING ROOM.

40.30

Road sign: LIFE'S MUSICAL SCORE—C SHARP, OR B FLAT.

40.31

A junk shop near a railroad crossing had a sign: GO AHEAD, TAKE A CHANCE. WE'LL BUY THE CAR.

40.32

Placard at a grade crossing in Pennsylvania: IT TAKES THE STREAMLINER 25 SECONDS TO PASS THIS POINT WHETHER YOUR CAR IS ON THE TRACK OR NOT!

40.33

Sign in a movie house: ELDERLY LADIES NEED NOT REMOVE THEIR HATS.

40.34

Forest-fire prevention: A huge match labeled THIS IS THE FOREST PRIME EVIL.

40.35

During the blitz on London during World War II, merchants put up such signs as: BOMBED OUT, BLOWN OUT, BURNT OUT, BUT NOT SOLD OUT; MORE OPEN THAN EVER; and perhaps best of all, DON'T BE ALARMED AT THIS; YOU SHOULD SEE OUR BERLIN BRANCH.

(*See also 19.16*)

SALESMEN AND CUSTOMERS

41. Traveling Salesmen

Anecdotes

41.1

The salesman reported back to his boss after several weeks on the road and said, "All I got was two orders."

"What were they? Any good?"

"Nope. They were 'Get out!' and 'Stay Out!' "

41.2

STORMS, FLOODS DELAYING ME FOR AT LEAST A WEEK. WIRE INSTRUCTIONS, telegraphed the traveling salesman.

BEGIN VACATION IMMEDIATELY, wired back the home office.

41.3

A salesman for a small manufacturer covered the Midwest territory and grossed increasingly larger sales. But finally it dawned upon him that although his orders were big ones and the concern's profits rising, his pockets were chronically short of money. He had to get a raise, and he was sure he was worth one. He wrote the boss three letters and received no reply and no raise. Finally he wired the boss: IF I AM NOT GIVEN A SUBSTANTIAL RAISE WITHIN TWO WEEKS, COUNT ME OUT.

The next morning the salesman received the following wire from the boss: ONE, TWO, THREE, FOUR, FIVE, SIX, SEVEN, EIGHT, NINE, TEN, AND YOU'RE OUT.

41.4

A new salesman on the third day out in his territory was dismayed to find that everywhere he called anywhere from three to ten salesmen from competing companies had already called. Despairing of making any sales, he wired his boss: THERE ARE FROM FIVE TO TEN SALESMEN FROM COMPETITORS ALREADY COVERING THIS TERRITORY. WHAT SHALL I DO? Within hours he got the boss's reply: KEEP ON GOING, BUT SPEED

UP. THERE ARE A HUNDRED SALESMEN AFTER YOU FOR EVERY ONE BEFORE.

41.5

"How come this big amount on your expense report?" asked the sales manager.

"That," replied the salesman, "is my hotel bill."

"Well," said the boss, "after this don't buy any more hotels."

41.6

Years before the westernization and modernization of Africa got into full swing, two salesmen for shoe manufacturers arrived there to sell their wares. Both salesmen immediately noticed that many—perhaps most—of the natives did not wear shoes.

One salesman cabled his company: RETURNING ON NEXT BOAT. NO BUSINESS HERE. NATIVES DON'T WEAR SHOES.

But the other salesman cabled his company: SEND QUICK MILLIONS OF SHOES ALL SIZES. NATIVES NOT WEARING SHOES.

41.7

Two salesmen for dry wallpaper paste arrived at a store simultaneously. One man went immediately into an eloquent account of his product which he climaxed by putting some of his paste in a bowl, adding water, and pouring the whole mixture on to a waffle iron which was connected to an electric outlet. When the "waffle" was cooked, the salesman ate it to prove to the shopkeeper how pure it was.

The second salesman watched all this without saying a word. Then when the first man's act ended, the second man said, "My paste is not for eating—in fact, I recommend it not be eaten; it's supposed to stick, and it might stick to one's insides." The second man got the order.

41.8

A traveling salesman arrived home after an extended road trip and was told by his wife that she had purchased half a dozen hens and two roosters.

"Why two roosters?" asked her husband.

"Oh," she said, "just in case one of the roosters should decide to go on the road."

41.9

A traveling salesman arrived in town and went immediately to one of his chief customers and asked if there were a telegram there for him.

"Here it is," said the customer.

The salesman opened the envelope, and his face fell.

"My wife," he said shakily, "has presented me with twins."

"Wonderful!" cried the customer. "Now you know how it feels to receive more goods than you order."

41.10

The traveling salesman stopped to pick up a good-looking young woman who had thumbed him for a lift. When she got in the car she explained that she had just escaped from the state mental institution. Looking the girl over appraisingly the young salesman asked her, "Can girls like you have children?"

"Certainly we can. Where do you think salesmen come from?"

41.11

A salesman boarded a train and took a roomette. He carried with him only a small grip. The porter inquired if he had other luggage.

"No."

"I thought you were a salesman," said the porter.

"I am. But I don't need a lot of luggage. I sell brains."

The porter scratched his head and said, "Well, you're the first salesman that ever rode this train without samples."

41.12

"And ladies and gentlemen," shouted the patent-medicine salesman at the county fair, "I have sold over a million bottles of this great Indian remedy, and I have never received one complaint. I ask you, what does that prove?"

Came a voice from the crowd: "That dead men tell no tales."

Definition

41.13

A star salesman is a man from the home office with authority to cut the price.

(*See also 43.1–43.22, 44.1–44.8*)

42. Retail Stores

Anecdotes

42.1

There is a grocer who is said to be so mean that he was seen to catch a fly off his counter, hold him up by the legs, and look into the cracks of his feet to see if he hadn't been stealing sugar.

42.2

"Boy, have I got myself a salesman," said the clothier to his friend. "The other day a woman came in whose husband had just died. She wanted to get some clothing in which to bury the poor fellow. And this salesman of mine not only sold her a suit but also an extra pair of pants!"

42.3

The summer resident at a resort went down to the local grocery store to buy a pound of coffee. After the coffee was given him, the proprietor asked him if he didn't want to buy some salt. "Why, no," said the customer.

"I can give you a bargain in salt," said the owner pointing with his hand to shelves sagging under the burden of packages of salt.

"Good Lord," said the customer, "you certainly must sell a lot of salt!"

"No," replied the proprietor, "hardly any. But the fellow who sells me salt! Can he sell salt!"

42.4

"Are those eggs fresh?" asked the customer.

"Boy," called out the grocer, "see if those eggs are cool enough to sell."

42.5

The man stopped to look at the display of beautiful fruit, and his eye was particularly caught by Golden Delicious apples. "How much are they?" he asked the proprietor.

"Twenty-five cents each."

"What! Twenty-five cents each for one apple?"

"That's right, Mister. But they are the finest. How much do you pay for aspirin when you have a headache?"

"Fifteen cents, but what has that got to do with it?"

"Well," said the shopkeeper, "you pay 15 cents when you have a headache, so why not pay a quarter for something you enjoy."

42.6

A customer went into an expensive food shop and asked the price of a peach.

"Fifteen cents."

The customer handed the clerk 25 cents.

"What is that for?"

"I stepped on a grape on my way in."

42.7

"How much are the peaches?"

"Ten cents each, madam."

"I'll have one."

"Oh, you're giving a party!"

42.8

A baker has invented a new kind of yeast. It makes bread so light that a *pound* of it weighs only *12* ounces.

42.9

A Chicago butcher named Louis Harris, disturbed because his Greek customers could not remember his name, had his name changed to Elias Haralampopoulos. (But why Mike Stench had his named changed to Joe Stench is not known.)

42.10

"Here you've only been in business for eight months, and already you're making a mint," said a customer to one Feigenbaum who ran a delicatessen on Sixth Avenue in New York.

"My friend," said Feigenbaum, "it's mostly because we eat so much herring. It does something for the brain."

Thereafter for days the customer came in and bought large quantities of herring. Finally he came in and said to Feigenbaum, "I don't think that herring does one a bit of good. Besides, I can get it for 15 cents less at the store three blocks down from here."

"You see," said Feigenbaum, "already you're getting smarter."

42.11

A man called on a friend of his in the clothing business, to buy a suit. The clothier picked out a suit, had the man put it on and examine himself in a mirror. "It is so beautiful," exulted the clothier, "that even your best friends wouldn't recognize you in it. It does things to you. Step outside and look at it in the daylight."

When the clothier's friend came back into the store only a few minutes later, the clothier walked up to him with a smile and said, "How do you do, stranger. What can I do for you?"

42.12

The clothing store was having a difficult time with a customer. No matter what one of the partners showed him, the customer didn't like it. No matter how many times he was pushed in front of a mirror and turned around before it so that he could see how well it looked, still the fellow would not buy. Finally the other partner took charge and sold the customer the first suit he was shown. "I hope you were watching me, Jake," said the second partner when the customer departed. "I sold that guy on the first try."

"Yeah, I know," said Jake, "but who first made the customer dizzy?"

42.13

A salesman was seeking employment in a clothing store. The proprietor said, "Here is the one suit I cannot sell. It's purple, green, and yellow. If you can sell it, I'll make you a partner."

"OK, I'll try it," said the applicant.

The owner came back and found the salesman in disarray, scratched and bleeding. "I got rid of the suit," said the salesman.

"But my God, what happened? Did you have to fight the customer?"

"No, it wasn't him—but I had a helluva time with his Seeing Eye dog."

42.14

"How did you lose your job at the dress shop?"

"Just because of something I said. After I had tried twenty dresses on a woman, she said, 'I think I'd look nicer in something flowing,' so I asked her why she didn't jump in the river."

42.15

The woman went into the store, sought the clerk that had previously waited on her, and said, "When I bought this sweater in here yesterday, you told me it was 100 percent wool, and now I find this tag on it reading 'All Cotton.' "

"Don't get upset, Madam," said the clerk. "That tag was put on to fool the moths."

42.16

Erskine Johnson, of the NEA, tells of the socialite who went to the salon of a fashionable milliner and said she needed a hat at once for a cocktail party. The milliner studied his client briefly, picked up a few yards of ribbon, twisted it expertly, put it on her and said, "There is your hat, madam."

The woman looked in the mirror and said, "It's perfect. What do I owe you?"

"Fifty dollars," said the milliner.

"Fifty dollars for a few yards of ribbon!" protested the woman.

"The ribbon, Madam, is free," said the milliner firmly.

42.17

"What'll I do with Simpkin?" asked the merchandising manager. "I've had him in five departments now, and in every one of them he dozes all day."

"Try him at the pajamas counter," suggested an assistant. "And put a tag on him reading: 'These pajamas are of such fine quality that even the man who sells them can't keep awake.' "

42.18

"I hear Jenkins has been transferred to the complaint department?"

"Yes, so they tell me. Seems he's losing his hearing."

42.19

The exhausted clerk had pulled down blanket after blanket from the shelf, but still the woman customer was not satisfied.

"There is one more blanket left," said the clerk. "Do you care to see it?"

"I'm not going to buy one today," said the woman. "I have only been looking for a friend."

"Well," said the clerk, "I'll take the last one down if you think your friend might be in it."

42.20

A man went into a New York department store and sought out a gift counselor, in this instance a clever, sophisticated young woman. "Could you suggest what I might buy as a present for an aunt of mine? She's in her eighties, and she's wealthy."

"What about some floor wax?" suggested the young woman with a slightly wicked smile.

42.21

Marshall Field, Chicago's great department store, prides itself on the variety and quality of merchandise it buys from all parts of the world.

On one of Mr. Field's frequent inspections of his store's goods he stopped at the linen department and was struck by a tablecloth. "Where did this come from?" he asked the buyer.

"It's from Italy, Mr. Field."

"What's it sell for?"

"Seven hundred dollars, Sir."

"Too high, even for the wealthiest in town. I don't think you'll sell it."

Several days later Mr. Field called in the

linen buyer. "I was wrong about the $700 tablecloth," he said. "The other evening I was dining at Mrs. R.'s home and was astonished to find it on her table. Congratulations!"

"Yes, Mr. Field, but the next morning she returned it. She'd only taken it on approval."

42.22

A woman was looking at toys to buy as a present for her young nephew. One that the salesman recommended seemed to her too complicated for a child of the age she had in mind.

"But, madam," said the salesman, "this toy is one of the latest educational devices invented for children. The authorities have approved it as being ideal for the conditioning of the child to the realities of this day and age. You see, no matter how the child puts it together, it will be wrong."

42.23

The proprietor of the store asked one of his clerks what he was doing in the sporting-goods department, when he was assigned to the greeting-card counter.

"Well, it happened this way," replied the clerk. "This fellow came in for a get-well card to send to his girl who had a broken hip. So I reminded him that he wouldn't be doing anything for six weeks and that he might as well go fishing. That led to a sale of fishhooks, then a line for the hooks, then a rod for the line, then a boat so that he could get into deep water, then a boat trailer. And of course I convinced him he would have to buy a car to haul the trailer. So I sold him my car."

42.24

Gilbert Barnhill, according to Bennett Cerf's *The Life of the Party*, related that the speech department of the State University of Iowa sent stutterers to a local establishment to purchase an item they would not be at all likely to have and to ask the store where such an item might be found and how to get there. The idea was to help the stutterer overcome his reticence in speaking to strangers.

For quite a spell the stutterers were sent to the campus bookstore and told to ask for Ping-Pong balls. The first dozen were, of course, turned away. But the thirteenth stutterer found they had an abundance of Ping-Pong balls. The clerk told the latest customer that it puzzled him why so many people thought a bookstore would stock Ping-Pong balls, but, he added, "We've never disappointed our customers. What gets me, though, is this: Why does everybody who plays Ping-Pong stutter?"

42.25

A farm boy had been hired to sell farm equipment. He was ambitious, earnest, worked hard at his new job, but sales were small and few. Finally the boss called him in and said, "Son, I'm afraid this isn't working out for us. You just can't sell."

The young man was surprised. "I'm selling all right," he said, "but the people just ain't buying."

42.26

A farmer who had just purchased a bushel of grass seed, asked, "Is this seed guaranteed?"

"It certainly is," replied the merchant. "If the seed doesn't grow, bring it back, and we'll refund the money."

42.27

A woman strode into the taxidermist's with a stuffed owl in her hand. "You stuffed this bird for me six months ago, and now look—all the feathers are falling off."

"My dear lady," said the taxidermist, "that is a tribute to our art. When we stuff a bird it moults in the proper season."

42.28

Seller of a used TV set: "This set's hardly been used. It was owned by an old lady with weak eyes."

42.29

Customer: "Gee, this cigar is rotten."

Proprietor: "You should complain—I've got a thousand of them!"

42.30

The owner of an optical shop was instructing a new man:

"First fit the glasses, and when the customer asks what the charge will be, say, 'The charge is $10.' Then pause, and watch carefully for the reaction.

"If the customer doesn't flinch, then you add, '. . . for the frames. The lenses will be another $10.'

"Then you pause again, this time only slightly, and watch again for the reaction. If the customer doesn't back away this time, you say, firmly, '. . . each.' "

42.31

The old shopkeeper was on his deathbed and knew it. His family had gathered at the bedside. "Is Momma here?" the old fellow asked weakly.

"Yes, Poppa, I'm here," said his wife.

"And Rebecca?"

"Yes, Father."

"And Sam?"

"Yes, Father."

"And Milton?"

"Yes, he is here, too."

The old man raised himself from his pillow, looked around despairingly, and in one pathetic cry said, "Then who's mindin' the store?"

42.32

A traveler entered a store in a small town in Georgia on a blistering hot day and found the proprietor asleep in a chair tilted against the wall.

"Say," called out the traveler, "I'm in a hurry. How about waitin' on me?"

"Mister," replied the storekeeper drowsily, "can't you come back when I'm standin' up?"

42.33

"Say, Harry, they tell me you're doing a whale of a business?"

"Are we doing a business!" replied Harry. "It has gotten to be so heavy that we now have one man just to insult new customers."

42.34

"Now that your opening sale has closed, what are you going to do next?" one shopkeeper asked the other.

"We shall now have the opening of our closing sale," replied the merchant.

42.35

A salesclerk asked his boss how he could handle women who complain about the prices compared to the low prices in the good old days. "Just act surprised and tell them you didn't think that they were old enough to remember them."

42.36

The market is the place set apart where men may deceive each other.

—Anacharsis

(*See also 17.3, 19.16, 23.7, 25.3, 25.4, 29.7, 30.8, 36.7–36.9, 36.11, 36.16, 37.4, 37.6, 38.5, 38.7, 38.24, 40.6, 40.7, 40.9, 40.10, 40.14, 40.17, 40.24, 40.25, 45.8, 46.3, 46.4, 48.1–48.3, 48.5, 48.6. 48.8, 48.9, 128.14. 135.4, 135.30, 177.14, 186.4, 190.3, 210.24, 227.1, 229.10, 234.10, 240.12, 264.4, 265.11, 266.20, 266.21, 268.27, 271.14, 274.10, 277.6*)

43. Salesmen-at-large

Anecdotes

43.1

A salesman, when asked why he always kept his hat on in the office, said he did it to remind himself that he has no business being there.

43.2

A high-pressure salesman was about to jump off the Brooklyn Bridge and was rescued by a policeman. However, the salesman sold the idea to the policeman, so together they jumped off the bridge.

43.3

Some years ago a magazine then considered daring and risque—with its gaudy makeup, pictures of somewhat naked women, and scandal stories—was trying to get the advertising of a famous manufacturer of pianos. But the piano manufacturer would have nothing to do with the magazine; it was much too correct and upper class to have its wares offered in such a disgraceful publication. Orders were given that the publication's salesman was not to be admitted to any of the company's executives.

Nevertheless, the space salesman pushed his way into the office of the company's president one day and immediately said, "I understand that yesterday at lunch you told my friend Brown that my magazine circulated chiefly in bawdy houses. Is that correct?"

"Well, er— er—, yes, I suppose so," said the piano executive.

"You are absolutely correct, sir," said the salesman. "Now let me ask you one more question: Have you ever been in a bawdy house that didn't have a piano?"

43.4

A star salesman, explained Walter Chrysler, needs something more than charm and perseverance. "Let me remind you that the stinger of a bee is only three-hundredths of an inch long. The rest of the 12 inches is pure imagination."

43.5

Gene Woods, Long Island's salesman of fire protection, relates that long ago he learned not to talk about the weather to customers, unless they persisted. He figures weather talk uses up too much time. "You talk weather for six minutes each day, for example. For five days a week and twenty years you have spent more than three months talking about weather. It's too expensive."

43.6

A wealthy man's son, with many social connections, went to a prominent bond house in Wall Street and offered his services as the best bond salesman in the nation. He was hired. He had not sold a bond after three weeks of work, and the boss called him in and said, "You said you were the best bond salesman in the nation, and here you have not sold a single $1,000 bond."

"Well, I guess I'll have to amend my statement. I am the second best bond salesman—the best one is the man that sold you this offering."

43.7

The salesman finally gained admittance to the plant manager and promptly told him he would like the opportunity to talk to the men in the plant about taking a correspondence course that would "put more fire and sparkle into their work."

"Beat it, Buster," said the plant manager. "This is a dynamite factory."

43.8

"I made some valuable contacts today," said one salesman.

"Same here," said the other salesman. "I didn't get any orders, either."

43.9

"It's a terrific buy," said the salesman on the big used-car lot. "Owned by an eighty-five-year-old school teacher who was half blind and hardly ever used it. Only got 90 miles on it. It's a steal for $1,600. Try it out—run it around the block."

The prospect got behind the wheel, drove the car around the block, and entered the lot at another entrance. Another salesman came out, and the prospect asked him, "How much will you give me for this car?" The salesman looked it over and said, "It's not worth a dime more than $550."

"Oh, hell," said the prospect as he got out and handed the keys to the salesman, "You can have it for nothing. I'm fed up with it."

And he walked away much pleased with his little joke.

43.10

Used-car dealer to fellow trying to sell him his old car: "Let me put it this way, if this was a horse it would have to be shot."

43.11

"Young man," said the busy executive to the salesman, "you are very fortunate to be in here. I've turned down ten salesmen today."

"I know. I'm them."

43.12

"Sam, you're only eating crackers and milk. On a diet?" one salesman asked the other.

"No," said Sam, "on a commission."

43.13

"You ought to be ashamed of yourself," said the boss to the office boy. "Do you know what we do with office boys who tell lies?"

"Yes, sir, you make salesmen of them," replied the bright young boy.

43.14

A life-insurance salesman entered the reception room of a company, offered his card and asked to see Mr. William Smith. He stood and watched as the receptionist weaved her way through aisles to an office with a glass partition. He saw the receptionist hand the card to the man, noticed the man frown and throw the card in the wastebasket.

The receptionist returned to the salesman and said that Mr. Smith was tied up in a meeting and could not see him. "That is too bad," said the salesman. "May I please have my card back?" The receptionist asked him to repeat his request, looked at him oddly, and went back to Mr. Smith. Again the salesman watched. He saw Mr. Smith bend over the wastebasket for a few seconds and then hand something to the receptionist. When the receptionist returned she handed the salesman a nickel, explaining that his card had become lost but that Mr. Smith did not want him to be out-of-pocket on the call.

The salesman thereupon took from his wallet four more cards and handed them to the receptionist. "Give these to Mr. Smith," he said, "because the cards are only 1 cent each."

The salesman watched the receptionist hand the cards to Mr. Smith, who burst out laughing. Then, in response to Mr. Smith's genial beckoning sign, he went in to see his man.

Definition

43.15

Supersalesman: A fellow who can sell double-breasted suits to a man with a Phi Beta Kappa key.

Aphorisms

43.16

There are two classes of people: those who work by the sweat of their brow, and those who sell them handkerchiefs, electric fans, air-conditioners, soft drinks, beer, refrigerators, tropical worsteds, and other lightweight fabrics.

43.17

I never knew an auctioneer to lie unless it was absolutely necessary.

—*Josh Billings*

43.18

Everyone lives by selling something.

—*Robert Louis Stevenson*

43.19

If the atomic bomb blows up America and sends us back to the caves, some man will come crawling out of the rubble, selling souvenirs of the disaster.

—*Sydney J. Harris*

43.20

Some salesmen electrify their prospects—others merely gas them.

43.21

Some sales talks are like steer horns—a point here, a point there, and a lot of bull in the middle.

43.22

The salesman who covers the chair all the time instead of his territory is always on the bottom.

(*See also 23.1–23.6, 23.9, 36.1, 36.9, 36.12, 36.13, 37.3, 37.4, 37.9, 41.1–41.13, 42.2, 42.3, 42.11–42.13, 42.17, 42.23, 42.25, 42.30, 45.1, 45.3–45.9, 45.11, 198.1, 198.4–198.7, 198.9–198.12, 210.3, 211.26, 215.1, 215.13, 234.7, 235.32, 244.19, 267.9, 272.5*)

44. Sales Managers

Anecdotes

44.1

"Herb is terribly forgetful," complained the sales manager to one of his assistants. "I don't see how he sells anything. Now wait, and I'll show you. I asked him to get me a pack of cigarettes, and I'll bet he returns without them."

Presently Herb sauntered back into the office and said to the boss, "Wait until I tell you what happened. During lunch I met old Graves—you know, the fellow who hasn't bought from us for four years. Well, we got talking, and by the time lunch was over he gave me this $250,000 order!"

"See what I mean," said the boss to his assistant. "Herb forgot all about the cigarettes."

44.2

A hunter who had borrowed a dog named Salesman bagged a record number of birds, and the next year returned to the same region and asked the owner if he could again borrow Salesman for some hunting.

"The critter's no good no more," said the owner.

"Why, what happened?" asked the hunter.

"Aw, some fool from the city came down here and called that dog Sales Manager, and now the damn hound don't do nothing but sit on his backside and howl all day."

44.3

The boss and his sales manager looked gloomily at the sales chart on the wall. In one corner was a graph showing the company's descending volume. The balance of the chart contained a map of the territory, with pins showing the location of the various salesmen.

The boss sighed, "I think we have only one hope. Let's take the pins out of the map and stick them into the salesmen."

44.4

A salesman whose bookings had slipped badly was called in by the sales manager, who pointed to his wall map and said, "Jones, don't misunderstand me. You are not in immediate danger of dismissal, but I want you to note that I have loosened your pin."

44.5

The sales manager returned from a trip over his territory and was about to commit suicide, when his secretary pointed out that the cleaning woman had turned his sales graph upside down.

44.6

The sales manager was giving one of his salesmen a severe going over, when finally the salesman blurted out, "Don't think you can talk to me like that. I'm not taking orders from any man."

"Now we're reading each other," said the

sales manager. "That is just why I'm giving you hell—you're not taking orders from any man."

44.7

The book salesman suggested the purchase of a book on salesmanship to a sales manager. "Why, young man," said the sales executive, "I've forgotten more about selling than you ever knew."

"Well then," said the book salesman, "I have here just the book for you—a five-volume course on memory training."

(*See also 23.3, 37.3, 41.1–41.13, 43.1–43.22, 205.19, 253.1*)

45. Peddlers and Canvassers

Anecdotes

45.1

An unusually successful door-to-door salesman begins his pitch by saying to the housewife, "I want to show you an article that several of your neighbors told me you can't afford."

45.2

A beautiful brunet opened the door in response to the salesman's knock. "Good morning, is your husband in?"

"No, I'm sorry. He's away on business. He won't be back for three weeks."

Taking another look at the gorgeous woman, the salesman said, "That's all right. I'll wait."

45.3

A fellow made a fortune going from door to door selling a sign reading NO SALESMEN ALLOWED, but right after each householder agreed to buy, he pulled open a sample case and said, "Now before you put up that sign let me show you this line of goods."

45.4

The Yankee peddlers were often an engaging lot. Richardson Wright tells how one would stop at a house and address the woman who came to the door: "Madam, are you in need of any pocket sawmills? Horn gunflints? Basswood hams? Wooden nutmegs? White-oak cheeses? Tin bungholes? Or calico hog troughs?" And when the woman burst out laughing, the peddler would get down to serious business and offer to sell her tinware, mats, glassware, brooms, washboards, clothes pins, matches, rolling pins, paddy irons, kettles, and pots.

45.5

Years ago a Yankee peddler of a quack nostrum arrived with his wares in Dallas, Texas, and began his selling campaign without first obtaining a license. The sheriff, anxious to trap the man, bought a case of the cure-all then demanded that the peddler show his license. When the drummer could not produce the document, the sheriff promptly fined him $5.

But the sheriff still had the case of cure-all medicine on his hands, for which he had paid $5, and offered to sell it back to the peddler for $3. The drummer bought it. Then the drummer asked the sheriff if he had a license to sell the stuff. The sheriff did not.

"Well," said the peddler, "I'll just have to have you brought into court for hawkin' and peddlin' without a proper document." And he did. The sheriff was fined $8.

45.6

One Yankee peddler became famous for his selling of clocks. He always sold a clock on the understanding that on his way back in two weeks he would replace the clock with another if the first one did not work. At the end of his route he would have one clock left. True to his promise, he would return to the first house where he had sold a clock and replace it with the one remaining clock. At the second house he replaced the unsatisfactory clock he had taken from the first house. And so over the entire route—selling and replacing and ending up with a big profit.

45.7

A Yankee peddler with his cart overtook another peddler on the road and called out, "Hello there, what you carrying?"

"Drugs and medicines," replied the other peddler.

"You go ahead, then," called out the first peddler. "I carry gravestones."

45.8

One day, according to P. T. Barnum, a peddler drove up to a New England store, but the storekeeper told him he wanted nothing to do with him, that he had been skinned enough by peddlers. The peddler thereupon offered to sell the shopkeeper anything on his wagon at wholesale prices and to take in payment anything from the store the storekeeper chose, and at retail prices. The store owner asked the peddler what he had on his truck and indicated he was interested only in whetstones. "How much?" asked the merchant. "The wholesale price of my whetstones is $3 per dozen," replied the peddler.

"I'll take a gross of them," said the shop owner.

When the 12 dozen whetstones were brought in the peddler said, "Now you owe me $36, for which I'm to be paid in whatever you choose to pay me in from your store—at retail prices. What's it going to be?"

"I'm paying you in whetstones at 50 cents each, which will add up to 6 dozen to pay you off," said the storekeeper. For a few seconds the peddler looked incredulous, then like the good sport who knew what he had coming to him, he burst out laughing and accepted the trade.

45.9

A peddler with a pushcart load of cheap socks parked at a busy corner in a poor neighborhood and hawked his wares in a loud voice. Some people looked, but no one bought anything from him. Presently another peddler appeared on the scene with a load of cheap socks and in an even louder voice began to advertise his merchandise at prices lower than his competitor. The first peddler glared at the new arrival, cursed him, and raised his cry an octave or two. The second peddler shouted back and then resumed calling out what a greater bargain he was offering.

Before very long the second peddler was doing a thriving business; in fact, all the business. After several hours he had sold his entire stock and happily departed. The other peddler sorrowfully pushed his burdened cart to possibly greener fields.

Some blocks away the two peddlers met, did some calculating, exchanged money, had lunch together, loaded up the empty pushcart with more socks, and moved off to another neighborhood.

45.10

For an interminable time the housewife pawed and fussed over the merchandise on a pushcart and then finally bought a fan for 1 cent. The next day she brought it back torn and demanded her money back.

The peddler asked what she had paid for it.

"One cent," was the reply.

"And how did you use it?" asked the peddler.

"Like a fan should be used, you stupid one," retorted the housewife. "I used it to fan myself."

"For that you should have bought a 5-cent fan," said the peddler. "The 1-cent fan you just hold in your hand and wave your head."

45.11

Several merchants were having lunch at a restaurant in New York's garment area, when a peddler came in and began to pester them with his line of handkerchiefs, blouses, shirts, and so on. The peddler was so noisy and so persistent that one of the merchants became annoyed and said to his companions. "I'm going to fix this guy; I'm going to make him miserable for the rest of the day." Whereupon he called to the peddler: "Have you any decent suspenders—best quality at a decent price?"

"Have I got suspenders!" cried the peddler. "You should see these beauties, the finest you could buy on Fifth Avenue."

"How much?" asked the merchant.

"A bargain at $3," said the peddler.

"OK," said the merchant, handing the peddler $3 and taking the suspenders, whereupon the peddler walked away with an obviously troubled look on his face.

"I don't get it," said one of the men at the table. "How did you ruin the guy's day by buying from him?"

"Simply by accepting his first price. He'll be out of his mind for the rest of the day, condemning himself because he didn't ask $4 instead of $3. It'll drive him nuts."

45.12

One housewife hit upon a method of discouraging door-to-door salesmen. When they indicate they are going to be persistent, she excuses herself with the remark that she is an amateur painter and has some of her work that they may be interested in buying. Most of the time when she returns to the door the peddler has disappeared.

(*See also* 43.1–43.22)

BUYERS

46. Bargains and Discounts

Anecdotes

46.1

The fuel merchant was asked how it was that he still made money when he not only quoted the lowest prices in town, but in addition gave discounts to his many friends.

"It's this way," said the coal merchant. "When I'm delivering to a friend, I knock off $1 per ton because he is a friend of mine, and then I knock off 200 or 300 pounds because I am his friend. It balances out."

46.2

George and John owned a tavern located at a small crossroads community. One day they ran out of whiskey and together drove into town to buy another barrel of it for their trade.

On the way back to the tavern with the whiskey, each man found his mouth watering for a drink of it. But neither wanted to violate their agreement not to do so.

Finally, George pulled a half dollar from his pocket and said, "John, I'd like to buy myself a drink of that whiskey."

John, being a good merchant, could not turn down a sale. But presently John's own thirst got the better of him and he used the same half dollar to buy himself a drink from George.

For the balance of the journey George and John kept on buying drinks for themselves with the same half dollar, until almost all of the whiskey was gone.

"Ish marvelous," chortled George thickly, "between us we get a whole barrel of whiskey for a half dollar."

46.3

Old Socks Moore entered Gibbon's store, in Dedham, Massachusetts, and handed over one of those large bottles in which the bottom had been driven up through the center and called for a quart of rum. "Why, Socks, this bottle won't hold a quart," cried Gibbon.

"Sam," said Socks, "if it won't I'll pay for it, and if it does then you pay for it."

"Agreed," said Gibbon. The bottle was filled to the brim, with a gill of rum left in the measure. Socks took a cork and drove it into the bottle, then turned the bottle over and ordered that the balance of the rum be poured into the bottom. Even after the remains of the quart had been poured into the bottom there was room left for more. Gibbon himself loved to tell this story.

46.4

In the old days in New England a good deal of trade in the small town was made by bartering.

One day the meanest man in the village came into the general store and asked for a darning needle, offering in exchange an egg, an offer the storekeeper accepted.

When the exchange was made, the crusty old character asked the storekeeper, "Aren't you goin' treat?" referring to a custom of the day and place.

"Treat! On that trade!" exclaimed the storekeeper.

"A trade is a trade," said the miser firmly.

"All right, what'll you have?" asked the storekeeper.

"A glass of wine," said the miser. The wine was produced, and the old fellow took a sip and then said, "If you put an egg in this wine it'll make it taste better."

Astonished at such cheek, but watched by loungers in the shop, the storekeeper reluctantly picked up the egg he had received in exchange, broke it and dropped it in the wine. Whereupon the drinker looked at the glass of wine and let out a whoop, "Hi! Look here! It's a double-yolk egg that I gave you. You ought to give me either another darning needle or another glass of wine."

46.5

A merchant, notorious for not paying his bills, was bargaining endlessly over a deal, when a friend came along and called him aside. "Why are you bargaining with this man so bitterly, when you seldom ever pay any of your bills?"

"Look," said the merchant, "I like the man, and I want to keep him from losing too much money on his deal with me."

46.6

When the colonists in America destroyed British stamp papers, the British ministry called in Benjamin Franklin, then a representative in London for Pennsylvania, and said they would repeal the act if the Americans would pay for the paper and other items destroyed by the colonists.

Franklin wrote this reply to the proposal: "I am put in mind of the Frenchman, who, having heated a poker until it was red hot, ran furiously into the street and addressed himself to the first Englishman he met. 'Aha, Monsieur! Voulez-vous give the pleasure, zee satisfaction if you pleez, to let me run zee pokair only one foot eento your rear?' The Englishman hesitated, whereupon the Frenchman amended his request, 'Veree well, zen perhaps six eenches?'

" 'I say, are you mad?' returned the Englishman. 'If you don't go about your business I shall be obliged to knock you down!'

" 'Well zen,' said the chastened Frenchman, 'weel you, good Sir, only zen be so obliging as to pay me for zee trouble and expense of heating zee pokair?' "

Definition

46.7

Bargain: Usually something that's so reasonable they won't take it back when you find out what's wrong with it.

Aphorisms

46.8

One of the difficult tasks in this world is to convince a woman that even a bargain costs money.

—*E. W. Howe*

46.9

There are very honest people who do not think that they have had a bargain unless they have cheated a merchant.

—*Anatole France*

46.10

A woman who has found a bargain usually gets something for which she has no use, at a price so low she can't resist it.

46.11

A discount is something sold instead of goods.

46.12

There is hardly anything in the world that some man cannot make a little worse and sell a little cheaper.

—*John Ruskin*

46.13

People will buy anything that's one to a customer.

—*Sinclair Lewis*

(*See also 10.3, 17.3, 17.13, 30.8, 35.9, 36.8, 38.17, 42.34, 43.9, 48.4, 48.9, 104.2, 161.2, 210.3, 214.2, 243.20, 248.20*)

47. Time Payments

Anecdotes

47.1

A collection agency, having difficulty with a particular account, wrote the laggard debtor and said: "What would your neighbors think if we came and took your car away?"

Presently they got a letter back from the man, in which he said: "I've asked my neighbors about this, and they all agree it would be a pretty lousy thing for you to do."

47.2

"I'm sorry I cannot make my installment payment this month."

"But you said that last month and the month before."

"Yes, and you must admit, I kept my word."

47.3

She was a reckless spender. Her husband was at his wits' end.

He said, "You're driving me to the poorhouse."

"Driving, nothing," she said, "You'll have to walk. The finance company took the car this morning."

Definition

47.4

Installment Buying: A method invented to make the months seem shorter.

Aphorisms

47.5

It has been said that the only reason a great many American families do not own elephants is because they have never been offered them for a $1 down and the balance in easy monthly payments.

47.6

Durable goods are those that last longer than the installment payments.

47.7

Many people who buy on time forget to pay that way.

(*See also 23.11, 25.1, 25.53, 202.15, 225.2, 225.12, 225.15*)

48. Customers-at-large

Anecdotes

48.1

The Quaker lady was incensed at a poultry dealer who, she felt, was overcharging her. As she made her dignified exit from the shop, she stopped at the door and called out, "I suggest when thee gets back to thy kennel, thee bring a bone for thy mother."

48.2

A woman, shopping for a lamb's-wool coat, encountered one priced $150 and another $175.

She asked why the price difference. The saleslady said the higher-priced one was virgin lambs' wool.

"For $25," said customer, "I should worry if the lamb was a virgin?"

48.3

"That's a delightful hat. It makes you look ten years younger," gushed the saleslady.

"Then I don't want it," said the customer. "I don't want to add ten years to my age every time I take off my hat."

48.4

"This hat," she explained to her husband, "cost me nothing. It was marked down from $20 to $10, so I bought it with the $10 saved."

48.5

A kleptomaniac addicted to S. Klein's Store at Union Square, in New York, repeatedly tried to steal something and just as often was caught in the act by one of the store's many detectives. They knew she was feeble-minded, so always let her go.

But finally the store detectives got sick of this compulsive thief and told her that if she did not stop bothering them they would have her sent up for five years. "Why don't you leave us alone and operate at some other store?" they asked her.

"Oh, but Klein's has such wonderful bargains!" exclaimed the nut.

48.6

Three devilish young boys went into Old Caspar's hardware store, and one of them asked for 10 cents' worth of BB shot—which was on a top shelf. Old Caspar creaked his way up and down the ladder to fill the order.

Then, to the old fellow's annoyance, the second kid said he wanted 10 cents' worth of BB shot, too. Again Caspar inched his way up and down the ladder, but before putting the box back on the shelf he asked the third boy if he wanted the same order. No, said the boy. But when old Caspar got down, the third boy said he wanted only a nickel's worth of BB shot.

48.7

The mountaineer on one of his rare visits to town stood looking at the products in a fruit store, and particularly at a stalk of bananas. "Those are bananas," said the proprietor. "Want to try one?"

"No, I reckon not," said the mountaineer. "I've got so many tastes now I kaint satisfy, I ain't aimin' to take on any more."

48.8

A man noticed a price tag of $100 on a scrawny and mean-looking parrot in a pet-store window. This gave him an idea. When he got home he rustled up a live turkey, put it in a cage, went with it to the pet store, and offered it to the proprietor for $200.

"You're kidding," laughed the store owner.

"No, I'm not," said the man with the gobbler. "If that mangy thing in the window is worth $100, then this chubby and beautiful bird is worth twice as much."

"But," said the merchant, "my parrot talks. What can a fool turkey do?"

"Sir," said the man proudly, "my turkey is a philosopher. He thinks."

48.9

"How much are these cigars?"

"Two for a quarter."

"I'll just have one," said the customer, paying 15 cents for it and departing.

A man standing nearby walked up to the cigar counter, pushed a dime across, and said, "I'll take the other cigar."

Definitions

48.10

Patron: A customer who doesn't ask prices.

48.11

Sales resistance is the triumph of mind over patter.

—*Anonymous*

Aphorisms

48.12

If you watch some women shop, you would think they were taking inventory of the store.

48.13

It makes no difference what it is, a woman will buy anything she thinks a store is losing money on.

—*Kin Hubbard*

48.14

An extravagance is anything you buy that is of no earthly use to your wife.

—*Franklin Pierce Adams*

(*See also 10.3, 13.7, 24.8, 24.17–24.19, 24.22, 24.24, 34.2, 42.6, 42.7, 42.9–42.16, 42.19–42.24, 42.26, 42.27, 42.29, 45.10, 46.3, 46.4, 46.13, 47.1–47.7*)

SERVICES AND DISSERVICES

49. Out of the Mouths of Cabbies

Anecdotes

49.1

A cab driver had knocked down a woman pedestrian, and the traffic cop on the corner began to bawl him out, yelling, "You must be blind!"

"Wassa matter with you," the hackie yelled back. "I hit her, didn't I?"

49.2

A pregnant woman crossing the street collided with a taxicab. The cab driver leaned out and said to the woman, "Lady, you can be knocked down, too."

49.3

A pedestrian stepped in the way of a New York taxicab in busy midtown. The driver leaned out of his cab and, in sweetest tones, asked: "Please, sir, may I ask what are your plans?"

49.4

"If you hit 'em you've gotta fill out a report," explained a New York taxi driver as he skillfully missed a pedestrian.

49.5

During an argument with a cab driver over the question of the fare, the woman passenger said, "See here, young man, don't try to tell me. I haven't been riding in cabs for five years for nothing."

"Maybe not," said the cab driver, "but I'll bet you sure tried to."

49.6

The elderly woman, disturbed by the way her taxi driver was whizzing around corners, finally said to him, "Why don't you do what I do when I turn corners—I just shut my eyes."

49.7

A wealthy New York widow customarily used the same cab from her apartment in the Waldorf-Astoria for her trips around Manhattan. When she planned to tour Europe she offered to pay all the costs, plus the usual meter charge, if the cabby would accompany her to Europe with his cab. So cab and cabby were aboard the ship when the widow left New York, and they were months touring Europe at a fantastic cost to the uncomplaining widow.

When they arrived back in New York the widow wanted to be driven direct from the pier to an ailing daughter who lived on the outskirts of Brooklyn and so instructed her cabby.

But the hackie reverted to type. "Brooklyn!" he screamed at her. "Are you crazy? Don't you know that every time a cab goes to Brooklyn he's got to come back empty. I can't afford no trip like that."

49.8

Two overdressed and overfed women sat in a New York cab smoking and deploring the large earnings of workers in general and of cab drivers in particular. "Some of the drivers," said one, "even own their own homes and send their children to colleges." The other woman agreed it was deplorable, then said, "There's not even an ash tray in this cab."

"Throw it on the floor, lady," called the up-to-this-point silent hackie. "I've a woman who comes in every week to clean up."

49.9

It was a windy, snowy, and bitterly cold day when a man got into a cab in New York and said to the driver, "Sure a terrible day, isn't it?"

"I guess you're right, mister," said the cabby. "I've been driving since sunrise, and I ain't seen a single butterfly yet."

49.10

A man wearing a hearing aid stepped into a cab, and the cabbie asked him, "Those things any good?"

Patron said, "I would be lost without it."

Hackie said, "Must be tough to be hard-of-hearing. Oh, well, nearly all of us have something the matter one way or another. Take me, for instance, I can hardly see."

49.11

Sign in a New York taxicab:

IF DROPPING ASHES ON THE FLOOR MAKES YOU FEEL AT HOME—THEN BE MY GUEST.

(*See also 70.17, 150.3, 175.4, 226.10, 229.14, 267.4*)

50. Waiters and Waitresses

Anecdotes

50.1

A customer refused to take a fried egg when it was served him, because he said the charge of 50 cents was too much. "But, my dear sir," said the waiter, "be reasonable and look at the other side of it. Remember that an egg represents a whole day's work for the hen."

50.2

The waiter placed the bill on the table, face down. The patron picked it up, looked at it, and demanded, "Waiter, what is this $5 charge for?"

"That, sir, is for the chopped liver."

"Whose liver did they chop—Rockefeller's?"

50.3

After years of back-breaking toil an old farmer came to New York City to see some of the sights and spend a few hard-earned dollars. He went to a few movies and then to a nice-looking restaurant for some cake and coffee. He dawdled over his food for an hour, enjoying it, the handsomely dressed people, and the beautiful decor of the place. When he was ready to leave he called a waiter over, handed him a 50-cent piece, and asked for his change.

The waiter said there was no change due him. "Why not?" demanded the farmer.

"Because," said the waiter with a touch of impudence, "cake and coffee costs 50 cents." When the farmer protested that this was exorbitant, the waiter replied that the charge included the beauty of the painting on the walls, the fine tables and chairs, the luxurious flooring. "You have to pay for these," said the waiter. "You've been looking at them and enjoying them."

"All right," said the farmer. He arose, went to another table, and again ordered cake and coffee. He then handed the waiter 20 cents. "I beg your pardon," said the waiter, "but the charge is 50 cents."

"Oh, you mean 30 cents more for the pictures and furniture and all that? Well, Mister, I've already paid for that. This time I'm just buying cake and coffee."

50.4

The headwaiter in a plush New York restaurant was horrified to notice that a diner had wrapped a napkin around his neck as he seated himself at a table.

The headwaiter called the waiter to him, pointed out the glaring breach of etiquette, and asked him to have it corrected without offending the guest. The waiter walked quietly to the offending diner, bowed, and said quietly: "Sir, will you have a shave or a haircut?"

50.5

A young woman entered the hotel dining room carrying an impudent-looking dog and sat down at a table. When the waiter handed her the menu and waited for her order, the dog began to yap irritatingly. In his most ingratiating manner the waiter asked, "Your first dog, Madam?"

50.6

A waiter standing against a post in a restaurant was asked the time by a patron. "This ain't my station," yawned the waiter.

50.7

Robert Q. Lewis reports he went into a restaurant for lunch and, after waiting twenty minutes for a waiter, called one over and told him that he had only one hour for lunch.

"I don't have time to discuss your labor problems now," replied the waiter coldly.

50.8

"May I help you with the soup, sir?" asked the waiter.

"What do you mean, help me? I don't need any help."

Waiter: "Sorry, sir. From the sound I thought you might want to be dragged ashore."

50.9

Diner: "Waiter, I want some oysters, but not too large or too small, too old or too tough, and they mustn't be salty. I want them cold and I want them at once."

Waiter: "Yes, sir. With or without pearls?"

50.10

A man ordered a lamb chop and peas in New York's costliest restaurant. The waiter returned and on the plate the customer saw only one pea.

"Where is the lamb chop?" he asked.

"Under the pea," said the waiter with dignity.

50.11

"Waiter, one of the legs of this chicken is shorter than the other?"

"You gonna eat it or dance with it, mister?"

50.12

"Waiter, look at this chicken; it's nothing but skin and bone."

"Whadda want? Maybe also the feathers?"

50.13

"Waiter, there's something wrong with these hot dogs."

"Don't bother me about it," said the waiter. "I'm not a veterinarian."

50.14

"Waiter, this bread isn't fresh. It's from yesterday."

"Wassamatter," replied the waiter. "Yesterday wasn't a good day?"

50.15

"Waiter, this water is cloudy."

"The water's all right," said the waiter. "It's the glass—it's dirty."

50.16

"Waiter, these oysters are not only too small, but they don't look healthy."

"Then you're lucky, mister, they ain't any bigger."

50.17

"Waiter, I don't like the looks of this mackerel?"

"If you want looks, why didn't you order goldfish?"

50.18

"Waiter, I don't find a single clam in this clam chowder."

"So what? You order cabinet pudding, you expect to find the Secretary of State in it?"

50.19

"Waiter, what is this thing in my soup?"

"Sorry, sir, I can't help you. I don't know nothin' about insects."

50.20

"Waiter, there's a fly in the ice cream!"

"Well, let him freeze to death. That will teach him a lesson."

50.21

"Waiter, there's a fly in my soup."—

"Shh—everyone will want one."

"Grab the fork. Maybe the trout will come to the surface."

"That's all right. No extra charge."

"Wait'll you see the coffee."

"What do you expect for a dime—a hummingbird?"

50.22

"Waiter, this food is terrible. I won't eat it! You'd better get the manager."

"Won't do any good, mister; the manager wouldn't eat it either."

50.23

Customer: "Why is it I never get what I ask for here?"

Waiter: "Perhaps, madam, we are too polite."

50.24

For years a veteran waiter had served a wealthy couple we will call the Johnsons. He was a model waiter, but after a while began calling them by their first names. "What are you having tonight, Sam?" he would ask cordially.

This irked Mrs. Johnson, and she demanded that her husband lay down the law to the waiter and insist that they be called Mr. and Mrs. Johnson. The next time they came to dinner the waiter said, "What looks good to you tonight, Jane?"

"From now on," said Mr. Johnson, "there will be no more first names. To you we are Mr. and Mrs. Johnson."

The waiter made an elaborate bow and said, "Pleased to meetcha."

50.25

Traveling by train, Albert Einstein decided to go into the diner for lunch. Arrived at his table, the great scientist discovered he had forgotten his glasses and could not read the menu. He asked the dining-car waiter to read it to him. The waiter fumbled with the menu and then said to Dr. Einstein, "Boss, I can't make it out either. I guess we're both ignorant."

50.26

Henry Ward Beecher is said to have gone into a short-order restaurant where he was amused by the way the waiters gave the orders to the cook—such as, "sinkers and a cow" (doughnuts and milk) and "one on the city" (a glass of water).

"I'll give the waiter an order that he cannot translate into his jargon," said Beecher to a friend. "Waiter, let me have two poached eggs on toast, with the yolks broken."

"Adam and Eve on a raft; wreck 'em," screamed the waiter.

50.27

The waitress was so dumb she thought hardening of the arteries was a highway project.

51. Barbershop Banter

Anecdotes

51.1

The customer sat himself down in the barber's chair and said, "Before you begin, I want you to know that I rather like the kind of weather we are having; I have no interest in either the N.Y. Mets or the N.Y. Yankees; I pay no attention to prize fights or horse races; I'm not interested in the latest newspaper scandals; and I never discuss my political opinions. Now, go ahead with your work."

"OK," said the barber. "And if it will not offend you, sir, I will be able to do my work better and faster if you don't talk so much."

51.2

A barbershop in Phoenix, Arizona, has a sign reading

TWENTY BARBERS—CONTINUOUS CONVERSATION.

51.3

The oldest recorded ad lib is said to go back hundreds of years B.C., when a barber asked a man how he wanted his hair cut. "In silence," was the reply.

(*See also 144.3, 178.11*)

52. Maids and Butlers

Anecdotes

52.1

"Bridget, for the first thirty minutes after six o'clock I want you to stand at the front door and call the guests' names as they arrive."

"Very well, ma'am, I've been wantin' to do that for years."

52.2

"Be careful, Bertha," said the mistress, "when you serve the guests this evening. I don't want you to spill anything."

"Don't worry," said Bertha. "I'll keep my mouth shut."

52.3

A man and his wife returning to the U.S. became interested in a Finnish girl migrating to the U.S. and uncertain as to what she would do when she got there. They decided she was a good prospect for a job in their home.

They questioned her. Could she cook? Could she do housework? Could she take care of young children? No, she said to each of these questions; her mother did the cooking; her sister did the housework; and the grandmother took care of the younger children in the family.

Nonplussed, they asked the girl, "Then what could you do if you worked for us?"

"Well," said the girl, "I could milk reindeer."

52.4

The new maid was relating some of the experiences she had had in service.

"You seem to have had a good many situations," said the mistress to whom she was talking. "How many different mistresses have you had all told?"

"Fifteen, all told," replied the maid; "all told exactly what I thought of them."

52.5

The new maid in a gourmet's home was instructed to serve the fish whole, with head and tail intact, and with a lemon in the mouth.

The maid did precisely as told. She served the fish with a lemon in her mouth.

52.6

The new maid dragged around the house on her chores with all the vim of an aging snail. "Heavens, you're slow," complained the mistress of the household. "Isn't there anything you can do quickly?"

"Yes, ma'am," said the maid indolently, "get tired."

52.7

"Mary, be careful when you dust those pictures," said the mistress to her new maid. "They are all old masters."

"Glory be!" said the maid. "I'd never have thought you've been married so many times."

52.8

When the phone rang the maid answered it, listened briefly, said, "Yes, I know it is," and then hung up.

"Who was that calling?" asked the mistress.

"Oh, some silly woman who said, 'It's a long distance from Chicago.' "

52.9

"Nellie, you only gave the eight-day clock a few turns," said the mistress to her maid.

"That's right, ma'am," replied the maid. "Have you forgotten I'm leaving tomorrow? I'm not goin' to do the new girl's work."

52.10

"Ma'am, this is my last day with you—I got myself a new job."

"What is this new job, Rebecca?"

"This new job don't allow me to work anymore. I'm going on relief."

52.11

When a woman pointed out to her maid how foolish some of her actions were, the maid retorted frankly but not unpleasantly: "Goodness, Miss Mae, you don't have to tell me what a fool I am. I wouldn't have been working here for twelve years if I wasn't foolish."

52.12

A servant, who was roasting a stork for his master, was prevailed upon by his sweetheart to cut off one of the bird's legs for her. When the stork was brought to the table the master wanted to know what had become of the other leg. The man answered that storks never have more than one leg. The master, very angry, but determined to strike his servant dumb before he punished him, took him the next day into the fields where they saw storks, standing each on one leg, as storks do. The servant turned triumphantly to his master, but the latter shouted, and the birds put down their other legs and flew away.

"Ah, Sir," said the servant, "you did not shout to the stork at dinner yesterday! If you had done so, he would have shown his other leg, too!"

(*See also 112.7, 118.7, 158.9, 160.1, 177.6, 179.8, 194.4, 226.1, 231.9, 240.26, 243.5, 248.14*)

53. Tips and Tippers

Anecdotes

53.1

A wealthy Chicagoan had taken his elderly aunt from Peoria to dinner at a posh restaurant. During their dinner a waiter passed with a portion of shishkebab (lamb on a flaming sword). "My goodness, what is that?" asked the startled lady. "Oh, don't get upset," said the man-about-town. "It's only a patron who failed to leave a large enough tip."

53.2

The old miser laid three pennies on the table as a tip for the waiter. The waiter, pretending thanks, said he would like to use the three pennies to tell the man's fortune. The old man agreed. "The first penny," said the waiter, "indicates that you are very frugal. The second penny tells me you are a bachelor."

"That is correct," said the miser. "Now what does the third penny tell?"

"It tells me," said the waiter, "that your father was a bachelor."

53.3

When a bellhop in a Miami hotel was asked to bring a deck of cards to a certain room, he did so by making fifty-two trips.

53.4

Although a generous tipper, Robert Benchley decided when leaving a swank resort hotel that he was not going to tip anyone because the service had been unsatisfactory. He managed to ignore all the outstretched hands as he was leaving, except for the final barrier—the doorman. This worthy thrust out his hand to Benchley and said, "You are not going to forget me, Sir?"

Benchley grasped the greedy palm and said, "No, I'll write you."

53.5

New guest: "I don't know why they call this hotel The Palms. I haven't seen a palm near the place."

Old-timer: "You'll see them before you go. They are reserved by the staff for the last day of your stay here."

53.6

A customer of a large department store complained to the management that the attendant in the ladies' room had stared coldly at her when she did not leave a tip.

"But we have no attendant in our ladies' room," insisted the manager. When the customer replied indignantly that she was not in the habit of lying, the manager promised an investigation would be made. It was then found that a woman had wandered into the ladies' room a year ago to rest. She took out her knitting and sat there to relax. When she found people giving her coins, she simply went there every day with her knitting and accepted the gratuities handed to her.

53.7

A pullman-car passenger asked the porter: "Tell me, what is the average tip you get from a passenger on this run?"

"One dollar, sir," was the reply. The traveler handed over $1, and the porter immediately burst into voluble thanks. "Sir," he said, "you are the first man who has ever come up to the average."

53.8

A true test of generosity is to give the hat-check girl a quarter without wondering if a dime would have been enough.

Definition

53.9

Service: The concept of doing something for nothing while doing someone for something.

(*See also 208.6, 208.16, 226.13*)

Part Two

POLITICS, GOVERNMENT, AND THE LAW'S DEFENDERS AND FLOUTERS

THE POLITICAL PARADE

HACKS, HECKLERS, WITS, AND WISDOM

54. The Game of Politics

Anecdotes

54.1

Several political hacks were discussing the merits of their respective candidates for an office that was open. The leader of the group finally said, "Let's not kid ourselves about these guys. None of them are much good, and every one of them would sell his mother if he got a good enough price."

"Yeah," said one of the men, "but my guy would deliver!"

54.2

A heckler accused a well-known politician of being two-faced. Without hesitation or change of expression the politician calmly replied, "I leave this to the audience. If I had two faces, would I be wearing this one?"

54.3

"I'm pleased to see so dense a crowd here this evening," said the politician as he began his speech.

"Don't be too sure of yourself, mister," cried out one man. "We ain't as dense as you think."

54.4

When a big power pump was installed in some dredging operation to replace several hundred Irish workers, a politician was asked what he thought of the new machinery.

"It's all right," he said, "it works fine—but it can't vote."

54.5

A politician, greeting a group of commercial artists, was asked his favorite color and replied, "Plaid."

54.6

The small town was shaken to its foundations by a political question. When one of the town's sages was asked for his opinion, he said, "I haven't yet decided which side I'm on. But I'll tell you this: When I do make up my mind I'm goin' to be damn bitter about it!"

54.7

Gerald F. Lieberman says that a Midwestern paper used to report the resignations and deaths of politicians under "Public Improvements."

54.8

In earlier days in America it was not unusual for politicians to take advantage of a public hanging to address the crowd of spectators. In one instance the condemned was told that a politician was going to speak on the grim occasion. "Hang me first," the poor fellow screamed. Another man about to be hanged thanked the speaker for making it easier to die.

54.9

Charles F. Murphy, the powerful and sometimes waggish leader of Tammany Hall, was continually being asked for help. On one occasion he was asked to help a city employee due to go on trial on a serious charge. Murphy got the record on this man, saw the evidence against him was conclusive, and decided to do nothing. Ten days later the seeker of Murphy's help phoned him and said, "You and your influence! My brother was convicted—look at his rogue's gallery picture in the paper!"

"I saw it," said Murphy. "But did you notice the nice low number I got him?"

54.10

The politician was mangling and misusing the facts during his political tirade. "He's murdering the truth," said a fellow newspaperman to Heywood Broun.

"Don't worry," said Broun. "He'll never get close enough to it to do it any harm."

54.11

Frederick Landis, speaking on the same program with Will Hays, wanted to have some fun with the then chairman of the Republican National Committee and said, "Will Hays has been successful in politics for twenty years—I know he has been successful because he has never been caught at it."

54.12

Three men were arguing—a doctor, an architect, and a politician—about whose profession was the oldest. The doctor said his was oldest since God created Eve out of Adam's rib and in fact performed a surgical operation.

The architect said, "My profession is the oldest since God, just like any architect, in creating the world, made it out of chaos."

"And who," asked the politician, "made the chaos?"

54.13

Two Politicians were exchanging ideas regarding the rewards for public service.

"The reward that I most desire," said the First Politician, "is the gratitude of my fellow citizens."

"That would be very gratifying, no doubt," said the Second Politician, "but, alas! in order to obtain it one has to retire from politics." For an instant they gazed upon each other with inexpressible tenderness; then the First Politician murmured, "God's will be done! Since we cannot hope for reward let us be content with what we have."

And lifting their right hands for a moment from the public treasury they swore to be content.

—*Ambrose Bierce,* Fantastic Fables

54.14

Robert Gordon Menzies, newly elected Prime Minister of Australia, was giving his first official interview. "I take it, Mr. Prime Minister," asked a left-wing correspondent, "that you will consult the powerful interests that control you before you choose your Cabinet?"

"Naturally," replied the Prime Minister, "but, young man, please keep my wife's name out of this discussion."

54.15

When a man said to de Gaulle, "My friends are not content with your policy," de Gaulle said, "Well, change your friends."

54.16

While I was in Paris there was a public debate between some steady-going Radical and the chivalrous, the magnanimous, the almost mythical Droulede.

"Your plebiscitary President," said the Radical to Deroulede, "would be just as likely as any other tyrant to knock you in the eye and make you see all the colors of the rainbow."

"I only wish to see three of them," retorted the Nationalist leader.

—*G. K. Chesterton*

54.17

A spokesman from a Bundestag delegation called on Chancellor Konrad Adenauer when he was the strong chief executive of West Germany after World War II. The head of the delegation said, "Herr Adenauer, we have not come here just to say 'Amen and Ja' to everything you propose." "Gentlemen," replied Adenauer, "'Amen' is not necessary—'Ja' will do fine."

54.18

The story is told of a Dutch farmer who was very proud of his young son. One day he slipped into the boy's room and put on his table a Bible, a bottle of whisky, and a silver dollar, and watched to see what happened—which the boy would choose and thus indicate his career.

The boy ran to the table, picked up the dollar and put it in his pocket, picked up the Bible and put it under his arm, and took a few drinks of whisky and smacked his lips.

The old man said "Mein gracious! He iss going to be a politician!"

—*Senator Bob Taylor,* Life Pictures

54.19

"Guver'mint," said an old Irish sage, "is half a dozen gintlemin an' the loikes, maybe, that meets an' thinks what's best for thimselves, and thin says that's best for the people."

54.20

During the rebellion in Ireland, an Irishman went to confession and said he had killed a British policeman. Hearing no comment from the priest, he said, "Father, are ye dead?"

"Dead I'm not," replied the priest. "I'm waiting for you to stop talking politics and start confessing your sins."

54.21

When asked what he considered the most essential qualifications for a politician, Winston Churchill said: "It's the ability to foretell what will happen tomorrow, next month, and next year—and to explain afterward why it did not happen."

54.22

Mother: "What makes you think Junior will be in politics one day?"

Father: "He says more things that sound well and mean nothing than any other boy I know."

—*The Tusco Tarian*

Definitions

54.23

Politics is the art of obtaining money from

the rich and votes from the poor, on the pretext of protecting each from the other.

—*Oscar Ameringer*

54.24

Politics is the art of looking for trouble, finding it everywhere, diagnosing it wrongly, and applying unsuitable remedies.

—*Sir Ernest Benn,* New York Times Magazine, 1946

54.25

Politics is perhaps the only profession for which no preparation is thought necessary.

—*Robert Louis Stevenson*

54.26

Politician: A man who identifies the sound of his own voice with the infallible voice of the people.

54.27

Politician: A person who can talk in circles while standing four-square.

—*Changing Times*

54.28

A politician is an animal who can sit on a fence and yet keep both ears to the ground.

54.29

A politician is a man who stands for what he thinks other people will fall for.

54.30

Politician: One who is willing to do anything on earth for the workers except become one.

—*Judge*

54.31

A statesman is a successful politician who is dead.

—*Thomas B. Reed*

54.32

A statesman is a man who can solve grave problems that wouldn't have existed if there were no statesmen.

54.33

A statesman is a man who knows the question. A politician is a man who knows the answers.

54.34

Imagination: What makes some politicians think they are statesmen.

—*Roberta Tennes*

54.35

When a politician was asked what he meant by a demagogue he said, "A demagogue is a man who can rock the boat himself and persuade everybody there's a terrible storm at sea."

54.36

A leader is one who watches which way the crowd is going and then runs and steps in front of it.

54.37

Influence: A power you think you have until you try to use it.

Aphorisms

54.38

Politics consists of two sides and a fence.

—*Herbert Dale*

54.39

The successful politician's first commandment is: Thou shalt not commit thyself.

54.40

In politics, as elsewhere, a nut goes with every bolt.

54.41

Politics makes strange bedfellows, but they soon get used to the bunk.

54.42

The fellow who stays home on election day because he doesn't want to have anything to do with crooked politics has a lot more to do with crooked politics than he thinks.

—Kingsport, Tenn., *Times-News*

54.43

The experienced politician can toss his hat in the ring and still talk through it.

54.44

A politician has to be able to see both sides of an issue so he can get around it.

54.45

A good politician is a fellow who has prejudices enough to suit the needs of all his constituents.

54.46

The typical politician, when he comes to the parting of the ways, goes both ways.

54.47

Some politicians repair their fences by hedging.

—*Hawley R. Everhart*

54.48

A politician stands on his record so that people may not be able to examine it.

54.49

A politician's opinions are subject to change, all except the one he has of himself.

54.50

Politicians are of two classes—the appointed and the disappointed.

54.51

Among politicians, the esteem of religion is profitable, the principles of it are troublesome.

—*Benjamin Whichcote*

54.52

Give a politician a free hand, and he'll put it in your pocket.

54.53

An honest politician is one who when he is bought will stay bought.

—*Simon Cameron*

54.54

The mistake a lot of politicians make is in forgetting they've been appointed and thinking they've been anointed.

—*Mrs. Claude Pepper*

54.55

A politician divides his time between passing laws and helping his friends evade them.

54.56

Politicians are the same all over. They promise to build a bridge even when there is no river.

—*Nikita Khrushchev*, 1963

54.57

If a politician found he had cannibals among his constituents, he would promise them missionaries for their Sunday dinner.

—*H. L. Mencken*

54.58

When a politician says the nation is due for a reawakening, it means he's running for office.

54.59

He's the kind of politician who follows you through a revolving door and then comes out ahead of you.

54.60

When in trouble, bad politicians go to good lawyers.

54.61

"Straight-from-the-shoulder" politicians should talk from a little higher up.

54.62

I am not a politician, and my other habits are good.

—*Artemus Ward*

54.63

Governor Robert Bradford of Massachusetts said that "the successful politician should have the hide of a rhinoceros, the memory of an elephant, the persistence of a beaver, the native friendliness of a mongrel pup, the heart of a lion, and the stomach of an ostrich. And it helps to have the humor and ubiquity of a crow. But all these combined are not enough, unless when it comes to matters of principle, you also have the stubbornness of an army mule."

54.64

If a politician tries to buy votes with private money, he is a dirty crook; but if he tries to buy them with the people's own money, he's a great liberal.

—*Pay Dirt*

54.65

The statesman shears the sheep, the politician skins them.

—*Austin O'Malley*

54.66

A politician thinks of the next election; a statesman, of the next generation.

—*James Freeman Clarke*

54.67

It seems like the less a statesman amounts to, the more he loves the flag.

—*Kin Hubbard*

54.68

You can always get the truth from an American statesman after he has turned seventy, or given up all hope of the Presidency.

—*Wendell Phillips*

54.69

The trouble with being a leader today is that you can't be sure whether the people are following you or chasing you.

54.70

A political war is one in which everyone shoots from the lip.

—*Raymond Moley*

54.71

Democracy is based upon the conviction that there are extraordinary possibilities in ordinary people.

—*H. E. Fosdick*

54.72

The man who pulls the plow gets the plunder in politics.

—*Huey P. Long*

54.73

A politician is like quicksilver: if you try to put your finger on him, you will find nothing under it.

—*Austin O'Malley*

(*See also 55.1–86.16, 154.32, 244.11, 269.63, 271.50*)

CAMPAIGNS AND CANDIDATES

55. From Coast to Coast

Anecdotes

55.1

When Franklin D. Roosevelt was running for a third term on the Democratic ticket, a Republican candidate for the Legislature in Vermont declared he was supporting F.D.R. for the Presidency. A Vermont Republican challenged this man's divided party loyalty. "What are you," he asked the candidate, "A Republican or a Democrat? I want an honest answer."

"I'll give you an honest answer," said the candidate. "I am a politician."

55.2

Senator Norris Cotton of New Hampshire tells about the time early in his career when he addressed a political rally. He gave it his best, pulled out all the stops, and got so involved with his own oratory that he forgot the passage of time. Finally he became aware that his audience was becoming restive and apologized for the time he had taken up. One of his associates in the rear of the hall, thinking he needed some encouragement, called out, "Come on Norris! Tell us the whole story."

The meeting chairman, glad of an opportunity to encourage the speaker to stop, leaned over and said, "Don't pay any attention to that blatherskite. He's the town drunk."

55.3

State Senator Ernest A. Johnson, seeking reelection, said, "I have made no wild promises, except one—honest government."

—Worcester, Mass., *Sunday Telegram*

55.4

Republican Senator John Sherman Cooper tells about the time he was campaigning in a fiercely Democratic area of Kentucky and was shaking every hand in sight. One old fellow seemed reluctant.

"I'm John Cooper," said the Senator.

"You're a Republican, ain't you?" challenged the man.

"Yes."

"Well," drawled the man extending a limp hand, "just press it light."

—*Paul F. Healy,* in Saturday Evening Post

55.5

After failing to win the nomination for sheriff in Jefferson County, Tennessee, a farmer advertised in the local paper: "I want to thank my forty-three friends . . . for casting their votes for me, and to the rest . . . I warn that I am now going armed with a sawed-off shot gun, because a man that has only forty-three friends in a county as big as Jefferson is definitely in need of extra protection."

55.6

A man campaigning for office in Virginia stopped one day on the outskirts of his district to talk to a farmer working in the fields. The farmer paid scant attention to him. The politician, in order to curry favor, picked up another hoe and began to work feverishly along with the farmer. Finally the farmer began to talk, and toward the end of conversation the farmer said, "Wa'al, I reckon you're pretty good at hoein', and if only I lived over the line in Old Virginny I'd vote for you." The politician hustled back from North Carolina to Virginia.

55.7

A candidate for the Georgia Legislature had years before been discharged from a mental hospital. His opponent learned of this and made it an issue in the campaign. This did not disturb the other man; he simply declared, "I am the only man running for office in Georgia who can prove he is not crazy."

55.8

When W. B. Hartsfield was mayor of Atlanta, he related that his first venture into politics was as a candidate for the City Council of Atlanta. On every crowded street corner and every public gathering he passed out cards and campaign material, greeting everyone. One day a friend told him a political meeting was being held on a certain residential street, but the fellow was not certain of the address. When Hartsfield came upon a number of parked cars and a crowd, he swung into action, dealing out cards and shaking hands. But he was stung by the cool reception he got; the more he smiled the more frigid. Finally on the steps of the house he mumbled, "This isn't much of a political rally—it's more like a funeral."

"Brother," a nearby voice retorted gruffly, "this is a funeral."

55.9

In the backwoods of Alabama two self-made lawyers were competing for the same office. One of them pointed out that he was a poor farm boy who had purchased some law books with money he earned working in the fields and had read those books whenever he found spare minutes night and day.

This made a strong impression, but his adversary got up and told the crowd that he had been an even poorer boy—too poor even to buy any law books. "But I obtained my knowledge of law by looking over this other man's shoulder."

55.10

A Southern politician, explaining how to make a safe and effective campaign speech, said that the speaker should make none of his points too distinct.

"A speech of this kind," he concluded, "should be blown up like a bladder, leaving no handle to be seized by the adversary."

55.11

"Private" John Mills Allen, later a famous senator from Mississippi, in the 1884 election took the stump against former Confederate General Tucker, who had two terms in Congress to his credit. Allen had not held office before. One night during the campaign Tucker wound up his speech with a rousing flourish, "My fellow citizens, twenty years ago last night, after a hard-fought battle on yonder hill, I bivouacked under yonder clump of trees. Those of you who remember, as I do, those times that tried men's souls will not, I hope, forget their humble servant when the primaries are held."

Allen went the general one better. He said, "My fellow citizens, what General Tucker says to you about bivouacking in yonder clump of trees on that night is true. It is also true, my fellow citizens, that I was a picket and stood guard over the general while he slept. Now then, fellow citizens, all of you who were generals and had privates stand guard over you while you slept, vote for General Tucker. And all of you who were privates and stood guard over the generals while they slept, vote for Private John Allen."

55.12

Congressman Johnny Allen, a famous wit from Mississippi, was once assailed by a man in the crowd who called out: "Allen, you're a faker. I'd rather vote for the Devil himself than for you."

"That's all right with me," said Allen. "But if your friend refuses to run, may I count on your vote then?"

55.13

When Congressman Johnny Allen was rebuked by a voter for talking "foolishly," Allen explained, "It was done, sir, only that you might better understand me."

55.14

One day when Mississippi Congressman Johnny Allen was campaigning, a stone was heaved through the air at his head. Allen ducked just in time.

"You see," said Allen, "if I had been an upright politician I would have been killed."

55.15

"Are you aware that Claude Pepper is known all over Washington as a shameless extrovert? Not only that, this man is reliably reported to practice nepotism with his sister-in-law, and he has a sister who was once a Thespian in wicked New York. Worst of all, it is an established fact that Mr. Pepper, before his marriage, habitually practiced celibacy."

—*Congressman Smathers,* of Florida, during an election campaign, 1949

55.16

A Texas candidate for office, speaking of his opponent, said, "That low-down scoundrel deserves to be kicked to death by a jackass—and I'm just the one to do it."

55.17

In 1950 Senator Robert Kerr of Oklahoma was campaigning for his junior colleague from Oklahoma, Mike Monroney, who was opposed by Rev. W. H. Bill Alexander.

Kerr told his audience that "Alexander one day said to his congregation, 'after communion with the Almighty, I have decided to enter the Democratic primaries and run for the Senate.' "

"Well," continued Kerr, "soon afterward Alexander switched over to win the Republican nomination. What I would like to know is this: If the Lord told Alexander to run as a Democrat, who, then, told him to run as a Republican?"

55.18

Some years ago Senator Homer Capehart, an

Indiana Republican, was campaigning for election and handshaking his way down a village street. He encountered one very old man, extended his hand, and went into his pitch: "I'm Homer Capehart, and I'd sure appreciate your vote for me."

"No, Sir," said the old fellow, "I'm not gonna vote for you. I'm a Democrat."

"My friend," said Capehart genially, "I've looked in all the books and talked to all the lawyers, and there's nothing that says a Democrat can't vote for a Republican."

"Maybe there's no law agin' it," said the old man firmly, "but there's a conscience against it, and I ain't gonna go against it."

55.19

Senator Jenner of Indiana spoke of the perils of campaigning in Indiana. At a political meeting in the southern end of the state, a campaign manager met a sad-eyed farmer leaving the hall where his candidate was making a bid for votes.

"Are you just going in?" the campaign manager asked diplomatically. "I hear the candidate for Congress is making a great speech."

"No, sir," said the farmer, "I've just come out. I heard the candidate."

"What's he talking about?"

"Well," said the farmer, "he didn't say."

55.20

During a primary campaign in Illinois a candidate touring the rural areas told a crowd, "I am a farmer, just like you men. I can plow, milk cows, shoe horses, harvest crops—do just about anything that needs doing on the farm."

"Can you lay an egg?" called a man in the audience.

55.21

Stanley Walker told about an old Mexican who stood at the curb of a public square in a New Mexico town just before election day, while a candidate for office ranted, raved, and rabble-roused with much arm waving, jumping up and down and generally acting like a political clown.

"Who is that?" Walker asked the old Mexican.

"*Es un hombre de muchas pulgas* (He's a man with many fleas)," said the Mexican.

55.22

The witty former Senator Azhurst from Arizona, illustrating the risks one takes employing wit in a political campaign, told about a colleague of his who was defeated when he explained why an opponent was burdened with a current indebtedness. The candidate said, "It is against his principle to pay the interest and against his interest to pay the principal."

55.23

Senator Henry M. Jackson, on a visit to his home state of Washington, was visiting a lumber mill when he stepped on a section of floorboarding that had rotted. Suddenly it gave way, and the Senator was buried up to his hips in the floor. Though cut up and bruised, he grinned up at the rest of the party and said, "This must have been one of the planks of the Republican platform."

(*See also* 54.2, 54.3)

56. From the Convention Hall

Anecdotes

56.1

A Republican convention in Chicago was opened by a clergyman who gave an exceptionally long prayer. As it went on and on, Heywood Broun in the press section listened in amazement then turned to a colleague and said, "My God, it's a filibuster!"

56.2

When the Republican convention of 1900 began, Finley Peter Dunne's astute bartender, Mr. Dooley, said of it: "Th' proceedins was opened with a prayer that Providence might r-remain undher th' protection iv th' administration."

56.3

William Allen White, covering a Democratic state convention, was spotted in the front row by the presiding officer, who leaned over and said to him, "Mr. White, since there is no clergyman in the audience we would like you to open the convention with a prayer."

White, annoyed by the attempt to get a well known Republican to open a Democratic meeting, said, "You will have to excuse me. I'm not much at public praying. Besides, I much prefer that the Lord doesn't know that I'm here."

(*See also* 60.19, 83.6)

57. Candidate versus Voter

Anecdotes

57.1

William Jennings Bryan, during the course of a political speech, shouted, "I wish I had the wings of a bird to fly to every village and hamlet in America to tell the people about this silver question."

"You'd be shot for a goose before you've flown a mile," cried out a man in the audience.

57.2

In a frothy peroration a candidate for Congress cried out: "And in conclusion, my fellow citizens, I want to state that I was born a Democrat, always have been a Democrat, and expect to die a Democrat."

A heckler called back: "Not very ambitious, are you?"

57.3

An old Civil War general, campaigning for public office, declared: "My proudest boast is that I was one of the men behind the guns."

"How far back, General?" asked someone in the audience.

57.4

"You cannot keep me down," shouted the orator at a political meeting on the New England seacoast. "Though I may be pressed below the waves, I rise again; you will find that I come to the surface, gentlemen."

"Yes," said an old whaler in the audience, "you come to the surface to blow."

57.5

An old politician making a speech shouted, "Fellow citizens, I know no North, I know no East, I know no West, I know no South."

A barefoot boy in the crowd yelled out, "You'd better go an' study jog-er-fey!"

57.6

The candidate for political office was in fine fettle, screaming and raving and ranting about the sins of the opposition. Finally he walked to the edge of the platform and called out, "Are you going to take this lying down?"

"We don't have to," called a voice from the rear. "The shorthand reporters are getting it all."

57.7

A man of dubious reputation had announced his candidacy for political office. One of his neighbors was asked by a townsman what he thought of the candidate—was he an honest man?

"Well," said the neighbor, "I wouldn't exactly call him a liar—but I have heard that when he wants his pigs to come home for their feed, he has to git somebuddy else to call 'em."

57.8

The candidate for office was up on the platform sounding off at great rate concerning his qualifications for office.

"Who is that man?" asked one man in the audience.

"I don't know," replied his friend, "but he sure recommends himself."

57.9

When James J. Curley was speaking during one of his many political campaigns in Boston, a heckler called out, "I wouldn't vote for you if you were St. Peter."

Without a moment's hesitation Curley replied, "If I were St. Peter you wouldn't be in my precinct."

57.10

Norman Thomas, during one of his campaigns for the Presidency on the Socialist ticket, was asked by a heckler: "You talk about the Socialist party. Then how come you were a Republican as an undergraduate at Princeton?"

"That proves," shouted back Thomas, "that you can learn something after you've graduated from Princeton."

57.11

"We must grow more wheat and . . .," said the politician when he was interrupted by a listener who called out, "What about hay?"

"I am talking about food for human consumption now," said the speaker. "I'll come around to your food in a minute."

57.12

A young man campaigning for office was hit with a ripe tomato while speaking to a hostile audience. He picked up the tomato, held it high, and said, "Folks, I take these kind of things with a grain of salt."

P.S. He was elected.

57.13

A congressman running for reelection was aware that the most stubborn opposition to him came from a certain farming region. He decided to campaign vigorously in that area. In order to reach the largest number of voters he had a loudspeaker installed in his car.

He then drove out to a remote part of the

countryside where he could try out the equipment in privacy. He parked his car beside a lonely road and over and over tested the volume of his voice. "Vote for Dr. Burnside for Congress," he kept repeating. The amplifier was powerful. The sound echoed up and down the valley.

The next day the congressman went into the grain and feed store of the nearby town and while there heard one Sam Jones urging some townspeople to vote for Burnside. Burnside was surprised because he knew that Sam had made no bones about being against his reelection.

"Why, Sam," said Burnside, "you've always argued against me. What did I say that made you change your mind?"

"Taint nothin' *you* said," Sam replied, shaking his head in wonder. "You think your way, and I'll think mine. But a powerful strange thing happened to me yesterday afternoon. I was out in my fields plowing when all of a sudden I hears a voice comin' right out of the heavens. 'Vote for Dr. Burnside' it said plain as could be and kept sayin' it over and over again. When I get a message from the Almighty, I don't aim to quarrel with Him."

57.14

A politician came upon a "poor white man" who had a vote and who did his own milking. Candidate Jones asked the farmer if he should hold the cow, which seemed to be uneasy. The old man said, "All right," and the politico took her by the horn and held her while they talked.

Finally the politician asked, "Have you had Robison (his opponent) around here lately?"

"Oh, yes," said the farmer. "He's behind the barn right now, holding the calf."

57.15

A co-ed on her way to a political rally said, "I'm going with an open mind, a complete lack of prejudice, and a cool, rational approach to listen to what I'm convinced is pure rubbish."

57.16

The Senator had just ended a long and tiresome speech to his constituents and was receiving congratulations from his loyal followers, when one man came up and said, "Senator, let me congratulate you. It was a great speech. I liked the straightforward way you dodged the issues."

57.17

A seasoned politician was seeking election to the State Senate. The voters were predominantly rural folk. One of the campaign issues was a recently enacted law regulating the shooting of deer. The office seeker had investigated this debated question and found that one-half of the voters favored the regulation; the other half were against it.

During the campaign the politician was making a speech on a wholly different subject when a rangy young man stood up and called out:

"You're talking right smart stuff, Senator, but we aim to find out how you stand on this here deer-shooting business. What you got to say about that?"

The politician stopped, squirmed, wiped his brow and his glasses, looked around with a smile and said: "I'm happy, my friend, to let you know exactly where I stand on that deer-shooting law. I made considerable study of it. I canvassed this county, and I find that half of my friends are for it and half of my friends are against it. And I solemnly promise you, here and now, that I am not going to let anyone down. I'll stand by my friends!"

57.18

"What about the tariff?" a listener asked Senator Tom Corwin. It was at that time a sensitive question, but the undaunted candidate replied: "I know some people in this audience are for a high tariff and others are opposed to a high tariff. After considerable thought, I want everyone here to know—so am I."

57.19

During a whirlwind campaign tour the candidate arrived late for one meeting, dashed onto the platform, and began a fervid speech on a subject he knew was close to the hearts of the people in this community. But after he had gone on at some length and then paused for a drink of water, the chairman of the meeting whispered, "The group sponsoring you here is on the other side of the question."

When the speaker resumed his talk he promptly said, "Now folks I've given you pretty much the picture as my opponents see it. I will now tell you the truth—and give you the real facts—about this question, and I'm confident when I'm through you are going to agree with me 100 percent."

57.20

Alben Barkley's favorite story concerned Farmer Jones, a man for whom Barkley had done innumerable favors when he was successively County Attorney Barkley, Judge Barkley, Congressman Barkley, and Senator Barkley from Kentucky. Barkley had visited Jones when he was in a hospital in France during World War I; he had interceded with high brass to get the man demobilized from the Army sooner than others; he waded through red tape to get the man's disability payments started; he helped Jones get loans on his farm, got him a Disaster Loan during the thirties after floods devastated his farm, and had Mrs. Jones appointed postmistress.

Several years after the last of these deeds in behalf of Jones, Barkley had a hot political fight on his hands and was astonished to hear that Jones was supporting the man opposing Barkley. Barkley descended on Jones and indignantly cited all the things that had been done for him over the years.

Jones listened to the end, then said to Barkley, "But what in hell have you done for me lately?"

(*See also* *54.2, 54.3, 55.2, 55.12–55.14, 55.20, 218.14*)

58. Candidates-at-large

Anecdotes

58.1

A candidate for sheriff called on the local minister for his support. "Before I decide," said the preacher, "I'd like to know if you partake of intoxicating beverages?"

Said the candidate, "Before I answer, tell me if this is an inquiry or an invitation?"

58.2

It was a bitter election campaign, and the candidate was dashing hither and yon madly. He was rushing from his office to address a meeting. On his way down the hall he was stopped by a friend who asked, "Well, what do you think about the political situation now?"

"Don't bother me!" screamed the candidate. "I've got to talk. This is no time to think."

58.3

Alben Barkley used to tell about the four candidates making an appeal for votes from the same platform. The first man had crutches, and an empty trouser leg conspicuously pinned to his stump. "I heard the call of duty," he said, "and I fought all during the war. I lost my leg at Shiloh." The second candidate related how he lost an arm at the Battle of Gettysburg. The third man pointed proudly to the patch over the eye he lost at Vicksburg.

Then the fourth man hobbled to the center of the platform and said, "I never fought in any war or got wounded. But, my fellow citizens, if physical disability is a qualification for office, I can tell you this: I am the doggondest most ruptured son of a gun you ever saw."

58.4

In questioning a political opponent's credibility, Alben Barkley told about the parson who was all wrought up about the sin of hatred. After dwelling on this most un-Christian fault, the preacher asked his congregation if anyone present had won out over the sin of hatred. One man—a feeble old fellow of ninety-nine years—arose.

"You do not hate anybody, Jasper?"

"No, Parson, I don't."

"That is most inspiring. Will you tell us how you did this."

"Well," spluttered the old man, "All them lousy rats that done me dirt—all them no-good scoundrels—they're all dead and burning in 'ell."

58.5

A man making a campaign speech said, "My candidate is as honest a man as money can buy."

The sudden laughter made him realize his slip, so in an attempt to recover he said: "I mean he never stole a dollar in his life—and all he asks is a chance."

58.6

A congressman on a trip back to his district met one of his supporters and said, "Well, George, I suppose you'll be voting the straight party ticket again this year?"

"No, not this year."

"Why, I thought you were a stanch party man," said the congressman.

"I have always been," said George, "but this year the stanch is more than I can stand."

58.7

At the close of a political meeting a young politician was asked if he was surprised to be nominated to run for the Legislature. "I'll say I was," replied the candidate. "I was so surprised that I almost dropped my acceptance speech."

58.8

A speech attributed to Davy Crockett went like this:

"Friends, fellow citizens, brothers and sisters: Carroll is a statesman, Jackson is a hero, and Crockett is a *horse!*

"Friends, fellow citizens, brothers and sisters: They accuse me of adultery—it's a lie. I never ran away with any man's wife that was not willing in my life.

"They accuse me of gambling—it's a lie—for I always plank down the cash.

"Friends, fellow citizens, brothers and sisters: They accuse me of being a drunkard; it's a d——d lie, for whiskey can't make me drunk."

58.9

Michael Dempsey had been the leader of the party in his county for years and years. He was the idol of all the Irish voters, and of some others, too. The Irish thought him one of the great leaders of the state, if not the nation.

Eventually it came time for a new courthouse to be built, and when the new cornerstone for it was laid, several of Dempsey's friends were there to witness the ceremony. One of them wondered what was the meaning of the Latin numerals on the cornerstone, MDCCCXCIX, and a more knowledgeable friend explained it this way:

"The MD stands for Michael Dempsey; the three C's in a row mean Clerk of the County Court—that's Mike's title you know—and the rest of the mark stands for the times the Democrats under Mike have beaten the Republicans."

58.10

A politician, to illustrate the deviations of a tricky opponent, told of the green hand who was employed to plow a field. "See that red cow, yonder? Well, just make a beeline for her, turn around when you get to her, and when you come back make another beeline for her, and so on until you get the field plowed."

Hours later the farmer found his field plowed in crisscross fashion like a crazy quilt and demanded to know how in the world the farmhand could do such a thing after the instructions given him.

"Well, I did just as you told me—I plowed right for that red cow, but the fool thing kept moving and shifting around and near drove me crazy."

58.11

In ancient Athens, when a man made a brilliant and showy speech, his opponent arose and said, "All that he *said,* I will *do.*"

Definitions

58.12

A candidate is a man who shrinks from the publicity of private life to seek the obscurity of public office.

58.13

A lame duck is a politician whose goose has been cooked.

Aphorisms

58.14

The election isn't very far off when a candidate can recognize you across the street.

—*Kin Hubbard*

58.15

The political candidate can either stand on his own record or jump on his opponent's record.

58.16

Some defeated candidates go back to work and others say the fight has just begun.

—*Kin Hubbard*

58.17

The chief difference between a horse race and a political race is that in a horse race the whole horse runs.

58.18

The war on privilege will never end. Its next great campaign will be against the special privileges of the underprivileged.

—*H. L. Mencken*

58.19

A lame duck is never so lame that he can't waddle as far as a new government job.

—*H. V. Prochnow*

58.20

A majority is always the best repartee.

—*Benjamin Disraeli*

58.21

Bad officials are elected by good citizens who do not vote.

—*George Jean Nathan*

58.22

When a man starts throwing dirt, it's a sign he's losing ground.

58.23

The most successful politician is he who says

what everybody is thinking most often and in the loudest voice.

—*Theodore Roosevelt*

58.24

The demagogue is one who preaches doctrines he knows to be untrue to men he knows to be idiots.

—*H. L. Mencken*

(*See also 54.1, 57.1–57.19, 59.1–59.7, 60.8, 60.9, 60.21, 72.1, 72.2, 72.6, 72.7, 73.7, 75.1, 76.8, 77.1, 78.4, 79.11–79.14, 79.46, 142.13, 154.31, 154.33, 154.34, 218.14, 248.21, 251.27*)

59. Candidates for Parliament

Anecdotes

59.1

When William Makepeace Thackeray was a candidate for Parliament, he was opposed by Edward Cardwell. The two competitors encountered each other in the course of the campaign and stopped to chat. At the close of the friendly conversation Thackeray said it would be a good fight and "may the best man win!"

"Oh, I hope not!" said his rival.

59.2

Beginning a political speech with "I am here . . ." and then pausing and then resuming with "I am here . . . ," Lloyd George was interrupted by a voice from the crowd: "So am I!" George then flung back, "Yes, but there is a difference. I am *all* here."

59.3

Some years ago Lloyd George was making a speech at a political rally.

"Will you free Ireland?" yelled a heckler.

"I will," was the unperturbed reply, followed by thunderous applause from the proponents of Irish freedom.

When the applause died down, Lloyd George added, ". . . not," which was again followed by applause, this time from the opponents of Irish freedom.

When the cheering had died down, he concluded, ". . . tell you."

59.4

During one of Lloyd George's campaign speeches a brick came hurtling through the air and landed at the speaker's feet. George picked up the brick and cried out: "Behold the only argument of our opponents."

59.5

During one of Nancy Astor's political campaigns, a heckler asked her if she did not think mothers ought to stay home with their children. Looking at the questioner with mock concern, Mrs. Astor said, "I think children ought to stay at home with their mothers."

59.6

During a campaign speech a young woman asked Nancy Astor whether she favored a reform of the divorce laws, obviously intending to embarrass the speaker because of her divorce sixteen years earlier. With pretended concern, Mrs. Astor said, "Madam, I am sorry to hear you are in trouble." The woman left the hall shortly thereafter.

59.7

Your husband is a millionaire," yelled a heckler derisively at Lady Astor when she was campaigning for political office.

"Let any man in this hall stand up who would not like to be a millionaire," replied Mrs. Astor. No one stood up.

(*See also 21.1, 54.2, 54.3, 54.5–54.8, 54.10, 54.23, 54.26–54.30, 54.35, 54.36, 54.38, 54.39, 54.43–54.48, 54.64, 54.70, 55.1–55.23, 65.6, 82.2–82.6, 83.6–83.8, 83.10, 83.11, 117.2, 272.16*)

PARTY LABELS AND LIBELS

60. Republicans versus Democrats

Anecdotes

60.1

A group of politicians were discussing old times when one man said, "There was a time when we had such control over this county that we could elect a jackass if we chose to nominate one."

"Can't you do that now?" asked a younger man.

"No, Sir, no more. The Democrats have beat us in the last two elections."

"How do you explain that?"

"I am inclined to conclude that when we

had the power, we simply elected too many jackasses."

60.2

I never said all Democrats were saloonkeepers; what I said was all saloonkeepers were Democrats.

—*Horace Greeley*

60.3

The story is told of a crowd of Democrats sitting one day on the porch of a hotel in northern New Hampshire during the Grant-Seymour campaign of 1868. An old traveler, ragged, dirty, unshaven, and unshorn, ambled up and stared vacantly at the crowd that began to ply him with questions. Finally someone asked him, "You're a Seymour man, aren't you, old fellow?"

Straightening up he answered, "From my present appearance you would probably take me for a Democrat, but I ain't. I learned my politics before I took to drink."

60.4

A good many Democrats are now threatening to read each other out of the Democratic Party. Quite a number of them will have to go to school before they can do that.

—*George D. Prentice*

60.5

In the early days many people in the United States thought that Thomas Jefferson was little better than anti-Christ. Some felt strongly that if the Federalists were overthrown and the Democrats elected, the Christian religion would be suppressed and atheism made dominant. It was even rumored that the Democrat platform called for the destruction of all Bibles.

An old lady, wondering how the Scriptures could be preserved in such an event, called on a Democrat friend in her town and asked him to hide her Bible.

After scoffing at the idea that the Democrats would suppress and destroy all the Bibles, the Democrat asked the old lady why she wanted him to hide her Bible.

"Because," she said, "they'll never think of looking for a Bible in the house of a Democrat."

60.6

John Sharp Williams told of the man engaged in selling eggs who went to market with one basket of eggs and another basket full of affidavits attesting to the freshness of the eggs.

But he had poor sales because of the affidavits—they made people doubtful about the eggs—a little suspicious of their soundness. Williams said this applies, too, to talk of Republican "prosperity."

60.7

When Republican leader of the House, Joe Martin, was twitted about his party's losses during a recent election, he was asked what the Republicans would do now.

Martin said the query reminded him of the two rabbits who were chased by two foxes and took refuge in the hole of a tree. Time passed but the two foxes remained on watch outside the tree.

"What shall we do?" asked one rabbit.

"It looks," said the bolder rabbit, "like we'll just have to stay here until we outnumber them."

60.8

During the presidential campaign of 1940 Harold Ickes called Wendell Willkie, the Republican candidate, "a simple, barefoot Wall Street lawyer." And when young Thomas E. Dewey announced he was entering the presidential race on the Republican ticket, the same Ickes observed that "Mr. Dewey has tossed his diapers into the ring."

60.9

Of a Republican prospect for the presidential nomination, House Speaker Reed said, "They could look much farther and do much worse—and I think they will."

60.10

In the campaign of 1900 Lieutenant Governor Bill Thorne, of Kentucky, told about the Republicans holding a big ratification meeting —brass bands, floats and banners, hundreds of men marching, also women and boys. A young girl claimed that while standing on her porch, which was covered with vines and foliage, she was repeatedly hugged and kissed by a young man she did not know. He was arrested.

At the trial the girl was closely questioned.

"What night was this?" thundered the defense attorney.

"Thursday night."

"What time of night?"

"About eight o'clock."

"That was about the time the parade was passing your house?"

"Yes."

"Did you ever cry or scream?"

"No, Sir, I did not."

"Will you tell this jury, with the streets

thronged with people and this man hugging and kissing you against your will, as you claim, why you never uttered a single cry for help or assistance?"

"Yes, Sir, I will tell the jury, and everybody else, that you'll never ketch me hollerin' at no Republican gatherin'."

60.11

A man said the Democrats paid him $3 to vote for their man and the Republicans paid him $2 to vote for their man, so he voted Republican because they were less corrupt.

60.12

As a new and bitter election approached and the campaign began to get underway, a representative from the Democratic party approached highly successful Republican campaigner Chauncey Depew and said, "Let's make it a clean, high-class campaign this year. Let us conduct this campaign without any mudslinging."

Depew said, "Why, of course, let us do so. You promise not to tell any lies about the Republican party, and I will promise you that I will tell only the truth about the Democratic party. It is as easy as that."

60.13

Senator Alben W. Barkley once read a letter alleged to have been written to Dorothy Dix, who conducted an advice-to-the-lovelorn column: "Dear Miss Dix: I am in love with a beautiful girl of fine character, and I want to marry her. But there are some things I am ashamed of. She knows about my sister who is a prostitute, my brother who is in the penitentiary, and my uncle who is in an insane asylum. But she doesn't know about my two cousins who are Republicans [or Democrats, if you prefer]. Should I tell her?"

60.14

Senator and later Vice President Alben Barkley, an incurable Kentucky Democrat, said that "the Republicans remind me of an old quack down in Graves County who was called to the bedside of an ailing farmer. After trying a lot of mumbo-jumbo, the quack admitted he couldn't cure the farmer's disease.

"But I'm powerful good on fits," boasted the quack. "I'll throw the patient into a fit, and then I'll cure him of that."

60.15

Republicans sleep in twin beds—some even in separate rooms. That is why there are more Democrats.

—*Will Stanton,* Ladies' Home Journal, 1962

60.16

A Republican has observed that Democrats were like an iceberg: 10 percent visible, 90 percent submerged, and a 100 percent all at sea.

60.17

A Kentuckian with seventeen children was asked, when they were all grown, why all but one of the children were registered Democrats.

"Couldn't do nuthin' with that one that became a Republican. He was all right until he took to readin'."

60.18

When an old-timer in a rock-ribbed Republican stronghold registered as a Democrat, it caused a great deal of consternation to have him break the community's Republican uniformity. When he was asked why, he said: "Well, you know I hate Democrats as much as anyone else, and since I'm gonna die pretty soon, I thought it would be better to have a Democrat dying than a Republican."

60.19

A small boy with four puppies for sale had been exhibiting them for some time at a large Democratic convention in a midwestern city, when he was approached by one of the delegates who asked, "Are these Democratic pups, son?"

"Yes, sir."

"Well, then," said the man, "I'll take these two."

About a week later the Republicans held their convention in the same city and among the crowd was the same boy with the two remaining puppies. He tried for hours to obtain a purchaser, but had no luck. Finally he was approached by a Republican, who asked, "What kind of pups are these?"

"They're Republican pups, sir." The Democrat who had purchased the two Democratic pups earlier was standing nearby and intervened, "See here, you rascal, last week you told me that those pups I bought were Democratic pups, and now you're saying these are Republican pups. How come?"

"Yes, sir, you are right, but now these pups have their eyes opened."

60.20

Shortly after the massive Democratic victory in the presidential election of 1964, Vice-President Humphrey was spending a few days at the LBJ ranch in Texas. One day Johnson was showing Humphrey over the pastures when Humphrey suddenly stopped, lifted a foot gingerly, and called out, "Mr. President, I just stepped into the Republican platform."

60.21

William Jennings Bryan during a political campaign was called upon for an impromptu speech, but the only available perch for him was a manure spreader in an adjoining field. So Bryan climbed aboard the spreader and began by saying that it "was the first time I have had occasion to speak to an audience from a Republican platform."

60.22

The girl brought her boyfriend home to meet her father, who was deaf, and a fiery Republican.

When the boy had left the old man growled, "That boy looks like a Democrat to me."

"Oh, no, Daddy," said the girl. "He's the son of a bishop."

"I know, I know," snapped the deaf parent. "They all are."

60.23

"Pappa, what is a traitor in politics?"

"A traitor is a man who leaves our party and goes over to the other one."

"What, then, is a man who leaves the other party and comes over to our party?"

"That is a convert."

(*See also 55.1, 55.4, 55.17, 55.18, 55.23, 56.3, 58.9, 61.4, 63.25, 70.21, 71.3, 72.9, 78.1, 78.2, 79.13, 83.6, 83.7, 142.8, 142.9, 211.34*)

61. From Left to Right

Anecdotes

61.1

"Mr. Clancy, we are making a survey and would like to know your political sympathies."

"I haven't got any," said Clancy. "I'm agin' all governmints."

"But that would be anarchy!"

"And I'm agin' that, too."

61.2

Asked to define communism, an Irishman said, "Well, you see, if you have two automobiles, under bolshevism you keep one for yourself and give up the other to the State."

"That's fine," said another.

"And if you have two pianos, you keep one and give one to the State."

"That's ideal," said another.

The first man continued, "Should you have two cows, likewise, you keep one and give the other to the State."

"I don't like that so well."

"Why not."

"You see, I have only one auto and one piano, but I do have two cows."

(*See also 61.8, 61.26, 61.31*)

61.3

An agitator was addressing a crowd of workingmen. "Comes the era of the common man," he said, "and you will enjoy the pleasures of the rich. You will walk down Park Lane wearing a top hat . . ."

"Excuse me," interrupted a member of his audience, "but Hi'd rather 'ave a cloth cap."

". . . or if you prefer it, a cloth cap," went on the speaker. "You'll wear a cutaway coat and pinstripe trousers . . ."

"Excuse me," interposed the fellow again, "but Hi'm more comfertabul in corduroys."

"Very well, corduroys, if you insist," continued the annoyed orator. "And you'll ride to work in a Rolls Royce . . ."

"Excuse me," said the cockney, "but Hi'd rather use me bike."

The agitator left his platform, grabbed the man by the sleeve and shook him roughly. "Listen, you!" he said between his teeth, "comes the revolution, and you'll do what you are bloody well told to do!"

61.4

"What is the political faith of your family?" asked the poll taker.

"It's mixed," replied the wife. "I am a Republican; my husband is a Democrat; the baby is Wet; the Cow is Dry; and the dog is a Socialist."

"The dog, a Socialist? Why do you say that?"

"Because," concluded the wife, "all that critter does is sit around all day and howl."

(*See also 57.10, 61.8, 61.11, 61.12, 61.27*)

61.5

In General Washington's time, there used to be a Congressman from Massachusetts by the name of Fisher Ames, and he had a way of explaining how a republic survives.

"A monarchy," he used to say, "is like a merchant vessel. It sails the seas proudly, but if it strikes a rock it will sink.

"A republic, however, is like a raft. It will never sink in any sea, but your feet are always wet."

—*James B. Reston*

61.6

Said Representative Charles S. Hartman of Montana, in 1896: "It is true that the Populist party has a number of different remedies for the situation. And I am advised that they are about to add three additional planks to their platform. One of them is to make a cross between the lightning bug and the honeybee for the purpose of enabling the bee to work at night. Another, that of breeding the centipede with the hog, for the purpose of having a hundred hams to each animal. And I am told they have a further visionary scheme of budding strawberry into milkweeds, so that everybody can have strawberries and cream from the same plant."

Definitions

61.7

Communism: The opiate of the asses.

—*Arthur C. von Stein*

61.8

Free Enterprise: You furnish your own ladder, the government merely stands by to steady it as you climb.

Socialism: The government furnishes you a ladder for free—but with no rungs.

Communism: The Comrades, finding you already well up on the ladder, jerk it from under you, break it up and beat you to death with the pieces.

—*Pathfinder*

61.9

Radicals: Those who advance and consolidate a position for conservatives to occupy a little later.

—Rochester *Times Union*

61.10

A radical is one who thinks he can get more if he makes more noise than others.

61.11

Socialism is the philosophy of failure, the creed of ignorance, and the gospel of envy. Why should queues become a permanent, continuous feature of our life? The Socialist dream is no longer Utopia but Queuetopia.

—*Winston Churchill*

61.12

Socialism: A system which is workable only in heaven, where it isn't needed, and in hell, where they've got it.

—*Cecil Palmer*

61.13

A liberal is one who has enemies right and left.

61.14

A liberal is a man who is right most of the time, but he's right too soon.

—*Gregory Nunn*

61.15

A Liberal: A man with his mind open at both ends.

61.16

A democracy is a form of government in which the majority gets at least two guesses concerning which minority will rule the rest.

61.17

Democracy is the hole that lets the sawdust out of the stuffed shirt.

61.18

Conservative: A statesman who is enamored of existing evils, as distinguished from the Liberal, who wishes to replace them with others.

—*Ambrose Bierce*

61.19

Conservative: One who admires radicals a century after they're dead.

—*Leo C. Rosten*

61.20

A conservative is a man who will not look at the new moon, out of respect for that "ancient institution," the old one.

—*Douglas Jerrold*

61.21

A conservative is a man who is too cowardly to fight and too fat to run.

—*Elbert Hubbard*

61.22

Conservative: A man who believes nothing should be done for the first time.

—*Alfred E. Wiggam*

61.23

Standpatter: A man whose most annoying trait is not his stand but his patter.

61.24

Extremist: A man who cries "Stop thief!"—and then shoots an innocent bystander.

—*Harriet Van Horne*

Aphorisms

61.25

Reforms come from below. No man with four aces howls for a new deal.

61.26

A Communist borrows your pot to cook your goose in.

61.27

Socialism thrives when people of thrift and initiative build something which other people decide is worth owning.

61.28

I can remember way back when a liberal was one who was generous with his own money.

—*Will Rogers*

61.29

If you have the right to complain when there is nothing to complain about, you are living in a democracy.

61.30

In a democracy you can say what you think without thinking.

61.31

The difference between communism and democracy is—plenty!

61.32

Describing a man of strong conservative character, Douglas Jerrold said that he would have opposed vaccination as interfering with the marked privileges of smallpox.

61.33

When a man opposes change, he probably has his.

61.34

Any party which takes credit for the rain must not be surprised if its opponents blame it for the drought.

—*Dwight W. Morrow*

61.35

Party government is like an hour-glass. When one side's run out, we just turn on the other and go on as before.

—*Douglas Jerrold*

61.36

All political parties die at last of swallowing their own lies.

—*John Arbuthnot*

61.37

Remember, it was a third party that spoiled things in the Garden of Eden.

(*See also 20.14, 75.5, 75.6, 75.7, 80.9, 83.14, 228.5, 229.1–229.28, 269.205, 272.1, 272.2*)

LEGISLATORS IN AND OUT OF SESSION

62. Senators: Stooges and Straight Men

Anecdotes

62.1

"Is it true, Senator, that you find public office an easy berth?"

"No, I don't think that is the correct term," said the Senator. "It's like a hammock, hard to get into comfortably and still harder to get out of gracefully."

62.3

When the Rev. Edward Everett Hale was chaplain of the United States Senate, he was asked if he prayed for the Senators.

"No," he said, "I look at the Senators and pray for the country."

62.4

During a debate in the Senate, Senator John J. Ingalls from Kansas arose to reply to a Senator from Pennsylvania who had referred scathingly to "bleak Kansas." "Pennsylvania," said the gentleman from Kansas, "has produced only two great men—Benjamin Franklin from Massachusetts and Albert Gallatin of Switzerland."

62.5

Alben Barkley took care of a Senator who was unable to get to the point, with the story about a minister who was fired by the board of deacons and who protested his dismissal. "Didn't I argufy?" he asked. "Didn't I magnify? Didn't I glorify?"

"Yes," they agreed, "you argufy, magnify, and glorify, but you don't tell us wherein. We want a preacher who will tell us wherein."

62.6

When presiding over the Senate as Vice-President, Alben Barkley was obliged to make a crucial ruling that was painful to him as a supporter of the Truman administration on the one hand, and as a Kentuckian on the other. Barkley later said his emotions were somewhat like the fellow who, before being ridden out of town on a rail, said that if it wasn't for the honor of the thing, he'd rather walk.

62.7

When Senator Alben W. Barkley was the majority leader in the Senate he sometimes clashed with President Truman when the latter failed to keep him in touch with legislative strategy. One day when Truman unexpectedly proposed some changes in the tax laws, Barkley blew up and said to a White House aide: "I feel like the catcher in a night ball game. They not only fail to give me signals from the bench, but sometimes they turn off the lights just as the pitcher throws the ball."

62.8

When a certain U.S. Senator died, a newspaperman asked the owner of the paper what, if anything, he wanted said about the Senator in an editorial.

"Oh," said the boss, "just write some generalities and say that he was faithful to his trust."

"OK, but should I mention the name of the trust?"

62.9

"Do you remember me?" a woman constituent asked Senator Dirksen.

"Madam," replied Dirksen, "If I remembered a woman of your beauty, I'd never be able to get any work done."

62.10

One day Congressman J. H. Tinkham of Massachusetts, who sported a luxuriant beard, was walking through the capitol corridors, when a woman stopped him and said, "Why Senator Lewis, it's been years since I've seen you!"

"No wonder," replied Tinkham, quickly recalling J. H. Lewis of Illinois and his beard; "You see, I died fifteen years ago."

62.11

Senator and later Secretary of State Cordell Hull was always a very cautious man; he was noted for his extreme accuracy of utterance. One day he was riding on a train through Montana when a companion pointed to a flock of sheep and said, "Those sheep have just been sheared."

Hull looked at the flock and said, "Yes. Sheared on this side at least."

62.12

Senator Margaret Chase Smith, Republican from Maine, is sometimes questioned about the possibility of a woman President. One day someone asked her, "What would you do if you woke up and found yourself in the White House?"

"I would go to the President's wife," said Mrs. Smith, "and apologize and then leave at once."

62.13

Pressed by party leaders to change his position on an issue before the Senate, Senator Azhurst of Arizona was congratulated by a colleague for having "seen the light." "I didn't see the light," replied Azhurst. "I felt the heat."

62.14

During the inspection of agricultural resources by a senatorial committee, the conversation was interrupted by the loud braying of a jackass.

Senator Azhurst looked up and said, "But for senatorial courtesy, I could tell you what Senator it was that just answered the roll call."

62.15

A visitor to Washington parked his car near the capitol, and as he stepped out he said to a man standing nearby, "If you are going to be here for the next few minutes, will you keep an eye on my car?"

"Do you realize I'm a United States Senator?" asked the bystander.

"No, I hadn't known it," said the motorist. "But it's all right. I'll trust you."

62.16

When William Jennings Bryan burst onto the political scene he was hailed as the "Boy Orator of the Platte." Senator Foraker promptly told the nation that the Platte River, in Nebraska, was "only 6 inches deep but 6 miles wide at the mouth."

62.17

A congressional opponent of Henry Clay's once said to him, "You, sir, speak for the present generation, but I speak for posterity."

"It seems you are resolved to speak until your audience arrives," Clay replied to the tiresome and redundant speaker.

62.18

Henry Clay: "This being, so brilliant yet so corrupt, which, like a rotten mackerel by moonlight, shines and stinks."

—*John Randolph*

62.19

Davy Crockett pilloried Martin Van Buren in the 1836 campaign. Crockett wrote a "biog" of Van Buren and in it said: "When he enters the Senate chamber in the morning he struts and swaggers like a crow in the gutter. He is laced up in corsets, such as women in town wear, and, if possible, tighter than the best of them."

62.20

Congressional fashion plate J. Hamilton Lewis one morning strolled into Congress with a paper and said, "Mr. Speaker, I rise to a question of personal privilege. I have here a copy of this morning's New York *Sun* in which I am referred to as a thing of beauty and a joy forever."

Retorted Senator Thomas B. Reed, "The point is well taken. It should have been a thing of beauty and a jaw forever."

62.21

During the Civil War, Senator Thaddeus Stevens warned Lincoln that Simon Cameron was not trustworthy as head of the War Department. "You don't mean to say you think Cameron would steal?" asked Lincoln.

"No," replied Stevens, "I don't think he'd steal a red-hot stove."

62.22

Once when Senator Thaddeus Stevens of Pennsylvania was propounding an important argument, he was interrupted several times by Kellian V. Whaley of West Virginia, with, "Will the gentleman yield?" On Whaley's third interruption, Stevens turned to him savagely, "I yield to the gentleman from West Virginia for a few feeble remarks."

62.23

Thaddeus Stevens in the United States Senate said, "There is in the natural world a little, spotted, contemptible animal, which is armed by nature with a foetid, volatile, penetrating virus, which so pollutes whoever attacks it, as to make him offensive to himself and all around him for a long time. . . . It is my purpose nowhere in these remarks to make personal reproaches; I entertain no ill will toward any human being, nor any brute, that I know of, not even the skunk across the way to which I referred."

62.24

U.S. Senator A. H. Stephens was very small in stature. During a congressional debate an opponent shouted at him: "You little know-nothing, I could swallow you whole and never know I had eaten anything."

"In that case," replied Stephens, "you would have more brains in your belly than ever you had in your head."

62.25

During a debate in Congress, A. H. Stephens said: "My opponent is not fit to carry swill to swine. . . ."

Other Senators cried out, "Order, order," and Stephens was told to apologize. He did so in this fashion:

"Mr. Speaker, I do apologize. The Senator is absolutely fit for the duty to which I referred."

62.26

Some years ago a U.S. Senator who had married a wealthy widow had just returned to the Senate and got into an elevator carrying other Senators. Acid-tongued Senator T. H. Caraway of Arkansas, who had scant respect for the newlywed one, said in a stage whisper, "It's astonishing what little value one gets for his money these days."

62.27

During a debate in the U.S. Senate Tom Hefflin, of Alabama, made the mistake of suggesting that John Sharp Williams, of Mississippi, took too much pleasure in alcohol. "At least," added Hefflin, "I am in complete command of my faculties."

Senator Williams arose to inquire, "And what difference does that make?"

62.28

Senator John J. Ingalls, of Kansas, said, when a Senator from Delaware gibed at Kansas: "Mr. President, the gentleman who has just spoken represents a state which has two counties when the tide is up—and only three when it is down."

62.29

The Senator droned on and on to little or no purpose. "That fellow," said one Senator to another, "abuses the privilege of being stupid."

62.30

Of Roscoe Conkling: "A becurled and perfumed grandee gaped at by the gallery-gapers."

—*James G. Blaine*

62.31

When Roscoe Conkling, a famous New York lawyer, was asked to campaign for Presidential candidate James G. Blaine, he replied, "I can't. I've retired from criminal practice."

62.32

Of General Benjamin F. Butler: "A lamentably successful cross between a fox and a hog."
—*James G. Blaine*

62.33

When someone mentioned to General U. S. Grant that Massachusetts Senator Charles Sumner did not believe in the Bible, the general said, "Why should he? He didn't write it."

Definition

62.34

Senate: A nice, quiet sort of place where good Representatives go when they die.
—*Thomas B. Reed*

Aphorisms

62.35

Trouble is there are too many Democratic and Republican Senators and not enough United States Senators.
—*Ed Ford*

62.36

You can reach any United States Senator simply by adding after his name S.O.B.—which stands for Senate Office Building.

(See also 55.4, 55.11–55.15, 55.17–55.19, 55.22, 55.23, 57.20, 58.3, 58.4, 60.13, 60.14, 64.1, 64.5, 65.1–65.15, 70.21, 71.4, 76.7, 76.8, 76.10, 76.11, 142.4, 154.35, 154.40, 214.18, 252.6)

63. The House Divided

Anecdotes

63.1

There is a congressional legend about a newly elected congressman making his maiden speech on the floor of the House, who said, "As Daniel Webster makes clear in his dictionary . . ."—when he was interrupted with "Noah Webster wrote the dictionary."

"Noah nothing," replied the greenhorn." "Noah built the ark."

63.2

An old fake from the Midwest habitually interrupted other congressmen early each day in Congress, to get his name in the record, and then left for the day. His usual practice was to rise and ask what the bill or resolution under consideration was. When Speaker Reed had the floor one day the man made his usual interruption, and when it was over Reed said, "Now, having imbedded that fly in the liquid amber of my eloquence, I will proceed."

63.3

The insistent chatter of two members of Congress annoyed Congressman Thomas B. Reed, who said in a loud voice to the nearby sergeant at arms, "They never open their mouths without subtracting from the sum of human knowledge."

63.4

During a furious attack on the Republican party by a member from New York, Speaker Thomas B. Reed took the wind out of the man with, "I cannot hope to equal the volume of the voice of the gentlemen from New York. This is only equaled by the volume of what he does not know."

63.5

Upon being complimented for a speech in Congress because it was not answered, John Randolph replied, "Answered, sir? It was not made to be answered."

63.6

John Randolph arose one day in Congress and in the course of his speech spoke eulogistically of a deceased member, and pointing to the member who had taken his place, he added, "That able and distinguished member of this House, whose place is now vacant."

63.7

During a bitter debate in Congress, Bourke Cockran answered a congressman from Virginia in the most excoriating terms, ending with a story about an old colored man down in Virginia who was riding a mule during a violent thunderstorm in the forest.

Unable to make any progress, except when fitful flashes of terrible lightning showed him the path, and becoming alarmed by the great peals of thunder, the old Negro raised his eyes to Heaven and said, "Lawd, if it's all right with you, I'd ruther hev a little less noise and a little mo' light."

63.8

In the post-Civil War days, when debates were unusually bitter, Congressman Pierce of Massachusetts was listed as having changed his vote. A colleague rushed over to him and demanded to know why he had switched his vote.

"My conscience finally broke loose," said Pierce.

63.9

Some statesmen go to Congress, and some go to jail. It is the same thing after all.

—*Eugene Field*

(*See also* 62.34, 67.4, 263.8)

64. In Committee

Anecdotes

64.1

Senator Henry Cabot Lodge, commenting on the ineffectiveness of some congressional investigating committees, said they reminded him of a certain Si Hoskins. Every day Si sat near a dam with a gun on his knee. One day he was asked, "Si, what are you doing?"

"I am paid to shoot muskrats, sir. They're undermining this dam."

"There goes one now," cried the questioner. "Why don't you shoot it?"

Old Si puffed away on his pipe. "Do you think I want to lose my job?" he said.

64.2

In the course of a Senate committee meeting, Senator Dirksen launched into a long and eloquent dissertation on the question being considered. But one of his colleagues kept interrupting him, until finally Dirksen turned on him and said, "My dear sir, you are interrupting the man I most love to hear."

64.3

During a legislative committee hearing on an involved fiscal question, one of the committee members began a tedious discourse on the problem by saying: "Gentlemen, I ask your patience if during this dissertation I seem to be wandering mentally."

One of the legislators turned to a companion and said, "Why should he have any such worry? With his mind he can't wander far."

64.4

During a committee hearing a Senator and a member of the House got into a violent argument, which continued out in the corridors with the representative saying, "As far as I am concerned, you can go straight to hell." Said the Senator, "I have no intention of becoming a member of the lower house."

64.5

When a constituent asked Alben Barkley why the House had a Foreign Affairs Committee and the Senate a Foreign Relations Committee, he replied: "When I was in the House I was told the difference was that Senators were too old to have affairs. They only have relations."

(*See also* 6.1–6.4, 6.7–6.9, 218.14)

65. Congressmen-at-large

Anecdotes

65.1

While a windbag was addressing Congress one of the members pointed to a colleague who was leaning forward with an ear trumpet to hear better and said, "Look at that fool over there, refusing to avail himself of his natural advantage."

65.2

The Washington *Daily News* reported: "Congress was asked to write a check for $23.48 to pay for replacing steel plates in the Capitol dome. They were buckled by hot air."

65.3

A foreigner, after sitting in the visitors' gallery at Congress, said, "The American Congress is strange—a man gets up and speaks and says nothing. Nobody listens—then everybody disagrees with him."

65.4

Two men were chatting in a train. "It's going to be tough for me when I get home," one man said. "I've just been discharged from the state prison.

"I know pretty much how you feel," said the other man. "I'm also returning home—from a long session in Congress."

65.6

A congressman, back in his home district for some visiting, met an old friend, who said, "Have you heard that old Tom True is planning to run against you?"

"Frankly," said the congressman, "I'm not surprised at anything that misnamed thief would do. Every day he's out of jail, he's away from home."

"I hear," added the friend, "that Ichabod

Dillinger is also going to announce his candidacy."

"There's another no-good louse," said the congressman. "Some day I'll tell you of the jams I've gotten him out of."

"Relax," said the friend to the congressman. "I'm only having some fun with you. In fact, both of those men are hoping to see you while you're back home."

"Now, that's no way to act," said the congressman. "You tricked me into saying nasty things about two of the finest men in my district—men of the highest character and loyalty it has ever been my privilege to know."

65.7

Advice often given to new congressmen is: "You must not feel too humble. You see, you spend your first six months wondering how you got here. After that you wonder how the other members made it."

Definitions

65.8

Congress: A body of men brought together to slow down the government.

65.9

Congress: The generation of wind by the winded generation.

Aphorisms

65.10

Every congressman should be compelled by law to try to make a living under the laws he has helped pass.

65.11

Reader, suppose you were an idiot. And suppose you were a member of Congress. But I repeat myself.

—*Mark Twain*

65.12

Washington is the only place where sound travels faster than light.

—*C. V. R. Thompson*

65.13

Some members of Congress would best promote the country's peace by holding their own.

—*George D. Prentice*

65.14

Representatives make the laws and senators talk them over.

65.15

There are two periods when Congress does no business: one is before the holidays, and the other after.

—*George D. Prentice*

(*See also 33.1, 58.6, 61.6, 62.1–62.36, 63.1–63.9, 72.4, 79.45, 80.6, 80.10, 142.5–142.7, 211.15, 218.14, 271.4, 272.11, 274.1*)

66. Uncommon Episodes in the House of Commons

Anecdotes

66.1

John Wilkes encountered Lord Sandwich, who was chiefly responsible for the first of Wilkes's several expulsions from Commons, and an argument ensued. In a rage, Sandwich said, "Sir, you will come to your end either upon the gallows or of a venereal disease!"

Wilkes replied smoothly, "I should say that depends upon whether I embrace your principles or your mistress."

66.2

When Disraeli was once asked to define the difference between a misfortune and a calamity he answered, "Well, if Gladstone fell into the Thames, it would be a misfortune. But if anybody dragged him out, that would be a calamity!"

66.3

Of Gladstone: "A sophisticated rhetorician inebriated with the exuberance of his own verbosity, and gifted with an egotistical imagination that can at all times command an interminable and inconsistent series of arguments to malign an opponent and to glorify himself."

—*Benjamin Disraeli*

66.4

Once, while in the Opposition party in Parliament, Disraeli depicted the Government ministers as they sat in their places in the House of Commons: "As I sat opposite the Treasury Bench, the ministers reminded me of those marine landscapes not unusual on the coasts of South America. You behold a range of exhausted volcanoes."

66.5

Of Lord John Russell: "If a traveler were informed that such a man was leader of the

House of Commons he may begin to comprehend how the Egyptians worshipped an insect."
—*Benjamin Disraeli*

66.6

Francis Burdett arose in the House of Commons during a debate with John Russell and said that there was nothing more odious than the cant of patriotism. Russell replied that the cant of patriotism was no doubt odious, but there was something more odious, and that was the recant of patriotism.

66.7

One day Richard Brinsley Sheridan, in the House of Commons, was much annoyed by a fellow member who kept crying out every minute, "Hear! Hear!" Finally, in describing a political contemporary, Sheridan said, "Where shall we find a more foolish knave or a more knavish fool than he?" Promptly the troublesome member shouted, "Hear! Hear!" Sheridan turned to him with thanks for the information and sat down amid a roar of laughter.

66.8

R. B. Sheridan, called upon in Parliament to apologize to a fellow member, arose and said, "Mr. Speaker, I said the honorable member was a liar it is true and I am sorry for it." He then added that the honorable member could place the punctuation marks where he pleased.

66.9

During a fiery debate in the House of Commons on the French Revolution, Edmund Burke flung a daggerlike carving knife on the floor of the House.

"Where's the fork?" asked Sheridan.
—*F. L. Lucas,* Literature and Psychology

66.10

When Nancy Astor was first elected to the House of Commons, a powerful faction determined to make her stay there as uncomfortable as possible. One day Lady Astor encountered in the corridors of Commons a Cabinet member who felt compelled at last to offer congratulations on her election.

"But I've been in the House for six months, and you have not taken the slightest heed of me," said the outspoken woman.

"No," he said. "I don't like women in Parliament, and when you took your seat I endured the same kind of embarrassment as I would had a lady invaded my bathroom."

"If I were as ugly as you," retorted Mrs. Astor, "I should have no fear of any lady invading my bathroom."

66.11

A verbose member of Parliament asked John Philpot Curran, "Have you read my last speech?"

"I hope I have," said Curran.

66.12

When Winston Churchill began his political career, retired Admiral and later Lord Charles Beresford in the House of Commons sneered at his lack of knowledge of the Navy. Said Churchill: "When my Right Honorable friend rose to his feet a few minutes ago, he had not the least idea of what he was going to say. Moreover, he did not know what he was saying when speaking. And when he sat down, he was doubtless unable to remember what he had said!"

66.13

Early in his career, when he was a member of the Liberal party, Winston Churchill arose in the House of Commons to defend the party against a charge of misrepresenting the Conservative party by asserting that they had condoned Negro slavery in South Africa. "I admit," said Churchill, "the term 'slavery' might be a terminological inexactitude."

"I prefer the ugly little English three-letter word l-i-e," retorted Joseph Chamberlain.

66.14

Speaking of Ramsay MacDonald, Winston Churchill said: "I remember, when I was a child, being taken to the celebrated Barnum's circus, which contained an exhibition of freaks and monstrosities, but the exhibit on the program which I most desired to see was the one described as 'the Boneless Wonder.' My parents judged that spectacle would be too revolting and demoralizing for my youthful eyes, and I have waited fifty years to see the Boneless Wonder sitting on the Treasury Bench."

66.15

Winston Churchill called Clement Atlee "a sheep in sheep's clothing."

66.16

Referring to Clement Atlee, Winston Churchill said: "A modest man, and I know no one with more to be modest about."

66.17

Pointing to Chancellor of the Exchequer, Sir

Stafford Cripps, Winston Churchill said: "There but for the grace of God, goes God."

66.18

In criticizing the Stanley Baldwin Government in England before World War II, Winston Churchill said: "They are decided only to be undecided, resolved to be irresolute, adamant for drift, solid for fluidity, all-powerful for impotence."

66.19

Stanley Baldwin occasionally stumbles over the truth, but he always hastily picks himself up and hurries on as if nothing happened.

—*Winston Churchill*

66.20

Winston Churchill, referring to Stanley Baldwin, who was noted for his honesty: "It is a fine thing to be honest, but it is also very important to be right."

66.21

Speaking of former Prime Minister Stanley Baldwin, Winston Churchill said, "He sat on the fence so long that the rust got into his soul."

66.22

Nothing is more dangerous in wartime than to live in the temperamental atmosphere of a Gallup poll, always feeling one's pulse and taking one's temperature. I see [it said that] leaders should keep their ears to the ground. All I can say is that the British nation will find it very hard to look up to the leaders who are detected in that somewhat ungainly posture.

—*Winston Churchill,* in Commons, September 30, 1941

66.23

Winston Churchill, in Commons, referring to R. H. S. Crossman, July, 1954: "The Honorable Member is never lucky in the coincidence of his facts with the truth."

66.24

Jeremy Thorpe, a Liberal in the House of Commons, when Prime Minister Macmillan took drastic measures against certain Cabinet members, said: "Greater love hath no man than this, that he should lay down his friends for his life."

66.25

In the reign of George II, Mr. Crowle, a counsel of some eminence, was summoned to the bar of the House of Commons to receive a reprimand from the Speaker, on his knees. As he rose from the ground, with the utmost nonchalance he took out his handkerchief, and, wiping his knees, coolly observed that it was the dirtiest house he had ever been in in his life.

66.26

Joseph Addison, a gifted writer of the eighteenth century, was making his first speech in Parliament and was so nervous he fumbled and stumbled for words. "Mr. Speaker . . . I con—con—conceive. I con— con . . . con— conceive . . ."

A voice from the gallery called out, "You've conceived three times and brought forth nothing."

66.27

A member of Parliament, giving a speech he had learned by heart, came to the exordium when his memory failed at the beginning of a sentence that started with "Necessity . . ." He repeated the word "necessity" three times, when Sir Robert Peel broke in and said, "Necessity is not always the mother of invention."

66.28

On the House of Commons:
To wonder now at Balaam's ass is weak;
Is there a day that asses do not speak?

(*See also 152.31, 225.1–225.21, 272.17*)

GOVERNMENT FUN AND FROLICS

TAXES: COLLECTORS, PAYERS, SPENDERS, AND WASTERS

67. Income Tax: A Poor Joke

Anecdotes

67.1

The business executive had spent eighteen months on a deserted island, the lone survivor when his yacht sank. He had managed so well he thought less and less of his business and his many investments. But he was nonetheless delighted to see a ship anchor offshore and launch a small boat that headed toward the island.

When the boat crew reached shore, the officer in charge came forward with a bundle of current newspapers and magazines. "The captain," explained the officer, "thought you would want to look over these papers to see what has been happening in the world, before you decide that you want to be rescued."

"It's very thoughtful of him," replied the executive. "But I think I need an accountant most of all. I haven't filed an income tax return for two years, and what with the penalties and all, I'm not sure I can now afford to return."

67.2

A man went to the local income tax office and handed a 25-cent piece to the startled clerk.

"What's this for?"

"Why, it's my income tax. They told me I could pay a quarter at a time."

67.3

A man who claimed income tax deductions for both his mother-in-law and his dog was curtly told by Internal Revenue that in no circumstances was a dog an allowable deduction. Undaunted, the fellow wrote back deploring the injustice of such a ruling, since he had spent $50 more on his dog than on the mother-in-law.

67.4

When a man was questioned by Internal Revenue for deducting his Uncle Herbert as a dependent, Uncle Herbert having died a year or so earlier, the taxpayer said that Uncle Herbert depended upon him to keep his grave decorated.

67.5

A man who listed as a charitable contribution the cost of a tombstone over his brother's grave was asked by Internal Revenue to explain this. He said that since his brother never did anything for him, the erection of the tombstone was an act of charity.

67.6

It is supposed to be true that a taxpayer on his income tax return deducted for the cost of 2 quarts of blackberry wine every week and 3 quarts of gin every month. When asked to explain this he said it was to conserve water during a protracted drought.

67.7

In the files of the Bureau of Internal Revenue it will be found that:

A railroad man tried to deduct for two wives and two homes—one at each end of the railroad line.

A man charged off $6,000 in cab fares and $12,000 in telephone calls as business expenses on an individual tax return.

A family corporation wanted to charge off the cost of a "water purification experiment" which investigators found to be the family swimming pool at their summer home.

A man deducted $30,000 in salary paid his secretary over three successive years. But it was disallowed because then he married her and paid her successor only $3,800 annually.

A stock-market operator wanted to deduct the cost of fees paid to an astrologer for market guidance.

A businessman with a part-time chicken farm was not allowed to deduct the cost of operating it because the IRS said he sold only 70 chickens, whereas his operating costs averaged out at $65 per chicken.

A man wanted to deduct, as a dependent on his previous year's return, a child born in February, explaining that it was "last year's business."

67.8

Charlie Rice says it's gospel truth that an irate citizen recently wrote the Bureau of Internal Revenue to this effect: "I realize it's a great privilege to pay my United States taxes, but if things go any higher, I'm going to have to give up that privilege."

67.9

A letter to the Internal Revenue Bureau: "Gentlemen, I have not been able to sleep nights account of worrying about not having reported on a good deal of income. So I'm enclosing my check for $1,000. If I find I still can't sleep, I'll send the rest of it."

67.10

The Bureau of Internal Revenue received a typed income tax return from a bachelor, who had listed one dependent. The examiner returned it with a notation: "This must be a stenographic error."

"You're telling me," the taxpayer answered in writing after the penciled notation.

67.11

Senator Harry F. Byrd stopped at a Virginia town where a circus barker offered a curious throng $100 if they could get a drop of juice from a lemon after a strong man had clutched it.

Several tried, none succeeded. Finally a man stepped up and got two drops of juice from the lemon after the strong man had squeezed.

The winner was paid the prize and asked to tell the people what his occupation was.

"I'm an Internal Revenue agent," said the winner.

67.12

Sign over the incoming door at the Los Angeles tax bureau: "Watch Your Step."

Sign over the Outgoing door: "Watch Your Language."

—*Jimmy Starr,* in Los Angeles Herald and Express

Aphorisms

67.13

Three R's of the tax collector: This is ours, that is ours, everything is ours.

67.14

You've got to hand it to income tax people. If you don't, they'll come and get it.

67.15

An income tax form is like a laundry list—in both instances you lose your shirt.

67.16

Someday the income tax return will be simplified to:

How much money have you got?

Where is it?

When can you get at it?

67.17

About the time a man is cured of swearing, another income tax falls due.

67.18

Next to being shot at and missed, nothing is quite as satisfying as an income tax refund.

—*F. J. Raymond*

67.19

The one thing that hurts more than paying an income tax is not having to pay an income tax.

—*Thomas Robert Dewar*

67.20

To produce an income tax return that has any depth to it, any feeling, one must have Lived—and Suffered.

—*Frank Sullivan*

67.21

According to the Internal Revenue Bureau, America is the land of untold wealth.

67.22

Psychologists say no person should try to keep too much to himself. The Internal Revenue Bureau is of the same opinion.

—*H. V. Prochnow*

67.23

Where there is an income tax, the just man will pay more and the unjust less on the same amount of income.

—*Plato*

(*See also 19.19, 27.16, 30.30, 31.40, 68.1–68.19, 71.2, 142.14*)

68. The Taxpayer Strikes Back

Anecdotes

68.1

In one of the newly created nations in Africa, an old native was told that he had to be taxed in order to support the government that was protecting him from his enemies, would care for him when he was sick, would see that he did not starve, would educate his children.

"I think I understand," said the native after a few moments. "It's like I have this dog, and the dog is hungry. He comes begging to me for food. So I take my knife, cut off the poor dog's tail and then give him the tail to eat. That I think is what taxation is like."

68.2

A young woman, after hearing an address by the Secretary of the Treasury, was puzzled. She asked her husband what was the difference between direct and indirect taxation.

"The difference," he replied, "is the same as the difference between asking me for money and going through my pockets while I am asleep."

Definitions

68.3

Taxpayer: One who doesn't have to pass a civil service exam to work for the government.

—*Business Executive*

68.4

Public: The people who pay the taxes and buy the goods had better damn well keep their noses out of politics and the way business is run.

—*Name Withheld by Request*

Aphorisms

68.5

If Patrick Henry thought taxation without representation was bad, he should see it with representation.

—*Handy News*

68.6

I dread crushing taxation: fewer and fewer people with enough financial independence for intellectual courage.

—*W. B. Yeats*

68.7

The art of taxation consists in so plucking the goose as to obtain the largest amount of feathers with the least amount of hissing.

—*Jean Baptiste Colbert*

68.8

There is one difference between a tax collector and a taxidermist—the taxidermist saves the skin.

—*Mortimer Caplan,* Time, February 1, 1963

68.9

In levying taxes and in shearing sheep it is well to stop when you get down to the skin.

—*Austin O'Malley*

68.10

Count that day won when, turning on its axis, this earth imposes no additional taxes.

—*Franklin Pierce Adams*

68.11

One of the things we have to be thankful for is that we don't get as much government as we pay for.

—*C. H. Kettering*

68.12

The art of government consists in taking as much money as possible from one class of citizens to give to the other.

—*Voltaire*

68.13

The best form of taxation is that which will be paid by somebody else.

—*Wealthy Taxpayer*

68.14

When you do wrong they fine you. When you do right they tax you even more than they fine you.

—*Delinquent Taxpayer*

68.15

No one has been able to make clear the distinction—if there is any—between nuisance taxes and ordinary taxes.

—*Anonymous*

68.16

He wanted his son to share in the business, but the government beat him to it.

—*Anonymous Taxpayer*

68.17

Instead of tearing down buildings to save taxes, it would be well for government to tear down taxes to save buildings.

—*Pro Bono Publico*

68.18

The general most certain of surviving a war is General Taxation.

68.19

When your ship comes in the government docks it.

(*See also 158.2, 223.12*)

69. Government Borrowers and Spenders

Anecdotes

69.1

Government Department Head: "We've got to get rid of this 300 million dollars or we'll be out of our jobs."

Assistant: "Let's build a bridge across the Ohio River?"

Department Head: "Wouldn't cost enough; we'd have too much left over."

Assistant: "I've got it—let's build it lengthwise!"

69.2

In combating welfare statism, Winston Churchill said: "What is the use of being a famous race and nation if at the end of the week you cannot pay your housekeeping bill?"

69.3

The Cabinet of a certain country met to consider the nation's grave financial difficulties. After much futile talk, one of the ministers suggested they declare war on the United States. "Of course we would be quickly defeated, but then America would shower money and supplies upon us, and we would then be over our difficulties."

"But," interjected the Prime Minister, "suppose by some chance we won the war? Then we would be in a terrible crisis."

69.4

When the King discovered that the finances of his kingdom were dangerously depleted, he called in his twenty-five chief deputies to examine and solve the crisis.

"Why," asked the King, "is our treasury empty when we collect so much in taxes? What happens to the money? Can it be large-scale thieving?" Everyone looked to the Secretary of the Treasury for a reply. This sage gentleman excused himself briefly and returned with a large piece of ice, saying, "This will answer your question."

The Secretary handed the ice to one man, told him to hold it briefly in his hands and then pass it along to the person next to him. The ice went from man to man, steadily melting. When it finally reached the King the ice was so diminished he could close his hand over it.

"That, Sire," said the Secretary of the Treasury, "is what happens to the taxes we collect."

69.5

Congressman "Uncle" Joe Cannon, from Illinois, liked to recall a Judge Holman of Indiana, a former congressman and auditor under President Grant. He was often referred to as "the watchdog of the Treasury," but it was said that he never growled when his friends were around.

69.6

A woman in Georgia, according to Julia Lowell, wrote the Federal government this letter: "I understand the government is to give loyalty checks to its employees. I think we deserve them. I worked for the War Department for two years during the war, and I had an excellent efficiency rating during that period. Please don't overlook me when the government starts to hand out those checks."

69.7

Julia Lowell reports that one U.S. Senator received a letter stating: "Last month I bought some United States government bonds. When do I pay interest on them?"

69.8

"Father," asked the serious young man, "do you think that the American Indians were superior to the white man who took this land from him?"

"Well, look at it this way," said the parent. "When the Indians were the sole occupants of this land, they had no taxes, no national debt, no centralized government, no military draft, no foreign-aid programs, no nuclear weapons, and their women did all the work. Could one ask for better than that?"

69.9

A man went to a small-town circus which was climaxed by a donkey that performed a number of feats and ended by bursting into tears. However, on this occasion the trainer simply could not get his donkey to do any weeping.

The man in the audience went down and offered to help the trainer. He bent down and whispered for a minute or so into the donkey's ear, whereupon the animal burst into weeping and wailing such as the trainer and the spectators had never before heard.

"What did you say to that animal?" asked the bewildered trainer.

"I just told him the facts of life," said the stranger. "I told him the size of the national debt, the annual interest charge on it, the tax rates on individual incomes, the cost of armaments and foreign aid, the cost of congressional junkets, and a few other figures. It's enough to make even a jackass weep."

Definition

69.10

Federal Aid: A system of making money taken from the people look like a gift when handed back.

—*Carl Workman*

Aphorisms

69.11

Won't our grandchildren have a swell time paying for the good times we didn't have?

69.12

National Debt: America's most outstanding public figure.

—*Joseph B. Young*

69.13

U.S. now stands for Unlimited Spending.

—Tampa *Tribune*

69.14

In national affairs a million is only a drop in the bucket.

—*Burton Rascoe*

69.15

Government trims expenses when there is nothing else left to trim.

69.16

Governments never cut off expenses that are capable of voting.

69.17

It has often been asked what this nation stands for, and the answer is easy—too much.

69.18

We have operated in red ink so long that the

pages of the Federal ledger look like a slaughter-house.

—*K. B. Keating*

(*See also 34.3–34.8, 80.1, 80.11, 82.5, 112.12, 210.20, 215.5*)

70. Bureaucrats and Red Tape

Anecdotes

70.1

"Our files are so crowded," said the chief clerk to a bureau head in a Federal government department, "that we'll simply have to destroy all correspondence more than six years old."

"Go ahead and do it," said the bureaucrat decisively. "But first be sure to make copies of everything marked for destruction."

70.2

A minor bureaucrat in Washington received from a higher bureaucrat a note reading: "The regulations state that you are not to initial documents before I have seen them. Therefore erase your initial, initial the erasure, and confirm this action by a memo to me with nine carbons to appropriate interested parties."

70.3

Hilaire Belloc, in his *Path to Rome,* tells a story about three men—strangers to one another—who were seated one evening at the same table in a crowded Parisian restaurant. They began talking of bureaucracy. One man denounced it as the curse of France: "Men are governed like sheep. The administrator is a despot, and most people will run toward him like a servile dog."

The second man disagreed; he argued that men are governed by the ordinary sense of authority—they recognize it and obey it.

The third man, who had introduced himself as the Duke of Sussex, said that the most subtle and powerful influence on men was the aristocratic feeling.

After dinner the first man offered to prove that bureaucracy governs mankind. He went up to the wall of the Credit Lyonnais, put the forefinger of either hand against it, about 25 centimeters apart, and at a level of about a foot above his eyes. A crowd gathered to watch him. In a few moments a pleasant, elderly, short, and rather fat gentleman in the crowd came forward and offered to help. The man against the wall explained that he was an engineer for the Public Works Department and had to take an important measurement with the apothegm of the bilateral, "which runs tonight precisely through this spot. My fingers now mark the concentric of the secondary focus whence the radius vector should be drawn, but I find that (like a fool) I have left my double refractor in the café hard by. I dare not go for fear of losing the place I have marked; yet I can go no further without my double refractor."

The stout little stranger agreed to hold the place marked until the man ran for his instrument. So the three men left the little man holding his fingers in the exact place, and well above his head. "Let us go to the theater," suggested the experimenter. "And when we come back I will warrant you will agree with my remarks on bureaucracy." Off they went and returned three hours later to find the little man still stretching his arms up against the wall and an enormous crowd watching him. The poor fellow was a pitiable sight—almost ready to collapse, but still faithful to his promise to help the engineer for the Public Works Department. "You will not match that with your aristocratic sentiments!" said the believer in the power of bureaucracy.

"I'm not so sure," replied the Duke of Sussex. "It is late and I must be off, but before I go let me tell you that you have paid for a most expensive dinner and behaved with admirable deference in the belief that I was the Duke of Sussex. As a fact, my name is Jerks, and I am a salesman of linseed oil. Good evening!"

"Wait a moment," said the man who believed in the power of authority. "I am a detective officer, and my theory of authority still holds. You will both be good enough to follow me to the police station."

The engineer was fined fr.50, and the Duke of Sussex was imprisoned for ten days.

70.4

At the foot of the stairway in the House of Commons there was an attendant who, it was said, had been standing there for twenty years. Nobody knew why. At last, someone checked into the matter and discovered that the job had been held by his family for three generations.

The job had originated forty-five years earlier, when the stairs had been newly painted and his grandfather had been assigned the job of standing at the foot of the stairway to tell people not to step on the wet paint.

70.5

"It took more than one hundred years to build these pyramids," said the guide to a party of tourists.

"Ah, a government project," said an American in the party.

P.S. It was a government job.

70.6

"I hear your husband tried to get a government post. What's he doing now?"

"Nothing—he got the post."

70.7

A heavy contributor to a winning candidate's campaign barged into the newly elected official's office. He had his empty-headed son with him and announced that he would like the boy to be given a job by the politician.

"What can he do?" asked the official skeptically.

"Nothing whatever," replied the father frankly.

"Oh," said the politician with relief, "that makes it easier. We won't have to break him in."

70.8

During World War II a Japanese spy in Washington reported to his superior that it was no use to think of bombing Washington. He said that if one building were destroyed, nothing would be accomplished. "For they already have two other buildings completely staffed doing exactly the same thing."

70.9

A meteorite fell into a field rented by a Middle Western farmer, and he promptly began to charge people who wanted to see it. When the owner of the land heard of this he pointed out that the rental of the land did not include mineral rights, therefore the meteorite was his. They compromised by sharing the proceeds. However, the Customs Service intervened, classed the meteorite as unmanufactured iron and confiscated it because it had entered the country without payment of duty.

70.10

A little boy who had lost his father and whose widowed mother was having a difficult time making ends meet, wrote a letter: "Dear God: Will you please send my mother $100 cause she is having a hard time."

The letter ended up in the General Post Office, and the employee who opened it was touched. He put a few dollars aside and collected a total of $50 among the other postal employees to whom he showed the letter, and the money was sent to the little boy.

Several weeks later the little boy again wrote, this time a letter of thanks. But he also pointed out that God had made the mistake of sending the letter through Washington and that they had deducted 50 percent of the money.

70.11

A Louisiana attorney applied to the government for an RFC loan in behalf of a client, offering certain land as collateral. The RFC informed him that the loan would be granted when he proved satisfactory title to the land. After several months of checking the attorney reported to the RFC that he had checked the title back to 1803. The government agency replied that in order for the loan to be approved it would be necessary for the title to be cleared for the years prior to 1803.

The lawyer, after some thought, wrote the RFC as follows:

"I am now able to satisfy your requirement that title to this land be cleared for the years previous to 1803. Louisiana was purchased from France in that year. France acquired title to the land from Spain by right of conquest. Spain obtained the land through right of discovery ensuing from voyages made by a sailor named Christopher Columbus. Columbus's expeditions were sanctioned and financed by the then reigning monarch, Isabella of Spain. Queen Isabella, a pious and cautious woman, took care to protect her rights by asking and receiving the blessing of the Pope upon Columbus's voyage before she pawned her jewels to finance Columbus. The Pope is the vicar on earth of Jesus Christ, the Son of God, and it is commonly agreed that God made the world, including that part of the United States known as Louisiana. Only God could give you title clearance prior to Creation."

70.12

An assistant rushed into the office of William S. Knudsen, in charge of war production during World War II, upset because a certain report was missing. "There are two kinds of reports," said Knudsen: "One says you can't do it. The other says you can do it. The first kind is no good. The second kind you don't need."

70.13

Many years ago the windows at Windsor Castle, England, remained dirty and unwashed because the outside of the panes belonged to the Department of Woods and Forests, and the inside of the panes to the Lord Steward's Department.

70.14

Some hunters stopped to ask an old farmer if he thought the weather would be good on the morrow, the opening of the deer season.

"When the Lord was running this country," replied the old fellow, "I could give you a good idea of the weather ahead. But now that this damn government has took over, there's no tellin' what's goin' to happen."

70.15

A door in a government building in Washington, D.C., is labeled: "4156; General Services Administration; Region 3; Public Buildings Service; Building Management Division; Utility Room; Custodial." It is a door to a broom closet.

—*Rep. Lester Johnson,* in Rice Lake, Wisc., Chronotype

70.16

The more I observed Washington, the more frequently I visited it, and the more people I interviewed there, the more I understood how prophetic L'Enfant was when he laid it out as a city that goes around in circles.

—*John Mason Brown,* Through These Men, 1956

70.17

The tourist riding in a cab past the National Archives Building in Washington read out the carved words "The Past is Prologue" and wondered aloud what it meant.

"It means," said the driver, "that you ain't seen nothin' yet."

70.18

A plumber wrote the U.S. Bureau of Standards that he had used and found hydrochloric acid excellent for cleaning out clogged drains and wanted to know if this was safe to do. The Bureau wrote back: "Our studies and research reveal that the efficacy of hydrochloric acid for the purpose stated in your letter is without question. However, the use of it results in a corrosive residue that is incompatible with metallic permanence." The plumber wrote back to the Bureau that he was glad they had found he was correct. The Bureau again wrote to him, stating, "We must point out to you without qualification that we can under no circumstances assume responsibility for the resulting toxic and noxious residues from the employment of hydrochloric acid in the plumbing uses to which you have put it, and we most strongly urge that you resort to alternative procedures that will not have the deleterious consequences we alluded to in our earlier communication." The plumber liked this letter, too, and wrote the Bureau to tell them so. The Bureau thereupon sent the plumber a final letter, which stated: "Stop using hydrochloric acid. It eats the hell out of pipes."

70.19

A small but successful boat builder during World War II was rebuked by a bureaucrat in Washington for manhandling official red tape.

"How," asked the government official, "do you chart production progress at your shipyard?"

"We have got it down to a science," replied the boat builder. "At the close of each day we weigh the boat and then we weigh the paper work you require. When the boat weighs as much as the paper we know the boat is completed."

70.20

B. A. Botkin's *Sidewalks of America* contains the following samples of Washington red-tapeese:

Confidential Work: We're so ashamed of what we're doing that we don't want anyone to know about it.

Expedite: Stop everything. Put my case through at once. To hell with the others.

File This: Lose, if possible. If anyone calls, we never heard of the case.

For Your Approval: You sign this, too, so if the boss kicks, you can share the blame.

Have You Any Remarks: Can you give me an idea of what this is all about?

I Approach the Subject with an Open Mind: Completely ignorant of the subject.

In Due Course: Never.

Prepare This for My Signature: You do the work, I'll take the credit, but if anything goes wrong, you take the blame.

Rush Job: You do something about this quickly. I haven't done a thing about it in three months and the boss is mad.

Submitted for Information: This means nothing to us; it may to you.

This Will Be Borne in Mind: No further action will be taken till you remind me.

Definitions

70.21

Kentucky Democrat Alben Barkley described a bureaucrat as "a Democrat who holds an office that some Republican wants."

70.22

Senator Albert W. Hawkes described a bureaucrat as "a person who proceeds in a straight line from an unknown assumption to a foregone conclusion."

70.23

Bureaucracy is a giant mechanism operated by pygmies.

—*Honoré de Balzac*

Aphorisms

70.24

The nearest thing to immortality in this world is a government bureau.

—*Hugh S. Johnson*

70.25

In government, where there's a vacancy, there's a relative.

70.26

Governmental machinery is the marvelous labor-saving device which enables ten men to do the work of one.

70.27

The way things are being done in Washington these days reminds one of the fellow who sawed off a board three times and it was still too short.

—*Jacob M. Braude*

70.28

There's nothing so permanent as a temporary job in Washington.

—*George Allen*

70.29

People only leave Washington by way of the box—ballot or coffin.

—*Claiborne Pell,* Vogue, 1963

70.30

If there's anything a public servant hates to do it's something for the public.

—*Kin Hubbard*

70.31

A man speaking of government alphabet agencies said it was OK with him so long as everything from ABC to XYZ took second place to USA.

(*See also 11.5, 68.3, 69.1, 69.4, 69.15, 69.16, 74.1, 79.29, 86.11, 142.9, 150.10, 213.6, 213.8, 214.15, 247.1, 247.4–247.8, 269.170*)

PRESIDENTIAL HUMOR

---

71. L.B.J. in the Saddle

71.1

President Johnson tells about a preacher back home who dropped his notes one day as he was leaving for church, and his dog jumped on them and tore them up. When the preacher stepped into the pulpit, he apologized to his congregation: "I am very sorry that I have no sermon today. I will just have to speak as the Lord directs. But I will try to do better next Sunday."

71.2

President Johnson tells about the Baptist minister who received a call from an Internal Revenue agent who said, "I am checking the tax return of one of the members of your church. He has listed a donation of $200 to your church. Can you tell me if he made the contribution?"

"I don't have my records in front of me," said the minister, "but if he didn't he will!"

71.3

After his sweeping victory over Barry Goldwater in the presidential elections, President Johnson said: "I think it is very important that we have a two-party country. I am a fellow that likes small parties and the Republican party is about the size I like."

71.4

President Johnson tells about the time Senator Tom Connally, of Texas, was speaking on home and started out on the beautiful piney woods of Texas, went on to the bluebonnets, then to the plains and down to the hill country, to the Gulf Coast, and then back to the piney woods again and started all over again. When he was well into his second time around the state of Texas one little fellow in the back of the hall arose and called out: "The next time you pass Lubbock, how about letting me off?"

71.5

One of President Lyndon Johnson's favorite stories is about the shiftless Texas farmer who was brought into court on a charge of blackening his wife's eye. The defendant told the judge that when he had appeared several days earlier before the same judge on a charge of being drunk, the judge had called him a drunken bum, and he had repeated the judge's remarks to his wife. "Your Honor," concluded the farmer, "when the wife heard what you called me, she became so abusive of you that I could not sit there and let her denounce you like that. I had to hit her a few."

71.6

Once President Johnson called in one of his bright young men and said sharply: "The people want to know—what are we going to do about the farm bill?"

"I don't have that file before me," replied the young man, "but you can tell the people: if we owe it, we will pay it."

71.7

When President Lyndon B. Johnson is given excuses why something cannot be done, he likes to tell about "a fellow down in Blanco County who wanted to find the courthouse. He asked the town drunk, who lurched up to the car and began to give directions. 'You go down to the creek, take a right past the bridge, then go left—no, you can't get to the courthouse that way.' He tried again. 'Let's see, you go on up to the top of the hill, turn left at the cedar grove and cross the bridge—no, you can't get to the courthouse that way either.' After a couple of more stabs at it, the drunk gave up, looked at the other fellow and said, 'You just can't get to the courthouse from here.' "

71.8

Two birds were sitting on a telephone pole, when one asked the other, "Are you for L.B.J. [or whatever politician you prefer to substitute]?

"Why not?" replied the other bird. "He's for us.

(*See also 229.13*)

72. Kennedy Wit

72.1

I have just received the following telegram from my generous Daddy. "Dear Jack: Don't buy a single vote more than necessary. I'll be damned if I'm going to pay for a landslide."

—*John F. Kennedy,* in an off-the-record speech at the Washington Gridiron Dinner, 1958

72.2

On this matter of experience. I had announced earlier this year that if successful I would not consider campaign contributions as a substitute for experience in appointing Ambassadors. Ever since I made that statement I have not received one single cent from my father.

—*John F. Kennedy,* October, 1960

72.3

I appreciate your welcome. As the cow said to the Maine farmer, "Thank you for the warm hand on a cold morning."

—*John F. Kennedy,* Los Angeles, November, 1960

72.4

A story President Kennedy liked to tell was about the time a group of newspaper publishers came to Joe Cannon, powerful congressional leader of some years ago, and promised to elect him President of the United States if he would agree to lower the tariff on newsprint from Canada.

"Two thousand years ago," Uncle Joe told the newspapermen, "a certain man was taken up on a high mountain by the Devil, who showed him the whole country below them and promised him all that real estate if he would adore him."

Uncle Joe removed the cigar stump from between his teeth, looked up at the publishers with a touch of belligerence, and said, "Now it so happened that the Devil who was offering all that property didn't own an inch of it, and neither do you."

72.5

Kidding Secretary of Labor Arthur Goldberg, in a speech before an AFL-CIO convention, President Kennedy told how Goldberg got lost while mountain climbing in the Alps. Search parties were sent out to find him. The Red Cross finally joined the rescue attempt, and their men went around calling out, "Goldberg! Goldberg! It's the Red Cross.' " Finally from the mountains came a voice: "I gave at the office!"

72.6

About a year after taking office as President, John F. Kennedy said, "When we got into office the thing that surprised us most was to find that things were just as bad as we'd been saying they were."

72.7

During the John F. Kennedy–Richard Nixon presidential campaign, the wits got together and suggested that ideally Kennedy's running mate should have been Martin Luther from Kansas, and Nixon's, "a Mississippi nun who belongs to a trade union."

72.8

Barry Goldwater, a good photographer, once took a picture of President Kennedy and sent it to him, asking the President to autograph it. The picture went back to Goldwater with this inscription:

"For Barry Goldwater, whom I urge to follow the career for which he has shown so much talent—photography. From his friend, John Kennedy."

72.9

"The Republican National Committee recently adopted a resolution saying that you were pretty much of a failure. How do you feel about that?" asked a reporter at a Presidential press conference in 1963.

"I assume it passed unanimously," replied President Kennedy.

72.10

I think this is the most extraordinary collection of talent, of human knowledge, that has ever been gathered together at the White House—with the possible exception of when Thomas Jefferson dined alone.

—*President John F. Kennedy*, at a White House dinner honoring winners of the Nobel Prize.

72.11

On a trip through the West, President Kennedy was asked by a little boy how he happened to become a war hero. "It was absolutely involuntary," replied the President. "They sank my boat."

73. The Light Side of Ike

73.1

President Dwight D. Eisenhower, referring to construction of reviewing stands for John F. Kennedy inauguration, December, 1960: "I feel like the fellow in jail who is watching his scaffold being built."

73.2

One of President Eisenhower's favorite stories concerns a man who was being importuned to make up a foursome by three golfing friends.

"I'm sorry, but I don't think my wife would like it," said the hesitant golfer.

"Aw, come on," entreated one of the friends, "are you a man or a mouse?"

"Oh, I'm a man all right," was the reply. "My wife is afraid of a mouse."

73.3

Senator Kerr, Democrat of Oklahoma, once described President Eisenhower as "the greatest living unknown soldier."

73.4

President Eisenhower was fond of telling about the monk who said there were seven reasons why he had left the Church. The first of these was that he was thrown out. In the light of this there was no use listing the other six reasons.

74. "Give 'Em Hell" Harry

74.1

When President Truman announced he was getting rid of some unnecessary government bureaus, a woman wrote him that since she was building a new house and needed furniture she would appreciate a few of the discarded bureaus.

Truman replied that he had disposed of the bureaus, but that if she was interested he had a secondhand, no-damned-good Cabinet he'd like to get rid of.

74.2

There is a legend that when Harry Truman was speaking at a Grange convention in Kansas City, Mrs. Truman and a friend were in the audience. Truman in his speech said, "I grew up on a farm and one thing I know—farming means manure, manure, manure, and more manure." At this, Mrs. Truman's friend whispered to her, "Bess, why on earth don't you get Harry to say fertilizer?"

"Good Lord, Helen," replied Mrs. Truman, "you have no idea how many years it has taken me to get him to say manure."

74.3

H. Allen Smith reports that Harry S. Truman once said that when he dies he wants to be buried in a coffin made of mulberry wood, "because I want to go through Hell a-crackin' and a-poppin'."

74.4

Harry S. Truman delights in telling about the Catholic priest who stopped at a cabin of an anti-Catholic farmer in Alabama and asked for a drink of water. The farmer took one look at the Roman collar, turned his back and refused. The priest, noticing a picture of Pope Pius XII hanging on the wall, asked why a man would refuse a drink of water to a priest when he had the Pope's picture in his house. "Pope!" snorted the farmer. "Why, the peddler what sold me that picture said it was Harry Truman in his Masonic robes."

74.5

President Truman, visiting show places in Mexico, was shown the new fiery Parícutin volcano. As he viewed it with keen interest, President Aleman of Mexico asked what he thought of it. Truman said, "It's quite a volcano, but it's nothing compared to the one I'm sitting on in Washington."

74.6

Speaking of Josef Stalin, Harry Truman said: "He was a little bit of a squirt. Whenever he had his picture taken with me he stood up on a step above me, so he'd be on a level with me."

74.7

If I'd known how much packing I'd have to do, I'd have run again.

—*President Harry S. Truman,* upon leaving the White House, January, 1953

74.8

Most of the visitors come here to see if the animal is still alive. But I fool 'em; I stay in my office most of the time.

—*Harry S. Truman,* referring to visitors to the Truman Library, Independence, Mo., 1959

75. F.D.R. Stories

75.1

When Franklin D. Roosevelt spoke in Denver, Colorado, during his first presidential campaign, in 1932, he was reminded by his introducer that "there are sitting with you on this platform men qualified to serve with you in the Cabinet, men of United States Senatorship size, men who would bring honor and high attainment to the highest diplomatic posts."

Candidate F.D.R. arose and said, "Mr. Chairman, members of the Cabinet, distinguished representatives of the nation in the Senate of the United States, and plenipotentiaries extraordinary in foreign lands!"

75.2

President Franklin D. Roosevelt liked to tell about the two young fellows from the Southern mountains visiting Washington. They were walking along Pennsylvania Avenue when they were startled by the roar of motorcycle cops escorting a black limousine. "It's the President!" they heard someone call out.

"Wonder what he's done, now?" asked one of the mountaineers.

75.3

President Franklin D. Roosevelt's favorite story was about a commuter in Westchester County, a Republican stronghold, who every morning before boarding the train for New York picked up the N. Y. *Herald-Tribune,* glanced at it hurriedly and handed it back to the newsboy. Finally the curious newsboy asked the man why he only glanced at the front page.

"I'm only interested in the obituary news," he replied.

"But that is on the inside of the paper," said the newsboy.

"Boy, the death I'm interested in will be on the front page!" roared the tycoon.

—*George Allen,* Presidents I Have Known

75.4

It is said that when Franklin D. Roosevelt was once confined to bed with a mild indisposition, one of the papers headlined it with PRESIDENT KEPT TO ROOMS BY COED. F.D.R. showed everyone the paper.

75.5

Franklin D. Roosevelt liked to tell about the young Naval officer who was a poor navigator. Once on a cruise off the English coast he was told to shoot the sun in order to determine the ship's position.

Shortly after the young officer's finding had been delivered to the captain, he was called into his superior officer's cabin. "Remove your cap and bow your head," said the captain. "We are upon a sacred spot."

"Sir," said the young man, "I don't believe I understand."

"Well," said the captain, "according to your calculations we are now in the middle of Westminster Abbey."

75.6

A radical is a man with both feet firmly planted in the air. A conservative is a man with two perfectly good legs who has never learned to walk.

—*Franklin D. Roosevelt*

75.7

A reactionary is a somnambulist walking backward.

—*Franklin D. Roosevelt*

75.8

Speaking of Franklin D. Roosevelt, Alice Longworth said: "Franklin is 90 percent mush and 10 percent Eleanor."

76. Cal Plays It Cool

76.1

On his return from church one Sunday, Calvin Coolidge was asked by his wife what the minister spoke about.

"Sin," said Coolidge.

"What did he say about it?" asked Mrs. Coolidge.

"He was against it," replied Coolidge.

76.2

When someone twitted Calvin Coolidge for his habitual silence, he replied, "Well, I found out early in life that you didn't have to explain something you hadn't said."

76.3

A Washington society leader, seated next to President Coolidge at a dinner party, said: "Mr. President, I made a bet today that I could get more than two words out of you this evening."

"You lose," replied the President.

76.4

When he was Vice President, Calvin Coolidge attended many social functions, but he was the despair of hostesses because he simply would not engage in conversation. One hostess thought she could break the silence by placing next to Coolidge at dinner the brilliant Alice Roosevelt Longworth. But even her sparkling talk and gay personality failed to thaw out Coolidge. Finally, Mrs. Longworth, with obvious exasperation, said to the Vice-President, "You must get terribly bored at all the dinners you attend."

"Well," said Coolidge, "a man must eat."

76.5

Even when he was campaigning, President Calvin Coolidge refused to comment on issues on the infrequent occasions that the press met him. At one so-called press conference he was asked, "Have you anything to say on prohibition?"

"No," replied Coolidge.

"What about unemployment?"

"No."

"Will you tell us your thinking about disarmament?"

"No."

"Can you give us some idea of what you will tell Congress in your message?"

"No."

As reporters started to leave in disgust, Coolidge called out, "And don't quote me."

76.6

When President Calvin Coolidge was asked by a visiting Governor how he, Coolidge, could see a long list of callers every day and still finish his day's work, whereas the Governor was at his desk until late at night.

Coolidge said, "Yes, but you talk back."

76.7

President Calvin Coolidge was often annoyed by his fellow Republican Senator Borah, of Idaho. One day while horseback riding with an aide in a Washington park, the aide pointed to another rider and asked: "Isn't that Senator Borah?"

"Can't be," said Cal, "the rider and the horse are going in the same direction."

76.8

A group of Republican congressmen were discussing legislation with President Coolidge, when the conversation turned to the blunt oratory of Senator Jim Watson of Indiana. One of them observed that he had recently heard Watson address a group of voters back home where he concluded by telling them, "Now you have the facts, and you know exactly where I stand on the issues. You can vote for me, or you can go to the devil."

Coolidge looked out the window briefly, then said, "He gave them a difficult alternative."

76.9

When Rupert Hughes's *Life of George Washington* was published, its debunking caused an uproar. A reporter asked President Coolidge if he did not deplore this aspersion of our first President.

Coolidge arose from his desk, went to the window, looked out and said, "I see the monument is still standing."

76.10

Senator George H. Moses went storming into the White House when Coolidge was President, to complain about a man under consideration for a Republican Senatorial nomination, and told the President the man was "an out-and-out s.o.b."

"That could be," said Coolidge, "but there's a lot of them in the country and I think they are entitled to representation in the Senate."

—*Walter Trohan,* Chicago Tribune Press Service

76.11

During a heated debate in the U.S. Senate, one man told another "to go to hell." The Senator so attacked appealed to the Vice President, who was presiding, concerning the propriety of the remark.

Coolidge, who had been idly leafing through a book, looked up and said, "I've been going through the rule book. You don't have to go."

76.12

In the Massachusetts Legislature a member spoke at great length against a bill supported by Calvin Coolidge. The speaker prefaced each of his many arguments with the statement: "It is." When Coolidge arose to refute his opponent, he simply said, "It isn't," and then he sat down.

76.13

When Calvin Coolidge was governor of Massachusetts he made a campaign speech in behalf of a colleague. After the speech an elderly woman came up to him and said, "Governor, I stood up all during your speech."

"So did I," said Cal.

76.14

Colonel Lindbergh urged President Coolidge to fly. "Why, Mr. President, it's the safest mode of passenger transportation. In 200,000 passenger miles only one casualty."

Said Cal, "Very little comfort for the casualty."

76.15

Calvin Coolidge was once asked, "Mr. President, do the people where you come from say 'a hen lays' or 'a hen lies'?" Coolidge said, "The people where I come from lift her up to see."

76.16

A visitor to the White House said to President Coolidge that he would greatly appreciate a Coolidge cigar to give to a friend who collected cigar bands from famous men of the world. Coolidge picked up a box of cigars, removed the band from a cigar, replaced the cigar in the box, and handed the band to the caller.

76.17

Calvin Coolidge, when asked, "How does it feel to be President of the United States?" replied, "Well, you got to be mighty careful."

76.18

Mrs. Coolidge once surprised the President by having his portrait painted without his knowledge and hung in the library. The President and a Cabinet member entered the room and both looked at the new portrait in silence. After a painful pause the President said, "I think so, too!"

76.19

President Coolidge had guests to dinner at the White House, friends from Vermont. They were worried about their table manners so decided to watch Cal and do whatever he did. When Cal poured his coffee into his saucer they did same; when he added sugar and cream to the coffee in the saucer, they did same. Then the President placed the saucer of coffee on the floor for the cat.

76.20

When Calvin Coolidge was Vice President of the United States he lived at a Washington hotel. Late one night there was a small fire in the hotel, and all the guests were assembled in the lobby and adjoining rooms.

As soon as the Vice President concluded there was nothing to be alarmed about he made a move toward the elevator to return to his suite.

"Hey, you, come on back here," called out a fire chief.

"I happen to be the Vice President," said the usually silent Cal.

"OK then, go ahead," said the fireman but then called out, "vice-president of what?"

"Of the United States, of course," replied Coolidge.

"Oh, that's different. I thought you meant vice-president of the hotel. Come on back, then."

76.21

Clarence Darrow characterized Calvin Coolidge as "the greatest man who ever came out of Plymouth Corner, Vermont."

76.22

When Wilson Mizner was told that Calvin

Coolidge was dead, he said, "How can they tell?"

(*See also 142.2, 142.3*)

said, "You look familiar to me, but I just can't place you."

"Why, Mr. President, I made your pants."

"Oh, yes, why how do you do, Major Pants."

77. Taft's Laughs

77.1

While campaigning for governor of Ohio, William Howard Taft was hounded with continual hissing and booing by a hostile audience. Suddenly someone threw a cabbage that landed at Taft's feet. Looking down at the smelly cabbage, Taft shook his head in mock horror. "I see," he commented with a grin, "that one of my hecklers has lost his head."

77.2

At a function Chauncey Depew was kidding William Howard Taft about his vast weight. He said he had worried whether Taft could make his scheduled address since he was obviously pregnant.

"It's true I look pregnant," said Taft, "and if it's a boy, I'll name it William; if a girl, I'll name it after my wife; but if it proves to be only wind, then I'll name it Chauncey Depew."

77.3

President Taft told about the time he was swimming in the ocean at a New England resort. "Let's go in the water," cried someone in a group near the exceptionally big and heavy President.

"We can't," said a youngster, "until the President stops using the ocean."

77.4

Following a review of the Grand Army of the Republic in Cincinnati, twelve of the marchers were presented to President William Howard Taft. One man proudly showed where a hand had been shot off at Shiloh, another a leg at Bull Run. Taft turned to an aide and said, "They told me this was to be a reception, but it's more of an organ recital."

77.5

President William Howard Taft gave a reception at the White House. It was attended by government officials, officers of the Army and Navy, members of the diplomatic corps, and leading Washington citizens. As they lined up to shake hands with the President, the President's tailor fell into line. When he came up to the President, Mr. Taft grasped his hand and

78. "Teddy" R.

78.1

When the New York *World* called him a "dude," "goo-goo," and "Lah-de-dah," Theodore Roosevelt characterized the paper in these words:

"The New York *World*—a local stock-jobbing sheet of limited circulation, of voluble scurrility and versatile mendacity—owned by the arch-thief of Wall Street and edited by a rancorous kleptomaniac with a penchant for trousers."

78.2

During one of his campaign tours Theodore Roosevelt, a Republican, encountered a stubborn fellow who said that his grandfather was a Democrat, his father was a Democrat, and he was a Democrat, and he wasn't going to change.

"Suppose," asked T.R., "your grandfather and father were horse thieves? What then would you have been?"

"In that case, I would have been a Republican."

78.3

American Jews were justly proud in 1906 when President Theodore Roosevelt appointed Oscar Strauss to his Cabinet—as Secretary of Commerce and Labor.

Shortly thereafter a private dinner was given to celebrate the event, attended by the President. In explaining his selection, the President told the diners that Mr. Strauss was chosen for his character and ability—without regard to race, creed, color, or party. And, added Mr. Roosevelt, "Jacob Schiff will confirm the fact that I sought only the best-qualified man for the post."

Mr. Schiff, presiding at the celebration—wealthy, respected, gently senescent, and quite deaf—nodded and said, "That's right, Mr. President, I remember you said to me, 'Jake, who is the best Jew I can appoint as Secretary of Commerce?' "

78.4

During one of his political campaigns, a delegation called on Theodore Roosevelt at his home in Oyster Bay, Long Island. The President met them with his coat off and his sleeves rolled up. "Ah, gentlemen," he said, "come down to the barn and we will talk while I do some work." Whereupon Theodore Roosevelt picked up a pitchfork, looked around for the hay, and then called out, "John, where's all the hay?"

"Sorry, sir," called back John from the hay loft, "but I ain't had time to toss it back down again since you threw it up here when the Iowa folks was here."

78.5

When Theodore Roosevelt was visiting Germany he asked if he could call on the Kaiser. Word came back that the Kaiser said he could give up only half an hour to see the former President of the United States. T.R. sent back word that he could only spare fifteen minutes.

78.6

Shortly after former President and trustbuster Theodore Roosevelt left on a lion-hunting safari in Africa, the following notice was posted on a wall in the New York Stock Exchange: "Wall Street expects every lion to do his duty."

(*See also 155.5, 188.5*)

79. Lincolnania

79.1

Abraham Lincoln disliked boisterous people who came to the White House with all kinds of poor advice. He related that they reminded him of a fellow out in Illinois who thought he could make a lot of money. He made arrangements with a merchant whereby he would catch a couple of carloads of frogs, ship them to big cities where frogs' legs were a table delicacy. "There are at least 10 million frogs in that marsh near me, judging by the noise they make," said the man.

However, at the end of two weeks of searching, the haggard hunter had only a small basketful of frogs. "According to the noise they make," said the frog merchant, "there were millions of 'em, but after two weeks' search I could only harvest six frogs."

"So," concluded Mr. Lincoln, "these boisterous people make too much noise in proportion to their number."

79.2

Abe Lincoln told this story: A fellow out in Illinois had better luck in getting prairie chickens than any one in the neighborhood, although he used a rusty old gun that no other man dared to handle and never seemed to exert himself when he went hunting.

When a sportsman asked the hunter why he was so successful, he at first demurred, then after getting his questioner to promise not to reveal his secret, he said: "All you got to do is to hide in a fence corner an' make a noise like a turnip. That'll bring the chickens every time."

79.3

Abraham Lincoln, failing to convince an opponent that his reasoning was faulty, said, "Well, tell me how many legs has a cow?"

"Four, of course," was the quick reply.

"That's right," said Lincoln. "Now suppose we call the cow's tail a leg, how many legs would the cow have?"

"Why, five, obviously."

"That's where you are wrong," replied Lincoln. "Simply calling a cow's tail a leg doesn't make it a leg."

79.4

When Lincoln was practicing law in Illinois, a New York firm wrote him for information about one of his neighbors. Lincoln made this reply:

"I am well acquainted with Mr. ———, and know his circumstances. First of all, he has a wife and baby; together they ought to be worth $50,000 to any man. Secondly, he has an office in which there is a table worth $1.50 and three chairs worth, say, $1. Last of all, there is in one corner a large rat hole, which will bear looking into. Respectfully, A. Lincoln."

79.5

In defending a client charged with assault, Lincoln told the jury his client was in the fix of a man who, in going along the highway with a pitchfork on his shoulder, was attacked by a fierce dog, which he killed with the pitchfork.

"Why did you kill my dog?" demanded the dog's owner.

"Because he tried to bite me."

"But why did you not go at him with the other end of the pitchfork?"

"Why didn't your dog come at me with his other end?"

79.6

Lincoln related that when he was practicing

law he had to walk about ten miles to the court. One day the judge overtook him in his carriage and invited Lincoln to get in. Presently the carriage struck a stump on one side of the road, then it hopped to the other side. Lincoln noticed that the driver was jerking from side to side on his seat and said to the judge, "I think your coachman has been taking a little too much this morning."

The judge put his head out of the window and shouted to his coachman, "Why, you infernal scoundrel, you're drunk!"

"That's the first rightful decision you have given for the last twelvemonth," replied the driver.

79.7

During a court trial in which Abraham Lincoln defended one of the parties, the lawyer for the other side talked at great length and often to no purpose. When Lincoln addressed the jury he said that his opponent was an all-right fellow but that he had one peculiarity—his habit of reckless assertion and statements without grounds. "But," added Lincoln, "one should not impute this to a moral fault of the man's. He can't help it. It is just that the moment he begins to speak his mental faculties cease to function. I never knew of but one thing which compared with my friend," said Lincoln. "Back in the days when I performed my part as a keel boatman in 1830, I made the acquaintance of a trifling little steamboat which used to bustle and puff and wheeze about the Sangamon River. It had a 5-foot boiler and a 7-foot whistle. And every time it whistled it stopped."

79.8

Abraham Lincoln, speaking of a strict judge, said, "He would hang a man for blowing his nose in the street, but he would quash the indictment if it failed to specify which hand he blew it with."

79.9

Speaking of a certain lawyer, Abraham Lincoln said, "He can compress the most words into the smallest ideas better than any man I ever met."

79.10

For a brief period in his career, Abraham Lincoln was notably successful as a corporation lawyer. In one case he defended a railroad in a suit involving hundreds of thousands of dollars. The opposing attorney's summation to the jury was long, detailed, and eloquent and took more than two hours.

When it came Lincoln's turn to address the jury in rebuttal, he arose and said only: "My opponent's facts are right, but his conclusion is wrong." The jury burst out in laughter and brought in a verdict favoring Lincoln's client.

When Lincoln had won this stunning court victory following his one-sentence summation to the jury, several attorneys asked him how he was able to do it.

Lincoln told his colleagues that the night before the case went to the jury, he had a few drinks with the judge and the gentlemen of the jury, and during the evening he told them about the little farm boy who came running to his father one night and said, "Father, the hired hand is out in the barn with the new serving maid, and they're keeping the hay warm." The farmer said, "Son, your facts are right but your conclusion is wrong." That, pointed out Lincoln, was just what he told the jury in rebutting his opponent's argument, and he suggested that the jury the next morning may have remembered the story of the previous evening.

79.11

In one of the famous debates, Stephen Douglas charged Lincoln with having failed at everything he attempted—farming, teaching, liquor selling, and the law. "It's true—every word of it," replied Lincoln. "But there's one thing that Douglas forgot. He told you I sold liquor, but he didn't mention that while I had quit my side of the counter, he has remained on his."

79.12

During one of the Lincoln-Douglas debates, Douglas was the first speaker and in the course of his talk remarked that in early life his father, who, he said, was an excellent cooper by trade, apprenticed him out to learn the cabinet business.

This was too good an opportunity for Lincoln to pass up. When his turn came, Lincoln arose and said: "I had understood before that Mr. Douglas had been bound out to learn the cabinet-making business, which is well enough, but I was not aware until now that his father was a cooper. I have no doubt, however, that he was one, and I am certain, also, that he was a very good one, for (here Lincoln bowed gently to the heavy-drinking Douglas) he has made one of the best whiskey casks I have ever seen."

79.13

When Lincoln was seeking reelection to Congress, in 1836, the opposing candidates spoke one day at the courthouse in Springfield, Illinois. One of Lincoln's platform opponents was George Forquer, a Democrat who lived in the largest and finest house in the city, to which he had added a lightning rod—a then-new appendage.

Forquer's remarks were directed against Lincoln, and he proceeded to ridicule the person, dress, and arguments of Lincoln in a most offensive manner.

When Lincoln arose his eyes were flashing with indignation, but he answered Forquer calmly, fully, and triumphantly. Lincoln pointed to Forquer and said, "Live long or die young, I would rather die now than, like the gentleman, change my politics, and with the change receive an office worth $3,000 a year, and then feel obliged to erect a lightning rod over my house to protect a guilty conscience from an offended God!"

79.14

In 1846, when Lincoln was preparing to run for Congress, he attended a service conducted by the Rev. Peter Cartwright, who called upon all those desiring to go to Heaven to stand up. All arose but Lincoln. Then Cartwright asked all those who did not want to go to Hell to arise.

All but Lincoln arose.

"I am surprised," said Cartwright, "to see our brother Abe Lincoln unmoved by my appeals. If Mr. Lincoln does not want to go to Heaven and does not want to avoid going to Hell, will he please tell us where he wants to go?"

Lincoln arose slowly, looked around, and said, "I am going to Congress."

79.15

During a conversation between President Lincoln and Petroleum V. Nasby, the humorist, the name came up of a recently deceased politician of Illinois whose merits were blemished by his great vanity. Lincoln, recalling the large crowd at the man's funeral, said, "If General ——— had known how big a funeral he would have had, he would have died years ago."

79.16

When Lincoln was going to attend a political meeting in Illinois he hired a horse from a political rival, who gave him a slow horse in the hope Lincoln would not arrive on time. When he returned the horse, Lincoln said. "You keep this horse for funerals, don't you?"

"Oh, no," replied the liveryman.

"Well, I'm glad of that, for if you did you'd never get a corpse to the grave in time for the resurrection."

79.17

Abraham Lincoln, asked what he thought was the best attribute for a politician, said he thought it "would be the ability to raise a cause which would produce an effect and then fight the effect."

79.18

A political party called the Know-Nothings was working to stop the influx of foreign immigrants. They asked Abe Lincoln if he wouldn't help them keep America for Americans.

"That depends on what you call an American," said Abe. "Now for instance take old Mike McCarthy who works for me in my garden. I asked Mike if he was an American.

" 'Sure, now,' he said, 'I'm an American citizen, same as you!'

" 'But, Mike, you weren't born an American, were you?'

" 'Faith—I wanted to, but me mither wouldn't let me!' "

79.19

When the Republicans lost an important election in New York State, Abraham Lincoln was asked how he felt about it. "Somewhat like the boy in Kentucky," said the President, "when he was running to see his sweetheart. He fell, and he said he was too big to cry and too badly hurt to laugh."

79.20

During the Civil War an old friend of Lincoln's called at the White House on official business, and in the course of their conversation the caller said, "Well, Mr. Lincoln, if anybody had told me that in a great crisis like this the people were going out to a little one-horse town and pick out a one-horse lawyer for President I wouldn't have believed it."

"Neither would I," replied Lincoln. "But it was a time when a man with a policy would have been fatal to the country. I have never had a policy. I have simply tried to do what seemed best each day, as each day came."

79.21

During one of his receptions as President, one of his constituents approached Lincoln and said, "Mr. Lincoln, I have watched you closely ever since your inauguration. As one of your constituents, I now say to you, do in the future as you damn please, and I will support you."

Lincoln said, "I haven't seen half enough of you. Sit down, my friend."

79.22

During the Civil War, guests to a reception at the White House were kept by guards from shaking hands with President Lincoln. But this did not cool the ardor of one man who waved his hat at Lincoln and called out, "Mr. President, I'm up from York State where we believe that God Almighty and Abraham Lincoln are going to save this country."

"My friend, you are half right," replied Lincoln.

79.23

During the Civil War a minister called on Lincoln, and during their conversation he said, "Let us have faith, Mr. President, that the Lord is on our side in this great struggle."

"I am not at all concerned about that," replied Lincoln, "for I know that the Lord is always on the side of the right; but it is my constant anxiety and prayer that I and this nation may be on the Lord's side."

79.24

Lincoln, with a "no offense, gentlemen," told some visiting ministers about the Negro boy who was making "mud pies" with his toes.

"What are you making," an onlooker asked him.

"A church," he said. "Can't you see the pews and the pulpit?"

"Why don't you make a minister?"

"Ain't got enough mud," the boy said.

79.25

During a discussion with a caller at the White House, Lincoln remarked that he had great reverence for learning.

"Men of force," replied his visitor, "can get on pretty well without books. They do their own thinking instead of adopting what other men think."

"Yes," said Mr. Lincoln, "but books serve to show a man that those original thoughts of his aren't new, after all."

79.26

When President Lincoln had smallpox in the mild form of varioloid, though slight, it kept callers away from the White House. Lincoln said he enjoyed it. "Now, while I have something to give everybody, no one comes near me."

79.27

When the name of the Reverend Dr. Shrigley, of Philadelphia, was sent to Congress for approval as a chaplain, a delegation called on Lincoln to protest that the man was not "sound in his theological opinions. He does not believe in endless punishment, but believes that even the rebels will be finally saved."

"Well, gentlemen, if that be so," replied Lincoln, "and there is any way under heaven whereby the rebels can be saved, then, for God's sake and their sakes, let the man be appointed." And he was appointed.

79.28

Soon after Lincoln took office as President, he was besieged by office seekers. When war broke out and the office seekers persisted, Lincoln said, "I feel like a man letting lodgings at one end of his house while the other end is on fire."

79.29

Harried night and day by office seekers, President Lincoln once said, "This human struggle and scramble for office, for a way to live without work, will finally test the strength of our institutions."

79.30

President Lincoln appointed a young dandy as the American consul in one of the South American countries. But a wag warned the fellow, who was on his way to the White House to thank the President, that the bugs in that country would make his life unbearable. This frightened the man.

When he arrived at the White House he told the President that he had heard that the bugs in that land would bore a hole clean through him before he was there a week. Lincoln looked at the young man's extravagant clothes and said, "Well, young man, if that's true, all I've got to say is that if such a thing happened they would leave a mighty good suit of clothes behind."

79.31

At a Cabinet meeting the advisability of putting a legend on greenbacks similar to the "In God We Trust" legend on silver coins was discussed. When Lincoln was asked his opinion, he replied, "If you are going to put a legend on the greenback, I would suggest that of Peter and Paul: 'Silver and gold we have not, but what we have we'll give you.' "

79.32

When a group of Senators called on Lincoln and asked him to change all seven of his Cabinet members, rather than just the one change proposed, Lincoln said:

"Gentlemen, your request for a change of the whole Cabinet because I have made one change, reminds me of a story I once heard in Illinois of a farmer who was much troubled by skunks. His wife insisted on his trying to get rid of them.

"He loaded his shotgun one moonlit night and waited. After some time the wife heard the shotgun go off, and in a few moments the farmer entered the house.

" 'What luck have you?' asked she.

" 'I hid myself behind the woodpile,' said the old man, 'with the shotgun pointed toward the hen roost, and before long there appeared not one skunk, but seven. I took aim, blazed away, killed one, and he raised such a fearful smell that I concluded it was best to let the other six go.' "

79.33

One day when Lincoln was in the minority on a serious question before his Cabinet, he told them about a fellow out in Illinois who happened to stray into a church while a revival meeting was in progress. The man was not quite sober but nevertheless walked down the aisle to the front pew. For a while he joined in the Amen's, but soon fell asleep.

At the close of the meeting the preacher asked, "Who are on the Lord's side?" and the congregation arose en masse. When he asked, "Who are on the side of the Devil?" the sleeper woke up, and seeing the minister on his feet, he too arose.

"I don't exactly understand the question," he said, "but I'll stand by you, parson, to the last. But it seems to me that we're in a hopeless minority."

"I'm in a hopeless minority, now," added Lincoln, "and I'll have to admit it."

79.34

When Thurlow Weed urged that a certain Marylander be appointed to the Cabinet, Lincoln remarked that "Maryland must be a good state to move from." Then he told the story of a witness in court in a neighboring county, who, on being asked his age, replied, "Sixty." The judge interrupted and said, "The court knows you to be much older than sixty."

"Oh, I understand now," was the rejoinder; "you're thinking of those ten years I spent on the eastern shore of Maryland; that was so much time lost and didn't count."

79.35

When an official of the War Department escaped serious punishment for a flagrant offense, because he exposed even more serious irregularities in the Department, Lincoln was reminded of the story about Daniel Webster when he was a boy.

Young Daniel, caught violating a school rule, was called to the teacher's desk for the customary "feruling" of the hand. On his way to the desk, young Webster spit upon the palm of his right hand, wiped it on the side of his pants, and then presented that hand to the teacher. The teacher looked at it and said, "Daniel, if you will find another hand in this schoolroom dirtier than this one, I will let you off this time."

Instantly Daniel brought his left hand from behind his back and presented it to the teacher.

"That will do," said the teacher. "Take your seat."

79.36

During the early days of the Civil War, General McClellan's waiting tactics and indecision irked Lincoln to the point where he finally wrote: "My dear McClellan: if you do not want to use the Army I should like to borrow it for a while."

79.37

In the summer of 1862 President Lincoln received a long letter from General McClellan in which Lincoln was advised how to conduct the affairs of the nation. When asked what reply he made to McClellan's letters, Lincoln said, "Nothing. But it made me think of the Irishman whose horse kicked up and caught his foot in the stirrup. 'Arrah!' said he. 'If you are going to get on I will get off.' "

79.38

Carl Sandburg in his biography of Lincoln, quotes Edward Dicey as follows:

"At the first council of war, after the President had assumed the supreme command-in-chief of the army, in place of McClellan, the General did not attend, and excused himself the next day by saying he had forgotten the appointment. 'Ah, now,' remarked Mr. Lincoln, 'I recollect once being engaged in a case for rape, and the counsel for the defense asked the woman why, if as she said, the rape was committed on a Sunday, she did not tell her husband till the following Wednesday? and when the woman answered she did not happen to recollect it—the case was dismissed at once.' "

79.39

"It seems to me," said Lincoln while reading some telegrammed appeals sent to him by General McClellan, "that McClellan has been wandering around and has sort of got lost. He has been hollering for help ever since he went South—wants somebody to come to his deliverance and get him out of the place he's got himself into.

"He reminds me of the story of a man out in Illinois who, in company with a number of friends, visited the state penitentiary. They wandered all through the institution and saw everything, but just about the time to depart this man became separated from his friends and couldn't find his way out.

"He roamed up and down one corridor after another, becoming more desperate all the time, when, at last, he came across a convict who was looking out from between the bars of his cell door. Here was salvation at last. Hurrying up to the prisoner he hastily asked:

" 'Say! How do you get out of this place?' "

79.40

When General McClellan was pursuing his "waiting campaign," Abraham Lincoln sent General Hooker to take charge of the forces. Hooker rushed into action. He reported his movements in an urgent dispatch from "Headquarters in the saddle." Abraham Lincoln smiled and said, "The trouble with Hooker is that he's got his headquarters where his hindquarters ought to be."

79.41

A Union general, who had allowed himself and his men to get trapped, reminded Lincoln of a man out West who was "heading" a barrel. He worked to drive down the hoops, but just when he thought he had the job done, the head of the barrel would fall in. Suddenly it occurred to him that he could put his young son, who was standing nearby, inside the barrel to hold the top in place, while he pounded the hoops down the side. This worked immediately, but the man could not figure out how to get his son out of the barrel.

79.42

When P. T. Barnum brought his show to Washington during the Civil War, he called on Lincoln, whereupon there was discussion about Barnum's two famous midgets, General Tom Thumb and Admiral Nutt. "You have some pretty small generals," said Lincoln, "but I think I can beat you."

79.43

An officer who had been disgraced and defeated in a Civil War battle sent in a report that slickly slid over the fact that he had been soundly beaten. Lincoln saw right into the heart of the fraud and made known what he saw simply by telling a story. A young fellow, he said, came up to a farmer out in the field, plowing.

"I want your daughter!" yelled the young man.

The farmer went on plowing as if the interruption was not worth stopping his work for. All he did was shout over his shoulder, "Take her."

The young man stood there on the edge of the field, looking puzzled, scratching his head, and saying dubiously, "Too easy, too durned easy!"

79.44

"Grant is a drunkard," protested powerful and influential political detractors of Lincoln's general. "Well," said Lincoln, "you just find out, to oblige me, what brand of whiskey Grant drinks, because I want to send a barrel of it to each of my generals." Lincoln judged Grant on his performance.

79.45

One day during the Civil War, Senator Wade, of Ohio, called on Lincoln at the White House to demand that General Grant be dismissed. When Lincoln refused and said, "Senator, that reminds me of a story," Wade thereupon burst out with: "It is with you all story, story! You are the father of every military blunder that has been made during the war. You are on the road to hell, sir, with this government, by your obstinacy and you are not a mile off this minute."

"Senator," replied Lincoln good naturedly,

"that is just about a mile from here to the capitol, is it not?"

79.46

When some enemies of General Grant called on Lincoln and urged that the "Silent One" was a no-good character, Lincoln replied that "Grant fights" and then told the delegation that this reminded him of a man out in Illinois who was nominated for the office of Sheriff—"a good man for the office, brave, determined, and honest, but not much of an orator. In fact, he couldn't talk at all; he couldn't make a speech to save his life."

Finally, however, the candidate's friends persuaded him to make a speech at a political rally. When called upon he arose, advanced to the front of the platform, glared at the crowd, and said: "Fellow Citizens, I'm not a speakin' man; I ain't no orator, an' I never stood up before a lot of people in my life before; I'm not goin' to make no speech, 'cept to say that I can lick any man in the crowd!"

79.47

When Union General Phelps took possession of Ship Island, near New Orleans, during the Civil War, he issued a pompous and elaborate proclamation, in which he declared that thereby the slaves were free. This he had no authority to do, and it was expected that Lincoln would repudiate the declaration. But when friends asked Lincoln about it, Lincoln said he was unable to take Phelps seriously, that the general was just blowing off steam. He said, "I feel about that a good deal as a man I call Jones, whom I knew once, did about his wife. He was one of those meek men—badly henpecked. One day his wife had been switching him out of the house. A day or two afterwards a friend met him in the street and said, 'Jones, I have always stood up for you, as you know. But I am not going to do it any longer. Any man who will stand quietly and take a switching from his wife, deserves to be horsewhipped.' Jones looked up with a wink, patting his friend on the back. 'Now don't,' said he; 'why it didn't hurt me any; and you've no idea of the power of good it did my Sarah Ann!' "

79.48

After listening to arguments and appeals of a committee which called on him not long before the Emancipation Proclamation was issued, Lincoln said: "I do not want to issue a document that the whole world will see must necessarily be inoperative, like the Pope's Bull against the comet."

79.49

A bustling society woman called on President Lincoln and told him, "My son must be given a commission. It is a right of our family's, sir, since my grandfather fought at Lexington, my uncle was one of the few who stood his ground at Bladensburg, my father was in the Battle of New Orleans, and my husband died in battle at Monterey."

"My dear lady," said Lincoln, "your family has done enough for the nation. It is time to give somebody else a chance."

79.50

A woman who refused to make further personal sacrifices in behalf of the Union cause during the Civil War, reminded Lincoln of a young man whose aged father and mother owned considerable property. This only son, concluding the old folks had outlived their usefulness, killed them both and was tried and convicted of murder. When he appeared before the judge for sentencing he was asked if there was any reason why the sentence of death should not be passed on him. The young man thereupon promptly said that he hoped the court would be lenient with him because he was a poor orphan.

79.51

A story about himself that Lincoln most enjoyed telling concerned two Quakeresses who were discussing the Civil War leaders, Lincoln and Jefferson Davis.

"I think Jefferson will succeed, said one.

"Why does thee think so?"

"Because Jefferson is a praying man."

"And so is Abraham a praying man."

"Yes, but," argued the first Quakeress, "the Lord will think Abraham is joking."

79.52

Hotheads yelped that Jeff Davis ought to be captured and hanged. Lincoln, eager to heal the nation's wounds as soon as possible, saw good reasons for refusing the demand. But it was not politic for him to say so. General Sherman told how Lincoln handled the matter:

"I asked Mr. Lincoln explicitly, when we were at City Point, whether he wanted me to capture Jeff Davis or let him escape, and in replying he told me a story. 'I'll tell you, General,' Mr. Lincoln began, 'what I think of taking Jeff Davis. Out in Sangamon County there was an old temperance lecturer who was very strict in the doctrine and practice of total abstinence. One day, after a long ride in the hot sun, he stopped at the house of a friend, who proposed making him a lemonade. As the mild beverage was being mixed the friend insinuatingly asked if he wouldn't like a drop of something stronger to brace up his nerves after the exhausting heat and exercise. "No," replied the lecturer, "I couldn't think of it; I'm opposed to it on principle; but," he added with a longing glance at the black bottle that stood conveniently at hand, "if you could manage to put in a drop unbeknownest to me, I guess it wouldn't hurt me much." 'Now, General,' Mr. Lincoln concluded, 'I am bound to oppose the escape of Jeff Davis; but if you could manage to let him slip out, unbeknownestlike, I guess it wouldn't hurt me much.' "

79.53

Several days before he was assassinated, Abraham Lincoln received a request from General Creswell for a pardon for a Confederate friend and made this reply:

"Creswell, you make me think of a lot of young folks who once started out and to reach their destination had to cross a shallow stream. They did so by means of an old flatboat. When the time came to return, they found to their dismay that the old scow had disappeared. They were in sore trouble and thought over all manner of devices for getting over the water, but without avail.

"After a time, one of the boys proposed that each fellow should pick up the girl he liked best and wade over with her. The masterly proposition was carried out, until all that were left upon the island was a little short chap and a great, gothic-built elderly lady.

"Now, Creswell, you are trying to leave me in the same predicament. You fellows are getting all your own friends out of this scrape; and you will succeed in carrying off one after another, until nobody but Jeff Davis and myself will be left on the island, and then I won't know what to do. How should I feel? How should I look, lugging him over?"

79.54

A man was praising a certain historian to Abraham Lincoln and said, "It may be doubted whether any man of our generation has plunged more deeply into the sacred fount of learning."

"Yes, or come up drier," remarked Lincoln.

79.55

Abraham Lincoln had little patience with men who were secretive about their own past. They reminded him, he said, of a little Frenchman out West one winter when the snow was exceptionally deep. Lincoln said his legs were so short that the seat of his trousers rubbed out his footprints as he walked.

79.56

A foreign diplomat unexpectedly walked in on Abraham Lincoln when he was shining his shoes.

"I am astonished, Mr. President," he said, "to find you blacking your own shoes."

"Whose shoes do you shine?" asked Lincoln.

79.57

President Lincoln, visited by two rival hatters who presented him with hats each had made, for a moment was uncertain how to compliment them. Finally, he said: "Gentlemen, both hats mutually excel each other."

79.58

A story which would seem very dubious to attribute to Abraham Lincoln, relates that he went one evening to the theater and thoughtlessly put his famous stovepipe hat on the seat next to him, with the open end of the hat upward. After the curtain had gone up and Lincoln's attention was riveted on the stage, an amply proportioned lady came down the aisle and plumped herself down on Lincoln's hat. She jumped up when she heard the crunch of the suddenly pancaked hat. "Madam," said Lincoln, "I could have told you that my hat would not have fit you before you tried it on."

79.59

Once when Abraham Lincoln was making a speech a drunk called out: "Did I have to pay a dollar to see the ugliest man in the whole U.S.A.?"

Lincoln said: "Yes, sir, I am afraid you were charged a dollar for that privilege. But I have it for nothing. Thank you."

79.60

A neighbor saw Abraham Lincoln striding past her house with his two sons, both howling.

"Why, Mr. Lincoln, whatever is the matter with the boys?"

"Just what's the matter with the world," smiled Mr. Lincoln, "I've got three walnuts, and each wants two."

79.61

My father taught me to work; he did not teach me to love it.

—*Abraham Lincoln*

79.62

I fear explanations explanatory of things explained.

—*Abraham Lincoln*

79.63

Die when I may, I want it said of me by those who know me best, that I have always plucked a thistle and planted a flower when I thought a flower would grow.

—*Abraham Lincoln*

(*See also 106.1, 212.7*)

80. Other Presidents

80.1

Blessed are the young for they shall inherit the national debt.

—*Herbert C. Hoover*

80.2

Once upon a time my political opponents honored me as possessing the fabulous intellectual and economic power by which I created a worldwide depression all by myself.

—*Herbert C. Hoover,* 1958

80.3

When Will Hays took Will Rogers to the White House to meet President Harding, Rogers said, "Mr. President, I would like to tell you all the latest political jokes."

"You don't have to, Will," said Harding with a touch of bitterness; "I appointed them."

80.4

One day President Harding invited Grantland Rice and Ring Lardner to join him in a game of golf. Rice was a good player, but Lardner tended to hit the ball low and with a hook. Harding, on the other hand, had the habit of making his shot and then moving on ahead before the others had taken their turns. Thus it was that one of Lardner's shots just whistled past Harding's head and struck the branches of a tree over the President's head. Harding looked around in surprise and then with puzzlement that no apology from Lardner was forthcoming.

Instead, Lardner said, "Well, I did my best to make Coolidge the President of the United States."

Harding roared with laughter.

80.5

President Woodrow Wilson liked to tell of the time he was sight-seeing in Hannibal, Missouri, the birthplace of Mark Twain, and decided to see to what extent the novelist was appreciated in his hometown. He asked an old-timer what he thought of Tom Sawyer.

"Never heard of him," was the reply.

"No doubt you have heard of Huckleberry Finn, then," said Wilson.

"Nope."

"Well what about Pudd'nhead Wilson?" asked the President.

"Oh, him," snorted the old fellow. "Yes, I made the mistake of voting for him."

80.6

President and Mrs. Wilson arrived in Washington from Europe one evening in 1919, and cheering crowds welcomed his return. When passing the national capitol in their car, Mrs. Josephus Daniels, wife of the Secretary of the Navy, deplored the failure of Congress to order the dome of the capitol illuminated, as was usually done.

"Do not let that trouble you, Mrs. Daniels," said the President. "There are domes underneath the capitol building that need illuminating more than the physical one."

80.7

Golf: A game in which one endeavors to control a ball with implements ill adapted for the purpose.

—*Woodrow Wilson*

80.8

Every man who takes office in Washington either grows or swells.

—*Woodrow Wilson*

80.9

A conservative is a man who just sits and thinks, mostly sits.

—*Woodrow Wilson*

(*See also 118.4*)

80.10

Members of the House of Representatives like to tell about the time Grover Cleveland was President and having his troubles with the Senate. One night he was awakened by a servant who said, "Mr. President, there are burglars in the house!"

Cleveland opened his eyes and said, "In the Senate, maybe, but not in the House."

80.11

A committee was appointed, and money was

raised to place a statue of ——— (whatever President you don't like) in the Hall of Fame.

There was a dispute about where the statue should be placed. It was agreed that the statue could not go next to George Washington, because Washington never told a lie. Nor could it be next to Lincoln because he was known as "Honest Abe," nor next to Jefferson because he was a statesman of the highest principles.

Finally it was decided to place the statue next to Christopher Columbus, because Columbus did not know where he was going, he did not know where he was when he got there, nor where he had been when he returned home. And he made the whole trip on borrowed money.

(*See also 154.5–154.7*)

81. Some Views of the White House

81.1

When I was a boy I was told that anybody could become President; I'm beginning to believe it.

—*Clarence Darrow*

81.2

Since television all a man needs to be elected President is the kind of profile that looks good on a postage stamp.

—*Gregory Nunn*

81.3

There's some folks standing behind the President that ought to get around where he can watch 'em.

—*Kin Hubbard*

81.4

An autocrat is a ruler that does what th' people wants an' takes th' blame f'r it. A Constitutional ixecutive, Hinnissy, is a ruler that does as he dam pleases an' blames th' people.

—*Finley Peter Dunne*

81.5

An Italian, applying for citizenship, was asked: Who is the President of the United States?

"Mr. Johnson."

"And who is the Vice President?"

"Mr. Humphrey."

"Now, tell us, could you be President?"

"No."

"Why not?"

"Mister, scusa me, please. I vera busy worka de restaurant."

POLITICIANS ON THE NATIONAL, STATE, AND LOCAL LEVELS

82. The Happy Warrior

82.1

A committee is a group of men who individually can do nothing but collectively meet and decide that nothing can be done.

—*Alfred E. Smith*

82.2

Early in his political career in New York, Al Smith asked the district attorney to give special consideration to a friend. "Depend on it, Al, I'll see that your man gets justice," said the D.A.

"Heck," replied Smith, "I can get that from anyone—I want you to give him a break."

82.3

During one of Al Smith's campaigns for governor of New York, when he walked onto the platform to begin an address, a voice from the crowd called out: "Tell us all you know, Al; it won't take long!"

"I'll tell 'em all we both know," retorted Smith; "it won't take any longer."

82.4

During one of his political campaigns an opponent charged Al Smith with telling lies about him. "You ought to be glad," replied Smith. "If I told the truth about you, they'd run you out of town."

82.5

Running to unseat Nathan Miller from the governorship of New York State, Al Smith had to come up quickly during the last days of the campaign with an answer to the boast that Miller had saved the people of the state 40 million dollars through economies. Smith replied by saying that he did not have the time to make an analysis of the Miller assertions, but he did wish to ask one question: "If it is true that Governor Miller saved the people 40 million dollars, then what became of the money? Who got it? Where did it go?"

82.6

At a nonpartisan dinner the chairman introduced Al Smith, then running for office. "And may the best man win!" said the toastmaster. "Oh, so you're against me, too," said Smith.

82.7

Al Smith avoided when possible the use of prepared speeches. He said they reminded him of the fellow who worked for six months forging a check, only to have it come back marked "Insufficient Funds."

82.8

When Al Smith was Governor of New York State, he once visited one of the state mental hospitals, and, walking through the grounds alone, he was accosted by one of the patients who asked who he was.

"I'm Al Smith, Governor of the State of New York," said Smith.

The patient looked him over carefully, then said, "Well, it won't take 'em long around here to knock that idea out of your head. When I came here I was Napoleon."

82.9

Al Smith, who delighted to show visitors around the Empire State Building, was plied with numerous questions by a woman visitor.

Smith bore up under the strain until, riding in an elevator at the end of the tour, she asked, "Suppose the elevator's cables broke, would we go up or down?"

"That depends, madam," replied Smith, "upon the kind of life you have been living."

83. Adlai Ad-libs

83.1

Man does not live by words alone, despite the fact that sometimes he has to eat them.

—*Adlai Stevenson*

83.2

During his campaign against Eisenhower for the Presidency, Adlai Stevenson said: "We were driving through the streets of a big city, and a little boy ran out in front of the crowd and shouted, 'Hooray for Stevenhower!' I am going to give that kid a job in the State Department."

83.3

I have sometimes said that flattery is all right —if you don't inhale.

—*Adlai Stevenson*

83.4

The relationship of the toastmaster to speaker should be the same as that of the fan to the fan dancer. It should call attention to the subject without making any particular effort to cover it.

—*Adlai Stevenson*

83.5

When Adlai Stevenson was practicing law in Chicago he had built for himself and family a handsome home at Libertyville, near Lake Forest. They had been in the new home less than two months when a fire burned the house and contents to the ground. While the fire raged Stevenson stood watching it helplessly with several neighbors. A bit of flaming debris drifted down at Stevenson's feet. He picked it up and calmly lit a cigarette. "As you can see," he said to a neighbor, "we are still using the house."

83.6

In welcoming the delegates of the Democratic National Convention to Chicago in 1952, Adlai Stevenson, then Governor of Illinois, referred to the just-concluded Republican National Convention in the same hall: "For almost a week pompous phrases marched over the landscape in search of an idea."

83.7

During the presidential campaign of 1952, Stevenson on the stump said: "The Republicans have a 'me, too' candidate running on a 'yes, but' platform, advised by a 'has been' staff."

83.8

Characterized as an "egghead" during the 1952 campaign for the Presidency, Stevenson said, "Eggheads of the world, unite! You have nothing to lose but your yolks!"

83.9

I have great faith in the people. As to their wisdom, well, Coca-Cola still outsells champagne.

—*Adlai Stevenson,* after he was defeated in 1952.

83.10

In the 1956 presidential campaign Stevenson said: "I have finally figured out what the Republican orators mean by what they call 'moderate progressivism.' All they mean is: 'Don't just do something. Stand there.' "

83.11

Soon after his second defeat for the Presidency, Stevenson said: "I think I missed my calling. As a matter of fact, I think I missed it twice."

83.12

Adlai Stevenson, objecting to some of the newspapers that he felt were picking a truth here and a truth there to build a case against him, said it reminded him of the old lawyer addressing a jury, who said: "And these, gentlemen, are the conclusions on which I base my facts."

83.13

A politician is a person who approaches every subject with an open mouth.

—*Adlai Stevenson*

83.14

Adlai Stevenson, deploring the attempts to measure everyone as either of the "Left" or the "Right," said it reminded him of the church seeking a new minister. One of the deacons said, "We want someone who is not too radical and not too conservative. Not too far to the right and not too far to the left—just someone mediocre."

83.15

Once when asked if he had ever thought as a boy that he might grow up to be President, Stevenson replied: "Yes, but I just dismissed it as a normal risk that any red-blooded American boy has to take."

84. Other Governors

Anecdotes

84.1

When Thomas E. Dewey was Governor of New York, he and a friend passed a political clubhouse in a rather drab neighborhood. Noticing black crepe on the building in honor of an old member who had just died, Dewey said, "It sure livens up the old place."

84.2

After he was defeated for the Presidency, Thomas E. Dewey said the best analogy of his feelings the day after—when he saw defeat snatched from the jaws of victory—was of the mourner who had passed out from too much drinking at a wake and was laid in a spare coffin in the funeral parlor, to sleep it off. When he came to and realized where he was, he asked himself, "If I'm alive, why am I in this coffin? And if I'm dead, why do I have to go to the bathroom?"

84.3

Former Governor James of Pennsylvania related that one day he boarded a train which was transporting about twenty men from one institute for the criminally insane to one in another part of the state. The Governor happened to get in the car carrying the twenty men, but since the distance was short decided to stay in his seat. Presently the conductor came through the car, counting one, two, three, etc., to check on the passengers. When he came to James he hesitated and then asked, "Who are you?" "I am the Governor of the state," said James. The conductor promptly resumed his count, "four, five, six, etc."

84.4

When protests were made to a governor for his neglect of the arts, he replied, "Gentlemen, you have been misled. Every single campaign expenditure in my behalf has included a brass band."

84.5

A state employee in New Jersey was driving a state truck along a highway when he was flagged down by a trooper. "Don't you know you were going 60 miles an hour?"

"No, I didn't," said the driver.

"Haven't you a governor on that truck?"

"No, sir," said the employee. "The Governor's in Trenton—that's fertilizer you smell."

84.6

I went to the store the other day to buy a bolt for our front door, for as I told the storekeeper, the Governor was coming here. "Aye," said he, "and the Legislature too." "Then I will take two bolts," said I. He said that there had been a steady demand for bolts and locks of late, for our protectors were coming.

—*Henry David Thoreau,* Journal, September 8, 1858

Definition

84.7

Governor: A device attached to a state to keep it from going ahead very fast.

(*See also 155.2, 155.3, 213.15, 216.1*)

85. Legislators-at-large

Anecdotes

85.1

A member of a legislative committee went to investigate an insane asylum. There was a dance at the institution when he arrived there, and he joined in the affair. He was introduced to a beautiful woman, one of the patients, who had frequent days of perfect lucidity and sanity. He danced with this woman, and she said to him: "I do not remember having met you before. How long have you been in the asylum?" The legislator explained that he had only just arrived as a member of a legislative committee of investigation.

"How stupid you must think me," said the woman, "I knew you must either be one of the inmates or a member of the Legislature the moment I met you, but I had no way of knowing which."

85.2

Much of the legislation passed these days reminds one of the official who asked a lawyer friend to draw up a dog law for him to present to the Legislature.

"What kind of a dog law do you want?" asked the attorney.

The legislator said, "I want a safe, comprehensive, kindly, and warmhearted one that will satisfy the voters and not interfere with the rights of dogs."

85.3

A young lawyer anxious to obtain a legislative post, asked Judge Samuel Seabury, of New York, to help with his influence. The judge, apparently a bit doubtful about the young man, said "I'll put in a good word for you, if you give me your word of honor that you will not get involved in any crooked dealings."

The young attorney bristled and said, "I will go to Albany unpledged, or I won't go there at all."

85.4

Courtland Nicoll was engaged in a controversy in the New York State Legislature with Jimmy Walker over the 5-cent transit fare in New York City. Nicoll worked for days on his speech, and it took him one hour to deliver it, exhausting both the subject and his listeners.

Walker arrived in the legislative chamber late, greeted his friends genially, and waved in friendly fashion to Nicoll. When it came time for Walker to reply, he arose, looked balefully at the Senate clock, and said, "My colleagues, it is late. You are tired after the day's legislative grind. You deserve a rest. You have listened to a great speech. I cannot hope at this time to reply in kind. I have just one thing to say to my good friend from the silk-stocking district of New York. You have gone pretty far for a Nicoll yourself."

Aphorisms

85.5

A great deal of this country's troubles come from legislators and lawmakers with too much bone in the head and not enough in the back.

85.6

Laws, like sausages, cease to inspire respect in proportion as we know how they are made.

(*See also 55.1, 55.7, 123.7*)

86. Mayors and City Councils

Anecdotes

86.1

When Jimmy Walker was mayor of New York an adversary trapped him in an outright lie. The reporters asked him what he had to say to this. Walker smiled and said, "Another good story ruined by eyewitnesses."

86.2

During an interview, Mayor Jimmy Walker began to speak strongly against a certain official.

"Would you say that he is a total loss?" asked a reporter.

"Oh, no," replied Walker. "The man is not that good."

86.3

Jimmy Walker, more than customarily late for a luncheon where he was to speak, finally arrived and said: "After all, everyone can't be first; even George Washington married a widow."

86.4

An incurable office seeker, upon learning of the death of a city official, went quickly to Mayor Walker and asked, "Can't I take Shanahan's place?"

"I have no objection," said Walker, "if the undertaker hasn't."

86.5

"All the politicians," said Jimmy Walker, "have three hats: one they wear, the other they throw into the ring, and the third they talk through."

86.6

When New York Mayor James J. Walker was unmercifully attacked by a politician, Walker said to a friend, "That's odd; I don't remember ever doing a favor for him."

86.7

A sympathetic constituent said to Mayor

Walker: "It must be a lot of work and strain being mayor of New York."

"Yes, madam," replied Beau James, "you can always see a light in my office long after I've gone for the day."

86.8

When Mayor John F. O'Brien, a Tammany candidate, was elected mayor of New York, he was asked by reporters who was going to be his police commissioner. "They haven't told me yet," he replied.

86.9

Old-timers in St. Louis tell about Mayor Sigenheim, when complaints were made of the dark streets while the street lamps were being changed from arc lights to gas mantles. "We got a moon yet, ain't we?" asked Sigenheim.

86.10

"My name is O'Flaherty," said the taxpayer to the mayor. "My cellar is full of water, and I want it fixed." The mayor explained and explained that it was not within his duties or power to do anything about O'Flaherty's cellar, but the taxpayer insisted it was the mayor's responsibility and that "my hens will drown if something isn't done."

"O'Flaherty," said the mayor finally, "the best thing for you to do is to keep ducks."

86.11

An American politician, returning home from a visit to London, said that when the lord mayor of London enters a room they call out, "My Lord, the Mayor," but when he, the American politician, comes into a room they say, "My God, the Mayor."

86.12

A party of Aldermen in the city barge, passing, a short time ago, from Staines to Kew Bridge, after dinner—a gentleman hailed the corporate crew with the following uncourteous exclamation, "Halloa! you Aldermen! I'll give you half-a-crown a-piece if you will come and disgorge in my hog-trough."

—*Cyclopedia Magazine,* England, September, 1807

86.13

Resolution passed years ago by the Board of Councilmen of Canton, Mississippi:

1. Resolved by this Council, that we build a new jail.
2. Resolved, that the new jail be built out of material of the old jail.
3. Resolved, that the old jail be used until the new jail is finished.

86.14

The members of the New York Board of Aldermen once visited Dan Mulligan's house en masse and were so well entertained they all fell asleep.

"Whatever will I do?" asked Mrs. Mulligan. "The aldermen are all sound asleep. Will I wake them?"

"Lave thim be," said Mulligan. "While they sleep the city's safe."

86.15

During a Chicago City Council meeting which was discussing the World's Columbian Exposition, it was suggested that a number of gondolas be brought from Europe for a Venice scene that was planned. But one economy-minded alderman said, "We've got a year yet. All we hafta do is buy two of 'em, a male and a female, and let 'em mate and then you'll have plenty of gondolas."

86.16

The meeting of the town council had been long, torrid, and tempers were badly frayed. "You," shouted one member to another, "are the most thickheaded ignoramus I've ever met!"

"Please, please, gentlemen," shouted the chairman, "you forget that I am here."

(*See also* *55.8, 155.13, 210.20, 252.3, 253.2*)

MONARCHS, OTHER RULERS, AND DIPLOMATS

---

87. Kings, Queens, and Dictators

Anecdotes

87.1

Demosthenes told General Phocion: "The Athenians will kill you some day when they are in a rage."

"And you," answered Phocion, "when they are in their senses."

87.2

When the philosopher Aristippus sought a hearing of Dionysius, he was ignored, whereupon he fell at the ruler's feet, was listened to, and had his request granted.

Following this incident Aristippus was chided for degrading philosophy by falling at a man's feet for private gain.

Aristippus retorted: "It was not my fault, but rather Dionysius's that his ears are in his feet."

87.3

Plutarch reported that King Philip of Macedonia wrote a threatening letter to rulers of Sparta which said, "If once I enter your territories, I will destroy you all, leaving you never to rise again."

The Spartans replied in a letter containing but one word, IF.

87.4

When Alexander the Great called on Diogenes, he found the famous Greek philosopher impoverished and sitting in the sunlight. "Is there anything I can do for you?" Alexander asked.

"Yes," replied Diogenes, "you can stand out of my sun."

87.5

When Tiberius succeeded Augustus he withheld a legacy to the people of Rome that his predecessor had willed. One day Tiberius noticed a man standing whispering into the ear of a corpse and asked him what he was up to. The man explained that he was asking the corpse to tell Augustus that Tiberius had not paid the legacy to the people of Rome. Tiberius thereupon ordered the whisperer slain so that he could take the message direct to Augustus himself.

87.6

The King was tired of his jester and of his puns. "If you don't make a pun at once—and a good one—you'll be hanged," declared the monarch.

"All right," said the jester. "Name a subject."

"Myself," said the King; "the King."

"The King," quipped the clown, "is not a subject."

"All right," said the King, still annoyed, "why do you make fun of my figure?"

"Because," said the jester, "everyone likes to have fun at someone else's expanse."

"Well then," continued the monarch, "why do you say that Queen Elizabeth was greater than Joan of Arc?"

"Because Joan was a wonder," replied the clown, "whereas Queen Elizabeth was a Tudor."

"Hang him!" cried the King.

But when the noose was placed around the jester's neck, the King relented to the extent of sparing his life if the jester would promise never to make another pun.

"I promise, Your Majesty," said the clown solemnly. "No noose is good news."

And so the jester was hanged.

87.7

Madame de Chevreuse visited the Tuileries splendidly arrayed in a blaze of diamonds.

"Are they real?" asked Napoleon.

"*Mon Dieu, Sire,* I really don't know, but at any rate they are good enough to wear here."

87.8

After exile in London, Napoleon returned to France and usurped power, and all Europe wondered how long he would remain dominant. At this time Napoleon met a woman he had previously known when he was in London.

"Are you staying in Paris long, Madame?" asked Napoleon.

"Not long. Are you?" asked the Englishwoman.

87.9

Napoleon to Talleyrand: "Sir, you are in love with yourself, and you don't have a rival on earth."

87.10

If I wished to punish a province, I would have it governed by philosophers.

—*Frederick the Great*

87.11

Several years before World War II, when Mussolini and his followers were making faces and gestures and deluding themselves into believing they were a great military power, a Fascist said to a Frenchman, "If Mussolini ordered his troops to march into France what could stop us?"

The Frenchman thought about this briefly, then replied, "The French Customs Service."

87.12

One day Mussolini, when at the height of his power, slipped unnoticed into a movie theater. When the newsreels came on and his own image appeared on the screen everyone, except Mussolini, arose and cheered. The man next to Mussolini tapped him on the shoulder and said, "You'd better stand up. We all feel the way you do, but it's not safe to show it."

87.13

When Nikita Khrushchev was Russia's top man, an admirer sent him a bolt of fine woolen cloth with a pattern he liked very much. He called in a Moscow tailor and asked him to measure him for a suit from the material. The tailor examined the bolt of cloth and told him there was not enough of it for a three-piece suit. A month or so later Khrushchev was due to go to East Germany so he took the cloth with him and called on an East German tailor. The tailor took measurements, looked at the cloth, and told Mr. K that the suit would be ready in six days. "How come," Khrushchev asked, "that the Moscow tailor couldn't make me a suit out of this cloth?"

"Comrade," said the tailor, "you must remember you are not so big a man in East Germany as you are in Moscow."

87.14

King Henry IV of England arrived in a small town, was greeted by the entire populace, and escorted to a spot where the town's leading official began an elaborate address of welcome. During the oration an ass began to bray, whereupon His Majesty turned to the animal and said, "Gentlemen, one at a time, please."

87.15

During the course of a serious disagreement with Francis I of France, Henry VIII asked Thomas More to carry a sharp note to the French King. More mentioned Francis I's temper and said, "Why, he might have me beheaded."

"Never fear," assured Henry, "if he does I'll have the head of every Frenchman in London."

"That is most kind, Your Majesty," said More, "but I do not think any of their heads would fit my shoulders."

87.16

Ben Jonson sent this message to King James I: "He despises me, I suppose, because I live in an alley; tell him his soul lives in an alley."

87.17

King Charles II, attended by only two persons, encountered the Duke of York, who expressed surprise that the King should be so indifferent to danger. "I'm in no danger," said the King. "No man is going to take away my life to make you king."

87.18

At a grand review by George III of the Portsmouth fleet in 1789, there was a boy who mounted the shrouds with so much agility as to surprise every spectator. The King particularly noticed it and said to Lord Lothian, "Lothian, I have heard much of your agility; let us see you run up after that boy."

"Sire," replied Lord Lothian, "it is my duty to *follow Your Majesty.*"

87.19

Dissolute, stupid George IV was widely believed to have illegally married his mistress, Mrs. Fitzherbert. But despite this he still pursued his legal spouse, Caroline of Brunswick, with continual malice and finally brought her before the House of Lords on a charge of adultery.

When asked to answer this charge, she replied, "The only time I ever committed adultery was with the husband of Mrs. Fitzherbert." She was acquitted.

87.20

The rather undiplomatic George IV of England encountered a notorious sport and loose liver at a seashore resort. "I hear you are the greatest blackguard in this place," was the King's salutation. The King's subject bowed graciously and said, "I trust Your Majesty has not come here to take away my reputation."

87.21

King George V once asked his grandson what he was studying so intently.

"About Peter Warbeck," replied the youth.

"Who was he?"

"Oh," said the grandson, "he pretended he was the son of a king. But he wasn't. He was really the son of respectable people."

87.22

When one of her courtiers told Queen Victoria that Prime Minister Gladstone was saying unkind things about her, she is reported to have said, "It doesn't matter a particle what he thinks of me. It is what I think of him that is important."

87.23

People wondered how Disraeli got along so much better with Queen Victoria than his bitter rival, Gladstone. When the quick-witted and acid-tongued Disraeli was asked how he ingratiated himself with Her Majesty, he said, "Gladstone speaks to the Queen as though she were a public institution. I treat her with the knowledge that she is a woman."

87.24

Of Adolf Hitler, Winston Churchill said: "No one can have a higher opinion of him than I do. I think he is a dirty little guttersnipe."

87.25

When the Nazis invaded Russia, Winston Churchill said: "If Hitler invaded Hell, I would make at least a favorable reference to the Devil in the House of Commons."

87.26

An actor was once married to Winston Churchill's daughter, Sarah. Churchill was not overly fond of the young man, who insisted upon calling Churchill "Papa" to the latter's extreme annoyance. One day toward the end of World War II the son-in-law said to Churchill, "Papa, who do you think was the greatest statesman of World War II?"

"Mussolini," said Churchill, "because he had the guts to shoot his son-in-law."

87.27

In 1952 Queen Elizabeth II became annoyed at persistent newspaper reports that she was pregnant. She summoned Prime Minister Churchill to Buckingham Palace and angrily told him, "I insist that these rumors be stopped."

When Churchill left the royal presence he was reported to have muttered, "She may not be pregnant, but she is certainly regnant."

87.28

A schoolboy explained that "one difference between a president and a king is that the king has no vice."

Aphorisms

87.29

Under a dictatorship everything that isn't forbidden is obligatory.

87.30

Only cowards insult dying majesty.
—*Aesop*

87.31

The people have always some champion whom they set over them and nurse into greatness. . . . This and no other is the root from which a tyrant springs; when he first appears he is a protector.
—*Plato*

(*See also 81.4, 91.9, 93.33, 110.14, 139.30, 151.3–151.5, 151.11, 152.7, 178.3, 178.8, 183.6, 199.4, 254.3, 268.10, 269.10, 270.8, 271.3, 272.6, 273.15, 273.16, 275.1*)

88. Diplomats and Diplomacy

Anecdotes

88.1

The Secretary of State called in one of his assistants concerning a conference soon to be held in Paris.

"I suppose," said the Secretary, "that you speak French?"

"A little," replied the assistant. "I can make myself understood to waiters and cab drivers."

"But," said the Secretary, "suppose there should be no waiters or cab drivers at the conference?"

88.2

Secretary of State Olney had a firm rule never to appoint anyone to the consular service who could not speak the language of the country to which he was assigned. When a politician called on him and asked to be appointed American consul at a Chinese port, Olney reminded him of the Department's new rule and added, "I don't suppose you speak Chinese, or do you?"

The politician grinned and said, "You just ask me a question in Chinese and I'll answer it."

P.S. He got the appointment.

88.3

Discussing the profession of diplomacy, John Foster Dulles suggested that J. P. Morgan once provided a key to its success.

It seems that the great banker was rebuking an associate in his firm for certain indiscretions that had become a matter of common knowledge in Wall Street.

"But, Mr. Morgan," said the young man, "what I have been doing has been quite out in the open. I have not been doing anything behind closed doors."

"Young man," snapped Morgan, "that is what doors are for."

88.4

An official in the State Department replaced a KEEP SMILING sign in his office with one reading KEEP SMILING ANYHOW.

88.5

"Diplomacy is nothing but a lot of hot air," said a companion to Georges Clemenceau as they rode to a peace conference.

"All etiquette is hot air," said Clemenceau. "But that is what is in our automobile tires; notice how it eases the bumps."

88.6

When Ramsay MacDonald was England's Prime Minister after World War I, he was discussing the prospects of permanent peace with another government official. The latter, an expert in foreign affairs, was cynical about MacDonald's idealistic hopes for lasting peace among nations. He reminded MacDonald that the mere wish for peace did not ensure it.

"True enough," said MacDonald. "But neither does the desire for food satisfy one's hunger. Nevertheless it can get you started toward a restaurant."

Definitions

88.7

Diplomacy is to do and say the nastiest thing in the nicest way.

—*Isaac Goldberg*

88.8

Diplomacy is the art of saying "nice doggie" until you have time to pick up a rock.

—*Francis Rodman*

88.9

Diplomacy: Lying in state.

—*Oliver Herford*

88.10

A diplomat is a person who can tell you to go to hell in such a way that you actually look forward to the trip.

—*Caskie Stinnett,* Out of the Red, 1960

88.11

Diplomat: A person who can be disarming even though his country isn't.

—*Sydney Brody,* Saturday Evening Post

88.12

A diplomat is a man who always remembers a woman's birthday, but never remembers her age.

88.13

A diplomat is a man who can keep a civil tongue in his cheek.

88.14

A diplomat is a man who can bring home the bacon without spilling the beans.

88.15

An ambassador is an honest man sent to lie abroad for the commonwealth.

—*Sir Henry Wotton*

88.16

Peace is that blessed period when it isn't your sacred duty to believe an official lie.

88.17

Disarmament: Agreement between nations to scuttle all weapons that are obsolete.

88.18

Alliance: In international politics, the union of two thieves who have their hands so deeply inserted in each other's pocket that they cannot separately plunder a third.

—*Ambrose Bierce*

Aphorisms

88.19

I have discovered the art of fooling diplomats—I speak the truth and they never believe.

—*Benso di Cavour*

88.20

The diplomat thinks twice before saying nothing.

88.21

It is fortunate that diplomats have long noses since they usually cannot see beyond them.

—*Paul Claudel*

88.22

An appeaser feeds the wild animal in the hope it will eat him last.

88.23

American diplomacy is easy on the brains but hell on the feet.

—*Charles G. Dawes*

(*See also 72.2, 79.30, 79.56, 83.2, 91.9, 142.10, 142.11, 156.20, 184.39, 225.1, 229.5, 230.12, 231.11, 232.1, 271.3, 271.10, 271.18, 271.28, 272.3, 272.6, 272.9, 272.11, 273.20*)

THE LAW AND THE LAWLESS

LAUGHTER IN THE COURTROOM

89. Called for Jury Duty

Anecdotes

89.1

A man who appeared for jury duty had been examined by both defense and prosecution and was about to be accepted, when the prosecutor asked, "Do you believe in capital punishment?"

The prospective juror hesitated and, after a moment's reflection, replied, "Well, sir, I do—if it ain't too severe."

89.2

During a murder trial the judge asked one prospective juror if he had formed any opinion concerning the guilt or innocence of the prisoner.

"No, Your Honor, I have not."

"Have you any conscientious scruples against the imposition of the death penalty if the prisoner is found guilty."

"Not in this case, Your Honor," replied the juror.

89.3

The man called to jury duty asked the court if he could be excused, explaining, "I owe a man $50. He is leaving town today, and I want to see him before he gets away so I can pay him the money."

"You are excused," said the judge. "I don't want anybody on the jury who can lie like you."

89.4

Conscientious Citizen: "Your Honor, I couldn't serve on the jury. One look at that man there convinces me he's guilty."

Judge: "Quiet! That is the district attorney."

89.5

The old fellow was an experienced jury man who had sat in on many trials. An attorney asked him, "Who influences you the most—the lawyers, the judge, or the witnesses?"

The old man pondered for a moment before replying. At last he drawled: "Well, I'll tell ye. I'm a plain and reasoning man, and I ain't influenced by anything the lawyers say, nor by what the witnesses say—no, nor by what the judge says. I just look at the man in the dock, and I asks myself, if he ain't done nothing wrong, why's he here? So I brings 'em all in guilty."

89.6

"Where did the car hit him?" the doctor was asked by the attorney.

"He was struck at the junction of the dorsal and cervical vertebrae," replied the physician.

A burly old fellow rose up in the jury box and called out, "I been livin' in this town for forty years, and I ain't never heard of any such place around here."

89.7

The young lawyer retained by a farmer to bring an action against a railroad company for the loss of twenty-four pigs did his best to impress the jury with the magnitude of the case.

"Twenty-four pigs, gentlemen," he said, "twice the number in the jury box."

89.8

The judge said, "Have you a lawyer?"

Prisoner said, "No, I don't need one. I have plenty of friends on the jury."

89.9

Thoroughly disgusted with a jury which seemed unable to reach a verdict in an absolutely cut-and-dried case, the judge said, "I discharge this jury."

One sensitive member, indignantly faced the magistrate. "You can't discharge me," he said firmly.

"And why not?" snapped the surprised judge.

"Because," and the juror pointed to the lawyer for the defense, "I'm hired by that man."

89.10

Mr. Justice Morris charged a jury in Calcutta, India, years ago, as follows: "Gentlemen of the jury: The prisoner has nothing to say, and I have nothing to say. What have you got to say?"

89.11

The efficiency of our criminal jury system is only marred by the difficulty of finding twelve men every day who don't know anything and can't read.

—*Mark Twain*

89.12

A Chinese description of American court trials: "One man is silent, another talks all the time, and twelve wise men condemn the man who has not said a word."

Definition

89.13

A jury is a group of twelve persons of average ignorance.

—*Herbert Spencer*

(*See also* 7.15)

90. Judge versus Lawyer

Anecdotes

90.1

In his very first address to the court, the young lawyer soared to the heights, and his imagination and enthusiasm threatened to keep him in this rarefied and unrealistic atmosphere for an inordinate time. Finally, the judge interrupted him and said, "Please, counselor, don't get up any higher; you are already beyond the jurisdiction of this court."

90.2

Detecting signs of the judge's boredom, the young lawyer stopped in the midst of a long and wearisome presentation to the court and asked, "Is it Your Honor's pleasure that I should continue?"

"Pleasure, my dear man," sighed the judge, "has long since ceased, but you may go on with your presentation."

90.3

Shortly after New Mexico was admitted to the Union, an old guide and Indian fighter was appointed a judge. The first case before him was a man charged with horse stealing. When all the witnesses and evidence against the alleged thief were heard, the attorney for the defendant stepped up to present the defense.

"There's no point in you saying anything now," said the old judge. "The evidence is all in, and you'd only confuse the jury if you got talkin'."

90.4

Justice Hitz, a witty jurist who presided over the Federal Court of Appeals in Washington, leaned over the bench one day and said to a lawyer, "My friend, this court is often in error, but never in doubt."

90.5

Sir Fletcher Norton was noted for his want of courtesy. When pleading before Lord Mansfield on some question of manorial right, he chanced unfortunately to say, "My Lord, I can illustrate the point in an instant in my own person: I myself have two little manors."

The judge immediately interposed, with one of his blandest smiles, "We all *know it,* Sir Fletcher."

90.6

The young lawyer's knees shook as he arose to present his first case before the great and witty Lord Ellenborough.

"My Lord, my unfortunate client—My Lord, my unfortunate client . . ."

"Go on, go on!" said Ellenborough, "as far as you have gone the court agrees with you."

90.7

Lord Bacon to Sir Edward Coke: "Mr. Attorney, I respect you, I fear you not; and the less you speak of your greatness, the more I will think of it."

90.8

It was the habit of Lord Eldon, when Attorney General, to close his speeches with some remarks justifying his own character. At the trial of Horne Tooke, speaking of his own reputation, he said: "It is the little inheritance I have to leave my children, and, by God's help, I will leave it unimpaired." Here he shed tears, and, to the astonishment of those present, Mitford, the Solicitor General, began to weep.

"Just look at Mitford," said a bystander to Horne Tooke; "what on earth is he crying for?"

Tooke replied, "He is crying to think what a small inheritance Eldon's children are likely to get."

90.9

Lord Birkenhead, a famous English lawyer, was not reluctant on occasion to make his personal point to the presiding judge. Once during an important trial when he had addressed the court sharply, the judge stopped him to ask, "Are you trying to teach me the law?" Birkenhead smiled and said softly, "My Lord, I never attempt the impossible."

90.10

When he was a young barrister, the Earl of Birkenhead protested a judge's obvious sympathy for his opponent's side. The judge rebuked Birkenhead, and their remarks developed a distinctly personal flavor. Finally the exasperated judge exclaimed, "Young man, you are extremely offensive."

"As a matter of fact," said the Earl, "we both are. But I am trying to be, and you can't help it."

90.11

Lord Clare, who was much opposed to John P. Curran, an eighteenth-century Irish patriot, one day brought a Newfoundland dog upon the bench and during Curran's speech turned aside and caressed the animal. Curran stopped. "Go, on, go on, Mr. Curran," said Lord Clare.

"Oh, I beg a thousand pardons," was the rejoinder; "I really thought your lordship was employed in consultation."

90.12

There is a celebrated reply of Mr. Curran to a remark of Lord Clare, who curtly exclaimed at one of his legal positions, "Oh! if that be law, Mr. Curran, I may burn my law books!"

"Better *read* them, My Lord," was the sarcastic and appropriate rejoinder.

90.13

During a trial in a country courthouse, a trial attorney so far forgot himself as to wave a volume of Blackstone in front of the judge while protesting a ruling from the bench. "Sit down," thundered the judge. "Don't try to say that I do not know the law."

"Your Honor," replied the attorney, "I do not for a moment suggest that you do not know the law. I simply wanted to read a few lines from Blackstone to show what a legal ass *he* was."

90.14

Thaddeus Stevens, one day in court, didn't like the ruling of the judge. The third time the judge ruled against Stevens, the old man got scarlet with rage and with quivering lips commenced tying up his papers as if to quit the courtroom.

"Do I understand, Mr. Stevens," asked the judge, "that you wish to show your contempt for this court?"

"No, sir, no, sir. I don't want to show any contempt; I'm attempting to conceal it."

90.15

Max Steur, a once prominent trial lawyer of New York, was requested to apologize to the court for some remarks he had made. Steur arose with dignity, bowed to the judge, and said: "Your Honor is right, and I am wrong, as Your Honor generally is."

The judge never figured out whether he should be satisfied with this remark or cite Mr. Steur for contempt of court.

90.16

There is a traditional story told around Lynchburg, Virginia, about Patrick Henry when he was practicing law.

A man stole a hog and dressed it, was caught, and asked Henry to defend him. Henry asked, "Did you walk away with that shoat?"

"Yessir."

"Have you got the carcass?"

"Yessir."

"You go home, you wretch; cut the pig lengthwise in half, and hang as much of it in my smokehouse as you keep in yours."

In court Patrick Henry said: "Your Honor, this man has no more of that stolen shoat than I have. If necessary, I'd kiss the Bible on this." The man was acquitted.

90.17

A young lawyer, in his first appearance before the Supreme Court, was citing at some length certain elementary principles of law in behalf of his client. Presently one of the justices leaned over the bench and with some asperity said: "Young man, apparently you give this court little credit for knowing the rudiments of the law."

"Your Honor," replied the brash young attorney, "I made that mistake in the lower courts."

90.18

A Scotch attorney, arguing a case before the House of Lords, repeatedly referred to "the watter of the mill."

"Do you Scotchmen spell 'water' with two t's?" asked the presiding judge.

"No, My Lord," he replied, "but we spell 'manners' with two n's."

90.19

During the proceedings in the court of a small town, Daniel O'Connell's address to the jury was several times interrupted by the braying of a donkey in a nearby field. "One at a time," quipped the presiding judge.

Later when the judge was charging the jury, the same donkey again began braying. O'Connell arose and said, "My Lord, there seems to be such an echo that I have difficulty understanding what Your Lordship is saying."

90.20

An Irish counselor having lost his cause, which had been tried before three judges, one of whom was esteemed a very able lawyer, and the other two but indifferent, some of the other barristers were very merry on the occasion. "Well, now," says he, "I have lost. But who could help it, when there were an hundred judges on the bench?—one and two ciphers."

90.21

The lawyer went on interminably in his address to the court, until the exhausted judge finally interrupted to ask: "Mr. O'Brien, is it any good for you to continue? At this point everything you say simply goes in one ear and out the other."

"Perhaps," said the counsel, "that is because there is nothing to stop it."

90.22

A clash arose between the judge and the attorney. The judge ordered the lawyer to sit down. The lawyer was deaf and didn't hear him and went on talking. The judge fined him $10.

The lawyer leaned toward the clerk of the court and cupped his hand behind his ear. "What did he say?"

"He fined you $10."

"What for?"

"Contempt of court."

The lawyer gave the judge a mean look and thrust his hand in his pocket. "I'll pay it now. It is a just debt."

90.23

A judge, joking with a young barrister, said, "If you and I were turned into a horse and an ass, which would you prefer to be?"

"The ass, to be sure," replied the barrister. "I've heard of an ass being made a judge, but a horse never."

90.24

"Your Honor," said the lawyer, "I submit that my client did not break into the house at all. He found the living-room window open, inserted his right arm, and removed a few trifling articles. Now, my client's arm is not himself, and I fail to see how you can punish him for an offense committed wholly by one of his limbs."

"Your argument," said the judge, "is very well put, but dubious. However, I will follow your tenuous logic. I sentence the prisoner's arm to one year's imprisonment. He can accompany the arm or not, as he chooses."

Whereupon the defendant calmly removed his artificial right arm, handed it to the speechless judge, and walked out.

90.25

On being informed that the judges in the Court of Common Pleas had little or nothing to do, an attorney remarked, "Well, well, they're *equal to it!*"

(*See also 79.6, 79.8, 211.25*)

91. Lawyer versus Lawyer

Anecdotes

91.1

In a Hackensack, New Jersey, court an attorney addicted to verbosity droned on and on in his summation to the jury, to the mounting anger of the twelve good men and true. When the opposing lawyer, Paul Huot, arose, he realized that the jury was now on his side, and he wanted to keep them with him. He therefore said, "Your Honor, I will emulate my worthy opponent and submit the case to the jury without argument." Whereupon Huot sat down—to await the jury's quick decision in favor of his client.

91.2

The attorney for the defense made a long and moving plea in behalf of his client, pulling out all the stops that would evoke sympathy. When he ended most of the spectators were in tears. But the jury of stern and experience-hardened countrymen sat apparently unmoved. The veteran prosecuting attorney took shrewd note of the jury's seemingly stony attitude and began his address to them with: "Gentlemen of the jury, I want you to understand at the outset that I am not going to bore for water."

91.3

The lawyer of the old school during a trial in Georgia arose to address the jury. He shook the rafters of the old courthouse with his booming voice, he flailed his arms like a man going down for the third time, his tie waved in the breeze created by his swinging arms, his hair was mussed and his clothes disarrayed. He sat down exhausted but satisfied he had won the jury to his cause.

His young opponent arose and gave a good imitation of his old-school adversary, then after a few minutes suddenly quieted down and said, "Now, gentlemen of the jury, having fully answered the arguments of my opponent, I would like to discuss with you the facts in this case."

91.4

"You're nothing but an ambulance-chasing phony," shouted one lawyer at another as the trial opened. "And you're so crooked you'd fit into a corkscrew," retorted the other attorney.

"Gentlemen," said the judge, "let us proceed now that you have identified each other."

91.5

The young Texas lawyer was trying his first case before a jury and resorted to the device of stacking formidable-appearing law books on the table before him. It was a harmless little stunt that often worked with rural juries. During his address to the jury the young lawyer turned often to one of the volumes of *Corpus Juris* and cited cases as authority for the position he was arguing.

The wily old lawyer who was opposing the young man, when it came time for him to address the jury, picked up one of the young lawyer's volumes, looked at it, pointed to the title as he held it before the jury, and said "As you can see, this is titled *Corpus Juris*. You all know that means *Dead Law!* Now don't let this young lad from the city fool you with a lot of stuff from dead law!" The young man lost his first case before a jury.

91.6

Joseph Choate, famous lawyer, was once defending a case in Westchester County, New York, with his usual skill and poise. The plaintiff's lawyer, ruffled and exasperated, finally said to the jury: "Gentlemen! I sincerely hope that your decision will not be influenced by the Chesterfieldian urbanity of my opponent."

Choate arose, smiled, and purred, "Gentlemen, I am sure you will not be influenced, either, by the Westchesterfieldian suburbanity of my opponent."

91.7

Once a lawyer interrupted Rufus Choate in the midst of a patent case: "Look here; there's nothing original in your patent; your client did not come by it naturally."

Choate, surprised, looked up at his opponent. "What does my brother mean by 'naturally'? We don't do anything naturally. Why, naturally, a man would walk down the street with his pantaloons off."

The laughter that followed obscured the point of the other lawyer's remarks, which was precisely what Choate intended.

91.8

Paul Huot was sitting quietly in the courtroom at Hackensack, New Jersey, while the attorney opposing him was addressing the jury. But the lawyer got so wrought up that he lost control of his teeth—his denture flew out of his mouth and toward the jury.

"I object," said Huot as he quickly arose and addressed the judge, "to my worthy opponent's attempt to intimidate the jury in this manner."

91.9

In one of his first cases in court, Clarence Darrow was irked by the efforts of his much older adversary to belittle him before the jury by referring to him as "this beardless attorney."

When it came Darrow's turn to address the jury, he said, "My opponent has been trying to discredit me because I haven't a beard. Let me tell you about a King of Spain who sent a young man to a neighboring monarch with an important message. The monarch was incensed by this and shouted, 'Does the King of Spain so lack men and respect for this court that he sends a beardless boy here?'

"The young ambassador replied, 'Sire, if my sovereign had supposed you imputed wisdom to a beard, he would have sent a goat to you.' "

91.10

A barrister entered an English court one day with his wig inadvertently stuck on the side of his head. Still unaware of the wig's amusing angle, the wearer of it was puzzled by the observations made concerning it. Finally he asked John Philpot Curran, "Do you see anything ridiculous in this wig?"

"Nothing except the head," said Curran.

91.11

He had just lost a lawsuit and was furious. He turned to the opposing attorney and said, "I look upon you, sir, as a scoundrel."

The lawyer looked at him coldly and said, "You have a right to look upon me in any character you care to assume."

(*See also* 79.7, 79.10)

92. On the Witness Stand

Anecdotes

92.1

"You seem to have plenty of intelligence for a man in your position," sneered the lawyer, in cross-examining a hostile witness.

"If I wasn't under oath I'd return the compliment," said the witness.

92.2

Clarence Darrow was having trouble getting a coherent story from a hostile witness.

Finally the witness said, "Mr. Darrow, how can you question my word? I am wedded to the truth."

"Ah," said Darrow, "and tell us how long you have been a widower?"

92.3

Prosecuting a case, the brilliant Sir Edward Carson asked an unfriendly witness, "Do you drink?"

"That's my business," snapped the witness.

"Do you have any other business?" asked Carson.

92.4

A browbeating counsel asked a witness how far he had been from a certain place. "Just 4 yards, 2 feet, and 6 inches," was the reply.

"How came you to be so exact, my friend?"

"Because I expected *some fool* or other would ask me, and so I measured it."

92.5

The famous Rufus Choate was questioning a witness in an assault case in which Choate's client was accused. He maneuvered the fellow into admitting that he hadn't actually seen the offense committed.

"So," purred Choate, "you say you didn't actually see him bite off this man's ear?"

"No," said the witness, "I didn't see him bite it off. I just saw him spit it out on the ground."

92.6

A lawyer, cross-examining a witness to a robbery, asked, "When did the robbery take place?"

"I think—" began the witness.

"We don't care what you think, sir. We want to know what you know."

"Then if you don't want to know what I think," retorted the witness, "I might as well leave the stand. I can't talk without thinking. I'm no lawyer."

92.7

George Jeffreys, a famous English lawyer and later a notorious judge, was once cross-examining a young woman, shortly after Jeffrey's wife had given birth to a baby much too soon after their marriage. During the cross-examination Jeffrey turned on the witness with a sarcastic, "Madam, you are very quick with your answers." "Quick as I am, Sir George," snapped the witness, "I am not as quick as your lady."

92.8

"Your testimony is completely contrary to that of the previous witness," said the cross-examining lawyer. "Do you mean to impeach her veracity?"

"Not at all," replied the witness. "I wish only to make clear what a colossal liar I am if she is telling the truth."

92.9

Timothy Healy, during a trial in London, was challenging a young woman witness whose testimony was proving damaging to Healy's client. Healy, in possession of facts which revealed the woman as one of loose morals, was intent upon bringing this to the jury's attention. The opposing lawyer, pretending outrage, declared, "This woman is as pure as the driven snow."

"Oh, a hoar frost," said Healy.

92.10

An elderly itinerant was being cross-examined by a young lawyer who was trying to cast doubt on the witness's credibility. Despite all the showy efforts of the young attorney, the man remained unruffled, though provoked by the lawyer's crude tactics. "What do you do for a living?" asked the lawyer.

"A little bit of everything," replied the witness. "I have a little farm I work, do some fishin', sometimes cut some wood, sometimes work a few days on Colonel Starling's big place, and then I'm a sort a jackleg preacher."

"What do you mean by a jackleg preacher?"

"Well, mister, so long as you ask me, I'd say a jackleg preacher is like to a real preacher man like what you are to a good lawyer."

92.11

A famous doctor was called to the witness stand in the course of an important trial and gave impressive testimony. The opposition lawyer then cross-examined the distinguished physician.

"Doctor, I understand you have treated many famous people?"

"Yes, I have attended perhaps more than my share of them."

"Was Andrew Carnegie one of them?"

"Yes, that is correct."

"And where is Mr. Carnegie now?"

"He died."

"And you treated President Harding, I believe?"

"Yes."

"And where is he?"

"Dead, of course!"

"And I believe that among others you attended John D. Rockefeller, Sr., J. Pierpont Morgan, Enrico Caruso, Alfred E. Smith, Cardinal Hayes, and Chief Justice Taft?"

"Yes, and every . . ."

"Now tell us, Doctor, what happened to all these men?"

"They died, of course, just as all men must eventually."

"Thank you, Doctor. That will be all," said the lawyer with a shrug as he looked at the jury.

The jury's subsequent verdict indicated it did not place the expected confidence in the famous physician's testimony.

92.12

The witness's testimony in a shooting affair was unsatisfactory. When asked "Did you see the shot fired?" he replied, "No, sir, I only heard it."

"Stand down," said the judge sharply. "Your testimony is of no value."

The witness turned around in the box to leave, and when his back was turned to the judge he laughed loud and derisively. Irate at this exhibition of contempt, the judge called the witness back to the chair and demanded to know how he dared to laugh in the court.

"Did you see me laugh, Judge?" asked the witness.

"No, but I heard you," retorted the judge.

"That evidence is not satisfactory, Your Honor," said the witness respectfully.

92.13

A lawyer, cross-examining a witness, asked:

"And you say you called on Mrs. Jones on June 1. Tell the jury just what she said."

"I object to the question," interrupted the lawyer on the other side.

There was nearly an hour's argument between the counsel, and finally the judge allowed the question.

"And as I was saying," the first lawyer began, "on June 1 you called on Mrs. Jones. Now, what did she say?"

"Nothing," replied the witness, "she wasn't home."

92.14

A rail-riding hobo was the witness in a railroad accident case.

"You saw this accident while riding the freight train?"

"Yes."

"Where were you when the accident happened?"

"Oh, about forty cars from the crossing."

"Forty car lengths at 2 A.M. Your eyesight is remarkable! How far can you see at night, anyway?"

"I can't exactly say," replied the hobo. "Just how far away is the moon?"

92.15

The prosecutor began his cross-examination of the witness. "Do you know this man?"

"How should I know him?"

"Did he borrow money from you?"

"Why should he borrow money from me?"

Annoyed, the judge asked the witness, "Why do you persist in answering every question with another question?"

"Why not?" asked the witness.

92.16

The district attorney was examining a colonel. Unable to shake his testimony he tried sarcasm, "They call you colonel. In what regiment are you a colonel?"

"Well," drawled the colonel, "it's like this. The 'Colonel' in front of my name is like the 'Honorable' in front of yours. It doesn't mean a thing."

92.17

"Do you understand what you are swearing to?" asked the judge of the not-too-bright witness.

"Yes, sir, I am swearing to tell the truth."

"And do you know what will happen if you do not tell the truth?"

"Yes, sir," replied the witness. "Our side will win the case."

92.18

During the trial of a suit for slander a witness was asked to repeat the exact conversation that occurred between the two parties. The witness replied, "I can't rightly remember, but I can tell you they wuz callin' each other names that they both is."

92.19

A wealthy cattleman appeared in court in his lawsuit with John Jones over a boundary-line fence. He saw Jones going over the case with his lawyer and four or five other men.

He stopped to look at the group and then said to Jones, "Are those your witnesses, John?"

"Yes, they are."

"Well, in that event, you win. Those were the witnesses I had the last time I was in court."

92.20

"Do you mean to imply that he is a thief?" asked the lawyer.

"Well, if I were a chicken I'd roost mighty high," was the reply.

92.21

A man charged with alienating the affections of another man's wife was on the stand. The attorney for the aggrieved husband began his cross-examination by asking: "Mr. Wolfe, what is your occupation?"

"I am in the house-wrecking business," replied Wolfe.

"That will be all," said the attorney with an amused glance at the jury.

92.22

A man was charged with feloniously kicking a fellow citizen in the stomach. The prosecutor demanded to know how the defendant could possibly claim to have delivered such a violent kick unintentionally. The accused thought for a moment and said:

"Well, he must have turned around too quick."

92.23

In opening his cross-examination of a witness who had obviously engaged in repeated acts of perjury, Attorney Ralph Lockwood said: "I just want to ask you one question: Would you believe yourself under oath?"

Definition

92.24

Perjury is a lie confirmed by oath.

—*Star Chamber Cases—Hobart Reports*

Aphorisms

92.25

Four-fifths of the perjury in the world is expended on tombstones, women, and competitors.

—*Thomas Robert Dewar*

92.26

After you've heard two eyewitness accounts of an auto accident, you begin to worry about history.

—*Changing Times, The Kiplinger Magazine*

92.27

It is not the oath that makes us believe the man, but the man the oath.

—*Aeschylus*

(*See also 71.5, 79.38, 121.4, 160.4, 165.58, 170.1–170.3, 170.5, 170.8–170.11, 170.13–170.15, 172.1, 173.5, 184.20, 184.21, 197.1, 198.9, 201.8, 201.11, 201.12, 203.3, 203.4, 212.5, 215.17, 218.17, 244.17, 271.46*)

93. Crime and Punishment

Anecdotes

93.1

A man in Chicago said he broke eight plate-glass windows because "it gave me a sense of fulfillment."

93.2

A man in Sheffield, England, was fined £50 for breaking a window. He said he did it in outraged innocence for a previous conviction and fine of £20 for breaking the same window.

93.3

A Wisconsin railroad road worker said he assaulted two bunk mates because they were plotting an attack on him by snoring in Morse code.

93.4

A man charged with assault was asked by the judge whether he was guilty or not. "How can I tell," was the reply, "till I have heard the evidence?"

93.5

The prisoner stood before the judge in court and was asked: "Are you guilty or not guilty?"

"Isn't that," asked the prisoner, "the very thing we are here to find out?"

93.6

An old fellow brought into court on a charge of stealing chickens was told by the judge that he should have a lawyer.

"But I don't want no lawyer."

"Why not?" asked the judge.

"Well, Jedge, because no matter what happens I want to enjoy those chickens myself."

93.7

The local chicken stealer had been tried and found guilty. But the judge was interested in the thief's technique—how he managed to steal the chickens right from under the window of the owner, and with a mean dog loose in the yard. The expert was not at all inclined to reveal his method to the judge. He said, "Your Honor, it wouldn't do no good to tell you how I did it. If you tried it, they'd catch you, or you'd git a backside full of shot. I think, Jedge, that you better just stick to the kind of rascality you know—the court kind."

93.8

There's the one about the thief in the chicken coop. When the farmer called out, "Who's there?" he replied, "Ain't nobody in here but us chickens." This story can be topped by some howlers from real life—such as the fellow who was accused of setting fire to a house in Alpena, Michigan, and replied, "No, not me. I was stealing a car that day in Detroit." Or, the elderly convict who was discovered trying an assortment of twenty-five keys on the door of a church rectory. "I was just trying to find a place to pray," he explained.

93.9

A man charged with horse stealing was found guilty and stood before the rural judge for sentencing. The judge said, "It is my intention to sentence you to five years in state prison, but before doing so I shall listen to anything you may care to say to the court."

"All I got to say, Jedge," said the prisoner, "is that you folks seem to be pretty generous with other people's time."

93.10

Pat was brought before the judge on a petty offense. During his examination the judge asked: "Is there any one in court who can vouch for your good character?"

"Yes, Your Honor," answered Pat; "the sheriff over there can do that."

"Why, Your Honor," exclaimed the sheriff in amazement, "I don't even know the man."

"There, you see," said Pat triumphantly, "I've lived in this country for over ten years, and the sheriff doesn't know me yet. Ain't that a character for you?"

93.11

"It seems to me," said the judge, "that you have been appearing before me for the last fifteen years."

"It's not my fault," said the lawbreaker, "if you don't get promoted."

93.12

"Have you anything to say before sentence is passed on you?" asked the judge.

"Yes, I have, Your Honor," said the still-truculent prisoner. "It's a miscarriage of justice for me to be identified as a housebreaker by a yellow-belly who kept his head under the bed-clothes all the time."

93.13

An old man was arraigned before a justice of the peace on a charge of larceny. As there was no one to defend him, the judged asked if he would like a lawyer appointed.

"No, sir, Your Honor," he replied. "I don't want no lawyer, but I certainly would like a couple of good witnesses, if you got 'em."

93.14

A young man was arrested for robbery. The case against him had been closed, and there was no testimony forthcoming from the defendant. The judge turned to him impatiently: "Where are your witnesses?"

"Witnesses? Not me. I never bring along any witnesses when I commit a robbery."

93.15

Judge: "Why did you steal $50,000?"

Defendant: (plaintively) "I was hungry."

93.16

A prisoner charged with embezzlement appeared in court without counsel.

"How does it happen you have no lawyer?" asked the judge.

"Well, I did engage an attorney," explained the prisoner, "but as soon as he found out that I had not stolen the $10,000, he would have nothing to do with my case."

93.17

A thief stood bewildered before the judge, listening but not understanding. Finally his attorney said, "You're acquitted."

"What does that mean?"

"It means you are free—you are not guilty."

"Oh! But what about the stuff I stole? Can I keep it?" the defendant asked.

93.18

"Your Honor," said the prisoner when asked for an explanation, "I do not see how I can be accused of forgery, when I can't even write my own name."

"You are not charged with signing your own name," replied the judge.

93.19

"You are a nuisance, and I'll have to commit you," said the judge.

"You have no right to commit a nuisance even if you are a judge," was the reply.

93.20

The man stood nervously before the bench, and to the judge's first question he sputtered and stammered, and all that came out was "s--s--s--sss--sss--sss."

"What in heaven's name is this man charged with?" asked the judge.

"Sounds like carbonated water," replied the assistant district attorney.

93.21

A little boy was brought before a magistrate, charged with throwing stones at motorists.

"What have you to say?" asked the judge.

"I didn't throw no stones, Sir, I was only going to," said the boy.

"Only going to!" echoed the magistrate. "Well, the intent was there, and as a deterrent I shall fine you $5."

The father took the youngster's hand and started to leave the courtroom when the judge called him back and reminded him that he had failed to pay the fine.

"Yes," said the father, "I should have, but since intent is just as good in the eyes of the law, why, you're paid."

93.22

Three men stood before the judge on a charge of disorderly conduct in the park.

"What were you doing?" the judge asked the first man.

"Just throwing peanuts into the lake," replied the defendant.

"That's seems harmless enough," said the judge. "Now, what about you?" the judge asked the second man.

"I was throwing peanuts into the lake, too," was the answer.

The judged turned to the third man before him. "And what about you? Were you also throwing peanuts into the lake?"

"No, Sir," said the third man. "I'm Peanuts."

93.23

"How did you get so terribly drunk," asked the judge.

"I got in bad company, Your Honor. I had a bottle of whiskey—and the other two fellows I was with don't touch the stuff."

93.24

A drunk, hauled into court on a charge of stealing a car, said: "I didn't steal the car. I saw it parked in front of the cemetery and just thought the owner was dead."

93.25

Some drunken drivers don't even make sense when they sober up. One of them told the court he was weaving down the highway in order to avoid all the other drunken drivers. Another, when asked by the judge if any of the passengers in his car could testify in his behalf, replied, "No, Your Honor. They were all drunker than I was."

93.26

Years ago a Texas bad man, reputed to have killed at least forty men, was shot in the head while standing at a bar in El Paso and died. There was immediately controversy about whether the desperado had been shot in the eye with the bullet exiting through the back of his head, or vice versa. However, the question was put into proper perspective when the local minister, who also served as coroner, took the stand and testified: "If he was shot in the eye, I'd say it was excellent marksmanship. If he was shot in the back of the head, then I'd say it was excellent judgment."

93.27

A man on trial for killing his wife with an arrow was asked why he had resorted to so primitive a method. "I didn't want to awaken the children," he explained.

93.28

The man had just been sentenced to life imprisonment and before being taken away said to the judge: "Your Honor, this is going to be a mighty hard sentence for me to do."

"Well," said the judge, "just do the best you can."

93.29

A lawsuit involving a large sum of money had been heard before a judge. In the corridor outside the courtroom the defendant, who was faced with financial ruin if the decision went against him, listened to his attorney.

"Well, it's up to the judge now, and frankly, I wouldn't attempt to read his mind."

"How about me sending the judge a box of cigars with my card," suggested the defendant eagerly.

"Good Lord, no!" snapped the attorney. "This judge is a stickler for ethical behavior. A stunt like that would prejudice him against you, and he would probably hold you in contempt of court. Don't even smile at that judge."

Several days later the judge rendered a decision in favor of the defendant.

As the defendant left the courthouse with his attorney he said, "Thanks for the tip about the cigars. It worked."

"I should say it did. We would surely have lost the case if you had sent them."

"But I did send them."

"You did?"

"Yes. That's why we won the case."

"I don't understand," said the puzzled attorney.

"It's easy. I sent the cigars to the judge but enclosed my opponent's card."

93.30

A judge in a rural area was presiding over a dispute concerning a large area of valuable grazing land that had an even more valuable mineral potential. Neither side was confident of either the legality or justice of its position. The attorneys involved in the case would not predict which side the judge would favor.

On the second day of the trial the judge began the proceedings by making the following statement: "Gentlemen, I believe it will be agreed that I have always been on the level in my decisions. And I intend to remain unswayed by anything except the evidence and the law. Now, last evening two envelopes were handed me. One contained $4,000 from one party in this case. The other contained $5,000 from the other party. But in order to remove any suspicion of influence, I am returning $1,000 to the party who gave me $5,000. That makes everything even. We will go on with the case."

93.31

"I am going to give you the maximum penalty," said the judge to the trembling and abject defendant who stood before him. "If you think you are going to be sent away to the security of a nice, safe, comfortable jail, then you are mistaken. Instead I am sentencing you back into the mainstream of life, where you will have to worry about making a living, the stock market, the uncertainties and chicanery of politics, the hazards of the highways, and the risk to life and limb involved in walking the streets of our cities."

93.32

The new warden was proud of the scientific principles of penology he had put into practice and of his program of rehabilitating the prisoners under his charge.

"Well, Hughie," he said when one of his first experiments was about to be released, "it has been a long time since I last heard you speak of crime. I hope you are determined to begin a new kind of life. After all, time is running out on you—this has been your fourth time here. What plans do you have?"

"Warden, I've got it all worked out," said Hughie. "My sister has a big place in the country—cows, chickens, and all. I'm going down there."

"Good for you," said the warden enthusiastically. "It encourages me to hear that you are reforming."

"Who said anything about reforming?" demanded Hughie. "To hell with reform—I'm just retiring."

93.33

When Frederick the Great visited a Potsdam prison, prisoner after prisoner told him he was innocent, the victim of schemers or police mistakes. But one man hung his head and said, "Your Majesty, I am guilty and deserve the punishment I am getting."

"Free this rascal," bellowed Frederick, "and get him out of our prison before he corrupts all the noble and innocent people here."

93.34

A distraught wife, visiting her husband in a prison waiting room, turned on him and said: "I'm fed up with you. Look at your record: attempted robbery, attempted robbery, attempted burglary, attempted murder. What a failure you've turned out to be; you can't succeed in anything you try."

93.35

A man under sentence of death wrote the Governor:

"Dear Governor: They are fixing to hang me on Friday, and here it is Tuesday."

93.36

A man about to be hanged, asked if he had anything to say, said: "Yes, sir, I want to say that this is going to be a lesson to me."

Definitions

93.37

A murderer is one who is presumed innocent until he is proved insane.

93.38

Criminal: A person with predatory instincts who has not sufficient capital to form a corporation.

—*Howard Scott*

93.39

A criminal is a person without sufficient means to employ expensive lawyers.

—*Henry Waldorf Francis*

93.40

Arson is a fire caused by the friction between the fire-insurance policy and the mortgage.

Aphorisms

93.41

No doubt Jack the Ripper excused himself on the grounds that it was human nature.

—*Alan Alexander Milne*

93.42

A man of courage never needs weapons, but he may need bail.

—*Ethel Watts Mumford*

93.43

A man who has never gone to school may steal from a freight car; but if he has a university education, he may steal the whole railroad.

—*Theodore Roosevelt*

93.44

Crimes are not to be measured by the issue of events, but from the bad intentions of men.

—*Cicero*

93.45

The reason there are so many imbeciles among imprisoned criminals is that an imbecile is so foolish even a detective can detect him.

—*Austin O'Malley*

93.46

Successful and fortunate crime is called virtue.

—*Seneca*

93.47

Nothing is more annoying than to be obscurely hanged.

—*Voltaire*

(*See also 12.5, 30.49, 35.7, 36.7, 48.5, 54.8, 54.9, 65.4, 79.50, 89.1, 89.2, 89.5, 89.12, 90.3, 94.2, 94.3, 94.5, 94.13–94.15, 99.1–99.16, 100.1–100.17, 155.45, 158.7, 158.8, 213.15, 227.8, 258.1, 266.19, 271.4*)

THE LEGAL PROFESSION

94. Attorney and Client

Anecdotes

94.1

A young lawyer in a small town made a specialty of personal-injury cases. He won two or three cases, got a good fee each time, and decided to go after a larger clientele. So he moved to the "blue grass" and opened up a pretentious office in the city of Lexington. After he had been there a month a friend met him on the street and asked how he was getting along.

"Well," he said, "it's not as good down here as I had expected to find it. I'm going to try it a little while longer, but if business doesn't pick up pretty soon, I'll be damned if I don't pack up and take my witnesses and move to Chicago."

94.2

Hansen was arrested and went to a lawyer.

"If I win this case, I will give you 1,000 kroner," said Hansen.

"Very well," said the lawyer. "Get some witnesses."

Hansen got his witnesses and the case was won. The lawyer said, "Well, I won your case. What about my 1,000 kroner?"

"That's right," said Hansen. "Get some witnesses."

94.3

"Although the evidence is against me," said the man charged with a crime, "I've got $50,000 in cash to fight the case with."

"You'll never go to prison with that kind of money," the lawyer assured him.

And he didn't. Before he entered prison the lawyer had the $50,000.

94.4

"How can I ever show my appreciation," gushed a woman to Clarence Darrow after he had settled her case to her satisfaction.

"Madam," said Darrow, "ever since the Phoenicians invented money there has been only one answer to that question."

94.5

A confidence man hired a lawyer to defend him on a criminal charge. The wily attorney asked him, "What about my fee?"

"My friend," replied the even wilier client, "If I get something, you get nothing; if I get nothing, you get something."

94.6

A lawyer had just won a damage suit for his injured client and presented his bill for one-half of the award. The client thumped and jumped and hollered. Finally, the lawyer said, "I furnish the skills, the eloquence, and the legal learning to win your case. After all, anybody can fall down a coal hole."

94.7

A lawyer had successfully handled a difficult law case for a wealthy friend. Following the happy outcome of the case, the friend and client called on the lawyer, expressed his appreciation of his work, and handed him a handsome morocco leather wallet.

The lawyer looked at the wallet in astonishment and handed it back with a sharp reminder that it could not possibly compensate him for his services. "My fee for that work," acidly snapped the attorney, "is $500."

The client opened the wallet, removed from it a $1000 bill, replaced it with a $500 bill, and handed it back to the lawyer with a smile.

94.8

"On what grounds," asked the judge, "do you ask for a new trial for your client?"

"On the grounds of newly discovered evidence, Your Honor," replied the lawyer.

"And what is the nature of this new evidence?"

"Your Honor, I have just learned that my client has dug up some $500 I was not heretofore aware that he had."

94.9

A young woman who lived in New York's plush Westchester County met a golf professional at a cocktail party and spent most of the time questioning him about her game and getting good advice in return. Several days later she got a bill for $200 from him. Thinking he was kidding her, she phoned him but was told that it was his customary fee, and he expected payment.

Determined to beat the charge, she asked a lawyer friend about it. He told her that in the circumstances the fee was preposterous, and if she heard further from the golf pro to let the attorney know about it.

The next day she received a bill for $200

from the lawyer friend. In despair, she paid both bills.

94.10

An agitated man called on his attorney and told him that he had loaned $500 to an acquaintance but had failed to get in return any written acknowledgment of the debt. "And," added the client, "when I asked him for his note or I.O.U., he became very angry. Now I am afraid he plans to ignore the debt. If only I had something in writing, I could sue him if he refuses to repay the loan."

"Leave it to me," replied the lawyer. "I think I can get something in writing from him."

When the client again called on his lawyer he asked, "How did you make out?"

"Just fine. I've got a letter from him. It was easy. I wrote asking that he drop me a line stating he had borrowed $1,000 from you."

"But that's wrong. It wasn't $1,000, only $500."

"I know," said the lawyer. "That's what he said in this letter. Here, read it."

94.11

A party to a suit was obliged to return home before the jury had brought in its verdict. When the case was decided in his favor, his lawyer wired him: RIGHT AND JUSTICE WON.

To which the client replied: APPEAL AT ONCE.

94.12

Patrick Murphy, beefy and florid, was brought into a Kansas court during Prohibition days, charged with selling whiskey.

When it came time to address the jury, Patrick's lawyer made his remarks brief, direct, and pointed.

He said, "Gentlemen, do you honestly think that if this defendant—look at him carefully—do you think that if he had a quart of whiskey he would sell it?"

Verdict a few minutes later: "Not guilty."

94.13

A young lawyer conducting a not-too-successful defense of an habitual criminal was allowed one hour for his final plea to the jurors. During a recess he conferred with a veteran attorney and mentioned he planned to use only fifteen minutes of his allotted hour.

"Take the full hour," said the older attorney.

"Why?"

"Because you owe it to your client; the longer you talk the longer you keep him out of jail."

94.14

In an address to students at the Harvard Law School, Chauncey Depew gave them this bit of witty counsel: "Everything you learn will go for naught if you forget this fundamental rule: When it becomes apparent in a case that somebody on your side is headed for jail, be sure it is your client!"

94.15

When a group of Wall Street financiers wired attorney John F. Johnson for advice about the possibility of their joining in a merger, the lawyer wired back: MERGER POSSIBLE, JAIL CERTAIN.

94.16

Senator Watson of Indiana was once trying a case when his client became alarmed because the other side had two lawyers. "We gotta have another lawyer," protested Watson's client.

"Why?" asked Watson. "Aren't you satisfied with my handling of this?"

"You're doing OK for one man," said the client. "But they got two lawyers, so when one is talking the other is thinking. But when you're talking, who's doing the thinking?"

94.17

An Indiana woman asked the Better Business Bureau for the name of the best shyster lawyer in town. Asked why, she said, "Because my case is so bad that only a shyster could get me off."

94.18

After conferring a long time with the estranged husband, the lawyer went to the wife, his client, and said: "Mrs. Ryan, I have finally arrived at an agreement with your husband that is entirely equitable and fair to both of you."

"Fair to both of us?" stormed the wife. "Who asked you to be fair? I could have made that kind of a deal without you. What do you think I hired a lawyer for?"

Aphorism

94.19

If a man dies and leaves his estate in an uncertain condition, the lawyers become his heirs.

—*E. W. Howe*

(*See also 93.16, 93.29, 93.39, 98.1, 215.17*)

95. High and Low Court

Anecdotes

95.1

Two judges were arrested for speeding. When they arrived in court no other judge was present, so each agreed to try the other. The first judge went up to the bench and said, "You are charged with exceeding the speed limit. How do you plead?"

"Guilty."

"You are hereby fined $5."

"Hm," said the other judge, "these cases are becoming far too numerous. This is the second case we have had of this kind this morning. I hereby fine you $10 or ten days in jail."

95.2

A couple who wanted to marry appeared before a cranky judge and showed him their license. The judge looked at it and said, "Take it back to the clerk. It has no date."

They returned with the corrected license, but now the judge noted that the bride's middle name had been omitted, and he sent them back again—and still again because the court seal had not been placed on the license. Finally the judge performed the ceremony.

When he finished he noticed a small boy standing nearby.

"Whose boy is that?" he asked.

"Ours," said the groom.

"Do you mean that you had him before—"

"Yes, Your Honor."

The judge said, "I suppose you realize that this child is a technical bastard?"

"That's funny," said the groom, "that's what the clerk just said about you."

95.3

During the first days of the U.S. Supreme Court the several justices lived in the same house in Washington, accommodations being too limited and unsatisfactory for their wives to be with them. The justices lived together pretty much as a family and discussed their cases most of the time. Saturday was their "consultation" day.

When there arose talk about the justices drinking too much, Chief Justice John Marshall decided that they would not drink on "consultation" day—"that is, except when it rains," added Marshall.

The next consultation day the justices assembled. Marshall asked one of them to step to the window and see if there was any sign of rain. The man came back and sadly reported there was no sign of rain. Chief Justice Marshall then said, "Justice Story, I think that is the shallowest and most illogical opinion I have ever heard you deliver; you forget that our jurisdiction is as broad as this Republic, and by the laws of nature, it must be raining someplace in our jurisdiction. Waiter, bring on the rum."

95.4

During the latter part of his life, Chief Justice John Marshall was up on a ladder in his law library searching for a volume on the top shelf, when he and a whole mess of books toppled to the floor. When his servant rushed into the room he found the great jurist sitting on the floor under the avalanche of books. He looked up, laughed and said, "Well, I've been laying down the law for a good many years, but this is the first time I have ever been laid down by the law."

95.5

When Charles Evans Hughes was Chief Justice of the U.S. Supreme Court, he took several of his colleagues from the Court on a cruise on Chesapeake Bay. But the Bay was rough—particularly so on Justice Benjamin Cardozo, who got an attack of seasickness. "Is there anything I can do for you?" Hughes asked solicitously.

"Yes," gasped Cardozo, "you can overrule this motion, Your Honor."

95.6

For some time court circles in Chicago were puzzled how a certain judge could mount his bench cold sober every morning and leave it half tipsy every noon. Mary Faith Wilson, of the Chicago City News Bureau did more than speculate or guess; she simply took a drink one noontime from the judge's carafe and found it to be straight gin.

Definitions

95.7

A judge is a vehicle of Justice who pokes holes through her with Law.

—*Henry Waldorf Francis*

95.8

Judge: A lawyer who knew a governor.

—*Judge Mahoney*

95.9

Court: A place where they dispense with justice.

—*Arthur Train*

95.10

A court is a place where what was confused before becomes more unsettled than ever.

—*Henry Waldorf Francis*

95.11

Dictum is what a court thinks but is afraid to decide.

—*Henry Waldorf Francis*

95.12

Appeal: An appeal, Hennessy, is when ye ask wan court to show its contempt for another court.

—*Finley Peter Dunne*

Aphorisms

95.13

The penalty for laughing in a courtroom is six months in jail; if it were not for this penalty, the jury would never hear the evidence.

—*H. L. Mencken*

95.14

On the upright judge, who condemned the printer of "The Drapier Letters":

In church your grandsire cut his throat;
To do the job too long he tarried:
He should have had my hearty vote
To cut his throat before he married.

—*Jonathan Swift*

95.15

No matter whether the Constitution follows the flag or not, the Supreme Court follows the election returns.

—*Finley Peter Dunne*

96. Lawyers-at-large

Anecdotes

96.1

A preacher was once asked if he always corrected his mistakes. He said he sometimes does, and sometimes does not. For instance, once when he was preaching he intended to say that Og was the king of Bashan, but by a slip of the tongue he said that "hog was the king of bacon," but he did not correct it because it was true. In another case, when he intended to say that the devil was the father of liars, he happened to say that "the devil was the father of all lawyers," but he let that stand also, because it was correct in a sense.

—*Congressman Jasper Talbert,* South Carolina, 1897

96.2

To be sold on the 5th of July, one hundred and thirty-three suits at law, the property of an eminent attorney about to retire from business. NOTE: The clients are rich and obstinate.

—*Advertisement in a New Jersey newspaper, 1821*

96.3

The household furniture of an English barrister, then recently deceased, was being sold, in a country town, when one neighbor remarked to another that the stock of goods and chattels appeared to be extremely scanty, considering the rank of the lawyer, their late owner.

"It is so," was the reply; "but the fact is, he had very few *causes,* and, therefore, could not have many *effects.*"

96.4

When a wealthy barrister argued that nobody should be admitted to the bar unless he owned land, John Philpot Curran said: "May I ask, sir, how many acres make a wiseacre?"

96.5

A famous trial lawyer had been asked to give a talk to the law class. He made it short, telling them that "when you are in court with the facts on your side, then hammer them at the jury. When you have the law on your side, then hammer that into the judge. And if you have neither facts nor law on your side, then simply hammer the table."

96.6

A visitor from out of town stopped in to see the police court in action. The stranger looked around for a moment and then said to a man sitting next to him, "My goodness, they've caught a tough-looking lot this morning."

"You're looking at the wrong bunch," said the other man. "They're the lawyers."

96.7

An eminent Scottish divine met two of his own parishioners at the house of a lawyer, whom he considered too sharp a practitioner. The lawyer ungraciously put the question,

"Doctor, these are members of your flock; may I ask, do you look upon them as white sheep or as black sheep?"

"I don't know," answered the divine drily, "whether they are black or white sheep; but I know, if they are long here, they are pretty sure to be fleeced."

96.8

Actual names of lawyers and law firms:

Ketchum and Cheathum was a well-known New York law firm in 1880. The firm's name was later changed to I. Ketchum and U. Cheatham—Israel Ketchum and Uriah Cheatham.

Abel Crook was once a prominent Manhattan lawyer.

Dilly, Daly, Doolittle, and Stahl was an Akron, Ohio, law firm of not too long ago.

Argue and Phibbs were law partners in Dublin, Ireland.

Wind and Wind, a law partnership, appropriately enough were located in Chicago, Illinois.

Stahl, Stahl, and Stahl were once located in Port Clinton, Ohio.

Definitions

96.9

A lawyer is a legal gentleman who rescues your estate from your enemies, and keeps it himself.

—*Lord Brougham*

96.10

A lawyer is a man who lives by litigation, declaration, replication, consultation, cross-examination, botheration, damnation (of others), and who, on the day of trial, proposes arbitration, keeps his fee, and returns his brief.

—*Attributed to Sir Andrew Allrealize in an old English comedy*

96.11

A counsel is an accomplice of a lawyer.

—*Henry Waldorf Francis*

Aphorisms

96.12

A lawyer's dream of heaven: Every man reclaimed his own property at the resurrection, and each tried to recover from all his forefathers.

—*Samuel Butler,* Notebooks

96.13

Beneath these stones a Lawyer lies,
Fame us assureth he was just and wise,
An able Advocate, and honest too,
How strange ye God? And can this tale be true?

—*Alexander Laing*

96.14

THE HANDWRITING ON THE CITY HALL

(In New York City, when the dome of the City Hall was graced by a figure of Justice)

The lawyers all, both great and small
Come here to cheat the people;
For be it known that Justice's flown,
And perches on the Steeple.

—*Anonymous*

96.15

Lawyers are the only persons in whom ignorance of the law is not punished.

—*Jeremy Bentham*

96.16

Ignorance of the law excuses no man—from practicing it.

—*Addison Mizner*

96.17

Ignorance of the law excuses no man who retains poor counsel.

96.18

If the laws could speak for themselves, they would complain of the lawyers in the first place.

—*George Saville, Marquis of Halifax*

96.19

If there were no bad people, there would be no good lawyers.

—*Charles Dickens*

96.20

The lawyers' favorite toast: To those who write their own contracts and wills.

96.21

When an irresistible force meets an immovable object, there's usually a lawyer who will take the case.

96.22

Lawyers earn their living by the sweat of their browbeating.

—*J. G. Huneker*

(*See also 24.5, 55.9, 79.4, 79.5, 79.9, 83.12, 89.5, 89.7, 90.1–90.25, 91.1–91.11, 92.1–92.27, 93.6, 93.13, 93.16, 93.39, 94.1–94.19, 95.1–95.5, 95.7–95.12, 98.1, 98.2, 106.4, 201.10, 211.21, 211.28, 211.34, 243.8, 246.3, 263.2, 265.4, 267.11, 269.31, 269.111, 271.45*)

97. Laws and Lawsuits in General

Anecdotes

97.1

Demosthenes told of an Athenian who hired an ass to take him to Megara and at midday dismounted and reclined in the shadow of the beast. The ass's owner came along and protested that he rented the ass, not its shadow. The men went to law over the question. Thus became current the saying, "If you quarrel, let it be for something more than an ass's shadow."

97.2

A man of the state of Cheng was one day gathering wood when he encountered and killed a deer, which he then concealed in a ditch and covered with leaves. In his joy he forgot where he hid the animal and on his way home he began to think he must have been dreaming.

Meanwhile a man who overheard his words got the deer. When this man reached home he said to his wife: "A woodman dreamt he had got a deer, but did not know where it was. Now I have got the deer, so his dream was reality."

"It is you," replied the wife, "who have been dreaming. You saw the woodman. Did he get the deer? And is there really such a person? It is you who have the deer; and then can his dream be a reality?"

"It is true I have the deer," said the husband. "It is therefore of little importance whether the woodman dreamt the deer or if I dreamt the woodman."

When the woodman reached home he became annoyed at the loss of the deer. That night he dreamt where the deer was and who had it. In the morning he went to the place indicated by his dream and found the deer and took legal steps to recover it.

The magistrate delivered the following judgment: "The plaintiff began with a real deer and an alleged dream. He now comes forward with a real dream and an alleged deer. The defendant really got the deer which the plaintiff said he dreamt, and is now trying to keep it; while, according to his wife, both the woodman and the deer were but figments of a dream, so that no one got the deer at all."

"However, here is a deer, which you had better divide between you." When the Prince of Cheng heard this story he cried out, "The magistrate himself must have dreamt the case."

—Translated from the Chinese by *Lionel Giles*

97.3

The sad story is told of an Englishman whose wife sued for a divorce on the grounds he was sterile, while at the same time their maid sued him for being the father of her child. All of which is bad enough. But, in addition, he lost both cases!

Definitions

97.4

Lawsuit: A method of collecting half the debt by compelling twice the payment.

97.5

Contract: An agreement to do something if nothing happens to prevent it.

Aphorisms

97.6

I was never ruined but twice: once when I lost a lawsuit, and once when I won one.

—*Voltaire*

97.7

When I hear a man talk of an unalterable law the only effect it produces upon me is to convince me he is an unalterable fool.

—*Sydney Smith*

97.8

Men fight for freedom, then begin to accumulate laws to take it away from themselves.

97.9

Laws are generally found to be nets of such a texture, as the little creep through, the great break through, and the middle-sized alone are entangled in.

—*Shenstone*

97.10

If you laid all our laws end to end, there would be no end.

—*Arthur "Bugs" Baer*

(*See also* 89.7)

98. Wills and Wails

Anecdotes

98.1

The wealthy old lady, aware of her approaching death, sent for her lawyer to make her will. She was very weak and distraught, and the lawyer was gentle and sympathetic.

He said to her, "Now, don't you worry about this. Just leave it all to me."

"Oh, well," sighed the old lady, "I suppose I might as well. You'll get it anyway."

98.2

The story is told of the lawyer who stayed up all night trying to break a widow's will.

98.3

"What are you looking so despondent about?" a man asked a friend.

"You know, two weeks ago my uncle Jake died and left me $40,000, and then last week a cousin died and left me $19,000. And here it is Friday, and so far nothing."

98.4

When the lawyer was asked where he got the beautiful diamond in the stickpin he wore, he said it was what might be called a testamentary stone.

"Testamentary stone? What's that?"

"Well, it's like this. A friend of mine left a provision in his will that his executor should take $3,000 of the estate and buy a stone to his memory. The will appointed me as the executor, and so this is the testamentary stone called for by provision of the will, in memory of the deceased."

98.5

Mike Connolly, the Hollywood reporter, tells about the young man who paid careful attention to his rich old aunt and was especially affectionate to the several dogs she liked so inordinately. When the old lady died, her will provided that the dogs should be left to the nephew.

98.6

Daniel O'Connell, the famous Irish patriot, was one day contesting a will in behalf of a client. O'Connell claimed that the will had a forged signature, written after the death of the benefactor. The opposing counsel insisted that the will was signed while the deceased "still had life in him."

"You mean that he had a fly in his mouth?" asked O'Connell.

98.7

I give all my deer to the Earl of Salisbury, who I know will preserve them, because he denied the King a buck out of one of his parks. I give nothing to Lord Say; which legacy I give him, because I know he will bestow it on the poor.

To Tom I give five shillings: I intended him more, but whoever has seen his history of the Parliament, thinks five shillings too much. I give Lieutenant General Cromwell one word of mine, because hitherto he never kept his own.

—*From the will of the Earl of Pembroke*

98.8

I give to John Abbot, and Mary, his wife, the sum of sixpence each, to buy for each of them a halter, for fear the sheriff's should not be provided.

—*From the will of Stephen Swain,* Parish of St. Olave, England

Aphorism

98.9

Where there's a will there's a way.
Where there's a will there's a fight.
Where there's a will there's a family.
Where there's a will there's a wail.

(*See also 19.17, 94.19, 154.38, 165.99, 167.9, 169.1, 264.9, 264.15, 265.8*)

COPS AND ROBBERS

99. On the Beat

Anecdotes

99.1

The police surgeon was called in to examine a motorist suspected of drunken driving. When his examination was concluded the doctor said, "This man isn't drunk. He's been drugged."

"I might as well admit," said the arresting officer, "that I drug him three blocks."

99.2

A zigzagging motorist told a cop in California, "It's all right, officer. I'm just shaving with my electric razor while driving."

99.3

A burglar told Washington, D.C., police that he held up liquor stores during the daytime because "I'm afraid to be out on the street at night with so much money."

99.4

A Buffalo man was caught stealing a car because instead of pressing the starter he pressed the siren.

99.5

An Evanston, Illinois, man arrested for stealing the same radio three times said, "I just love that radio."

99.6

During a race riot in Detroit some years ago, the police stopped a car which was speeding through the battle area. A white pillowcase was dangling from the center of the car, for all to see.

"What's that for?" asked the cop. The driver grinned and explained: "It's a white pillowcase. That's to show I'm neutral, boss."

The policeman quickly frisked the driver and discovered a .45 in his pocket.

"Neutral, eh?" said the cop. "Then what's this gun for?"

"I'm neutral, boss," vowed the driver. "But that gun's in case somebody don't believe me."

99.7

The police of a Midwestern town raided a gambling house and held four men on a charge of playing poker. But they were unable to make the charge stick.

The first man said, "I walked in right after the cops. I'm a stranger here myself."

The second man stated that he had just dropped in to sit and chat with some of the fellows.

The third man said he was waiting for a bus and went in to keep out of the cold until the bus arrived.

Then the police turned to the fourth man with: "Well, we've got you anyway. You had the cards in your hand and all the chips in front of you on the table."

"Me?" blandly asked the fourth man. "Why you can't pinch me for playing poker because I wasn't playing. I had no one to play with, and you can't play with yourself."

99.8

One day a policeman appeared at the establishment of Mike McDonald's, Chicago's longtime gambling czar, and asked for $5 toward a fund for the burial of a policeman. "Good!" said Mike. "Here's $25. Bury five of 'em."

99.9

A Chicago police officer was testifying in a case against a saloon keeper who had encouraged prostitution. The officer said that during his investigation he found that a prostitute made the bar her base of operations, had a room over the bar, and took her customers up the backstairs to her room.

"How often did this happen?" the officer was asked.

"I'd say she took men up to her room about fifteen times a day."

"Good Lord," exclaimed the judge, "what cruel self-inflicted punishment."

"That's right, Your Honor," agreed the policeman. "I figure all that stair climbing must be a terrible strain on the girl's heart."

99.10

Patrick Murphy was an honest, brave, and efficient St. Louis policeman. This powerful son of Erin could and would do everything expected of a sterling officer of the law—except spell. He could read and write, but he could not spell. That was his great difficulty.

One day Officer Murphy was on patrol when he came upon a dead horse at the corner of Pestalozzi Street and Kosciusko Avenue. Officer Murphy knew the rules of the department required that he make an immediate report of this to the Health Department so that the carcass could be hauled away promptly. He began to write out his report but stopped in perplexity when he came to the names of the streets where the dead horse could be found.

With a sigh massive Patrick Murphy reached down, grasped the dead horse's tail, and dragged the animal two blocks to the corner of Broadway and Locust Street, and then completed his report to the Health Department.

99.11

Norton Mockridge, New York World-Telegram columnist, told about a taxi delivering a man with a knife stuck in his back to the emergency entrance of a New York hospital. A cop helped the man into the hospital then returned to the door. Another taxi thereupon roared up, and a man leaped out in some agitation.

"What's bothering you?" asked the cop.

The man gestured angrily and said to the cop, "I came to get my knife."

99.12

Before the new breed of police came on the scene, a New York cop swore to the following affidavit: "I hereby solemnly swear that the prisoner set upon me, calling me an ass, a precious dolt, a scarecrow, a ragamuffin, and an idiot, all of which I certify to be true."

99.13

The man was just about to jump off the Brooklyn Bridge one night when a cop pulled him down from the railing and began to talk to him. "Please have a little consideration," urged the cop. "If you jump, I'll have to go in after you. Now it's a cold night, and I could freeze to death before an ambulance arrived. Besides I don't swim so good and might drown. And I've got a wife and five kids. Be a good fellow and go home and hang yourself."

99.14

"I'm just looking for flora and fauna," explained the biologist to the inquiring cop in the park.

"Get along with you, or I'll run you and your girl friends in for loitering," replied the cop.

99.15

Two cops were quarreling about the division of some graft. "You never heard of my honesty being questioned, did ya?" yelled one of the men.

"I never even heard it mentioned," said the second and sharper man.

99.16

It was a quiet night in the station house, and the desk sergeant was getting worried. "Sort of gives me the creeps," he said to several other men on the force. "Why a whole week has passed and we've not had any murders, muggings, rapes, or holdups—just a few traffic violations and some drunks."

"Don't let it get you down," said a veteran on the force. "A whole mess of trouble is bound to pop up any minute—murders, rapes, muggings, and all the rest. I have complete faith in human nature."

Aphorism

99.17

One has to admit that the local police department has the most magnificent collection of clues in existence.

(*See also 93.45, 155.9, 158.7, 165.19, 184.23, 201.10, 202.7, 203.3, 203.4, 215.8, 218.7, 229.12, 229.16, 230.13, 231.2, 235.13, 239.15, 251.3, 268.12*)

100. Assorted Lawbreakers

Anecdotes

100.1

One day a fellow started through the gate of a large factory wheeling a wheelbarrow full of sawdust and was stopped by the guard. He told the guard he had permission to take the sawdust. The guard checked and found out that this was correct, and so he let the fellow go on his way that day—and for many days thereafter.

Finally, a fellow worker asked the sawdust collector what he was up to. "Are you stealing all this sawdust, or what?"

"No," was the reply, "not sawdust—I'm stealing wheelbarrows."

100.2

Years ago in Arabia a man riding an ass passed beneath a fig tree, the fruit-laden branches of which hung invitingly over the road. As he passed the rider reached up with both hands to grasp some fruit, while the animal kept on going, leaving the rider suspended in air. At that moment a farmer came up and demanded to know what the man was doing. "I fell off my ass," said the thief.

100.3

The young tough walked up to the teller's window in a bank and handed across a note which read: "This is a holdup. Fill this bag with tens and twenties if you don't want to get shot."

The teller instead wrote out a note and handed it to the robber. It read: "Comb your hair and straighten your tie, stupid. They're taking your picture."

100.4

It is rather pleasant to be alone in a bank at night.

—*Willie Sutton,* famous bank robber, 1953

100.5

An elderly woman was held up on the street by a massive thug with a gun. She handed over the $7.92 in her purse and said to the crook, "You should be ashamed of yourself holding up a poor old lady like me. A man of your size ought to be holding up a bank."

100.6

An attendant at a funeral home in Fort

Wayne noticed a mourner tearfully squeeze the hand of the deceased and later found a $150 ring missing from the corpse's finger.

100.7

The Canadian National Exhibit at Toronto has a CRIME DOES NOT PAY exhibit, from which two wax hands from two dummies were stolen.

100.8

Los Angeles burglars broke into a home and stole only the burglar alarm.

100.9

Sometimes the laugh is on the thief, as when one broke into a New York songwriter's apartment and walked away with two hundred phonograph records, all of which were various styles of hog calls. But when an Illinois hardware dealer stenciled on his safe a sign reading POSITIVELY NOT LOCKED. NO MONEY IN SAFE. TURN HANDLE AND OPEN, burglars followed instructions and removed $700 from the safe.

100.10

Some thieves bring a conscious sense of humor to their work. A Costa Rican chicken thief left this note around a rooster's neck: "I was made a widower at 2 A.M." New Jersey burglars stole $500 from a safe and before leaving took a motto from the wall and hung it on the safe. It read SMILE.

100.11

There is a counterfeiter who does exquisite work, but he still has the first dollar he ever made. Some attribute it to his thrift, others to his cowardice.

100.12

J. Edgar Hoover (and Al Smith long before him) tells the story of a prisoner who spent months mastering a signature, only to have the first forged check he submitted come back marked "Insufficient Funds."

100.13

A counterfeiter was going out of business. Just for kicks he made a $15 bill and gave it to a clerk in a cigar store when he bought a few cigars. The clerk looked over the bill carefully and gave him two $7 bills in change.

100.14

A counterfeiter—famous as a craftsman—made what he thought was a perfect $10 bill. When he finished he put it under a microscope and minutely compared it with the one he had copied from and found not a single deviation or imperfection. But as soon as he tried to test pass it before running off a batch he was picked up. He challenged the Secret Service man to find a single flaw in it; to find any difference between the two ten spots.

"No difference," said the Secret Service man. "But the one you used to copy from is a counterfeit."

100.15

Two prisoners were talking of their future, what they would do after they had served their time. One of them said, "I am spending all the time I can to improve myself. And when you're still an ordinary thief, I'll be a prominent embezzler."

100.16

Excuses offered by lawbreakers include:

A California motorist said he was speeding because a tail wind pushed him along.

A woman arrested for shoplifting said she had tried the hat on, but it was so tiny she had forgotten she was wearing it.

A North Carolina man arrested for stealing said he took the money because he needed it to repay $10 he had stolen.

A Midwestern motorist said he was driving without a license because it was impossible for him to get one since he was receiving a pension for blindness from the state.

Aphorisms

100.17

Thieves respect property; they merely wish the property to become their property that they may more perfectly respect it.

—*G. K. Chesterton*

100.18

A counterfeiter is a man who gets into trouble by following a good example.

100.19

He is so crooked he'd steal two left shoes.

—*Wilson Mizner*

100.20

He'd steal a hot stove and come back for the smoke.

—*Wilson Mizner*

100.21

"You sparkle with larceny," said Wilson Mizner to a man.

100.22

Be careful, and you will save many men from the sin of robbing you.

—*E. W. Howe*

100.23

Much as he is opposed to lawbreaking, he is not bigoted about it.

—*Damon Runyon*

100.24

When Willie Sutton, the notorious bandit, was asked why he robbed banks, he replied, "Because that's where the money is."

(*See also 5.5, 7.19, 7.21, 8.5, 11.3, 11.11, 12.2, 12.5, 13.11, 17.5, 19.57, 25.11, 27.15, 28.21, 30.28, 32.2, 35.4, 35.6–35.8, 35.14, 35.27, 36.27, 42.8, 46.9, 48.5, 49.1, 54.8, 54.9, 54.13, 58.5, 65.4, 92.20, 92.22, 93.1–93.48, 99.1–99.16, 126.4, 128.14, 145.4, 158.7, 158.8, 160.4, 165.48, 165.57, 213.15, 219.1, 226.2, 234.28, 239.3, 242.1, 243.5, 243.18, 244.17, 246.4, 251.3, 268.17, 277.1*)

Part Three

MEDICINE, SCIENCE, AND THE CAMPUS

THE PRACTICE OF MEDICINE

101. Diagnosis

Anecdotes

101.1

A man bothered with continual ringing in his ears and a pronounced bulging of his eyes went to the doctor. The physician was puzzled but suggested that maybe the removal of his tonsils would help.

The tonsils were removed, but the condition persisted. Another doctor thought that extraction of all the man's teeth would clear up the trouble, so they were duly removed, but still no alleviation of the condition; his ears continued to ring, and his eyes kept bulging. A consultation of doctors decided that the man had some obscure and unknown condition, and they told him plainly they could do nothing for him, and that they feared he was not destined long for this world.

The poor man decided to write off all the doctors and to at least live it up during the few months apparently left to him. So he took what money he had from the bank, checked into a plush hotel, and proceeded to live as he had always wanted to. He ordered several expensive made-to-order suits and decided to have custom-made shirts to match the stylish new suits. When the haberdasher was measuring him for the shirts he put down collar size 15½. The customer noticed this and told him he was in error—that he always wore 14½-inch collars. The shirtmaker again measured the man's neck and said, "No, it is 15½." The customer still insisted that 14½ was the correct size and demanded that the new shirts be that size.

"All right," said the shirtmaker resignedly. "You're going to wear them. But I'll tell you right now, don't come back here complaining to me because your ears are ringing and your eyes are popping."

101.2

A young executive went to an orthopedic surgeon and complained of a sore back. Examinations, tests, and x-rays failed to reveal any trouble.

"When did this begin?" asked the doctor.

"Oh, about two weeks ago, shortly after we moved to our new offices," replied the patient.

The doctor told the patient he could do nothing for him and suggested he come back in a week or so if the trouble persisted. But several days later the patient phoned that he had discovered the difficulty. It seems that the new offices he had moved to were equipped with ultra-modern furniture, and the executive had, unwittingly, been sitting in the wastebasket.

101.3

An old man who came into a modest fortune went to the big city to have his eyes examined. He visited an oculist who had been highly recommended and asked him to fit him with glasses so that he could read. After elaborate examinations and the trying on of every type of glasses, in spite of the man's apparently fine sight, the oculist gave up and said he was unable to find any reason why the man could not read. The old fellow then went to two other oculists, with the same results. When he returned to his hometown he called on an elderly general practitioner. After a few questions, the family doctor told the old fellow why he could not read: He was illiterate, and in addition he was slightly stupid.

101.4

A doctor's daughter wanted to marry a young fellow the M.D. did not like, and he told her so. He said the fellow was worthless, inclined toward obesity, and would be a burden to any young woman who married him. But the daughter kept on seeing the young fellow.

"Apparently what I said," said the doctor to the daughter one day, "carries no weight with you. I wish you would tell that fellow my opinion of him."

"I did."

"And what did he say?"

"He said it wasn't the first wrong diagnosis you have made."

101.5

"Doctor," complained the patient, "all the other physicians called in on my case seem to disagree with your diagnosis."

"Yes, I know they do," said the doctor, "but the autopsy will prove that I am right."

101.6

"I can't find the cause of your complaint," said the doctor as he ended his examination. "Probably it's due to drinking."

"That's all right, Doctor," said the patient understandingly. "I know how it is. Suppose I come back when you're sober?"

101.7

He was the young doctor's first patient; he had an ugly rash. The M.D. looked it over in puzzlement.

"Did you ever have this before?" he asked.

"Yes, several times over the past few years."

"Well, you've sure got it again," said the doctor.

101.8

Signs reading GOK hung over hospital beds. A doctor, visiting, asked what it meant. He was told: GOD ONLY KNOWS.

101.9

A doctor filled out a death certificate and signed his own name in the space marked "Cause of Death."

101.10

A patient complained to the doctor that he was unable to sleep at night. The doctor told him to eat something before going to bed. "But," said the patient, "two months ago you told me *not* to eat anything before going to bed."

"My dear man, this just illustrates the great strides science is making."

101.11

A woman phoned her doctor one evening and said, "Now I know what's wrong with me. I've got hyperinsulism."

"I know," said the doctor. "I was watching the same TV program."

101.12

George Jessel mentioned that one of his relatives was suffering from chronic frontal sinusitis.

"Good Lord," exclaimed a friend, "Where did she get that?"

"From a recent issue of *The Reader's Digest*," replied Jessel.

101.13

A doctor examining an attractive young woman finally said, "Well, Mrs. Atherton, I have good news for you."

"Pardon me, Doctor, but it is *Miss* Atherton."

"Well, in that case, Miss Atherton, I have bad news for you."

101.14

He finally went to a doctor complaining of persistent headache. The physician examined him and questioned him. No, he never drank, never smoked, never overate, never bothered with women.

"Well," said the M.D., "perhaps your halo is on too tight."

101.15

A well-known diagnostician was cornered by a wealthy matron at a cocktail party. She promptly launched into lengthy details about her latest complaint and wondered if the doctor might have some suggestions concerning what she might do.

"I think," said the doctor with his best professional air, "that you should give up smoking and drinking, get more sleep, and drink much warm milk."

The woman thanked him and then added, "I suppose since this is a social occasion that you would be offended if I sent you a check for your advice."

"Don't think of it," said the doctor. "I never charge for advice given on such occasions. But then, it's not worth anything, either."

101.16

Dr. Abernethy, a famous London diagnostician, was once approached at a social function by a dowager who tried to wangle some free medical advice. "Oh, Dr. Abernethy," she said, "if a patient came to you with such and such a symptom, what would you recommend?"

"My dear Madam," he replied, "I would recommend Dr. Abernethy."

Definitions

101.17

Diagnosis: A preface to an autopsy.

101.18

Virus: A Latin medical term, meaning, "Your guess is as good as mine."

(*See also 28.1, 102.10, 103.4, 184.46*)

102. Patients

Anecdotes

102.1

A farmer complained about "the damned scientists"—he knew they would keep foolin' around until they did something they hadn't oughta.

"Now look what they have gone and did."

"What's that, Paw? You mean the atom bomb?"

"No, I mean they fooled around until now they discovered something besides likker that will cure colds."

102.2

"You are in amazingly fine condition," said the doctor after making a thorough physical examination of a man. "How old did you say you were?"

"Seventy-nine."

"Well, you have the health of a man of sixty. How have you managed to keep so fit?"

"I think," said the patient, "my condition is due to an agreement me and the missus made when we got married. We agreed not to argue. She promised if she got mad around the house she'd keep quiet but stay in the kitchen until she calmed down. And I promised that when I got mad I'd keep quiet too and jest go out-of-doors until I calmed down."

"But why would that give you such a sound constitution?" asked the doctor.

"Well, Doc," replied the man, "I think you could say that I've lived what you might call an outdoor life."

102.3

It was a busy morning in the doctor's office. One elderly patient had to wait an inordinate amount of time. The doctor apologized to the elderly gent, and the old man said, "I didn't mind the wait so much, Doctor, but I thought that you would prefer treating my ailment in its earlier stages."

102.4

A National Health Service patient in England went to see his doctor. He walked through the front door and found himself facing two more doors marked "Male" and "Female." He walked through the door marked "Male" and saw another corridor with two doors, one marked "Under 20" and the other "Over 21." He walked in the first one and found two more doors, one marked "Married" and the other "Single." He went through the "Married" door and was confronted with another choice: "Socialist" or "Conservative." He went through the door marked "Conservative" and found himself in the street.

102.5

"I think," said the doctor, "that although you are a very sick man I will be able to pull you through."

"Doctor, if you do that, when I get well I'll donate $500,000 for your new hospital."

Months later the doctor met his former patient, "How do you feel?" he asked.

"Wonderful, Doctor, fine—never better."

"I've been meaning to speak to you," said the doctor, "about that money for the new hospital."

"What are you talking about?" said the patient.

"You said that if you got well you would contribute $500,000 to the hospital."

"I said that?" asked the patient. "That just shows how sick I was."

102.6

A man phoned his doctor, "Doctor, my wife has just dislocated her jaw. If you should happen to be in the neighborhood during the next two or three months and have the time, I would like you to stop in and have a look at her."

102.7

When Sydney Smith's doctor told him he should take a walk every morning on an empty stomach, Smith said, "Gladly. Upon whose?"

102.8

An elderly man, hard-of-hearing, went to the doctor.

"Do you smoke?"

"Yes."

"Much?"

"Sure, all the time."

"Drink?"

"Yes, just about anything at all. Anytime, too."

"What about late hours? And girls, do you chase 'em?"

"Sure thing; I live it up whenever I get the chance."

"Well, you'll have to cut out all that."

"Just to hear better? No thanks."

102.9

A devotee of mental healing met a young friend who seemed disconsolate. "It's my pa," said the youth when questioned. "He's ailin' bad. Doctor says he's not goin' to get well, and it sure seems like he's right."

"That's nothing but medical quackery," asserted the believer in mental healing. "My boy, it is a purely mental condition—that's what's bothering your father. Now you just go home and tell him what I said—tell him it is all in his mind and that he will be all right if he simply thinks himself well."

Several weeks later the same youth met the

same man again. "How's your father getting along?" asked the older man.

The youth sighed and said, "He thinks he's dead now."

102.10

"Cheer up!" said the doctor. "I have the same complaint as you."

"True enough," said the patient, "but you don't have the same doctor."

102.11

When a man died and appeared before St. Peter at the gate of Heaven, the records were consulted and the man told that the schedule did not call for his appearance at that time. The man went to Hell and Satan told him the same thing. Back to Heaven went the man, and again St. Peter went over the records and finally said: "Well, I've finally found your record. But you're not due here for another ten years. Who's your doctor?"

102.12

A medical student spent his summer vacation at a variety of jobs, one of which was an assistant to a butcher, and another as an orderly at night in a nearby hospital. On both jobs the young man wore a long white coat.

One evening he was wheeling a patient into surgery. The nervous woman looked up at the young man and screamed, "My God! It's the butcher!"

—*Betty Ware,* Journal of the AMA

102.13

A motorcycle driver one winter evening reversed his jacket so that the bitter winds would not come through the gaps between the buttons. As he sped along the road, he skidded on an icy spot and crashed into a tree.

When the ambulance arrived, the first-aid man pushed through the crowd and asked a man who was standing over the victim what happened. He replied that the motorcycle rider seemed to be in pretty good shape after the crash, but by the time they got his head straightened out he was dead.

102.14

An elderly man waiting in a doctor's reception room was disturbed when a nun came from the doctor's office weeping tears of alarm and bitterness. When the man went into the doctor he rebuked him for causing the poor nun to become so upset.

"Don't get so excited," said the doctor. "The poor woman had a severe case of hiccups, and the only way I could cure her was to shock her; I simply told her she was pregnant."

Aphorisms

102.15

Doctors think a lot of patients are cured who have simply quit in disgust.

—*Don Herold*

102.16

The patient is not likely to recover who makes the doctor his heir.

—*Thomas Fuller*

102.17

The only way to keep your health is to eat what you don't want, drink what you don't like, and do what you'd rather not.

—*Mark Twain*

102.18

There's another advantage of being poor—a doctor will cure you faster.

—*Kin Hubbard*

(*See also 101.1–101.3, 101.5–101.7, 101.10–101.16, 103.1–103.4, 103.6, 104.1–104.3, 104.6–104.9, 104.11, 104.12, 104.14–104.18, 105.1, 105.2, 106.3, 106.7, 106.9–106.14, 106.19, 106.21, 107.3, 107.6, 107.7, 108.3–108.6, 109.1–109.8, 110.1–110.8, 110.10–110.13, 110.16, 111.1–111.28, 111.30–111.33, 111.40–111.43, 117.8, 126.15, 165.35, 184.46, 213.10, 225.3, 232.3, 243.3, 259.6, 263.7*)

103. Hypochondriacs

Anecdotes

103.1

A hypochondriac, in listing his current complaints to his doctor, added that he was also losing his hearing. "It's getting so bad," he said, "that I can no longer hear myself coughing."

The doctor handed the patient a prescription. "Will this improve my hearing?" asked the patient.

"No," said the doctor, "but it will make you cough much louder."

103.2

The hypochondriac called on her doctor and said, "There is something wrong with my neighbor. She never has the doctor in."

103.3

A fellow tormented by a succession of imaginary ills consulted a psychologist, who suggested that he keep saying to himself: "Every day in every way I am feeling better and better."

Several weeks later the patient again met the psychologist who asked how the formula was working with him. "Fine in the daytime," said the unhappy man. "But at night I still feel pretty bad."

103.4

Jittery Jake went to his doctor and told him that he had a fatal liver condition.

"Nonsense," said the doctor. "You couldn't tell whether you had it or not. With that condition there is no discomfort whatever."

"Those are my symptoms exactly," said Jake.

103.5

You have two chances: one of getting the germ, and one of not. If you get the germ, you have two chances: one of getting the disease, and one of not. If you get the disease, you have two chances: one of dying, and one of not. And if you die—well, you still have two chances!

103.6

The overwrought man called on his doctor, afraid that he was developing something serious, maybe fatal. The doctor examined him carefully, told him there was nothing wrong with him, but picked up a bottle from his desk and said, "Here are some pills that should help you. Try three every day, and come back in a month."

The patient came back on schedule, told the doctor that the pills had done him a world of good—no more tension, headaches, stomach pains, trembling, or sleeplessness. "That's the greatest thing any doctor ever gave me—and believe me I've tried plenty of different medicines."

"I'm not going to kid you," said the doctor. "The whole thing has been mental with you. There's nothing in those pills but bread—they are bread pills."

"My God, Doctor," screamed the patient in alarm, "were they whole wheat or rye?"

103.7

"Did you have a good sleep last night?" a friend asked an insomniac.

"I slept all right, but it didn't do me any good; I dreamed that I was awake all night."

Definition

103.8

Insomnia is what a person has when he lies awake all night for an hour.

—*Paul H. Gilbert*

Aphorisms

103.9

There's lots of people in this world who spend so much time watching their health that they haven't the time to enjoy it.

—*Josh Billings*

103.10

You can tell how healthy a man is by what he takes two at a time—stairs or pills.

—*Kin Hubbard*

104. Bills, Paid and Unpaid

Anecdotes

104.1

Doctor: "You had a pretty close call. It's only your strong constitution that pulled you through."

Patient: "Well, Doctor, it would be nice if you remembered that when you make out your bill."

104.2

The great specialist had just completed his medical examination of the brassy professional beggar and told him the fee was $25.

"The fee is too high. I ain't got that much," said the beggar.

"Well make it $15, then."

"It's still too much. I haven't got it."

"All right," said the doctor, "give me $5, and beat it."

"Who has $5? Not me," said the beggar.

"Well give me whatever you have, and get out," said the doctor.

"Doctor, I have nothing."

By this time the doctor was in a rage and said, "If you have no money you have some nerve to call on a specialist of my standing and my fees."

The beggar, too, now got mad and shouted back at the doctor: "Let me tell you, Doctor, when my health is concerned nothing is too expensive for me."

104.3

Mrs. Brown complained to the doctor about the size of her bill.

"But, Mrs. Brown," said the doctor, "You must remember that I made eleven visits to your home on the case."

"Yes," said Mrs. Brown, "But you seem to be forgetting that my son infected the whole school."

104.4

"This bill is exorbitant," protested the doctor to the service station. "For a few hours' work you're charging me more than a physician gets."

"But, Doctor," said the service-station manager, "you must remember that you are all the time working on the same old piece of machinery, while we fellows have a whole flock of new models every year and have to learn all over again each time."

104.5

The doctor pulled into the service station and said to the attendant, "I'm having a devil of time with my steering; the car won't respond to the wheel."

The attendant took one quick look and noticed that the car had a flat tire. "Doctor," said the service man, "you've got here a case of flatulency of the perimeter due to an extreme decline of pressure, resulting in a dangerous lesion of the epidermis and a possible rupture of the internal tube. We will have to charge you accordingly."

104.6

Doctor: "The check you gave me the other day came back."

Patient: "So did my arthritis."

104.7

"Mr. Greenhouse," said the doctor with becoming solemnity but with ill-disguised pleasure, "yours is a case which will enrich medical science."

"Good Lord!" cried Greenhouse, "I thought I was going to get off easy—with maybe something like a fee of $50."

104.8

"I can't pay your bill, Doctor," said the businessman. "I followed your instructions; I slowed down, and they fired me."

104.9

"What an outrageously high bill, Doctor, for only two weeks of treatment," protested the patient.

"Calm yourself, my dear man. If you knew how interesting and difficult your case was, and if you knew how tempted I was to let it go on to postmortem, you would be grateful rather than complaining; you'd be glad to pay three times as much."

104.10

"Why, sir, do you always ask patients what they have had for dinner?" asked the young assistant of the older man.

"It is an important question, young man. I make out my bills for them according to their dinner menus."

104.11

"Doctor," said the patient, "I must say you kept your promise when you said you'd have me walking within two months."

"I'm glad to hear that," replied the doctor warmly.

"Yessir," said the patient, "when I got your bill I had to sell my car."

104.12

The small-town doctor, hoping to ease the usual difficulty of securing payment from his patients, posted a sign in his waiting room:

TEN DOLLARS FOR THE FIRST VISIT. SEVEN-FIFTY FOR THE SECOND VISIT. FIVE DOLLARS FOR ALL SUBSEQUENT VISITS.

Soon after a total stranger went to the doctor one evening, read the sign carefully, and then breezed confidently into the doctor with: "Well, Doctor, here I am again for the third visit."

The doctor looked at the patient appraisingly, then said, "You're looking just fine. Continue with the same treatment. That will be $5."

104.13

A young doctor had just opened his office. His first caller, a stranger, entered. The ambitious doctor asked to be excused as he hurried to the phone. Lifting the receiver he said: "Yes, this is Dr. Bumble. Yes, I'll expect you at ten past two. Please be prompt because I'm very busy. Yes, the fee will be $500."

Putting down the receiver, he turned to the strange visitor and said, "Now, Sir, what can I do for you?"

"Nothing," said the visitor, "I've come to install the phone."

Aphorisms

104.14

The doctor felt the patient's purse and said there was no hope.

104.15

Unto our doctors let us drink,
Who cure our chills and ills,
No matter what we really think
About their bills and pills.

—*Philip McAllister*

104.16

We live on one-third of what we eat, and the doctors live on the rest.

—*Royal S. Copeland*

104.17

When a doctor looks me square in the face and kant see no money in me, then I am happy.

—*Josh Billings*

104.18

Take your fee while the patient is still in pain. —*John of Salisbury* (twelfth century)

(*See also 25.20, 101.15, 102.5, 107.3, 109.1–109.3, 111.33, 111.40, 243.3*)

105. Prescriptions

Anecdotes

105.1

When the celebrated Beau Nash, a famous Welshman, was ill, Dr. Cheyne wrote a prescription for him. The next day the doctor, coming to see his patient, inquired if he had followed his prescription. "No, truly, Doctor," said Nash; "if I had I should have broken my neck, for I threw it out of a two-pair-of-stairs window."

105.2

A doctor was called in for a fellow who was pretty sick. He said the man must get absolute rest and quiet. While he was there the wife kept fussing and jabbering all the time. The doctor left sleeping pills.

"When do I give them to him?" she asked the doctor.

He said, "They are not for him—they are for you—you take them."

105.3

A woman sent a dinner invitation to a doctor friend. When she received his hurried reply written on a prescription form, she could not read his writing. Knowing that the local druggist would be able to decipher the writing, she took the note to him. The pharmacist looked at it, excused himself, and presently returned with a bottle, saying "That will be $1.50."

105.4

A fellow driven nuts by a severe attack of hiccups, asked a druggist what he could do for him. The druggist mixed a preparation in a glass and said, "Now don't ask any questions—just drink this down quickly without stopping." The customer did and then said, "Now what am I supposed to do?"

"Well," said the druggist, "that was a huge dose of castor oil. Now just take a long walk, and before long you'll find yourself hanging onto a telephone pole or lamp post. You won't *dare* hiccup, and you'll be cured."

105.5

A woman, incensed that her favorite cure-all could not be purchased without a prescription, stormed at the druggist. "But, Madam," explained the druggist, "it cannot be obtained except by prescription because it is habit-forming."

"It is not," retorted the woman. "I know, because I've been taking it regularly for fifteen years."

Aphorism

105.6

I firmly believe that if the whole *materia medica, as now used,* could be sunk to the bottom of the sea, it would be all the better for mankind—and all the worse for the fishes.

—*Oliver Wendell Holmes,* Address, May, 1860.

(*See also 41.12, 103.1, 103.6, 106.1, 115.1, 224.9*)

106. Doctors-at-large

Anecdotes

106.1

When Lincoln was making a political speech one day in Illinois, a Dr. Hamburgher, a Democrat, forced his way to the front to reply. As Hamburgher launched into an emotional, supercharged speech, a little man with a limp came over to Lincoln and said, "Don't mind him. I live here, and I know him. I'll take care of him. Watch me." He took the platform, and his remarks brought from Hamburgher the cry, "That's a lie." To this the little fellow with the limp called out defiantly, "Never mind, I'll take that from you—yes, I'll take anything from you, except your pills." At the mention of pills the doctor snorted, "You scoundrel, you know I've quit practicing medicine." Whereupon the little man dropped to his knees, raised his hands heavenward, and fervently called out, "Then, thank God! The country is safe."

106.2

Twin brothers entered professional life, one as a clergyman and the other as a physician. The one who was a doctor was stopped one day by a woman who said, "That was a fine sermon you preached last Sunday."

The physician said, "Madam, I am not the brother that preaches; I am the one that practices."

106.3

Jake Bentley fell off a load o' hay t'day an' had t' crawl all th' way t' th' golf links to have his leg set.

—*Kin Hubbard*

106.4

Returning to his birthplace Clarence Darrow met a doctor friend.

"If you had listened to me," said the doctor to Darrow, "you, too, would now be a doctor."

"What's wrong with being a lawyer?"

"Well, I don't say all lawyers are crooks, but even you will have to admit that your profession doesn't exactly make angels of men."

"No," said Darrow, "you doctors have the better of us there."

106.5

Sir Richard Burton, the famous translator of *The Arabian Nights,* was visiting at the home of Dr. George Bird, of London. After dinner Burton gave an account of some of his exploits in the East, when Dr. Bird asked him, "What does it feel like to kill a man?"

"Why," said Burton, "that is a funny question for a medical man to ask. Now, what does it feel like? Do tell us."

106.6

"Can you come right over and make a fourth at bridge?" one doctor asked another on the phone.

"Yes, Doctor, by all means; I'll rush right over."

"Is it important, dear?" asked the sympathetic wife as she helped him on with his coat and got his medical bag.

"I'm afraid it is, my dear," said the doctor. "Sounds serious—there are three doctors there already."

106.7

A doctor vacationing at a seashore resort was walking the beach when he came upon a first-aid squad trying to revive a man who had been pulled from the surf. He was being worked over with a stomach pump at the water's edge. As the crew worked desperately over the inert figure, the doctor saw seaweed, small shells, sand, and saltwater come out of the victim's mouth. Finally he felt he had to intervene and tell them, "It would help if you took that fellow's behind out of the water."

106.8

"This letter from your father indicates he's an undertaker."

"Yes, that's right."

"But you said he was a doctor."

"Oh, no; you must have misunderstood. I said that he followed the medical profession."

106.9

The wind was howling, the snow flying, and the thermometer dropping when the doctor received a call at 3 A.M. to drive five miles out in the country on an emergency.

When he got to his destination the patient said, "I'm not in any particular pain, but I just got an idea that death is about to take me off."

The doctor said not a word but examined the man's heart and blood pressure. "Have you got a will?" asked the doctor.

"At my age—is it going to happen to me?" whined the patient.

"You heard me," said the doctor. "You'd better get your lawyer right away."

Trembling in terror, the man phoned the lawyer to come right out.

"And what about your pastor?" asked the doctor. "You'd better get him instantly."

"But doctor—do you really—"

"And your parents should be called," added the doctor.

The man began to blubber, "I just can't die tonight!"

The doctor looked at the man with cold contempt. "No, you're not going to die tonight. There's nothing whatever the matter with you, except your character. But I'm damned if I'm going to be the only man you've made a fool of on a night like this."

106.10

"Is there any hope, Doctor?" asked the patient's wife.

"It all depends upon what you're hoping for," replied the doctor.

106.11

"Doctor, isn't it somewhat out of your way to visit me here?"

"Not at all. I have another patient nearby, and so I'll kill two birds with one stone."

106.12

"I was in such great pain, Doctor, that I wanted to die."

"You did right, Madam, to call me in," said the doctor.

106.13

"Doctor," called a frantic young man over the phone, "my father's at death's door!"

"Now don't get excited, son," soothed the doctor. "I'll be right over and pull him through."

106.14

There is a young and popular doctor who always subtracts ten beats whenever he takes a woman's pulse.

Definitions

106.15

From a schoolboy's examination paper: "M.D. stands for Mentally Deficient."

106.16

Dentist: A prestidigitator who putting metal into your mouth, pulls coins out of your pocket.

—*Ambrose Bierce*

Aphorisms

106.17

Women doctors have the advantage of being able to combine medical guesswork with feminine intuition.

106.18

Is there any significance in the fact that doctors are always described as "practicing"?

106.19

One doctor single, like the sculler plies,
The patient struggles, and by inches dies;
But two physicians, like a pair of oars,
Waft him right swiftly to the Stygian shores.

—*Joseph Jekyll*

106.20

TO SIR JOHN HILL, PHYSICIAN AND PLAYWRIGHT

For physic and farces
Thy equal there scarce is;
Thy farces are physic,
Thy physic a farce is.

—*David Garrick*

106.21

I am dying with the help of too many physicians.

—*Alexander the Great*

106.22

Doctors will have more lives to answer for in the next world than even we generals.

—*Napoleon Bonaparte*

106.23

A doctor gets no pleasure out of the health of his friends.

—*Michel de Montaigne*

106.24

The most dangerous physicians are those who, being born actors, imitate born physicians with perfect imposture.

—*Friedrich Nietzsche*

106.25

The best doctor is the one you run for and can't find.

—*Denis Diderot*

106.26

Dr. Myerbach knows less of urine than a chambermaid.

—*Dr. I. Lettsom*

(*See also 40.22, 54.12, 60.14, 92.11, 101.1–101.16, 102.3, 102.5, 102.10, 102.11, 103.1, 103.2, 103.4, 103.6, 104.1–104.18, 105.1–105.3, 107.1–107.11, 108.1–108.8, 109.1–109.13, 110.2, 110.12, 110.14, 111.1–111.10, 111.12–111.40, 112.7, 124.28, 150.6, 155.23, 180.3, 184.46, 184.47, 184.61, 188.2, 188.11, 197.2, 213.10, 215.3, 225.3, 235.25, 240.12, 243.3, 248.11, 259.6, 263.7, 266.18, 266.28, 268.15, 271.43, 271.46, 272.27*)

107. Specialists

Anecdotes

107.1

At the Mayo Clinic in Minnesota you are bound to hear about the time a bustling woman stopped Dr. Will Mayo and asked, "Are you the head doctor here?"

"No, Madam," replied Dr. Will. "My brother is the head doctor. I'm the belly doctor."

107.2

The teacher read to her class the famous story of the three blind men who examined an elephant. One of the men said the elephant was like a tree; another said it was like a wall, and the third man said it was like a rope. "Now," asked the teacher, "what kind of men were they?"

"Specialists," called out one boy—whose father no doubt was a general practitioner.

107.3

The janitor of a Park Avenue building mentioned to a prominent nose and throat specialist that his little child was very sick with a bad throat. The good doctor volunteered to look at the child, drove to the man's address on the East Side, climbed five flights of a run-down tenement, carefully examined the child, said he would have a prescription filled and sent to the home by his druggist, and on the way out—moved by the family's dire poverty—dropped a $20 bill on the table.

The next afternoon the doctor met the janitor and asked how the baby was. "Just fine, Doctor. That $20 bill you left so kindly, well my wife she used it to bring the baby to a specialist."

107.4

The young doctor completing his internship was asked by an older doctor what his plans for the future were. "I intend to specialize on the nose."

"You mean nose and throat, don't you?"

"No, just the nose," replied the young man firmly.

"Oh, I see," said the older doctor. "Tell me, which nostril are you specializing in?"

107.5

"I thought your son was going to study to be an ear specialist," said one Scotsman to another. "But now he tells me you have influenced him instead to take up dentistry."

"I left it pretty much to him," said the second Scotsman. "I simply pointed out to him that people have thirty-two teeth and only two ears."

107.6

A dermatologist said he chose his specialty because: his patients never get him out of bed at night; his patients never die; his patients never get well.

Dermatologists understandably resent the observation that they are engaged in "the skin game."

Definitions

107.7

A specialist is a doctor whose patients are expected to confine their ailments to his office hours.

107.8

Consultation is the seeking of approval of a course already decided upon.

Aphorisms

107.9

A chiropodist makes money hand over foot.

107.10

Pediatricians eat—because children don't.
—*Carleton Fredericks*

107.11

Internists know everything and do nothing. Surgeons know nothing and do everything. Obstetricians know nothing and do nothing.
—*Anonymous*

(*See also 104.2, 117.8*)

HOSPITALS AND NURSES

108. The Bedpan Brigade

Anecdotes

108.1

A conceited young man recuperating in the hospital had an extremely pretty nurse. He said to her one morning, "Nurse, I'm in love with you; I don't want to get well."

"Don't worry, you won't. The doctor is in love with me, too, and he saw you kissing me yesterday."

108.2

When an intern tried to take liberties with a pretty young nurse, she turned on him and said, "Thermometers are not the only things that are graduated and get degrees without having any brains."

108.3

"Why," asked a visiting doctor, "do you nurses call that patient in room 123 the 'old sardine'?"

"If you knew how many times he wants to go to the can you'd know why," said the nurse.

108.4

When Grandma developed diabetes she rebelled at the rigid diet imposed upon her, and finally—after a particularly risky spell of cheating on her food—she had to be sent to the hospital for careful supervision. But because of the crowded conditions it was necessary to put her in the maternity ward.

When her granddaughter went to the hospital and walked down the corridor, a nurse stopped her and asked what she was doing in the maternity ward. "I'm visiting Grandma," replied the girl.

"Your grandmother! What is she doing in the maternity ward?"

"Oh," said the innocent child, "She's been cheating again."

108.5

Day after day the husband asked the nurses at the hospital how his wife was doing. Each time he got the standard reply, "She's showing improvement." But each day she seemed to be a bit worse. But still they kept telling him, "She's showing some improvement." Finally the poor man's wife died. When asked the cause of her death, he shook his head in bewilderment and replied, "It seems she just couldn't stand all that improvement."

108.6

Coming out of the ether after his operation, a man found the blinds in his hospital room drawn and asked his nurse why they were drawn so that he could not see out.

"Oh, take it easy," said the nurse. "There's a big fire burning across the street, and we didn't want you to wake up and think that the operation was a failure."

108.7

A doctor, speaking of practical nurses, said the most practical one he ever knew married a wealthy patient.

Definition

108.8

Hospital Bed: A parked taxi with the meter running.

—*Frank Scully*

(*See also* 155.22, 232.3)

109. The Surgeon's Scalpel

Anecdotes

109.1

"Have you ever been operated on?" asked the doctor.

"Yes," replied the patient.

"What for?"

"$300."

"I mean, what did you have."

"Only $250."

"You still don't understand—what was your complaint."

"The bill was still too high."

109.2

A doctor in a clinic examining a patient said, "If I find it necessary to operate, would you have the money to pay for it?"

"Listen, Doc," said the man, "if I didn't have the money, would you find it necessary to operate?"

109.3

"Will this be a dangerous operation?" asked the patient as he was wheeled into the operating room.

"Ridiculous. No $80 operation is dangerous."

109.4

"Doctor, is it safe to perform this operation?" asked the nervous patient.

"That, my dear lady," said the doctor, "is one of the things we intend to find out."

109.5

A man coming out of ether in a ward after an operation said amiably, "Thank God, that's over."

"Don't be too sure," said the patient in the next bed. "They left a sponge in me and had to cut me open again."

And the patient in a bed on the other side said, "Why they had to open me, too, to recover one of their instruments."

Just then the doctor stuck his head in the door and called, "Anyone seen my hat?"

The man fainted.

109.6

Senator Everett Dirksen tells about a man who insisted there was a cat in his stomach. Shortly after, the man was rushed to the hospital for an emergency appendectomy, and his doctor thought it was a good time to cure the man of his cat obsession. So when the man came out of the ether the doctor held up a black cat and said, "Well, we got him out of you, all right."

"You've got the wrong one," screamed the man. "It was a white cat."

109.7

An old fellow had just been returned to his room after a rejuvenation operation. The kind-faced nurse bent over him and told him not to be so alarmed, that the surgery was successful, and the pain would subside in a day or so.

But still the old fellow continued to weep bitterly.

Finally the nurse pleaded with him not to carry on so, that everything would be all right —the pain would go away, and soon he would be in good shape again.

"It's not that," sobbed the old man. "What worries me is that I'm late for school already."

109.8

"I sure was lucky," said the surgeon as he emerged from the operating room. "I was just in time. In another hour the patient would have recovered without the operation."

109.9

Surgeons wear masks, according to one young student, so that if a mess is made of the operation, the patient won't know who did it.

109.10

A surgeon out walking with his wife passed a vivacious young blond who hailed him gaily. The doctor's wife eyed him narrowly, "Where," she asked, "did you meet that person, my dear?"

"Just a young woman I met professionally."

"Whose profession? Yours or hers?"

Aphorisms

109.11

The practice of medicine is a thinker's art, the practice of surgery, a plumber's.

—*Martin H. Fischer*

109.12

Once a surgeon, Dr. Baker
Then became an undertaker,
Not so much his trade reversing,
Since for him its just re-hearsing.

—From *Martial*, of ancient Rome

109.13

Culture is what your butcher would have if he were a surgeon.

—*Mary Pettibone Peele*

(*See also* 102.12, 247.9)

110. The Psycho Ward

Anecdotes

110.1

A bishop, visiting an insane asylum, was told by his guide that one of the inmates insisted he was God. The bishop expressed interest in meeting the man, who proved to be a venerable and dignified figure, with a flowing white beard.

"I understand that you are God?" said the bishop.

"That is correct," replied the old man with a gentle bow.

"Well, there is one thing I would like very much to know. When you speak in the Bible of creating the world in six days, do you mean this literally or metaphorically? Do you mean six days of twenty-four hours each, or do you mean aeons, or ages?"

"I am sorry," replied the old fellow, "but I make it a practice never to talk shop."

110.2

One of the residents of an asylum fancied himself a painter, and with the help of his understanding doctors was given a room for a studio and supplied with the necessary equipment.

After a time the patient invited the superintendent and doctors to come to the unveiling of a just-completed masterpiece. With a flourish, the painter pointed to an untouched piece of canvas, mounted on an easel. "How do you like it?" asked the proud artist.

"Fine," said one of the doctors. "But what is it?"

"It represents the passage of the Children of Israel through the Red Sea."

"But where is the sea?"

"It has been driven back—as related in the Bible."

"And where are the Israelites?"

"They have already crossed over."

"What about the pursuing Egyptians—where are they?"

"They haven't yet arrived," explained the artist.

110.3

The pilot of the plane began to laugh uncontrollably.

"What's so funny?" asked the passenger.

"Oh," said the pilot, "I was just wondering what they'll say at the asylum when they discover I've escaped."

110.4

A fellow pushing a wheelbarrow upside down at an insane asylum was asked why—and he said, "I suppose you think I'm crazy. Well, I'm not so crazy as to push this thing right side up and then have somebody fill it up."

110.5

A patient in a mental hospital placed his ear to the wall of his room, listening intently. "Quiet," he whispered to an orderly and pointed to the wall. The attendant pressed his ear against the wall, listened, and then said, "I don't hear anything."

"No," replied the patient, "it's awful; it's been this way for days!"

110.6

An inmate of a mental institution was trying to drive a nail into the wall, but he had the head of the nail against the wood and was hammering the point. After a while he threw it down in disgust and said, "Bah! Idiots! They gave me a nail with the head at the wrong end."

Another inmate who had been watching began to laugh. "It's you that's the idiot," he said as he jerked his thumb toward the opposite wall. "That nail was made for the other side of the room."

110.7

"There is nothing in the world impossible to me," said a mental patient. "I have conquered space and time."

"I'll bet you can't walk up on a beam of light from my flashlight," said the other mental patient.

"I could do it, but I won't," replied the first patient. "When I got halfway up you'd turn off the light—then where would I be?"

110.8

Two patients in a mental institution were walking through the grounds and stopped to watch a gardener. "What are you doing?" one of them asked.

"I'm putting fertilizer on these strawberries," replied the gardener.

"Humph!" exclaimed one of the patients. "We put sugar and cream on our strawberries, and they call us crazy."

110.9

A distinguished politician customarily began his speeches with, "Why are we here?" He had occasion to address the inmates of a mental hospital and finally said, "Ladies and Gentlemen, why are we here?" One of the inmates called out, "We are all here because we're not all there."

110.10

When Franklin D. Roosevelt was Governor of New York State, his wife, Eleanor, arrived one day unannounced to inspect a state mental institution. A distinguished-looking man recognized her when she came to the entrance and at once offered his services as guide on her tour.

In the course of several hours of careful inspection Mrs. Roosevelt became impressed by the knowledge and intelligence of her guide, and pleased by his gentle manners and obvious good breeding. In taking her leave she thanked him and expressed her belief that the hospital was in good hands.

"Oh, I'm not an official here. I am a patient," explained her guide. He told her how he had been unjustly committed by greedy members of his family who had designs on his personal fortune and a greater fortune he was soon to inherit. His detailed and reasonable account of the conspiracy which had resulted in his commitment caused Mrs. Roosevelt to promise to have the Governor make an immediate investigation and correct whatever injustice had been done. The patient thanked her gravely for her kindness.

As she turned to go down the steps a vigorous kick in the posterior caused Mrs. Roosevelt to stumble and nearly fall down the flight.

Gasping with shocked indignation she demanded: "Why did you do that? You might have hurt me seriously."

The patient smiled gently. "I don't want to hurt you. I did that so that you would not forget to tell the Governor about my case."

110.11

The social worker was interviewing a man about to be released from a mental institution after a three-year confinement. "What are your plans when you get out?" she asked.

"I've been thinking of resuming the practice of law, if I can build up a practice."

The social worker thought that was good, and she agreed, too, when he said that as alternative he could go into business or become a certified public accountant.

"Well," said the social worker, "apparently you will not lack for choices of occupation."

"No," said the patient. "In fact, since I have a medical degree I might take up the practice of medicine, specializing in psychotherapy because of my experience here. And," concluded the patient with a sudden gleam in his eye, "if worst comes to worse, I can always be a teakettle."

110.12

A new psychiatrist was making his rounds of a mental institution when he encountered a patient he had previously talked to. He asked the man his name. "George Washington," was the reply.

"But," said the psychiatrist, "the other day you told me you were Abraham Lincoln."

"That," said the patient with a touch of melancholy, "was by my first wife."

110.13

A farmer, visiting a mental institution, stopped to watch one of the patients cultivate a flower bed. "Did you ever do any farming?" he asked the worker.

"Sure, I've farmed," said the patient. "Were you ever in an asylum?"

"Nope."

"Well," said the patient, "It's lots better than farmin'."

110.14

The popular and democratic Queen of the Belgians visited the United States after World War I. She wanted to show her appreciation for the help the American people had given the Belgians.

One day the Queen went unheralded, unaccompanied, and unannounced to visit the Henry Phipps Psychiatric Clinic of Johns Hopkins Hospital. The Queen inquired where she might find Doctor Adolf Myer, the famous director of this clinic.

When she located Dr. Myer, the Queen introduced herself as the Queen of the Belgians.

Dr. Myer bowed, smiled gently, and then soothingly replied, "That's very interesting. Tell me, how long have you thought so?"

110.15

A distinguished visitor to a mental institution had occasion to use the telephone, but he had difficulty in getting his connections. Exasperated, he shouted to the operator, "Do you know who I am?"

"No," said the operator, "but I know *where* you are."

110.16

Harry Hershfield tells about the young man who was given a boomerang for his birthday and in the course of time became expert at throwing it and having it return to him. After several years of skillful development in the art, he was given a new boomerang, but the poor lad finally ended up in a mental institution—he had lost his mind trying to throw away the old boomerang.

110.17

Phillippe, an eighteenth-century French physician noted for his studies of mental illness and a pioneer advocate of humane treatment for mental patients, one day was accosted by a Parisian literary celebrity.

"I am writing an *Encyclopedia of Atheists,*" said the writer to the doctor, "and I plan to give you a place in it that shall be worthy of you."

"I thank you for the honor," replied the doctor, "and in return I shall, in the next edition of my volume on lunatics and idiots, be certain to add your case."

(*See also 24.4, 82.8, 84.3, 85.1, 122.6, 130.3, 165.30, 165.97, 205.21*)

FROM THE PSYCHIATRIST'S COUCH

111. Patient Talk

Anecdotes

111.1

A woman went to the doctor and said she was in a terrible state over her husband.

"He thinks he is a horse; he sleeps standing up, and he neighs instead of speaking. He even insists on being fed oats in a bag. It is terrible," said the woman.

"How long has this been going on?" asked the doctor.

"Six, maybe eight, months."

"You have let things go too far," said the psychiatrist. "Your husband will require a great deal of treatment. I would have to give him most of my time for two or three months to begin with, and it would be very expensive."

"I care nothing for the expense," said the wife. "Anything—anything at all to make my husband stop thinking he is a horse."

"But it would cost several thousand dollars," said the doctor.

"What is that to us?" replied the wife.

"But can your husband afford this amount of money?"

"Why of course he can," said the woman. "He's already won three races this season at Aqueduct."

111.2

A psychiatrist thought he would try group therapy with three businessmen. For his initial probing, the psychiatrist held up a handkerchief and then let it fall to the floor. "What does that remind you of?" he asked the first man. "It makes me think of a beautiful mountain suddenly disintegrating because of a volcano."

The second man said it made him yawn by suggesting the bed clothing dropped on him late on a winter night.

The third man said, "It makes me think of sex."

Immediately interested, the psychiatrist asked, "Why does it make you think of sex?"

"Because," explained the third man, "that is all I ever think of."

111.3

A successful businessman consulted a psychiatrist after having the same dream night after night. "In my dream," he said, "we're seated in chairs facing each other, and one of me is giving advice to the other me. Doctor, am I losing my mind?"

"No," said the doctor, "as long as you just dream, you're all right. But if you heed that advice . . . you're sunk."

111.4

Smoke poured through the apartment building, fire engines came clanging to the scene, tenants ran to the street in night clothes carrying whatever possessions they could grab. One of the tenants noticed that the man who lived in the apartment next to her's was carrying a covered bird cage and asked, "What have you in the cage?"

"That's my pet rooster," he replied.

"Rooster!" the woman gasped. She told a solicitous neighbor, "Can you beat that; here I've been going to a psychiatrist for months to cure me of the delusion that I kept hearing a rooster crow."

111.5

"So," said the psychiatrist, "you think you are a dog. How long have you been subject to this dangerous hallucination?"

"Ever since I was a puppy."

111.6

A fellow who thought he was a dog went to a psychiatrist and took a series of treatments. When it was all over a friend asked him how he felt, and he said, "Fine; feel my nose."

111.7

"Doctor," said a patient to one of Dr. Freud's disciples, "I'm in love with a horse."

"That is not too unusual," said the doctor. "Millions of people are horse lovers."

"Yes," said the patient, "but I love this horse romantically."

"Well, that is not so common. Tell me, is it a male or a female horse?"

"I'd have you understand, Sir, it is a female horse," said the patient angrily. "Do you suggest that I am queer?"

111.8

A man asked a psychiatrist, "Can a fellow be in love with an elephant?"

"No," said the doctor.

"Where, then, can I get rid of an extra-large engagement ring."

111.9

A man walked into a psychiatrist's office snapping his fingers frantically and incessantly. "Calm down," said the doctor. "What are you doing that for?"

"It keeps away the elephants."

"There are no elephants around here!"

"See, it works," said the finger snapper.

111.10

No amount of friendly persuasion could convince the man that he was not dead, so his family took him to a psychiatrist. The latter placed him in front of a large mirror, telling him to stand there for three hours and repeat, "Dead men don't bleed."

At the end of that time the psychiatrist pricked the man's finger with a needle, and holding up the bleeding digit he said triumphantly, "There, now, see, what does that prove?"

"Dead men do bleed," said the patient.

111.11

A fellow who lived with his mother celebrated his fortieth birthday and his completion of four years of psychoanalysis on the same day. Mother had an elaborate dinner celebrating the two occasions. At the close of the meal the man was presented with two ties by his mother. He put one on, and the mother's eyes filled with tears. "What is the matter, dear," she asked, "don't you like the other tie?"

111.12

One of the yarns that Henny Youngman gets guffaws with concerns the mother who brought her son to the psychiatrist and said that he insisted upon emptying the ash trays all the time.

"That is not at all unusual; lots of people empty ash trays," said the psychiatrist.

"In their mouths?" asked the mother.

111.13

A distraught mother went to the psychiatrist and said her son was always making mud pies, and when he had finished them he ate them.

"That's not too unusual," said psychiatrist.

"Lots of boys make mud pies and try to eat them."

"I'm not so sure of that," said the mother, "and neither is my son's wife."

111.14

A man went to the psychiatrist and said, "Every night when I get into bed I have the conviction there is someone under the bed. I get up, and there's never anyone there. When I get under the bed, then I get the idea there is someone on top of the bed. And then there is never anyone on top of it. So it goes all night long—either someone under the bed, or on top of the bed, depending on where I am. It's driving me out of my mind."

The psychiatrist thought he could help the man if the patient would agree to two visits a week at $20 per visit, for a two-year period. "That is an awful lot of money for a man of my means," said the patient. "I'll have to talk it over with my wife and let you know."

The next week the patient phoned the psychiatrist and told him that his wife had solved his problem. "My wife," explained the patient, "simply cut off the legs of the bed."

111.15

Psychiatrists are likely to encounter just about anything—such as the man who walked into one's office stark naked and said, "I wish you could tell me why it is that whenever I walk through the streets people keep staring at me."

111.16

"Doctor, my trouble is that I dream the same dream over and over; I'm in a girl's dormitory, and the girls run from room to room stark naked."

"Very interesting," said the psychiatrist. "No doubt you want me to help you get rid of these dreams about naked women?"

"Oh, no," said the patient, "not that. I just want these girls to stop slamming doors and waking me up just when I'm about to catch one of them."

111.17

"Do dreams of escapades with half-naked men ever bother you?" asked the psychiatrist.

"No," sighed the young woman. "In fact, I rather like them."

111.18

After months of treating a patient, the psychiatrist said, "Now you are cured. You will no longer have delusions of grandeur and imagine that you're Napoleon."

"That's wonderful," said the patient. "The first thing I'm going to do is to call Josephine and tell her the good news."

111.19

A man with severe pains went to a psychiatrist, who asked, "Where is your pain?"

"In my navel," replied the patient.

"What does it feel like?" asked the doctor.

"Like a big screw in my navel."

"I would suggest you go home, take a screwdriver, and remove the screw." The patient agreed to do this.

The next day the patient phoned the doctor that he had done what he was told and removed a large screw from his navel.

"How do you feel now?" asked the doctor.

"I feel all right," said the patient, "but the damnedest thing happened; when I took out the screw my legs fell off."

111.20

A woman said to a psychiatrist, "I wish you'd see my husband. He's out of his mind. He blows smoke rings all the time."

"That's not unusual," said the doctor, "I do that myself."

"But, Doctor, he doesn't smoke."

111.21

A man addicted to collecting spaghetti went to a psychiatrist to be cured of the messy habit. He explained that the spaghetti was all over his living room.

"Why don't you put it in the closet?" suggested the psychiatrist.

"There's no room," said the patient. "That is where I keep the meat balls."

111.22

"I had a strange case recently," said the psychiatrist. "A man came to me under the delusion that he was to receive a huge fortune. The tension of it was destroying him. He kept waiting for two letters that would inform him he was being given title to some valuable oil-producing lands in Oklahoma. It was an unusual case, and I worked hard on him."

"What was the outcome?" asked the second psychiatrist.

"Well, just when I had effected a complete cure, the two letters actually came to him—but after I had presented my bill to him."

111.23

A psychiatrist examining a soldier asked, "Do you ever hear voices without being able to tell who is speaking or where the voices are coming from?"

"Sure."

"And when does this occur?"

"When I answer the telephone."

111.24

A timid little man went to the psychiatrist and asked if the good doctor couldn't split his personality.

"Split your personality?" asked the doctor. "Why in heaven's name do you want me to do a thing like that to you?"

"Because," said the little man weepingly, "I'm so lonesome."

111.25

Hy Gardner tells of a fellow who went to a psychiatrist with such an inferiority complex that when he got into an elevator and gave his floor number, he always added, "If it isn't out of your way."

111.26

A psychiatrist once asked his patient if the latter suffered from fantasies of self-importance. The patient replied: "No; on the contrary, I think of myself as much less than I really am."

111.27

A society woman went to a psychiatrist, and at the first interview he said, "Now just go ahead and tell me about yourself." She needed no urging—in fact after two hours the doctor had to tell her to stop and resume the account the next week. This went on for some weeks, but still the woman kept on talking about herself. Finally the doctor told her, "I've done just about all I can for you now. I think the best thing for you to do is to go to Niagara Falls and spend as much time as possible looking at something bigger than yourself."

111.28

A man went to a psychiatrist and revealed his life story, all the details about his childhood, love life, hobbies, etc. At length the doctor said, "There doesn't seem to be anything wrong with you. You're as sane as I am."

"But, Doctor," said the patient, "it's these butterflies. I can't stand them. They're all over me," whereupon he began brushing himself off with his hand.

"For heaven's sake," cried the psychiatrist, "Don't brush them off on me."

111.29

Two psychiatrists encountered each other on the street. One said, "Well, it's good to see you."

As he got a few steps along, the other psychiatrist came to a halt and said to himself, "I wonder what he meant by that?"

111.30

A psychiatrist was unusually scornful of a patient who got into a panic every time he heard thunder. "It is absurd to get into a fright over thunder—a harmless manifestation of nature. Get a hold of yourself the next time you hear it. Do what I do—I simply put my head under the pillow and close my eyes until the thunder passes away."

111.31

A West Coast psychiatrist practices what he calls "socialized psychiatry"—he lies down on the couch with his patient.

111.32

Morey Amsterdam says he met a psychiatrist walking down the street with a couch on his back. "Where are you going with that?" asked Amsterdam. "I'm making a house call," said the psychiatrist.

111.33

A New York University professor, deciding he should consult a psychiatrist, picked out one on Park Avenue and entered the doctor's reception room, beautifully appointed but devoid of a receptionist. There were two doors—marked "Men" and "Women." He went through the door marked "Men" and encountered two other doors marked "Extrovert" and "Introvert." He decided he was an introvert, opened that door, and found himself in a room with two more doors—one marked "Those Making $10,000 and Over" and "Those Making Less than $10,000." He knew he made less than $10,000 and so opened that door—and found himself back on Park Avenue.

—*Dr. Wm. L. Pressly,* quoted by Hugh Park in Atlanta Journal

111.34

When a secretary was asked why she had resigned her position with a psychiatrist, she said that when she was late for work she was considered hostile, when on time she was diagnosed as having an anxiety complex, and when exactly on time she was charged with having acted compulsively.

111.35

Psychoanalysis is the disease it purports to cure.

—*Karl Kraus*

111.36

A psychiatrist had his office decorated with new furniture made of overwrought iron.

111.37

Louis Ginsberg, English instructor at Rutgers University, wrote New York *World-Telegram* columnist Norton Mockridge: "Many psychiatrists live on Park Avenue, in what is known as the mental block. They have plush offices with overwrought furniture. Theirs is the only business where the customer is *always* wrong. One psychiatrist told an architect he had an edifice complex, and another told a wrestler to get a grip on himself. But the prize of the year goes to the psychiatrist who told a taxidermist that his ailing pet monkey was suffering from mounting apprehension."

Definitions

111.38

A psychologist is a man who, when a good-looking girl enters the room, looks at everybody else.

111.39

Psychiatrist: A doctor who doesn't have to worry so long as other people do.

111.40

A neurotic is a man who builds a castle in the air. A psychotic is the man who lives in it. And a psychiatrist is the man who collects the rent.

—*Lord Webb-Johnson,* Look, 1955

111.41

A neurotic is a person who, when you ask how she is, tells you.

111.42

Harold Rome says that a psychotic asserts, "Two and two are five and I'll fight any man who says me nay." The neurotic says, "Two and two are four, and I simply can't stand it."

Aphorisms

111.43

There's nothing wrong with the average person that a good psychiatrist can't exaggerate.

—*Toronto Star*

(*See also 103.3, 173.2, 215.15, 272.22*)

THE HUMOR OF SCIENCE

112. Scientists-at-large

Anecdotes

112.1

Scientists at the U.S. Bureau of Standards had some sport with mathematics by proving Heaven is hotter than Hell. The heavenly temperature is determined by combining Biblical data from Isaiah with the Stefan-Holzmann "fourth power law" for radiation, resulting in a temperature of 977°. Hell, they argued, must be cooler than 832°, because higher temperatures would evaporate brimstone into gas. Thus Heaven is 145° hotter than Hell.

112.2

Dr. Karl Compton of M.I.T. tells about the time his sister lived in India and hired a native electrician to do some work in her home. But the man kept coming to her for instructions concerning how to do this and that. Finally, exasperated, she said, "You know what has to be done. Why not just go ahead and use your common sense?"

"Madam," said the young Indian with becoming gravity, "common sense is a gift of God, and I have only a technical education."

112.3

One summer evening an engineer and inventor drove up to his summer cottage but when he got to the door realized his house key was on the ignition key ring and that it was in the car which had locked from the inside when he closed the car door. He tried the windows of the house, but they were all locked. He went back to the car at the road side and started to break a window to get the keys, when a truck pulled up. The truck driver got out, learned the man's plight, returned to his truck for a coat hanger, which he bent into a hook with a long handle. He snaked this through a small opening in the car window next to the driver's seat and manipulated it until he retrieved the keys in the car. When he handed the keys to the grateful inventor and engineer, he said, "It's brain work, Mister—you gotta use the old bean!"

112.4

Thomas A. Edison, never a social lion, one day found himself at an unusually boring affair and gradually worked his way toward the door in order to make his escape at the first opportunity. At this point his host came up and said, "It's certainly a great honor to have you with us, Mr. Edison. What are you working on now?"

"On my exit," said Mr. Edison.

112.5

One day Thomas A. Edison was showing guests through his summer home, taking pride in pointing out the various labor-saving devices he had installed. At one point of the tour of the grounds the guests had to pass through a turnstile which took quite a bit of force to move.

"Mr. Edison," said one of the guests, "it is strange that the turnstile is so difficult to push when all the other devices here work so well."

"Oh," laughed Edison, "every time one pushes through the turnstile, he pumps 6 gallons of water into the tank on the roof."

112.6

Two little boys decided one day to play a joke on their friend, Charles Darwin. They caught a butterfly, a grasshopper, a beetle, and a centipede, and from various parts of these creatures they carefully constructed a weird-looking composite insect, put it in a box and brought it to the famous scientist.

"What kind of a bug is this, Mr. Darwin?" they asked with a show of innocence.

Darwin looked at the "bug," smiled, and asked: "Did it hum when you caught it?"

"Yes, Sir, it did."

"Well, then," declared the scientist, "I would call it a humbug."

112.7

One day the phone rang in the home of Robert A. Millikan, the famous physicist. Mrs. Millikan went to answer the phone, but the maid had already picked up the receiver. Mrs. Millikan heard her say, "Yes, Ma'am, this is where Dr. Millikan lives, but he ain't the kind of doctor that does anybody any good."

112.8

When a new night watchman for an astronomical observatory arrived for work, he watched one of the astronomers aiming a gigantic telescope at the heavens. Suddenly a shooting star swung out and fell through space.

"That was a good shot, sir," said the simple lad.

112.9

When Benjamin Franklin was U.S. Ambassador to France he witnessed one of the first balloon flights over the city of Paris. As the large bag drifted slowly out of sight, a man turned to Franklin and said, "What possible good could a balloon be?"

"What good is a newborn baby?" countered Franklin as he still gazed skyward.

112.10

The pretty but not-quite-bright sophomore in college was seated next to a famous astronomer at a dinner party and asked him what work he was engaged in.

"I study astronomy," said the scientist.

"My goodness, I finished that last year," said the young woman.

112.11

One of the marvels for the home now being perfected in the scientific laboratories of modern industry is an ingenious device whereby when one presses a button two sticks spring into action—they automatically rub against each other and light the gas in the kitchen stove.

112.12

In opposing funds for education, a backwoods legislator said, "Science is making education useless. For example, I took up larnin' so's I could read, then they come along with talkin' pictures, so what use was the readin' education?"

Definitions

112.13

Science: An orderly arrangement of what at the moment seem to be facts.

—*Research Viewpoints*

112.14

Science: The creation of dilemmas by the solution of mysteries.

112.15

Science: A first-rate piece of furniture for a man's upper chamber if he has common sense on the ground floor.

—*Oliver Wendell Holmes*

Aphorisms

112.16

Scientists animated by the purpose of proving that they are purposeless are an interesting subject for study.

—*Alfred North Whitehead,* The Function of Reason

112.17

Scientists are men who prolong life so we can have time to pay for the gadgets they invent.

112.18

Technological progress has merely provided us with more efficient means for going backwards.

—*Aldous Huxley*

112.19

One humiliating thing about science is that it is gradually filling our homes with appliances smarter than we are.

—*Anonymous*

112.20

The highest explosive known to science is made by combining idle hands and addled minds.

112.21

Science is resourceful. It couldn't pry open the Pullman windows, so it air-conditioned the trains.

—Montreal Star

(*See also 113.1–113.3, 113.5, 113.6, 114.3, 114.4, 115.3–115.5, 117.1, 205.14, 205.15, 269.47*)

113. The Jargon of Science

Anecdotes

113.1

Albert Einstein, asked to explain his theory of relativity in language the layman could understand, said: "I was walking once in the country with a friend who was blind. I observed that I would like a drink of cool milk. 'Milk?' asked my friend. 'Drink I know—but what is milk?'

"'It is a white liquid,' I told him.

"'Liquid, yes—but white—what is that?'

"'White is the color of a swan's feathers.'

"'Feathers I know—but swan I do not.'

"'A swan is a bird with a crooked neck.'

"'Neck, of course, but what is meant by crooked?'

"I took his arm and straightened it, then bent it at the elbow, and told him that is crooked.

"'Oh,' exclaimed my blind friend, 'now I know what you mean by milk.'"

113.2

Albert Einstein was fond of telling about the time the question of relativity came up during the meeting of a debating society. One of the members volunteered to explain the profound theory of Einstein's, and he tried to do so for an hour, getting himself and his listeners hopelessly involved in words, jargon, and misinformation.

Finally one of the listeners spoke up: "I think you are really greater than Einstein on relativity. It is said that only ten men in the world thoroughly understand Einstein's theory of relativity. But no one understands you."

113.3

Albert Einstein is reported to have explained relativity in this fashion: "When you are with a pretty girl for three hours, and it seems like only three minutes, and then you sit on a hot stove for a minute and think it's a hour—well, that is relativity."

113.4

Relativity: The fly tiptoeing at one foot a minute across the bald head of the brakeman staggering at three miles an hour along the top of a freight train high-balling at forty miles an hour on a world spinning at 900 miles an hour and chasing its orbit at eighteen and one-half miles a second in a solar system scurrying toward the Hercules constellation at twelve and one-half miles a second.

—*Burton Crane*

113.5

Robert Sommer in an article titled "Einstein's Girl Friday" wrote, "It is axiomatic that a lab can produce only as fast as its secretary can type. When four or five people share the same secretary, everyone hovers over the secretary's desk to see if she is typing his work rather than someone else's." This caused Mr. Sommer to formulate a law of productivity for any laboratory, expressed thus:

P (productivity) equals number of secretaries times average typing speed divided by number of scientists.

In other words, the lab with only one scientist and four secretaries, typing say sixty words a minute, is much more efficient than the lab with four scientists and one secretary typing at the same speed. Or—

$$P = \frac{4 \times 60}{1} = 240$$

compared with

$$P = \frac{1 \times 60}{4} = 15$$

Mr. Sommer's final conclusion is: "One interesting feature of this equation is that when the number of scientists is zero, productivity becomes infinite."

113.6

William Gilman, in an article "Science Laughs at Itself," New York *Times Magazine,* March 18, 1962, speaks of scientists developing the so-called Laws of Murphy, also known as Finagle's Laws. These travesties on the laws of thermodynamics are:

"First Law: If anything can go wrong with an experiment, it will.

"Second Law: No matter what result is anticipated, there is always someone willing to fake it.

"Third Law: No matter what the result, there is always someone eager to misinterpret it."

113.7

An article in the *Arkansas Engineer* was titled "The Stress Analysis of a Strapless Evening Gown" and later was used as the title of a book of scientific humor.

113.8

The *Industrial Bulletin* issued by Arthur D. Little, Inc., in discussing electroencephalography, referred to the process as "decoding the code in the head."

113.9

A student at the University of Pennsylvania, fascinated by jargon, sketched an imaginary "vector injector" and ended up with a bucketful of vectors, which he captioned "Vector injector reflector sector reflector selector director erector rejector corrector deflector inspector connector collector ejector." This performance was later published in the magazine *CQ*.

114. Atoms and Electrons

Anecdotes

114.1

When the atomic bomb was being developed in the utmost possible secrecy at Oak Ridge, Tennessee, the workers—most of whom had no idea what it was all about—often explained to questioners that "this is where the front end of horses are made. Then we ship them to the Pentagon for final assembly."

114.2

Leonard Lyons tells about some Indians in the Las Vegas area who, for old times' sake, still communicated with one another through smoke signals. One day in July, 1945, an Indian sent up smoke signals asking another one a question. He did not get a reply immediately, but presently the sky was alight from a terrific explosion in the direction of Almagordo—the most spectacular signal the Indian had ever seen. When all had once again quieted down, the Indian signaled back to his friend—"All right, I got your message, but you didn't have to get so mad about it."

114.3

Ralph Cooper, a theoretical physicist at Los Alamos, in a waggish moment but not without a certain seriousness, suggests a "neutrino" bomb, the explosion of which would create a vacuum; into it would rush the surrounding air with a terrifying bang. Mr. Cooper said the bang would be so loud that the world would stop, listen, and consider where it is heading.

114.4

During a convention of atomic scientists at Las Vegas, one of the professors spent all his free time at the gambling tables.

"Hotchkiss gambles as if there were no tomorrow" observed one of his colleagues.

"Maybe," said another, "he knows something."

—*E. E. Kenyon,* American Weekly

114.5

In his highly readable *Deadlines and Monkeyshines,* John J. McPhaul tells about Sam X, a newspaper photographer who was sent to cover a reunion of nuclear scientists at the University of Chicago in 1952. These were the men who ten years earlier had achieved the first self-sustaining chain reaction, thereby controlling the release of nuclear energy. Sam X had but the scantiest background information. However, he rounded up such giants as Vannevar Bush, Enrico Fermi, Arthur H. Compton, and Harold C. Urey and told them he had three pictures in mind: one of them putting the atom in the machine, another of the splitting of the atom, and finally a picture of the scientists looking at the pieces of the split atom.

114.6

When the world was destroyed by nuclear warfare the sole survivors were two monkeys in an African jungle. They discussed the situation, and one of them asked the other, "Shall we start the whole thing all over again?"

Definition

114.7

Atom: A subdivision of matter that is likely to be the death of the subdivision business.

(*See also 43.19, 211.13, 218.15, 268.34*)

115. Tales from a Test Tube

Anecdotes

115.1

Frantic chemist to his boss: "We can't conform to these specifications. We've combined trillium, chlorophyll, irium, phosphate and X 29, but there's no room left for toothpaste!"

—*Bernhardy* in Christian Science Monitor

115.2

In illustrating how "correlation" can misguide the scientific method, Anthony Standen in his *Science Is a Sacred Cow* writes:

"A man gets drunk on Monday on whisky and soda water; he gets drunk on Tuesday on brandy and soda water, and on Wednesday on gin and soda water. What caused his drunkenness? Obviously, the common factor, the soda water."

115.3

A manufacturer of insecticides asked a research laboratory to make a study of fleas. The task was given to an earnest young man who first read all the literature he could find on fleas, then carefully selected a particular flea to be trained. His report stated in great detail how he trained the flea to leap over his finger when commanded to "jump." Then he pulled off one of the flea's legs, but still the creature jumped upon command. Two more legs were removed, and still the flea jumped. Finally the earnest researcher pulled off the flea's remaining legs, but after this the flea did not jump when commanded. "One of our major findings," read the research man's report, "is that when all a flea's legs are removed, the insect becomes deaf."

115.4

Reporting to a conference the results of his years of research, the scientist said that the findings could best be summed up by saying eventually man would be born without teeth. A young and much less learned man at the conference observed that men are already born without teeth.

115.5

The head of the research department of one of the big pharmaceutical houses said to his boss:

"Something's got to be done about our research so that we can develop new products at least one-third as fast as does our publicity department."

115.6

In one issue of *The Worm Runner's Digest, An Informal Journal of Comparative Psychology,* published irregularly by the Planaria Research Group, department of psychology, the University of Michigan, appeared "Research Man's Prayer," which begins: "Help me to be Manic so I may be joyous though results are equivocal; help me be Depressive, for when a prediction is verified I must know that it will not later be confirmed." The prayer ends with, "Finally, help my wife get a job! For when I cross over the shadowy border of normalcy, someone will have to support the kids."

Definition

115.7

Research is something that tells you that a jackass has two ears.

—*Albert D. Lasker*

Aphorism

115.8

Basic research is what I am doing when I don't know what I am doing.

—*Werner von Braun*

OUT OF THIS WORLD

116. Astronauts

Anecdotes

116.1

A man with precognition reports that when the first Americans landed on the moon a man sent out to reconnoiter reported by walkie-talkie that a weird-looking character was coming toward him. "He's got a head like a corkscrew; he's comin' closer, and I'm going to incinerate him with my ray gun!" said the advance man. "Relax," radioed the commanding officer. "One with a corkscrew head is not likely to be bringing bad news."

116.2

Astronauts in training asked a veteran occupant of space capsules what his advice to them would be. "Don't look down," he replied.

116.3

A commentator on the Armenian radio, speaking of the orbital flights of Russian astronauts, said they must be crazy, since "nobody in his right mind would fly around the world so many times and then land in the Soviet Union."

116.4

During a cocktail party at Cape Kennedy, the wife of a man working on the space shots said to him, "You've had enough martinis; you'd better fire your retro-rocket."

116.5

Overheard at Cape Kennedy: "He's a fine fellow practically all of the time, but he is inclined to blow up without any countdown."

116.6

O Moon, when I gaze on thy beautiful face,
Careering along through boundaries of space,
The thought has often come into my mind,
If I ever shall see thy glorious behind.

—*Anonymous,* from the nineteenth century

116.7

Space is very large. It is immense, very immense. A great deal of immensity exists in space. Space has no top, no bottom. In fact, it is bottomless both at the bottom and at the top. Space extends as far backwards as it does forward, and *vice versa.* There is no compass of space, nor points of the compass, and no boxing of the compass. A billion million miles traveled in space won't bring a man nearer than one mile or one inch. Consequently, in space, it's better to stay where you are, and let well enough alone.

—*Bill Nye*

Definition

116.8

Astronaut: A cloud hopper.

Aphorisms

116.9

When we get to the point of sending three men up in one space capsule, there is bound to be an argument about who sits by the window.

116.10

If athletes suffer from athlete's foot, do astronauts get mistle toe?

(*See also 229.28, 230.6*)

117. Martians and Little Green Men

Anecdotes

117.1

Scientists of the University of Chicago have lately detected something that looks like moss growing on the planet Mars. Perhaps Mars was once inhabited by beings like ourselves, who had the misfortune, some millions of years ago, to invent television.

—*Robert M. Hutchins*

117.2

A new arrival from Mars wandered into Las Vegas and watched a group of people grasping the arm of a slot machine. When the crowd drifted away the Martian went up to the machine and said, "Listen fellow, if you're going to get elected you'll have to show more personality and smile when you greet the voters."

117.3

A Martian wandered from his space ship in the desert into Las Vegas and arrived when one of the slot machines was spewing forth a batch of nickels. When the exploding gadget had subsided, the Martian went over to it and said, "With a cold like that, you ought to take some aspirin and get into bed."

117.4

A Martian, reporting to his home headquarters after a visit to earth, told about a new electronic computer. "She's a knockout, and besides she's got some brain."

117.5

Joey Adams said that when a truck rounded a corner too fast, and a package fell off, a Martian ran after it yelling, "Hey, lady, you dropped your purse!"

117.6

A Martian visitor, who had availed himself of all the comforts and conveniences of our civilization and had done some traveling about the country, was getting restless, and since his space ship had returned home, he went to a travel agency for suggestions.

"Where do you want to go?" the travel man asked the Martian.

"Let's see your globe," said the Martian.

He looked over the globe carefully, shook his head, and said to the travel man, "Is this all there is? Haven't you anything else to offer?"

117.7

Gerald F. Lieberman looked into his crystal ball and reported that in the year 2100 a visitor to Venus saw a Venusian place a coin into what appeared to be a cigarette machine, and out popped a baby. They explained to him that it was their baby machine and asked him, "Don't you make babies that way on earth?"

The man from earth then explained to the Venusian the way in which babies are conceived on earth—sparing no detail.

"Oh," said one of the Venusians, "That's how we make trucks up here."

117.8

A strange-looking creature from outer space—one with small feet attached directly to the abdomen, arms of appalling length and thinness, a head that appeared to operate on a swivel, and a back and a front eye—walked into a small hospital in midtown New York and asked for the head doctor.

"We can do nothing for you," said the receptionist. "You better go over to the Hospital for Special Surgery."

117.9

Two arrivals from outer space arrived quietly in Manhattan and set out to explore the city. One of them went up to a traffic stanchion on Fifth Avenue and noticing the changing lights asked, "Where is your leader?" When no reply was forthcoming, the second man from outer space said, "Come on, let's try someone else; this guy is stupid."

117.10

Two monsters from far out in space wandered into New York City one night late and began prowling for some food. They spotted some garbage cans and began to chew them up. After a few minutes one of the repulsive characters said, "The outside is all right—nice crust—but the filling is too rich."

ON THE CAMPUS

118. Prexies and Presidents

Anecdotes

118.1

An English headmaster received a letter from a mother who said that before she sent her boy to the school, she must ask whether the school was very particular about the social background of the students.

The headmaster wrote Mrs. Snob: "Dear Madam: As long as your son behaves himself and his fees are paid, no questions will be asked concerning his social background."

118.2

In the early 1920s Harvard University became alarmed by the influx of Jews and decided on subtle measures to impose a quota system. One day the Harvard Admissions Board was examining the application of a young man who looked Semitic. They did not want to tip their hand by a direct question, so they asked him, "What language do you speak in your home?"

"Oh," said the candidate, "we always speak English. But I think I could learn enough Yiddish to find my way around the campus."

118.3

One day President Neilsen of Smith College received a letter from a Southern woman, stating she wanted to register her daughter for Smith, but that she had heard Smith had colored girls in its student body. Neilsen replied to the anxious lady and told her that Smith did have Negro girls, but that the college had no objection—nor did the colored girls—to the woman sending her daughter to Smith.

118.4

Woodrow Wilson, who was president of Princeton University before he was President of the United States, used to tell about a group of college professors who were considering the misconduct of a certain student. One of the professors urged that severe punishment be given the lad. "After all," he said, "God has given us eyes."

"Yes," replied another professor, "and he has also given us eyelids!"

118.5

A college president, pestered by parental questions concerning the college course and the treatment of students, finally in exasperation wired: SATISFACTION GUARANTEED OR WE RETURN THE BOY.

118.6

A small but venerable New England college had invited a great number of scholars from all over the nation to attend its centennial celebration. They arrived, of course, with their gowns and bright hoods.

The academic procession was to march to the chapel, headed by the president of the college.

As the procession came to the chapel entrance, the president hesitated, for he realized he would be sitting on the platform for close to three hours. He turned to the two men back of him, then stepped out of line.

But the two men back of him misunderstood him. They followed him, the whole academic procession followed them; and they all headed for the men's room.

118.7

A university president was brought before the board of trustees charged with drunkenness. The houseman employed by the president was called as a witness. "Did you ever see the president intoxicated?"

"No, Sir."

"Don't you know that he was drunk on Commencement Day last?" asked the examiner.

"I know he was *not* drunk," said the houseman.

"How do you know that?"

"You know them three flights of stairs in the president's house, two of them curving? No man is drunk who can slide down all those bannisters without losing cap or gown or hood or balance."

118.8

Harvard President C. W. Eliot, congratulated for making Harvard a "storehouse of knowledge," agreed it was true but said it was primarily a result of the fact that the freshmen bring so much knowledge in, and the seniors take so little out.

118.9

One day President Neilsen of Smith College received a letter from an irate resident who complained that her family was annoyed by Smith girls disrobing in the dormitories without drawing the shades. Neilsen wrote back that the college would much prefer that the girls drew their shades when undressing, but he suggested that the residents of the town were not compelled to look at the girls—that the residents could simply draw their own shades.

118.10

The grassplots in the college courts or quadrangles are not for the unhallowed feet of the undergraduates. A master of Trinity had often observed a student of his college invariably to cross the green. One day the master determined to reprove the delinquent for invading the rights of his superiors, and for that purpose he threw up the sash at which he was sitting and called to the student: "Sir, I never look out of my window but I see you walking across the grassplot."

"My lord," replied the offender instantly, "I never walk across the grassplot, but I *see you* looking out of your window." The master, pleased at the readiness of the reply, closed his window, convulsed with laughter.

118.11

The freshman dean had dark circles under his eyes when he came to breakfast. His wife asked him what was wrong.

"Had a terrible dream last night," he said. "I dreamed that the trustees required that—that I should—that I should pass the freshman test for admission," sighed the dean.

118.12

Some years ago Annie Besant, a noted theosophist, took an East Indian named Krishnamurti under her wing. He was at that time believed by many to be an avatar of the Eternal Vishnu. Mrs. Besant wanted Krishnamurti entered at Oxford University. She told the dean of Christ Church, Oxford, that Krishnamurti was nothing less than the Messiah, but the dean thought that this would render the young man a bit too conspicuous. At Balliol she was again turned down, for substantially the same reason. Finally Mrs. Besant spoke to the dean of Magdalen, the snootiest of all the Oxford colleges. She retracted nothing concerning Krishnamurti, even going so far as to state that he was nothing less than the Everlasting God Himself, and wondered if this could be an objection.

"By all means," said the dean, "let him come to Magdalen. Our undergraduates will accept him on terms of almost perfect equality."

118.13

The dean of women at a large coeducational college began her announcement to the student body with: "The president of the college and I have decided to stop necking on the campus."

118.14

During a discussion among college executives concerning what they would like to do when they reached retirement, one said he would like to run a prison or a school of correction because the alumni would never come back to visit. Another chose an orphan asylum so that he would not be plagued with the advice of parents.

118.15

In the first place God made idiots; this was for practice; then he made school boards.

—*Mark Twain*

(*See also 154.6, 207.13*)

119. Classroom Capers

Anecdotes

119.1

The absent-minded professor of biology said to the class: "I have in this package an excellent specimen of a frog I dissected." Upon opening the package he found it contained a sandwich and a piece of pie.

"Strange," said the bewildered man, "I know I've already eaten lunch."

119.2

Sir James M. Barrie's favorite story was about the professor of biology who explained to his class the spawning of fish. "So you see," he concluded, "the female fish deposits her eggs, the male fish comes along and fertilizes them, and later the little fish are hatched."

One of the girls raised her hand. "You mean, Professor, that the father and mother fish—that they—that before that nothing happens?"

"Nothing," said the professor, "which doubtless explains the expression, 'poor fish.' "

—*Henry P. Moriarty,* Coronet

119.3

"You can't sleep in my class," said the professor sternly.

"I could if you didn't talk so loud," said the student.

119.4

It's an old story, the one about the professor who dreamed he was lecturing his class—and woke up to find that it was true.

119.5

Professor: "I won't begin today's lecture until the room settles down."

Voice from the rear: "Go home and sleep it off, old man."

119.6

"When does a book become a classic?" asked the English teacher.

"When people who haven't read it begin to say they have," replied the astute pupil.

119.7

"I don't think we'll do too bad," said the student to the professor in referring to an upcoming football game.

The professor chided him for his bad grammar, pointing out that he should have said badly.

"Oh," said the student, "what difference does an 'ly' make?"

"Well," said the professor, "suppose you see a girl coming down the street; it makes a difference whether you look at her stern, or sternly."

119.8

"Now, Mr. Adams," said the professor, "what can you tell us about French syntax?"

"I didn't know they had to pay for it," replied the student.

119.9

Professor: "If I saw a man beating a donkey and stopped him from doing so, what virtue would I be showing?"

Voice from the Rear of the Classroom: "Brotherly love."

119.10

Professor: "Name a product the supply of which always exceeds the demand."

"Trouble," answered one young scholar.

119.11

Professor: "Why don't you answer me?"

Student: "I did, professor—I shook my head."

Professor: "You don't expect me to hear it rattle way up here, do you?"

119.12

The bell rang when the professor was in the middle of his closing remarks. As the students began to close their books and arise from their desks, the professor called out, "Please, just a minute more. I have a few more pearls to cast."

119.13

The professor wanted to make a point in logic to his class, so he said: "The United States is bound on the south by Mexico, on the north by Canada, on the east by the Atlantic Ocean, and on the west by the Pacific Ocean. Now how old am I?"

"You are forty-eight," called out one of the students.

"How did you arrive at that?" asked the surprised professor.

"It was easy," said the student. "My twenty-four-year-old brother is only half crazy."

119.14

Those who have panaceas for the world's ills should remember the professor who was approached by a student who said, "I have invented a universal solvent. This chemical will dissolve anything and everything."

"Fine," said the professor, "but what are you going to keep it in?"

119.15

Professor: "What is the most important fact about nitrates?"

Student: "They are lower than day rates."

119.16

"What does HNO_3 stand for?" asked the professor of chemistry.

"It stands for . . . er . . . er . . . oh, I've got it on the tip of my tongue," said the student.

"Well," snapped the professor, "you better spit it out; it's nitric acid."

119.17

"Young man," said the professor to a student who kept interrupting, "are you trying to instruct the class?"

"No, Sir," said the student.

"Well then, don't talk like an idiot."

119.18

"If there are any morons in the room I would like them to stand," said the professor at the beginning of the term.

After a brief pause, one student stood up.

"Do you consider yourself a moron?" asked the professor in surprise.

"Not really," said the student. "But I felt sorry for you standing up there alone."

119.19

In Wilmington, Delaware, the local Power Squadron class was taking an oral quiz, and the instructor asked a female student, "What signal would you give if you were coming out of your slip slowly stern first?"

—*Ellen Crossman,* Wilmington Sunday Star

119.20

Student: "Sir, I don't think that I deserve a zero on that examination."

"You don't, but it's the lowest mark I can give."

119.21

One of the questions on a college examination was: "How would you determine the height of a building through the use of an aneroid barometer?"

An ingenious but not studious pupil gave this answer: "I would lower the barometer on a string and then measure the string."

119.22

The professor in going over examination papers encountered one that had only two or three answers to the simpler questions asked, followed by the drawing of a tombstone on which the student had written: "Sacred to the memory which always deserts me on occasions such as this."

119.23

On an examination paper just before Christmas, one of Yale professor William Lyon Phelps's students wrote across his paper, "God only knows the answers to these questions. Merry Christmas," and handed in the paper.

Professor returned the paper with his notation: "God gets an A. You get an F. Happy New Year."

119.24

A medical student under examination, being asked the different effects of heat and cold, replied: "Heat expands and cold contracts."

"Quite right; can you give me an example?"

"Yes, Sir, in summer, which is hot, the days are longer; but in winter, which is cold, the days are shorter."

119.25

The medical student struggled frantically and desperately over a tough examination. When he came to the question, "How would you induce copious perspiration?" He promptly replied, "I would have the patient take this medical examination."

119.26

An Oxford medical student dug up an ancient University regulation that said he was entitled to a pint of beer as refreshment while cramming for final exams. He was so persistent that the authorities finally gave in and provided him with his pint.

They also searched the regulation, and fined him five pounds for not wearing a sword.

—*The Lancet,* quoted by UP

119.27

The professor called on a student in medical school to state how much of a certain drug he would give a patient, and the young man promptly said, "Five grains."

A minute later the student raised his hand and told the professor he wanted to correct his answer. The professor looked at his watch and said, "It is too late. Your patient died thirty seconds ago."

119.28

The professor in the medical school exhibited a diagram and said, "The subject here limps, because one leg is shorter than the other. Can one of the students tell me what he would do in such a case?"

"I'd limp, too," replied the first boy to answer.

119.29

Legend has it that a candidate for a doctorate at the University of Rochester had his subject matter approved and the research work given the official OK. But the title of his paper, he was told, would have to be changed. It had been titled "The Position of Women under King Henry VIII."

119.30

The story has been pinned on several undergraduates, but there is no question that the beloved Charles Townsend Copeland, English Professor at Harvard and spiritual father of many authors, set it up.

A Radcliffe student, counting on "Copey" being late to his lecture, slipped into her front-row seat after Copey was seated behind his desk. He looked at her over his glasses for a long moment. When she seemed sufficiently cowed, he inquired, "And how will you have your tea, Miss Parks?"

"Without lemon, please, Professor Copeland."

119.31

A student in the class of C. T. Copeland, Harvard's famous professor of English literature, was indignant at a scathing criticism the professor had given of one of the student's efforts. "Professor," said the young man in class, "I glued several pages together in the middle of my paper, which apparently was never noticed by you. This proves you don't read that far."

"My boy," replied Copeland, "one does not have to eat a whole egg to know that it is bad."

119.32

Maxwell Droke says it actually happened in Boston College: A young priest was delivering a long and complex lecture, when a student arose and asked the professor for documentary evidence in support of the various statements he had made. The professor explained that there was an abundance of evidence which he could easily enough produce, but that of course he did not have it with him. "Well, sir," said the obnoxious show-off, "until you produce the documentary evidence, do you mind if for the time being I call you a liar?"

Amid the stunned silence, the professor asked the young man for his parents' marriage certificate. The student of course was unable to produce it. "Well, sir," said the professor coldly, "until you can produce documentary evidence, would you mind if I called you an impudent bastard?"

119.33

Some years ago Dr. Francis Wayland was speaking to a class at Brown University and praised the Proverbs of the Old Testament. A supercilious student interrupted to say that he didn't think much of the Proverbs—"They are rather commonplace remarks of common people."

"All right," said Wayland, "make *one*."

119.34

Teacher: "Can anyone in the class give the number of tons of aluminum exported by the U.S. in any given year?"

Student: "The year 1492—none."

Definition

119.35

Lecture: A process by which the notes of the professor are passed to the pupils without passing through the brains of either.

—*Anonymous*

(*See also 174.1–174.36*)

120. Professors-at-large

Anecdotes

120.1

A University of Texas ichthyologist, walking across the campus with a colleague, was greeted cordially by several students, but answered them with marked impersonality. "How is it that you don't know the names of those friendly students of yours?" asked the colleague.

"I have made it a point," said the ichthyologist, "never to learn the names of my students. Whenever I remember a student I forget a fish."

120.2

The professor of economics stood in his bathing suit at the edge of the college pool when a co-ed's camera fell into the water. She asked the professor to help her retrieve the camera, which he did without too much difficulty. When he handed it to her, he said he was curious to know why she had called on him when there were so many young and expert swimmers at hand. "But, Professor," she replied, "I'm in one of your classes, and I know you can go down deeper and come up drier than any other man in the college."

120.3

"Curious how Napoleon's greatest detractors have all come to horrible ends. Castlereagh cut his throat. Louis the Eighteenth rotted to death on his throne. And Professor Saalfeld still teaches at Gottingen."

—*Heinrich Heine*

120.4

Another absent-minded professor said, "I have three pairs of glasses. One pair is for short sight, another for long sight, and the third to look for the other two."

120.5

They say that Gotthold Lessing, the German poet, was coming home one dark night, but discovered that he had forgotten his house key. He knocked at the door. A servant opened an upper window and called out, "The professor hasn't come home yet."

"Oh, I'm sorry," called back Lessing. "Tell him I'll stop by later."

120.6

A pretentious college professor was being rowed across a stream out West and asked the boatman: "Do you understand philosophy?"

"Never heard of it," said the boatman.

"Well," said the professor, "one-fourth of your life is gone. What do you know about geology?"

"Nothing at all," said the boatman.

"Then that makes one-half of your life gone," declared the professor.

Just then the boat tipped over. The boatman asked, "Can you swim?"

"No," gasped the professor.

"Then your whole life is gone," said the boatman.

120.7

When various professions met at a convention, there was conversation in the lobby just before dinner.

"My name is Rodale. I'm a painter, work in water colors chiefly."

"I'm particularly happy to know you," replied another. "I'm an artist, too. I work in bronze."

"Now, isn't this a coincidence," chimed a third. "I happen to be a sculptor. I work in marble."

Then a quiet little fellow, who had kept apart, stepped up and extended his hand, "Glad to make the acquaintance of you gentlemen, for I have a common interest with all of you. I work in ivory. I am a college professor."

120.8

A professor of mathematics was bitterly opposed to coeducation. He said it was difficult and often impossible to teach a boy mathematics if there were girls in the class.

Someone who opposed this theory said to the professor, "This may be true of some boys, but there are exceptions."

"There might be an exception," the professor snapped back, "but he wouldn't be worth teaching!"

Definitions

120.9

A professor is a man whose job is to tell students how to solve the problems of life which he himself tried to avoid by becoming a professor.

120.10

A professor is one who talks in someone else's sleep.

—*W. H. Auden*

120.11

A teacher is a person who swore he would starve before teaching and has done both ever since.

Aphorisms

120.12

A.M. after a professor's name means absent-minded.

120.13

College professors divide up what's left after the football coach is paid.

120.14

A retired mathematics professor called his house After Math.

(*See also 15.3, 118.6, 118.10, 118.11, 119.2–119.5, 119.20, 119.22, 119.23, 119.27, 119.30–119.33, 119.35, 196.11, 205.14, 267.3, 271.25, 271.29, 271.49*)

121. The Big Game

Anecdotes

121.1

One of the more spectacular Notre Dame football teams had the experts puzzled at half time of an important game when it trudged back to the dressing room, a badly whipped and bewildered aggregation of young men.

When the team returned to the field for the last half of the game, the young collegians played as though enraged, tearing through their opponents like inspired madmen, and winning the game by a wide margin. It was a surprising transformation from a first-half lacklustre team to a second-half maniacal rushing machine.

Between halves the team had sat morosely in the dressing room awaiting Coach Knute Rockne and the inevitable thunder.

Shortly before time to go on the field for resumption of play the door opened. Rockne stood at the threshold, glanced swiftly over the players, bowed gently but unsmiling, then turned and left as he said over his shoulder, "I beg your pardon, girls, but I thought this was the Notre Dame football team."

121.2

One of Notre Dame's football stars had gone in for some fancy footwork and showboating during a game and as a consequence was repeatedly thrown for losses by a player on the opposing team. When he was lifted from the game, the star sat crestfallen on the bench and turned to Coach Knute Rockne, saying "I'm sorry I messed things up like that. I had no idea that guy was so fast and smart."

"Oh, it's not your fault," said Rockne. "The only thing is, you should have shown him your press clippings. Then he wouldn't have dared put a hand on you."

121.3

A reporter accompanied the Notre Dame football team on one of its game trips. He asked the coach, "I understand you always take a chaplain with you on these trips?"

"That's right," said the coach.

"I would like to meet him," said the reporter; "would you introduce me?"

"Sure—I would be glad to," said coach. "Which one did you want to meet—the offensive or the defensive chaplain?"

121.4

A Notre Dame football star was subpoenaed to appear in a South Bend court as a witness in a civil suit. "Are you on the Notre Dame football team this year?" asked the judge.

"Yes, Your Honor."

"What position?"

"Center, Your Honor."

"How good a center?"

The player squirmed in his chair, but in confident tones admitted, "Sir, I'm the best center Notre Dame ever had."

Coach Frank Leahy, in the court, surprised by this statement from an always modest and unassuming lad, later asked him why he had made such a statement.

"I hated to, Coach, but I had no choice. I was under oath."

121.5

During the 1952 Notre Dame–Oklahoma football game the Oklahoma team suddenly developed an epidemic of fumbling; they just couldn't hold on to the ball. As the team waited on the field to resume play for the second half, the band was finishing its routine on the field, in the course of which the Oklahoma drum major threw his baton in the air—and failed to catch it when it descended.

"Look at that!" yelled a fan. "Wilkinson [the Oklahoma coach] even coaches the band."

121.6

When Hugh Devore was coaching New York University's football team, and the team was going downhill rapidly, someone suggested that he change his psychology and tell the boys exactly how bad they were. "It might do something to them," added the adviser.

"Too risky," said Devore. "If I tell them how bad they are, they are very likely to believe it."

121.7

When Bernie Bierman was coach of the University of Minnesota football team, he said that he found prospects for the team by driving through the country and, when he saw a young fellow plowing, stopped and asked him the direction to town. If the fellow pointed with his arm, Bierman drove on. But if the fellow lifted the plow and pointed with it, then Bierman signed him up for the University.

121.8

During one of the traditional Cornell-Columbia football games the Columbia players were being bowled over easier than tenpins. Columbia coach Lou Little called time to make a substitution, but before the replacement went into the game, he was put on the field phone to take instructions from the Columbia spotter high up in the stands. While the player stood listening with the phone to his ear, a fan yelled out, "The poor guy's saying good-bye to his mother."

121.9

The Yale football team was returning from Georgia after taking a fearful beating that afternoon at Athens. While the Yale men lounged in the car, nursing their bruises, a Yale rooter staggered through the car, so drunk that he seemed not to mind the loss. He stumbled over the feet of one of the Yale linemen. "Where you goin'?" the drunk asked the lineman.

"I'm not going any place," said the player.

"Hey, Coach," called the drunk, "put him in the Yale backfield."

121.10

When Yale coach Herman Hickman addressed a group of Yale old grads, he discussed the team and his coaching problems, then, with that engaging charm of his, said that he could win more games than he did, but that he did not like to establish a standard that some years might be difficult to duplicate. "My aim," he concluded, "is to lose just enough games to keep the alumni sullen, but not mutinous."

121.11

In asking the state legislature for more funds for the University of Oklahoma, president George L. Cross said, "We're working to develop a university the football team will be proud of."

—*Time*

121.12

On his way out of the stadium after his team was badly beaten, the coach was stopped by an old grad. "How many students are there in our university?" he asked the coach.

"About 14,000," replied the coach.

"Well why in hell can't two of them be put in front of the man who is carrying the ball?" asked the alumnus.

121.13

The big star had played a poor first half during the college football game. When he came back to the bench the coach said, "You're out of shape, Arbuthnot. Looks like you've been studyin' again."

121.14

The quarterback of the college team was having his hair cut six days after his team had lost a close game played on the home grounds. The barber got discussing the game and began to condemn the team's quarterback, unaware of the identity of his customer. "That quarterback shoulda hit the line more instead of trying those long passes."

"You know," said the quarterback, "I might have done that if I had had a week to think about it."

121.15

"What position does your son play on the football team, Mrs. Jones?"

"I'm not sure," replied Mrs. Jones, "but I think he's one of the drawbacks."

121.16

When a coach was asked if all the praise heaped by the press on a star athlete would not go to the young man's head, the coach said, "No, he can't read."

121.17

A dumb star athlete was instructed by his coach to sit next to the class grind for a crucial examination and to copy the grind's answers. On the thirty-fifth question the brilliant scholar wrote down, "I do not know the answer to this question." The dumb athlete wrote down, "I don't know the answer either."

121.18

The college football team was on its way home after a big victory. When the train stopped at a small town the star of the team, whose considerable vanity had been nourished by the crowds at the game, stepped out on the platform during the brief stop and responded to a ripple of applause with all the eagerness of a man running for office. As the train began to pull out the applause increased. "Too bad," said the star, "the stop here isn't longer. But it's real kind of them to keep on cheering."

"They're not cheering you," said a teammate. "They're applauding the engineer."

121.19

During one of the big college football games there had been a record number of fumbles, most of them by one team. The fumbling team's coach ordered a substitute back to warm up; during the warm-up the substitute dropped a ball that was tossed to him.

"Send him in, Coach; he's ready," called a man in the stands.

121.20

"What's the new halfback's name?" asked the coach.

"Szczuckowski," said an assistant.

"Good," said the coach, "Put him on the first team. Now watch me get back at those reporters."

121.21

During a college football game in Texas one of the co-eds, noticing that the coach was in almost constant telephone conversation with his spotters high up in the stands, said, "No wonder we're losing. Our coach is spending all his time on the telephone."

121.22

A college football coach died and by a decree of divine justice was turned over to Satan. The devil told the coach that he had been so wicked on earth he was going to be given preferred treatment in the nether regions. He was assigned to an area where some fifty football coaches were standing on tiptoe in a cesspool to their chins.

"Gosh," gasped the coach, "this is really Hell!"

"If you think this is Hell," said one of the coaches in the cesspool, "just wait until the alumni come along in their motorboats."

Aphorisms

121.23

Colleges often have an end in view when they lower their entrance requirements—or a halfback or quarterback.

121.24

A college has 2,000 seats in its classrooms and 50,000 seats in its stadium.

(*See also 119.7, 120.13, 123.6, 123.9, 125.1–125.19*)

122. The Sheepskin Parade

Anecdotes

122.1

The proud parent mentioned that his son had just earned his M.A. degree.

"I guess the next step is a Ph.D.," remarked the friend.

"Oh no," said the parent, suddenly becoming stern. "From now on he will be after a J-O-B."

122.2

"You should be ashamed of yourself to be afraid of that illiterate beast—and you with your fine education!" she declared.

"Do you expect me to beat him to death with my diploma?" he asked.

122.3

A woman had a horse she thought very smart, but her friends thought the beast stupid. To prove her point she wrote several universities and offered $50,000 to the university that would confer an honorary degree on the horse. One university accepted, and at the commencement exercises the horse was provided with cap and gown and led to the platform to receive the honorary degree—which was presented by the university president, who said, "This is the first time in the University's entire history that a degree has been conferred on a whole horse."

122.4

A Yale graduate, encountering a want ad that read, "Wanted, a Harvard man, or equivalent," answered it with this inquiry: "Do you mean that if you do not get a Harvard man, you will accept two Princeton men, or one Yale man working half-time?"

122.5

Robert Frost said that one of his granddaughters, who had attended a progressive school, told him: "At the progressive school we learned to talk about everything. And now at college we have to find out what we were talking about."

122.6

A man mistook an insane asylum for a college. When his error was pointed out to him, he said to the guard, "Well, I don't suppose there's much difference."

"There's a big difference, Mister," said the guard. "Here you have to show improvement before you get out."

122.7

"Pop, what does 'college-bred' mean?"

"They make college bred, my boy, from the flower of youth and the dough of old age."

122.8

Why study? The more we know, the more we forget. The more we forget, the less we know. The less we know, the less we forget.

The less we forget, the more we know. So why study?

—*Evan Esar,* The Humor of Humor

122.9

A pretender to knowledge one day was boring a Talmudic scholar to the point of distraction. Finally the scholar, completely out of patience, said, "You should have lived in the time of Maimonides."

"I am flattered to have you say that," replied the bore. "But just why do you say that?"

"Because," sighed the scholar, "you would have bored him instead of me."

122.10

A few centuries ago a scholarly man at a parish meeting made some proposals which were objected to by a farmer. Highly enraged, he said to the farmer, "Sir, do you know that I have been at two universities, and at two colleges in each university?"

"Well, sir," replied the farmer, "what of that? I had a calf that sucked two cows, and the observation I made was the more he sucked, the greater calf he grew."

122.11

In a certain town were four Brahmans who lived in friendship. Three of them had reached the far shore of all scholarship and lacked sense. The other found scholarship distasteful; he had nothing but sense.

One day they met for consultation. "What is the use of attainments," said they, "if one does not travel, win the favor of kings, and acquire money? Whatever we do, let us all travel."

But when they had gone a little way the eldest of them said, "One of us, the fourth, is a dullard, having nothing but sense. Now nobody gains the favorable attention of kings by simple sense without scholarship. Therefore we will not share earnings with him. Let him turn back and go home." Then the second said, "My intelligent friend, you lack scholarship. Please go home." But the third said, "No, no. This is no way to behave. For we have played together since we were little boys. Come along, my noble friend. You shall have a share of the money we earn."

With this agreement they continued their journey, and in a forest they found the bones of a dead lion. Thereupon one of them said, "A good opportunity to test the ripeness of our scholarship. Here lies some kind of creature, dead. Let us bring it to life by means of the scholarship we have honestly won."

Then the first said, "I know how to assemble the skeleton," the second said, "I can supply skin, flesh, and blood," the third said, "I can give it life."

So the first assembled the skeleton, the second provided the skin, flesh and blood. But while the third was intent on giving the breath of life, the man of sense advised against it, remarking: "This is a lion. If you bring him to life, he will kill everyone of us."

"You simpleton!" said the others, "It is not I who will reduce scholarship to a nullity."

"In that case," came the reply, "wait a moment, while I climb this convenient tree."

When this had been done the lion was brought to life, rose up, and killed all three. But the man of sense, after the lion had gone elsewhere, climbed down and went home.

—*Panchatantra*

Definitions

122.12

Education is what remains when we have forgotten all that we have been taught.

—*George Savile, Marquis of Halifax*

122.13

Education: That which discloses to the wise and disguises from the foolish their lack of understanding.

—*Ambrose Bierce*

122.14

Education is that which enables you to get into more intelligent trouble.

122.15

Education consists in pounding abstract ideas into concrete heads.

122.16

A "New Thinker," when studied closely, is merely a man who does not know what other people have thought.

—*Frank Moore Colby*

122.17

Highbrow: A man who has discovered something more interesting than women.

—*Russell Lynes*

122.18

A highbrow is a person educated beyond his intelligence.

—*Brander Matthews*

122.19

University: An institution for the postponement of experience.

Aphorisms

122.20

The college graduate is presented with a sheepskin to cover his intellectual nakedness.

—*Robert M. Hutchins*

122.21

A college education isn't essential. Just being a graduate sometimes will do.

—*Glenn R. Bernhardt*

122.22

A college education is one of the few things a person is willing to pay for and not get.

—*William Lowe Bryant*, president emeritus of Indiana University

122.23

It took her four years to get a sheepskin—and one day for her friend to get a mink.

122.24

When a young man steps out of college and says, "World! here I am with my A.B.!" the world softly replies, "All right, my lad, now I'll teach you the rest of the alphabet."

122.25

Still, if nobody dropped out at the eighth grade, who would hire the college graduates.

—Chatham (Ont.) *News*

122.26

You can lead a boy to college but you cannot make him think.

—*Elbert Hubbard*

122.27

College is like a laundry—you get out of it what you put into it—only you never recognize it.

122.28

One without education is compelled to use his brains.

(*See also 15.3, 22.2, 22.3, 112.2, 123.1–123.11, 142.17, 221.1, 275.1*)

123. Students-at-large

Anecdotes

123.1

A wife told her husband that the economy lessons he had been giving their son, now in college, were bearing fruit. She had just heard from the son, and he said that all he wanted them to spend on his birthday was 75 cents.

"Well, well," beamed the father, "but what can you get for 75 cents?"

"Just one little thing," said the wife, "He wants his own set of keys for the car."

123.2

William had returned home after his first year at college. He was resplendent in college finery. His father looked at him in disgust and said, "You look like a silly fool."

Later William called on an old major who lived next door, who greeted the young man heartily. "William," he said, "you look exactly as your father did twenty-five years ago."

"Yes," said William with a smile. "Father was just telling me that."

123.3

In discussing an upcoming debate he was to engage in, a college student said to his roommate, "This is going to be a real battle of wits."

"I think," said his friend, "that it is very courageous of you to go into it unarmed."

123.4

Hesketh Pearson related that when historian Philip Guedella was president of the debating society at Oxford he primed a friend to ask him two specific questions before the debate began—a usual practice at that time. The friend agreed, and when he asked the two questions Guedella gave brilliant answers because of his preparations for the planned encounter. However, Guedella's friend was not through; he gravely arose and asked Guedella, "I'm sorry I've forgotten—but what was that third question you wanted me to ask you?"

123.5

The rather awkward freshman at a prom finally got up nerve enough to ask a sultry young beauty for a dance. "I never dance with a child," said the pretty little snob. The freshman looked her over critically and said, "Please forgive me; I didn't realize you were pregnant."

123.6

A student from the Orient attended one of the big state universities in the U.S. and wrote home that it was "a vast athletic association where some studies are maintained for the benefit of the feeble-bodied."

123.7

A lobbyist fighting the appropriation of funds for the expansion of a state university, approached one backwoods legislator of severely limited education. "Do you realize," said the lobbyist ominously to the legislator, "that at our state university men and women students are using the same curriculum? And that boys and girls often matriculate together? And that a young lady student can be forced to show a professor her thesis?"

"I won't vote them a damn cent," said the backwoods legislator.

123.8

Yale Man: "Say, my boy, I'm a stranger here in Cambridge. Could you tell me where I might stop at?"

Harvard Man: "I would suggest you stop before the at."

123.9

"How's your son doing in college?"

"Pretty well—he's a halfback."

"But I mean in his studies."

"In that he is away back," said the not-so-proud parent.

123.10

Nowadays they spend $15,000 for a school bus to pick up the kids right at the door so they don't have to walk. Then they spend $100,000 for a gym so they can get some exercise.

Aphorism

123.11

A senior always feels the university is going to the kids.

—*T. L. Masson*

(*See also 57.10, 57.15, 112.10, 118.2, 118.4, 118.8–118.10, 118.12, 119.2, 119.3, 119.5, 119.8–119.11, 119.13, 119.15–119.18, 119.20–119.34, 120.1, 123.1–123.28, 160.3, 190.8, 191.7, 191.9–191.11, 201.1, 211.12, 243.9, 243.11, 269.47, 275.1*)

Part Four

ATHLETICS, GAMBLING, THEATRE, LITERATURE, ART

SPORTS AND SPORTSMEN

124. Hits, Runs, and Errors

Anecdotes

124.1

Rocky Colavito made a great try for a ball hit down the right-field line but, instead of catching it, slipped and fell—and was sitting on the ball without being aware of that fact.

Manager Joe Gordon stood up in the dugout and screamed out, "Somebody tell that guy to get off the ball before he hatches it!"

124.2

They arrived during the fifth inning of the game. "What is the score?" she asked her escort. "Nothing to nothing," he replied.

"Oh, aren't we lucky," she exclaimed. We haven't missed anything."

124.3

One young woman at her first baseball game said she liked the pitcher best, "because he hit the bat every time."

124.4

The story is told of a screaming, jumping dame who kept yelling all through the game, "Kill the umpire—kill the umpire!"

Finally a fan called to her to "pipe down! The ump ain't done nothin' wrong."

"That's what you think," snapped the dame. "He's my husband—kill the umpire!"

124.5

One year when the Philadelphia baseball team was reaping more than its share of blunders there was a sign on the right-field fence of Shibe Park reading:

THE PHILLIES USE LIFEBUOY SOAP.

The day after one of their more disastrous games the team came out on the field and found that during the night someone had written under the soap sign:

AND THEY STILL STINK.

124.6

Frank Chance, the famous manager of the Chicago Cubs of earlier days, took baseball seriously. The Cubs were fighting hard for a certain game. It was a pitcher's battle all the way, and the enemy finally won. Chance was gloomy after the defeat, and when he got home his wife said, "Cheer up, Frank, you still have me."

"Yes," shouted Chance, "and there were a couple of times this afternoon when I would have traded you for a base hit."

124.7

The young man realized that his continual preoccupation with baseball was disrupting his life. He imagined himself on the mound for the Yankees in the World Series, or hitting in the cleanup spot in an All-Star Game, or making spectacular catches that ruined home runs for Roger Maris and Mickey Mantle, and so on. He thought he should take his problem to a psychiatrist. "The thing has got so bad," he told the doctor, "that I can't get to sleep anymore thinking about baseball and the part I play in it."

"Try this," said the doctor; "when you get into bed imagine you have a beautiful and warm young woman in your arms."

"But if I do that," said the young man, "I'd miss my turn at bat."

124.8

"Who would you save if both your brother and Mickey Mantle were drowning?" a man asked a New York Yankee fanatic.

"What a question!" exclaimed the fan. "Why my brother never even played baseball."

124.9

The young boy was showing off to his father what a hitter he was; three times he tossed the ball into the air and swung at it and missed each time. At the third miss he said, "Boy, what a pitcher I am!"

124.10

An unusually obnoxious grandstand manager got on the nerves of Frank Frisch when he was managing the Pittsburgh Pirates. The fellow continually kept yelling to Frisch what he should do next, until during the later innings Frisch walked over to the man's box seat and with a straight face pretended to seek his advice concerning plays and strategy. At the end of the game Frisch returned to the man and asked him his name and where his office was located.

"Why do you ask?" asked the grandstand strategist.

"Because," said Frisch in a loud voice, "tomorrow morning I'm coming down to your joint, and I'm going to lean over your shoulder all day and tell you how to run your business."

124.11

It had been a terrible season for the local baseball team, and a friend trying to cheer up the manager said, "At least you've taught the boys fine sportsmanship. They're certainly good losers."

"Good!" crowed the manager. "They're perfect."

124.12

Walter Johnson, the famous speed-ball pitcher for the Washington Senators, was on the mound in an exhibition game against a minor-league team. Washington was in the lead when the other team came to bat in the ninth inning. Two men were out, and the batter had two strikes on him. It had been growing dark, the field had no lights, and there was danger the batter might not see Johnson's blazing pitch and thus get hit and seriously injured.

Gabby Street, the catcher, walked out to the mound and explained the matter to Johnson. He appeared to hand the ball to Johnson, but instead concealed it in his big glove. He told Johnson to pretend he was pitching, and that he would bang the ball in his catcher's mitt as if he had just caught it, and they'd see what happened.

So Johnson went through his pitching motion; Street feigned to catch the ball; and the umpire called, "Strike Three!" At almost the same instant the batter roared, "You blind bum!" and he ran his hand across his face, "that ball was way up here."

124.13

When Yogi Berra was a rookie in spring-training camp, measurements were being taken for uniforms, and he was asked his cap size. "How do I know?" replied Yogi. "I'm not in shape yet."

124.14

One of the great batting stars of the major leagues took over the management of a minor-league team when he began to lose his fleetness of foot. But every so often he put himself into the game as a pinch hitter when a critical situation arose and his still-keen batting eye could be of use to his team.

In midseason this minor-league manager had a serious dispute on the field with one of the umpires. The umpire said little despite the abuse showered on him. He was a patient man.

Some weeks later the manager's team was losing by a score of 15 to 2 in late innings. His team had one man on base, with two out, when the manager, by some peculiar process of reasoning, decided to put himself in as a pinch hitter.

As the manager moved to the plate swinging his bat, the umpire picked up a megaphone (as was done in the days before public address systems) and called out to the people in the stands: "Joe Blank now batting for exercise!"

124.15

Before a Fourth of July game in New York a contralto from the Metropolitan Opera stood at home plate to sing "The Star Spangled Banner." When she finished the first verse the fans resumed their seats. But she began to sing the second verse, and everyone again stood up, and sat down again when she finished it. But when the singer at the home plate began the third verse of the national anthem, a fan yelled out, "Why don't somebody give that broad a base on balls?"

124.16

Ping Bodie, a New York Yankee outfielder of other days, was slow-footed on the bases. Once when he was thrown out stealing second, Arthur "Bugs" Baer said, "His heart was full of larceny, but his feet were honest."

124.17

During spring training the team was performing very badly at bat. Finally the manager got so irate that he picked up a bat and said, "Now I'm goin' to show you guys a thing or two." Whereupon the manager struck out pitch after pitch. When the pitcher began to get weary—and the manager remained hitless—he flung the bat aside and said, "Now you see what I mean? That's what you've been doing. Now come out of it and connect with the ball."

124.18

When Charlie Grimm was managing the Braves they played a night game in Milwaukee. The game was lost when the Braves' Danny O'Connell tripled but was left there stranded when the next three batters failed to bring him in. After the game the team had to rush to the airport for a plane to New York. All the men showed up on time except O'Connell. Grimm said to the traveling secretary, "You better rush out to the stadium and see if O'Connell is still on third base."

124.19

During a game between the St. Louis Cardinals and the Chicago Cubs, the St. Louis center fielder, Heinie Mueller, was instructed to watch the catcher's sign for pitches, so that on slow balls he could move in 20 feet and go back to the fence when a fast ball was called for. The bleacherites soon caught on to this and began chanting "Slow ball" when Mueller moved in, and "Fast ball" when he moved back to the fence. This began to get on Mueller's nerves, especially when the Cubs got three men on base and the St. Louis catcher called for a fast ball. Although Mueller should have moved back to the fence, instead he moved in, and the batter drove the ball over Mueller's head and won the game.

When Mueller's manager asked him why he did not obey instructions he said, "I thought I would cross up those wise guys in the bleachers."

124.20

It was a doubleheader at Ebbets Field, Brooklyn, August 15, 1926. In the seventh inning the Dodgers had filled the bases. Babe Herman was at bat and sent a high fly into right field, then put his head down and lit out for first base. The man on third scored; the man on second reached third and stopped. Herman rounded first and headed for second; the man on second had to run to third, even though the runner there refused to race on for home plate. Herman rounded second and headed for third, right behind the man who had been on second, and with the man on third still standing there wondering what to do. Suddenly all three men were on third base. The ball was thrown to the third baseman, and he started to tag all three men out. But one of the men on third headed for center field so they couldn't tag him—and of course he was out for leaving the base path.

124.21

One day the Brooklyn Dodgers arrived in the wrong town for a game.

124.22

One day in Brooklyn a Dodger first baseman singled but was picked off first base by the ancient hidden-ball trick. The rival first baseman simply tucked the ball under a corner of the bag, then pretended a return throw to the pitcher. When the runner took a lead off the base, the first baseman reached down for the ball and tagged the man out. A week or two later the victimized first baseman thought he would try the same trick on the Boston Braves. When a Boston player reached first base the Dodger first baseman tucked the ball under the bag and simulated a return of the ball to the pitcher. The Boston runner thereupon took a generous lead off the base. The Dodger first baseman then reached down to the bag for the ball, but he had tucked it so securely under the bag that he couldn't get it. By the time he found the ball, the Boston runner was safe on third base.

124.23

During a rare World Series Game at Ebbets Field, in Brooklyn, a reporter in the press box draped his topcoat over the railing, but during the game the coat slipped and landed on a Dodger rooter below. The fan looked up and called up, "Where's de pants?"

124.24

When Tony Cuccinello was playing for the Dodgers he hit a towering ball to deep right field. The ball was brilliantly fielded, and the throw into third was a beauty. Casey Stengel, coaching at third for the Dodgers, yelled, "Slide! Slide!" to Cuccinello. But the runner preferred to come in standing up and was tagged out. "I told you to slide!" yelled Stengel.

"I heard you," said Cuccinello. "But I didn't want to bust my cigars."

124.25

One day when Casey Stengel was managing the Brooklyn Dodgers he wanted the game called because of approaching darkness. There were no lights for the field at that time. The umpire refused and ordered the game to continue. Casey, a few minutes later, used a flashlight to signal the bullpen to send in a new pitcher, for which he was thrown out of the game.

124.26

Clay Felker, in his *Casey Stengel's Secret*, dwells delightfully on the famous baseball manager's wild and wonderful talk and relates that one day a reporter called on Casey to talk about a big trade made between the Red Sox and the White Sox. "It goes this way, Case," said the reporter. "The Red Sox get Ray Scarborough and Bill Wight from the White Sox for Al Zarilla, Joe Dobson, and Dick Littlefield. What do you think of the trade?" After a long pause, Casey said. "Well, the feller ought to help them."

On another occasion, in spring training, Casey said, speaking of his regular third baseman: "Well, the feller I got on there is hitting pretty good, and I know he can make the throw, and if he don't make it that other fellow I got coming up has shown me a lot, and if he can't, I have my guy, and I know what he can do. On the other hand, the guy's not around now. And, well, this guy may be able to do it against left-handers if my guy ain't strong enough. But I know one of my guys is going to do it."

124.27

During a New York Yankee game manager Casey Stengel had to yank a pitcher. Casey walked to the mound with the bad news, but the pitcher pleaded that he be allowed to continue the game. But the Yanks were being clobbered, and Casey was adamant. "Why do I have to go out?" asked the pitcher. Casey pointed to the stands and said, "Up there people are beginning to talk."

124.28

The baseball manager was being examined by the doctor, who told him he had high blood pressure and would simply have to be more philosophical about the game. "Just keep calm, hold your temper, and when you leave the park, leave the team and the game there. Stop mulling it all over when you get home." As the manager was leaving the doctor said, "Before you leave, I want to know why in yesterday's game you called for a squeeze play when your runner on third was so slow and the man at bat a weak hitter?"

124.29

Umpires Bill McGowan and Roy Van Graflan worked as a team, and one evening in their hotel room were practicing their calls and their gestures before a mirror. "Out!" one would yell and make the proper gestures, while the other man watched and criticized. This went on for some time, each man taking his turn before the mirror calling "Out!" and practicing the appropriate gestures.

After a hour or so of this performance the phone rang in their hotel room. McGowan answered and a voice said, "Say, I'm the man in the next room, and I'd like to know if you guys ever call anybody safe?"

124.30

In his *Baseball Is a Funny Game,* Joe Garagiola recalls the time when Nick Altrock was quarreling with umpire Bill McGowan on every call he made, until a foul ball was hit into the stands, immediately after which a woman in the stands was carried out on a stretcher. McGowan asked Altrock if the ball had hit the woman. "No," said Altrock, "you called that one right, and she fainted."

124.31

"Strike three!" called out the umpire on Jimmy Foxx, Philadelphia's great batter.

Foxx turned on George Moriarty and said, "You missed on that one."

"Well you missed on the other two," said Moriarty.

124.32

"Ball one," called out Tim Hurst, the famous major-league umpire of earlier days.

"Wait a minute, Ump," snapped the catcher. "That plate's got corners on it."

"Yes, I know," said Hurst, "but it ain't got bay windows on it."

124.33

When Pepper Martin was managing the Miami baseball teams he disagreed violently with an umpire's decision. During an inquiry into the incident by the league president, Pepper was asked: "When you had your hands on that umpire's throat, what could you have been thinking?"

"I was thinkin'," Martin replied, "that I'd choke him to death."

124.34

During a Yankee-Senator game plate umpire Bill Guthrie called Babe Ruth out on strikes. Ruth began to call the umpire names and was ordered to the clubhouse by the umpire. Yankee manager Miller Huggins then got into the argument, and he was ordered out of the game. As Ruth walked toward the clubhouse Huggins stood on the field, obviously reluctant to leave the field as ordered. Whereupon Umpire Guthrie yelled to Ruth, "To the clubhouse, Babe—and take the bat boy with you," he added, pointing to the diminutive Miller Huggins.

124.35

When a batter began to protest too vigorously about a called third strike, Umpire Bill Guthrie said to him, "Pipe down, and nobody but you and me will know you can't see any more."

124.36

A slugger, called out on strikes, started to raise hell with Beans Reardon, the umpire.

Finally Reardon said, "Son, no matter what you think, when you pick up the paper tomorrow morning you will find that you struck out."

124.37

It was a close play at home plate as the runner and the ball came into the catcher at almost the same instant. The two players—and everyone else in the ball park—waited tensely for Umpire Charlie Moran's decision. "Is it safe or out?" cried the catcher in anguish as Moran hesitated. Then Moran spoke up, "It ain't nuttin' until I call it."

124.38

I occasionally get birthday cards from fans. But it's often the same message: they hope it's my last.

—*Al Forman,* National League umpire, 1961

124.39

Satchel Paige's rules for staying young:

Avoid fried meats which angry up the blood. If your stomach disputes you, lie down and pacify it with cool thoughts. Keep the juices flowing by jangling gently as you move. Go very light on the vices such as carrying on in society. The social ramble ain't restful. Avoid running at all times. Don't look back. Something might be gaining on you.

—*Collier's Magazine,* 1953

124.40

The great Roger Hornsby was at bat. "Ball one!" called the umpire when the first pitch was made. The pitcher dashed to the plate and protested that he had thrown a strike to Hornsby.

"Mr. Hornsby," retorted the umpire, "will let you know when it is a strike."

And Mr. Hornsby did—on the next pitch; he hit it out of the ball park.

(*See also 24.4, 62.7, 131.7, 213.14, 273.17, 277.3*)

125. Gridiron Grins

Anecdotes

125.1

Some years ago a rookie with the Chicago Bears yearned to get into a game as a pass receiver, and day after day practiced catching balls thrown by quarterbacks in practice. But week after week passed, and still the earnest rookie failed to get the word from coach George Halas.

Finally, during the last quarter of a game the rookie was told to get ready to get into the game. Just before leaving the bench he turned to Halas for instructions. "We've run out of time-outs," said Halas. "Go in there and get hurt."

125.2

Dixon Ryan Fox said, "I listened to a football coach who spoke straight from the shoulder—at least I could detect no higher origin in anything he said."

125.3

Noticing that just before the football game started both teams gathered together and prayed briefly, a fan seated next to a priest asked what he thought would happen if both teams prayed with equal faith and fervor.

"In that event," replied the priest, "I imagine the Lord would simply sit back and enjoy one fine game of football."

125.4

Herman L. Masin tells about the mastodonic tackle who became increasingly annoyed at the elbows being thrown at him by an opponent in the line. Finally the massive tackle rose to his full height, looked his tormentor in the eye, and said: "If you want to play rough, it's OK with me. But don't forget, you've got a mighty pretty face, and I've got nothin' to lose."

125.5

There is a rumor about a football coach who had to resign because of the severe persecution complex he developed. Every time his players went into a huddle, the coach thought they were talking about him.

125.6

The late Herman Hickman, a great football player and wit, told about the time he became enraged at a referee who he thought had made a number of bad calls during a game and yelled at him, "You stink!"

The referee picked up the football, marked off another penalty of 15 yards, turned toward his abuser, and yelled, "How do I smell from here, Hickman?"

125.7

A substitute was rushed into a hard-fought football game and in his excitement forgot to remove his glasses. As he came up to the line of scrimmage a beat-up lineman looked at him in disgust and said, "Hey, four eyes, beat it back to the bench. We don't need any peacemakers out here."

125.8

Just before the game began the football coach said to his men: "Now remember that football depends on and develops individuality, courage, leadership, and above all initiative. And don't forget to do exactly what I tell you."

125.9

All during the skull sessions preceding a big game, one of the star backs spent most of the time reading a comic book, to the mounting fury of the coach. But he said nothing. On the day of the game this particular back sat it out on the bench, until in the last quarter when things began to get critical the coach called to him and said, "Warm up!" The back jumped up and went through a series of warm-ups and turned expectantly to the coach. "Here," said the coach as he reached into his pocket and pulled out a comic book, "sit over there at the end of the bench and read it."

125.10

When Knute Rockne, Notre Dame's famous football coach, and Heywood Broun, New York journalist, were both at the height of their fame, they were introduced. "Nice to meet you," said Rockne. "I never miss a column of yours in the New York *Journal*."

"Thank you, Mr. Rockne," said Mr. Broun of the New York *World*, "and I always try to see your Yale basketball teams."

125.11

The great running back had snaked his way down field on a kickoff return. When he was just opposite the Philadelphia Eagle bench he stopped short, and an Eagle tackler flew past him harmlessly and landed at the feet of Eagle coach Greasy Neale. Neale looked down at the tackler in disgust and snapped, "Get up quick. That guy will be back any moment."

125.12

Fred Russell, Nashville sportswriter, tells about a mountainous tackle who was being taken apart verbally by a coach for his miserable playing during the first half of a game. "If I were as big as you," snarled the coach, "I'd be heavyweight champion of the world."

The man-mountain looked down on the coach casually and said, "Why don't you be lightweight champion?"

125.13

A coach of one of the professional football teams had spent a good part of the game needling one of the referees from the sidelines. But he picked the wrong man, as he discovered late in the game when he was caught illegally shouting instructions to his players.

The needled, but not nettled, referee called time, paced off 10 yards, and said to the coach, "That's for coaching from the sidelines."

"That proves you don't know your business," shouted the coach. "The penalty for illegal coaching is 15 yards."

"I know," said the referee. "But your kind of coaching is worth only a 10-yard penalty."

125.14

During a kick from scrimmage, a Chicago Bear's tackle blundered in his moves, and the ball caught him in the seat of his pants. An opposing player recovered the ball and dashed for a touchdown. Back on the bench Bear's coach George Halas came over to the tackle and asked, "You feel all right?"

"Sure," said the player with surprise.

"I'm glad to hear it," said Halas. "I was a little worried—thought you might have a brain concussion."

125.15

Bronko Nagurski, as every football fan knows, was the terror of the field. Few who had played against him escaped some kind of injury, and none ever forgot his power and drive. When one team went onto the field to play the Chicago Bears, a rookie halfback, aware of Nagurski's reputation, said to his coach, "Tell me what this Nagurski looks like and how he moves, so I'll have some idea how to play him?"

"Don't worry," said the coach, "about finding Nagurski. He'll find you!"

125.16

During the intermission of the game between the Chicago Bears and an Army All-Star Game in 1942, Ludmila Pavichenko was introduced to the crowd as a female Soviet sharpshooter who had killed 309 Nazis. Then the announcer introduced another Soviet woman sharpshooter who he said got 150 Nazis with 152 bullets.

"What she'd do with the other two bullets?" yelled a man in the crowd.

125.17

During a New York Giants football game, one of the backs on the opposing team ripped through the Giant line time and time again, until the ball was within a few yards of the goal line. On the next play the same back again tore through the Giants, shaking off one man after another, and at the goal line was finally brought down by several Giants just as the timer's gun sounded.

"My God!" shouted a spectator. "They had to shoot him to stop him!"

Definition

125.18

Coach: A fellow who is always willing to lay down your life for his job.

—Texas *Longhorn*

Aphorism

125.19

God is always on the side which has the best football coach.

—*Heywood Broun*

(*See also 121.1–121.4*)

126. Par for the Course

Anecdotes

126.1

Four men were on the golf course and had just reached the seventh hole, alongside of which ran a highway. As the men moved on to the green a funeral procession passed along the road, and one of the men removed his cap and stood solemnly as the procession passed by. One of his friends was touched by this gesture of respect for the dead and said so. "Oh, it's the least I could do," replied the man. "Just think, in ten more days we would have been married twenty-five years."

126.2

A golfer caught up with a foursome ahead of him and asked if he could play through. "I've just received word that my wife has had a serious heart atttack."

126.3

"You think so much about your golf game that you don't even remember when we were married," complained the wife.

"I certainly do; it was the day I sunk that 35-yard putt."

126.4

A man was brought into court on a charge of beating his wife. The defendant's attorney pleaded: "My client is by no means wholly at fault in this matter. His wife has been constantly nagging him for years, and finally in exasperation he beat her into silence with a golf club."

The judge leaned over the bench and asked, "How many strokes?"

126.5

"I would like to buy a low handicap," said the woman to a clerk in New York's Abercrombie and Fitch.

"A low handicap? I do not understand, Madam," said the clerk.

"Yes, a low handicap—I want to give it to my husband for his birthday. He's always wishing for one."

126.6

A golfer was having a bad day on the famed Monte Carlo course. Not one of his shots went right. At the eighteenth hole he made a last swipe at the ball, missed completely, and tore up about a yard of turf.

He strolled disgustedly from the tee and looked down at the blue Mediterranean, hundreds of feet below. Several sailboats were gliding lazily about. "How can anyone be expected to shoot a decent game," demanded the golfer passionately, "with those infernal ships rushing back and forth."

126.7

After a series of disastrous holes, the strictly amateur golfer, in an effort to smother his rage, laughed hollowly and said to his caddy, "This golf is a funny game." "It's not supposed to be," said the boy gravely.

126.8

"If you laugh at me again, I'll knock your block off," snarled the golfer at the caddy.

"Why you wouldn't even know what club to use," said the caddy.

126.9

Hollywood actor John Payne grew a beard for his role in a Western but found time to try his skill on the toughest golf course in town. However, he soon ended up in a sand trap and spent many minutes profanely trying to blast his way out of it.

Another actor, hearing the abusive language, stopped by to see what the trouble was and recognized Payne in spite of the whiskers flapping in the breeze.

"My Lord, John," gasped the actor, "how long have you been in this trap?"

126.10

A clergyman was engaged in a closely contested game of golf. He teed up to his ball, raised his driver, and hit the ball a tremendous clip, but instead of soaring down the fairway, the ball went all of 15 feet and stopped. The clerical fellow pursed his lips, bit his lips, sighed, but said nothing.

One of the players turned to him and said, "That was the most profane silence I have ever heard."

126.11

Two men were beginning a game of golf. The first man stepped to the tee, and his first drive gave him a hole in one. The second man stepped up to the tee and said, "OK, now I'll take my practice swing, and then we'll start the game."

126.12

"What's your golf score?" the recreation director asked.

"Well, not so good," replied the golfer. "It's 72."

"That's not so bad at all. In fact, it's real good."

"Well, I'm hoping I do better on the next hole," said the golfer.

126.13

Opie Read, the humorist, was playing golf in a foursome when his ball landed in a sand trap. Hidden from view, his repeated hacking finally enabled him to get the ball out. "How many strokes, Opie?" asked his friends.

"Three."

"But we heard six strokes!"

"Three," said Read, "were echoes."

126.14

Two men playing golf had just reached one of the greens when a ball came over a knoll and landed on the green. "Let's give the guy a big thrill," said one of the players, as he kicked the ball into the cup. "When he gets here we'll tell him his ball landed in the cup and he'll think he made a hole in one." When the unseen player arrived they told him of his luck. He smiled and said to a man with him, "Look! I made it in five."

126.15

"Why are you so down-in-the-mouth?"

"The doctor told me I can't play golf."

"Oh, you didn't have to go to the doctor for that. I could have told you that the other day on the links."

126.16

Joe E. Lewis said he shoots golf in the low 70s. "When it gets any colder, I quit."

126.17

Mark Twain accompanied a friend over the golf course. The other man repeatedly tore up more turf than golf balls and sent the dirt flying after every stroke. Finally he asked Twain how he liked the links.

"Best I ever tasted," said Mark Twain, wiping dirt off his face.

Definitions

126.18

A golfer is one who totes 25 pounds of equipment several miles, but who has Junior bring him the ash tray.

126.19

Golf is a game where a little white pill is chased by a lot of gaffers too old to chase anything else.

Aphorisms

126.20

When a man's golf score is below 90, he is neglecting his business; if above it, he is neglecting his game.

126.21

By the time a man can afford to lose a golf ball, he just can't hit it that far.

126.22

May our stocks go up and our game go down —to par!

(*See also 16.34, 17.7, 73.2, 80.4, 80.7, 94.9, 106.3, 148.1, 195.5, 196.14, 267.7*)

127. Hooks and Jabs

Anecdotes

127.1

The willing but only so-so club fighter had been carried to his dressing room after taking a terrible beating from his rival from the adjoining ward. When the young pug gained consciousness and vaguely recalled what had happened to him in the ring, he turned to his manager and said: "Get me another fight with that lousy bum, and you'll see what a real beating is. I'll knock your empty head loose from your shoulders."

127.2

The two fighters circled the ring cautiously, striking out at each other in light and tentative fashion but never landing a blow, while making fierce faces at each other and grunting as though striving desperately. This went on for several dreary rounds when a voice from the gallery called out, "Come on, hit him, ya bum! Ya got the wind with you!"

127.3

Damon Runyon told about the time the famous Sam Langford became annoyed at one "Beanie" Walker, a Los Angeles sports editor who declared Fireman Jim Flynn the heavyweight champion of the world on the strength of his no-decision fight with Langford.

Flynn and Langford were rematched. Sam maneuvered Flynn so that he was right over Walker's seat at the ringside, and then Langford went to work on Flynn with his powerful fists. After dealing out the proper amount of punishment to Flynn, Langford called out, "Mister Beanie, here comes yo' champion," and with that Sam knocked out Jim Flynn.

127.4

A fighter was taking a terrific beating in the ring. He stumbled back to his corner at the end of a round; his manager looked at him and said, "Let him hit ya with his left for a while. Your face is crooked."

127.5

A fighter was knocked to the canvas in the fifth round. Although receiving only a light punch, he did not get up until after the count reached 10. "Whassa matter, you crazy?" asked his trainer. "You wasn't hit hard. Why didn't you get up in time?"

"I was so mad at being floored," said the pug, "that I thought I'd better count to 10 before I did anything."

127.6

"Just think," said the conceited heavyweight fighter, "millions of people will watch me fight on TV tonight."

"Yes," said a sportswriter, "and they'll all know the result at least ten seconds before you will."

127.7

As the bell rang for the first round, the prizefighter made the sign of the cross before advancing to the center of the ring. A fellow in the audience turned to a priest seated next to him and asked, "Father, will that help him win the fight?"

"Yes," said the priest, "if he is in condition and knows how to fight."

127.8

After winning a dubious victory over Bob Fitzsimons, heavyweight Tom Sharkey opened a saloon in New York. On a visit to Chicago he was telling some sportswriters about his new place. "You ought to have a big chandelier to go with that layout," suggested one of the writers.

"I would," said Sharkey, "except I haven't a damned soul that could play it."

(*See also* ***154.48, 244.14***)

128. Hunting

Anecdotes

128.1

A Southerner fond of deer hunting decided one day to take with him his faithful old Negro servant and let him have a shot at a deer for a change.

As luck would have it, the colonel located a deer run immediately. He gave old Mose the rifle and told him to stay right there behind a bush while he circled around and tried to drive a buck past him.

After a while the Southerner located and frightened a large buck out of a clump of trees, throwing rocks at him to speed up his escape. The deer took off at terrific speed, leaping boulders and tree stumps, and ran within a few yards from where old Mose stood ready with his rifle.

But the old servant froze—he could not so much as lift the gun when the buck came into sight. Annoyed, the hunter asked the servant why he didn't shoot.

"It's this way, Colonel," said the old fellow. "There's no point wastin' shot on that buck—he was coming so fast I thought I'd just let him go and he'd kill himself."

128.2

A hunter began to have suspicions of his wife's affection when she bought him a deerskin coat for a hunting trip.

128.3

A newly rich American and his wife were guests at an English country home—an atmosphere new and uncomfortable to them. In addition, they were exceptionally awkward when it came to hunting; so clumsy in fact that the American narrowly missed shooting the wife of their host. When the Englishman sputtered his rage at such dangerous ineptness, the American handed his gun to the Englishman and said,

"Well, here, take my gun; it's only fair that you have a shot at my wife."

128.4

The sportsmen were sitting around recounting their experiences, when one man told how he came upon a large branch of a tree that had on it ninety-nine squirrels. "Yessir," he said, "ninety-nine squirrels of various colors and sizes, and I got every one of 'em."

"Oh, come now," said one of the listeners, "why not make it an even hundred."

"No, Sir, not me," replied the hunter. "I'm not telling a lie for the sake of one damn squirrel."

128.5

Two fellows out hunting were stopped by a game warden. One of them took off, and the game warden went after him and caught him, and then the fellow showed the warden his hunting license.

"Why did you run when you had a license?"

"Because the other fellow didn't have one."

128.6

The game warden was strolling through the mountains when he encountered a hunter with a gun. "This is good territory for hunting, don't you think?" suggested the warden.

"You bet it is," said the hunter enthusiastically. "I killed one of the finest bucks yesterday—weighed at least 200 pounds."

"Deer are out of season now," said the warden. "Do you know that you are talking to a game warden?"

"No, I was not aware of that," said the hunter. "And I'll bet you didn't know that you've been talking to the biggest liar in the state."

128.7

Two hunters on a safari cornered a lion. But the lion fooled them; instead of standing his ground and fighting the two men, the lion took to his heels and escaped into the underbrush. One of the terrified hunters was finally able to stammer out to the other, "You go ahead and see where the lion has gone, and I'll trace back and see where he came from."

128.8

The big-game hunter had just returned from Africa and was relating some of his adventures. "The most astonishing experience I had," he said, "was once, when passing through the bush, I turned to find a lion just about to spring on me. He sprang, but I fell flat, and the beast passed right over me, and, presumably disgusted, bolted into the bush.

"I then had a goat tethered near the spot as bait and went back the next day in the hopes of catching the lion feeding.

"What do you think were my feelings when, as I approached the spot cautiously, I saw the lion practicing low jumps."

128.9

Sir Reggie Cholmondley, big game hunter, has been missing for ten days. It is feared that something he disagreed with ate him.

—*Anonymous*

128.10

After a day's hunting in India the young Englishman said to his native guide, "I sure missed a lot of shots today."

"Oh, no, Sir, you did not do so badly; but God was merciful to the birds."

128.11

A visitor to India was told he should by all means go on a tiger hunt before he returned to the United States.

"It's easy," he was assured. "You simply tie a bleating goat in a thicket as night comes on. The cries of the animal will attract a tiger. You are up in a nearby tree. When the tiger arrives, aim your gun between his eyes and blast away."

When the visitor returned from the hunt he was asked how he made out. "No luck at all," said the neophyte. "Those tigers are altogether too clever for me. They travel in pairs, and each one closes an eye. So, of course I missed them every time."

128.12

Bore: "This bear on the floor I shot in Alaska. It was a case of him or me."

Bored: "Well, the bear certainly makes a better rug."

128.13

A gentleman on circuit, narrating to Lord Norbury some extravagant feat in sporting, mentioned that he had lately shot thirty-three hares before breakfast. "Thirty-three *hairs!*" exclaimed Lord Norbury. "Zounds, Sir! Then you must have been firing at a *wig*."

128.14

Two elegant confidence men met a wealthy sportsman who invited them to his Southern estate for some hunting. Although never having hunted for anything but easy marks, the two men readily accepted the invitation for the value such a friendship would be to them in future operations.

Before daylight on their second day at the hunting preserve, the two men were routed out of bed and directed to take a skiff and paddle out to a blind that had the previous night been stocked with wooden decoy ducks. There the guide left them for a while.

As the sun began to come up, one of the confidence men saw the wooden ducks bobbing before them in the water. He quickly raised his gun and let both barrels go at the flock of decoys.

"You big dope!" screamed the other man. "You've gone and shot the boosters!"

128.15

The tall-tale teller was speaking about a thick forest he had been passing through. It was so thick, he said, that often he had to move sideways in order to get through the trees, and while there he encountered a fully antlered buck.

"Wait a minute," interjected a listener. "If you had to move sideways, how could a fully antlered buck get through the forest?"

"Easy," replied the tall-tale teller. "He had to pull in his horn, just as all of us have to do sometimes."

128.16

Partridge had a gun with a crooked barrel, and it was said that when he shot at a man behind the house, he had to jump quick inside or the shot would get him behind.

128.17

Poggius the Florentine told about a physician of Milan who developed a cure for madmen. He had a pit of water in the front of his house in which he kept his patients. They were placed in water to their knees, or waist, or chin, according to their condition.

One of these patients who had recovered was standing at the door when a man rode by on a horse. He had a hawk on his fist, and his dogs ran alongside. When asked what he was up to, the man on horseback said he was out to kill certain fowl. The patient asked the value of the fowl he killed, and the hunter named a modest sum. When asked the total cost of the hunting expedition, the horseman named a sum greatly in excess of the value of the fowl killed. Whereupon the patient urged the man to speed on his way, lest the doctor seize him and put him in water up to his chin.

Definitions

128.18

Fox Hunting: The unspeakable in full pursuit of the uneatable.

—*Oscar Wilde*

Aphorism

128.19

The Puritan hated bear-baiting not because it gave pain to the bear but because it gave pleasure to the spectators.

—*Thomas Babington Macaulay*

129. Fishing

Anecdotes

129.1

An old-timer sat on the river bank, obviously awaiting a nibble though the fishing season had not officially opened. The game warden stood behind him quietly for several minutes.

"You a game warden?" the old-timer asked.

"Yep."

Unruffled, the old man began to move the fishing pole from side to side. Finally, he lifted the line out of the water.

"Just teaching him how to swim," he said, pointing to the minnow wiggling on the end of the line.

129.2

Joe Jefferson once was fishing when a game warden came up and examined his catch, which consisted of one beautiful black bass. The warden said, "It will cost you, Sir, $25 for catching this black bass out of season."

"I—take a black bass out of season?" exclaimed Jefferson. "Never! Such an idea never occurred to me. I'll tell you how it happened. That black bass was eating the bait off my hooks as fast as I could put it on, so I thought I would just tie him up where he couldn't get at it until I got through fishing."

129.3

He had been fishing with no luck. On his way home he went to the local fish store and asked the fellow to pick out the two largest trout he had and throw them to him while he stood at the door.

"What's the idea of throwing them?"

"Well, I've been fishing and had no luck—but I'm no liar—I want to arrive home and show them the fish I caught."

129.4

Irvin S. Cobb used to tell of walking along a country road in Georgia after a hard rainstorm when he came upon Henry sitting in an easy chair by the kitchen door, fishing in a puddle of water.

"Henry, you old fool," said Cobb, "what are you doing there?"

"Fishin' a little," said Henry.

"Well, don't you know there are no fish there?"

"Yes, Sir," said Henry, "I know that, but this here place is so handy."

129.5

A man relates he was fishing in the Tar River, North Carolina, when he got a splendid bite and hauled in one of the biggest chubs he ever saw. He was bending over, admiring the fish, when a $10 gold piece dropped out of his vest pocket and fell into the fish's mouth. The chub instantly swallowed the coin, then gave one lively flip, jumped out of the boat, and was gone.

"A year later," the fisherman related, "I was fishing in the same place and got the same chub. Instantly I thought of my $10 gold piece. When I opened the fish there was the shining coin, and with it six dimes, interest on my money for one year."

129.6

The angler trod wearily and uncertainly through the field on his way home from an unsuccessful day. His knapsack was empty of fish, and his flask was empty of the whiskey he had started out with. In the course of his wavering journey he encountered a scarecrow in the field—a battered hat and sleeves of a ragged coat thrust through the wooden crosspieces.

The befuddled angler stared at this for a few seconds then said sternly, "Don't try to hand me that. You know damned well you ain't got no fish that size."

129.7

Spike Jones tells about the irate wife of a movie star who had gone off fishing and left her alone. Asked where her husband was she said, "Just go down to the bridge and look around until you find a pole with a worm at each end."

129.8

The fisherman was explaining to a friend the size of a fish he almost caught. Stretching his hands wide apart, he said, "It was at least this long. I never saw such a fish."

"I guess not," said his friend drily.

129.9

The sportily dressed, expertly equipped angler hauled in a good-sized trout, turned to a country boy standing nearby, and asked, "Did you ever have a trout this size at home?"

"Naw," said the boy quietly. "The old man always throws the little ones back in."

129.10

Two fishermen were exchanging their experiences of the previous day. One man said he had caught a 300-pound salmon. "But salmon never weigh as much as 300 pounds," said the other man. "Nevertheless—I caught one weighing 300 pounds. What did you catch?"

"Not much," answered the second man. "Only a rusty old lamp, but on the bottom of it was inscribed 'Property of Christopher Columbus, 1492.' When I opened the lamp, I was surprised to find it still held a candle in it, and you know that the candle was still lit."

"Now let's get together on these stories," urged the first fisherman. "If you will put out that damn candle, I'll take a couple hundred pounds off that salmon."

Definitions

129.11

Fishing is a delusion entirely surrounded by liars in old clothes.

—*Don Marquis*

129.12

Angler: A man who spends rainy days sitting around on the muddy banks of rivers doing nothing because his wife won't let him do it at home.

—*Irish News*

129.13

Fishing is just a jerk at one end of the line waiting for a jerk at the other end.

—*Ernie Ford*

129.14

A fishing rod is a stick with a hook at one end and a fool at the other.

—*Samuel Johnson*

Aphorisms

129.15

This would be a fine world if all men showed as much patience all the time as they do when they're waiting for a fish to bite.

—*The Hub,* Tampa, Fla.

129.16

Sign beside a Maine pond: PRIVATE. ANYONE FOUND NEAR THIS TROUT POND WILL BE FOUND THERE NEXT MORNING.

129.17

Here's to our fisherman bold;
Here's to the fish he caught;
Here's to the one that got away,
And here's to the one he bought.

129.18

The biggest fish he ever caught were those that got away.

—*Eugene Field*

129.19

I would rather fish than eat, particularly eat fish.

—*Corey Ford*

129.20

There are more fish taken out of a stream than ever were in it.

—*Oliver Herford*

(*See also 79.2, 142.15, 168.1, 211.29, 211.34, 231.4, 268.4, 268.7, 269.164, 269.168*)

130. Win, Place, and Show

Anecdotes

130.1

A woman seeking a divorce charged that her husband "thinks only of horse racing. He talks horse racing; he sleeps horse racing and the racetrack is the only place he goes. It is horses, horses, horses all day long and most of the night. He doesn't even know the date of our wedding."

"That is not true, Your Honor," cried the husband. "We were married the day Dark Star won the Kentucky Derby."

130.2

An incurable horse player, whose wife bitterly opposed his betting, continued to bet on the sly. One day a friend stopped by at his home and asked, "How did you make out with Susie-Q yesterday?" The bettor's wife heard the remark and flounced out of the room in obvious anger.

"Now you've blown it!" said the husband. "My wife thinks I've given up betting. You've got to square it somehow."

When the wife returned to the room several minutes later, the visitor said to her, "I think I gave you the wrong impression. Susie-Q isn't a racehorse; she is a waitress in the restaurant where the fellows in the office go to lunch."

130.3

A man on his way to the horse races stopped to watch a man painting the inside fence that surrounded a mental institution. When he noticed the worker had no paint in his bucket or on his brush, he asked him why, but was given a curt reply. "Oh, well," said the questioner, "I'll get along to the races."

"Are you going to bet?" asked the man 'painting' the fence.

"Sure, I am, and I'm going to win a bundle on a hot tip I got," said the man.

"You're a sap," said the worker. "You'll lose your shirt."

"I don't need a guy in your position to tell me I'm off my rocker," said the bettor as he walked on his way.

Later in the afternoon the bettor was straggling home from the races, and when he passed the institution the worker was still "painting" the fence. "How'd you make out?" asked the worker.

"Lost every bet I made," said the racing fan.

"OK," said the patient of the mental institution. "Here, take the brush and start painting the fence."

130.4

An old racetrack devotee was asked why he had refused to contribute to a statue honoring Paul Revere. "Why," he said, "Revere don't deserve no credit. He just had a great horse under him."

130.5

A butcher and tailor went to the racetrack. The butcher decided to place a hunch bet on Chopped Meat. On his way to the betting window he encountered a tout who talked him into betting on Tug of War since, said the tout, "Chopped Meat doesn't have a chance." So Chopped Meat won, and Tug of War came in last.

The next race the tailor decided to play a hunch and bet on a horse named Overcoat. On his way to the window he met the same tout, who convinced him Overcoat did not have a chance and talked him into betting on Flying Feet. So Overcoat won, and Flying Feet came in last. On their way to the parking lot for the return trip, winnerless, the two men decided to buy some peanuts. The tailor said he'd get them. He came back with popcorn.

"What's the idea?" said the butcher. "I thought we agreed to buy peanuts."

"Yes, I know," said the tailor, "but I met that man again."

130.6

A man owned a single horse, a horse not addicted to speed. Nevertheless, the owner was perfectly willing to pay the high costs of stalls, feed, trainer, and all the rest. And the horse was entered in race after race, usually ending up last and never coming near the money. After each such race, the owner made elaborate notations on a large chart he carried with him.

After this had gone on for some time the trainer pointed out to the owner that the horse had run in just about every kind of race, and at various tracks, but never gave any indication that he would win.

"Stay with him," said the owner to the trainer. "I'm keeping a very careful record, every time he beats one or two horses, as sometimes happens, I mark it down. One of these days we are going to have our horse in a race where all the other horses will be ones he has already beaten—and then he'll win."

130.7

When Dave Woods was handling publicity for Belmont Racetrack he heard about a fanatical New York Yankee fan who went to the races one afternoon to bet on Yankee Winner, and he watched the race while listening on his portable radio to the account of the Yankee game on the road. However, he forgot about the ball game when Yankee Winner came closing fast down the stretch. Just before the horses came to the finish the baseball fan screamed, "Slide, you fool, slide!"

130.8

A blind man went to the racetrack to bet on a horse named Bolivar. A friend stood next to him and related Bolivar's progress in the race.

"How is Bolivar at the quarter?"

"Coming good."

"And how is Bolivar at the half?"

"Running strong!"

After a few seconds, "How is Bolivar at the three-quarter?"

"Holding his own."

"How is Bolivar in the stretch?"

"In there running like hell! He's heading for the line, driving all the other horses in front of him."

130.9

One horse player told another horse player of the sudden death of a mutual friend. He went on to mention the funeral arrangements, then added, "I can't remember the name of the cemetery, but it's the third one on the way to Aqueduct after you leave La Guardia Airport by cab."

130.10

Joe Palmer, the late racing expert, told about a man from Idaho who breezed into Kentucky with a six-year-old horse that had never raced before, but which he entered for a race. The horse won easily and paid a whopping price.

The racing stewards did not like the look of the thing and questioned the owner. "Is this horse unsound?" they asked.

"Not a bit," said the owner.

"In that case," asked the stewards, "why have you never raced him before?"

"Mister," said the man from Idaho, "we couldn't even catch the critter until he was five years old."

130.11

Alben W. Barkley told about the fellow at the racetrack who made three separate trips to the windows to place bets on the same horse—Bluebells in the fifth race. On the man's fourth trip to the betting window he was tapped on the shoulder by a man who said, "It's none of my business, but if I was you I wouldn't put so much money on Bluebells. That horse hasn't got a chance."

"Thanks, pal," said the bettor, "but confidentially I own Bluebells, and I'm sure we're goin' to win it."

"If you do," said the stranger, "it's going to be a mighty slow race. I own the other four horses in the race."

Aphorisms

130.12

The race is not always to the swift, nor the battle to the strong—but that's the way to bet.

—*Damon Runyon*

130.13

The only man who makes money following the races is the one who does so with a broom and shovel.

—*Elbert Hubbard*

130.14

Horse sense is what keeps horses from betting on what people will do.

—*Raymond Nash*

(*See also 58.17, 111.1, 134.15, 276.18*)

131. Swimming

Anecdotes

131.1

Two fellows were sitting idly on the beach watching the bathers when they were attracted by the perfect swimming and diving of an elderly man. And when the swimmer began to tread water in such a fashion that he seemed literally to walk back and forth through the water, one of the observers exclaimed aloud how wonderful he was.

"It's no surprise to me," said the other man. "I would expect that he would do that. He used to be a letter carrier in Venice."

131.2

Two young women came to a deserted part of the seashore and decided to take a swim and a sun bath. They disrobed, dashed nude into the surf, swam around for a while, and then stretched out on the sand naked. Presently an elderly gentleman came along, and, seeing no one about, he undressed and left his clothes and his camera behind a sand dune while he went swimming.

Meanwhile, another man sitting behind some boulders on the beach had witnessed the actions of the girls and of the elderly gentleman. This young man realized each was unaware of the presence of the others. So he got up and walked behind the sand dune until he came to where the elderly gentleman had left his clothing. He took the other man's camera, set it, walked over the dune, snapped a close-up picture of the girls sleeping on the beach, and replaced the camera among the elderly gentleman's effects.

131.3

Norman Ross, who had won many swimming titles, was in the habit of swimming in Lake Michigan early every morning before reporting for his job on the sports desk of a Chicago newspaper. Ross sometimes would spot a solitary person walking along the lakeside. He would then swim to the shore and call out, "What town is this?"

"Chicago," the startled pedestrian would reply.

"Oh, I want Milwaukee," Ross would call out and then plunge back into the water and swim away.

132. Other Sports

Anecdotes

132.1

A basketball coach told an associate of a "wonderful" dream he had had the previous night. "I met this beautiful dame," he said. "Her face was adorable, her figure breathtaking, and she promptly said she had always liked me more than a little, and wouldn't I come up to her room, where she had a surprise for me. Well, when I got there she introduced me to her kid brother—he's 7 feet 6 inches tall. Boy, what a dream!"

132.2

The young wife weepingly told her friend that her husband had walked out on her after a quarrel.

"Oh, don't let it upset you. Men often do that sort of thing. He'll be back," assured her friend.

"No, he won't," wailed the wife. "I can tell. He took his bowling ball with him."

132.3

A stout, bald gentleman was discussing his tennis game with a friend. This rather awkward individual said, "My brain barks out a command to my body: Run forward speedily. Start right away. Land the ball gracefully over the net."

"And then what happens?" asked the friend.

"And then," the heavy-set fellow concluded wistfully, "my body says, 'Who, me?' "

Definitions

132.4

Professional Athlete: One who goes through the motions without the emotions.

—*College Humor*

132.5

Athlete: A dignified bunch of muscles unable to split wood or sift the ashes.

—*Indiana Bored Walk*

132.6

Bowling: Marbles for grown-ups.

132.7

Skiing: Whoosh! Then walk a mile.
—*Anonymous Indian*

Aphorisms

132.8

The only exercise some women get is running up bills.

The only exercise some men get is wrestling with their conscience.

The only exercise some people get is stretching the truth, bending over backwards, running out of cash.

132.9

A hobby is hard work you wouldn't do for a living.

132.10

Whenever I feel like exercise, I lie down until the feeling passes.
—*Robert M. Hutchins*

132.11

I get my exercise acting as a pallbearer to my friends who exercise.
—*Chauncey M. Depew*

(*See also 42.24, 77.3, 138.3, 191.7, 196.3, 211.29, 229.11, 231.10, 238.9, 244.6, 246.3, 263.12*)

133. Poker and Bridge

Anecdotes

133.1

The weekly poker group was in the midst of an exceptionally exciting hand when one of the group fell dead of a heart attack. He was laid on a couch in the room, and one of the three remaining members asked, "What shall we do now?"

"I suggest," said the senior member of the group, "that out of respect for our dear departed friend, we finish this hand standing up."

133.2

A man troubled with a puzzling abdominal condition, which caused his stomach to rumble in strange fashion, was playing poker with some friends, and of course the tension of the game caused his innards to misbehave in customary manner. A drunk standing nearby heard the strange noises and said, "Mister, you sound like you're haunted."

133.3

An all-night poker game in a hotel room kept a man in the next room from getting to sleep. Finally he began to pound on the wall to protest to the revelers.

"What's the idea," shouted back one of the gamblers, "of hanging pictures at two o'clock in the morning?"

133.4

In a poker game in a Western mining town, luck favored the stranger from the beginning; he won steadily. Finally he drew four aces, and after the stakes had been run up to a considerable figure, he magnanimously refused to bet further.

"This is downright robbery," he exclaimed. "I don't want to end the game by bankrupting you. So here goes." He threw down the four aces and reached for the money.

"Hold on!" cried an antagonist. "I'll take care of the dust, if you please."

"But I held four aces—see?"

"Well, what of it. I've got a looloo."

The stranger was dazed. "A looloo? What is a looloo?"

"Three clubs and two diamonds," coolly replied the miner, taking in the stakes. "I guess you ain't accustomed to our poker rules out here.

"See there?" he said pointing to a sign on the wall:

A LOOLOO BEATS FOUR ACES.

The game resumed. The stranger presently threw down his cards with an exultant whoop and cried out, "There's a looloo for you—three clubs and two diamonds."

"Tut, Tut," said the miner. "Really this is too bad. You still don't understand our rules. Look at that rule over there!"

THE LOOLOO CAN BE PLAYED BUT ONCE IN A NIGHT.

133.5

A common belief among poker players in the West is that one would have bad luck playing with a one-eyed player. This led to the expression "There's a one-eyed man in the game," meaning, "Look out for a cheat." The bad repute of the one-eyed player is said to have come about in this way:

There was a little game of draw poker in Omaha. Among the players was a one-eyed man. He was playing in rather remarkable luck, though no one could find any fault with that. Presently, there came a jackpot, and it was the one-eyed man's deal. He opened the pot, and while he was giving himself cards a certain bellicose gentleman named Jones thought he detected the one-eyed man in the act of palming a card. Quick as a flash Jones whipped out a revolver and placed it on the table in front of him. "Gentlemen," he said decisively, "we will have a fresh deal; this one doesn't go."

The players were surprised, but they consented.

"And now that we start a new deal," said Jones, "let me announce that we are going to have nothing but square deals. I am not making any insinuations or bringing any charges, and I will say only this, that if I catch any son of a gun cheating, I will shoot his other eye out."

133.6

The card game was tense, the stakes high. Suddenly the dealer threw his cards down on the table and said, "This game is crooked."

"Where do you get that idea?" asked one of the players.

"Because," said the dealer, "you're not playing the cards I dealt."

133.7

One Baron Newman, a celebrated gambler in London years ago, was detected in rooms at Bath secreting a card. The company threw him out the window of a one-pair-of-stairs room. The Baron, meeting Sam Foote some time afterwards, loudly complained of this usage and asked him what he should do to repair his injured honor.

"Do?" asked Foote. "Why 'tis a plain case—never play as high again as long as you live."

133.8

During a bridge tournament a fierce argument broke out with the result that one of the men arose abruptly and left the table. An opponent turned to the man's partner and asked, "Is that your husband?" "Of course it is," she snapped back. "Do you think I'd be living in sin with a man like that?"

—*Madeline Anderson,* The Bulletin, American Contract Bridge League

Definition

133.9

Bridge is a game in which a good deal depends on a good deal.

(*See also 99.7, 106.6, 182.6, 182.7, 240.24, 241.14, 268.2*)

134. Gamblers-at-large

Anecdotes

134.1

Cohen was showered with congratulations when his number 38 won first prize in the lottery. "Say, Cohen," asked his friend Hyman, "how did you happen to pick number 38?"

"It was easy," said Cohen. "I saw it in a dream. Six 6s appeared and jumped before my eyes. Six times 6 is 38. That's all there was to it."

"But, Cohen, six times 6 is 36, not 38," protested Hyman.

"All right, all right," snapped Cohen. "You be the mathematician."

134.2

A seller of lottery tickets, after many attempts, finally sold a 50-cent ticket to Baron Rothschild, who bought it to get rid of the pest. A week or two later the seller of the ticket came to Rothschild and excitedly told him that the ticket had won the Baron $200,000.

The Baron, pleased to be a winner, said to the seller of the ticket, "I'll give you your choice of $10,000 outright in cash or $2,000 a year for the rest of your life. Which will it be?"

"I'll take the $10,000," said the seller. "With your luck, I wouldn't live another year."

134.3

"Brother," said the minister to one of his parishioners, "I understand you have been gambling heavily—and on Sunday, too."

"Yes, Reverend, "I must admit that is true, and I regret it."

"Don't you think, brother, that you should atone for this transgression by making a generous contribution to the church?"

"To tell you the truth, Reverend, what I've lost already is atonement enough—more atonement than I could afford."

134.4

"I'll bet anyone here that I can fire thirty shots at 200 yards and call each shot correctly without waiting for the marker. Who'll wager a ten spot on this?" challenged the lieutenant.

"I'll take you," cried a major.

They went immediately to the target range, and the lieutenant fired his first shot. "Miss," he calmly and promptly announced.

A second shot. "Missed," repeated the lieutenant.

A third shot. "Missed," snapped the lieutenant.

"Hold on there!" said the major. "What are you trying to do? You're not even aiming at the target. And you've missed three shots already."

"Sir," said the lieutenant, "I'm shooting for that ten spot of yours. And I'm calling my shot as promised." He got his ten spot.

134.5

Dr. Paul Hifferman was fond of laying, or rather offering, wagers. One day in the heat of an argument he cried out, "I'll lay my head you are wrong on that point."

"Well," said Sam Foote, "I accept the wager. Any trifle, among friends, has a value."

134.6

Herbert Asbury says it was Canada Bill who originated the story of the gambling partners marooned in a little river town a few years before the Civil War. Bill found a faro game and began to play. His partner urged him to stop. "The game is crooked," he said.

"I know," replied Bill, "but it's the only one in town."

134.7

A man who mentioned that he had a brother 12 feet tall was challenged to prove it by several men who heard the remark. Bets were made, and the challenged one asked, "Gentlemen, do you agree that two halves make a whole?" Yes, they agreed that this was a fact.

"OK," said the man with the brother 12 feet tall. "I have two brothers—they are twins; each is 6 feet tall. And 6 and 6 make 12. Now pay me."

Definition

134.8

Hunch: What you call an idea that you're afraid is wrong.

—*Carter Dickson*

Aphorisms

134.9

No wife can endure a gambling husband unless he is a steady winner.

—*Thomas Robert Dewar*

134.10

A warnin' is all the average American needs t'make him take a chance.

—*Kin Hubbard*

134.11

The only sure thing about luck is that it will change.

—*Wilson Mizner*

134.12

The gambling known as business looks with severe disfavor upon the business known as gambling.

—*Ambrose Bierce*

134.13

The urge to gamble is so universal and its practice so pleasurable that I assume it must be evil.

—*Heywood Broun*

134.14

Gambling promises the poor what property performs for the rich—something for nothing.

—*George Bernard Shaw*

134.15

Anybody can win, unless there happens to be a second entry.

—*George Ade*

134.16

There may come a time when the lion and the lamb will lie down together, but I am still betting on the lion.

—*Josh Billings*

134.17

The best throw of the dice is to throw them away.

—*Austin O'Malley*

(*See also 17.11, 35.16, 35.20, 35.21, 114.4, 117.2, 117.3, 130.2, 130.3, 130.5, 130.7, 130.11–130.14, 133.1–133.8, 214.9, 239.14, 240.24, 243.16, 244.13, 268.26, 277.3*)

SHOW BIZ AND SHOW PEOPLE

135. On and Off Broadway

Anecdotes

135.1

A fellow after much hustling finally got a small part in a show. All he had to do was to memorize and call out, "Hark, I hear a cannon," when the cannon backstage was fired. Came the first night, and the novice was all atwitter over his one line, repeating and repeating it to himself over and over. Came the big moment—he was on the stage—and off went the cannon —Boom! He turned around and called out, "What in hell was that!"

135.2

Maurice Evans relates an amusing incident that took place when he was starring in *Dial M for Murder*. It's the kind of drama in which the audience quickly becomes involved and tries to solve the mystery—which turns on who has a certain key. At a high point in the play, the key is surprisingly found in a woman's purse. When this happened on the Broadway stage one evening, a man in the third row half rose from his seat and said in a loud voice, "Well, I'll be a son of a bitch!"

135.3

An obnoxious young man was trying out for a part in a play, and the director knew immediately this was one man he did not want in the cast. "Would you please step back a little farther," said the director as the applicant stood at the footlights. The actor stepped back a few feet. "Go back a little farther, please," said the director, and then again, "I want you to go back still farther."

"But," protested the actor, "if I go back any farther I'll be off the stage."

"Exactly," said the director curtly.

135.4

Johnny Carson recalled a play in which an important courtroom scene included a hurriedly recruited group to play the jury. All they had to do was sit quietly until asked for their verdict and give it as instructed by the play's director.

But this jury, on this evening, was by no means apathetic; the jurors became utterly absorbed in the drama being played before them. So absorbed, in fact, that instead of following instructions and saying, "Guilty," they arose and firmly said, "Not guilty!"

135.5

"Would you really commit suicide if I refuse to marry you?" the gushing girl asked the veteran actor.

"That," replied the actor with unrehearsed dignity, "has been my usual custom."

135.6

A Broadway director was annoyed by an actress who rolled her r's excessively. He reached the breaking point when she said, "You want me to cr-r-oss the stage. But I'm behind a table. How shall I get ac-r-r-oss?"

"Why, my dear," said the director, "just r-r-oll over on your r's."

135.7

An actor fell off a ship as it was passing not too far from a lighthouse. But the poor fellow drowned because he persisted in swimming in circles in order to keep within the spotlight.

135.8

An actor and a banker found themselves seated next to each other at a fund-raising dinner. "I'm ashamed to admit it," said the banker, "but I have not been to the theater in five years."

"Don't let it embarrass you," said the actor. "I haven't been in a bank in ten years."

135.9

A handsome young actor developed extreme hoarseness and became alarmed because he was to be on TV that night. He went early in the morning to a doctor's home a few doors away, and the M.D.'s lovely young wife opened the door. The actor said in a low voice, "Is the doctor in?"

"No," she whispered back, "come on in."

135.10

"Man, have I got a sensation," said the agent to a theatrical producer. "Built like Burt Lancaster, sings like Goulet, and acts like Gielgud."

"Wonderful," said the producer. "Bring him in!"

"Trouble is," said the agent, "it's a girl."

135.11

A ventriloquist, down to his last dollar, used it to buy a little dog which he carried under his arm to the nearest bar. He said to the bartender, "This talking dog is all that I have left. How about $25 for it?"

"Whaddya mean, a talking dog?" asked the barkeep.

The ventriloquist went into his act. Apparently from the mouth of the dog came a shrill bark, and then, "Yeah, I talk! I could say plenty about this cheap joint and its lousy liquor. I know; I've been here before."

The bartender was astonished. The ventriloquist looked fondly at the dog, and said: "I hate to give him up, but I need the money. What do you say?"

"Twenty-five dollars is too much, even if it does talk. I'll give you $15." The bartender reached into the cash register for the money.

The ventriloquist, in no position to bargain, took the money, handed over the dog, and hastened to the door. But when he reached the door, the dog called to him: "I'm only worth $15, eh? Well, just for that I'm never going to say another word." And he didn't.

135.12

In the days when vaudeville was the rage, two actors met after an absence of months and began to discuss their experiences on the vaudeville circuit. One of them said he had been having considerable success with his act everywhere he played. But he added, "Poor Joe Blow, he's having it pretty rough. Last week we were on the same bill, and his act preceded mine. He didn't get over at all. In fact the crowd didn't like him—they booed and hissed the poor fellow right off the stage. It was so bad that right in the middle of my act they started in booing poor Joe again."

135.13

A small-time vaudeville couple, playing in hand-me-down theaters, just barely making a living, eating skimpy meals, traveling in coaches or buses, was waiting for a bus one day for the next booking in some miserable joint. Suddenly a swanky limousine turned the corner; two well-dressed and overstuffed persons were in it.

"Looks pretty wonderful!" sighed the actress.

"Yes," admitted her partner, "but remember they can't act!"

135.14

A neurotic actor was traveling with a show which contained an act of three midgets, two of whom were in love with the third—a female midget. Traveling from one town to another, the actor complained he couldn't get any sleep the night before—seems one of the midgets got the girl, and the third midget was so upset he was pacing back and forth in his upper berth all night—right over the sleepless actor.

135.15

A showman, in the days when nudity on the stage was daring, produced a woman in the garments of Eve on the platform of a small-town hall, claiming she was "the Naked Truth."

A country man, craning his neck and examining her carefully, called out. "She ain't naked truth. That's Molly Smith from over the hill a piece."

135.16

For years a man worked for the circus as a human cannon ball. He was shot out of a big cannon so often that his eardrums were shattered and his nerve was gone. He went to his boss and said he was quitting. "We'll miss you," said the boss. "It's not easy to find a man of your caliber."

135.17

Edward H. Sothern, famous American actor of earlier days, was quite a joker on occasion. One day he passed an ironmonger's shop and noticed a mopey-looking young clerk at the counter. Sothern entered and asked, "Do you have a good second-hand copy of Cicero's *Orations?*"

"This is an ironmonger. We got nothing like that."

"I'm not interested in the kind of binding."

"But, Mister, this ain't a book store."

"I don't care what kind of wrapping paper you have. I'll take it in a bag."

"We don't sell books in here," the young man shouted at Southern.

"OK, I'll wait," smiled Sothern pleasantly and sat down. The clerk rushed into the back of the shop excitedly and returned with the proprietor. "What are you after?" asked the boss irritatedly.

"All I want is a small file—about 4 inches long," said Sothern.

"Certainly," said the proprietor, as he turned to glare at the bewildered clerk.

135.18

Minnie Maddern Fiske, a famous and imperious American actress, was in her home one day when an irate author called on her and began accusing her of losing the manuscript of a play he had submitted to her. Mrs. Fiske rang for the butler, while she said firmly, "I have never mislaid a manuscript." When the butler arrived she turned to him and said, "Wilkins, it's getting chilly in here. Throw a few more manuscripts on the fire, please."

135.19

In the second act of a drama, the beautiful young heroine was disrobing—properly. Slowly she turned off the various lights, leaving only the bedside lamp. She slipped into her negligee and loosened her unmentionables, which fell to the floor, stepped out of them, placed them on a chair, walked around to the side of the bed, took off her shoes and stockings, and then tucked herself into bed amid a breathless audience. But just then came a voice from the audience, "What, without first brushing your teeth?"

135.20

Finley Peter Dunne was asked what he thought of the dancing of a once-famous ballerina, now become heavy and less graceful.

"She," said Dunne, "reminds me of Grant's Tomb in love."

135.21

Alfred Lunt has his head in the clouds and his feet in the box office.

—*Noel Coward*

135.22

Earl Wilson reports that a show girl was overheard speaking about her latest beau—a rich fellow. "All right, he's got a Rolls Royce with a phone in it—but he's a penny pincher; the phone is on a party line."

135.23

Florenz Ziegfeld was trying out a version of his famous Follies in the Midwest before bringing it to Broadway. While there he encountered an old school friend who was operating a fairly successful little business in a nearby small town. Ziegfeld thought the friend would enjoy watching a rehearsal of the Follies and took him to the theater. Of course a dazzling succession of beautiful girls appeared on the stage, most of them in scanty costumes. The merchant just sat there next to Ziegfeld and kept muttering, "Phui!" Finally Ziegfeld got annoyed and said to him, "What's the idea? Here you see some of the most beautiful women in America—and you see a lot of each one—and you sit there saying 'Phui!' at every one of them."

"I'm not saying 'Phui!' to the girls, I was thinking of my wife."

135.24

Marshall Foch when he first went to the Follies said, "I never saw such sad faces and gay behinds."

135.25

Yul Brynner, who costarred with Gertrude Lawrence in the play *The King and I,* related that during a heat wave in New York the producer put an air-conditioner in Miss Lawrence's dressing room. The thought that the other girls in the show suffered just as much from the heat, moved Miss Lawrence to pay for the installation of an air-conditioner in their dressing room.

On the following evening, in a scene where all the King's wives appear on stage and bow to the King, Brynner noticed that Miss Lawrence standing back of the girls had all she could do to keep from laughing. Later he heard that the girls had taken lipstick and written across their underpants W-E L-O-V-E Y-O-U—a message Miss Lawrence got when they bowed to the king and flounced up the backs of their dresses.

135.26

If it is possible to believe that Victor Borge ever played to an apathetic audience, then you will believe the story about a time when, after he finished his act without any response from the audience, he stepped to the footlights and said, "What time do you want to be called in the morning?"

135.27

Raymond Massey, as playgoers well remember, gave an extraordinary performance as Abraham Lincoln in a play. In fact, Massey looked the part even without makeup, and scornful characters began to remark that Massey never stepped out of the character of Lincoln even when he was on the street.

"Massey won't be satisfied until he's assassinated," said George S. Kaufman.

135.28

Ethel Barrymore was in her dressing room when an attendant knocked and said, "A couple of gals to see you, Miss Barrymore; they say they went to school with you."

"Wheel them in," said Ethel Barrymore.

135.29

Ethel Barrymore invited some old friends to her birthday party.

"Are you going to have candles on the birthday cake?" she was asked.

"This," said Miss Barrymore, "is to be a birthday party—not a torchlight procession."

135.30

At the height of his fame, John Barrymore went into a Hollywood haberdashery shop and bought some shirts and ties. "Charge it as usual," said Barrymore.

"The name is?" asked the clerk.

"Barrymore."

"The first name?"

The great Barrymore was furious. "Ethel," he said.

135.31

During a matinee performance of John Barrymore in *Hamlet,* Jane Cowl was in the audience and was by no means reluctant to make her presence manifest. Barrymore, of course, soon became aware of Miss Cowl's verbal performance but concealed his irritation.

However, when the play ended Barrymore made a curtain speech, which closed with an elaborate bow toward Miss Cowl, and he said: "In conclusion, may I take this opportunity to thank Miss Cowl for the privilege of costarring with her this afternoon."

135.32

Scene stealing is one of the oldest games in the theater. Walter Winchell tells of a certain performance of *Hamlet* where Gravedigger No. 1 customarily diverted the audience from Hamlet himself by peeling off a coat every time Hamlet made a speech. One night Gravedigger No. 2 stole the scene from Gravedigger No. 1. Every time the first Gravedigger removed a coat, the second gravedigger put it on. The whole thing became so uproarious that poor Hamlet was ready to jump into the grave himself.

135.33

An actor playing the role of Hamlet in an English theater got into conversation with a scene shifter, who said that he had once played the part of Hamlet.

"Tell me," said the actor. "What was your interpretation of Hamlet's relation to Ophelia? Did you feel that Hamlet loved her too well but not wisely?"

"I don't know," said the scene shifter, "what 'Amlet did, but I can tell you that I did."

135.34

A high schooler wrote on an examination paper: "The Merchant of Venice was a famous Italian who bought and sold canal boats."

135.35

"A horse! A horse! My kingdom for a horse!" called out the actor dramatically in a rendering of Shakespeare's *King Richard III*.

"Wouldn't a jackass do?" called out a clown in the gallery.

The actor stepped to the edge of the footlights, peered up toward the gallery, and said with dignity, "Why yes—come right down."

135.36

During the rehearsal of an *avant-garde* play for off-Broadway production, one of the actors protested that he didn't know what it all meant.

The director replied: "You don't know what it means. Neither do I. The author himself doesn't know what it means. That is what makes it art."

135.37

One of the off-Broadway shows had music composed by a member of the musician's union, who was also a partner in the show's production. Funds were limited and the prospects not too good. They felt if they could lay off two musicians, they might make a go of it. The composer was asked to take it up with union.

He made a strong plea at a union meeting, ended up in tears over the fate of some thirty families if the union did not agree to the proposal. When he ended his plea he stood up again and said, in an entirely different mood, "I was speaking to you as a producer. Now I tell you as a member of the union, 'To hell with them! Turn 'em down.' "

135.38

Murray Robinson in the New York *World-Telegram* several years ago wrote about the Yiddish actors in New York, to whom top billing was often more important than to their colleagues on big-time Broadway. One minor actor named Max was always given the last position on the billboards, a position he appeared to be resigned to.

But one summer the entire company set sail for Europe, arranging their return to coincide with their reopening in New York on Labor Day. When the boat was to pull out of the European dock, the manager spotted Max on shore. "Come on!" screamed the manager. "If you miss the boat, you'll miss the opening!"

"I ain't going back," yelled Max. "I want to see whose name will now be last on the billboards!"

135.39

One day Professor Benjamin Jowett of Oxford learned that a junior play-producing don had deleted some lines about the Athenian code of morals from an ancient Greek drama. He sent for the don and said to him: "I hear you have been making cuts in a Greek play. Aristophanes wrote it. Who are you?"

135.40

Following World War I, Winston Churchill's political career was at its lowest point, and his popularity by no means great. A strictly apocryphal story is that during this period George Bernard Shaw sent Churchill two tickets for the opening night of Shaw's latest play. Shaw suggested in a note that one ticket was for Churchill, the other one "for your friend, if any."

Churchill returned the tickets, with this note: "I regret I am unable to attend the opening of your play. Please send me two tickets for the second performance, if any."

135.41

When the curtain rang down on the first-night performance of *Arms and the Man* the audience set up a cry for the author. George Bernard Shaw went up on the stage amid applause, except for the hissing of a man in the gallery.

Shaw looked up at the gallery and said, "I agree with you, Sir, but what can we two do against so many?"

135.42

Oscar Wilde, when asked about the first night of a play of his, said: "Oh, the play was a great success, but the audience was a failure."

135.43

While playing one of his favorite roles in a country theater in England, actor John Kemble was continually interrupted by the squalling of a young child in the audience. Finally he could stand it no longer. He walked to the footlights and in his most tragic tones said, "Ladies and Gentlemen, unless the play is stopped the child cannot possibly go on." The audience saw to it that the child stopped.

135.44

Herbert Tree visited his friend Colonel Lowther, who lived in a famous English castle. A party of tourists walking through the grounds stopped Lowther and asked him if he was Colonel Lowther. "No," said Lowther, and he pointed to Tree as being the proprietor. The tourists walked over to Tree, who greeted them cordially and told them to help themselves to as many peaches from the trees as they liked. Lowther heard this, then introduced himself to the tourists as Herbert Tree of His Majesty's Theatre, and said, "I should be delighted to place a box at your disposal whenever you care to apply."

Later Lowther told Tree that some of the tourists asked if they could not instead have tickets for the Coliseum.

135.45

An English actor, down to his last few dollars, went into a run-down hash house on a side street for a cheap meal. He was amazed to find an actor friend of his behind the counter. "My Lord," he exclaimed, "you a counterman in a joint like this!"

"True," replied the other actor with dignity, "but I don't eat here."

135.46

Several eighteenth-century actors were discussing the marriage of a well-known woman whose premarital escapades were notorious. "They say that she has given her husband a full account of her past," remarked one of the group. "What courage!" said one. "What honesty!" observed another. "And what a memory!" said Sam Foote.

135.47

Nepomucene Lemercier, a playwright, and Napoleon were first good friends, then quarreled. Nevertheless Napoleon sent his old friend one of the first Crosses of the Legion of Honor, which the writer returned. Napoleon thereupon forbade any performances of Lemercier's plays, which forced the playwright to live in a garret. Sometime later Napoleon encountered Lemercier among a group of people. He waved the crowd aside, went up to Lemercier, and asked, "When are you going to write a new tragedy?" "I am waiting, Sire!" replied Lemercier—a prophetic remark to make to Napoleon in 1812, the eve of the disastrous Russian campaign.

135.48

Schopenhauer tells about an actor named Unzelmann who was notorious for adding remarks of his own to the lines written by the playwright. At one Berlin theater he was strictly forbidden to improvise. Soon afterwards he had to appear on stage on horseback, and in the course of the performance the horse was guilty of serious misconduct—certainly of conduct unbecoming to a public stage. The audience began to laugh; but Unzelmann severely reproached the horse with, "Do you not know that it is forbidden to improvise?"

135.49

After producing plays for a young author, the producer and playwright decided to form a partnership for joint production. When the papers were drawn up and signed, the manager turned to the author and said, "Now there is one thing I want you to remember now that we are in partnership. That is for goodness' sake don't let anybody impose on you the way I've been doing these past three years."

135.50

A playwright, unable to attend the opening night of his drama, wired the producer: HOW IS IT GOING?

IT IS GONE, was the producer's sad reply.

135.51

An Irish-American had written a musical show with an Irish theme and an Irish title and deemed it fitting that the chorus girls should also be Irish.

The director of the show's dance numbers was a man of exceptional gentleness and politeness and was never known to lose his temper during rehearsals—uncommon conduct for Broadway. But this man's patience was severely tested as a result of the producer's hiring of chorus girls on the basis of Irish ancestry rather than talent.

Finally, after a particularly frustrating rehearsal the dance director called the girls together and said to them:

"I believe the great majority of you girls belong to the wonderful Irish race. That being the case, I would suppose most of you are Catholics and as a consequence go frequently to confession."

By a show of hand the girls confirmed the dance director's conclusion.

"Now I want you girls who raised your hands to do me a very special favor. I want each of you Irish Catholic girls to promise that you will go to confession over this weekend. And I want you to confess to the good priest that you lied when you told me you could dance.

"That will be all. Thank you."

135.52

Mrs. Rabinowitz loved the theater, but she could never persuade her husband to accompany her. He always had several excuses: too tired, too busy, another engagement. But finally one day she insisted he come with her to a certain popular drama.

During the performance Rabinowitz squirmed uncomfortably, and when it was over his wife said with a note of triumph: "And what do you say now about it?"

"Lousy—that's what I say."

"What do you mean 'lousy'?"

"I'll tell you," said Mr. Rabinowitz. "It's the same old thing on the stage. When he wants, she doesn't want. When she wants, he doesn't want. And then when they both want, what happens? Boom—they pull down the curtain!"

135.53

A man bought a ticket to a show and walked away without picking up his change. The girl in the box office was asked by the next man what she did in such cases. She said she always knocked on the window with a feather to call the man back.

135.54

From an Ohio newspaper: EASTER MATINEE FOR CHILDREN. EVERY CHILD LAYING AN EGG IN THE DOORMAN'S HAND WILL BE ADMITTED FREE.

135.55

A schoolboy wrote: "Flotsam and Jetsam were a famous team of comedians."

Aphorisms

135.56

What a glorious garden of wonders the lights of Broadway would be to anyone lucky enough to be unable to read.

—*G. K. Chesterton*

135.57

Broadway is America's hardened artery.

—*Mark Kelly*

135.58

In a drama the villain is simply thrown over by the heroine. In a melodrama she throws him over a cliff.

135.59

The artistic temperament is a disease that afflicts amateurs.

G. K. Chesterton, Heretics

135.60

Talent is an infinite capacity for imitating genius.

—*Benjamin De Casseres,* The Muse of Lies

135.61

Every crowd has a silver lining.

—*P. T. Barnum*

135.62

A good musical comedy consists largely of disorderly conduct occasionally interrupted by talk.

—*George Ade*

(*See also 24.14, 36.2, 139.1–139.46, 140.1–140.23, 150.39, 150.41, 158.9, 171.6, 171.9, 212.6, 274.6*)

136. Hollywood

Anecdotes

136.1

In the film *Harlow* a Hollywood producer, modeled after Louis B. Mayer, says, "The time has come for us to start making sex films for the family."

136.2

Legend has it that when Mrs. Patrick Campbell was introduced to Mary Pickford, when the latter was known as America's Sweetheart, she said, "My, what beautiful golden hair, and what lovely eyes. Really, my dear, you should try to get into the movies."

"But I am in the movies," protested Miss Pickford. "I am Mary Pickford."

"Oh, well, you could change your name," said Mrs. Campbell consolingly.

136.3

When Katharine Hepburn was assigned her first role at MGM she was awed at the prospect of playing opposite Academy Award winner Spencer Tracy. But, determined not to betray her fright, she breezed onto the set and anxious to get in the first word said to Tracy, "Oh, Mr. Tracy, I'm really afraid that I am too tall for you."

Tracy turned to her slowly an expressionless face and calmly said, "That's all right, my dear, I'll soon cut you down to my size!"

—*Motion Picture Magazine*

136.4

On the radio a fashion editor was interviewing a Hollywood star who said: "I think women's clothes are very interesting. I've been successful with them, on and off, for ten years."

136.5

A movie star after a trying day at the studio came home exhausted. After dinner she changed to a strapless evening gown to attend a party and then said, "I'm so tired, I'd rather stay home."

"OK," said her husband. "Put something on, and let's go to bed."

136.6

Dan Duryea advises young women desiring to break into the movies: "Change your hair style, learn how to walk, buy a sexy wardrobe, and before you know it you'll be married, have six kids and forget about all this nonsense."

—*Gene Sherman,* in Los Angeles Times

136.7

The Los Angeles telephone directory contained the name of actress Giselle Werbischek Pfiffle. One evening Nunally Johnson phoned her number, and when Miss Pfiffle came to the phone, he said, "This is Nunally Johnson. Do you remember me?"

"No, I don't believe I do," she replied.

"Oh, I'm sorry," said Johnson. "I must have the wrong Giselle Werbischek Pfiffle."

136.8

The wife of a Hollywood actor told him that their marriage was on the rocks. When he asked in surprise why, she said it was the eternal triangle.

"That is untrue," said the actor. "You know very well that I hardly even look at other women."

"It's not that kind of a triangle. It is that both you and I are in love with you."

136.9

The once-great movie lover was escorting some friends over the large estate upon which he was living in his old age. They strolled through a pasture where a flock of sheep gathered about him affectionately as he tossed tidbits of food to them. "See how they love me!" exclaimed the old actor.

"Of course they do," said one of the visitors. "That's because you feed them."

"When you get to my age," said the actor wistfully, "you will call it love, too."

136.10

While visiting a Hollywood studio the professor of literature was introduced to one of the actors in his dressing room. Noticing a picture of Longfellow on the wall he said, "I see you are an admirer of Longfellow."

"Who?" asked the actor.

"Longfellow," said the professor, pointing to the picture.

"Oh, him," said the actor. "Never knew his name. But he got's a beautiful beard, and it helps me when I make up for the role I'm playing."

136.11

Orson Welles was doing a scene in which he was about to be burned to death in bed and became increasingly nervous when the director repeatedly called for "takes" in order for it to be precisely as desired. Welles said, "I'll sure be glad when this thing is finished."

"Don't let it get you down," quipped Joan Fontaine. "We'll let you know if we get the odor of burning ham."

136.12

Walter Winchell, in 1946, told about one actor wondering to another one about a certain movie executive: "I understand he's changing his faith."

"Is that right?" added the other actor. "You mean to say he no longer thinks he's God?"

136.13

A bit player in Hollywood was offered the chance to play a more important role—as a participant in a simulated jungle scene with a performing lion in a camouflaged cage.

The young fellow was not at all enthusiastic—in fact he demurred.

"What's the matter with you," said the brave director, "this is a tame lion that was raised on milk."

"I was brought up on milk, too," said the extra, "but I like a bit of meat myself now and then."

136.14

During a conference in Hollywood a producer got himself into a towering rage. One of his assistants pleaded with him to be calm, adding, "If you're not careful you'll get ulcers."

"Get them? Nonsense! I give them."

136.15

The Hollywood movie executive opened the conference with, "Now don't anyone say 'Yes' until I have finished speaking."

136.16

A Hollywood producer brags he arrived in the U.S. without a cent and now owes more than $50,000.

136.17

Earl Wilson tells about a Hollywood party of movie-colony people during which one man mentioned that he had just seen what was perhaps the worst picture ever made. When he named it another man said, "I wrote it." The first man began to apologize, saying that actually he had exaggerated, that really he had seen worse pictures and particularly one horror which broke all records for sheer drivel. When asked to name it, which he did, the other man said, "I wrote that one, too."

136.18

Samuel Goldwyn met his match when he attempted to dicker with George Bernard Shaw for film rights to some of Shaw's plays. The Irish playwright was not interested in Goldwyn's proposal. But Goldwyn persisted. "Think, Mr. Shaw," he said, "think of the millions of people who would have the opportunity to become acquainted with your art."

"Ah, Mr. Goldwyn," said Shaw, "you think only of art, while I think only of money."

136.19

The scenario writer went to his Hollywood producer and said, "I've been going over this play that you just bought, but it's impossible for the movies. The story deals entirely with Lesbians."

"So what?" snapped the producer. "Make them Americans—or any other nationality."

136.20

For years the Hollywood movie executive complained that he never saw any stories with true originality. "Always the same old thing," he said repeatedly. One day an unknown young man was brought into his office. "I hear you have a new play," said the movie man. "Relax and read the whole thing to me."

The author had not expected so cordial a reception, and although he stammered badly he decided to brave it through and began to read—stuttering scene by scene to the very end. The excited movie executive stood up and shouted for his secretary: "Sign this gentleman up right away. He's got an angle that will be a sensation. Every one of his characters stutters!"

136.21

A movie house showing a popular thriller-diller was being picketed, but crowds continued to walk past the pickets into the movie. Union officials then decided on a new tactic: they posted a lone picket who stood silently by the box office, with a sign reading "The hero's uncle did it."

—*Jim Lowe,* CBS

136.22

Hollywood lines designed to wilt their victims: "Get a stick and I'll help you kill it," and, "Follow him and see what he eats."

136.23

Jean Cocteau described Hollywood as "an insane asylum run by its own inmates." Ferenc Molnar called it "a sunny place for shady people." J. B. Priestley said it was "a series of suburbs in search of a city."

Definitions

136.24

Hollywood: A place where everyone is a genius until he loses his job.

—*Erskine Johnson*

136.25

Hollywood: A place where they shoot too many pictures and not enough actors.

—*Walter Winchell*

136.26

Hollywood: Ten million dollars' worth of intricate and highly ingenious machinery, functioning elaborately to put skin on baloney.

—*George Jean Nathan*

Aphorisms

136.27

I've had several years in Hollywood and I still think the movie heroes are in the audience.

—*Wilson Mizner*

136.28

American motion pictures are written by the half-educated for the half-witted.

—*St. John Ervine*

(*See also 126.9, 129.7, 137.1–137.36, 141.9, 142.8, 142.9, 146.3, 146.5, 148.4, 149.1, 149.2, 152.58, 155.20, 162.42, 179.10, 179.11, 183.2, 199.6, 216.6, 259.2*)

137. Goldwynisms

NOTE: There is no doubt that Hollywood producer Samuel Goldwyn committed *some* of the malaprops and tangle talk attributed to him. But it is equally certain that the blunders of other Hollywood moguls have been ascribed to Goldwyn. Which are genuine Goldwynisms is apparently beyond determination.

137.1

During a conference of producers, directors, and studio executives a strong effort was being made to persuade Samuel Goldwyn to agree to a project he had previously disagreed with. Goldwyn heard them out, then said, "Gentlemen, the best I can give you is a definite maybe." Goldwyn left the room, but a few minutes later he said firmly, "Gentlemen, I've thought it over. You can include me out."

137.2

Dorothy Parker was suggested to Samuel Goldwyn as a writer he should get to come to Hollywood. "But," objected an assistant, "she's rather caustic."

"What do I care about how much she costs?" said Goldwyn. "Send for her."

137.3

"Gentlemen," said Samuel Goldwyn at a scenario conference, "I may not always be right—but I'm never wrong!"

137.4

During Truman's worst days, Samuel Goldwyn said that "if F. D. R. were alive he'd be turning over in his grave."

137.5

Movie director Michale Curtiz reputedly gave Samuel Goldwyn some competition when he instructed Gary Cooper, "Now ride off in all directions," and while a script was being filmed snarled, "Don't talk to me while I'm interrupting."

137.6

Other Goldwynisms:

What a wonderful day to spend Sunday.

A verbal contract isn't worth the paper it's written on.

Every Tom, Dick, and Harry is named William.

I want to go where the hand of man has never set foot.

Now, gentlemen, listen slowly.

For your information, I would like to ask a question.

I have been laid up with intentional flu.

I'll tell you my opinion of that picture in two words: Im Possible.

(*See also 156.1–156.25, 182.1–182.10*)

138. Radio and Television

Anecdotes

138.1

"We've got to put some conflict into this script," demanded the television producer.

"Conflict?" said the scriptwriter. "Isn't there conflict in it, now?"

"Not the kind I want," said the producer. "When I say conflict I mean something like maybe where one man wants to be a wrestler and the other man wants to be a salesman in Tiffany's. And they are Siamese twins. There you got conflict."

138.2

A television gagwriter was conversing with a sponsor when another writer came in and said, "I want to speak to you."

"Go ahead," said the first man.

"Not in front of the client."

"Well, spell it, then."

138.3

Rumor hath it that one night in Buffalo, through a confusion of transmission lines to a television station—where there is one line for the picture and another for the sound—two wrestlers came on the TV screen, and while they strove to tear each other apart, there came the softly vibrant tones of a man's voice saying, "Darling, we were made for each other."

138.4

Broadcasting land tells of the contestant on a quiz show who was asked the difference between amnesia and magnesia.

The young fellow thought about it for a few moments, then said, "The fellow with amnesia doesn't know where he's going."

138.5

When a quiz contestant was asked if he could name a product the supply of which exceeds the demand, he answered, "Trouble."

138.6

From the land of television comes the story about a quiz program on which a young man was asked to complete the line, "Humpty Dumpty sat on a ———." The contestant was obviously reluctant to answer. "Come on, give us the answer. Surely you know what Humpty Dumpty sat on?"

"I know, all right," said the young man, "but I don't think I should say it on the air."

138.7

On a quiz program a soldier took his place before the microphone. "Here's your question," said the M.C., "How many successful jumps must a paratrooper make before he graduates?"

"All of them," said the soldier.

138.8

Although they are usually composed of stupid husbands, smug wives, and ill-mannered children, there is one thing you have to admire about the families in the TV serials—they don't waste their time watching TV.

—Denver *Post*

138.9

Many a child who watches television for hours will go down in history—not to mention arithmetic, English, and geography.

—*Rotopics,* Belleville, Ont., Canada

138.10

Early to bed and early to rise is a sure sign that you're fed up with television.

—The Richmond (Ind.) *Rotor*

138.11

During an interview program on station WMGM, in New York, a woman guest told Bill Silbert that she had four children, age two, three, five, and six.

"How come you missed having a four-year-old child?" asked the interviewer.

"Oh," replied the mother, "that was the year we got our television set."

138.12

The Reader's Digest reports that a farm editor on a Western radio station, tired of "citified" commercials, said, "Well, now here's something we can really get our teeth into—*fertilizer.*"

138.13

Earl Wilson relates that a woman on the radio referred to a person as "an inveterate streetwalker," though meaning to say "an inveterate sleepwalker." And of course there is the famous fluff of the announcer who presented "Hoobert Heever."

And the usually reliable Bob Trout years ago said to the radio audience, "You have just listened to Herbert Hoover, the only formerly living President of the United States." At least once Ruperts Beer was called "Buppert's Rear" by a broadcaster.

Songwriter Dave Clark, according to Earl Wilson, once said, "I don't like him, and I always will." When Wilson Mizner asked Clark how he liked a certain show, he said, "It's a great show. Don't miss it if you can." Clark is also supposed to have said, "I may be crazy, but I'm not far from it."

138.14

Famous radio fluffs include: the commentator who said, "The battle of the Bulgian Belch"; Lowell Thomas's reputed reference to "Sir Stifford Crapes"; and Harry von Zell's report that "the RAF dropped four ton blondes on Berlin." Jimmy Wallington, so they say, did as well or better when at the end of a program in the Famous Romance series, while the "Wedding March" was being softly played, said, "So ends another virgin."

138.15

The radio interviewer was so impressed by having Walter Pidgeon as his guest that in his excitement he said, "Mr. Privilege, this is indeed a pigeon." And one sleepy announcer said one morning, when beginning a commercial, "Does your husband wake up dill and lustless?"

138.16

A radio correspondent reported that a congressman referred to a certain diplomat as a "pushie cooker."

138.17

Evan Esar, in his excellent *Humorous English,* reports the following radio tangle talk: An announcer doing a commercial for a drugstore's prescription department said, "This is typical of the scare and kill shown by the Main Street Drug Store." One unfortunate came out with, "I am happy to speak over this nationwide hiccup." And then the Governor of the Virgin Islands was introduced as "the Virgin of Governor's Island."

138.18

H. Allen Smith says he heard a radio announcer say, "And now here's the Girls' Bum and Droogle Corps."

138.19

Graham MacNamee once referred to Texaco Fire Chief Gasoloon.

138.20

A radio announcer once referred to General Dwight Eisenhowever.

138.21

If that radio announcer doesn't get off the air, I'll stop breathing it.

—*Wilson Mizner*

Definitions

138.22

Radio: A device which permits speakers to state without fear of contradiction.

138.23

Television is a medium of entertainment which permits millions of people to listen to the same joke at the same time and yet remain lonesome.

—*T. S. Eliot*

Aphorisms

138.24

Television comedians in capitalist countries, with their dubbed-in laughter and trained audiences, function in the same false popularity as Soviet Russian leaders with their trained audiences.

138.25

The ideal voice for radio may be defined as having no substance, no sex, no owner, and a message of importance to every housewife.

—*H. V. Wade*

(*See also 81.2, 117.1, 138.8, 141.13–141.15 141.22, 196.5, 205.17*)

139. Sharps and Flats

Anecdotes

139.1

One day Serge Koussevitzky was driven into a frenzy while rehearsing his symphony orchestra by one of the players who persisted in coming in at the wrong moments and then not playing precisely as the conductor desired. Finally Koussevitzky screamed at the faulty musician: "You're fired! Get out right away!"

The player got up and left the stage with his instrument, walked to the door, turned to the conductor and called out, "Nuts to you, Koussevitzky!"

"It's too late," retorted Koussevitzky. "I won't take you back."

139.2

One of the legends enjoyed by musicians concerns the symphony orchestra that was playing the *Lenore No. 3* overture of Beethoven at an outdoor concert. During this piece the first trumpeter steals from his place and moves offstage where he gives a fanfare heralding the arrival of the Minister of Justice. The trumpeter got up at the right time and stood waiting the correct distance from the orchestra, his trumpet raised awaiting the cue. But the expected fanfare did not come. A policeman rushed up when the man was about to blow and yelled, "You can't do that! Don't you know there's a concert going on!"

139.3

Arturo Toscanini thought it would be nice to offer the faithful chambermaid in a hotel he was staying at two tickets to one of his concerts. "Would you like to go to the concert next Friday evening?" he asked her.

"Is that the only night you have off?" she asked.

139.4

During a concert one evening, the soloist in an orchestra under the direction of Arturo Toscanini began properly enough but soon wandered from the score, and the more he wandered, the more flustered he became. Just before the end of his solo the performer got control of himself and ended up in the correct key. Toscanini bowed to him and said, "Welcome home, Mr. Goldsmith."

139.5

British conductor Sir Thomas Beecham and a friend went to an all-Mozart concert under the direction of a rival conductor. Beecham, famous as an interpreter of Mozart, began to squirm uncomfortably soon after the performance began and was obviously disappointed.

"What's the trouble," asked his friend. "I thought Mozart was your favorite composer."

"He is," said Beecham, "when I conduct him."

139.6

After one of his performances an excited woman spectator dashed backstage and said to Serge Koussevitzky, "Maestro! You—you are God!"

"Yes, Madam," replied Koussevitzky with great solemnity, "and it is such a responsibility."

—*Time*

139.7

A symphony orchestra on tour under the auspices of a skinflint impresario arrived in Pittsburgh for a concert, when the leader discovered the second oboe player was missing; he had been fired by the impresario. The leader protested vehemently, but the impresario said, "Don't get so excited over nothing. Who's buying a ticket to hear a second oboe!"

139.8

The conductor rehearsing his band gave special attention to the tuba player. After this player had made a mess of several difficult passages, the irate conductor demanded, "What's the matter with you?"

"It's not me," said the worried musician. "It's this damn horn. I blow in it so sweet, and it always comes out so rotten."

139.9

Former Ambassador James G. McDonald tells about the Israel Philharmonic giving a concert. Mrs. Ben-Gurion nudged her husband and pointed, "See, Ben Zvi is sleeping."

Ben-Gurion snarled, "So you wake me up for this?"

139.10

Some years ago when Jascha Heifetz, the famous violinist, made his triumphant debut in New York one spring evening, Mischa Elman, the great violinist, and Josef Hoffman, the celebrated pianist, were in the audience.

As the concert proceeded the audience was spellbound by the genius of young Heifetz. But the more the great artist played, and the greater became the audience's reception, the more Elman fidgeted and squirmed in his seat and nervously mopped his brow. During a pause in the program Elman turned to Hoffman and said, "It's terribly hot in here, isn't it?"

Hoffman smiled and whispered, "Not for pianists."

139.11

Walking with a friend one day, violinist Fritz Kreisler passed a large fish shop where a fine catch of codfish, with mouths open and eyes staring, were arranged in a row in the window.

"That reminds me," said Kreisler in some alarm, "I should be playing a concert."

139.12

For years the first violinist in an orchestra sat during performances making the most agonizing faces. He was a silent man, and his colleagues concluded he was either in considerable physical pain or had a great sorrow he could not conquer. But finally the man and his grimaces got on the nerves of the conductor of the orchestra, who called him aside one day after a performance and said, "For heaven's sake, what is the matter with you? For years now you have been making the most painful faces all during the performances."

"There's nothing the matter," said the violinist. "I feel all right, It's just that I don't like music."

139.13

The young but expert violinist was playing at a private musicale, rendering a difficult concerto which contained some particularly long rests for the soloist. During one of the intervals, the kindly hostess leaned over to him and whispered, "Don't get upset, my boy; just play something that you know; we'll all understand."

139.14

Rachmaninoff waged a one-man war against music watchers—those who sit in the audience with the score in their hands, following it to be sure the performer is faithful to the score. Once when he was playing his famous *Prelude in C-sharp Minor,* Rachmaninoff noticed a man in the hall reading the score. Just before the end of the *Prelude,* the pianist began to improvise a cadenza, and out of the corner of his eye enjoyed watching the man frantically turning the pages of his score to find what Rachmaninoff was playing. The pianist walked off the stage in the happy knowledge he had ruined the evening for at least one music watcher.

139.15

A young lady called on Rubinstein, the great pianist, and asked if he would listen to her playing and give her a judgment on it. He consented, reluctantly.

When she had finished playing a piece she turned to him expectantly. "Get married," said Rubinstein.

139.16

"I will now play 'Liebestraume,' by Franz Liszt," announced Victor Borge. "The Steinway Company has asked me to announce that this is a Baldwin piano."

139.17

When Victor Borge was asked why the keys of his piano were yellow, he said, "It's not because the piano is old, but because the elephant smoked too much."

139.18

During an orchestral performance the piccolo player stepped forward and played a solo. When it was ended somebody in the audience called out that the piccolo player was an s.o.b.

Before resuming with the music, the enraged conductor stepped forward and angrily asked, "Who called that piccolo player an s.o.b.?"

Once more a voice came from the audience: "Who called that s.o.b. a piccolo player?"

139.19

Enrico Caruso, the world-famous operatic tenor, was driving through the Wisconsin countryside while on a concert tour when he realized he was lost. He stopped at a farmhouse for directions and a drink of water and became friendly with the farmer. The great singer was invited to stay for the midday meal then being put on the table. As he was preparing to leave after a fine meal, Caruso thought it would please the kindly old farmer and his wife to know that they had entertained so celebrated a personality, so he told them his name.

The farmer was wide-eyed. "This is a great thing," said the farmer. "Who would have thought that I would have as a guest that great explorer—Robinson Crusoe!"

139.20

A small opera company was playing *Faust* in the provinces, with poor equipment and make-do scenery. At the point in the opera when Mephistopheles descends to the underworld—through a trapdoor in the stage—the trapdoor became stuck, and poor Mephistopheles could neither get in or out of it. The audience's tension was broken by a voice from the gallery, "By gad, 'Ell's full up!"

139.21

Adelina Patti, in an argument with an impresario about a fee, was reminded by the producer, "You are already making more money than the President of the United States!"

"Then go and get the President to sing for you," said Madame Patti.

139.22

Opera singer Jan Kiepura complained to his agent that another singer was receiving more publicity. When the agent boldly told the Polish singer that the newspapers considered him conceited, Kiepura said in astonishment: "Me conceited? The Great Kiepura?"

—*David Green,* Cosmopolitan

139.23

Geraldine Farrar, a famous Metropolitan Opera star of other days, made the first pages with her feuds with Caruso and others but met her match in Arturo Toscanini. She told him during a rehearsal, "Maestro, I am a star." Toscanini, without raising his voice, replied, "*Madame,* I know only the stars in heaven."

Farrar's riposte, incidentally, was pretty good, too. She snapped back with: "But the public pays to see my face and not your back!"

139.24

A young tenor with a good voice, but a greater ego, was engaged by a small opera company to sing the role of Canio in *Pagliacci.* When he finished the famous lament, there was moderate applause. The singer signaled the conductor he would repeat the aria, and then sang it a third time, each rendition followed by greater applause. The tenor, concluding he was really good, said to the audience, "Thank you so much, but we must go on with the opera. I can't sing the same aria all evening."

"You'll sing it until you learn it," called a man in the gallery.

139.25

A foreign pianist was employed to accompany an amateur soprano at her first concert. After his first rehearsal with the ambitious but untalented woman, the pianist was in despair over her repeated flatting of notes. Finally, he said to her, sadly, "I must resign. I play the black keys, I play the white keys—and always you sing in the cracks."

139.26

A stupid fellow, employed in blowing a cathedral organ, said, after the performance of a fine anthem, "I think we performed very well today."

"*We* performed!" answered the organist; "I think it was *I* who performed, or I have been much mistaken."

Shortly after, another celebrated piece of music was to be played. In the middle of the anthem the organ stopped; the organist cried out in a passion, "Why don't you blow?"

The fellow popped out his head from behind the organ and said, "Shall it be *we* then?"

139.27

A young man called on Mozart and asked him how to write symphonies.

"You're still very young," replied the great composer. "I think you should start out by composing simple ballads."

"But," protested the young man, "you were composing symphonies at age ten."

"True," replied Mozart, "but I did not have to ask how."

139.28

At a dinner party a woman turned to Sir William S. Gilbert and asked, "Who composed *The Magic Flute?*"

"Mozart," replied Gilbert.

"Mozart! I never heard of him," said the woman. "Is he still composing?"

"No, Madam," replied Gilbert; he is decomposing."

139.29

Composer Richard Wagner refused to cater to hostesses who expected their talented guests to perform for their supper.

At one such dinner party, the hostess asked the violinist to play, and he did. She asked a pianist to perform, and he complied. Then she turned to Wagner.

"I am sorry, madam," said the composer, reaching for the champagne, "I play the orchestra."

139.30

When Philip of Macedon insisted that his opinion about music be accepted, a musician said to him: "God forbid, Sire, that your fortunes should be so bad that you know more about the subject than I do."

139.31

The family was gathered around the piano in a Northern home, while "Swanee River" and other Stephen Foster favorites were played and sung. A visitor sat in the corner of the room sobbing.

The hostess hurried to him and said, "You must be a Southerner? No doubt the singing has made you homesick."

"No, it isn't that," he replied. "I'm a musician."

Definitions

139.32

Classical music is the kind we keep hoping will turn into a tune.

—*Kin Hubbard*

139.33

Music Lover: A man, who upon hearing a soprano in the bathroom, puts his ear to the keyhole.

—*Kalends*

139.34

Impresario: A promoter with an opera cape.

139.35

The rumba is a fox-trot with the backfield in motion.

139.36

A schoolboy wrote: "A lyric is something written to be sung by a liar."

139.37

Another schoolboy wrote: "Tin Pan Alley is a street in a New York slum."

Aphorisms

139.38

Swans sing before they die—'twere no bad thing
Should certain persons die before they sing.

139.39

She was a singer who had to take any note above A with her eyebrows.

—*Montague Glass*

139.40

She was a town-and-country soprano of the kind often used for augmenting the grief at a funeral.

—*George Ade*

139.41

Music hath charm to soothe a savage beast—but I'd try a revolver first.

—*Josh Billings*

_139.42_

The English may not like music, but they absolutely love the noise it makes.

—*Sir Thomas Beecham,* 1961

_139.43_

It's an ill wind that blows a saxophone.

_139.44_

In order to compose, all you need to do is to remember a tune that nobody else has thought of.

—*Robert Schumann*

_139.45_

I know only two tunes: one of them is "Yankee Doodle," and the other isn't.

—*Ulysses S. Grant*

_139.46_

Wagner's music is better than it sounds.

—*Edgar Wilson Nye*

(*See also 36.3, 37.19, 40.17, 40.30, 43.3, 84.4. 100.9, 124.15, 127.8, 135.37, 135.62, 140.7, 141.1, 148.11, 149.5, 149.7, 149.11, 149.14, 152.40, 154.2, 155.18, 155.43, 163.1, 179.7, 179.9, 181.3, 199.8, 208.11, 225.14, 233.14, 236.6, 236.14, 243.16, 243.19, 244.10, 244.22, 245.21, 270.5, 274.4, 276.6*)

140. Critics Crack Their Quips

Anecdotes

_140.1_

An actor named Steyne sued Heywood Broun for saying in a play review that the actor "gave the worst performance on the contemporary stage."

When the actor appeared in a new show there was much speculation about what Broun would have to say. Broun simply said, "Mr. Steyne was not up to his standard."

_140.2_

A noted New York drama critic had eaten too heavily and too quickly before rushing to the theater for a first night. At the end of the second act he belched loudly several times. A young woman seated in front of him turned around and said, "Would you mind waiting until you get back to your office before writing your review?"

_140.3_

An Iowa court ruled the following was not libelous. It is from a review of a theatrical performance by the Cherry Sisters:

Effie is an old jade of fifty summers, Jessie is a frisky fille of forty, and Addie, the flower of the family, a capering monstrosity of thirty-five. Effie is spavined, Addie is stringhalt, and Jessie, the only one who showed her stockings, has legs with calves as classic in their outlines as the curves of a broom handle.

—*Cherry v. Des Moines Leader,* 114, Iowa 298

_140.4_

Eugene Field said of the actor, Creston Clarke: "He played the king as though he were in constant fear that somebody else was going to play the ace."

_140.5_

Mr. X played Hamlet. He played it until one o'clock.

—*Eugene Field*

_140.6_

In a review of *Uncle Tom's Cabin,* Eugene Field wrote: "The Irish wolfhound was very poorly supported by the cast."

_140.7_

Reviewing a new musical show, Eugene Field said, "I wouldn't leave a turn unstoned."

_140.8_

The House Beautiful is the play lousy.

—*Dorothy Parker*

_140.9_

Commenting on one of the earliest performances of Katharine Hepburn, Dorothy Parker said, "She ran the gamut of emotions from A to B."

_140.10_

When Mr. Wilbur calls his play *Halfway to Hell,* he underestimates the distance.

—*Brooks Atkinson*

_140.11_

This short play review is attributed to Brooks Atkinson: "Such and such opened last night. Why?"

_140.12_

I only work in my leisure hours.

—*Henry Clapp, Jr.,* New York Drama Critic.

_140.13_

When a member of the *Comédie Française* was rebuked for falling asleep while an author was reading a play, he said, "Sleep is a criticism."

_140.14_

Jimmy Cannon reported that a certain play was so bad that "the audience hissed the ushers."

140.15

In ripping a new Broadway play to shreds, George S. Kaufman concluded with, "Of course, I saw it under unfortunate circumstances. The curtain was up."

140.16

In reviewing one of the last, and no doubt the worst, play that John Barrymore ever appeared in, George Jean Nathan sadly commented: "I always said that I'd admire Barrymore's acting till the cows came home. Well, ladies and gentlemen, last night the cows came home."

140.17

Tallulah Bankhead barged down the Nile last night as Cleopatra—and sank.

—*John Mason Brown,* New York Post

140.18

Percy Hammond ended a review of a new show with: "I have knocked everything except the knees of the chorus girls, and nature has anticipated me there."

140.19

The human knee is a joint, not an entertainment.

—*Percy Hammond*

140.20

A dull eighteenth-century dramatic writer, who had often felt the severity of the public, was complaining one day to actor-playwright Sam Foote of the injustice done to him by the critics; but he added, "I have, however, one way of being even with them, by constantly laughing at all that they say."

"You are perfectly right, my friend," said Foote, "for by this method you will not only disappoint your enemies, but lead the merriest life of any man in England."

140.21

Playwright Sophie Treadwell returned home to find that while she was away on a vacation, squirrels had eaten up the manuscript of three of her unproduced plays. "Being squirrels isn't bad enough," she said. "Now they have to be critics."

Aphorisms

140.22

Detraction is the tribute which the little pay to the great.

—*Beerbohm Tree*

140.23

A drama critic is a person who surprises the playwright by informing him what he meant.

—*Wilson Mizner*

(*See also* 135.2)

FOOTLIGHTS AND FANCY-FREE

141. Down Allen's Alley

141.1

During a vaudeville tour, Fred Allen played in Toledo where the orchestra leader was a gloomy little man who never so much as cracked a smile when Allen stood on the stage delivering his witticisms. After several days of this, it irked Allen to the point where he walked to the footlights, leaned over to the orchestra leader, and asked, "How much would you charge to haunt a house?"

141.2

Fred Allen said Ray Bolger, the dancer, was so thin that if he had an ulcer he would have to carry it in his hand.

141.3

A celebrity is a person who works hard all his life to become well known, then wears dark glasses to avoid being recognized.

—*Treadmill to Oblivion,* 1954

141.4

Referring to an actor he disliked, Fred Allen said: "I don't know what became of him. The last time I saw him he was walking down Lover's Lane, holding his own hand."

141.5

Fred Allen said: "He is so narrow-minded that if he fell on a pin, it would blind him in both eyes."

141.6

The only thing he ever takes out on a moonlit night is his upper plate.

141.7

He was not brought by the stork; he was delivered by a man from the Audubon Society personally.

141.8

The man was so small, he was a waste of skin.

141.9

Fred Allen defined an associate producer as "the only man in Hollywood who will associate with a producer."

141.10

Fred Allen said: "A vice-president is a man who doesn't know what his job is until he's been there six months, and by that time he's no longer with the organization."

141.11

The average vice-president is a form of executive fungus that attaches itself to a desk. On a boat this growth would be called a barnacle.

141.12

Advertising agency: Eighty-five percent confusion and fifteen percent commission.

141.13

Fred Allen once suggested a television quiz show where a panel of doctors would be confronted with contestants wearing long hospital gowns. The show would be called, "What's My Disease?"

141.14

Television: A device that permits people who haven't anything to do to watch people who can't do anything.

141.15

Television: A kind of radio which lets people at home see what the studio audience is not laughing at.

141.16

Fred Allen announced on one of his radio shows: "Next Sunday the Rev. Dr. Jones will preach on 'Skiing on the Sabbath,' or 'Are Our Young Women Backsliding on Their Weekends?' "

141.17

The Philadelphia Chamber of Commerce, press, and hotels became quite agitated years ago when Fred Allen said over the radio that he had once checked into a hotel in Philadelphia where the rooms were so small that the mice were humpbacked.

141.18

Fred Allen told about a girl who made her living crushing grapes with her feet. But she got fired for sitting down on the job.

141.19

Gentleman: A guy who wouldn't hit a woman with his hat on.

141.20

California is a fine place to live in—if you happen to be an orange.

141.21

That city is so dead that a four-way cold tablet wouldn't have any place to go.

141.22

One day on the radio, Fred Allen was asked who Mr. Hooper was. Allen, aware that Hooper conducted a radio rating service where samplings were made to determine the popularity of radio programs, said, "Mr. Hooper is a fellow who can look in the bottom of a bird cage and tell you how many grains of sand there are in the Sahara Desert."

142. The Wit of Will Rogers

142.1

Will Rogers was scheduled to speak at a meeting in California. The Governor was to have introduced him but became ill. The lieutenant-governor, substituting for the Governor, preceded Rogers and in an inept effort to kid him said, "Mr. Rogers is the biggest joke in California. Like all conceited actors, instead of listening to me, I see he is whispering to his companion."

Rogers, annoyed by this clumsy effort at humor, arose and said: "First of all, ladies and gentlemen, I want to apologize. It is quite true that I was whispering to the lady next to me, and I feel very bad about it. I am sorry. The reason it made such a disturbance was that I had asked a question. I said: 'Who is that man talking?' And she said, 'I don't know.' And then she turned and asked the gentleman next to her, and then he turned and asked the lady next to him, and then—well, it had to go all the way down the aisle and over by the door, and then when they found out, it had to come all the way back. 'Why, it's the lieutenant governor.' That sounds pretty big when you say it, and that's why it made such a disturbance. And then I says to the lady, I says, 'Oh, it's the lieutenant governor, is it? Well, what does *he* do?' 'Oh, he don't do anything,' she said. 'What do you mean?' I said, 'don't do anything? Don't he even get up in the morning?' 'Oh, yes,' she said, 'he gets up every morning and inquires whether the Governor's any worse.' "

142.2

When Will Rogers was introduced to President Coolidge, the poker-faced President said something through tight lips as they shook hands. Rogers leaned over as if he had missed some words and said: "Pardon me. I didn't catch the name."

142.3

Will Rogers on a radio program announced the President of the United States and mimicked Coolidge's nasal twang saying, "It gives me great pleasure to report on the state of the nation. The nation is prosperous on the whole, but how much prosperity is there in a hole?"

Later Rogers met Mrs. Coolidge, who told him she could imitate her husband's voice better than the comedian could. "Well, Grace," said Rogers, "you can imitate Cal's voice better'n me, but look what you had to go through to learn it."

142.4

Some years ago Huey Long conducted a one-man filibuster in the Senate, during which he read, among other things, the U.S. Constitution. Of this Will Rogers said, "He read 'em the Constitution. A lot of 'em thought he was reviewing a new book."

142.5

Will Rogers said: "With Congress, every time they make a joke, it's a law; and every time they make a law, it's a joke."

142.6

I never went to West Point because I was too proud to speak to a congressman.

142.7

I never lack material for my humor column when Congress is in session.

142.8

Anybody can be a Republican when the market is up; but when stocks is selling for no more than they're worth, I'll tell you, being a Republican is a sacrifice.

142.9

You take a Democrat and a Republican and you keep them both out of office, and I bet you they will turn out to be good friends and maybe make some useful citizens and devote their time to some work instead of 'lectioneering all the time.

142.10

The United States never lost a war or won a conference.

142.11

Our foreign dealings are an open book—generally a checkbook.

142.12

I don't make jokes; I just watch the government and report the facts.

142.13

One of the evils of democracy is that you have to endure the man you elect whether or not you like him.

142.14

The income tax has made more liars out of the American people than golf has.

142.15

Will Rogers told about a friend of his who was as fond of hunting as he was poor at it. One day Rogers met this friend returning from a hunting expedition. "Get anything?" asked Rogers.

"Nothing," said the hunter with disgust. "But worse than that, I was ashamed to go home without something so I stopped at the butchers and asked them to tie a live rabbit to a tree so I could kill it and bring it home without too great a lie. But then I hit the rope through the middle, and the damn rabbit escaped."

142.16

Will Rogers, acting as toastmaster, arose after a tediously long talk by one of the speakers and said, "You have just been listening to that famous Chinese statesman, On Too Long."

142.17

Will Rogers said: "Maybe ain't ain't correct, but I notice that lots of folks who ain't using ain't, ain't eating."

142.18

A holding company is a thing where you hand an accomplice the goods while the policeman searches you.

142.19

Will Rogers once said that when Gabriel blows his horn half of the American people will be at a convention, and the other half will be packing their bags to go to one!

142.20

So live that you wouldn't be ashamed to sell the family parrot to the town gossip.

142.21

People who fly into a rage always make a bad landing.

142.22

I always like to hear a man talk about himself because then I never hear anything but good.

143. Bea Lillie Leaves 'Em Laughing

143.1

Beatrice Lillie (Ladv Peele in private life) has a sharp tongue when properly provoked.

One day while playing Chicago she went early to a beauty parlor and was told she could be taken care of immediately and the work completed before the wife of a wealthy meat-packer arrived for her appointment with the same operator Miss Lillie preferred.

But Mrs. Moneybags arrived ahead of schedule and fretted because she had to wait. "Tell that actress to hurry up," called out the meat-packer's wife.

And over the partition came the more genteel but equally firm reply: "Tell that butcher's wife that Lady Peele will be out in a few minutes."

143.2

A catty socialite is reported to have stared at a string of pearls Beatrice Lillie was wearing and asked, "Are they real?"

"Of course," said Miss Lillie.

The questioner fingered the pearls and said, "You can tell if they are genuine by biting them."

"Don't you dare try it," said Miss Lillie. "It's unfair to test real pearls with false teeth."

143.3

During a luncheon at Sardi's, in New York's theatrical district, an actress, noted for her jealousy, looked at Beatrice Lillie and said, "I dread the thought of life at forty-five."

"Oh," said Miss Lillie, "what happened to you then?"

144. Herb Shriner's Hoosier Humor

144.1

Herb Shriner said that the only hotel in his hometown in Indiana wasn't much, but it did have a bridal suite. You could tell it because it was the only room with a lock on the door.

144.2

Herb Shriner said that his spinster aunt in Indiana got a husband when she saw a poster on the wall of the post office, showing the man's picture and marked "Wanted." The aunt offered $100 more than the government offered for him.

144.3

Herb Shriner said that back in his Indiana hometown it was pretty quiet on weekdays, but that on Saturday things livened up when all the fellows went down to the barbers' to watch them give haircuts.

145. Stories of Sam Levenson

145.1

Sam Levenson tells about a garment manufacturer, obviously foreign-born, who was being challenged on his Americanism by a bigoted blue blood. "You call yourself an American," sneered the self-elected aristocrat. "You can't come up to my standards; my ancestors came over on the Mayflower."

"Lucky for you they did," replied the naturalized citizen. "When I arrived in this great country, the immigration laws were much stricter."

145.2

Parental discipline, or the lack of it, is a theme which Sam Levenson often employs both as a humorist and as a commentator on the social scene. For example, he explains why parental discipline today is so often not effective: "When a child disobeys his mother, he is sent to his room. When he goes to his room, he has a radio, a television set, a seventeen-year-old baby sitter. His father didn't have it so good on his honeymoon."

145.3

Sam Levenson recalls that when he came home and showed his mother his report card with a mark of 98 in algebra, his mother wanted to know who had gotten the other two points.

145.4

On "Two for the Money" Sam Levenson said that he read recently of a fellow walking down the street minding his own business, when a man ran up to him. "Hey, buddy," said the stranger, "did you see a cop around here?"

"No," said the pedestrian.

"How long you been walking?"

"About twenty minutes," replied the one questioned.

"Okay, buddy, this is a stickup," said the accoster decisively.

145.5

When he was M.C. on "Two for the Money," Sam Levenson recalled that every one of the eight children in his family knew the value of money. For a penny a kid could get a paraffin whistle; he blew on it all week and on Sunday ate it.

145.6

Sam Levenson says that a light sleeper is one who sleeps until dark.

145.7

Sam Levenson tells about a fellow who quarreled with his wife and moved to a hotel. He brooded all day over the matter, but by dinner time he was both hungry and sorry. He phoned her. "Hello, Sarah, what are you making for dinner?"

"Poison I'm making."

"So make only one portion. I'm not coming home."

146. W. C. Fields's Funny Bone

146.1

W. C. Fields's nimble wit was put to good use one evening when he was playing in Earl Carroll's *Vanities*. During one of his scenes a backdrop collapsed backstage with a resounding crash. Fields lifted his head inquiringly and said, "Mice."

146.2

Any man who dislikes children and dogs can't be wholly bad.

—*W. C. Fields*

146.3

When W. C. Fields determined to locate permanently in Hollywood he decided upon a grand entry. Choosing one of the most plush hotels, and arrayed in cutaway and morning trousers and a gold-headed cane, he strode jauntily to the desk and asked for "the bridal suite." The astonished hotel manager told him that the bridal suite was reserved for gentlemen with brides.

"I'll pick one up in town," said Fields grandly.

146.4

"Do you believe in clubs for women?" an interviewer asked W. C. Fields.

"Only," replied the comic, "when all other means of persuasion fail."

146.5

When W. C. Fields was engaged in movie work, it was his custom to arrive each day with an outsize shaker of martinis, which he insisted contained pineapple juice, an amusing deception Hollywood accepted good humoredly. But one afternoon a prankster got hold of the huge cocktail shaker and substituted real pineapple juice for the more potent contents. Field returned soon after for a few stimulating drinks, then roared out, "Somebody's been putting pineapple juice in my pineapple juice."

146.6

W. C. Fields said that if he could live his life over—he would live over a saloon.

146.7

In one of his characteristic outbursts, W. C. Fields said, "What a nitwit. When I said hello to this moron, he couldn't even think of an answer."

146.8

"How about a Bromo Seltzer?" W. C. Fields was asked one morning when he had a bad hangover.

"Good God, no!" said Fields. "I couldn't stand the noise."

147. Beerbohm Tree

147.1

Beerbohm Tree, the actor, liked to have vivid posters of himself made up to advertise his shows and admitted he liked to look at them when he went through the streets. When twitted about this, Tree said, "When I pass my name in such large letters I blush, but at the same time instinctively raise my hat."

147.2

Beerbohm Tree related that he was traveling in a train that was full, except for the seat opposite him. Tree was smoking a cigar. Much to his annoyance a young clerk boarded the train, sat in the opposite seat, and lighted up a cigarette. Tree said to him, "Are you aware that this is not the smoking car?" Upon this the young fellow stamped out his cigarette then looked up and found Tree still smoking his cigar.

"But you are smoking," said the passenger.

"Yes," replied Tree. "But I thought maybe you had conscientious scruples."

147.3

Sitting at the window of a London Club, Beerbohm Tree bet other members that the next hundred people who passed by would all have the appearance of unhappy souls. Ninety-nine melancholy persons passed by, then followed the hundredth, a man skipping along. "You lose," said one of the members to Tree. "Oh, no," replied Tree, "that last fellow was a victim of Saint Vitus's dance."

147.4

An actor who was to play Caesar was told to lie supine as the murdered Emperor throughout the Forum scene. The actor protested that he was subject to colds in the winter and the drafts on the stage would kill him. "What," protested the actor, "will people in the audience think if the corpse sneezes?"

"If that happens," said Beerbohm Tree, "you will be called Julius Cnaesar."

147.5

Beerbohm Tree, asked by a gramaphone company for a testimonial, gave them the following: "Sirs, I have tested your machine. It adds new terror to life and makes death a long-felt want."

147.6

Beerbohm Tree, the actor, stood gazing at a portrait of David Garrick and remarked, "They say I look more and more like Garrick every day."

"Yes, and less and less like him every night," someone observed.

147.7

When someone laid on flattery with a trowel, Beerbohm Tree said: "He has his tongue in his cheek and his cheek in his tongue."

147.8

Referring to an actress whose reputation as a lover was higher than her reputation as an artist, Beerbohm Tree said: "She kissed her way into society. I don't like her. But don't misunderstand me: my dislike is purely platonic."

147.9

Beerbohm Tree encountered a man on a London street staggering under the weight of a grandfather's clock and said to him: "My dear man, why not carry a watch."

147.10

Beerbohm Tree said: "The only man who wasn't spoiled by being lionized was Daniel. The process of acquiring a swollen head is a pleasant one; it is only the subsequent shrinkage that hurts."

147.11

Our domestic morality is founded on the axiom that boys must be boys but that girls mustn't be girls.

147.12

Every man is a potential genius until he does something.

147.13

I can stand any amount of flattery so long as it is fulsome enough.

148. Comedians-at-large

148.1

Bob Hope was golfing one day when his shirt tail popped out from his trousers, whereupon some moron yelled, "Hey, Hope, your slip is showing."

Hope stopped his game long enough to call back, "Your father's slip is showing."

148.2

The program is nearly over! I can feel the audience is still with me—but if I run faster I can shake them off.

—*Bob Hope*

148.3

A gentleman, according to Bob Hope, is a fellow who, when his wife drops anything, kicks it to where she can pick it up more easily.

148.4

George Jessel was giving a graphic account of how he had told off a certain Hollywood movie magnate.

"What happened when you finished your tirade?" a listener asked Jessel.

"Nothing," replied Jessel. "We parted good friends. He boarded his yacht, and I took a bus home."

148.5

George Jessel relates that one evening in New York a man gave him a hearty thump on the back and said, "Well, Goldblatt!"

"I'm not Goldblatt," said Jessel. "And if I were Goldblatt that's no way to greet a friend —punching him on the back like that."

"Say, mister," replied the stranger, "who are you to tell me how to greet Goldblatt?"

148.6

During one of his television shows, Jack Benny said that a friend of his to whom he customarily gave a bottle of bourbon was forbidden to drink by orders of his doctor. So that Christmas Benny gave him, instead of the usual bottle, the name of a new doctor.

148.7

Henny Youngman said he was driving one of the small cars and got into trouble when he put out his hand turning a corner and ruptured a policeman.

148.8

Milton Berle says that sometimes Bing Crosby's checks come back marked "Insufficient Banks."

148.9

Either this man is dead, or my watch has stopped.

—*Groucho Marx*

148.10

Sir, I would horsewhip you if I had a horse.

—*Groucho Marx*

148.11

"Ladies and gentlemen," said Ed Wynn, "the next act will be a couple of jugglers, accompanied by a little music in a jugular vein."

148.12

Happiness is your dentist telling you it won't hurt and then having him catch his hand in the drill.

—*Johnny Carson*

(*See also 135.55*)

149. Insults and Feuds

149.1

Upon leaving the overdone home of a Hollywood movie mogul after a weekend visit, Mrs. Patrick Campbell was asked to sign the visitors' book. She wrote: "Quoth the Raven—Stella Campbell."

149.2

Some years ago the Hollywood movie colony decided to even the score with Mrs. Patrick Campbell, who had been devastating them with her acid comments. As a result, an actress seated next to Stella Campbell at a dinner party said to her, in a carefully rehearsed speech, "You know, Mrs. Campbell, for years I have been eating your soups and find them delicious."

"Of course you have, my dear," said Mrs. Campbell. "Bean soup, no doubt, from the sallow color of your skin."

149.3

During an argument with a movie director, one aspiring actress new to the movie colony said to the director, "I'll have you know I'm a lady."

"OK, baby," said the director genially, "I'll keep your secret."

149.4

W. S. Gilbert, of Gilbert and Sullivan fame, had scant liking for Sir Charles Alexander, a prominent theatrical producer. Sitting in his club one day, Gilbert picked up a newspaper and noticed that Alexander was advertising his newest show, giving top billing to an actress with whom Alexander was generally supposed to be living with. "Well," said Gilbert, "I see Alexander is blowing his own strumpet."

149.5

Sir Thomas Beecham was conducting a rehearsal of Massenet's *Don Quixote* in which Chaliapin, the Russian basso, was starring. At one point in the last act the singer playing Dulcinea persistently failed to come in on the beat and blamed it on Chaliapin. "He always dies too soon," she explained.

"You are in error," said Beecham. "No opera singer dies soon enough for me."

—*Stephen William,* New York Times Magazine

149.6

Maurice Barrymore, father of the famous John, Ethel, and Lionel, and an actor with wit with few superiors in his day, enjoyed a profound contempt for an actor who was soon to appear on Broadway in the revival of a classic play.

When the posters were put outside the theater announcing the play and cast, they read something like this: HIRAM BLOO ANNOUNCES A REVIVAL OF "THE RIVALS," STARRING JOHN ROE, RICHARD DOE, JANE DOE, GEORGE DOE, GEORGE SPELVIN, JOAN DASH AND JAMES WASHOUT.

Barrymore went immediately to a hardware store, purchased a carpenter's pencil, returned to the theater, crossed out the "And" before James Washout's name, and for it substituted the word "But."

149.7

During rehearsal for a Broadway musical, a no-longer-young actress was given the leading role and sought to impress a younger woman in the cast. "In case you don't know it," she said, "I insured my voice for $50,000." "Really," said the younger woman. "And tell me, what did you do with all that money?"

149.8

Leonard Lyons in 1946 told about the film star who had had a series of unhappy marriages. She mentioned to Mark Connolly that she was getting married the following week.

"Against whom?" asked Connolly.

149.9

Walter Winchell tells about the Hollywood actress who sat at a nightclub table and proceeded to cut up the reputation of a rival. When she ordered a chicken sandwich and a glass of milk, a friend of the backbiter's victim asked, "Wouldn't you prefer the milk in a saucer?"

149.10

An actor named Priest was playing at one of the principal theaters. Someone remarked at the Garrick Club that there were a great many men in the pit. "Probably clerks who have taken Priest's orders," said Mr. Poole, one of the best punsters as well as one of the cleverest comic satirists of the day.

149.11

Composer Igor Stravinsky, when asked for his opinion of the music of a prominent colleague, said, "I will tell you when he has written some."

149.12

To a Dramatist

They say, O'Keefe,
Thou art a thief
That half thy works are stol'n,
or more;
I say, O'Keefe
Thou art no thief,
Such stuff was never writ before!

—*Peter Pindar* (John Wolcot)

149.13

Lady Diana Manners, herself an actress, once thought to deflate Noel Coward. She said to him, "I saw you in your play *The Vortex*, and I didn't think you very funny."

Coward, no man to exchange insults with, said, "My dear Lady Manners, I saw you as the Madonna in *The Miracle*, and I thought you were a scream!"

149.14

"What do you think of the violinist?" asked the hostess.

"He reminds me of Paderewski," replied George Bernard Shaw.

"But Paderewski is not a violinist."

"Neither is this gentleman," said Shaw.

149.15

An actor, suddenly realizing that he was talking to some companions in a loud voice, turned to Don Marquis and asked, "Are you conscious of my voice?"

"Yes," said Marquis, "but I'm about to be unconscious."

149.16

Berton Braley recalled that one day at the Players Club bar he heard a young actor speak woefully to Don Marquis about how whenever he started to talk among a group of Club members, the group would fade away, one by one. "Do you think I'm a bore, or something?" he asked Marquis.

"Or something," said Marquis.

149.17

Douglas Jerrold was always nervous on the first night of one of his plays. One of his colleagues, noted for his plagiarism, said to him, "Why not be like me? I'm never nervous at my first nights."

"Why should you be," replied Jerrold. "Your new plays have already been successful."

149.18

A rumor had been very general that a certain actor was laboring under an inflammation of the brain.

A friend, having mentioned the report to Douglas Jerrold, was reassured in the following words: "Depend upon it; there is not the least foundation for the report."

149.19

"When I came out on the stage the audience just sat there open-mouthed," boasted the actor.

"Oh," said a rival, "audiences never yawn all at once."

149.20

That fellow is so conceited that every time it thunders he dashes to the window and takes a bow.

149.21

When Oscar Wilde was asked what he thought of Beerbohm Tree's Hamlet, he said, "It was funny, but not vulgar."

149.22

Some of the greatest love affairs I've known have involved one actor—unassisted.

—*Wilson Mizner*

149.23

When actress Carol Landis depreciated Gypsy Rose Lee's leg art, Miss Lee said that no one would object if Miss Landis played Salome in long underwear and a fire helmet.

149.24

"What did you think of my last picture?" an actor asked Carol Landis.

"I was certain it was," she replied.

149.25

"If you posed with two more monkeys, you would look like one man's family," was the way in which Larry Nixon squelched a nuisance.

149.26

"Why don't you get a toupee with brains in it?" an actress asked a bald-headed wolf who was bothering her.

149.27

"Find yourself a home in a wastebasket," Larry Kent advised a heckler.

149.28

"Go out and play in the traffic," said Morey Amsterdam to a nightclub pest.

149.29

Professional insulter Jack E. Leonard, spotting a star in the crowd at a nightclub, called out to him, "I saw your show. When are you going to make a comeback?"

149.30

Of a star who has blossomed into the big time: "Two years ago she couldn't get arrested."

149.31

Wendie Barrie, annoyed by the antics of a ham, said of him: "That man has got the first penny ever thrown at him."

(*See also 140.1, 140.2, 140.8, 140.9, 140.15, 140.17, 141.4, 143.3, 152.1–152.59, 153.1–153.10, 154.22, 171.7, 171.8, 175.3, 273.1–273.25*)

ARTISTS AND WRITERS

FROM THE LITERARY SALON

150. Writers-at-large

Anecdotes

150.1

When a cub reporter asked George Bernard Shaw for an interview, the dramatist named a large sum as the price. The astonished youth explained that his paper could not pay any such amount. "Won't you give us just a few little ideas?"

"No," said Shaw, "I have no little ideas. All my ideas are great."

150.2

Rummaging among volumes in a secondhand book store, George Bernard Shaw encountered one of his own books and found that he had inscribed it "To X, with kind regards." He bought the book, wrote under the first inscription, "To X with renewed regards," and mailed the book to X.

150.3

One day Sir Arthur Conan Doyle arrived in Paris and asked a cab driver to take him to a certain hotel. The cab driver, recognizing his passenger as the famous creator of Sherlock Holmes, said, "I perceive, Sir, that you have recently visited Constantinople, and there are strong indications you have been in the neighborhood of Milan. I further deduce that you have recently been at Buda."

"Wonderful! Very clever! I'll give you five francs extra if you tell me how you arrived at so accurate a conclusion," said the great author of detective fiction.

"It was easy," smiled the cab driver proudly. "I simply looked at the labels pasted on your baggage."

150.4

Lexicographer Noah Webster was, of course, very discriminating in his choice of words. One day Mrs. Webster came upon him when he was kissing the young maid. "Mr. Webster!" the wife exclaimed. "I am surprised!"

"No, my dear," replied the great compiler of dictionaries, "you are astounded. It is I who am surprised."

150.5

"Mr. Webster," said a prim lady to the great lexicographer, "I was disgusted to find an obscene word in your dictionary."

"Madam," said Webster, "you would not have known it was there if you had not looked it up."

150.6

Gustave Flaubert, who once practiced as a physician before turning novelist, asked Balzac what he thought of a certain Flaubert book. "You always diagnose and prescribe for your characters who are obviously your patients," said Balzac. "And then like every good physician you end in putting them all to death."

150.7

Bret Harte, a very well-known writer of short stories and popular poetry, was erroneously believed by many to be the author of John Hay's poem "Little Breeches." One day when a woman was introduced to him, she gushed, "Oh, Mr. Harte, you have no idea how much I enjoy your poem 'Little Breeches.'"

"Thank you, madam," replied Harte, "but you are putting the breeches on the wrong man."

150.8

Editor Bob Davis one day received a manuscript from a mining town in Montana. He did not recognize the name of the sender, but in reading the story he recognized it as Bret Harte's "The Luck of Roaring Camp"—word for word it was Harte's story. Davis wrote the plagiarist, "Much as I admire the story you have submitted, I am unable to publish it for a very peculiar reason. Many years ago I promised my old friend, Bret Harte, never to print 'The Luck of Roaring Camp' by anyone else but himself."

A week later Davis received a postcard from the Montana "author." It read, "You are a damn fool to make any such promise."

150.9

When it was reported that Rudyard Kipling was being paid a shilling a word, an Oxford student sent him a shilling with the request he send him a word. Kipling sent back "Thanks."

150.10

As long as I live under the capitalist system, I expect to have my life influenced by the demands of moneyed people. But I will be damned if I propose to be at the beck and call of every itinerant scoundrel who has two cents to invest in a postage stamp. This, sir, is my resignation.

—*William Faulkner,* to the Postmaster General

150.11

Gertrude Stein, being interviewed by the press on her shipboard arrival from Europe, was asked, "Miss Stein, why don't you write the way you talk?"

"Why don't you read the way I write?" she replied.

150.12

Foes of censorship like to recall that *Godey's Lady's Book,* a famous nineteenth-century magazine in the U.S., in advising readers how to arrange their bookshelves, said: "The perfect hostess will see to it that the works of female and male authors are strictly separated. Their proximity on the shelves—unless they happen to be married to each other—should not be tolerated."

150.13

Edith Wharton was escorted to a railroad station by Ambrose Bierce—a sullen and vain host—and while waiting for the train to arrive he tried to kiss her. She burst out laughing and said, "The great Bierce—trying a kiss a woman by a pigsty."

There was a pigsty right next to the railroad station.

150.14

When G. K. Chesterton was asked what book he would most like to have with him if he were stranded on a desert island, he replied, *Thomas's Guide to Practical Shipbuilding.*

150.15

When Rex Beach was asked for the secret of his success as a novelist, he said the best way to answer was to remind them of the Swede who had made a fortune in Alaska gold mining. The Swede said that all he did was to keep digging holes.

150.16

This morning School said to me something amusing about Barriere: "Yes, yes, he has talent; but he doesn't know how to make people forgive him for having it."

—*Journal of E. and J. Goncourts*

150.17

When Westbrook Pegler was a rapidly rising young newspaperman he sold a short story to a magazine for the modest price of $75. The story drew so much attention that editors of other magazines ordered pieces from Pegler at much higher prices. With all these high-price assignments on his desk, Pegler received a note from the publisher of the original story, offering to buy ten more stories at the same price of $75.

"Sorry, I've turned pro," replied Pegler.

150.18

The editor of one of Ernest Hemingway's early books objected to the author's use of a certain strong four-letter word and asked that it be removed. Hemingway, knowing his editor to be a man of puritanical sensibilities, decided to have some fun with him by pretending not to understand what word in particular the man was referring to. Finally the editor wrote the word out on a pad, and then the two men went to lunch.

Upon his return from the lunch the editor turned to Hemingway and said, "My God, my secretary always checks my desk after I leave for lunch to see what work I have left for her. Look at this," and he handed the scratch pad to Hemingway. It read, "Things to do this afternoon:" then followed the offending word in the manuscript.

150.19

Sinclair Lewis, Sherwood Anderson, and Ernest Hemingway, over dinner one evening, began to speculate whether there was a surefire formula for the best-selling novel. They finally decided that, if such a formula existed, it would consist of sex, adventure, and success. They went on to devise a plot that contained these three basic ingredients and agreed upon a three-way collaboration to produce this novel that could not miss becoming a best seller. Anderson was to specialize on the sex aspect, Hemingway on adventure, and Lewis on success.

The three writers worked hard for several months and were well pleased with the smoothness of the finished product. They turned it over to an agent for marketing under a pseudonym and swore him to secrecy about the identities of the real authors.

Publisher after publisher promptly rejected the novel. A certain eminent editor wrote to the agent:

"I am astonished that you would handle so amateurish a work. Your author shows neither talent nor promise. The three basic ingredients of a successful novel are sex, adventure, and success. This writer is obviously incapable of handling any one of them."

150.20

An editor told a beginning author that a best seller should arrest the reader's attention immediately and that preferably the first paragraph should have in it: sex, society, and unconventionality.

Shortly afterwards the editor received a manuscript from the young writer, which began with: " 'Dammit, King,' said the Duchess, 'leggo my leg.' "

150.21

Bob Cousins said that when he was a young kid he used to put books inside of his trousers whenever he felt that he was soon to get a good spanking. From that time, the editor says, he has learned the advantage of a literary background.

150.22

Among an American family's treasured possessions was a letter written by Thomas Jefferson. When financial reverses were suffered, the owner of this letter was obliged to offer it for sale.

In examining and appraising the letter a dealer said: "It's too bad someone tampered with this letter. Apparently ink eradicator was used to remove writing at the bottom of it. If they had let it alone it would bring at least $100 additional."

"Oh?" said the owner weakly. "I did that. It was only a notation reading 'I agree with you' and signed 'Button Gwinett.' " (Gwinett was one of the signers of the Declaration of Independence.)

150.23

An author wrote a chapter titled: Snakes in Ireland. Beneath this he wrote: "There are no snakes in Ireland." That was the total text of his chapter. He knew when he had exhausted his subject, and there he stopped.

Definitions

150.24

Diary: A daily record of that part of one's life, which he can relate to himself without blushing.

—*Ambrose Bierce*

150.25

Autobiography is fiction written by the one who knows the facts.

150.26

An Historical Novel is like a bustle, a fictitious tale covering up a stern reality.

—*Augusta Tucker,* The Man Miss Susie Loved

150.27

A historical novel has been described as a book with a wench on the jacket, and no jacket on the wench.

150.28

Historians are gossips who tease the dead.

—*Voltaire,* Scribbling Books

150.29

Repartee: any reply that is so clever that it makes the listener wish he had said it himself.

—*Elbert Hubbard*

150.30

Repartee is something we think of twenty-four hours too late.

—*Mark Twain*

150.31

The faux pas is repartee which has become accidentally entangled with hara-kiri.

—*Jack Goodman and Albert Rice*

150.32

A classic is something that everybody wants to have read and nobody wants to read.

—*Mark Twain*

150.33

A Proverb is a short sentence based on long experience.

—*Miguel de Cervantes,* Don Quixote

150.34

An epigram is a half-truth so stated as to irritate the person who believes the other half.

—*Shailer Matthews*

Aphorisms

150.35

Lives of great men oft remind us
As we o'er their pages turn,
That we too may leave behind us
Letters that we ought to burn.

150.36

Through and through the inspired leaves,
Ye maggots, make your windings;
But, oh! respect his lordship's taste,
And spare his golden bindings!

—*Robert Burns*

150.37

God cannot alter the past; that is why he is obliged to connive at the existence of historians.

—*Nicholas Murray Butler*

150.38

Most writers regard truth as their most valuable possession, and therefore are most economical in its use.

—*Mark Twain*

150.39

Shakespeare was a dramatist of note who lived by writing things to quote.

—*Henry Cuyler Bunner*

150.40

In modern life nothing produces such an effect as a good platitude. It makes the whole world kin.

—*Oscar Wilde*

150.41

Artistic temperament is a disease that afflicts amateurs.

—*G. K. Chesterton,* Heretics

150.42

The difference between the right word and the almost right word is the difference between lightning and the lightning-bug.

—*Mark Twain*

150.43

When you take stuff from one writer, it's plagiarism; but when you take from many writers, it's research.

—*Wilson Mizner*

150.44

Biography is one of the new terrors of death.

—*John Arbuthnot*

150.45

A good many young writers make the mistake of enclosing a stamped, self-addressed envelope, big enough for the manuscript to come back in. This is too much of a temptation to the editor.

—*Ring Lardner*

150.46

The learned fool writes his nonsense in better language than the unlearned, but still 'tis nonsense.

—*Benjamin Franklin*

150.47

The art of writing is the art of applying the seats of the pants to the seat of the chair.

—*Mary H. Vorse*

(*See also 28.7, 28.22, 29.3, 53.4, 66.26, 80.5, 106.20, 135.18, 136.10, 137.2, 149.12, 149.17, 151.1–151.25, 152.1–152.59, 153.1–153.18, 154.1–154.69, 155.14, 158.5, 171.7, 171.8, 176.8, 184.9, 184.10, 186.9, 186.10, 186.18, 188.9, 191.13, 193.5, 199.6, 244.28, 246.1–246.16, 252.5, 259.5, 265.5, 268.6, 270.6, 273.11, 271.12, 271.19, 273.11, 273.23*)

151. Philosophers and Poets

Anecdotes

151.1

Diogenes, the famous cynic philosopher, argued that to be happy one must rid himself of all riches, honors, powers, and of all the enjoyments of life. And he practiced what he preached, going barefoot through Athens, never wearing a coat, eating coarse foods and inveighing against corruption and comfort. Diogenes was, in fact, convinced of his superiority and did not hesitate to abuse those who disagreed with him. It is reported, but not proved, that Socrates once said to him, "I see your vanity through the holes in your garments."

Even more telling is the incident of Diogenes's visit to Plato at his home. When the grumpy cynic walked across Plato's beautifully and richly carpeted floors he stopped, glared at his host, stamped his foot scornfully on the carpet, and said, "Thus do I tread on the pride of Plato!"

"Yes," said Plato, "and with a greater pride."

151.2

Diogenes, taunted by the query concerning why philosophers follow the rich, whereas the rich ignore philosophers, replied: "Because philosophers know what they have need of; the rich do not."

151.3

One day the tyrant Dionysius asked Aristippus, a pupil of Socrates but a cringing toady to the King, "Why do you philosophers always come to the rich, while the rich never, never return your calls?"

"Because," said Aristippus, "we philosophers want money which the rich can give us, but the rich want brains which we can't give them, even if they return our visits."

151.4

Aristippus was a most un-Socratic disciple of Socrates. He founded a school of philosophy dedicated to the practice of refined voluptuousness. In order to live in the luxury he advocated and preferred, Aristippus flattered and played the sycophant to one Denys, a rich tyrant. Moreover, Aristippus compounded his vice by treating less prosperous but more honest men with contempt and scorn.

One day Aristippus came upon Diogenes who was serenely sorting out and preparing some vegetables for a meal. "If you would learn to flatter Denys you wouldn't have to eat lentils," sneered the sensualist. "And you," retorted Diogenes, "if you had learned to eat lentils, you would not have to lower yourself to flatter Denys."

151.5

Aristippus wrote Diogenes that Alexander the Great, then at the height of his great power, desired the "ragged cynic" to visit him in Macedon. Diogenes, in a brief reply, said, "I am subject to nobody, and if that great prince has a mind to be acquainted with me and my manner of life, let him come hither, for I shall always think Athens as far distant from Macedon as Macedon is from Athens."

Some time later Alexander the Great did visit Athens and while there encountered Diogenes seated on the ground enjoying the sunshine. The world conqueror went up to Diogenes and stood between him and the sun and asked what he could do for him. "You can stand out of my light," replied Diogenes. The reply deeply impressed Alexander.

151.6

Sidonius, who had a great reputation at Athens as a teacher, was boasting that he was conversant with all the philosophic systems: "Let Aristotle call, and I follow to the Lyceum; Plato, and I hurry to the Academy; Zeno, and I make my home in the Porch; Pythagoras, and I keep the rule of silence." Then rose Cemonax from among the audience: "Sidonius, Pythagoras calls."

151.7

A scholar, discussing the Stoics and Epicureans, asked Benjamin Jowett, master of Balliol College of Oxford, "Do you really think a good man could be happy on the rack?"

"Well," replied Jowett, "perhaps a good man on a *very* bad rack."

151.8

"I have the greatest contempt for Aristotle," declared William Wordsworth.

"But not," replied a listener," the contempt bred by familiarity."

151.9

A few years ago Dr. Harper exposed the fact that Wordsworth in his youth had had a love-affair with a French girl, who had borne him a child and whom he then deserted. In most of the comments I read on this incident the critics wrote as if Wordsworth had magnanimously suspended his celibacy as part of a general programme for the renovation of humanity; or had at worst committed a slight error of judgment in his anxiety to get into line with the finer spirits of the French Revolution.

—*Hugh Kingmill*

151.10

Edmund Waller, the poet, shown the Duchess of Newcastle's verses on the death of a stag, said he would have given all his compositions to have written them. Later, being charged with exorbitant adulation, Waller replied that "nothing was too much to be given that a lady might be saved from the disgrace of such a vile performance."

151.11

Edmund Waller praised Oliver Cromwell in his verse, then later praised King Charles II in less fulsome verse. Knowing that Charles II was a bit miffed by this, Waller explained to the King that "poets succeed better in fiction than in truth."

151.12

When Robert Frost was asked what most influenced him in his life, he said, "When I was twelve I worked in a little shoe shop, and all summer I carried nails in my mouth. I owe everything to the fact that I neither swallowed nor inhaled."

151.13

When Henry Wadsworth Longfellow was introduced to a man named Longworth, the latter commented on the similarity of their names. "Here is a case," replied Longfellow, "where Pope's line applies: 'Worth makes the man, and want of it the fellow.' "

151.14

The cleaner of cesspools, in spite of his occupation, was a man given to a love of the poetic and was fond of quoting from the poets on every occasion.

Consequently, when he was called in on a particularly messy job, he looked at it grimly, rolled up his sleeves, sighed, turned to the person employing him, and said, "Oh, well, faint heart ne'er won fair lady."

151.15

A very young student of literature wrote on an examination: "An epicure is a poet who writes epics."

Definitions

151.16

A Philosopher is a fool who torments himself while he is alive, to be talked of after he is dead.

—*Jean D'Albert*

151.17

Philosophy: A route of many roads leading from nowhere to nothing.

—*Ambrose Bierce*

151.18

Philosophy is saying what everybody knows in language which nobody understands.

—*Muirhead*

Aphorisms

151.19

It is indeed a pity that our great public knows so little about poetry; almost as little, in fact, as our poets.

—*Heinrich Heine*

151.20

A poet must use his imagination. He must imagine people are going to read his poems.

—*Judge*

151.21

Nothin' makes a poet as mad as a late spring.

—*Kin Hubbard*

151.22

Writing a book of poetry is like dropping a rose petal down the Grand Canyon and waiting for the echo.

—*Don Marquis*

151.23

A married philosopher belongs to comedy.

—*Friedrich Nietzsche*

151.24

For there was never yet philosopher
That could endure the toothache patiently.

—*William Shakespeare*

151.25

A poet in history is divine, but a poet in the next room is a joke.

—*Max Eastman*

(*See also 31.8, 87.2, 87.4, 87.10, 120.5, 120.6, 165.62, 174.11, 181.4, 210.7, 216.1, 219.1, 240.16, 242.21, 269.59, 273.16*)

152. Literary Insults and Feuds

Anecdotes

152.1

When Clare Boothe Luce and her husband called on George Bernard Shaw, it is said that she opened the conversation with uncharacteristic coyness and said, "Oh, Mr. Shaw, if it weren't for you I wouldn't be here."

"Let me see," said Shaw with his usual agility on the pickup, "what was your dear mother's name?"

And, not to play favorites, he sent Clare

Boothe Luce a note which ended with: "Kindest regards to you and Mr. Boothe."

152.2

While visiting London, Mark Twain was invited to attend a small literary group at a dinner. Over the coffee and brandy one of the learned critics began speaking of the Bacon-Shakespeare controversy and asked Twain his opinion of it. "No doubt, Mr. Clemens, you have your own ideas about it," added the scholar.

"Oh, I think I'll wait until I get to Heaven and then ask Shakespeare and Bacon," replied Mark Twain.

"I doubt very much, Mr. Clemens," said the critic emphatically, "that you will meet either one of them in Heaven."

"Then you ask them," snapped Twain.

152.3

When asked his opinion of a book in manuscript, Samuel Johnson said, "This ought to be sent to the House of Correction."

152.4

Of Lord Chesterfield's *Letters to His Son,* Samuel Johnson said, "They teach the morals of a whore, and the manners of a dancing master."

152.5

Someone asked Samuel Johnson whether he reckoned Herrick or Smart the better poet and got this answer: "Sir, there is no settling the point of precedency between a louse and a flea."

152.6

A boring author, hoping to wring a compliment from William Dean Howells, said to him: "I don't know how it is, but I do not seem to write as well as I used to."

"Oh, yes you do," replied Howells. "You write as well as you ever did. But your taste is improving."

152.7

Louis XIV proudly showed some of his verses to Boileau and asked for a judgment of them. The poet said, "Ah, sire, I am more convinced than ever that nothing is impossible to Your Majesty. You desired to write some very poor rhymes, and you have succeeded in making them positively detestable."

152.8

Voltaire, asked to comment on Jean Baptiste Rousseau's poem "To Posterity," said, "This poem will not reach its destination."

152.9

Epistle Dedicatory

My Lords,

Your *uncommon attention* to my late Publications demands a return of Gratitude. Permit me to present to your Lordships the following Lyric Trifles, which, if possessed of Merit sufficient to preserve them from Oblivion, will inform Posterity that you existed.

I am, my Lords
and etc.
Peter Pindar.

Expostulatory Odes to a Great Duke, and a Little Lord, by *Peter Pindar* (John Wolcot), 1789, London.

152.10

On Colley Cibber

In merry old England it once was a rule,
The King had his poet, and also his fool:
But now we're so frugal, I'd have you to know it,
That Cibber can serve both for fool and for poet.

152.11

Macaulay has occasional flashes of silence that make his conversation perfectly delightful.
—*Sydney Smith*

152.12

Reverend Sydney Smith, speaking of Thomas Babington Macaulay, said: "He not only overflowed with learning, but stood in the slops."

152.13

Samuel Rogers once entered a drawing room in London during a sudden silence and said, "I see Hallam has just been telling a joke."

152.14

The painter James McNeill Whistler and the playwright Oscar Wilde were engaged in a continual duel of wits, often at social occasions in London. Once when Whistler had made an unusually brilliant observation, Wilde sighed and said, "I wish I'd said that."

"You will, Oscar, you will," replied Whistler.

152.15

When Sir Lewis Morris protested to Oscar Wilde that there was a conspiracy of silence against his work and asked what he should do, Wilde said: "Join it."

152.16

Frank Harris was telling as his own an anecdote which everyone in the party recognized as a paraphrase of a story by Anatole France. When Harris finished his account,

Oscar Wilde said, "Frank, Anatole France would have spoiled that story."

152.17

When Harriet Martineau professed her atheism, Douglas Jerrold said, "There is no God, and Harriet Martineau is His Prophet!"

152.18

Somebody told Douglas Jerrold that a friend of his, a prolific writer, was about to dedicate a book to him.

"Ah!" replied Jerrold, with mock gravity. "That's an awful weapon he has in his hands!"

152.19

Douglas Jerrold was seriously disappointed with a certain book written by one of his friends. This friend heard that Jerrold had expressed his disappointment and questioned him, "I hear you said ——— was the worst book I ever wrote."

"No, I didn't," came the answer, "I said it was the worst book anybody ever wrote."

152.20

A literary gentleman once said pretentiously to Douglas Jerrold, "My dear Jerrold, you know, of course, what guano is?"

"No," Jerrold replied; "but I can understand your knowledge, you've had so much thrown at you in your time."

152.21

One day Douglas Jerrold encountered a bore while walking down the street.

"Hello there, Jerrold. What's going on?"

"I am," said Jerrold as he kept on walking.

152.22

"I passed your house the other day," said an acquaintance to John Wilmot Rochester.

"Thanks," said Rochester.

152.23

Lord Byron, referring to his contemporary Robert Southey, said, "Southey's poetry will be read after Virgil and Homer are forgotten, but not until then."

152.24

When Alexander Pope, in his attack on Lord Hervey wrote:

"Yes, I am proud, and must be proud to see
Those not afraid of God, afraid of me,"

Lord Hervey scored nicely with:

". . . the great honor of that boast is such,
That hornets and mad dogs may boast as much."

152.25

Said S. T. Coleridge to Charles Lamb: "I think, Charles, that you have never heard me preach."

"My dear boy," said Lamb, "I have never heard you do anything else."

152.26

Thomas Carlyle characterized Samuel Taylor Coleridge in this manner: "He mounts scaffold, pulleys, and tackle, and gathers all the tools in the neighborhood with labor, with noise, demonstration, precept, abuse—and sets three bricks."

152.27

When Thomas Carlyle was asked to meet Algernon Swinburne, he said that he did not care to be introduced to one "who was sitting in a sewer and adding to it."

152.28

Henry James, Senior, said Carlyle was "the same old sausage, fizzing and sputtering in his own grease."

152.29

Samuel Butler said: "It was very good of God to let Carlyle and Mrs. Carlyle marry one another and so make only two people miserable instead of four, besides which it is very amusing."

152.30

Sir John Lubbock. He is trying about this time (May 1884) to teach his dogs to converse. If I was his dog and he taught me, the first thing I should tell him would be that he is a damned fool.

—*Samuel Butler,* Notebooks

152.31

When asked by a redundant fellow member of Parliament, "Did you hear my last speech?" John P. Curran replied, "I hope so." When a poet asked him if he had seen the author's *Descent into Hell,* Curran said, "No, but I should like to."

152.32

A notorious hack sent Thackeray a copy of his book. Thackeray acknowledged it with a note: "Your volume has arrived. I shall lose no time reading it."

152.33

Algernon Swinburne mentioned to Edmund Gosse that he had been quarreling with Ralph Waldo Emerson by mail.

"I hope your language was moderate," said Gosse.

"Perfectly moderate," replied Swinburne. "I merely informed him, in language of the strictest reserve, that he was a hoary-headed and toothless baboon, who, first lifted into notice on the shoulders of Carlyle, now spits and sputters from a filthier platform of his own finding and fouling. That is all I said."

152.34

Of Lord Brougham: "It is quite the worst and very nearly the ugliest physiognomy in existence. It has, however, one advantage over its proprietor—it does not lie."

—*Walter Savage Landor*

152.35

August Wilhelm von Schlegel: "A little pot-bellied pony tricked out with stars, buckles and ribands, looking askance from his ring and halter in the market, for an apple from one, a morsel of bread from another, a fig of ginger from a third, and a pat from everybody."

—*Walter Savage Landor*

152.36

Nature, not content with denying to Mr. Y. the faculty of thinking, has endowed him with the faculty of writing.

—*A. E. Housman*

152.37

Discussing the writings of Arnold Bennett, Oliver Herford said: "When Bennett published his first novel—*Buried Alive*—I reviewed it for the New York *Times;* and that review so prejudiced me against the man that I have never read another word he wrote."

152.38

Oliver Herford was strolling across the lobby of his club when he felt a thump on his back. He turned to recognize a man whom he did not much like. "Hello, Ollie, old boy! How goes it?"

Herford looked at the man with cold curiosity and said, "I don't recall your face, but your manners are familiar."

152.39

Edward Simmons, a painter, came to Oliver Herford at the Players Club one day and said he had been insulted by a tipsy member who had offered him $50 if he would resign from the Club. "Don't take it," counseled Herford. "If you hold out, I'm sure you can get $100."

152.40

At a social club to which Douglas Jerrold belonged, the subject turned one evening to music. The discussion was animated, and a certain song was cited as an exquisite composition.

"That air," exclaimed an enthusiastic member, "always carries me away when I hear it."

Looking round the table, Jerrold anxiously inquired, "Can anybody whistle it?"

152.41

When Lord Londonderry asked Winston Churchill if he had read his last book, Churchill replied, "No, I only read for pleasure or profit."

152.42

"I have had great pleasure in reading Jean-Paul Sartre's latest novel," commented Francois Mauriac, "and in finding that it was extremely bad."

152.43

Speaking of Alexander Woollcott, Edna Ferber said the New Jersey-born author was "a New Jersey Nero who mistakes his pinafore for a toga."

152.44

A young author, reading a tragedy he had just written, perceived his listener very often pulled off his hat at the end of a line, and asked him the reason. "I cannot pass a very old acquaintance," replied the critic, "without that civility."

152.45

A famous author attending a party was buttonholed by an unsuccessful writer who deprecated himself and admitted he was a poor scribbler, a hack who shouldn't be in a great man's company.

The famous author listened patiently for several minutes, then said, "Why do you make yourself so small? You have never been big enough to do that."

152.46

A well-known author received a batch of manuscripts from a young English writer whom he did not know and had never heard of. The unknown one asked advice as to the "best channel" for marketing his effusions.

The famous writer returned the manuscripts with this note: "The only channel I can think of as appropriate for these pieces is the English Channel."

152.47

"I have finished reading your manuscript, my dear lady," said the pretentious publisher, "and I must say it has some merit, but there are also many parts of it that are obscure and vague. You must learn to write so that even the most ignorant can understand you."

"Yes, I understand," said the authoress coolly. "Tell me, which parts gave you the most difficulty?"

152.48

When a novelist sent in a book manuscript, he attached a note stating: "The characters in this novel are entirely fictional and have no resemblance to any person living or dead."

Within a short time he got the manuscript back, and also the note on which the editor had written: "That's what is wrong with them."

152.49

"Here is the manuscript I offered to you last year," said the writer.

Said the editor, "What's the idea of bringing this thing back when I rejected it last year?"

Writer: "Well, you've had a year's experience since then."

152.50

"What do you think of my story?" the young author asked the editor. "Give me your honest opinion."

"It isn't worth anything," said the editor.

"I know," conceded the author, "but give it to me anyway."

152.51

We have nothing more to say of the editor of the Sweetwater *Gazette.* Aside from the fact that he is a squint-eyed, consumptive liar, with a breath like a buzzard and a record like a convict, we don't know anything against him. He means well enough, and if he can evade the penitentiary and the vigilance committee for a few more years, there is a chance for him to end his life in a natural way. If he don't tell the truth a little more plentifully, however, the Green River people will rise as one man and churn him up till there won't be anything left of him but a pair of suspenders and a wart.

—*Bill Nye*

152.52

"That editor," wrote the editor of the *Daily Blah,* "is mean enough to steal the swill from a blind hog."

The next day the competing editor said in his columns: "The editor of the *Daily Blah* knows right well that we never stole his swill."

152.53

Newspaper feuds in the old days were neither unusual nor gentle. One day the most proper and correct New York *Post* dropped its manners and called its rival the New York *Sun* a yellow dog. The *Sun,* never reluctant to trade blows, said, "The *Post* calls the *Sun* a yellow dog. The attitude of the *Sun,* however, will continue to be that of *any* dog toward *any* post."

152.54

Newspaper publisher William Randolph Hearst once had an advertising manager named John Eastman who resigned and took over the ownership of another newspaper. They apparently remained friendly, but when Eastman's mother died Hearst's paper carried an obituary of only thirty words. Eastman felt that his onetime friend had personally affronted him.

Some years later Mr. Hearst's mother died. Mr. Eastman caused to be printed in his paper the following obituary: "Mrs. Phoebe Hearst died today. She was the mother of a newspaper publisher and weighed 95 pounds."

152.55

When a frequent contributor but rare visitor to the offices of the *New Yorker* came in and flounced around in petulant fashion, one of the men on the staff said, "Oh my, a butterfly in heat."

152.56

The elderly and very proper lady stopped in to a bookstore down South some years ago and asked what they could recommend for reading on a train trip she was about to take.

"Well," said the clerk, "here is a novel that is very popular at present—it's James Lane Allen's *The Cardinal.*"

"No," said the lady, "I don't care to read about any Roman ecclesiastics."

"But, madam," said the clerk, "this Kentucky cardinal was a bird."

"Nevertheless," said the prim lady, "I have no desire to read about the unchaste peccadillos of the clergy. If you don't have what I want, I will go elsewhere."

152.57

When Jean Harlow, a flashy, platinum blonde, Hollywood star of the 1930s, met Margot Asquith, the Englishwoman whom Kipling once referred to as "the woman with the serpent's tongue," something was bound to happen.

Miss Harlow, in an effort to be pleasant, said to Mrs. Asquith, "I have always wanted to meet Margot Asquith,"—which was all right except that she pronounced Margot exactly as it is spelled. True to her reputation, Mrs. Asquith replied with characteristic sweetness, "My dear child, my name is pronounced Margo —the 't' is silent just as it is in 'harlot.'"

Definition

152.58

An author is a fool who, not content with having bored those who have lived with him, insists on boring future generations.

—*Baron de Montesquieu*

(*See also 140.1, 140.2, 140.8, 140.9, 140.15, 140.17, 141.4, 143.3, 152.1–152.58, 153.1–153.10, 154.22, 171.7–171.8, 175.3, 273.1–273.25*)

153. From the Critics' Circle

153.1

Thomas Babington Macaulay wrote this one-sentence review of Atterbury's *A Defense of the Letters of Phalaris:* "The best book ever written by a man on the wrong side of a question of which the author was profoundly ignorant."

153.2

Of A. A. Milne's *Winnie-the-Pooh,* Dorothy Parker said, "Tonstant Weader fwowed up."

153.3

Dorothy Parker, reviewing the author of a series of best sellers of questionable value, said, "He is a writer for the ages—the ages of four to six."

153.4

Speaking of Katharine Brush's novel *You Go Your Way,* Dorothy Parker said it was "elfin in a spastic sort of way."

153.5

In reviewing Margot Asquith's autobiography, Dorothy Parker said: "The affair between Margot Asquith and Margot Asquith will rank as one of the prettiest love affairs in Literature."

153.6

George Saintsbury had this to say of Edward Young's *Night Thoughts:* "An enormous soliloquy addressed by an actor of superhuman lung power to an audience of still more superhuman endurance."

153.7

On Sir Walter Scott's Poem of Waterloo

On Waterloo's ensanguined plain,
Full many a gallant man lies slain;
But none, by bullet or by shot,
Fell half so flat as Walter Scott.

153.8

Two literary critics got into an argument about a certain book. "Stop talking so absurdly," said the first critic. "I know what I'm talking about. I reviewed the book."

"I know you did," said the second critic. "But I read it."

153.9

The mass interview of the much-publicized author was over. "He's not quite as conceited as I had expected," observed one critic.

"True," said the other critic. "But he has so much to be modest about."

153.10

"I dream my stories," said a well-known novelist.

"How you must dread going to bed," replied the literary critic.

Definitions

153.11

A critic is a legless man who teaches running.

—*Channing Pollock*

153.12

Critic: A eunuch—he knows what to do but can't do it.

—*Esquire*

153.13

Criticism: A profession by which men grow important and formidable at very small expense.

—*Samuel Johnson*

Aphorisms

153.14

Nature, when she invented, manufactured, and patented her authors, contrived to make critics out of the chips that were left.

—*Oliver Wendell Holmes*

153.15

I never read a book before reviewing it; it prejudices one so.

—*Sydney Smith*

153.16

A poem read without a name,
They justly praise, or justly blame:
For critics have no partial views
Except they know whom they abuse.

—*Jonathan Swift*

153.17

A critic is a necessary evil, and criticism is an evil necessity.

—*Carolyn Wells*

153.18

Criticism comes easier than craftsmanship.

—*Plato*

(*See also 140.1–140.23, 151.10, 151.11, 152.3, 152.5, 152.19, 152.23, 152.26–152.28, 152.32, 152.36, 152.37, 152.41, 152.42, 152.44, 152.46, 153.7, 153.11, 153.12, 157.13*)

FINAL EDITION

154. Reporters and Editors

Anecdotes

154.1

The owner of a newspaper instructed his managing editor to hire the proprietor's son, just out of college, as a reporter. The young man was promptly assigned to cover a big society wedding—an atmosphere in which he would be thoroughly at home.

Late in the day the managing editor came upon the new reporter deep in a mystery story.

"Where's the wedding story? It's almost press time," asked the editor.

"Oh, there's no story," said the reporter casually. "The whole thing blew up. The bride eloped last night with some local jerk—a drummer in some band, I think that's what he is."

154.2

The cub reporter was sent out to check on a report that there was a man who could sing tenor arias without interruption while he was eating a seven-course meal. The reporter came back and told his editor, "There's nothing to it; the guy has two heads."

154.3

Gene Fowler used to tell about a cub reporter on a Denver paper who on his third day on the job rushed in to Joe Ward, the editor, and said, "Mr. Ward, I've got a big story!"

"What is it? Murder?" asked Ward with sudden interest.

"No, sir," said the cub. "It's like this: I was walking past the East Denver High School last night and I saw a lot of young people and they were doing—well, they were—well, you know what I mean."

"You mean like Adam and Eve?" asked Ward.

"Yes, sir. I counted twenty couples—right there next to the high school."

"Son, this thing has been going on for thousands of years," said Ward. "You can criticize it, denounce it, preach against it from every pulpit, write books condemning it, produce plays exposing it, mobilize the armies of the Lord to suppress it. But, son, mark my word, you will never succeed in making it unpopular with the masses."

154.4

A cub reporter sent to cover the annual class play of the local high school described the event in glowing terms, concluding with ". . . and the auditorium was filled with expectant mothers, eagerly awaiting their offspring."

154.5

A young reporter on the Providence, Rhode Island, *Journal* was sent to one of the local Catholic churches to interview the pastor concerning some new improvements in the parish.

At the rectory, the reporter was told that the pastor was hearing confessions in the church. He entered the confessional and said, "Father, I'm a reporter for the Providence *Journal.*"

"Young man," said the priest, "I have listened to confessions for many years, but yours is the most shocking I have ever heard."

154.6

When the *New Yorker* sent a woman to interview Dean Gildersleeve, dean of Barnard College, Miss Gildersleeve indicated her annoyance that they had not sent a college graduate to interview her, then added, "I had hoped the *New Yorker* would send a man to interview me. Why didn't they send a man?"

"Probably for the same reason they haven't got a man as dean of Barnard," said the young woman interviewer.

154.7

The cub reporter was emphatically told by his editor never to make any statement for print that could not be verified from personal investigation. Soon afterwards the young man was assigned to cover a local social event, attended by many of the town's bigwigs. His story ran about like this: "A woman asserting she was named Mrs. John Smith, and said by others to be the town's society leader, gave what is purported to be a lavish party to a group of alleged ladies. The hostess claims she is the wife of a reputedly prominent banker."

154.8

The first news of the disastrous Johnstown, Pennsylvania, flood of 1889 reached the office of a Pittsburgh paper at a time when the only reporter on hand was a young cub awaiting his first assignment. The editor rushed the young fellow to Johnstown to cover the scene until more experienced members of the staff could be located and put on the job. "This is a big break for you, kid," said the boss. "If you have anything on the ball, now's the time to show it. Give it all you have."

Quite a few hours later the first account of the flood came over the wires from the young cub reporter. It began, "God sits broodingly on the hillside overlooking the disaster and desolation of Johnstown. The roaring waters seem but to echo the mind of the Creator. . . ."

The editor took one look at these opening words and then wired the youthful reporter: "Don't bother with the flood, interview God."

154.9

A visiting bishop delivered a speech at a banquet on the night of his arrival in a large city. Because he wanted to repeat some of his stories at meetings the next day, he requested reporters to omit them from their accounts of his speech. A rookie reporter, commenting on the speech, finished with the line: "And he told a number of stories that cannot be published."

—*Sign Magazine*

154.10

When Dorothy Ducas was a student at Columbia University, she applied to Dwight Perrin, editor of the New York *Tribune,* for the post of the paper's correspondent at the University.

"Suppose," asked Perrin, "there was a fire in one of the dormitories—what good would you be?"

"Suppose," countered Miss Ducas, "there was a fire in the dormitories at Barnard [the women's college affiliated with Columbia]; what good would a man be?"

154.11

The Springfield *Republican,* long a famous Massachusetts newspaper, once printed the obituary notice of a local citizen, who promptly and indignantly insisted that he was still very much alive. He demanded that the newspaper print a retraction.

The editor of the paper replied that he could not print the retraction because it would sully the paper's established reputation for accuracy.

"People who know you, know you are alive," added the editor, "and to those who don't know you, it won't make a bit of difference. Besides, we said some very flattering things about you in that obituary."

The citizen became abusive and insisted that his death be officially rescinded.

"All right," said the editor finally, "I give in. Tell you what I'll do. Tomorrow we'll run a notice of your birth on the front page."

154.12

Hammond Lamont, managing editor of the New York *Post* in the days when the paper was dominated by aristocrats and scholars, asked Rheta Childe Dorr, a steady contributor to the press, if she would like to edit the paper's woman's page. He wanted first to know if she had a college degree. "No," said Mrs. Dorr.

Lamont then said that the *Post* required its editorial workers to be of good breeding and education—people of impeccable character. While Lamont was talking, Mrs. Dorr noticed a picture of the paper's founder, Alexander Hamilton, on the wall, and remembered that Hamilton was of illegitimate birth.

"It gives me a certain sense of superiority," said Mrs. Dorr, "to think that I am to have a job that Alexander Hamilton himself couldn't have aspired to."

154.13

A reporter, out for vengeance on Charles Chapin, an editor of the New York *World* who was addicted to firing reporters on the least provocation and without notice, phoned Chapin.

"Do you have a reporter working for you named Charles Hogan?" asked the reporter in a disguised voice.

"Yes," replied Chapin.

"You're a damn liar, Chapin," yelled Hogan over the phone. "I just resigned!"

154.14

A young reporter covering a fire phoned New York *World* editor Charles Chapin and asked him for further instructions.

"Find the hottest place and jump in!" yelled Chapin over the phone.

154.15

When a reporter phoned later in the day than instructed and told editor Charles Chapin that he had failed to get the story he was sent out on, Chapin asked sweetly, "Your name is Smith, isn't it?"

"Yes," said the reporter.

"Do I understand that you work for the *World*?" inquired Chapin.

"That's correct," said the reporter.

"You're a liar," screamed Chapin. "Smith got fired from the *World* an hour ago."

154.16

A New York *World* reporter phoned in and told tyrannical editor Chapin he would not be in that day because he had fallen in the bathtub and scalded his foot. When he returned, he worked only a few days when Chapin fired him, saying, "I waited to see how long it would be before you forgot to limp."

154.17

In his early days, Irvin S. Cobb worked as a reporter for the New York *World* under Charles E. Chapin. One day Cobb arrived for work and asked where editor Chapin was. When told Chapin was home sick, Cobb said, "I trust it's nothing trivial."

154.18

A newspaperman, on a South Pacific tour of duty during World War II, was captured by a tribe of cannibals and prepared for the inevitable feast. He asked to see the chief and, brought before that eminence, told him that, since he was employed by a big United States paper, there would be serious consequences if he were roasted alive.

The chief asked him what his job was on the paper.

"I am an assistant editor," replied the newspaperman.

"Well," said the chief smacking his lips in relish, "you will soon be promoted to editor-in-chief."

154.19

The editor of a successful small-town paper was asked how he managed to sell so many copies in a town where everybody seemed to know what everybody else was doing.

The editor laughed and said, "They don't buy the paper to find out what people are doing. They buy it to find out who's been caught."

154.20

A scoop-minded newspaper editor out West ran a big first-page story one day about a disaster in a nearby town. No other paper in the nation carried a line about the tragedy. The next day the same editor had another scoop. His paper said: "We were the first to announce the news about the destruction of Jenkins's paint store last week. We are now the first to announce that the report was absolutely without foundation."

154.21

"Our paper is two days late this week," wrote a Nebraska editor, "owing to an accident to our press. When we started to run the press Wednesday night, as usual, one of the guy ropes gave way, allowing the forward glider fluke to fall and break as it struck the flunker flopper. This, of course, as any one who knows anything about a press will readily understand, left the gang-plank with only the flip flap to support it, which also dropped and broke off the wooper-chock. This loosened the fluking between the ramrod and the flibber-snatcher, which also caused trouble. The report that the delay was caused by the over-indulgence in stimulants by ourselves is a tissue of falsehoods, the peeled appearance of our right eye being caused by our going into the hatchway of the press in our anxiety to start it, and pulling the coppling pin after the slap bang was broken, which caused the dingus to rise up and welt us in the optic. We expect a brand new glider fluke on this afternoon's train."

154.22

Robert J. Casey tells about Sam Makaroff, a much-loved editor on a Chicago paper, a man with a limited acquaintance of the finer points of the English language, but one with a talent for puncturing stuffed shirts. One day he tried to board a special train carrying a batch of society notables on a mission of no particular consequence. A dignified gentleman tried to keep Makaroff from boarding the train.

"I am Charles Harkness Harkness-Clifford," said the gentleman sternly.

"You're a son of a bitch," retorted Makaroff.

154.23

When Guy Pollock was on the editorial staff of a London paper owned by Lord Beaverbrook, he was instructed by the boss to write an article on his belief in God. Pollock hesitated because he did not care to give the impression he was exploiting his religious beliefs.

"You believe in God, don't you?" asked Beaverbrook, sensing Pollock's reluctance.

"Yes," replied Pollock, "but I'm not sure it is quite the same God you believe in."

"What do you mean by that?" demanded Beaverbrook curtly.

"Well," said Pollock decisively, "I don't believe in a God that shaves every morning."

Whereupon Beaverbrook, getting the point and choking with rage, fired Pollock.

154.24

A pundit in control of a Chicago paper once ruled that no story in the paper should begin with "A," "An," or "The." When Delos Avery was assigned to write a piece about the discovery of the body of an unidentified woman in the river, he pondered briefly, and then began with this: "Hello, everybody. Take a look at this! The body of an unidentified woman. . . ."

When that got in type, the rule was quickly changed.

154.25

Chicago newspapermen tell the yarn about a son being born to an unmarried woman in a taxicab. When a photo of the cab came to a picture editor who was feuding with the city editor of his paper, he captioned the picture: "Birthplace of a future city editor."

154.26

When William Randolph Hearst heard that James Gordon Bennett's New York *Herald* was for sale, he wired Bennett, "Is the *Herald* for sale?"

"Price of *Herald*," replied Bennett, "is 3 cents daily, 5 cents Sunday."

154.27

Here is a Castle. It is the Home of an Editor. It has stained Glass Windows and Mahogany stairways. In front of the Castle is a Park. Is it not Sweet? The lady in the Park is the editor's wife. She wears a Costly robe of Velvet trimmed with Gold Lace, and there are Pearls and Rubies in her Hair. The editor sits on the front Stoop smoking an Havana Cigar. His little Children are playing with diamond Marbles on the Tesselated Floor. The editor can afford to Live in Style. He gets Seventy-five Dollars a month wages.

—*Eugene Field,* 1882

154.28

Eugene Field, a frequent forgetter of debts he owed, was sought out by a New Yorker visiting Chicago and was reminded that he had not paid the New Yorker $25 borrowed several months before.

"You are absolutely right," said Field, "and I promise to do something about it tomorrow."

The next day Field in his newspaper column mentioned the New Yorker's arrival in Chicago and added that the man "was in town to look after one of his permanent investments."

154.29

Joe William tells about the laziest newspaper columnist he ever heard of. Seems this fellow took a column by Arthur Brisbane and reprinted it word for word. The only contribution he made was to add at the end of it: "What on earth does Brisbane mean by all this?"

154.30

Cleveland Amory, in *The Proper Bostonians,* tells of a Boston paper that had a rule against any reference to the anatomy in its columns. One reporter ignored the tradition and used the word "navel." The edition was already running off the press but it was stopped so the offensive word could be removed. Unhappily the full context was not considered in removing the word, so the paper appeared in the street referring to a concert musician who had been in a "state of repose as complete as that of a Buddhist contemplating his ———."

154.31

The reporter returned to the office after covering a speech by the paper's favorite candidate. "What did our man have to say?" asked the editor.

"Nothing," said the reporter.

"Well, keep it to a column," requested the editor.

154.32

In reporting on the activities of a county political organization, an idealistic young reporter wrote a blanket indictment of the organization and everyone in it. It added up to the characterization of all the members as either crooks or morons, and sometimes both. The editor told the reporter the copy would have to be toned down somewhat. "No matter what you think," he said, "you can't say everyone of them is an idiot."

"How should it be handled, then?" asked the reporter.

"The way to do it," said the veteran editor, is to say that 'every member of the outfit is a nincompoop—except one.' Then everyone will think that he is the exception and all the others the dunderheads."

154.33

Tom White of the *Baltimore News American* relates that a newspaper reporter paid his respects to a political candidate in this way: "Congressman M spoke at the town hall last night. The best that can be said for his address is that it was nothing more than a cowardly attack on the English language."

154.34

A politician was enraged when he read what he regarded as a slanderous attack on his character and competence, but one of his advisers urged him to calm down and consider the question analytically.

"Bear in mind," he said, "there are 20,000 people in this town. One-half of them don't get this paper. That leaves 10,000. One-half of those who get the paper didn't see the story; that leaves 5,000. One-half of those who saw it don't believe it. That leaves 2,500. One-half of those who believe it don't know you. That leaves 1,250. One-half of those who know you are your friends. That leaves 625. One-half of those felt that way about you before they read the story. So there's really nothing to get excited about."

154.35

Ruby Black, a noted Washington correspondent, was in an elevator in the Capitol at Washington one day when a Senator turned to her and asked, "Is everything you are writing today the truth?" "Everything not enclosed in quotation marks," replied Miss Black.

154.36

In the days when American horse racing reached its peak at Saratoga in August, an elderly operator at the Western Union office became accustomed to the daily appearance of a grizzled veteran sportswriter to file his racing story. Then one day he failed to come in. The Western Union man inquired about him from the other writers and learned that he had disappeared. He had not been seen at the racetrack or at his hotel.

"Oh, we're not worried about him," a man from another paper told the operator. "Old Mac is just off on one of his benders again."

"But won't his paper fire him?" the operator asked anxiously.

The man from the opposition paper shrugged.

For six days a story was filed from the Western Union office in the name of the absentee. The sympathetic operator studied the stories of the opposition papers that were filed for transmittal, selecting a paragraph here and a paragraph there, rewording them fairly skillfully into reasonably good racing stories.

After six days, a disheveled man with a bad case of the shakes made his way into the Western Union office and asked in a trembling voice to see the man who had been filing his stories. The old operator looked up at him with an expectant smile.

"You're the guy that's been filing my stuff? Well, get this straight. It's lousy copy. If you don't do a better job, I'll give my business to Postal." (Postal was then a competing telegraph system, later merged with Western Union.)

154.37

When Gene Fowler was a reporter on a New York newspaper he was sent to northern Canada to find several lost aviators, and in the course of his work he spent some $3,000. But it was a great deal more difficult to account for all this money in his expense account than it was to spend it. Fowler, however, proved equal to the task: he put down the expense of buying a mythical dog team, the imaginary illness of one of the dogs which required expensive medical treatment, and finally, the death and burial of the dog. Finding still quite a few dollars unaccounted for at this point, Fowler made up the difference with this entry: "Flowers for bereft bitch—$60."

154.38

A reporter covering the lingering death of the famous millionaire railroad magnate E. H. Harriman submitted an enormous expense account when his assignment ended with the man's death. The city editor looked over the big expense account, then handed it back to the reporter, saying, "If this is the will, it's worth a story."

154.39

During World War II, a correspondent began to get a bit heady from the wine of quick success, and sent in a monthly expense account which included $150 for taxicab fares. His boss, knowing that the man spent the entire month aboard an aircraft carrier, cabled: HOW CAN YOU SPEND TAXICAB MONEY ON A CARRIER?

The correspondent replied, IT'S A BIG CARRIER.

154.40

Heywood Broun, when he was a reporter for the New York *World,* once called on Senator Smoot to interview him. "I have nothing to say," said the Senator from Utah.

"I know that," said Broun. "Now let's get down to the interview."

154.41

Mark Twain developed an aversion to newspaper interviewers because he claimed that they too often garbled or misrepresented what he said. At one point in his career he refused to grant interviews.

But when he went to his boyhood home in Missouri he made an exception and granted an interview to a young reporter, who asked him what was the most interesting event he had ever witnessed during his life.

Mark Twain thought for a few moments and then said, "The funeral of Aaron Burr."

"Excuse me, sir," stammered the young cub, "but didn't Burr die a good many years before you were born?"

"Young man," exclaimed Twain, "come over and let me clasp your hand. You're the first newspaperman I've seen in years who discovered a mistake before he printed it."

154.42

When the late Canon Elliott of Westminster visited the United States, he was asked by a reporter upon his arrival what his views were on nightclubs. To obtain breathing space, the Canon answered with another question: "Are there any nightclubs here?"

The next day the journal in question appeared with the caption: CANON'S FIRST QUESTION—"ARE THERE ANY NIGHTCLUBS IN NEW YORK?"

154.43

When Robert Bridges, the English poet, arrived in the United States, he refused to be interviewed by the American reporters. One of the American papers captioned the incident: KING'S CANARY REFUSES TO SING.

154.44

"Keep in mind," said newspaper-owner James Gordon Bennett to his reporters, "that many good stories have been ruined by over-verification."

154.45

American newspapers of other days had such names as: *Corn Stalk Fiddle, Warring Words, Evening Caterwaul, Run and Read, Bazoo, Rough Hewer, Hot Blast,* and *Astonisher and Paralyzer.* And a 1662 English newspaper was titled: *News from the Land of Chivalry, by a Knight of the Squeaking Fiddlestick.*

154.46

Married—At York, Mr. John Young, age 83 years, to Miss Naomi Hill, aged 75, after 38 years of *courtship* and *cohabitancy!* Well done ye old faithful servants, your offspring has been numerous! Your love constant! And your vows unbroken!

—*Castine Journal and Eastern Advertiser,* Castine, Maine, January 9, 1801

154.47

On Monday last, the Presbyterian minister at Epsom broke his leg, which was so miserably shattered, that it was cut off the next day. This is a great token that these pretenders to sanctity do not walk so circumspectly as they give out.

—*The Weekly Packet,* November 12, 1715

154.48

An indignant man strode up to the newspaper editor and said, "You have libeled me, by referring to me as the lightweight champion."

"But your name is Pugnacious, isn't it?"

"Yes, it's my name, but my brother is the one who is a boxer. I'm a coal merchant."

154.49

Edith Wharton said of a rich and very fat California woman: "She looks as if she carried her wealth in her stomach." For which Edith Wharton lost her job on a San Francisco newspaper.

154.50

During a dinner party Christopher Morley was discussing with a newspaper editor a sensational murder triangle then spread over the nation's press. Commenting on this and other top news, the editor said, "The first page certainly makes strange bedfellows."

"No," said Morley, "it's the other way around."

154.51

Methuselah lived 969 years and all they said about him was that he died. But what was he doing for 969 years? What a story, and all the reporters missed it!

—*Francis Albert "Bee" Behymer,* St. Louis journalist

154.52

Headline from show-biz weekly *Variety:*
CHI COOL, PIX HOT: "BIRDIE" WOW 47 G, "EAGLES" BOFFO $24,000, "SAM" FAIR 17 G; "IRMA" SOCKEROO $28,000 IN 2ND.

Translated, the above means that cool weather helped the box office in Chicago for *Bye Bye Birdie, A Gathering of Eagles,* and *Irma La Douce* in its second week. *Savage Sam* grossed only $17,000.

—*Herbert Greenhouse,* How to Double Your Vocabulary

154.53

A classic *Variety* headline: STIX NIX HIX PIX

154.54

Variety has called teen-agers "juves" or "the soft-drink set," and refers to their weekly allowances for records as "teen-coin."

154.55

Charles A. Dana, editor of the New York *Sun,* wrote in January, 1871: "It is announced that Mrs. Grant will receive every Tuesday afternoon during the winter, beginning with January 1. President Grant will receive any time and anything whenever anything is offered."

154.56

The New York *Sun* published a story about the sale of "the Rutherford B. Hayes Gin Mill" for $41,000—but quickly denied the story's accuracy, adding, "Whoever heard of President Hayes selling anything from a hydrosulphated hen's egg down to his good name and personal honor—for a copper less than its market value."

154.57

If Mr. Tyler is to be believed, it is unconstitutional for him to hold the office of President; for he says in his last message that the Constitution never designed that the executive should be a cipher.

—*George D. Prentice*

154.58

Tilford Moots wuz over t' th' Henryville poor farm th' other day t' see an ole friend o' his that used t' publish a newspaper thet pleased ever'buddy.

—*Kin Hubbard*

Definitions

154.59

News is anything that makes a woman say, "For heaven's sake!"

—*E. W. Howe*

154.60

A newspaper is a circulating library with high blood pressure.

—*Arthur "Bugs" Baer*

154.61

Editor: A person employed on a newspaper, whose business it is to separate the wheat from the chaff, and to see that the chaff is printed.

—*Elbert Hubbard*

154.62

Journalism consists in buying white paper at 2 cents a pound and selling it at 10 cents a pound.

—*Charles A. Dana*

154.63

A tabloid is a newspaper with a permanent crime wave.

Aphorisms

154.64

In the old days men had the rack; now they have the press.

—*Oscar Wilde*

154.65

The art of newspaper paragraphing is to stroke a platitude until it purrs like an epigram.

—*Don Marquis*

154.66

If words were invented to conceal thought, newspapers are a great improvement on a bad invention.

—*Henry David Thoreau*

154.67

He had been kicked in the head by a mule when young, and believed everything he read in the Sunday papers.

—*George Ade*

154.68

Except the Flood, nothing was as bad as reported.

—*E. W. Howe*

(*See also 30.5, 32.5, 37.5–37.7, 37.31, 37.32, 54.7, 54.10, 54.14, 56.1, 56.3, 62.8, 72.4, 76.5, 83.12, 114.5, 121.20, 125.10, 127.3, 127.6,*

140.1–140.23, 150.1, 150.11, 152.3–152.5, 210.19, 224.8, 229.18, 230.8, 231.11, 232.1, 232.7, 240.14, 248.15, 251.4, 257.4, 264.5, 270.18, 271.13, 272.4, 273.1)

155. Slips That Pass in the Type

155.1

Social note in Ohio paper: Mr. and Mrs. Pratt drew the first blush at the Aurora volunteer fireman's ball when they skidded on a slippery spot and fell on their last name.

—*Cedric Adams,* Minneapolis Star

155.2

Columbia, Tennessee, which calls itself the largest outdoor mule market in the world, held a mule parade yesterday, headed by the governor.

—A newspaper report quoted in *Successful Farming*

155.3

After Governor Baldridge watched the lion perform, he was taken to Main Street and fed twenty-five pounds of raw meat in front of the Fox Theater.

—*Idaho paper*

155.4

It has been fifteen years since Tipton, California, has had a mayor who smoked. Mayor North never smoked, ex-Mayor Calman doesn't smoke, and Mayor Chapman never smoked when living.

—The trade magazine *Tobacco*

155.5

Said a paper reporting Theodore Roosevelt's inauguration as President of the United States: "It was a scene never to be forgotten when Roosevelt, before the Chief Justice of the Supreme Court and a few witnesses, took his simple bath."

155.6

The New York *Times* reported: "Walter P. Reuther said today that the next major bargaining goal of the Automobile Workers Union was a shorter work week with no reduction in say."

155.7

The Post Office Department is never questioned. Every person who presents a letter for mailing is fully confident it will be safely carried to its destruction.

—*Minnesota paper*

155.8

From a government report: "This report is made impossible through the cooperative efforts of three agencies of the Department of Agriculture." —*Quoted by AP*

155.9

Some years ago a New Zealand newspaper stated that a Mr. X was a "defective in the police force." The next day an attempt was made to correct the error, but it came out, "Mr. X is a detective in the police farce."

155.10

When a drink calls for sugar, add a dash of money instead. Blends smoothly and is a great pepper-upper.

—Chicago *American*

155.11

A paper that referred to a war veteran as "bottle-scarred" retracted with: "Last week we spoke of a certain veteran as 'bottle-scarred.' We are deeply mortified, and we apologize. We meant to say 'battle-scared.' "

155.12

A famous misprint: "The general will remain unequaled in history for his accomplishment on the bottlefield."

155.13

Captioning a story about attempts to solve budget problems, the Parkersburg, Pennsylvania, *Post,* came up with BOROUGH FATHEADS HAVE BUDGET TROUBLE.

155.14

The Tulsa, Oklahoma, *Daily World* reported: "Kathleen Winsor has written another book, *Star Money,* that is called a 'Twentieth-century *Amber,*' and is supposed to outsmell the two million copies of the first book."

155.15

COUNTY OFFICIALS TO TALK RUBBISH

—*Headline, Los Angeles paper*

155.16

HEAVY RAINS ASSURE CITY'S MILK SUPPLY

—Atlanta *Journal*

155.17

FATHER OF TEN SHOT—MISTAKEN FOR RABBIT

—*Newspaper headline*

155.18

News item: "Rudy Vallee, the well-known crooner and radio singer, was shaken up and bruised when his car left the highway and turned over. It is feared that his vocal cords were not injured."

155.19

The motorist approached the coroner at 55 miles per hour.

155.20

Reporting an accident involving movie star Greer Garson, the Monterey, California, *Peninsula Herald* said, "The area in which Miss Garson was injured is spectacularly scenic."

155.21

William Andrews returned home yesterday from the hospital, where his left leg was placed in a cast following a fracture of the right ankle.

—New York *Telegram*

155.22

On July 11, 1934, he suffered a stroke, but with the loving care of his family and his kind and efficient nurse, he never fully recovered.

—*Wisconsin paper*

155.23

DR. ISRAEL KAPLAN ELECTED BOARD OF HEALTH CHAIRMAN. HEARING ON CEMETERY EXPANSION NEXT WEEK.

—Headline, Salem, Mass., *Evening News*

155.24

There was a strawberry festival at the Union church Thursday evening for the benefit of the cemetery.

—*Massachusetts paper*

155.25

Social item in the press: "Mrs. Robbins, president of the Women's Club, announces that on Wednesday, June 15th, the final meeting will be hell."

155.26

Henry Watterson tells of a New York paper that transposed the heading of its obituary column with its shipping news, which chanced to be on the same page. As a result, a number of respected and deceased citizens were listed as "Passing through Hell Gate," the channel between Long Island Sound and the East River.

155.27

When Bret Harte was editor of a California mining-town paper, he had to write an obituary for the highly respected wife of a leading citizen. He concluded his obit with "She was distinguished for charity above all the ladies in town." When the proof of this landed back on his desk, he found it rendered "She was distinguished for chastity above all the ladies in town." Carefully Harte corrected the wording by referring the compositor to the original copy by a large query in the margin. To his horror the following day the paper appeared with the statement: "She was distinguished for chastity (?) above all the ladies in town."

155.28

In 1903 the London *Daily Mirror* carried a story about the marriage of two members of a cast playing at the Drury Lane Theatre. It mentioned that the newlyweds did not go away for a honeymoon. The story concluded with, "The usual performance took place in the evening."

155.29

According to the complaint, Mrs. O'D—— says her husband started amusing her three days before the marriage.

—*Texas paper*

155.30

When a veteran salesman retired, he married again and settled down in his home town of Lansing, Michigan. The Lansing paper had a story on the wedding, but somehow the headline for another story appeared over the wedding account: OLD POWER PLANT REACTIVATED.

—*Kenneth Nichols,* Akron Beacon Journal

155.31

Obviously meaning to speak of a bridge, a Kansas paper said: "The bride is twenty feet wide from buttress to buttress."

155.32

At the Ladies Aid Society meeting many interesting articles were raffled off. Every member brought something they no longer needed. Many members brought their husbands.

155.33

Recovering from a head injury and shock caused by coming into contact with a live wife, Arthur E—— left Mercy Hospital Wednesday.

—*Ohio paper*

155.34

WILD WIFE LEAGUE WILL MEET TONIGHT

—*W. Va. paper*

155.35

If linotypers must make errors, it was appropriate that one of them, setting a story about a man seeking a divorce, made it read that the plaintiff asked the court for a change of Venus.

—*Buffalo Evening News*

155.36

House and Garden is supposed to have missed this misprint: "Nothing gives a greater variety to the appearance of a house than a few undraped widows."

155.37

POCATELLO MATTRESS FACTORY PLAYS IMPORTANT ROLE IN CITY'S GROWTH

—*Idaho State Journal*

155.38

Picture caption in *Kiwanis Magazine:* "There is a picnic during the two-day outing which practically doubles the population of the town each year."

155.39

Adjacent to the library is another completely equipped lovatory.

—*Washington, D.C., paper*

155.40

Reverend Horace G—— returned from his Twin Cities visit yesterday and will take up his cuties at the church.

—*North Dakota paper*

155.41

The Junior Ladies Aid will serve an oyster at the church Saturday evening.

—*Iowa church bulletin*

155.42

The next meeting of the Legion will take place on February 10. Every man who died for his country is cordially invited.

—*North Dakota paper*

155.43

"TANNHAEUSER" SUNK BY METROPOLITAN

—*Philadelphia paper*

155.44

HOTEL BURNS, TWO HUNDRED GUESTS ESCAPE HALF GLAD

—*Boston paper*

155.45

TWO CONVICTS EVADE NOOSE, JURY HUNG

—*California paper*

155.46

The dangers of communication are illustrated by the man who encounters a friend and says, "I hear your brother has just left Penn State and is now living at the Park Central."

"Well, it isn't quite like that. My brother just left the State pen and is living in Central Park."

(*See also 156.1–156.25*)

PUNS, MALAPROPS, AND SPOONERISMS

156. Word Wranglers

156.1

A customer stopped in at his Greek tailor with a pair of ripped trousers.

"Euripedes?" asked the tailor.

"Yes; Eumenides," replied the customer.

156.2

A writer who was an incurable punster visited an orphanage and said, "Thus far and no father." While breakfasting, he could not help saying, "The bun is the lowest form of wheat." And when he saw the Grand Canyon, he was almost thrown in it after he said, "Gorgeous."

156.3

Four philologists were walking through town when they were solicited by several hussies. The scholars, ignoring the overtures, wondered how best to describe the group of girls.

One suggested, "A jam of tarts."

"How about a flourish of strumpets?" said the second man.

"Or an essay of Trollopes," added the third philologist.

The fourth man hesitated, then offered, "An anthology of pros."

To which Conrad Aiken has added, "A pride of loins."

156.4

Herb Greenhouse tells this story: A workman who had just completed the sidewalk in front of a new home was admiring it, saying to the new owner, "It's as smooth as glass." At that moment a neighborhood kid waded right through the center of it. The man broke out in profuse profanity.

"Please," said the lady, "I thought you were fond of children?"

"I am, in the abstract; but not in the concrete."

156.5

Edward Anthony tells about the time George Martin, editor of *Farm and Fireside,* was lunching in a restaurant where the adjoining table was occupied by an ink manufacturer. When Martin heard the man say, "There ain't nobody makes the quality ink I do," Martin leaned over and said, "You say you're an ink manufacturer?"

"I sure am," was the reply.

"Then why don't you speak Inklish?" asked Martin.

156.6

The prideful Tern, about to be a mother,
Reflects that two good Terns deserve another.

—*Clifton Fadiman*

156.7

Douglas Jerrold was once challenged by a friend to make a pun on any subject which should be given, and upon his engaging to do so, the friend added, "Well, I'm sure you can't pun on the Zodiac."

"By Gemini, I can-cer," said Jerrold.

156.8

Reverend Sydney Smith, while walking down the street in a residential neighborhood, came upon two women who stood in their respective yards and howled insults at each other. "They will never agree," said Smith, "because they are arguing from different premises."

156.9

Lord Russell, small in stature, married a very tall widow and was thereafter often referred to as "the widow's mite."

156.10

The things my wife buys at auction are keeping me baroque.

—*Peter De Vries*

156.11

The late Senator Charles B. Farwell claimed this was the only perfect triple pun in the English language: A woman's three sons went to Texas to raise beef cattle, sheep, and hogs. Stumped for a good name for their ranch, they wrote home to Mother for suggestions. NAME IT FOCUS she telegraphed. Puzzled, they wired for an explanation. The reply came immediately: FOCUS—WHERE THE SUN'S RAYS MEET.

—*Otis Chatfield Taylor,* Croton-on-Hudson (N.Y.) News

156.12

The more waist the less speed.

—*Oliver Herford*

156.13

When Sir Charles James Napier captured Scinde (or Sind), in India, he was supposed to have cabled the War Office a one-word message, PECCAVI—which is Latin for "I have sinned." Actually, reports Clifton Fadiman, the pun was originated by *Punch.*

156.14

Clifton Fadiman records what might be called a medical pun, originated by Jim Hawkins in 1927, when he said "There's a *vas deferens* between having children and no children."

156.15

An Oxford scholar met a porter who was carrying a hare through the street and accosted him with this extraordinary question:

"Prithee, sir, is that thy own hare or a wig?"

156.16

A woman writer who suffered during an Atlantic crossing cabled, *Sic transit.*

156.17

The dying Mercutio saw himself as a "grave man."

156.18

Henry Erskine said a pun was the lowest form of wit—therefore the foundation of all wit.

156.19

"I would like to meet a humorist who is not an exhumist," said the tired editor, after looking over a batch of old jokes suggested for publication.

156.20

Diplomat Henry Villard recently told of a punning career foreign service officer who was hounded out of the service when he mocked his superior, a dairy tycoon, by saying: "All I have I owe to udders."

156.21

Mrs. Malaprop, a character in R. B. Sheridan's play *The Rivals* (1775), from whom the term derives, said:

"No delusions to the past" should be made.

"Precipitate one down the prejudice" (instead of "precipice")

"As headstrong as an allegory on the banks of the Nile."

156.22

Mrs. Malaprop's successor was describing the adventure of her husband when he was in Messina, Italy, at the time of the earthquake.

"It was awful," she said in awed tones. "When Jim went to bed, everything was perfectly quiet. And then when he woke up, all of a sudden, there beside him was a yawning abbess!"

156.23

Another "malaprop": During a debate one man rose to his feet and called out, "That allegation is false and the alligator knows it."

156.24

Spoonerisms, the transposition of the initial sounds of words that result in a laughable combination, are named after the Reverend W. A. Spooner (1844–1930), an English clergyman addicted to this unconscious humor. It was he who said, "We all know what it is to have a half-warmed fish within us" (meaning "a half-formed wish"); and "Yes, indeed; the Lord is a shoving leopard"; and "Kingkering Kongs their titles take." He once asked a waitress for a "glass bun and a bath of milk." Intending to rebuke the congregation for its small attendance and to refer to the "weary benches," instead he said, "I am tired of addressing these beery wenches."

156.25

On other occasions the Warden of New College, Oxford, is supposed to have said: "Sir, I believe you are under the affluence of incahol"; "Now Rababbas was a bobber"; "blushing crow" (instead of "crushing blow"); "It is kisstomary to cuss the bride"; and finally, perhaps most famous of all, "Mardon me, Padam, but I am afraid that you are occupewing the wrong pie. May I sew you to another sheet?"

(*See also 26.12, 37.34, 40.17, 58.6, 77.4, 85.5, 86.16, 87.6, 90.5, 92.9, 93.19, 93.20, 95.4, 95.5, 96.3, 96.4, 102.7, 113.8, 130.13, 133.7, 134.5, 135.16, 139.28, 147.4, 149.10, 149.11, 136.19, 137.1–137.6, 138.12–138.20, 139.28, 155.1–155.46, 157.2, 164.1, 164.2, 165.11, 184.34, 184.39, 188.10, 191.7, 199.1, 207.12, 217.17, 219.11, 226.9, 226.19–226.46, 227.9, 231.7, 231.8, 234.12, 235.32, 235.37, 235.40, 236.3, 236.12, 236.13, 237.2–237.4, 240.6, 240.13, 240.14, 240.17, 244.7, 245.3, 247.2, 249.6, 253.1, 253.9, 264.10, 264.13, 264.18, 264.20, 266.3–266.7, 266.26, 266.34, 266.37, 268.22, 268.23, 268.39, 270.14, 271.18, 271.23, 271.32, 271.34, 272.15*)

FROM THE ART GALLERY

157. Brushers and Chiselers

Anecdotes

157.1

Raphael had painted a picture of Saints Peter and Paul. A group of Cardinals examined the work, declaring the faces were "too ruddy."

"They blush," explained the artist, "upon seeing the Church governed by such men as you."

157.2

George Bernard Shaw was introduced to James McNeill Whistler, the artist, by a mutual friend who said jocularly that Shaw was "a fellow artist." "Indeed!" said Whistler with ominous courtesy. "And what particular branch of art do you practice, Mr. Shaw?"

"Practically all of them," said Shaw. "But I am particularly good at blowing my own trumpet."

"Ah, yes," said Whistler, "one of the braggarts."

157.3

Whistler once succeeded in getting a work by a fellow artist hung during the autumn salon, in London. Whistler and his friend went to the exhibit, but the artist exclaimed in dismay, "Good heavens! They're exhibiting my picture upside down."

"Hush," said Whistler, "the committee refused it the other way."

157.4

When Whistler completed the portrait of a celebrity, the artist asked him how he liked it.

"I can't say I do, Mr. Whistler; you must admit it's a bad work of art."

"Yes," replied Whistler, "but then you must admit that you are a bad work of nature."

157.5

The art world is amused by the legend of the animal painter who was found rubbing raw meat on a painting of a dog. "What's the idea?" asked his friend.

"A wealthy woman is coming in this afternoon to see this painting. I happen to know she never goes out without her poodle. When she finds that her dog gets excited about this picture, she will probably buy it." And that is what happened.

157.6

Samuel Morse was not only an inventor but a painter of considerable talent. At one time he was quite proud of a canvas depicting Christ riding an ass into Jerusalem and asked a friend to tell him frankly what he thought of it. The friend inspected it carefully and said, "Your donkey is the savior of your picture."

157.7

Hogarth once painted an ugly and aged peer who was noted for his parsimony. The artist did an excellent if wholly unflattering likeness of the old man, who refused to pay for it when it was shown to him. Whereupon Hogarth wrote to him, "If you do not call and pay for the portrait, I shall add a tail to it, along with other simian appendages, and exhibit it at your club." The portrait was called and paid for promptly.

157.8

Gilbert Stuart, famous early American portrait painter, met a lady on a Boston street who said, "Oh, Mr. Stuart, I have just been admiring your miniature and found it so much like you that I kissed it."

"And did it return the kiss?" asked Stuart.

"Of course not!" laughed the woman.

"Then it was not like me," said Stuart.

157.9

An eminent painter was once asked what he mixed his colors with in order to produce so extraordinary an effect.

"I mix with my brains, sir, my brains."

157.10

A young man, grown rich, wanted a portrait done of his father, of whom he had no picture. So he gave the painter a detailed description of his parent and asked the artist to go ahead on that basis.

When the portrait was unveiled, the young son looked at it and said, "Yes, that's the old geezer. But my, how he's changed!"

157.11

A middle-aged man, visiting an art museum with his wife, stood for minutes rapturously looking at a painting of a woman dressed only in a few leaves.

Finally his wife snapped at him, "What are you waiting for, autumn?"

157.12

"Sculpture seems such a simple thing to do," observed the young woman on a visit to the studio of a sculptor.

"Nothing to it," said the artist. "All you need is a block of marble and a hammer and chisel. Then you simply knock off all the marble you don't want."

157.13

Leonard Lyons relates that two elderly artists, who had shared a studio in Paris years earlier, met in New York one day. "I hear you have just had an eye operation," one artist said to the other. "Will you be able to see well enough to continue with your painting?"

"If I can't," said the second artist, "I'll become a critic."

157.14

"Have you seen how Smearman, the critic, massacred my last work?" asked the struggling artist.

"Don't mind him," consoled a friend, "he just repeats like a parrot what everyone else is saying."

157.15

Note from an art critic's column: "They could not find the artist, so they hung his picture."

157.16

"This," said the artist to his visitor, "is my latest work. I have called it 'Builders at Work.' It is a piece of realism."

"But," said the visitor, "I don't see any of the men at work."

"Of course not—that is the realism of it."

157.17

If my husband would ever meet a woman on the street who looked like the women in his painting, he would fall over in a dead faint.

—*Mrs. Pablo Picasso,* 1955

157.18

"It's horrible," said the viewer of a work of modern art. "I only paint what I see," explained the artist.

"When in that condition, you shouldn't paint," said the critic.

Aphorisms

157.19

One reassuring thing about modern art is that things can't be as bad as they are painted.

—*M. Walthall Jackson*

157.20

It is only an auctioneer who can equally and impartially admire all schools of art.

—*Oscar Wilde*

157.21

An art school is a place for young girls to pass the time between high school and marriage.

—*Thomas Hart Benton*

(*See also 25.14, 27.1, 54.5, 76.18, 110.2, 152.39, 166.17, 175.26, 177.15, 178.10, 184.36, 207.2, 207.3, 215.7, 232.11, 241.2*)

Part Five

MALES AND "FRAILS": SINGLE, MARRIED, DIVORCED, AND FREE LANCE

THE SINGLE LIFE

158. Bachelors and Bachelorettes

Anecdotes

158.1

"How come you never married?" a man asked an old friend.

"I really don't know," replied the bachelor. "I've come close a number of times. Just the other day I fell in love with a girl at first sight."

"And you're not going to marry her?"

"No, I took a second look."

158.2

"Are you in favor of a tax on bachelors?" the heckler called out to the political candidate.

"I had supposed," replied the speaker, "that I had already made it perfectly clear that I am opposed to any tax on raw material."

158.3

"If I had my way, Miss Arbuthnot," said the slightly bitter man, "I'd put every woman in the nation in jail—and keep them there."

"And what kind of a nation would you have then?" demanded Miss Arbuthnot.

"Stag-nation, my dear lady," said the cynical man.

158.4

Brander Matthews suggested that the tenacity of the British army is due to the prevalence of spinsterhood in Great Britain. The conclusion is arrived at in this way: The British soldier is nourished on beef; the quality of the beef is due to an abundance of clover, which is fertilized by bees. Bees can only live and multiply when protected against field mice. Field mice are kept down only if there are enough cats to catch them. Cats are the favorite pets of old maids in England. Thus the spinsters keep the cats that destroy the field mice, which in turn prevents the bees from being destroyed, as a consequence of which clover flourishes and the cattle grow fat and strong on clover, and the soldiers in turn grow strong because they eat the beef.

158.5

Sir Walter Scott's diary comments on disclaimers which are sincere yet sound affected and recalls the story about an old woman who, "when Carlisle was taken by the Highlanders in 1745, chose to be particularly apprehensive of personal violence, and shut herself up in a closet, in order that she might escape ravishment. But no one came to disturb her solitude, and she began to be sensible that poor Donald was looking out for victuals, or seeking for some small plunder, without bestowing a thought on the fair sex; by and by she popped her head out of her place of refuge with the petty question, 'good folks, can you tell me when the ravishing is going to begin?' "

158.6

Mary O'Holloran was given a piece of wedding cake and told to place it under her pillow so that she would have dreams of the man she would wed. When asked about her dream the next day, she said she dreamed about the 69th Regiment.

158.7

When the old maid found a robber under her bed, she covered him with a gun while she called the police and told them to send a cop over in the morning.

158.8

A burglar who was caught looting the room of an old maid pleaded, "Please, lady, let me go. I ain't never done anything wrong."

"Well," said the old maid, "you just stay here. It's never too late to learn."

158.9

One day Maude Adams, the famous actress, was asked by her maid when she was going to get married.

"Oh," laughed the star, "I don't think I'll ever get married."

"Well," replied the faithful maid, "they say an old maid is the happiest person once they quit strugglin'."

158.10

When a spinster was asked why she had traded in her double bed for twin beds, she said: "Because every night I look under the bed to see if a man is there. With two beds, my chances are doubled."

158.11

During World War II, a lonely little lady made a pair of pajamas for use by the Red Cross. They were beautifully made, but the inspector noticed there was no opening in the front of the pajamas. As discreetly as possible he pointed out this omission to the nice old lady. At first she was crestfallen, but then she looked up and said, "Couldn't you give them to a bachelor?"

158.12

Two gentle maiden ladies sat rocking on the front porch when they noticed a rooster chasing a hen. The hen dashed into the road and was killed by a passing car. "How beautiful," said one of the women. "She'd rather die."

Definitions

158.13

A bachelor is a fellow who believes it is much better to have loved and lost than to have to get up for the 2 A.M. feeding.

158.14

A bachelor is a man who prefers to cook his own goose.

158.15

A Confirmed Bachelor: One who thinks that the only thoroughly justified marriage was the one that produced him.

—*Harlan Miller*

158.16

Bachelor: A man who is dancing when he walks the floor with baby.

158.17

A bachelor is a man who never makes the same mistake once.

158.18

A bachelor is a rolling stone that gathers no boss.

158.19

Bachelor Girl: A girl who is still looking for a bachelor.

158.20

A bachelor is a man who can be miss-led only so far.

158.21

Bachelor: A man who comes to work each morning from a different direction.

158.22

A bachelor is a man who has taken out many a girl, but has never been taken in.

Aphorisms

158.23

A bachelor wants to have a girl in his arms but not on his hands.

158.24

A bachelor is a permanent public temptation.

—*Oscar Wilde*

158.25

The trouble with being a bachelor is by the time you've played the field you're too old to make a pitch.

158.26

To the Bachelor, who is always free!
To the Husband, who sometime may be!

158.27

What a pity it is that nobody knows how to manage a wife but a bachelor.

—*George Colman*

158.28

Here's to the bachelor, lonely and gay,
For it's not his fault he was born that way,
And here's to the spinster, lonely and good,
For it's not her fault—she hath done what she could.

158.29

Pass me the wine. To those that keep
The bachelor's secluded sleep
Peaceful, inviolate and deep,
I pour libation.

—*Austin Dobson*

158.30

A smart man is one who hasn't let a woman pin anything on him since he wore diapers.

158.31

Wise is the young man who is always thinking of taking a wife, and never takes one.

—*Pietro Aretino*

158.32

In Genesis it says that it is not good for a man to be alone, but sometimes it is a great relief.

—*John Barrymore*

158.33

Here's to the girl who never drinks,
Who from the cursed liquor shrinks,
Who never once forgets herself
As she sits alone on her lonely shelf.

158.34

The only good husbands stay bachelors; they're too considerate to get married.

—*Finley Peter Dunne*

158.35

A bachelor never quite gets over the idea that he is a thing of beauty and a Boy forever.

—*Helen Rowland*

158.36

Never trust a husband too far, or a bachelor too near.

—*Helen Rowland*

(*See also 53.2, 67.10, 144.2, 159.1–159.3, 159.7, 159.10–159.20, 159.22–159.28, 161.1–161.31, 162.2, 162.7, 165.1, 168.11, 175.34, 181.1, 184.4, 250.15, 272.23*)

159. The Dating Game

Anecdotes

159.1

Harold was a painfully shy young man who wanted to date girls and dance with them, but who did not quite know how to go about it. When a friend told him there were a number of books of guidance on the subject of dating and romancing, he went to a bookstore. But because he was too shy to state what he wanted, he made his own selection: a large and beautifully bound volume titled *How to Hug*. It was, he felt certain, just what he needed. He bought it and took it home. But when he began to read it he discovered he had bought volume four of an encyclopedia!

159.2

An eligible young bachelor was asked by a friend why he never took the same girl out twice. "Because most of them keep diaries," said the cautious one.

"Why does that frighten you?" asked the friend.

"It's this way," said the bachelor. "My dates are strictly conventional. Nothing happens on them that would make interesting comments in the diaries. So there is always the risk that the girls might invent highly romantic happenings—even torrid ones. On the other hand, if they tell their diaries the truth and simply state 'Went out with Jim last night' a reader of that is liable to think that something went on that the girl would not dare record. So either way you lose if you keep dating the same girls."

159.3

"Young man," said the father severely, "considering your age and your income, do you think you should be taking my daughter to a nightclub?"

"No, sir," said the young man, "I do not. Let us both try to reason with her!"

159.4

A scientist arrived at a party with a young woman of much beauty but little brains. They were so interested in each other that they ignored others at the party.

"What can they have in common?" one guest wondered to the hostess.

"Only a difference in sex," said the hostess.

159.5

The boy looked at the prices on the menu, turned to his date, and said: "What will you have, my plump little doll?"

159.6

"I don't ask or expect much of life," said the beautiful young woman. "Like every other young woman, all I want is a handsome man to love and understand me. That isn't too much to expect of a millionaire, is it?"

159.7

A young girl was debating whether to keep a date with a rich, old bachelor.

"Don't you think he is too old to be considered eligible?" she asked her mother.

"My child," said the mercenary mother, "he is a little bit too eligible to be considered old."

159.8

A wealthy New York lawyer several years ago had some difficulties with a very troublesome and by no means conventional young lady. He had sent her off to Europe. Before long he received a note from her reading: "I am sitting here looking at Vesuvius. Vesuvius is looking at me. We are both burning."

159.9

"Did you ever catch your husband flirting?" the young woman was asked.

"I certainly did," was the reply. "That's how I caught him."

159.10

The young woman smiled sweetly as she brushed past others waiting for the use of the telephone booth and said, "I'll only be a minute. I just want to hang up on him."

159.11

A young man wrote his beloved this letter:

"There is nothing I would not do to reach your side. I would climb the highest mountain. I would cross the trackless desert. I would swim the widest ocean to be near you, my beloved."

Then at the end appeared this: "*P.S.* See you Saturday night, if it doesn't rain."

159.12

"Do you really love me, or do you just think so?" he asked.

"Yes, honey, I really do love you," she replied. "I haven't done any thinking at all about it, yet."

159.13

"Don't you love driving on a night like this?"

"Yes," he said, "but I thought I'd wait until we get farther out in the country."

—Tulane University *Urchin*

Definitions

159.14

Gold Digger: A woman after all.

159.15

Platonic friendship is the interval between the introduction and the first kiss.

159.16

Platonic friendship is one that half the town says isn't.

—*Raymond Duncan,* Ellaville, Ga., *Sun*

Aphorisms

159.17

In the spring boys begin to feel gallant and girls begin to feel buoyant.

159.18

A good line is the shortest distance between dates.

159.19

He's got a good head on his shoulders, but it's a different one every night.

159.20

The trouble with being a bachelor is that a man has to get up so early to make the money to stay out so late.

159.21

Here's to man: he can afford anything he can get; here's to woman: she can afford anything she can get a man to get for her.

—*George Ade*

159.22

Few things are more expensive than a girl who is free for the evening.

—*Earl Wilson*

159.23

She was a grasping gal—when I promised her a pearl necklace, she grew a goiter.

—*Arthur "Bugs" Baer*

159.24

It takes all the fun out of a bracelet if you have to buy it yourself.

—*Peggy Hopkins Joyce*

159.25

A thing of beauty is a great expense.

159.26

Show me a genuine case of platonic friendship, and I shall show you two old or homely mugs.

—*Austin O'Malley*

159.27

That's a lot of fish in any language—thirty-nine pounds—and all in one piece. Still, as Fred Simmons says, "For sheer tricks, fight and stamina, give me a small-mouthed lass at sundown, any time."

—*Northwest Organizer*

159.28

Here's to the Chaperone,
May she learn from Cupid
Just enough blindness
To be sweetly stupid.

(*See also 31.1, 35.4, 99.14, 154.3, 155.39, 161.1, 161.6, 183.7, 190.14, 191.3, 191.7, 191.17, 191.18, 191.32, 272.23*)

160. Love and Kisses

Anecdotes

160.1

The mistress was chiding her maid for being so fickle with her men friends, and asked, "Do you allow just any man to kiss you?"

"No," replied the maid, "I just allow those I know and those I love."

"That could mean a lot of men," said the mistress, "just about every man you go out with. What's the difference between the ones you know and the ones you love?"

"Well, those I know, I let. And those I love, I help."

160.2

The girl said, "'Erbert, you really shouldn't have kissed me like that, with all those people around, even if it was dark in that air raid shelter."

"I didn't kiss you," said the boy, looking angrily around in the crowd. "I'd like to find out who it was—I'd teach 'em."

" 'Erbert, you couldn't teach him anything."

160.3

Co-ed: "Is it natural to shrink from kissing?"

Professor: "If it were, my child, most of you girls would be nothing but skin and bones."

160.4

A woman appeared in court against a man she had had arrested. Taking the witness stand she said: "This fellow came into the movie theater and sat down beside me. Pretty soon he's holding my hand, and the next thing he's stroking my arm, gently and smoothly for quite a while. Then he started kissing me, and then squeezing and caressing me. Suddenly he was gone—and so was my purse."

"Why," asked the judge, "didn't you move away or call for help when he was doing all this kissing and hugging?"

"Your Honor, I had no idea he was after my money."

160.5

A famous actor riding in a train was recognized and pestered by two elderly women. It was a long trip and the actor wondered how he could put an end to their boring chatter. Presently the train entered a tunnel, but the train lights were not put on. During this brief interval the actor put the back of his hand to his mouth and made a loud smacking sound.

When the train emerged into daylight both women stared at each other in icy silence. The delighted actor thought he would insure continued silence, so with a charming smile he said, "Ladies, I will always regret not knowing which one of you kissed me while we were going through the tunnel."

160.6

Two elderly men, with some remaining traces of youth, stood on a street corner deploring the state of the world. One of them attributed most of the current troubles to women taking over men's work. "They work in factories, in service stations, on buses; they drive taxis, and they are policemen and judges. They are in just about every job a man ought to be in."

Just when this tirade ended, two young women met each other and embraced and kissed each other in delight.

"See what I mean," said the elderly man. "Women doing men's work."

160.7

The sun was dropping behind the horizon. The moon was beginning to rise. All was quiet on the farm, and the gentle breeze hinted at romance. The farm boy and the pretty girl from the village strolled hand in hand through the pasture. They stopped to watch the calf and its mother rubbing noses.

"I'd like to be doing that," said the farmer boy wistfully.

"Well, it's your cow," said the young lady.

Definitions

160.8

The philosopher asked to define the difference between life and love, said: "Life is just one fool thing after another. Love is two fool things after each other."

160.9

Platonic love is the gun you didn't think was loaded.

160.10

Love is the last word in a telegram.

160.11

Love is the delusion that one woman differs from another.

—*H. L. Mencken*

160.12

Love is the delightful interval between meeting a beautiful girl and discovering that she looks like a haddock.

—*John Barrymore*

160.13

Oliver Herford defined a kiss as: "A course of procedure, cunningly devised, for the mutual stoppage of conversation at a moment when words are superfluous."

Aphorisms

160.14

It is the same in love as in war; a fortress that parleys is half taken.

—*Marguerite de Valois*

160.15

The love game is never called off on account of darkness.

—*T. L. Masson*

160.16

Adam invented love at first sight, one of the

greatest labor-saving machines the world ever saw.

—*Josh Billings*

160.17

Nothing is potent against love save only impotence.

—*Nicholas Murray Butler*

160.18

A lover without indiscretion is no lover at all.

—*Thomas Hardy*

160.19

Before marriage a girl has to kiss a man to hold him; after marriage she has to hold him to kiss him.

160.20

Kissing don't last. Cookery do.

—*George Meredith*

160.21

When a rogue kisses you, count your teeth.

160.22

When the girl you kiss gives as good as you give, you are not getting firsts.

160.23

May we kiss those we please and please those we kiss.

160.24

Here's to the lasses we've loved, lad;
Here's to the lips we've pressed;
For kisses and lasses, like liquor in glasses,
The last is always the best.

160.25

Here's head first, in a foaming glass!
Here's head first, to a lively lass!
Here's head first, for a bit of kissing.
For the good don't know the fun they're missing!

160.26

Here's to the red of the holly berry,
And to its leaf so green;
And here's to the lips that are just as red,
And the fellow who's not so green.

160.27

I ne'er could any lustre see
In eyes that would not look at me;
I ne'er saw nectar on a lip
But where my own did hope to sip.

—*Richard Brinsley Sheridan*

160.28

Here's to the light that lies in a woman's eyes,
And lies, and lies, and lies.

160.29

To the ladies:
Our arms your defense.
Your arms our recompense.
Fall in!

160.30

Many a man in love with a dimple makes the mistake of marrying the whole girl.

160.31

To each man's best and truest love—unless it be himself.

160.32

Here's to love and unity, dark corners and opportunity.

160.33

Here's to love—the disease which begins with a fever and ends with a pain.

160.34

Here's to the land we love and the "love" we "land."

160.35

Here's to love—the only fire for which there is no insurance.

—*Anonymous*

160.36

He who loves and runs away may live to love another day.

—*Carolyn Wells*

160.37

Love is said to be blind, but I know lots of fellows in love who can see twice as much in their sweethearts as I can.

—*Josh Billings*

160.38

Love is the state in which man sees things most widely different from what they are.

—*Friedrich Nietzsche*

160.39

After all, doesn't free love cost the most?

—*T. L. Masson*

160.40

Love is like the measles; we can have it but once, and the later in life we have it, the tougher it goes with us.

—*Josh Billings*

160.41

To a woman the first kiss is just the end of the beginning; to a man it is the beginning of the end.

—*Helen Rowland*

160.42

A man snatches the first kiss, pleads for the second, demands the third, takes the fourth, accepts the fifth—and endures all the rest.

—*Helen Rowland*

160.43

You can always get someone to love you—even if you have to do it yourself.

—*T. L. Masson*

(*See also 24.13, 31.24, 108.1, 111.7, 111.8, 118.14, 147.1, 150.4, 150.13, 157.8, 158.23, 159.1, 159.6, 159.12, 159.13, 159.27, 160.1–160.18, 160.20–160.27, 160.30–160.43, 161.23, 161.25, 161.30, 164.26, 165.31, 168.7, 171.13, 173.2, 173.3, 176.8, 184.68, 185.5, 188.22, 217.10, 228.4, 260.5, 268.24, 268.37, 269.5, 269.53, 269.115, 269.196*)

161. Wolves of Both Sexes

Anecdotes

161.1

The old roué had tried without success to date his pretty secretary. She was polite but firm. Undeterred, the old fellow tried once more on his birthday, and to his surprise she agreed to dine with him that evening.

The old gaffer behaved himself as correctly as a choir boy. He even escorted the young lady to her apartment early in the evening. To his astonishment she said, when they got to the door, "Why don't you come up for a nightcap?"

"Excellent idea," he said with a sudden anticipatory gleam in his wayward eyes.

When they entered the apartment the secretary said, "Why don't you go in the other room and make yourself comfortable. That dinner jacket must be a nuisance."

Jumping to conclusions, the confident old wolf stripped down to nothing whatever and headed for the living room. As he entered the lights were turned up and there were all his employees singing "Happy Birthday! Happy Birthday to You!"

161.2

A roué in an elevator spotted a gorgeous blonde, sidled up to her and asked, "Would you for $100?"

"Why yes, certainly," she said.

"Would you for $5?"

She snatched her hand away from his and snapped, "What do you think I am?"

He said, "That we settled; now we're arguing price."

161.3

The Sultan maintained a harem 5 miles from where he lived. When he wanted one of the girls from the harem to stay with him he sent his messenger to bring the girl. The Sultan died at age ninety-eight. The messenger died at age forty. Which proves that it is not the women who kill you, it is chasing them that does it.

161.4

There is a girl who said she would do anything for a mink coat, and now she can't button it.

161.5

"A man," she said bitterly, "wants everything he can get."

"A woman," he retorted, "wants anything she can get."

161.6

A Midwestern furniture dealer in New York for his first buying trip met a beautiful young woman in the elevator of his hotel. She smiled and he smiled, and in trying to get acquainted with her found she spoke only French, a language he did not know. However, he drew a picture of a taxicab, and she nodded agreeably, and they went for a taxi ride. In the taxi he then drew a table in a restaurant, and she nodded yes. At a plush restaurant he drew the picture of dancers, and she smiled agreement, and off to a nightclub they went.

At the nightclub the girl took her turn at drawing and sketched a four-poster bed. The man was astonished at her intuition. He was never able to figure out how she knew he was in the furniture business.

Definitions

161.7

Sex: Something that children never discuss in the presence of their elders.

—*Arthur Somers Roche*

161.8

Debauchee: One who has so earnestly pursued pleasure that he has had the misfortune to overtake it.

—*Ambrose Bierce*

161.9

Chivalry is a man's inclination to defend a woman against every man but himself.

161.10

Honor: What a girl loses when she gains experience.

Aphorisms

161.11

One pretty girl is quoted as saying, "To err is human but it feels divine."

161.12

Familiarity—
Breeds contempt—and children.
Breeds attempts.
Breeds.

161.13

The thing that takes up the least amount of time and causes the most amount of trouble is Sex.

—*John Barrymore*

161.14

The trouble with being able to read a woman like a book is that you are liable to forget your place.

161.15

If men knew all that women think, they'd be twenty times more daring.

—*Alphonse Kerr*

161.16

She would rather be looked around at than up to.

—*Phil Robinson*

161.17

Lovely female shapes are terrible complicators of the difficulties and dangers of this earthly life, especially for their owner.

—*George du Maurier*

161.18

A fox is a wolf who sends flowers.

—*Ruth Weston*, 1955

161.19

In the spring a young man's fancy turns to thoughts of what the girls have been thinking of all winter.

161.20

Every line in her face is the line of least resistance.

—*Irvin S. Cobb*

161.21

Men who do not make advances to women are apt to become victims of women who make advances to them.

—*Walter Bagehot*

161.22

Women begin by resisting a man's advances, and end by blocking his retreat.

—*Oscar Wilde*

161.23

The man's desire is for the woman; but the woman's desire is rarely other than for the desire of the man.

—*Samuel Taylor Coleridge*

161.24

Vice is a creature of such hideous mien that the more you see it, the better you like it.

—*Finley Peter Dunne*

161.25

The only difference between a caprice and a lifelong passion is that the caprice lasts a little longer.

—*Oscar Wilde*

161.26

The weaker sex is the stronger sex because of the weakness of the stronger sex for the weaker sex.

161.27

Most women dress on the theory that a man can't think while he's looking.

—*Dan Bennett*

161.28

Men think women cannot be trusted too far; women think men can't be trusted too near.

161.29

She laughed when I sat down to play—but how did I know she was ticklish.

161.30

Here's to the wings of love—
May they never moult a feather,
Till my big boots and your little shoes,
Are under the bed together.

161.31

Here's to old wine and young women.

(*See also 3.7, 21.2, 23.1, 24.6, 35.1, 38.3, 45.2, 55.15, 79.10, 111.12, 111.16, 111.17, 135.9, 135.33, 147.8, 158.5, 159.4, 160.1–160.43, 199.1, 207.20, 208.7, 228.1, 235.22, 244.6, 244.23, 246.3, 246.4, 263.1, 263.3–263.5, 263.33, 271.15, 274.7, 276.20*)

162. Courtship and Proposals

Anecdotes

162.1

"Come, come," said Tom's father, "at your time of life,
"There's no longer excuse for thus playing the rake—
"It is time you should think, boy, of taking a wife."

"Why, so it is, father—whose wife shall I take?"

—*Thomas Moore*

162.2

A young woman was twitting a bachelor for his reasons for remaining single.

"No," he replied, "I was never actually disappointed in love. You might say that I was discouraged. Some years ago I was badly smitten by a young woman, and finally got enough courage to propose to her. I made it brief, simply saying, 'Let's get married?'

'Who'd have us?' she replied."

162.3

"I'm sorry, I didn't get your name," snipped the young girl who was introduced to a former suitor at a party.

"I know you didn't," said the young man, "but you sure tried hard enough."

162.4

"Mother, I can't marry him," moaned the love-stricken maid. "Last night he told me he was an atheist and he doesn't believe in Hell."

"Now you go right ahead and marry him," replied the mother, "and between the two of us we'll show him he's wrong."

162.5

Speaking of an improbable romance, one girl observed that the fellow in question worshipped the very ground the girl's father had discovered oil on.

162.6

One girl to another: "They are made for each other. He owns oil wells and she's always gushing."

162.7

"Is Jim a confirmed bachelor?"

"He is now. He sent his picture to a lonely hearts club, and they sent it back with a note saying, 'We are not that lonely.' "

162.8

A mother, worried because her twenty-six-year-old daughter was not yet married, urged her to insert the following in the classified ad columns: "Beautiful young heiress desires contact with easy-going playboy who wants some fast action."

"Any answers?" asked the mother several days later.

"Only one," sighed the daughter.

"From whom?"

"It's confidential. I'm not allowed to tell," replied the nervous girl.

The mother screamed and ranted that she must know who answered the ad.

"All right," said the daughter defiantly. "If you must know, it was from Daddy!"

162.9

The romantic young woman dreamed one night that a handsome prince came on horseback to her house, climbed a vine to her bedroom window, took her in his arms and down the vine and onto the waiting horse. As they rode off in the moonlight the breathless young woman whispered to her dashing prince, "Where are you taking me?"

"That's up to you," said the prince. "It's your dream!"

162.10

"Wilmer, dear, you told me your office is on Broad Street."

"That's right, it is."

"There must be some confusion; Daddy said he has been looking you up in Bradstreet."

162.11

"I'm sure you will like Jack," said the chick home from college. "He's a fine young man."

"Has he any property?" asked the old man.

"You men are all the same," said the daughter. "You're always wondering about property. Jack asked me the same question about you."

162.12

The marriage broker was escorting his client through the home of the woman he was offering to arrange a marriage with. "Of course the house looks a little run-down," he said, "but these people are really well-fixed. Notice the classy furniture; look at these fine pieces of china, this expensive table silver, and this beautiful linen."

"Yes," said the client, "but how do I know these things weren't borrowed just to impress me?"

"Borrowed!" said the marriage broker. "Are you crazy? Who'd lend anything to these miserable beggars?"

162.13

"You don't have to worry about this young woman's family," said the marriage broker to the client. "It is one of the community's finest families. But you'll never have to support them; the girl is an orphan."

Several days later the engagement was announced, and several days after that the young man descended upon the marriage broker. "You liar!" he shouted. "You told me she was an orphan, and now I find out her old man is not only alive but in prison."

"Oh, that," said the marriage broker. "You call that living?"

162.14

Upon the advice of the local *shadchen* a young Jewish fellow met and took for a walk a girl recommended to him by the matchmaker. Upon his return the *shadchen* asked him what he thought of the girl as a prospective bride.

"She limps," replied the youth tersely.

"So what?" replied the *shadchen.* "It's only when she walks."

162.15

The son of a strictly orthodox Jewish family told his mother that he was planning to marry Peggy Malone, the sweet Irish Catholic girl in the next block. When the mother regained her composure she said, "That's for you to decide, Milton, my boy. But please for a while don't say anything about it to your father. He has a bad heart, business is bad, and it would be too much of a strain. And for a while say nothing to Judith—you know how strong she feels about religion. And your brother Arnold with his temper would probably smack you good if he heard about it. But me you should tell. Anyway, I'm committing suicide."

162.16

"It's time for Susan's friend to go home," said the father.

"Now, Joe," said the wife, "remember how it was with us before we were married."

"That's exactly what I am remembering. Get him out!"

162.17

"My dearest love," exclaimed the love-stricken young man, "just think, tomorrow is your birthday, and I didn't even know you a year ago."

"Sweetheart," she purred, "let's not talk about the past. Let's talk about my present."

162.18

Rube Brown was too bashful to propose to his girl in person, so he phoned her.

"Mandy, I got me a little farm out in the country, I got a cow, a dozen chickens, a pig, a mule, and a hoss and buggy. What I want to know—will you marry me?"

"Co'se I will, honey—and who is this calling?"

162.19

"Dearest, will you marry me?"

"I'm sorry," she said, "the answer is no. But I shall always admire your taste."

162.20

A girl got an engagement ring, and on little or no provocation would call attention to it. In a group with girl friends no one noticed it. Finally, when her friends were sitting around talking she got up suddenly and said, "It's awfully hot in here. I think I'll take my ring off."

162.21

A rich old man fell in love with a young show girl and asked the doctor if he thought he would have a better chance to marry her by telling her he was sixty, or knocking ten years off his age.

"No," said the doctor, "your best chance would be to tell her you are eighty."

162.22

"Go to Father," she said
  When I asked her to wed,
Though she knew that I knew
  That her father was dead;
And she knew that I knew
  What a life he had led!
So she knew that I knew
  What she meant when she said
"Go to Father! Go to Father!"

162.23

"I did not accept George the first time he proposed," said the young lady with a touch of haughty assurance.

"Of course not, my dear. You were not there," said her friend gently.

162.24

After many false starts and much fumbling and stumbling, a Scotchman finally proposed marriage to a young woman. The girl accepted.

The Scot was silent; he said not a word. The girl asked, "Aren't you going to say anything?"

"I've said enough already," said the Scot sadly.

162.25

When a young woman was asked why her engagement to a man had been broken, she replied: "I want no part of a fellow like that. Everything was going along nicely until he bought a car and had only one seat belt installed in it."

162.26

"What can I say that will convince you of my love and cause you to marry me?" asked the ardent lover of a beautiful show girl.

"Only three little words," she replied.

"Yes, and what are they?" asked the man anxiously.

"One million dollars."

162.27

The local paper mentioned that a certain young woman had expressed interest in marrying any man who would pay the debts of her recently deceased father. Sandy MacTavish was young and interested. He called on the young lady, found her beautiful and charming, was immediately interested, and promptly told her so. "But first," said Sandy, "before I agree to marry you and pay your father's debts, I want you to tell me: who put your old man in debt in the first place?"

162.28

"Oh well," she said, "he may be old enough to be my father, but on the other hand he is rich enough to be my husband."

162.29

The cute-looking young chick came to work one morning sporting an engagement ring. One of the older women, after admiring it, said, "Take my advice, and don't give in to him too easily. Demand your rights. When I got married I made my husband quit smoking and drinking."

"And did he?" asked the sweet young thing.

"I don't know," said the older woman. "I haven't seen him for ten years."

162.30

GI: "Let's get married, or something."

Girl: "We will get married, or nothing."

162.31

On a bitterly cold night in January the young man trudged through the knee-high snow, entered his girl's home, and during the evening asked her to marry him. "When you have a few thousand dollars I will seriously consider it," said the very practical young woman.

Five months later—in mid-June—the young woman and the same young man strolled hand in hand through a grove of trees alongside the river. He stopped to kiss her and to ask her, "When are we going to get married?"

"How much money have you saved?" she wanted to know.

"Exactly $70," replied the youth boldly.

"Oh well," sighed and smiled the young woman, "I guess that's enough."

Definitions

162.32

Courtship is the period during which the girl decides whether or not she can do better.

162.33

An engagement is a period of urge on the verge of a merge.

Aphorisms

162.34

The worst of having a romance is that it leaves one so unromantic.

—*Oscar Wilde*

162.35

In courtship a man pursues a woman until she catches him.

162.36

The hardest task of a girl's life is to prove to a man that his intentions are serious.

—*Helen Rowland*

162.37

When a girl begins to count on a man, his number is up.

162.38

Don't try to marry an entire family or it may work out that way.

—*George Ade*

162.39

When a couple of young people strongly devoted to each other commence to eat onions, it is safe to pronounce them engaged.

—*James Montgomery Bailey*

162.40

Man is like a worm: he comes along, squirms a little, then some chicken gets him.

162.41

Advice to persons about to marry: Don't.

—*Punch,* 1845

162.42

Thornton Wilder believes every American woman wants to be a good wife for a man, if only he'd step down from the movie screen and propose to her.

162.43

A man is never so weak as when some woman is telling him how strong he is.

162.44

When a young man complains that a young lady has no heart, it is pretty certain that she has his.

—*George D. Prentice*

162.45

A fool and her money are soon courted.

—*Helen Rowland*

162.46

That man that hath a tongue, I say, is no
man,

If with his tongue he cannot win a woman.
—*William Shakespeare*

(*See also 8.8, 79.43, 101.4, 111.8, 135.5, 159.1–159.28, 160.1–160.43, 164.1, 164.26, 234.24, 245.17, 270.1*)

THE MATRIMONIAL MERRY-GO-ROUND

163. Weddings and Honeymoons

Ancedotes

163.1

A handsome playboy decided to settle down and narrowed his choice between a beautiful but dumb doll and an opera singer. He finally chose brains and culture and married the singer. They spent their wedding night at a swanky hotel. When he opened his eyes the next morning and the dawn's early light began to shine upon his bride, the groom looked at her and shuddered and cried out, "Sing, for God's sake, sing."

163.2

A couple wanted to get married in a hurry. The man, a soldier on a 48-hour pass, took his blushing bride to see the vicar. "Impossible," said the latter. "Even a special license would take too long."

The would-be bride and bridegroom exchanged a look of misery. Then a smile spread across the soldier's face. "Well," he suggested brightly, "couldn't you say a few words just to tide us over the weekend?"
—*Indiana Horizon*

163.3

An Illinois justice of the peace, newly elected but not yet formally commissioned, issued a marriage license which read as follows:
"State of Illinois:
Peoria County:

Know all men by this presents that John Smith and Polly Myers is entitled to go together and do as all folks does anywhere in Coppers precinct and when my commission comes I am to marry em good and date em back to kiver accidents.

O—— M—— R——
Justis of Pease."

163.4

An Irishman asked leave of his boss to attend a wedding. He returned to work with two black eyes. The foreman asked him what had happened.

"When I got there," said the Irishman, "I saw a fellow dressed up like a peacock. 'An' who are you?' says I. 'I'm the best man,' says he. An' he was, too!"

163.5

Everything was in readiness for the marriage ceremony. The groom and best man had arrived at the church in plenty of time, but the groom was uneasy, apprehensive.

"What's worrying you, Tim?" asked the best man. "Have you lost the ring?"

"No," he answered with a sigh, "I've got the ring, but I've lost my enthusiasm."

163.6

A schoolboy's version of matrimony: "As she is going to be married next month, she is very busy getting her torso ready."

163.7

When the minister came to the "love, honor, and obey" part of the ceremony, the bridegroom interrupted with, "Parson, please read that again so that this lady will get the full meaning and seriousness of it. You see, I've been married before."

163.8

After the minister had married the young couple, the groom asked him what the fee was.

"Oh," said the minister, "you can give me whatever you think it is worth."

The groom looked his bride over from top to bottom, then slowly rolled his eyes and said, "Good Lord, Sir, you have ruined me for life; you have, for sure."

163.9

The Sunday School teacher was explaining to the children the significance of the color "white" and added that white stands for joy. "That is why a bride wears white when she is married. Her wedding day is the most joyous one in her life."

"Then why," asked a shrewd little boy, "does the groom wear black?"

163.10

During the wedding ceremony, when the bridegroom knelt at the altar, it was noticed that someone had painted on the soles of his shoes HE LP.

163.11

The young gangster and his equally tough

sweetheart had just been pronounced man and wife, before a glittering array of the best people from the top gangs. As they marched through the hall where the wedding reception was to be held, the bridegroom turned and slapped his bride resoundingly on the face.

"That," he said, "is for nothin'. It's a warnin'—be careful!"

163.12

Heywood Broun was standing next to a prim old lady at a wedding. "Can you imagine," she said as the couple met at the altar, "they've known each other scarcely two weeks, and here they are getting married."

"Well," said Broun philosophically, "it's one way of getting acquainted."

163.13

During the elaborate wedding reception the bashful groom, who sat at the head table with his bride, was told he would be expected to say a few words in response to the several toasts and congratulations. When he demurred, his forceful and self-possessed bride told him he would simply have to get up and speak briefly.

At last the poor fellow arose, looked around helplessly, stumbled and stumbled over his opening words, and finally rested a trembling hand on the shoulder of the bride and said, "This thing has been forced upon me!"

163.14

As the newlyweds were driving away from the church, the bridegroom put an arm around the bride, and said, "Now, sweetheart, about this talk about your quitting your job. . . ."

163.15

"I trust," said the father of the bride, "you appreciate that my daughter is a deeply sympathetic and generous young woman."

"I do, sir," replied the bridegroom, "and I trust that she has inherited those fine qualities from her father."

163.16

The bride wanted to disguise the fact that they were honeymooning and asked her husband while on the plane if there was any way they could make it appear that they had been married for a long time.

"Sure," said the husband, "you carry the bags."

163.17

The bride and groom boarded the Pullman and asked the porter to keep their newly wedded status a secret. The next morning the newlyweds were aware of being stared at when they headed for the diner. The groom, angry, sought out the porter and rebuked him for passing word along that they had just been married.

"I never told them that at all," said the porter. "I just said that you two were good friends."

163.18

A newly married couple boarded a train late at night. Shortly after they entered their berth, she started to say in a loud voice, "Johnny, I just can't convince myself that we are really married."

For a long time the bride kept repeating over and over again in a loud voice, "Johnny, I just can't convince myself that we are married."

Finally a voice called out, "Go ahead, Johnny, for heaven's sake, really convince her so we can all go to sleep."

163.19

A honeymoon couple were at an airport. Through force of habit the bridegroom bought a single ticket.

"Why, John, you bought only one ticket!"

"How stupid of me, darling," he said. "I'd completely forgotten myself."

163.20

The honeymoon couple reached their seashore hotel room late in the evening after the wedding. The bride modestly changed into her new nightgown and climbed expectantly into bed.

The husband, in his pajamas, sat at the window looking out at the sea and up at the skies. The bride waited and waited and finally said, "Honey, what's the matter with you? Aren't you coming to bed?"

"Not right away; not for a while. After all, my mother always told me this would be the most beautiful night of my life—and I'm not going to miss a bit of it."

163.21

The honeymooning couple walked arm in arm along the seashore, when the young groom looked poetically out at sea and eloquently cried, "Roll on, thou deep and dark blue ocean—roll!"

His bride gazed at the water a moment, then adoringly at him as she gasped, "Oh, Jim, you wonderful man! It's doing it."

163.22

A honeymooning couple checked into the hotel, and the bride went out to do some shopping. Upon her return to the hotel she forgot their room number, so she walked along the corridor, gently tapping at various doors, calling softly at each, "Honey, let me in." Finally she came to one door and called out as usual, only to be met with the gruff response of a man on the other side of the door: "This isn't a beehive—it's the bathroom."

163.23

The first evening after the newlyweds came back home from their honeymoon the husband came home from work and found his bride studiously going over his bankbooks.

"Why, darling," said he, "this leads me to fear you married me for my money."

"Don't be silly," said she, "I worship the very ground you walk on—and any other property you may acquire in the meantime."

163.24

"Rudolf is wonderful to me, mother. He has given me everything I have asked for," said the bride.

"That goes to show," replied the mother, "that you are not asking for enough."

Definitions

163.25

Honeymoon: The time during which the bride believes the bridegroom's word of honor.

—*H. L. Mencken*

163.26

A honeymoon is a thrill of a wife time.

163.27

Honeymoon is the vacation a man takes before beginning work under a new boss.

163.28

Housewarming: The last call for wedding presents.

—*June Provines*

Aphorisms

163.29

Women like to attend weddings, to hear the big, sweet, juicy promises the bridegroom makes.

—*E. W. Howe*

163.30

People seldom think alike until it comes to buying wedding presents.

—*Wall Street Journal*

163.31

The honeymoon is not actually over until we cease to stifle our sighs and begin to stifle our yawns.

—*Helen Rowland*

(*See also 3.10, 32.1, 32.4, 38.1, 40.15, 60.13, 95.2, 135.2, 144.1, 145.2, 146.3, 154.1, 154.46, 155.28–155.31, 156.9, 158.6, 165.93, 190.13, 190.14, 211.24, 212.6, 230.3, 251.22*)

164. The Marital State

Anecdotes

164.1

A friend was describing to Douglas Jerrold the story of his courtship and marriage—how his wife had been brought up in a convent and was on the point of taking the veil, when his presence burst upon her enraptured sight.

Jerrold listened to the end of the story and by way of comment said, "Ah! She evidently thought you better than nun."

164.2

Discussing Mrs. Grundy and her "set," a member of the Museum Club said, "They'll soon say marriage is improper."

"No, no," said Douglas Jerrold, "they'll always consider marriage good breeding."

164.3

George Ade related that an eight-year-old girl stopped reading a fairy tale and asked him, "Does m-i-r-a-g-e spell marriage?" "Yes," replied Ade.

164.4

When a forty-year-old man married a twenty-year-old girl it caused a sensation in their community. One day when an unkind reference was made to the man concerning his marriage to one so young, he replied, "It is really quite a nice arrangement. When my wife looks at me it makes her feel ten years older, and when I look at her I feel ten years younger. So we are both thirty—and what's wrong with that?"

164.5

Francis Leo Golden, in his *Laughter Is Legal*, reported that in Cleveland, May Dye married and became May Linger, and in Arizona Wayne Flowers married Martha Trees.

Other amusing coincidences are the marriage in Omaha of Frank Frost and Dorothy Snow, and Lillian Rentmeister of Paterson, New

Jersey, to Harry Fivehouse; and in Prior, Montana, a marriage license was issued to Owen Smells and Mary Knows.

Definitions

164.6

Marriage: An institution which is popular because it combines the maximum of temptation with the maximum of opportunity.

—*George Bernard Shaw*

164.7

Marriage: The state or condition of a community consisting of a master, a mistress, and two slaves, making in all, two.

—*Ambrose Bierce*

164.8

Marriage: A ceremony in which rings are put on the fingers of the lady and through the nose of the gentleman.

—*Herbert Spencer*

164.9

Marriage is a public confession of a strictly private intention.

Aphorisms

164.10

Marriage entitles women to the protection of strong men who steady the ladder when they are painting the ceiling.

164.11

Marriage is a great institution—but who wants to live in an institution?

164.12

Marriage is like a tourniquet: it stops your circulation.

164.13

Though marriage makes man and wife one flesh, it leaves them still two fools.

—*William Congreve*

164.14

A good marriage would be between a blind wife and a deaf husband.

—*Michel de Montaigne*

164.15

Twenty years of romance make a woman look like a ruin, but twenty years of marriage make her something like a public building.

—*Oscar Wilde*

164.16

Statistics prove that 50 percent of the married people in the United States are women.

164.17

Here's to matrimony, the high sea for which no compass has yet been invented!

—*Heinrich Heine*

164.18

Here's to economy, that enables two to live as cheaply as one thought he could.

—*Anonymous*

164.19

The wonderfully warm and reassuring thing about marriage is that you know that no matter what comes along you'll always have somebody at your side to blame it on.

—*Bill Vaughan,* Sorry I Stirred It, 1964

164.20

I think if people marry it ought to be for life; the laws are altogether too lenient with them.

—*Finley Peter Dunne*

164.21

When a girl marries she exchanges the attentions of many men for the inattention of one.

—*Helen Rowland*

164.22

When you see a married couple coming down the street, the one who is two or three steps ahead is the one that's mad.

—*Helen Rowland*

164.23

Socrates being asked whether it was better to marry or not, replied, "Whichever you do, you will repent it."

—*Diogenes Laertius*

164.24

The only time that most women give their orating husbands undivided attention is when the old boys mumble in their sleep.

—*Wilson Mizner*

164.25

Matrimony is a bargain, and someone has to get the worst of the bargain.

—*Helen Rowland*

164.26

When billing and cooing result in matrimony, the billing always comes after the cooing.

—*T. L. Masson*

164.27

Before marriage a man will lie awake all night thinking about something you said; after marriage, he'll fall asleep before you finish saying it.

—*Helen Rowland*

164.28

There is one advantage in a plurality of wives; they fight each other instead of their husbands.

—*Josh Billings*

164.29

If men knew how women pass the time when they are alone, they'd never marry.

—*O. Henry*

164.30

Most wives are nicer than their husbands, but that's nothing. I am nice to everybody from whom I get money.

—*Don Herold*

(*See also 7.12, 8.3, 8.9, 19.5, 19.32, 23.8–23.10, 28.9, 28.19, 34.1, 35.12, 38.18, 41.8, 47.3, 48.4, 54.14, 68.2, 71.5, 73.2, 79.47, 87.19, 93.27, 93.34, 102.6, 105.2, 106.6, 106.10, 124.4, 124.6, 126.1–126.5, 130.1, 130.2, 132.2, 133.8, 134.9, 136.5, 136.8, 139.9, 155.33, 156.10, 157.11, 166.1–166.17, 168.1–168.30, 170.1–170.23, 171.1–171.12, 173.20, 173.23, 173.30, 145.7, 148.3, 158.1, 160.19, 160.30, 162.1–162.46, 163.1–163.30, 182.10, 182.40, 182.42, 183.8, 184.5, 185.42, 187.1, 188.1, 190.17, 190.18, 192.1, 202.1, 203.2, 203.7, 205.16, 207.2, 207.3, 210.11, 210.17, 210.18, 211.15, 217.14, 218.12, 243.4, 251.22, 263.5, 263.10, 266.8–266.17, 268.26, 274.11, 274.12, 276.7, 276.10, 276.13, 278.2*)

165. Husbands: Devilish and Bedeviled

Anecdotes

165.1

"What is it a sign of when a married man dreams he is a bachelor?"

"It is a sign he is going to wake up disappointed."

165.2

"Don't let it get you down, Si," consoled the minister on the drive back from the cemetery. "You and Millie have been together thirty years. It has been a long and fruitful marriage."

"You're right, Parson," said Si. "Millie was a good woman and made a right nice wife. But you know, somehow or other I never liked her very much."

165.3

A man in the jewelry business, astonished by the size and quality of a diamond ring worn by a woman on a Florida-bound plane, became friendly with the woman's husband in the hope of learning about the dazzling stone.

After a few minutes' conversation he mentioned the ring and said that it seemed to him almost as fine a stone as the famous Hope Diamond. "But, of course," he added, "the Hope diamond has bad luck attached to it."

"Well, my friend," replied the husband, "that stone is known as the Rosenberg diamond and it has bad luck with it, too."

"I never heard of it before," replied the jewelry man. "Who is Rosenberg, and what is the bad luck?"

"I'm Rosenberg," replied the husband. "The bad luck is that I had to buy it."

165.4

The ruler of an ancient kingdom wanted to disprove the statement that the men of his domain were ruled by their wives. He had all the males in his kingdom brought before him and warned that any man who did not tell the truth would be punished severely. Then he asked all the men who obeyed their wives' directions and counsel to step to the left side of the hall. All the men did so. That is, all but one little man who moved to the right.

"It is good to see," said the king, "that we have one real man in the kingdom. Tell these chicken-hearted dunces why you alone among them stand on the right side of the hall."

"Sire," came the reply in a squeaky voice, "it is because before I left home my wife told me to keep out of crowds."

165.5

"What did you tear out of the evening paper?" asked the wife.

"An account of a man being granted a divorce because his wife continually searched his pockets."

"And what," pursued the wife in a subdued voice, "are you going to do with it?"

"I'm going to put it in my pocket," he said.

165.6

Their first quarrel was about that old devil, money.

"Before we were married you told me you were well off," she protested bitterly.

"And so I was," he snarled, "but I didn't have enough sense to know it."

165.7

"My wife drives me crazy with her constant demand for money, money, money!"

"What does she do with all the money?"

"I don't know. She never gets it."

165.8

"My wife dreamed last night that she was married to a millionaire."

"You're lucky—my wife dreams that in the daytime."

165.9

"It's pitiful the way we are forced to live," said a wife to her husband. "Daddy pays our rent; Aunt Sophie buys our clothing; and my sister's husband sends us money for food. I hate to complain, but I'm sorry we can't do any better than this."

"You should be," said the husband. "After all, you've got three uncles and a brother who never send us a red cent."

165.10

"Should I go to a palmist or a mind reader?" she asked.

"Try the palmist; your palm is much more obvious," he said.

165.11

An actor who had left his wife without any money in London wrote glowing letters from America, but still sent no supplies. One of these letters was read aloud in the greenroom of the Haymarket.

"What kindness!" exclaimed Douglas Jerrold, with strong emphasis.

"Kindness!" ejaculated one of the actresses indignantly. "When he never sends the poor woman a penny?"

"Yes," replied Jerrold, "unremitting kindness!"

165.12

In the spring of the year in which Douglas Jerrold died, Mr. Benjamin Webster had a pleasant gathering of friends at his quaint old home by Kensington Church to celebrate the birthday of his daughter. Jerrold was there, playing whist; in the adjoining room they were dancing. Touching him on the shoulder, a friend asked, "Who is that man, Jerrold, there, dancing with Mrs. Jerrold?"

He looked round, for an instant, through the open door. "God knows, my dear boy!" he replied. "Some member of the Humane Society, I suppose."

165.13

Two old friends who had not seen each other for years met by accident. "I suppose you are married by this time?" one fellow asked the other.

"No," said the one questioned, "I managed to escape that fate."

"George, you must be off your rocker," said the first man. "You don't know what you're missing. Take me: I come home at the end of a hard day's work, my loving wife meets me at the door, she mixes me a drink while I rest before sitting down to an exquisite home-cooked meal. After dinner I sip a liqueur while my wife cleans up the dishes, and then she hands me my pipe and slippers, and she snuggles down next to me and starts to talk. She talks, and talks, and talks. I wish she'd drop dead."

165.14

"Doctor, my husband has a serious mental affliction. I notice when I have talked to him for an hour or so that he hasn't heard a word I said."

"Madam," soothed the doctor, "that is not an affliction. It's a gift."

165.15

A talkative woman was telling her husband about a visitor: "If that woman yawned once, while I was talking, she yawned twenty times."

"Maybe," said the husband, "she wasn't yawning; maybe she wanted to say a word."

165.16

"How are things going at home, Frank?"

"Well," replied Frank, "the old ball and chain ain't talkin' to me—and I'm certainly not goin' to interrupt her."

165.17

A quarreling couple saw a team pulling a heavy load. Asked the wife: "Why can't we get along and pull together in harmony like that team?"

"Because," said the husband, "those horses have only one tongue between them."

165.18

The conversation turned to wives. Simkin said, "When my wife and I have an argument, I always have the last word."

"Really?" asked an interested listener.

"Yes," came the reply, "I apologize."

165.19

The drunk was fumbling with his key at the front door of his house one morning at the time other men were leaving to go to work. The cop on the beat, who knew the man, called out jokingly, "Where are you going at this hour?"

"To a lecture," called back the drunk.

165.20

It was their twenty-fifth wedding anniversary and the man of the house started out for his office as usual. "John," his wife said, "don't you know what day this is?"

"Yes, indeed I do," said John.

"Well, how are we going to celebrate it?" persisted his wife.

"Sure and I don't know, Maggie," said John scratching his head in puzzlement. "How about two minutes of silence?"

165.21

John J. Daly says this was Victor Herbert's last story:

A family of four left Ireland. The parents and one boy settled in Boston. The other boy went to Chicago. Two years later while the parents were visiting the son in Chicago, the father died. News of the tragedy was telegraphed to the boy in Boston. Grief-stricken, he wired back to his brother:

WHAT WERE FATHER'S LAST WORDS?

The reply was: FATHER HAD NO LAST WORDS. MOTHER WAS WITH HIM TO THE END.

165.22

A young wife found it impossible to handle her wayward husband, who continually arrived home drunk. She decided to change her tactics and to treat him with kindness.

The next time he came home drunk, she addressed him tenderly: "Sit down, honey, I'll get your slippers and then I'll sit on your lap."

The husband looked at her in bewilderment. "Oh, I might as well," he said. "I'll get hell anyway when I get home."

165.23

The Kiwanis Club luncheon ended with an eloquent talk by a local clergyman on the love of a man for his wife and stressed that the passing years should enrich and enhance that love, and a man should keep that love glowing.

One man at the luncheon was deeply impressed by the talk—so impressed that on his way home he stopped and bought a dozen roses and a box of candy for his wife.

When he presented these gifts to his wife, instead of being delighted she burst into tears. "Oh, I can't take much more of this. Bobby broke his arm, the maid smashed our new lamp, the oil burner quit working, and now you come home drunk!"

165.24

A beggar stopped a prosperous young man and asked for a dollar for a meal. "I'll buy you a drink, instead," said the other man.

"Thanks, sir, but I don't drink," said the beggar. "Just give me something for a meal."

"Have a cigar," said the prosperous man.

"Thanks, again, but I don't smoke," replied the beggar. "I'm just hungry."

"Well," countered the well-heeled fellow, "how about some girls? I know some nice ones you'd like."

"Please, mister, I have no desire for anything but food. Even half a buck would help."

"Suppose I give you two bucks, if you'll come home with me? I want my wife to see what happens to a man who does not drink, smoke, or chase women."

165.25

Cicero told about a man who came weeping to his friend and said that his wife had just hanged herself on a fig tree in his garden. The friend, also a married man, said, "I wonder if I might procure some slips of the same tree to plant in my garden?"

165.26

"Dad, why is a man allowed to have only one wife?"

"My boy, when you get older you will understand that the law must protect those who are unable to protect themselves."

165.27

A husband was heard to confess that in the early months of his marriage he was so in love with his wife that he wanted to eat her—and that as the years rolled by he increasingly regretted that he had not.

165.28

A shiftless husband joined some of the other loafers sitting on the curb of the courthouse square. He announced he was leaving town—he just couldn't live in it any longer.

"What's the matter?"

"Well, the town's all right," he replied, "but there just ain't no place where a woman can find work."

165.29

A Frenchman was invited to the silver wedding anniversary of a well-known couple.

"I do not understand," he said. "What this means: silver anniversary?"

"It means they are celebrating twenty-five years of living together happily."

"Ah," said the Frenchman, smiling broadly. "Now they marry! Wonderful!"

165.30

A farmer's wife lost her mental balance completely—from a quiet woman she suddenly went berserk—and had to be taken to a mental institution in a straitjacket.

"I can't understand it," said her husband. "Nobody ever bothered her. Why she hadn't been out of the kitchen in almost twenty years."

165.31

A couple celebrating their twentieth wedding anniversary went to the movies and saw a torrid picture. When they got home, the wife said, "Why don't you ever make love to me like that?"

"Do you know what those fellows get paid for doing that?" replied the husband.

165.32

The serene old man was being interviewed on the occasion of his seventy-fifth birthday, and the reporter remarked upon the fact that his friends and neighbors unanimously agreed that his married life had been singularly free of acrimony.

"Yes," agreed the old fellow, "that's the truth. I'll tell you how it came about. When we were driving home from our honeymoon the mare stumbled. 'That's once,' I said. Then the poor mare stumbled agin', and I said, 'That's twice.' Well, when that fool horse stumbled a third time I pulled out my gun and killed it. The wife, well she got pretty het up about this for a while and raised plenty of cain. I let her go on until she ran out of words and air. Then I said to her, 'That's once.' And you know, Son, I ain't had a bit of trouble with that gal ever since then."

165.33

"Alfred, wake up, there's a mouse in the bedroom!" called the wife to her sleeping spouse.

"What of it?" said the husband.

"I can hear it squeaking," said the wife frantically.

"What do you expect me to do? Get up and oil it?" asked the husband before he went back to sleep.

165.34

"My wife's memory is driving me out of my mind," complained a husband.

"Yeah, mine's the same way—always forgettin'," said his friend.

"That's not it," said the first man. "My wife remembers everything."

165.35

"I'm not at all pleased with the way your wife looks," said the doctor to the husband as he gravely emerged from the sickroom.

"I'll go along with that, Doc," said the husband. "I never did think much of her looks, but she's a good housekeeper and good with the kids, so I guess it all balances out."

165.36

"I was a fool when I married you," said the angry wife.

"I don't doubt it," said her husband. "But I was much too infatuated to notice it."

165.37

Art Buchwald, a man with a talent for uncovering unusual stories, tells about a Frenchman named *Formidable* as a kind of jest by his parents. He never grew past five feet in height, was married early in his life, and lived to be eighty years old. When he was dying he called his wife, with whom he had had a long and happy life, to his bedside and made one last request: Do not put his name on his tombstone. All his life he had been the butt of jokes because of his name; in death he wished the jokes to end.

True to her promise the wife put over the grave simply this:

Here Lies a Man
Who for Fifty-seven Years
Was True to His Wife.

But when people passed the tombstone they would chuckle and say, *"Ah, çà, c'est formidable."*

165.38

A lady, walking with her husband at the seaside, inquired of him the difference between exportation and transportation. "Why, my dear," he replied, "if you were on board yonder vessel leaving England, you would be exported, and I should be transported!"

165.39

Loud brayed an ass. Quoth Kate, "My dear,"
(To spouse, with scornful carriage)
"One of your relatives I hear."
"Yes, love," said he, "by marriage."

165.40

A man always went out on his own on Tuesday night. But one day he never came back, until seven years later when he returned unexpectedly. His forgiving wife was delighted, and immediately began to make numerous phone calls. "What's the idea?" the husband asked.

"Why, I'm calling some old friends so we can have a party to celebrate your return."

"What, on my night out? Don't you know this is Tuesday?"

165.41

She had just tried on a beautiful new skunk coat her husband had given her for her birthday. As she stood admiring herself in it, she said, "I can't see how such a lovely coat comes from such an evil-smelling brute."

"I don't ask for thanks," the husband snapped, "but the least I should get is some respect."

165.42

"That's a beautiful mink coat your wife has. It sure ought to keep her warm."

"I didn't buy it to keep her warm—but to keep her quiet."

165.43

"Do you think I'm going to wear this squirrel coat the rest of my life?" she asked.

"Why not—squirrels do," he said.

165.44

A woman, who had been previously married, went for a walk in deep mourning and encountered a neighbor. "My dear," said the neighbor, "I did not know that you had suffered a death in the family."

"Well, I have not," said the woman in mourning. "But my husband so annoyed me this morning that I decided to pay him back by paying my respects to my first husband."

165.45

During a revival meeting the evangelist had worked himself up to such a pitch of emotion over the weaknesses of man that he finally called out, "Who is the perfect man? Is there such a being? If anyone has seen the perfect man let him stand up and say so."

A timid little man arose and said he knew of a perfect man.

"Who may he be?" asked the evangelist.

"My wife's first husband," said the meek little fellow.

165.46

A woman talking to Dorothy Parker and others boasted at great length about the success of her marriage and the sterling qualities of her husband, a fellow many others considered a dull person.

"I've kept him for seven years!" said the proud wife.

"If you keep him long enough," said Miss Parker, "he'll come back in style."

165.47

When the husband drifted into his home at 5 A.M. one morning, his irate wife demanded an explanation. He told her he had been sitting up with a sick friend.

"What is his name?" she demanded.

"I really don't know," said the husband. "The fellow was too sick to tell me."

165.48

"I'd like to talk to the burglar who broke into my house last night," requested a caller at the police station.

"What for?" asked the officer at the desk.

"I want to find out how he got into the house without waking up my wife."

165.49

"Did you ever see one of those machines that can tell when a person is telling a lie?"

"See one? I married one!"

165.50

"I guess your wife will hit the ceiling when you arrive home like this," said one drunk to the other.

"I guess she will—she always does because she's a lousy shot."

165.51

One day Oliver Herford walked into the Players Club wearing an absurd-looking hat. Twitted about it, he said that the hat was one of his wife's whims.

"Oh, don't be intimidated," said a friend. "Throw the thing away and forget about your wife's whims."

"See here," said Herford, "my wife has a whim of iron."

165.52

"I'd like to go to the mountains this summer," said the dominating woman to her meek husband. "But I'm afraid that the mountain air would not agree with me."

"My dear," said he, "it wouldn't dare disagree."

165.53

"In our house my orders are obeyed," boasted the fellow at the office. "For example, last night there was no hot water, so I raised Cain about it. And I got hot water—in a hurry!" The speaker paused for breath and possibly for reflection. Then he added in a softer voice, "You can't wash dishes in cold water, you know."

165.54

A man married to a veritable termagant was ordered and pushed around the house like an abject slave. One day several women called on the wife, and in order to show them how she ruled the roost, she ordered her husband to get under the table.

Without a word of protest the man obeyed her.

"Now!" she cried out, further to demonstrate her authority, "come out from under that table, you fool!"

"I will not!" he retorted with vigor. "I'll show you who's master in this house!"

165.55

He was a meek little man. He chased no women, nor was he chased by them. He rarely drank, and he never argued with his wife. Nevertheless, one day his wife spent most of the evening berating him unmercifully and without justification. The next day, still brooding, he stopped by on his way home to fortify himself with strong drink, but this made him dreadfully sleepy so when he passed the zoo he crawled into the lion's cage and fell asleep at the feet of a lion.

The next day the wife instituted a search for him and found him still asleep in the lion's cage. "Come out of there, you coward!" she screamed at him.

165.56

"I couldn't help hearing you and your wife quarreling last night," said one neighbor to another while they were waiting for a bus. "How'd you make out?"

"Just fine," replied the husband. "By the time it was over she came crawling to me on her hands and knees."

The neighbor, who knew the man's wife, asked in astonishment, "How come?"

"I'm not kidding," said the husband. "She got down and called out to me 'Come on out from under that bed, you big coward.' "

165.57

"Young man," said the judge sternly, "you are charged with brutally beating your wife—blackening her eyes, knocking out seven of her teeth, and breaking her arm. What do you have to say to these charges?"

"Your Honor," said the defendant, "all I can say is that you shouldn't pay no attention to what she says. She's punch-drunk."

165.58

"Why did you hit your wife?" asked the judge of the slight little man who stood before him, next to his large and vigorous-looking wife.

"It was a matter of circumstances, Your Honor," replied the man. "She stood with her back to me, I still had the broom in my hand after sweeping the floor, and the door was open. It was a temptation, an opportunity, and a risk. I took it."

165.59

"Is there a man in this hall," demanded the lecturer, "who would allow his wife to be slandered without lifting a finger?"

A meek little fellow raised his hand. The speaker thundered at him, "Do you mean to say that you are so lacking in manhood that you would allow your wife to be slandered and that you would not retaliate?"

"Oh," said the timid little soul, "I beg your pardon. I thought you said 'slaughtered.' "

165.60

"I have no sympathy for a man who beats his wife," said the big, muscular man in the bar.

"Let me tell you," said the timid little man, "a man who can beat his wife needs no sympathy."

165.61

Ad in Ohio paper: FOR SALE, COMPLETE SET OF ENCYCLOPEDIAS, NEVER USED. MY WIFE KNOWS EVERYTHING.

165.62

The schoolboy who confused the philosopher's marriage with his trial wrote: "Socrates died of an overdose of wedlock."

Aphorisms

165.63

Every man who is high up loves to think that he has done it all himself; and the wife smiles, and lets it go at that.

—*James M. Barrie*

165.64

You can never trust a woman; she may be true to you.

—*Douglas Ainslie*

165.65

The most effective water power in the world —women's tears.

—*Wilson Mizner*

165.66

American women are the best yessed women anywhere.

165.67

A bad woman raises hell with a good many men while a good woman raises hell with only one.

—*E. W. Howe*

165.68

Give a woman an inch and she'll think she's a ruler.

165.69

Women, when they have made a sheep of a man, always tell him that he is a lion with a will of iron.

—*Honoré de Balzac*

165.70

Sometimes a wife drives a man to distinction.

165.71

A husband should tell his wife everything that he is sure she will find out, and before anyone else does.

—*Thomas Robert Dewar*

165.72

Behind every famous man stands a woman to tell him he's not so good.

165.73

My notion of a wife at forty is that a man should be able to change her, like a bank note, for two twenties.

165.74

The wife who drives from the backseat is no worse than the husband who cooks from the dining room table.

165.75

A man is in general better pleased when he has a good dinner upon his table than when his wife talks Greek.

—*Samuel Johnson*

165.76

Second Marriage: the triumph of hope over experience.

—*Samuel Johnson*

165.77

The ideal will be reached when all women are married and all men are single.

165.78

Imagination is that which sits up with a woman when her husband comes home late at night.

165.79

Nobody works as hard for his money as the man who marries it.

—*Kin Hubbard*

165.80

When a wife asks for pin money, the first pin she wants has diamonds in it.

165.81

A wife is an illogical creature who asks, "Where did you have it last?" and goes there, and there it is.

—*H. V. Wade,* Detroit *News*

165.82

All husbands are alike, but they have different faces so we can tell them apart.

—*Anonymous*

165.83

The man who brags, "I run things in my home" usually refers to the lawn mower, the washing machine, the vacuum cleaner, the baby carriage, and errands.

—*Jacob M. Braude*

165.84

Every famous man's wife has an uneasy feeling that something will happen to open the public's eyes.

165.85

While Adam slept, from him his Eve arose:
Strange his first sleep should be his last repose.

—*Anonymous*

165.86

A wise woman will always let her husband have her way.

—*Richard Brinsley Sheridan*

165.87

Canine experts say: "Treat a dog with kindness, pet him often, feed him well, and he'll never leave you." The same methods work well with husbands.

165.88

Before marriage a man declares that he will be the boss in his home or know the reason why; after marriage he knows the reason why.

165.89

Before marriage a man thinks nothing is good enough for his wife; after marriage he still thinks nothing is good enough for her.

165.90

American women expect to find in their husbands a perfection that Englishwomen only hope to find in their butlers.

—*Somerset Maugham*

165.91

Petroleum V. Nasby said: "As it is now arranged, man and wife are one, and the man is the one."

165.92

Give a husband enough rope, and he'll want to skip.

165.93

Mrs. Artie Small talks some o' moving t' Niagary Falls, where she wuz so happy when first married.

—*Kin Hubbard*

165.94

After such years of dissension and strife,
Some wonder that Peter should weep for his wife:
But his tears on her grave are nothing surprising,—
He's laying her dust, for fear of its rising.

—*Thomas Hood*

165.95

When Eve upon the first of Men
The apple pressed with specious cant,
Oh! what a thousand pities then
That Adam was not adamant!

—*Thomas Hood*

165.96

When we go home late, may we find our wives where Cain found his—in the land of Nod.

165.97

There are more men than women in mental institutions—which goes to show who's driving who nuts.

165.98

Here's a beautiful toast
To the feminine host—
Here's a swing to "The ladies—
God bless 'em";
But the women should cry
With their glasses on high,
A toast to the men who dress 'em!

165.99

Men dying make their wills—but wives
Escape a work so sad;
Why should they make what all their lives
The gentle dames have had?

—*J. G. Saxe*

165.100

Toast: Here's to the ladies. Bless them. First in our hearts and first in our pockets.

165.101

The way to fight a woman is with your hat—grab it and run.

—*John Barrymore*

165.102

The dearest object to a married man should be his wife but it is not infrequently her clothes.

—*James Montgomery Bailey*

165.103

A husband is what is left of the lover after the nerve has been removed.

—*Helen Rowland*

165.104

When a man makes a woman his wife, it's the highest compliment he can pay her, and it's usually the last.

—*Helen Rowland*

165.105

When a man's dog turns against him it is time for a wife to pack her trunk and go home to mama.

—*Mark Twain*

165.106

Married men live longer than single men, or at least they complain more about it.

—*Don Herold*

(*See also 3.18, 3.19, 23.8, 23.9, 48.14, 135.23, 158.34, 158.36, 159.9, 164.1–164.30, 166.1–166.17*)

166. The Wives Strike Back

Anecdotes

166.1

A man stepped on a weighing machine. His wife picked up the card that fell into the slot and read aloud: "You are a brave, strong leader of men, endowed with unusual creative powers and striking appearance." Then the wife looked again at the card and said, "It's got your weight wrong, too."

166.2

"Oh, am I tired and worn out," said Mike as he arrived home from work.

"There you go again," replied his wife. "Always complaining. Here I've been standing over a hot stove all day while you've been down in that nice cool sewer."

166.3

The man and wife were in the midst of a violent quarrel, and the husband found his temper getting the best of him. "Be careful," he warned his wife, "or you'll bring out the beast in me."

"What of it!" scoffed the wife. "I'm not afraid of mice."

166.4

"I haven't done anything," protested the husband meekly and plaintively. "I have sat here and listened in silence to you for more than an hour."

"Yes," said the wife, "but your silence is impudent."

166.5

Caspar Milquetoast had been advised by his psychiatrist to go right home and assert himself. "Don't let your wife bully you any more. Go home and show her who's the boss."

So the timid soul went home, banged the door shut, and said in a loud voice, "Now get this! From now on I'm the boss in this joint, and I'm giving the orders and you're obeying them. Now get busy and get my supper on the table right away and after that lay out my clothes because I'm going out tonight—alone—in my tuxedo. And do you know who's going to dress me in my tuxedo and black tie?"

"Yes, dear," replied the wife softly. "The man next door. The undertaker."

166.6

They had had an argument over a certain investment.

"But you must admit," said the husband, "that men have better judgment than women."

"Oh, yes," replied the wife. "You married me, and I married you."

166.7

The son of the house was reading about an escaped lunatic and stopped to ask, "How do they catch lunatics?"

The boy's father, who was writing checks in payment of numerous household bills, looked up and said, "They catch them with absurd hats and ridiculous dresses, with silks, laces, feathers, jewelry, perfume, and a number of other costly articles, plus smiles and sweet words."

"That reminds me," said the mother of the family, "I used all those devices until I married you."

166.8

"Mama, what is a second-story man?"

"Your father is one; if I don't believe his first story he tells a second one."

166.9

"I'm glad, my dear," said the young husband, "that you are interested in what I have been telling you about the Federal Reserve System and banking."

"Really, sweetheart," replied the wife, "it is amazing that one should know so much about money and yet not have any."

166.10

Mr. Jones staggered into his home one evening, trembling and obviously shaken. "I'm going to fire that damn chauffeur," he moaned. "For the third time in six days he's nearly killed me with his insane driving."

"Dear, don't get so upset," soothed his young wife. "Just give him one more chance."

166.11

A woman declared that she could always tell when her husband was lying, and when asked how she could perform so remarkable a feat replied that it was easy. "If his lips are moving, he's lying," she said.

166.12

A White Elephant party was announced. Every guest was to bring something that she could not find any use for, yet was too good to throw away. Eleven of the nineteen women brought their husbands.

166.13

A woman's husband disappeared. She did nothing about it until friends prevailed upon her to go to the police station and report him missing. One friend went with her, and she gave the police a description of him that more befitted a matinee idol than her husband. When they left the police station, the friend said to the wife, "Morris isn't like your description at all—he is fat, short, bald, toothless, and ugly. With that description they will never find him."

"Who wants him?" said the wife.

166.14

Man to his wife: "Do you know, dear, that the biggest idiot always marries the prettiest woman?"

Wife: "It is high time you paid me a compliment, but I must admit you did it very nicely."

166.15

A visitor to Fruitland, Bronson Alcott's attempt at Utopia, asked Mrs. Alcott, "Are there any beasts of burden on the place?"

Mrs. Alcott, who labored from sunup to sundown and said little, replied with a touch of understandable bitterness, "Only one woman."

166.16

Eyebrows were raised and tongues wagged

when old Obadiah, the village miser, seemingly went berserk and bought a new car, a television set, a new refrigerator, and had a phone installed in his home. But the gossips found out in due course what had happened. Seems the old man's wife learned from an actuarial table that, according to the figures, she would live three years longer than her husband. This set her to listing some of the things she would buy when old Obadiah passed on to his eternal reward. But the old skinflint saw the list—whether by his wife's design or otherwise was not determined—and he went out and made some of the purchases.

166.17

A woman making arrangements with an artist to sit for her portrait said to him, "Although I have only a few items of jewelry, nevertheless I want this painting to show me wearing diamond rings and earrings, an emerald brooch, and a multistrand necklace of pearls that look like they are priceless."

"I can do this all right," said the artist. "But do you mind telling me why you want this when apparently you do not particularly care for jewelry?"

"You see, if I die first," said the woman, "and my husband marries again, I want that second wife to go out of her mind trying to find where he hid the jewels."

(*See also 3.8, 3.9, 9.6, 124.4, 155.32, 159.9, 165.3, 165.4, 165.39, 165.65, 165.72, 165.88, 266.18*)

167. Husband versus Mother-in-law

Anecdotes

167.1

The domestic quarrel had escalated to torrid proportions. "I wish," said the aroused wife, "that I had taken my mother's advice and not married you."

"Do you mean to assert that your mother tried to prevent your marrying me?" asked the husband in astonishment.

"Yes, she most emphatically did," said the wife.

"God forgive me," said the husband with a touch of reverence. "How I have wronged that fine woman."

167.2

A fear-stricken cave woman called to her husband, who was up in a tree, "A saber-toothed tiger has gone into our cave where my mother is."

"I don't care what happens to a tiger," said the husband.

167.3

"I am going home to Mother," asserted the wife. "I should have listened to her ten years ago."

"Go ahead. When you get there you'll find she's still talking."

167.4

"Jim," pleaded the dying wife, "my last wish is that you promise me my mother will ride in the same car with you at my funeral. Surely you cannot deny me this."

"Oh, all right," said the husband. "But it's going to ruin my whole day."

167.5

"What do you think, John? Mother says she wants to be cremated."

"OK. Tell her to put her things on, and we will be right over."

167.6

An undertaker wired a man whose mother-in-law had died, and asked whether he should bury, cremate, or embalm her. DO ALL THREE; DON'T TAKE ANY CHANCES, the man wired back.

167.7

A large crowd gathered for the funeral of the farmer's mother-in-law, who had been kicked to death by the farmer's mule. But the predominance of men among the mourners was a cause of comment, even by the minister who asked why there were so many men present.

"Oh," said the farmer, "they all want to buy that mule."

167.8

"I hate my mother-in-law," said one cannibal to the other during dinner.

"Well," replied the other cannibal, "just eat the vegetables."

Aphorisms

167.9

The mother-in-law hated him so much that she grieved she was too poor to disinherit him.

167.10

If you're uncertain about the definition of "mixed emotions," then think of your mother-in-law going off a bridge while driving your new Chrysler.

167.11

Be kind to your mother-in-law, and if necessary pay for her board at some good hotel.

—*Josh Billings*

167.12

Peter remained on friendly terms with Christ notwithstanding Christ's having healed his mother-in-law.

—*Nicholas Murray Butler*

167.13

Here's long life to the mother-in-law,
With all her freaks and capers,
For without our "dear old ma,"
What would become of comic papers?

167.14

There are three basic jokes, but since the mother-in-law joke is not a joke but a very serious question, there are only two.

—*George Ade*

(*See also 67.3, 162.4, 168.29, 188.3, 192.1*)

168. Philanderers and Bigamists

Anecdotes

168.1

Adam told Eve he was going out hunting and would return soon. However, he did not come home until a long time afterward. Eve was angry. "What have you been doing all this time?" she demanded. "I am sure you are hiding something from me. Did you meet anybody or see anyone?"

"You know as well as I do that there is no other human being here," Adam insisted.

He was tired and went quickly to sleep. As soon as he was asleep, Eve began to count his ribs.

168.2

A man and his jealous wife were sitting on the beach. "Just look at that girl over there," he said, "in the blue bathing suit. Now that is what I call a decent suit for a woman to wear on the beach. It makes her look very modest and proper."

Said the jealous wife, "Some women will do anything to attract attention."

168.3

One night a fellow arrived home very late, and his wife called out, "Is that you, Bill?"

"Yes, whom were you expecting?"

168.4

"I don't know what to do about Joe," said the wife to her pastor about her philandering husband. "Every night he is out on the town, drinking and running after women."

"You have my deepest sympathy," said the clergyman. "Your husband is a miserable sinner."

"Miserable sinner!" cried the wife. "Sinner, yes, but he is not miserable. He's having the time of his life."

168.5

An old fellow wanted to marry a young chick. He asked the doctor what he thought about the idea. "OK," said the doctor, "but since this is a young girl you are marrying I think it might be a good idea for her to take in a young boarder for company." So she did.

Sometime later the M.D. ran into the old man and was told, "My wife is going to have a baby."

"Good," said the doctor, "and by the way, did she ever take in a young boarder?"

"Sure did, and she is going to have a baby, too," replied the antique lecher.

168.6

"Your Honor, when I entered my home, there was my wife in the arms of this strange man."

"What did your wife say when you surprised her in these circumstances?" asked the judge.

"She turned to me and then to this other man, and she said, 'Oh, here's Old Blabbermouth! Now the news will be all over the neighborhood.' "

168.7

A Quaker was caught by his wife when he was kissing the cook. Undaunted, the husband said to the wife, "Rebecca, if thee don't stop thy peeking, thee will cause trouble in the family, and there will be scandalous talk."

168.8

When a warrior in ancient times was called off to battle, he put his beautiful and much-loved wife in a suit of armor, secured it with lock and key, and handed the key to his best friend with instructions to use it if the husband did not return in six months.

The warrior was only a few miles along the road toward the battle when his friend dashed up on horseback and excitedly handed him the key, saying, "It must be the wrong key; it won't work."

168.9

Maud Tree, speaking of her philandering

husband, Herbert Tree, said: "Poor Herbert! All his affairs begin with a compliment and end with a confinement."

168.10

Indignant woman to a luscious-looking librarian: "Strange you haven't that book. My husband told me you have everything."

168.11

A man, aroused by the increasing flirtations of his beautiful young wife, decided to put an end to it by writing to a handsome bachelor who was more attentive to the man's wife than others under suspicion. The letter said: "I am aware of, and I demand that you explain, your undue attentions to my wife. I will expect you to be at my office at 11 A.M. Monday."

The bachelor replied in this way: "I am entirely willing to join my fellow citizens at the meeting you have arranged in your office this coming Monday."

168.12

An actor noted for his numerous affairs of the heart was seated gloomily one day at his favorite bar. A friend came up and asked him what was bothering him.

"It's really quite disturbing," said the actor. "This morning I received a letter from a man who promises to kill me if I don't terminate my relations with his wife."

"Surely you should be able to do that—if only to save your life," said the friend.

"Of course, I'd gladly leave the fellow's wife alone—but the man did not sign his name."

168.13

A fellow who had lost a new hat and could not remember where he had mislaid it decided that if he went to church he could probably find one to fit him in the cloakroom. But by the end of the services he did not feel the necessity to take another man's hat, because during the sermon he remembered where he had left his own. The sermon was on adultery.

168.14

The preacher spoke at length about Solomon and his wives and related that the wise man fed his numerous wives ambrosia. After the service one fellow stopped the minister and said that what he wanted to know was what Solomon himself ate.

168.15

Three men argued as to the meaning of *savoir faire.* One man suggested it could be defined by imagining he came home to find his wife kissing another man and thereupon taking off his hat to the man and saying, "'Excuse me!' "That is *savoir faire.*"

"No, I don't think so," said the second man. "But if I got home and found my wife kissing another man and I tipped my hat and said, 'Excuse me, continue'—that would be *savoir faire.*"

"I don't agree with either one of you," said the third man. "Now if I came home and found my wife kissing a man and tipped my hat and said, 'Excuse me, continue'—and if then the man continued—then he has *savoir faire.*"

—*Irving Hoffman,* Hollywood *Reporter*

168.16

A hard-working husband came home from the shop early one day, and found his wife in bed with another man.

"Don't shoot him, Jim!" cried the wife. "When you were out of work so long, who do you think paid the bills? And that wristwatch I gave you for Christmas—where do you think I got the money? And the time I needed money for an operation—where do you think I got money for that?"

The husband looked on in amazement and puzzlement, then said tenderly to his wife, "Cover him up, darling, before he catches cold."

168.17

An optimist is a man who concludes his wife has given up cigarettes because when he got home from a trip he found cigar butts all around the house.

168.18

Charged with bigamy, the wealthy businessman won a quick acquittal.

"You're free," said the judge. "Go home to your wife."

"Which one?" asked the acquitted.

168.19

An immigrant applying for citizenship wrestled with questions asked by the clerk and became a good deal excited and discouraged. At the question, "Do you believe in polygamy?" he threw up his hands and said, "I no understan'! I no understan' not'ing."

"Well," said the clerk, "I'll put it this way: Do you believe in plural marriage?"

That was still worse.

"No capisco. I no understan' not'ing. I no Americano!" he shouted and picked up his hat as though to walk out.

The judge leaned forward helpfully.

"Let me ask this question: Benito, what do

you think of the idea of having two or three, or perhaps four, wives?"

Benito's face relaxed in a most comprehending smile.

"I tink pretty good, Judge. What you tink?"

168.20

Mark Twain got into an argument with a Mormon on the subject of polygamy, and was challenged to cite a single passage of Scripture condemning polygamy. "No man can serve two masters," quoted Mark Twain.

168.21

A man who had married three wives was brought before the king for punishment. The king called in his counselors and asked them to devise the worst possible punishment for the offender, even death itself. But they did not order his execution, ruling it would be still worse for him to live with all three wives at the same time. Two weeks later, the man committed suicide.

168.22

An Irishman was once brought up before a magistrate, charged with marrying six wives. The magistrate asked him how he could be so hardened a villain.

"Please, Your Worship," says Paddy, "I was just trying to get a good one."

Definitions

168.23

Bigamy is when two rites make a wrong.

168.24

Bigamy is having one wife too many, and in some instances monogamy is the same thing.

Aphorisms

168.25

Most of the love triangles turn into wrecktangles.

168.26

To our sweethearts and wives—may they never meet.

168.27

Here's to those who'd love us
  If we only cared,
Here's to those we'd love,
  If we only dared.

168.28

The chain of wedlock is so heavy that it takes two to carry it, sometimes three.

—*Alexandre Dumas*

168.29

When a judge was asked what was the extreme penalty for bigamy, the jurist smiled and said, "Two mothers-in-law."

168.30

One man's folly is another man's wife.

—*Helen Rowland*

(*See also 38.1, 38.2, 87.19, 97.3, 149.4, 150.4, 165.22, 170.10, 170.11, 218.12, 235.48, 236.9, 269.61*)

169. Widow Take All

Anecdotes

169.1

When a man is born people ask, "How is the mother?" When he marries they exclaim, "What a lovely bride!" And when he dies they inquire, "How much did he leave her?"

—*Mexican-American Review*

169.2

A worker on a tugboat in New York harbor fell overboard and was drowned. Company insurance and other benefactions resulted in the widow getting a total sum of $70,000. When consolation was offered the widow, she said, "Poor Paddy never learned how to swim, thanks be to God."

169.3

There was astonishment in knowledgeable art circles when a widow, executrix of her wealthy husband's estate, sold a Van Gogh at an absurdly low price. But to those in the know it made sense, because they realized the will provided that the proceeds of this sale must go to the deceased man's secretary.

169.4

The owner of a monument company was commissioned by a young widow to carve on her husband's monument: "My sorrow is more than I can bear."

A month later, the monument company received a note from the widow asking that one word be added to the inscription: "alone."

169.5

"He was a man of principle," said Mrs. O'Flaherty to the widow at the wake.

"That he was," sighed the widow. "Every Saturday night for these twenty years the poor man would come home and faithfully hand me his pay envelope—that he never missed doing. Of course the envelope was always empty—but mind you, he was loyal to the principle of the thing."

169.6

In her loneliness a recently widowed woman attended a spiritualist meeting in the hope of being able to communicate with her late husband. She was delighted but a bit skeptical when the medium told her he was in communication with the deceased.

"Is it really you, George?"

"It's me, all right, Mildred," came the voice from beyond.

"Are you happy?" asked the widow.

"Very happy," came the ghostly voice.

"Happier than when you were with me?" asked the widow.

"Yes, much happier."

"Heaven must be wonderful, George," sighed the widow.

"Who said I was in Heaven?" demanded the voice from beyond the grave.

169.7

"Mrs. Jones," asked the census taker, "I wonder if there is a mistake here. It says you have a child two years old and another four years old, and yet your husband has been dead five years?"

"No, that is correct. I'm still alive."

169.8

Two former neighbors met after an interval of some months. "And how are things with you?" asked one of the women. "Oh," said the other, "I'm managing well enough, although I lost my husband several months back."

"What happened?" asked the friend.

"Well," explained the widow, "I was getting dinner ready and asked him to go out to the garden and pick some tomatoes. He was gone such a long time, and when I went to see what the trouble was, there he was dead—a heart attack."

"Oh, how terrible! What did you do?"

"Oh, I had a can of tomatoes in the house, and just opened that," said the widow.

169.9

An ironworker fell from a New York skyscraper to his death, and one of his fellow workers consented to break the news to the dead man's wife. The other men warned him to be as gentle and as tactful as possible.

When the delegation of workers arrived at the home and the door was opened, the properly brief spokesman said, "How do you do? Are you the widow Murphy?"

"Certainly not! I'm no widow!" replied the woman at the door.

"The hell you ain't," said the head of the delegation. "Whadda you think they're dragging up the steps?"

Aphorisms

169.10

The comfortable estate of widowhood is the only hope that keeps up a wife's spirits.

—*John Gay*

169.11

Rich widows are the only secondhand goods that sell at first-class prices.

—*Benjamin Franklin*

169.12

Easy-crying widows take new husbands soonest; there's nothing like wet weather for transplanting.

—*Oliver Wendell Holmes*

169.13

To be two years a widow exceedeth a college education.

—*Gelett Burgess*

(*See also 86.3, 98.2, 265.2, 265.3, 266.8–266.10, 266.12–266.17, 266.20*)

170. Divorce and Alimony

Anecdotes

170.1

During a Nebraska divorce case the judge, noticing the stubbornness displayed by both husband and wife and concluding that it was impossible to reconcile them, said, "All right, go ahead and be divorced, but understand that everything you possess will have to be divided equally."

"What about the three children?" asked the wife.

"You'll have to figure that out yourself," said the judge.

The wife thereupon suddenly seized her husband by the collar and said, "Come on home, you no-good loafer."

And as she went through the door she looked back and called to the judge, "We'll be back here in a year with four children."

170.2

A woman was granted a divorce when she told the judge that since their marriage, her husband had spoken to her only three times. She was given custody of their three children.

170.3

"Why," asked the judge hearing a divorce action, "have you not spoken to your wife in more than three years?"

"Because," said the husband, "I didn't want to interrupt her."

170.4

Two fellows were talking about a divorce one of them had just obtained.

"What about the house the two of you lived in?" asked the friend.

"We split it fifty-fifty."

"How could you divide a house fifty-fifty?"

"This fifty-fifty means that she gets the inside and I get the outside."

170.5

Judge: "Mrs. Glitter, the court grants you a new divorce. How does that make you feel?"

Mrs. Glitter: "Like a new man."

170.6

"Despite the increasing number of divorces," asserted the lawyer specializing in such actions, "it does prove that this is still the land of the free."

"On the other hand," replied the other lawyer, "the persistence of marriage proves that it is also the home of the brave."

170.7

When the judge suggested to a woman she might as well go ahead and grant her husband the divorce he was asking for, she shouted: "What! I have lived with this bum for twenty years and now I should make him happy?"

170.8

"No, he never struck me," testified the wife in a divorce action. "But he went around the house slamming his fist into doors and walls and saying, 'I wish it was you.' "

170.9

A man seeking a divorce on the grounds his wife didn't love him, testified that recently when he fell down the cellar steps his wife called out, "Henry, when you come up, will you bring an armful of wood for the fireplace."

170.10

"We were happy for years," testified the wife during a divorce trial, "and then Baby came."

"Boy or girl?" asked the judge.

"A girl—a brunette who moved in next door."

170.11

The attorney for the plaintiff in a divorce case put him on the stand.

"Now as I understand it," the attorney began sympathetically, "every night when you returned home from work, instead of finding your wife alone and waiting for you, you found a different man hiding in the closet."

"Yes, that's right."

"And this, of course, caused you untold anguish and unhappiness."

"Why sure! I never had any room to hang up my clothes."

170.12

"I hear your marriage broke up," one woman said to the other. "Was it the old story of May being married to December?"

"No, not that," said the other woman. "It was worse—it was Labor Day married to the Day of Rest."

170.13

A man brought before the court on a charge of deserting his wife, explained that she talked too much.

"That's no excuse," said the judge. "Most women talk a great deal and every woman has the right to talk whenever she wants to."

"But, Your Honor," said the defendant, "my wife never stops talking, day or night, day in and day out, week after week, month after month, and year after year."

"What does she talk about?" asked the judge.

"I swear, Your Honor, she has never said."

170.14

When a man was reprimanded by the judge for having deserted his wife, he replied, "Judge, if you knowed that woman like I do, you wouldn't call me no deserter. You'd say I was a refugee."

170.15

"Your Honor," said the irate wife to the court, "this no-good husband of mine is always drinkin'."

"Yes, sir, Judge," replied the husband, "I do drink some. But, Your Honor, this woman doesn't treat me right. Why, I pawned the kitchen stove to git a little money, and my wife she don't miss that cookin' stove for two weeks."

170.16

Judge: "Your wife says you keep her continually terrorized."

"But honestly, Your Honor—"

Judge (whispering): "Now, not in my official capacity, but just between us, what is your system?"

Definitions

170.17

Alimony is like buying oats for a dead horse.

—*Arthur "Bugs" Baer*

170.18

Alimony is a system whereby when two people make a mistake, one of them continues to pay for it.

170.19

A divorcee is a woman who gets richer by decrees.

170.20

Alimony is the cash surrender value of a husband.

—*Anonymous*

170.21

Alimony is the high cost of leaving.

170.22

Alimony: Paying an installment on a car after the wreck.

—*Gordon Gordon*

Aphorism

170.23

No one knows the worth of woman's love till he sues for alienation.

—*Oliver Herford*

(*See also 94.18, 130.1, 155.35, 165.5, 173.30*)

STRICTLY FEMININE

171. Cat Fights

Anecdotes

171.1

After a bitter argument the two old crones decided, over their drinks, to call a halt and make peace.

"Mrs. Higgins, I bear you no malice," said Mrs. Brown. Whereupon she raised her glass and said, "So here's looking at you, though heaven knows it's an effort."

171.2

Mrs. Stuyvesant Fish, a society leader of malicious wit, vivid personality, and quick temper, was confronted one day at the Newport Casino by Mrs. Belmont who cried out in a great rage, "I just heard what you said about me at Tessie Oelrich's last night. She told me herself that you said I looked like a frog!"

"A toad, my dear, a toad," said Mrs. Fish without raising her voice.

171.3

Two women met on a New York-to-Washington train. One woman greeted the other by name. The second woman, though realizing she had met the first woman, could not for the life of her remember the name. She fumbled for a way to identify the woman and found it when the woman said she was going to visit her brother.

"Oh, yes," said the second woman. "Tell me, what is your brother doing with himself these days?"

"My brother," icily said the first woman, "is still the President of the United States."

171.4

Mrs. O'Rourke was not in a pleasant humor when she returned from a shopping trip. On the way to her apartment house she spotted Mrs. Shannahan sitting next to the window on the first floor and said, "I say, Mrs. Shannahan, why don't you take that ugly mug of yours away from the window and give the neighbors a treat once in a while by letting your pet monkey sit there instead."

"Strange you should mention it," replied Mrs. Shannahan, "because I did that very thing this morning, and the postman came along and said, 'Well, Mrs. O'Rourke, when did you move downstairs?' "

171.5

When Margaret Fuller was teaching in Rhode Island, she boarded at a home where another teacher, Mrs. Nias, also lived. One day a group of women were discussing mythology, and Mrs. Nias spoke of it as if it were a new phase of animal magnetism.

"Why, Mrs. Nias," said Margaret Fuller to the woman she disliked, "you would have been worth educating."

171.6

After she divorced much-married Louis Calhern, Ilka Chase found a box of calling cards engraved "Mrs. Louis Calhern." She sent them to socialite Julia Hoyt, who was Calhern's next wife, with a note reading: "Dear Julia, I hope these reach you in time."

171.7

The feud between Clare Boothe Luce and Dorothy Parker is said to have arisen from an incident that may be purely apocryphal. It is said that the two women happened to be entering the same restaurant at the same moment.

"Age before beauty," said Mrs. Luce as she stepped aside.

"Pearls before swine," said Mrs. Parker as she swept through the door.

171.8

When there was a rift between Clare Boothe Luce and Dorothy Parker, a friend of Mrs. Luce spoke generously of her and emphasized that "Clare is always kind to her inferiors."

"Where does she find them?" asked Mrs. Parker.

171.9

The chorus girl was telling the other girls in the dressing room about her birthday party. "You should have seen the cake! There were seventeen candles."

"Seventeen candles!" exclaimed one of the girls. "Burning them at both ends, no doubt."

171.10

"That's a lovely coat you are wearing, Mrs. X."

"Oh, thank you. My husband gave it to me for my thirty-fifth birthday."

"My! How well it has stood up."

171.11

"My goodness," she said, "it's been seven years since we've met. I must say you've aged."

"Really, I would not have recognized you but for the coat you're wearing."

Aphorisms

171.12

It goes far toward reconciling me to being a woman when I reflect that I am thus in no danger of marrying one.

—*Lady Mary Wortley Montagu*

171.13

When women kiss, it always reminds me of prizefighters shaking hands.

—*H. L. Mencken*

(*See also* 3.8)

172. Beauty before Age

Anecdotes

172.1

The appearance of the beautiful blonde on the witness stand was to be the high point of the trial. "Where were you on the night of June 22nd?" asked the prosecuting attorney.

"Please don't ask me that," pleaded the witness shamefacedly.

"You must answer," said the prosecutor sternly.

"All right," said the young woman with difficulty. "I was at home reading a mystery story."

"Why are you ashamed about that?" demanded the prosecutor.

"Because," said the witness, "a beautiful girl like me should not have to admit that she was wasting her time on a lousy mystery story on such an evening."

172.2

"I'm not happy about those pictures you took of me," said the woman to the photographer. "I do not think they do me justice."

"Madam," said the photographer, "you want mercy, not justice."

172.3

To a young girl who confessed she had incurred the sin of vanity, the late Father Healey of Dublin asked: "Why do you think so?"

She replied that every time she looked in the mirror she was impressed by her beauty.

"Never fear, my child," said the priest. "That's not a sin; that's only a mistake."

172.4

A much-loved old jurist occupied the place of honor at a reception. When an exceptionally lovely young woman passed by he said, almost involuntarily, "What a beautiful girl!"

She heard the observation, smiled at him, and said, "What an excellent judge!"

172.5

A judge asked a woman her age.

"Thirty," she said.

"You've given that age now for the last three years," said the judge, looking at the record.

"Yes, I'm not one who says one thing today and another thing tomorrow," replied the woman.

172.6

A woman was filling out an application for credit.

When she came to the space for age, she hesitated a long time. Finally, the clerk leaned over and said: "The longer you wait, the worse it gets."

Aphorisms

172.7

Women never git th' benefit o' a doubt. If they don't look good they might as well be bad.

—*Kin Hubbard*

172.8

Cosmetics are a woman's way of keeping a man from reading between the lines.

172.9

Here's to powder and lip stick;
Here's to mascara and curls;
Here's to sun tan and swim suits;
In other words—
Here's to the girls!

172.10

The ten best years in a woman's life come between twenty-eight and thirty.

172.11

A woman is as young as she feels like telling you she is.

172.12

A woman begins lying about her age when her face begins to tell the truth about it.

172.13

Never trust a woman who tells you her real age. A woman who would tell that would tell anything.

—*Oscar Wilde*

172.14

If you want to know how old a woman is, ask her sister-in-law.

—*E. W. Howe*

172.15

A woman is as old as she looks before breakfast.

—*E. W. Howe*

172.16

A woman is as old as she looks to a man who likes to look at her.

—*Finley Peter Dunne*

172.17

When a man has a birthday he sometimes takes a day off. When a woman has a birthday she sometimes takes a year off.

172.18

The years that a woman subtracts from her age are not lost. They are added to the ages of other women.

—*Countess Diane of Poitiers*

172.19

When the candles are out all women are fair.

—*Plutarch*

(*See also 3.1–3.3, 3.8, 3.10, 3.15, 173.19, 173.32, 180.4, 268.5*)

173. Girls-at-large

Anecdotes

173.1

An obviously pregnant woman was asked by another woman, "Are you going to have a baby?" "Oh, no," replied the mother-to-be, "I'm just carrying this for a friend."

173.2

A young woman said to a friend that her mind was troubled, perhaps because she had so many unsolved problems.

"Why don't you see a psychiatrist?"

"Oh, you mean one of those men who has you lie down on a couch and tell him about your personal life?" said the young woman who had been around. "Who has to go to a doctor for that?"

173.3

Two young ladies were dining together and talking about their boyfriends. One asked, "Is your boyfriend a freethinker?" The other replied, "I'll say he is; he hardly ever thinks of anything else."

173.4

The young matron sat quietly during her first attendance at a meeting of the League of Women Voters, and upon leaving expressed her thanks, adding, "I am awfully glad I came to hear this discussion of international trade. Of course, I'm still confused, but on a much higher plane."

—*Warner Oliver,* Saturday Evening Post

173.5

The flashily dressed young woman was on the stand in a casualty case.

The lawyer for the insurance company, hoping to confuse or irritate her into a contradictory statement, sneeringly asked her, "And when the elevator started to fall, I suppose all the sins of your past flashed before you?"

"Don't be absurd," she said. "The elevator only fell nine stories."

173.6

"How much are those cocker spaniels in the

window?" asked the nice little lady of the clerk in the pet shop.

"The bitch is $25, and the other one $35."

The little old lady was obviously shocked by the clerk's remark, and he was quick enough to notice it. "Madam, you seem disturbed. Aren't you familiar with the term 'bitch'?"

"Yes," admitted the little old lady, "but it's the first time I ever heard it applied to dogs."

173.7

A reporter asked Winston Churchill: "Do you agree with the prediction that women will be ruling the world by the year 2000?"

"Yes," said Churchill, "they will still be at it."

173.8

TO WOMAN:

Human intelligence cannot estimate what we owe to woman, sir. She sews on our buttons; she mends our clothes; she ropes us in at the church fairs; she confides in us; she tells us whatever she can find out about the little private affairs of the neighbors; she gives us good advice, and plenty of it; she soothes our aching brows; she bears our children—ours as a general thing.

I repeat, sir, that in whatever position you place a woman she is an ornament to society and a treasure to the world. As a sweetheart she has few equals and no superiors; as a cousin, she is convenient; as a wealthy grandmother with an incurable distemper, she is precious; as a wet nurse, she has no equal among men. What sir, would the people of the earth be without woman? They would be scarce, sir, almighty scarce.

—*Mark Twain*

Definitions

173.9

Woman: Someone who reaches for a chair when answering the telephone.

—Detroit *News*

173.10

Woman: A person who will look in a mirror any time—except when she's pulling out of a parking space.

—Atchison, (Kan.), *Globe*

173.11

Intuition is that uncanny second sense that tells a woman she is absolutely right—whether she is or not.

—*Harlan Miller*

Aphorisms

173.12

If my girl said what she thought, she'd be speechless.

—*Judge*

173.13

You can never tell about women, and if you can, you shouldn't.

173.14

Woman—she needs no eulogy; she speaks for herself.

173.15

Women's minds are cleaner than men's—they change them more often.

—*Oliver Herford*

173.16

Women most enjoy receiving the kind of letters that should never be written.

173.17

It always puzzles me to hear of professional women—are there any amateurs?

—*Arthur Godfrey*

173.18

She was suffering from fallen archness.

—*Franklin Pierce Adams*

173.19

In the beauty parlor women let their hair down while it is being put up.

173.20

It was so cold I almost got married.

—*Shelley Winters,* 1956

173.21

Women have a much better time than men because there are more things forbidden them.

—*Oscar Wilde*

173.22

Women without principle draw considerable interest.

173.23

A career woman earns a man's salary instead of remaining home and taking it from him.

173.24

Sir, nature has given women so much power that the law cannot afford to give her more.

—*Samuel Johnson*

173.25

Being a woman is a terribly difficult trade, since it consists principally of dealing with men.

—*Joseph Conrad*

173.26

Woman learns how to hate in proportion as she forgets how to charm.

—*Friedrich Nietzsche*

173.27

I know the disposition of women: when you will, they won't, when you won't, they set their hearts upon you of their own inclination.

—*Terence*

173.28

To find out a girl's faults, praise her to her girl friends.

—*Benjamin Franklin*

173.29

Some girls never know just what they are going to do from one husband to another.

—*T. L. Masson*

173.30

A woman marries the first time for love, the second time for companionship, the third time for support, and the rest of the time just from habit.

—*Helen Rowland*

173.31

Woman was God's *second* mistake.

—*Friedrich Nietzsche*

173.32

Beauty that doesn't make a woman vain makes her very beautiful.

—*Josh Billings*

173.33

The intellect of the generality of women serves more to fortify their folly than their reason.

—*La Rochefoucauld*

173.34

Women's intuition is the result of millions of years of not thinking.

—*Rupert Hughes*

173.35

It takes one woman twenty years to make a man of her son, and another woman twenty minutes to make a fool of him.

—*Helen Rowland*

173.36

There is no such thing as a dangerous woman; there are only susceptible men.

—*Joseph Wood Krutch*

(*See also 21.1, 31.1, 46.8, 46.10, 48.3, 48.12, 48.13, 124.2, 124.3, 136.6, 146.4, 155.25, 155.34, 156.3, 157.17, 158.3, 158.4, 158.19, 158.27, 159.8, 159.22, 160.6, 160.11, 160.28, 160.29, 160.60, 161.15–161.17, 161.23, 161.26–161.28, 162.29, 171.1–171.19, 181.9, 187.11, 187.12, 207.11, 226.8, 228.1, 233.18, 244.6, 271.20, 274.7, 274.8, 276.11*)

Part Six

THE YOUNG AND OLD FOLKS AT HOME AND AWAY FROM HOME

SMALL FRY

174. In School

Anecdotes

174.1

Teacher: "If your mother gave you a large apple and a small one, and told you to divide with your brother, which would you give him, the large one or the small one?"

Boy: "Which brother do you mean, my big one or my little one?"

174.2

Teacher: "If you have seven apples and I asked for three, how many would you have left?"

Pupil: "Seven."

174.3

Teacher: "Can any bright pupil tell me why a man's hair turns gray before his mustache?"

Pupil: "'Cause his hair has a twenty-year start on his mustache."

174.4

"Suppose there were fifteen sheep in a field, and nine of them jumped a fence; how many sheep would be left?"

"None," called out little Willie.

"Willie, I'm surprised at you," said the teacher. "Surely you know your arithmetic better than that."

"You may know arithmetic, teacher," replied Willie, "but you don't know sheep. If one jumped, they'd all jump the fence."

174.5

During a temporary exchange of teachers between a city school and a rural school, the city teacher asked her rural class, "If a farmer had 4,000 bushels of wheat, and wheat is $1.60 a bushel, what will he get?"

"A government loan!" replied the class almost in unison.

174.6

The teacher in a rural school rebuked her class of young farm boys for hesitating when she asked them, "If a dog can run 4 miles in an hour, how far would the dog run in two hours?"

One youngster raised his hand and said, "But teacher, you ain't told us what the dog was runnin' after."

174.7

A farm boy arrived late for school and explained that he had taken the family cow to the bull. "Couldn't your father have done it?" asked the irate teacher.

"I guess so," said the kid, "but I think the bull will do a better job."

174.8

A teacher in an ultraprogressive school asked a seven-year-old girl student: "What would you say you are—a boy or a girl?"

"I'm a boy," replied the little girl.

The teacher related this to the mother and said that the child was maladjusted and needed special treatment.

The mother asked her child why she told the teacher she was a boy.

"Because," said the child, "when anybody asks me a dumb question, I give them a dumb answer."

174.9

The mother wished to enter her five-year-old daughter in a kindergarten, but was told the minimum age was six. The mother urged the superior intelligence of her child and suggested she could easily pass a six-year-old test.

"We will determine that," said the principal. Then turning to the child, she said, "Just say whatever comes into your mind."

"Mother," said the five-year-old, "does she mean that I should address her in grammatically correct and logical sentences, or does she want purely irrelevant words?"

174.10

A mother called at the progressive school to inquire about entering her child. It was at a time when the school day was ending, and the poor woman was almost bowled over by the young savages tearing pell-mell out of the building. That is, all except one child who walked sedately and politely out of the building. "You must excuse her," said one of the teachers. "She's new here and has not yet become adjusted."

174.11

The lad was asked to write a brief essay on Socrates, and came through with this: "Socrates was the wisest man of ancient Greece. He knew everything about everybody, and he told everything he knew, and so they poisoned him."

174.12

The school system's visiting psychologist, to prove to a young teacher that she had failed to train her class to pay attention, went to the blackboard and asked for some one to suggest a number. "Thirty-five" called out one student. The psychologist thereupon wrote 53 on the board. "Another number?" "Nineteen." So he wrote 91. And then followed 47, which was written 74. "How about sixty-six; see what you can do with that!" called out one student who was paying attention.

174.13

"Suppose you took 75 cents out of one pocket of your trousers and then 75 cents out of the other trouser pocket; what would you have?" asked the teacher.

"Someone else's pants," said the realistic child.

174.14

The yokel in back of the room appeared to be paying attention, for a change, when the teacher was explaining arithmetic on the blackboard. This pleased the teacher, who thought that at last she was getting through to the boy and he was beginning to take some interest. He looked inquiringly at her, and she asked, "Yes, Cicero, what is your question?"

"Where do them numbers go when you rub 'em off the board?"

174.15

"Children, there is a lesson to be learned from the ant," said the teacher. "The ant works every day and all day. The ant is always working. And in the end what happens?"

"Somebody steps on him," called out one of the boys.

174.16

Little Claude's mother reluctantly agreed to send her precious child to the public school. "My child is so sensitive," she told the teacher, "he should not be punished. Just slap the boy next to him. That will frighten Claude."

174.17

A teacher taking her class of young children on a tour of the zoo pointed to a deer and asked if anyone knew what it was. No one answered. "What does your mother call your father?" she asked by way of a hint.

"Oh," said one of the boys, "I didn't know a louse was that big!"

174.18

The class had been assigned the writing of a composition on "What I Would Do if I Had a Million Dollars." All the boys and girls set busily to work—all except one, who sat at his desk doing nothing. "Don't you know how to answer the question?" the teacher asked the apparently indolent one.

"Yes, teacher," was the reply. "This is what I would do if I had a million dollars—nothing."

174.19

Teacher: "Why is Lapland so thinly populated?"

Pupil: "Because there are so few Laps to the mile."

174.20

"Where," asked the teacher, "was the Declaration of Independence signed?"

"At the bottom," replied the brightest boy in the class.

174.21

Teacher: "We have been discussing inventions. Who can tell me the name of something that did not exist fifteen years ago?"

Pupil: "Me."

174.22

The little boy was late for school and was running as fast as he could go to beat the bell. "Please, God, get me there on time, please God," he prayed. As he staggered exhausted up to the door, the bell began to ring, and he stumbled and fell over the threshold as he attempted a final leap. He arose deliberately, stuck his head out the door, looked heavenward, and said, "But You don't hafta push me!"

174.23

Teacher: "What did Archimedes mean when he leaped from his bath and yelled, 'Eureka! I have found it!' What did he find?"

Pupil: "The soap."

174.24

Teacher: "What month has twenty-eight days in it?"

Pupil: "All of them."

174.25

The teacher carefully explained to her class the subject of gravity and then asked the students to write an essay on the subject. All turned to the task with vigor, even the usually slow-witted Adolph, who eventually raised his hand and asked, "How do you spell 'poverty'?"

"Poverty?" said the teacher. "Why that, Adolph?"

"Because," said Adolph, proud that he still remembered something of what the teacher had said, "you said poverty is what holds man down to earth."

174.26

"Do you have trouble hearing?" asked the teacher of a youngster who sat dreamily at his desk.

"No, ma'am," replied the boy. "I have trouble listening."

174.27

A little girl in a Sunday School, asked to draw her idea of the flight into Egypt, handed in a picture of four people in an airplane, explaining, "There are Joseph, Mary, the infant Jesus, and Pontius the Pilot."

174.28

Said the Sunday School teacher, "Now, children, I have told you the story of Jonah and the whale. Can someone tell me what lesson it teaches?"

"I can," called out Johnny. "It shows that you can't keep a good man down."

174.29

An archbishop visited a small Catholic parish to administer the sacrament of confirmation. During the course of the exercises, he asked one nervous little girl what matrimony was.

"It is a state of punishment which those who enter are compelled to undergo for a time to prepare them for a brighter and better world."

"No, no," remonstrated her pastor. "That isn't matrimony. That's the definition of purgatory."

"Leave her alone," said the archbishop. "Maybe she is right. What do you and I know about it?"

174.30

"Billy, do you know what happens to little boys who tell lies?"

"Sure, they ride for half-fare."

174.31

A teacher, hoping to instill a bit more patriotism in her class, asked one of the young students what he would think if he saw the Stars and Stripes flying over a battlefield.

"I should think," replied the boy, "that the wind was blowing."

174.32

A small boy, asked to name the first man, promptly replied, "George Washington."

When he was reminded of Adam, the youngster replied, "Oh, I didn't think you were counting foreigners."

174.33

The school board was visiting various classrooms, and the teachers put their pupils through some oral tests. In one of them the teacher asked, "Who signed the Declaration of Independence?"

"Teacher, it wasn't me," called out one of the less-than-bright students.

The teacher, about to call on another student, was interrupted by one of the men on the school board. "Call that boy again," he said. "I don't like his looks. Maybe he did sign it."

174.34

SCHOOL—DON'T KILL A CHILD read the sign. Beneath it was a youthful scrawl: "Wait for a teacher."

Aphorisms

174.35

There is now less flogging in our schools than formerly—but then, less is learned there. So what the boys gain at one end, they lose at another.

—*Samuel Johnson*

174.36

The man who gets into a cage full of lions impresses everyone except a school-bus driver.

—*Rotary Booster,* Fairbury, Ill.

(*See also 79.35, 175.4, 175.6, 175.10, 175.18, 175.28, 177.16, 228.6, 228.7, 230.11, 235.41*)

175. At Home

Anecdotes

175.1

"When I was your age," the father told his eight-year-old son, "I was up at five every morning. I fed the chickens, cleared the snow from the house, and then did my 4-mile paper route. And I thought nothing of it."

"Don't blame you, Dad. I don't think much of it, either."

175.2

A family sat down to dinner with a guest at the table. The young son said, "Mother, isn't this roast beef?"

"Yes; what of it?"

"Well, Daddy said he was bringing a big fish home tonight."

175.3

A mother had been lecturing her young son about the necessity for him to help others, reminding him that we are in this world for that purpose.

The youth considered the mother's words, then asked: "Well, what are the others here for?"

175.4

When the poor little rich boy was informed by his parents that it would not be possible for him to be driven to school in the family's chauffeured Cadillac, he protested, "But how will I get to school?"

"You will get to school," said the mother firmly, "like any other American child—in a taxicab."

175.5

Four-year-old David was crushed and furious because he had gotten a sound spanking for repeated misbehavior. He decided the only course left to him was to leave home. He announced his decision to his mother. She made no objection. So David packed a few precious belongings and struck out on his own to face the world.

Half an hour later a neighbor noticed David walking up and down the street and asked him where he was going. "I'm running away from home," said the young rebel.

"Well," said the neighbor, "you'll never get very far just by walking up and down this street."

"Yes," replied David, "but I'm not allowed to cross the street."

175.6

The fifth grade teacher, imbued with hands-across-the-seas ideas, asked each child in the class to write to a child in a foreign land, the boys to write to girls, and the girls to write to boys.

Late that same afternoon, one of the boys said to his mother while she was preparing dinner, "Hey, Mom, you hear what happened? I got a girl in Dutch!"

175.7

The late Peter Marshall's favorite story was about a little boy in Scotland whose mother, when disciplining him, used to say, "God would not like that." And when the little boy really got out of hand, the mother would say, "God will be angry."

Usually these reminders were sufficient. But one evening at supper the youngster rebelled—he would not eat the prunes provided for desert. He would yield neither to persuasion or warnings. Finally he was sent to bed with the reminder that "God will be angry."

Soon after the child had gone to bed, a violent thunderstorm arose and the mother went to her son's room to quiet him, expecting that he would be in terror at God's anger. But to her surprise she found him at the window, looking out on the terrible storm.

"It's an awful fuss to be making over a few prunes," the boy said to his mother.

175.8

Little Alfie had never spoken a word, though his parents tried every way to get him to speak. Several doctors failed in their efforts to come up with a solution. But one day at breakfast Alfie looked at his plate of pancakes, turned to his mother, and said, "There's not enough butter on these pancakes."

Delighted with this first speech, the mother asked the child why he had never spoken before. "Because," said little Alfie, "I never had anything to complain about before."

175.9

When a little girl told her grandmother she was interested in penguins, the kind old lady carefully selected the best book she could find on penguins and sent it to her grandchild. Presently the polite child wrote her grandmother: "Thank you very much for the book about pengiums. It tells me more about them than I want to know."

175.10

Little Willie handed his report card to his father. "A stands for excellent," he explained. "And B is good. C is fair. And D is what I got."

175.11

A quiet, perfectly behaved little girl, who had always kept her room neat and was mother's little helper, suddenly burst forth as a noisy, careless, and saucy miss.

"You used to be such a help around the house," protested the mother.

"Yes," said the child, "that was when I was bored."

175.12

A little girl asked her mother if liars ever went to Heaven. "I suppose not," said the cautious mother.

"Well, did Grandpa and Uncle Jim and Aunt Lucy ever tell a lie?"

"Oh, I suppose at sometime in our lives all of us have said something that wasn't exactly true," replied the mother.

"Well," said the little girl with decisiveness, "I guess it is awful lonesome up there in Heaven with only God and George Washington."

175.13

Gabby woman at the door: "There was something I wanted to say before leaving, but I can't recall it just now."

Small daughter of the hostess: "Maybe it was good-bye."

175.14

It had been a particularly rough day at the office and the father was trying to rest a bit before dinner, but his son was bent on asking question after question. After numerous other queries, the youngster finally asked, "Daddy, what do you do all day at the office?"

"Nothing!" shouted the exasperated father.

"How can you tell when you're through, Daddy?" was the final question.

175.15

The sweet little girl had a violent fight with her friend. Her mother reprimanded her and said, "It was Satan who urged you to pull Jenny's hair."

"But," the child replied proudly, "kicking her in the shins was my own idea."

175.16

The greatest surprise of little Mary's life was receiving half a dollar on her fourth birthday. She carried the coin about the house, and was seen sitting on the stairs admiring it.

"What are you going to do with your half-dollar?" her mother asked.

"Take it to Sunday School," said Mary.

"To show your teacher?"

Mary shook her head, "No, I'm going to give it to God. He'll be as surprised as I am to get something besides pennies."

175.17

The little girl was inordinately proud of herself and the new gown that she had put on for the first time. As she stood admiring herself in front of a mirror, she said to her mother: "Did God make Papa?"

"Yes, dear."

"And did he make you, too?"

"Yes, dear."

The child looked again in the mirror, studied herself for a few moments with great satisfaction, and then turned to her mother and said, "Don't you think, Mother, that God is really doing much better work these days?"

175.18

Mother: "And what did Mama's little baby learn today?"

"I learned the boys not to call me Mama's little baby."

175.19

Mother had just given Mary Jane a severe talking-to on the waywardness of some of her playmates. "Now tell me," concluded the mother, "where do bad little girls go?"

"Just about everywhere," said worldly wise Mary Jane.

175.20

Boy about to be spanked: "Did Grandpa spank you when you were little?"

"Yes, he did."

"And did Grandpa's father spank him?"

"Yes."

"And did Great-Grandpa's father spank him?"

"Yes, I presume he did," said the father, by this time softening a little.

"Well," said the boy firmly, "don't you think it's about time to stop this inherited brutality?"

175.21

"This is going to hurt me more than you," said father to son.

"Then don't be too rough on yourself," answered the boy; "I'm not worth it."

175.22

"Dad, where were you born?"

"Chicago."

"Where was Mommy born?"

"Dallas."

"And where was I born?"

"Philadelphia."

"Certainly is funny how we three people got together, isn't it?"

175.23

The modern child quizzed her mother as to her own origin, and was given the traditional answer: "God sent you."

"And how did you get here, Mother, did God send you too?"

"Yes, dear." "And grandma?" "Yes, dear." "And great-grandma?" "Yes, dear."

"Do you mean to say, Mother, that there have been no sex relations in this family for over 200 years?"

—*Mary Ware Dennett,* The Reader's Digest, August, 1938

175.24

When the mother had given her young son the usual information about the birds and flowers and bees, and then pointed out that their dog was going to have puppies, the young child said, "Oh, she must have been stung by a bee."

175.25

When grace was about to be said before dinner, the little boy visitor said, "We don't have to say a prayer before we eat in our house. My mother is a good cook."

175.26

A little girl sat drawing a picture.

"What are you drawing, dear?" asked her mother.

"I am drawing God," said the child.

"But how can you do that? No one knows what God looks like."

"They'll know," said the girl quietly, "when I get finished."

175.27

A little child's prayer: "Dear God, I hope you'll take care of yourself. If anything happened to you, we would all be in a terrible fix."

175.28

Mary Jones was saying her prayers: "And please," she implored, "make Bangor the capital of Connecticut."

"Why, Mary, what made you say that?"

"Because I wrote it on my examination paper and I want it to be right."

175.29

Johnnie listened for a moment to his baby brother yelling in his crib. "Mom, did he come from Heaven?" he asked.

"Yes, dear," his mother answered.

"No wonder they put him out!"

175.30

A small child down South was continually complaining to her nursemaid, until finally the nursemaid said, "Child, you have to learn to want and not get."

Definitions

175.31

Baby: An alimentary canal with a loud voice at one end and no responsibility at the other.

—*Elizabeth I. Adamson*

175.32

A baby is an angel whose wings decrease as his legs increase.

Aphorisms

175.33

When a kid misbehaved fifty years ago to get attention, he really got it.

—*Grit*

175.34

Bachelors' wives and old maids' children are always perfect.

—*S. R. N. Chamfort*

175.35

The hand that rocks the cradle charges a dollar an hour.

175.36

Every time a boy shows his hands, someone suggests that he wash them.

—*E. W. Howe*

(*See also 150.21, 164.3, 189.3, 189.5, 189.6, 189.8, 192.7, 219.13*)

176. At Large

Anecdotes

176.1

One Sunday a man took his young son to the zoo and they stopped to look at the lion. "He's the king of the beasts," said the father.

"Why do they call him that, Daddy?"

"Well, he's the big boss. He can lick any other animal. He's a real man-eater, too!"

"Would he even eat you?"

"I guess he would—if he got out."

Little Willie studied the lion with interest, then turned to his father and said, "Daddy, if he does get out, what bus should I take home?"

176.2

"My father is an Elk, Lion, Moose, and Eagle," boasted the youngster.

"Oh yeah?" They got him in the circus?" asked another boy.

176.3

A man took his seven-year-old son to the circus. The youngster was fascinated by some African tribesmen whose glistening black skins showed above their costumes. After gazing long at these men from Africa, the boy asked his father, "Are they black all over?"

"Yes," said the parent.

"Gee, Pop, you know everything."

176.4

Three little boys were boasting about their

fathers. One youngster said, "My father writes some words under pictures and they call it an ad and he gets paid lots of money."

"My father," said the second boy, "writes dots and other funny marks on a sheet of paper and calls it a song and sometimes he gets thousands of dollars for it."

"That's nothing," said the third boy. "Once a week my father writes a sermon out on a piece of paper, gets up and reads it, then it takes three men to carry all the money in."

176.5

At a meeting of a troop of Boy Scouts, three of the members admitted they had failed to perform their good deed that day. The Scoutmaster reprimanded them and suggested they still had time to do their good deed. The youngsters hustled out to make up for their dereliction.

They returned quickly, explaining the deed was done. "Fine," said the Scoutmaster. "Tell us what you did."

"We helped an old lady across the street," explained the first scout.

The second scout said he had helped the first scout, and the third scout said he had assisted the other two scouts.

"Did it take the three of you to help one lady across the street?" asked the Scoutmaster.

"Yes, sir," replied the first scout. "You see, she didn't really want to cross."

176.6

A little boy was in the habit of sucking his thumb all the time. His mother tried every way to break him of the habit. Finally, one day she pointed to a fat man with a very large stomach and said that the man had grown his big stomach because he did not stop sucking his thumb.

The next day the child was with his mother in a supermarket, and he kept staring at a woman with a stomach that was obviously not at all normal—in fact she was very pregnant.

Finally the annoyed woman said to the child, "Stop staring at me like that. You don't know who I am."

"No," said the boy, "but I know what you have been doing."

176.7

In checking over the equipment of a new arrival at a boys' summer camp, the counselor came upon a tightly rolled umbrella. The tenderfoot was asked why the umbrella, since it was not part of the equipment listed as required.

"Did you ever have a mother?" asked the boy.

176.8

Ten-year-old Archibald was discussing the girl problem with his friend Jonathan. "I've walked Susan Smith to school five times, always carried her books, bought her an ice-cream cone twice, and did her homework once. Now do you think I ought to kiss her?" asked Archibald.

"Naw," replied Jonathan, "you've done enough for her already."

176.9

On one occasion Charles Lamb was invited to a party where the room was crowded with children. Their noise and tricks plagued him not a little, and at supper, when toasts were flying to and fro, he rose to propose the health of the "m-much ca-ca-calumniated g-g-good King Herod!"

(See also 42.22, 48.6, 108.4, 112.6, 124.9, 145.6, 156.4, 204.7, 211.29, 226.2, 235.44, 238.9, 276.2)

THE SOCIAL WHIRL

THE "400"

177. Snubs and Snobs

Anecdotes

177.1

During a fashionable dinner party in New York years ago, a visiting Englishman remarked how much he liked the things he saw in America but he added that he did miss one class in America that he found everywhere in England. "I mean," he explained, "that class of people who are not occupied in any particular trade, business, or profession, and whom we call gentlemen, you know."

"Oh," replied an American woman, "we

have a great number of such people here; but we call them bums."

177.2

He looked every inch the high society man when he checked into the Hotel Plaza in New York; everything about the gentleman was correct: his clothes, his speech, and even his arrogance were just the right quality. He went to the room given him on the twentieth floor, locked the door, opened the window, and leaped out. But his death was to him a social disaster when he discovered that he was falling toward 59th Street instead of on Fifth Avenue as he had planned.

177.3

"I never vote," said the town snob. "Really it's such a comfort not to feel that one is responsible for the terrible goings-on in Washington."

177.4

"That fellow acts as though he were born with a gold spoon in his mouth."

"Yeah, I know; but if so, it must have had someone else's initials on it."

177.5

The chauffeur of a new Rolls-Royce pulled up at a New York office building. The car door was opened and out stepped Mr. Importance himself. The chauffeur looked carefully at the tires of the car, got behind the wheel, moved the car a few inches, and got out again to examine the tires, this time appearing satisfied.

"What's it all about?" asked a curious bystander.

"Oh, 'e likes the name on the 'ub-caps right side up so people and 'e can read 'em when 'e's getting' in."

177.6

It was considered a social triumph to be invited to the great estate of a certain grande dame of regal bearing and icy aloofness to mundane affairs; and it was the highest honor to be her weekend guest.

A group of enthusiastic young people were invited to the famous country home for the first weekend in September. They arrived with visions of golf, swimming, tennis, exquisite food, and rare wines—nor were they disappointed, even though they saw very little of the great lady herself.

But at 10 A.M. on Monday morning, while preparing for a final day of fun and frolic, the young guests received a rude shock when the butler informed them that cars would be at the door in a few minutes to take them to the station for the 10:40 train back to New York City. They told the butler the day was a national holiday—Labor Day—and that there must be some mistake. The butler icily replied that "Madame makes no mistakes."

Finally one of the men belligerently insisted that the butler inform the lady that this was Labor Day—a part of the weekend—and that her guests had planned to remain until Tuesday. The butler reluctantly consented to deliver the message and retired with obvious trepidation.

Five minutes later, the butler returned and haughtily said, "Madame says she never heard of Labor Day."

177.7

A Park Avenue matron went into a fashionable pet shop and asked for the finest dog in the shop. The man showed her a poodle pup. She asked if it was pedigreed.

"Pedigreed?" smiled the dealer. "Why if this dog could talk, he wouldn't speak to either of us."

177.8

"Conceited? Why, I'd just love to buy him at his worth and sell him at what he thinks he's worth."

177.9

Jacob Blitzstein was awakened late one night by the phone. "Is this Mr. Astorbilt Van Rensselaer Terwilliger?"

"Oh," laughed Jake, "have you got a wrong number!"

177.10

Years ago, the conductors on Fifth Avenue buses walked down the aisles with a metal device into which passengers inserted their dimes in payment of their fares.

One day a wealthy dowager boarded a bus for the first time in her life. When the conductor came to her with his dime collector extended, she waved him away haughtily with, "Nothing, my good man. I have my own private charities."

177.11

A Philadelphia society leader, after having it pointed out to her by the rector of her church that she really ought to recognize a newcomer, still demurred.

"But you will have to meet her in Heaven," said the rector.

"Heaven will be quite soon enough," said the society leader.

177.12

A dying society woman requested: "Don't ask my friends to the funeral, because I can't return the call."

177.13

The wealthy and self-elected social leader of the town was admittedly generous in providing funds for civic enterprises. On one occasion there was to be unveiled her latest project—a sculptured birdbath in the little park adjoining the town square. A crowd gathered to witness the unveiling of the birdbath—a handsome piece of work. But astonishment was great when it was found that the base of the work bore this inscription: NOT TO BE USED BY SPARROWS.

177.14

A wealthy dowager barged into a flossy New York shop to buy a hat. After the salesgirl had shown her numerous models in the latest fashions, the old lady said sharply: "Now listen to me, young lady. I wear drawers and I wear corsets, and I want a hat to match."

177.15

The painter James McNeill Whistler's conceit was boundless. One day a duchess, in a polite gesture, said, "I believe you know King Edward, Mr. Whistler."

"No, I do not," said Whistler curtly.

"That is strange," said the duchess. "I met the King at a dinner party the other evening, and he said he knew you."

"Oh," said Whistler, "the man was just boasting."

177.16

Sarah Franklin Bache, Benjamin Franklin's daughter, overheard a schoolmaster rebuke her children and remind them they were "young ladies of rank."

"There is no rank in this country but rank mutton," Mrs. Bache told the schoolmaster.

Definitions

177.17

Dignity: Window dressing for a vacant store.

177.18

Socialite: A clubwoman whose husband advertises.

177.19

The Upper Crust is a lot of crumbs held together by dough.

—*Jean Webster*

Aphorisms

177.20

The fellow who stands on his dignity has poor footing.

177.21

It is only people of small moral stature who have to stand on their dignity.

—*Arnold Bennett*

177.22

He looked at me as if I was a side dish he hadn't ordered.

—*Ring Lardner*

177.23

Early to bed and early to rise, and you'll meet very few of our best people.

—*George Ade*

177.24

Exclusiveness is a characteristic of recent riches, high society, and the skunk.

—*Austin O'Malley*

177.25

Society is now one polished horde, form'd of two mighty tribes, the Bores and Bored.

—*Lord Byron*

177.26

Men ain't apt to get kicked out of good society for being rich.

—*Josh Billings*

177.27

If you wish to be agreeable in society, you must consent to be taught many things which you know already.

—*J. K. Lavater*

177.28

To get into the best society one has to feed people, to amuse people, or to shock people—that is all.

—*Oscar Wilde*

177.29

Snobs talk as if they had begotten their own ancestors.

—*Herbert Agar*

(*See also 118.1, 149.1–149.31, 171.1–171.13, 178.1, 178.2, 179.3, 179.9, 179.10, 179.15, 179.16, 181.1, 181.5–181.7, 181.18, 208.4, 221.2, 225.2, 231.1, 240.4, 244.25, 265.19, 268.3, 273.1, 273.8, 273.11, 273.19, 273.25*)

178. Ancestor Worship

Anecdotes

178.1

The wife of the Canon of Worcester Cathedral, when told years ago of Darwin's theory of evolution, is reported to have exclaimed, "Descended from the apes! My dear, we hope it is not true. But if it is, let us pray that it may not become generally known."

178.2

Several Baltimore social leaders were chatting one afternoon over a cup of tea. One said, "Did it ever occur to you that if Our Lord had come to Baltimore we wouldn't have met, since his father was a carpenter?"

"Yes, but He was well-connected on his mother's side."

178.3

"King William," boasted the Englishman, "struck one of my ancestors on the shoulder with the tip of his sword and made him a knight."

"Yeah," said an American, "and Sitting Bull conked my grandfather with a tomahawk and made him an angel."

178.4

Two friends met after a rather long interval. "You're looking pretty down in the mouth since last I saw you. Are you ill?"

"Not exactly, but I'll admit I've been worried of late. You remember I hired a man to trace my ancestry?"

"Yes," said the other. "What's the trouble? Hasn't he been successful?"

"That's just it—too successful—I'm having to pay him hush money."

178.5

A young woman who became tired of hearing a group of women talk about their ancestry put a stop to it all when she declared, "I am descended from a long line my mother fell for."

178.6

"My dear," said Mrs. Lowell Saltonstall Lodge, "we trace our ancestors back to—to—to—oh, well, we've been descending for centuries."

178.7

Paul Bourget once said to Mark Twain, "When an American has nothing else to do, he can always spend a few years trying to discover who his grandfather was."

"Yes," replied Twain, "and when all other interests fail for a Frenchman, he can always try to find out who his father is."

178.8

"My family traces back to Henry VIII," said the socially ambitious lady during a tea. Then turning to a woman nearby, she asked in a patronizing manner, "Tell me, my dear, how old is your family?"

"Oh heavens!" exclaimed the woman casually. "I have no idea. The family records were lost in the Flood."

178.9

During a luncheon a self-important woman said to the rabbi seated next to her, "Did you know that one of my ancestors signed the Declaration of Independence?"

"Very interesting," said the rabbi. "One of my ancestors signed the Ten Commandments."

178.10

One of the grande dames of Charleston, South Carolina, was visited by her grandchildren who had just returned from a trip to Europe. In relating their experiences, they told her of the great number of people who visited one of the museums to look at "Whistler's Mother." The old lady listened for a few minutes, then with all gentility said, "Strange, isn't it? You know she was only a McNeill of North Carolina."

178.11

Lord Thurlow, the son of a barber, was twitted by a noble peer about his lowly origin.

"Yes, of course, I am the son of a barber," said Thurlow. "And if Your Lordship had been the son of a barber, you would have been a barber, too."

Definitions

178.12

Heredity is an omnibus in which all our ancestors ride, and every now and then one of them puts his head out and embarrasses us.

—*Oliver Wendell Holmes*

178.13

Ancestor Worship: The conviction that your family is better dead than alive.

Aphorisms

178.14

Send your noble blood to market and see what it will buy.

178.15

He walks as if balancing the family tree on his nose.

—*Raymond Moley*

178.16

A man can't very well make a place for himself under the sun if he insists upon taking refuge under the family tree.

178.17

Nearly every man is a firm believer in heredity until his son makes a fool of himself.

178.18

It is indeed desirable to be well descended, but the glory belongs to our ancestors.

—*Plutarch*

178.19

The man who has not anything to boast of but his illustrious ancestors is like a potato—the only good belonging to him is underground.

—*Thomas Overbury*

178.20

The pride of ancestry increases in the ratio of distance.

—*George W. Curtis*

178.21

You can't choose your ancestors, but that's fair enough; they probably wouldn't have chosen you.

178.22

The trouble with some people who brag of their ancestry is in their great descent.

—*Josh Billings*

178.23

Snobs talk as if they had begotten their own ancestors.

—*Herbert Agar*

(*See also 7.7, 79.49, 145.1, 154.12, 177.7, 177.29, 220.1, 220.9, 269.133, 271.17, 273.12*)

179. The Nouveau Riche

Anecdotes

179.1

A man invented, produced, and sold a roach poison, making a large fortune. His wife, anxious to hit the social high spots, gave a big, lavish party. But all through the dinner her husband uttered not a word. As they were leaving the table, the wife got a chance to snarl at him:

"What's the matter with you tonight? Why don't you talk?"

The husband shrugged his shoulders in disgust and snapped back, "Aw, what's the use of talking? None of these people know anything about roaches."

179.2

A woman of scant education but wonderful pretensions when her husband suddenly became wealthy was entertaining some old friends in her palatial new home. During the course of a tour of the home, the hostess said they were having trouble with rats that had gotten into the house. "I suppose," she said to her old friend, "that even you are troubled with mice in your little house."

179.3

The young man who had made a fortune in a hurry promptly bought himself a small yacht and decked himself out in the regalia of a captain. He wanted his grandmother to be his first guest aboard the vessel. The perceptive, no-nonsense, little old lady boarded the vessel and was met by her grandson, who took her around the boat. While doing so, he pointed to his cap with its crossed anchors and said, "This signifies that I am a captain." The old lady made no comment.

"You don't seem very impressed," protested the young owner of the yacht.

"All right," replied grandma almost petulantly, "I'll be impressed. To yourself, you're a captain. To me, you're maybe a captain, too. But to *captains,* you're no captain!"

179.4

They were telling friends about their first time out of the United States—about their world trip to Asia, Africa, and Europe. They dwelt at length on the Orient, particularly China and India.

"Did you see the pagodas?" asked one listener.

"We not only saw them, we dined with them!" exclaimed the lady traveler grandly.

179.5

A young woman was sent to a fancy finishing school by her rich, uneducated parents. They wanted the girl to learn good manners. At the end of the term she arrived home pregnant, to the acute distress of her parents. When the girl insisted she didn't know the name of the fellow, the mother came to the end of her patience and screamed, "We've spent a young fortune to educate you and see that you have good manners. And now look! You go out with a man, permit a thing like this to happen to you, and don't even have the manners to ask, 'With whom do I have the pleasure?' "

179.6

The wealthy businessman went South for a vacation. He had his entire floor in the hotel cleared of guests, and paid for it. He demanded that the dining room be emptied when he was eating there—he had to have absolute quiet—and cheerfully paid for it. On the beach all bathers were removed from his vicinity—at a cost to the wealthy man of $1,500. He sat back and relaxed in his beach chair, soaked up the sun, and sighed, "This is the life. Who needs money?"

179.7

Mr. Newrich wanted the best of everything for his home. He went into a music shop and asked to see their most expensive violin. The clerk brought out a fine instrument and told him it was made in 1760.

"Is the outfit that made this still in business?" asked the rich man.

"Oh, no," said the clerk. "The maker has long since died; he had no successors."

"Then it's no good," snapped the customer. "You think I'm a sucker to buy a thing I couldn't get spare parts for?"

179.8

The cultured maidservant announced to her mistress, Mrs. Newrich: "If you please, madam, there's a mendicant at the door."

"Tell 'em there's nothin' to mend today," retorted Mrs. Newrich imperiously.

179.9

Mrs. Richbitch asked Fritz Kreisler what his fee would be to play at a private affair the woman was giving.

"$1,000," said Kreisler.

"It's rather high," said Mrs. Richbitch, "but I suppose we'll have to pay it. But of course you will be there as an entertainer and you will be expected to refrain from mingling with the guests."

"Well," said Kreisler, "in that case the fee would be only $500."

179.10

A movie mogul bought a large ranch and equipped it with luxurious stables and barns and chicken houses. When a friend asked, "Are the hens laying?" he replied, "Yes, but in my position they don't have to."

179.11

A suddenly rich movie colony figure was showing his ultramodern, electronically equipped mansion to a friend. Everything was done with buttons.

"Now here," said the proud owner, "is the big surprise. Here in California when it gets hot I like to take my daily bath in the open, so I get into the bathtub in the bathroom and press a button and out comes the bathtub to the patio. There are buttons here for both the entry and return of the bathtub. Now watch, I'll press the button and you'll see those doors open and the bathtub come right at us."

He pressed the button, the doors opened, and out rolled the bathtub—with the man's wife in it.

179.12

The wealthy illiterate always signed his checks with a simple X, but one day the bank phoned him to say they had a check with three X's—was it a forgery?

"No, that's OK," said the illiterate. "I meant to tell you from now on my signature will be three X's. My wife's got big ideas and thinks I should have a middle name."

179.13

During a luncheon for a charitable cause, a woman who had sat next to a bejeweled and overdressed woman said to a friend as they were leaving, "Do you know how much her husband makes?"

"Yes, half," said the other woman.

179.14

Mr. and Mrs. Climber were preparing to entertain some very special guests. After looking over all the appointments carefully, the hostess put a note on the guest towels, "I'll murder you if you use them." It was meant for her husband. In the excitement she forgot to remove the note and after her guests left she discovered the towels in perfect order, with the note still on them.

179.15

Two women met in a fashionable café. One said, "Mrs. Tobey isn't in your set any more, is she?"

"No, indeed," replied the other. "She had to drop out of our set."

"Drop out!" exclaimed the first speaker. "Why, she told me she climbed out."

179.16

"We are going to move—we're going to be living in a better neighborhood."

"So are we," said their neighbor.

"Oh, are you also moving?"

"No, we're staying here."

Definition

179.17

Deluxe: Mediocre in a big way.

Aphorisms

179.18

When you try to make an impression, that is the impression you make.

(*See also 15.3, 215.7*)

GUESTS AND HOSTS

180. The Cocktail Hour

Anecdotes

180.1

At a cocktail party a woman captured a distinguished man of learning and engaged him in a long conversation, during which a bystander, impressed with the woman's apparent grasp of her subject, complimented her.

"Oh, not really," smiled the woman. "I've just been concealing my ignorance."

The distinguished listener turned to her, smiled, and said, "Not at all, my dear lady. Quite the contrary, I assure you." From last reports the woman is still trying to figure out the man's exact meaning.

180.2

An elderly and well-heeled woman at a cocktail party was introduced to Dr. So-and-So. She immediately latched onto the poor man and began to give him the details of a medical problem that had her worried, replete with all her symptoms.

"But, my dear lady," said the doctor, "you are mistaken about me. I am not a physician. I am a doctor of economics."

"Oh, how interesting," pursued the lady. "In that case can you tell me whether I should hold on to my Chrysler stock?"

180.3

During a cocktail party a physician was captured by an overstuffed matron who launched into an endless monologue concerning her medical history, with all her current symptoms and self-diagnosis. Finally the doctor interrupted, pointed to a man on the other side of the room who was yawning, and said, "I think he must be eavesdropping on you."

180.4

I looked in at Mrs. Screaming's cocktail party yesterday afternoon. Lady Cabanleigh was there. "I have just come from the new beauty parlor," she said to me.

Mrs. Screaming, who happened to overhear this, cried loudly, "I suppose it was shut."

—*J. B. Morton*

Definitions

180.5

A cocktail party is a gathering where olives are speared and friends stabbed.

180.6

A cocktail party is where they cut sandwiches and friends into little pieces.

Aphorism

180.7

"Hear no evil, see no evil, and speak no evil," and you'll be a failure at a cocktail party.

(*See also 112.4, 274.1*)

181. Dinners and Teas

Anecdotes

181.1

A supercilious bachelor failed to acknowledge the dinner invitation of a woman friend. Several days later he met her on the street and said, "If I'm not mistaken, you asked me for dinner last Monday?"

The woman looked at him in puzzlement for a moment, then her face brightened, and she said, "Oh, yes—I did at that. And were you there?"

181.2

Lady Randolph had invited George Bernard Shaw, a well-known vegetarian, to a luncheon, and received in reply a curt note, saying: "Certainly not. What makes you think I would alter my well-known habits."

Lady Randolph, however, was not at a loss for a reply. She wrote: "Know nothing about your habits. Hope they are not as bad as your manners."

181.3

Rossini, the eighteenth-century actor, had dined thinly, for his host's table afforded only a snip of this and a snack of that. As coffee was being served, the host said, "I hope you will soon do us the honor of dining here again."

"Certainly," said the hungry Rossini briskly. "Let's start now."

181.4

A nobleman dining with a man prominent for his philosophical interests noticed that he took great relish in the dishes that were served.

"I am surprised to find a philosopher taking so much pleasure in delicacies," said the nobleman.

"Do you suppose, my lord," replied the scholarly one, "that delicacies are only for blockheads?"

181.5

The youth Curzon, in an after-dinner speech, said that he always tried to associate with his intellectual superiors.

Monckton Milnes, Lord Houghton, interjected in a loud voice, "My God, that would not be difficult."

181.6

During a dinner party in London one evening, Frank Harris was boasting that he had been invited to dine with every prominent social leader in England.

"Once," said Oscar Wilde.

181.7

One of the members of the Hooks and Eyes Club was expatiating on the fact that he had dined three times at the Duke of Devonshire's, and that on no occasion had there been any fish at table. "I cannot account for it," he added.

"I can," said Douglas Jerrold, "they ate it all upstairs."

181.8

During a dinner party, Frederick Townsend Martin related to Mrs. Stuyvesant Fish, society leader and wit, that he had spent the afternoon bringing cheer to the inmates of an asylum for the blind and that at the close of an inspirational address he asked them whether they preferred blindness or deafness.

"And," concluded Martin, "they were unanimous in choosing blindness."

"What!" exclaimed Mrs. Fish, "after hearing you talk for an hour?"

181.9

It was a formal tea, with footmen in attendance as if it were a banquet, and the elegant gentlemen were seated opposite the women, silent and ill at ease. The conversation was dreary and platitudinous.

Mrs. Stuyvesant Fish could stand it no longer. "They say in Europe," observed Mrs. Fish, "that all American women are virtuous. Well, do you wonder? Look at those men!"

181.10

Out on his boat with a lady guest one day, banker Frank Higginson ordered his steward to serve tea. The banker's tea was cold and in a rage he threw the cup overboard. Some moments later when he calmed down and new tea had been procured and quaffed to his satisfaction, he graciously offered to relieve his guest of her cup and return it to the tray.

"Oh, don't bother, Frank," she said, and with a smile tossed not only her cup but her saucer and sandwich plate along with it into the sea.

181.11

A woman, annoyed because she was seated to the left of her host rather than to the right, said, "I guess it's not always possible to seat people in their proper places."

"Oh," said the hostess, "those who matter don't mind and those who mind don't matter."

181.12

When Samuel Johnson returned from a trip through Scotland a hostess had a special Scotch dish prepared for him when he went to her home for dinner. During the meal she asked the blunt old man how he liked the dish. It was, he said, "a dish fit for pigs."

"Pray, sir," smiled the hostess sweetly, "let me help you to some more."

181.13

A society woman, noted for the way in which she collected celebrities for her parties, some years ago gave a large dinner at which Oliver Herford and a famous military man were the guests of honor. Toward the end of the meal the beaming and bulging hostess arose and said, without previous warning to Herford, "Mr. Oliver Herford will now improvise a poem in honor of the hostess."

Although embarrassed and distressed, Herford kept his wits, turned to the hostess and said, "I will do that after the general has fired his cannon."

181.14

Visiting some friends in the country who served honey at breakfast, Oliver Herford said, "I see you keep a bee."

181.15

At a debutante ball given at Boston's Copley Plaza, Mrs. S. Huntington Wolcott was informed of the presence of a young lady who had not been invited. Mrs. Wolcott gave the girl just time enough to remove her coat and join her friends. Then she moved quickly to the scene, extended her hand, and said in her most pleasant voice, "I hear you've been looking for me, dear—to say good night."

181.16

A young man who had crashed a party found himself in the line of guests who were bidding good-bye to their hostess.

"It's been a marvelous party," gushed the gate-crasher.

"So glad you liked it," said the hostess. "Remind me to invite you the next time."

181.17

Wolcott Gibbs, once a star member of the *New Yorker* editorial staff, was visiting a rich friend in the country. However, he was not impressed by the swimming pool, or the tennis courts, stables, horses, and all the numerous luxuries on display. At the main house the proud host pointed to a magnificent elm tree and said, "That tree stood for thirty years on the top of that hill over there. But I had it moved to this place so that I can sit out here on nice mornings and work in its shade."

"Just think," said Gibbs, "what God could do if He had the money."

181.18

Julia Ward Howe wished Senator Charles Sumner to meet Edwin Booth, the great actor. One evening at her home, Mrs. Howe mentioned this to Sumner.

He said, "I don't know that I should care to meet him. I have outlived my interest in individuals."

"Fortunately, God Almighty has not, by last reports, got so far," added Mrs. Howe in her journal.

181.19

A man invited to a friend's wedding anniversary party was given very explicit directions: "The address is 245; take the elevator to the tenth floor; turn to the right to Apartment H; and when you get there, push the bell with your elbow."

"With my elbow?" Why that?" asked the guest.

"Well, you're certainly not coming empty-handed, are you?"

Definition

181.20

Pink Tea: Giggle, Gabble, Gobble, Git.
—*Oliver Wendell Holmes*

Aphorisms

181.21

Speaking of houseguests, Oliver Herford said: "Many are called, but few get up."

181.22

Some people can stay longer in an hour than others can in a week.
—*William Dean Howells*

(*See also 52.1, 52.2, 52.5, 76.19, 165.74, 165.75, 175.2, 182.1, 182.4, 186.17, 210.23, 217.9, 227.4, 240.6, 240.13, 243.8, 244.25, 249.3, 254.1–254.3, 271.10, 271.11, 271.44, 272.26, 274.4, 274.13*)

182. Faux Pas

Anecdotes

182.1

J. P. Morgan went one day to dinner at the home of his junior partner, Dwight D. Morrow. Before Mr. Morgan arrived, Mrs. Morrow gave her several children very careful instructions not to stare at Mr. Morgan's extremely large nose, to make no comments about it, and not even to mention the word "nose" in Mr. Morgan's presence.

The children behaved perfectly; all went smoothly during dinner. Mrs. Morrow was beginning to relax, when she turned to the distinguished guest and said, "And now, Mr.

Morgan, will you have cream or lemon in your nose?"

182.2

At a party one fellow turned to his neighbor and said, "I just made a terrible mistake. I told one of the men here that the host must be a terrible tightwad, and he turned out to be the host." His neighbor replied, "Oh, you mean my husband."

182.3

At a party one man turned to the other and said, "Who is that awful-looking lady in the corner?"

"Why, that's my wife," said the second man.

"Oh, I don't mean her," recovered the first man. "I mean the lady next to her."

"That," cried the second man, "is my daughter."

182.4

A pretty young bride was frequently embarrassing her conservative husband by the pungency of the remarks she made when they were socializing. Before leaving for an ultra-plush and ultra-stuffy dinner party, the husband pleaded with her to avoid a running conversation. "Just confine your remarks to 'Oh, is that so?' 'Really!' 'How interesting,' 'Imagine that!' "

The young woman was seated next to a gracious old bishop, who was struck by her beauty. During the dinner he turned to her and said, "You look like one of those fine old paintings."

Up to this point the young woman had behaved with the greatest propriety. But this remark was too much for her. She forgot the promise she made her husband and snapped back at the bewildered cleric, "I like that! You don't look so damned hot yourself!"

182.5

A visitor from South America was dining with some friends in Baltimore and was encouraged to talk about his country and family. He spoke most complimentarily about his wife, then added, "But alas, we have no children." When an awkward silence seemed to follow, he went on, "My wife, you understand, is unbearable." He noticed puzzled looks on his listeners' faces, so elaborated with, "You see, she is inconceivable." Thinking that this, too, was not clear enough, he plunged on into more struggles with the English language, until finally on a note of triumph he said, "In short, my good wife is impregnable!"

182.6

"It's happened," cried the bishop in anguish as he sat playing bridge one evening with some charming people.

"What's happened?" asked the young woman next to him.

"A stroke: my left side is paralyzed."

"Are you sure?" asked the young lady.

"Yes, yes," groaned the bishop. "I've been pinching my left leg for the past few minutes and I feel no sensation whatever."

"Relax," laughed the young lady. "That was my leg you were pinching."

182.7

A student, invited out to dinner on Christmas Day, was asked by his hostess if he would care for a little more plum pudding. He said, "No, thank you; I have enjoyed immensely what there was of it."

Then, realizing his reply suggested a shortage, he sought to mend matters and said, "I mean there is plenty of it, such as it is."

182.8

A scientist working on a critical project stopped long enough to recall that he had forgotten a dinner engagement the previous Monday at the home of some new acquaintances. He phoned them immediately to express his apologies and to explain that his work had claimed all his attention, and asked to be forgiven. For a few brief seconds there was an ominous silence on the other end of the phone, and then the hostess said: "But you were here for dinner last Monday."

182.9

"Please don't trouble yourself," said the departing guest to the exhausted host. "I can see myself to the door all right."

"It's no trouble," said the host. "In fact, it's a pleasure."

182.10

Ernest Raymond, an English author, tells about the time he was lecturing at women's clubs in the United States and at one town was picked up at his hotel by one of his hosts, a large, overdressed woman who ushered him to a luxurious car driven by her husband. After the customary amenities were dispensed with, the woman launched into high praise of her guest's book and continued to dwell at length on *Sorrel and Son*. Raymond let the woman go on—which she did—but finally, in an effort to get her to change the subject, Raymond decided to correct the woman and tell her that Warwick Deeping was the author of *Sorrel and Son*.

The husband, who up to this point had said nothing, kept his eye on the road as he called to his wife in the back seat, "Caught again, Emily!"

(*See also 4.4, 18.1, 23.1, 52.2, 55.8, 55.16, 58.5, 78.3, 86.8, 86.16, 87.21, 89.7–89.9, 92.17, 93.13, 93.14, 93.17, 93.25, 99.12, 99.14, 101.9, 106.11–106.13, 108.4, 118.3, 119.17, 124.33, 136.4, 136.17, 136.19, 138.12–138.20, 150.7, 150.31, 152.1, 154.9, 154.42, 159.14, 163.13, 163.17, 171.3, 172.5, 174.7, 174.27, 174.33, 179.3, 179.7, 179.8, 179.14, 184.77, 188.4, 189.1, 189.7, 195.4, 205.18, 207.3, 207.6, 208.13, 215.7, 217.6, 226.7, 233.1, 233.2, 233.13, 233.14, 236.1–236.3, 236.7–236.11, 236.13, 236.15–236.18, 237.1–237.7, 237.9, 237.10, 240.3, 240.18, 243.7, 244.2, 244.6, 244.11, 244.20, 244.25, 245.10, 245.11, 245.13, 246.13, 248.17, 249.9, 251.2, 251.6, 252.1–252.8, 265.7, 265.12, 271.1–271.14, 275.6*)

183. Dining Out

Anecdotes

183.1

A woman sat at the table in a fashionable New York restaurant during the luncheon hour with a poodle dog in her lap. She smothered the creature with caresses and talked to it in the most endearing terms. A waiter came over, looked disdainfully at the dog, and with cool courtesy said, "Your first dog, Madame?"

183.2

New York restaurateur Toots Shor was not to be intimidated by any patron, no matter how rich or famous. One evening a prominent Hollywood magnate stood waiting with others for a table, when Shor passed by. Almost genially the movie man called over to Shor, "I hope your food is up to my standard." Shor looked at him unsmilingly and said, "I've seen some of your pictures."

On another occasion a four-star general complained to Toots Shor that the cheesecake was spoiled. Shor questioned the waiter, who told him that the general wanted Shor to taste it. "I should say not," said Shor. "Let him get sick."

183.3

They laughed and laughed when I spoke French to the waiter—but they didn't know I told him to give the check to the other fellow.

183.4

One day Colonel Ethan Allen of Connecticut entered the dining room of a plush New York hotel and walked to a table where the chair had been turned up.

A waiter hurried over and told him that the seat had been reserved.

"For whom?" asked Allen.

"For a gentleman," said the waiter.

"He's come," said Allen as he sat down and began to order his meal.

183.5

Oscar Wilde and a friend both ordered lobster at lunch. The friend said to the waiter, "Bring them quick!"

"I'll have mine dead," said Wilde.

183.6

Entering one of New York's elegant restaurants on a steaming hot day, the customer promptly removed his jacket and sat down at his table. The headwaiter rushed over and said, "Sir, you cannot do that in here."

"But the Queen of England gave me permission to do this," exclaimed the customer.

"The Queen of England? I don't know what you're talking about."

"Well, when I was at her court and started to remove my coat, she said, 'Sir, you can do that in America, but you can't do it here.' "

183.7

A gal ordered the most expensive things on the menu. When the waiter asked the guy, "What do you wish, sir?" he said, "I wish I hadn't brought her."

183.8

A fellow went into a restaurant and asked the waitress to bring him some orange juice, half water, with the seeds in; toast burnt to a crisp; scrambled eggs, mushy; coffee, weak and cold. The waitress looked at him quizzically. "Anything else?" she asked.

"Yes," groaned the man, "sit opposite me at the table and nag me. I'm homesick."

183.9

A fellow sat down at a lunch counter and ordered and ate four hamburgers, two dozen clams, a steak, doughnuts, pie a la mode, and coffee.

"You must be hungry," said the waiter.

"Far from it," said the customer. "In fact, I hate all this food, but I just love bicarbonate of soda."

183.10

Note clipped to menus in a Reno cafe: "If you are one of those who douse cigarettes in coffee cups, let the waitress know. She'll serve your coffee in an ashtray."

183.11

"I'm so hungry I could eat a horse!" said the fellow as he plumped himself down at a stool in the diner.

"You sure came to the right place," said a dour patron.

Definition

183.12

Banquet: A $2 dinner served in sufficient numbers to enable the caterer to charge $10 for it.

Aphorisms

183.13

Nowadays we are told that most of the food which is provided on the stage during a play is eatable. The idea may possibly be copied by some of our restaurants.

183.14

He who indulges, bulges.

183.15

To eat is human; to digest divine.

—*C. T. Copeland*

(*See also 30.3, 37.17, 40.11, 40.12, 40.20, 50.1–50.27, 53.1, 53.2, 76.4, 117.10, 159.5, 175.25, 179.5, 182.1, 182.4, 182.7, 182.8, 184.17, 184.19, 184.32, 186.1, 205.12, 206.2, 206.6, 206.14, 210.19, 211.5, 213.13, 214.9, 218.9, 222.4, 225.7, 228.2, 231.10, 238.2, 249.3, 249.18, 268.8, 270.7, 271.45, 273.13, 274.7*)

DRINKERS AND SMOKERS

---

184. The Imbibers

Anecdotes

184.1

A drunk accidentally fell down the subway steps, staggered along the platform, and reached the street by another entrance. When he finally caught up with his fellow drunk, he said to him, "I've been in the basement of a friend's house—and boy, has he got a set of trains!"

184.2

"Gimme a shot of bourbon and a shot of water," said the obviously heavy drinker to the bartender. When the order was placed before him on the bar, the lush pulled a worm from his pocket and dropped it into the glass of water. After watching it swim around for a few seconds, the man drew the worm from the water and dropped it into the whiskey. It wriggled briefly, then curled up and died.

"You see that?" said the lush to the bartender. "It proves that if you keep on drinking whiskey you'll never have worms."

184.3

A fellow came into a bar and ordered martini after martini, each time removing the olives and placing them in a jar. When the jar was filled with olives and the martinis all consumed, the fellow started to leave, but a stranger asked him if he would mind explaining his actions.

"Don't mind a bit," said the martini-minded man. "My wife just sent me out for a jar of olives."

184.4

Two old drunkards were in the habit of coming to Lebanon, Kentucky, twice a week to get drunk together. After years of this, one of them died. His old friend came in on Saturday and they told him his pal had died—that the whiskey had been taken into his circulation and so saturated his blood and his breath that one night before going to bed the old man went to blow out the candle and his breath caught fire and he was burned to death. The other man promptly called for a Bible and took an oath that from that time forward he would never blow out another candle.

184.5

A man was in the habit of spending his evenings after supper at the local tavern. He would stay there for hours. His wife was unhappy about this, and one evening she determined to go herself to this tavern and see what he was doing there.

She found her husband sitting at the bar, drinking liquor. She sat beside him, asked him what he was drinking, and he told her bourbon.

She ordered some bourbon and drank a large gulp from the glass placed before her. Then she made a face and gave every evidence that the whiskey was most distasteful to her. Her husband noticed her expression and said, "And you thought I came here every evening to enjoy myself."

184.6

When Eugene Field worked on a Kansas City paper, he and other choice spirits frequently gathered at the bar of George Seaton. Seaton had a rule that a customer's bill should never exceed his weekly paycheck—a rule never enforced against Field.

One time when Field's bill at the bar came to something like $110, Field ran a flattering item in his column about Seaton. Seaton considered this evened the score and so presented Field with a bill stamped PAID IN FULL.

After some sparring, Field asked, "Do I understand, George, that I have actually paid this bill?"

"That's right," said Seaton diffidently.

"In full?"

"In full," said Seaton.

"In that case," said Field, raising his voice and recovering his nerve, "It is the custom in Missouri, when one man pays another in full, to set up the drinks."

Seaton gasped but finally was able to mutter, "Gentlemen, this is on the house."

Whereupon all of Field's cronies gathered at the bar and called out, "Make it a case, George." And he did. And they made a night of it.

184.7

A group of men in an English pub were discussing the wartime closing hours. Most of them protested the early closing hour, but one red-nosed old-timer saw no harm in the new regulation.

"After all," he said, "if a bloke ain't drunk by 10:30 in the evening, he ain't trying."

184.8

An elderly gentleman went into a neighborhood bar and ordered two Scotches on the rocks. He drank one, then the other. He did this every day for weeks. Finally, the bartender said, "Why don't you order one at a time? Then the ice in the second drink would not be melted before you got to it."

The gentleman said, "I order these two Scotches because for years I lunched with my partner and we always each had a Scotch on the rocks. Before he died, he asked me always when I had a drink to have one at the same time as a silent toast to him."

Weeks later, the fellow came in and ordered only one drink. "How come?" asked the bartender. "I'm on the wagon now—I'm not drinking."

184.9

A fellow at the Players Club bar was drinking gingerale and going on at great length about his redemption from booze and claiming it was great to be off the stuff. He turned to Don Marquis, who had been on the water wagon from time to time, and wondered why people drank alcoholic beverages at all. Taking a sip of his whiskey and soda, Marquis said to the bore, "I drink only to make my friends seem interesting."

184.10

After riding the water wagon for several months, Don Marquis walked up to the bar of the Players Club and said for all to hear: "I've finally conquered my damn will power. A double Scotch, please."

184.11

Identical twins, dressed exactly the same, stopped in a bar for a drink. A man staggered past them, stopped to look at them in puzzlement, then ordered another drink.

Finally one of the twins laughed and said, "Don't let it upset you, old man; you're really not in such bad shape. We're twins."

The drunk took another look and said, "All four of you?"

184.12

A drunk sitting at the bar belched loudly and emphatically. A man seated next to the drunk said, "How dare you belch before my wife?" The drunk looked up, bowed to the woman seated next to the protesting man, and said, "I beg your pardon, I did not know the lady wanted to belch."

184.13

They had been having a series of temperance revivals and Pat had signed the pledge. Not long afterward, he was seen coming out of a saloon.

A friend said, "Pat, I thought you were a teetotaler?"

"Indeed," said Pat, "I am the same, but I am not a bigoted teetotaler."

184.14

An Irishman about to stop in a bar was halted by a temperance zealot who said, "If you go in there the Devil goes with you."

"If he does," retorted the Hibernian, "he'll have to pay for the drinks."

184.15

A man bumped into an acquaintance at a bar and remarked, "I thought you'd given up drinking. What's the matter? No self-control?"

"Sure, I've got plenty of self-control. I'm just too strong to be a slave to it."

184.16

A fellow was drinking a Tom Collins of second-rate gin.

"Don't you know that stuff's slow poison?"

"Oh, that's all right. I'm in no hurry."

184.17

During a fashionable banquet, one of the guests, feeling no pain, suddenly picked up a bottle of champagne and heaved it at a chandelier. When asked to explain his action the next day, he said, "At the time it seemed like a good idea."

184.18

Alexander Woollcott arrived at a friend's home one day during a severe storm and said, "I want to slip out of these wet clothes and into a dry martini."

184.19

At dinner the great drinker was offered grapes for dessert. "No, thank you," he said, "I don't take my wine in pills!"

184.20

"Your record is a disgraceful one," said the judge to the prisoner before him, "and there is only one explanation: alcohol, alcohol, and alcohol."

"I'm glad to hear you say that," said the prisoner, "because everybody else says it's my own fault."

184.21

An Irishman was called to the stand to testify concerning whether a certain Mr. A was drunk or not. Twenty other witnesses had already testified that A was drunk. So when Pat got on the stand he was asked how he could tell whether or not a man was drunk. "I never think a man drunk," said Pat, "as long as he can lay on the ground and hang on to the grass."

184.22

"How, with all this drunkenness, do you manage to support yourself?" the judge asked the town drunkard who stood before him.

"Well, Your Honor," said the drunk, "usually I leans against a fence."

184.23

"How do you know this man was drunk?" asked the police court judge.

"Well, Your Honor," said the policeman, "when I came up to him he had just dropped a penny in the mailbox and was looking up at the clock on the church tower, muttering, 'My God, I've lost 11 pounds.' "

184.24

A drunk driver going the wrong way on a one-way street was stopped by a cop. The drunk supposed that he was being stopped for speeding. He told the cop that he had to drive fast because he was late since everyone else was already on the way home.

184.25

A man was arrested recently for drunkenness when he stood with his arm around a lamppost, shouting, "Let me in!" When told that nobody lived there, he said, "Don't lie. There's a light upstairs."

184.26

A man obviously very drunk staggered up to a car and somehow got behind the wheel. A cop stepped up and said, "Are you going to drive that car?"

"Certainly I am," said the man behind the wheel. "I'm in no condition to walk."

184.27

It was a dark, rainy night when the policeman came upon a man down on his hands and knees pawing over the sidewalk.

"What's wrong?" asked the cop.

"I'm looking for a $10 bill I lost," replied the fellow rather thickly.

"Too bad," said the policeman. "Is this where you lost it?"

"No, it was over on Third Avenue and 49th Street," replied the searcher.

"Then why are you trying to find it here on Fifth Avenue and 49th Street?"

"Because, Officer," replied the befuddled fellow, "the light is better here."

184.28

A California woman, arrested for drunkenness, said she drank to relieve the pain of her rings, which were too tight.

184.29

A man telephoned the police that thieves had

stolen the steering wheel, the brake pedal, the clutch, and the dashboard of his car. The man was told the police would be there to investigate.

A few minutes later, the police got another call from the same man, who told them between hiccups, "It's all a mistake. I got into the back seat."

184.30

A drunk wandered aimlessly into the park one evening and stopped at the edge of a lake. He looked into the water and was astonished at the reflection of the moon in the lake. "What is that?" he asked a passing cop.

"That," said the cop, "is the moon."

"Well," said the troubled drunk, "how in hell did I get up here?"

184.31

A very drunken fellow staggered through a cemetery one night, looking for a shortcut to his home, but he fell into an open grave that had been prepared for a burial the next day. As chance would have it, another drunk came wandering through the cemetery and heard the man down in the grave call out, "Hey, up there, help me, I'm freezing!" The good-hearted drunk still above ground called back, "No wonder you're cold." And he picked up a shovel and filled up the grave.

184.32

When Fred Pabst headed the famous Milwaukee brewery bearing his name, he was proud of the beer-drinking capacity of his workers. One day some dignitaries toured the plant. Pabst pointed to a fire bucket and said, "One of our men can drink this bucket full of beer in one gulp."

The visitors were skeptical, so Pabst called in his man, a big upstanding German. The worker, when told of the challenge, excused himself for a minute, then returned, took a deep breath, and promptly swallowed the entire bucket of beer.

Later Pabst asked the worker why he had excused himself before drinking the beer.

"Oh, I wasn't sure that I could do it in one swallow, so I tried it first in the next room."

184.33

A drunk met a friend outside a distillery one evening. The drunk was, of course, drunk. His friend said, "Why don't you lay off the stuff? You'll never be able to lap up all the booze they're making in there."

"Maybe not," said the drunk, "but look—the place is all lighted up. I got them working nights!"

184.34

A drunken fellow coming by a shop asked an apprentice boy what the sign was. He answered that it was *a sign* he was drunk.

184.35

A drunk wandered into the Automat for the first time. He got a pocketful of nickels and in fascination began putting them into the slot for apple pie. As the pieces of pie stacked up on his table, the manager came over and suggested to him that maybe he had enough pie by this time. Said the drunk: "Whatdya mean quit? I can't afford to quit when I'm winning like this!"

184.36

George Cruikshank, having become a teetotlar, showed all the vehement zeal of a convert. Douglas Jerrold, meeting him shortly after his conversion, exclaimed, "Now, George, remember that water is very good anywhere—except upon the brain."

184.37

Once Boswell stated that drinking drives away care and then asked Samuel Johnson: "Wouldn't you allow a man to drink for that reason?"

"Yes," said Dr. Johnson, "if he sat next to you."

184.38

Representative James A. Garfield told about a war speech he made in 1864 to a crowd at Ashtabula, Ohio. "Gentlemen," he said, "we have taken Atlanta, we have taken Savannah, we have taken Charleston, and we are about to capture Petersburg and Richmond. What remains for us to take?"

An Irishman in the crowd called out, "Let's take a drink."

184.39

Secretary of State Evarts once was asked if drinking many different kinds of wine did not make him feel seedy the next day.

"No," he replied. "It's the indifferent wines that produce that result."

184.40

Returning home from a meeting late one evening, the minister noticed one of his congregation staggering down the street. "Let me help you to your door," the minister said. When they arrived at the fellow's house, the drunk urged the minister to come on in. "Please," he said, "just for a minute. I want the missus to see who I've been out with tonight."

184.41

Two drunks were straggling along the street. One asked the other, "What'll your wife shay for you staying out so late?"

"Haven't got a wife," mumbled the other man.

"Well, whassa idea staying out so late as this?"

184.42

"Every time I see you," said the irate wife, "you have a bottle in your pocket."

"So what?" replied her husband. "Do you expect me to have it in my mouth all the time?"

184.43

The two drunks boarded a train at London, and after a while one of them asked, "Is this Wembley?"

"No," replied the second drunk. "This is Thursday."

"I'm with you," said the first drunk. "I'm thirsty, too. Let's get off at the next station and have a drink."

184.44

Two drunks got on a bus. There was a naval officer standing near the door, and one of the drunks handed him two fares.

Scandalized, the man in blue said, "I'm a naval officer, not a conductor."

"Come on," called out the drunk to his companion, "We're on a battleship, not a bus."

184.45

A fellow in a state of total inebriation put the pommel toward his horse's tail. When it was pointed out to him, he said, "Mind your business. How do you know which way I am going?"

184.46

An elderly farmer went to the doctor and complained that he was losing his hearing. After a routine examination the doctor asked the patient if he did much drinking. "Some," said the farmer. "Things get fermenting on the farm and a man gets to drinking it—you know, prunes and grapes and other things."

"Well," said the doctor, "you'll have to cut out drinking or go stone-deaf."

Several months later, the doctor met the farmer on the street, and it was obvious that the man's hearing had become a great deal worse. After some difficulty, he got through to the farmer and asked him why he had not heeded the medical advice.

"Because," said the farmer emphatically, "the stuff I was drinkin' was so much better than the stuff I was hearin'."

184.47

A physician observing Charles Bannister, the great English actor, about to drink a glass of brandy, said: "Don't drink that filthy stuff; brandy is the worst enemy you have."

"I know that, but we are commanded by Scripture to love our enemies."

184.48

"If you drink too much, you'll hate yourself in the morning."

"OK—I'll just sleep later."

184.49

Some seasoned drinkers say: I always drink standing up, 'cause it's much easier to sit down when I get drunk standing up than it is to get standing up when I get drunk sitting down.

184.50

A Chinese visitor said, "Funny people, you Americans. You take a glass, put sugar in it to make it sweet, and lemon to make it sour. You put gin in it to warm you up, and ice to keep you cool. You say, 'Here's to you,' and then you drink it yourself."

184.51

The most perfect gentleman I ever saw: He turned his back on me—while I poured myself a drink from his own decanter.

Aphorisms

184.52

Absinthe makes the heart grow fonder.
—*Addison Mizner*

184.53

We drink to one another's health and spoil our own. —*Jerome K. Jerome*

184.54

Always remember, that I have taken more out of alcohol than alcohol has taken out of me.
—*Winston Churchill,* quoted by Quentin Reynolds, 1963

184.55

The veneer of some people is easily removed with a little alcohol.

184.56

Nothing can be more frequent than an occasional drink.
—*Ohio State Journal*

184.57

Drinking makes such fools of people, and people are such fools to begin with, that it's compounding a felony.

—*Robert Benchley*

184.58

Eat, drink and be merry, for tomorrow ye diet.

184.59

When you find you can't stand the terrible crashing of snowflakes as they hit the ground, you've had enough.

—*Gerald Barzan*

184.60

A soft drink turneth away company.

—*Oliver Herford*

184.61

There are more old drunkards than old doctors.

—*Benjamin Franklin*

184.62

Liquor talks mighty loud when it gets loose from the jug.

—*Joel Chandler Harris*

184.63

Toast: "Here's to us that are here, to you that are there, and the rest of everywhere."

—*Rudyard Kipling*

184.64

Here's to wine, the great magician, that can make a monkey out of an ass.

184.65

May the bloom of the face never extend to the nose.

184.66

There's many a toast I'd like to say,
If I could only think it;
So fill your glass to anything,
And, thank the Lord, I'll drink it!

—*Wallace Irwin*

184.67

A toast to the fellow
Who when he drinks deep
Gets royally mellow
And then falls asleep;
But not to the varlet
Who as he grows tight,
Turns noisy and scarlet
And starts in to fight.

—*W. E. S. Fales*

184.68

Here's to good old whiskey,
So amber and so clear;
'Tis not so sweet as woman's lips,
But a d——d sight more sincere.

184.69

Here's to a temperance supper
With water in glasses tall,
And coffee and tea to end with—
And me not there at all.

184.70

Here's to champagne, the drink divine,
That makes us forget our troubles;
It's made of a dollar's worth of wine
And three dollars' worth of bubbles.

184.71

Wine and women, mirth and laughter—
Sermons and aspirin on the day after.

184.72

Drink today and drown all sorrow;
You shall, perhaps, not do it tomorrow.

184.73

Drink to life and the passing show,
And the eyes of the prettiest girl you know.

184.74

If on my theme I rightly think,
There are five reasons why I drink,—
Good wine, a friend, because I'm dry,
Or lest I should be by and by,
Or any other reason why.

—*John Sirmond*

184.75

Not drunk is he, who from the floor
Can rise alone, and still drink more:
But drunk is he who prostrate lies,
Without the power to drink or rise.

—*Thomas Love Peacock*

184.76

Corn Licker: It smells like gangrene starting in a mildewed silo, it tastes like the wrath to come, and when you absorb a deep swig of it you have all the sensations of having swallowed a lighted kerosene lamp. A sudden, violent jolt of it has been known to stop the victim's watch, snap his suspenders and crack his glass eye right across.

—*Irvin S. Cobb*

184.77

The difference between chirping out of turn and a *faux pas* depends on what kind of a bar you're in.

—*Wilson Mizner*

184.78

Many a man keeps on drinking until he hasn't a coat to either his back or his stomach.

—*G. D. Prentice*

184.79

Never drink from your finger bowl—it contains only water.

—*Addison Mizner*

(*See also 26.2, 26.13, 28.20, 40.19, 40.21, 46.2, 46.3, 58.1, 60.3, 67.6, 71.5, 71.7, 79.11, 79.12, 79.44, 79.52, 84.2, 92.3, 93.23–93.25, 94.12, 95.3, 95.6, 101.6, 102.1, 115.2, 116.1, 116.4, 118.7, 118.9, 119.5, 119.26, 129.6, 133.2, 146.5, 146.6, 146.8, 148.6, 155.10, 158.29, 158.33, 160.24–160.27, 161.31, 165.19, 165.22, 165.23, 170.15, 180.1–180.7, 201.4, 201.19, 202.6, 210.8, 211.6, 211.7, 212.4, 216.7, 217.4, 226.4, 227.9, 229.5, 235.7, 235.11, 236.5, 240.1, 240.8, 240.11, 240.19, 240.23, 243.19, 244.24, 245.15, 246.7, 248.15, 251.23, 259.3, 263.11, 268.14, 271.44, 272.4, 272.12, 272.14, 276.9, 277.6*)

185. The Inhalers

Anecdotes

185.1

"Have you got a cigarette?" one man asked his friend.

"How come?" queried the friend. "The last time I talked to you, you had sworn off the weed for good."

"Well," said the first man, "I'm still in the first stage: I've quit buying them."

185.2

Phyllis Diller says there is one cigarette on the market with a filter so thick than when a smoker inhales too deeply he gets a hernia.

Aphorisms

185.3

It is now proved beyond doubt that smoking is one of the leading causes of statistics.

—*Fletcher Knebel,* 1961

185.4

Cheap cigars come in handy; they stifle the odor of cheap politicians.

—*Ulysses S. Grant*

185.5

To smoke a cigar through a mouthpiece is equivalent to kissing a lady through a respirator.

(*See also 111.20, 147.2, 155.4*)

CLOTHES HORSES AND TONGUE WAGGERS

186. Fashions

Anecdotes

186.1

A gay young woman wore a new and eccentric hat to luncheon in a smart restaurant. While dining, she noticed a woman at a nearby table wearing an exact duplicate of the hat she had just bought. Undismayed, she caught the other woman's eye, pointed to her head with a circular movement of her index finger, and smiled. The other woman immediately looked alarmed, hurried through her meal, and left rather precipitately. Later in the ladies' room, the gay young woman looked into a mirror and discovered she had not worn her new hat after all.

186.2

When the Bishop of London was taken to a fashionable ball at which the ladies' dresses were cut very low, he was asked if he had ever before seen such a sight.

"No, not since I was weaned."

186.3

The carefully protected young lady, looking for the first time at a fig tree, said: "Gracious, I surely thought the leaves would be larger than that."

186.4

A man at a nudist colony had a beard that reached to his knees and covered his front almost entirely. When asked why he was so well covered, he said that someone had to go to the store.

186.5

A farmer, returning home from a visit to the high spots in New York City, was asked what he thought of the clothes worn by the city women. He said they put him in mind of a barbed-wire fence around his farm. They appear to protect the property without obstructin' the view.

Definitions

186.6

Fashion is that by which the fantastic becomes for a moment the universal.

—*Oscar Wilde*

186.7

Fashion is gentility running away from vulgarity, and afraid of being overtaken.

—*William Hazlitt*

186.8

Jewelry: Something people use in order to make out that they're better than other people.

—*Hugh Roy Cullen*

Aphorisms

186.9

The worst way to torture the average woman is to lock her in a room with a hundred hats and no mirror.

—*John P. Medbury*

186.10

Eve ate the apple that she might dress.

186.11

As soon as Eve ate the apple of wisdom, she reached for the fig leaf; when a woman begins to think, her first thought is of a new dress.

—*Heinrich Heine*

186.12

Women wear evening gowns so that they will be seen in all the best places.

186.13

Miss Tawny Apples is confined t' her home by a swollen dresser drawer.

—*Kin Hubbard*

186.14

She looked as if she had been poured into her clothes and had forgotten to say "when."

—*P. G. Wodehouse*

186.15

She wears her clothes as if they were thrown on her with a pitchfork.

—*Jonathan Swift*

186.16

Women's styles may change, but their designs remain the same.

—*Oscar Wilde*

186.17

Ask a woman to a tea-party in the Garden of Eden, and she would draw up her eyelids and scream, "I can't go without a new gown."

—*Douglas Jerrold*

186.18

It is an interesting question how far men would retain their relative rank if they were divested of their clothes.

—*Henry David Thoreau*

186.19

Old lace is one of those graceful perquisites of her sex whereby the mate of man has made herself something different from the mate of the gorilla.

—*Henry Arthur Jones*

186.20

We smile at the women who are eagerly following the fashions in dress whilst we are as eagerly following the fashions in thought.

—*Austin O'Malley*

(*See also 13.10, 13.16, 24.8, 32.6, 42.16, 79.30, 113.7, 123.2, 165.43, 165.98, 165.102, 166.7, 177.14, 243.15, 263.1, 265.12, 265.13, 269.69, 271.47, 272.26*)

187. Gossips and Scandalmongers

Anecdotes

187.1

"Everyone is talking about the Smith's quarrel," said his wife. "Some are taking his part and others are taking her part."

"And," replied the husband, "I suppose a few eccentrics are minding their own business."

187.2

For twenty minutes three women tore apart a mutual acquaintance, until finally one of them said, "I tell you she's a menace. You don't know her like I do."

"Oh, yes, I do," countered another. "I know her every bit as well as you do."

"Nonsense," snapped back the first woman. "You couldn't possibly know her as well as I do. I'm her best friend."

187.3

"As you know," she said, "I never say anything about a person unless it is good. But, oh boy, is this good!"

Definitions

187.4

Scandal is what one half of the world takes pleasure in hearing, and the other half in believing.

—*Horace Smith,* The Tin Trumpet

187.5

A secret is something you tell to one person at a time.

187.6

Gossip is the art of saying nothing in a way that leaves practically nothing unsaid.

—*Walter Winchell*

187.7

Scandal: Something that has to be bad to be good.

Aphorisms

187.8

A gossip puts two and two together and gets whee!

—Francis Rodman

187.9

The things most people want to know about are usually none of their business.

—George Bernard Shaw

187.10

The difference between conversation and gossip: Three women talking is conversation. When one woman leaves, the two remaining are gossiping.

187.11

When it comes to spreading gossip, the female of the species is much faster than the mail.

187.12

When a woman says, "I don't wish to mention any names," it ain't necessary.

—Kin Hubbard

187.13

What people say behind your back is your standing in the community.

—E. W. Howe

187.14

Half the world does not know how the other half lives, but is trying to find out.

—E. W. Howe

187.15

It's easy for folks to make monkeys of themselves just by carrying tales.

—T. Harry Thompson

187.16

If we all said to people's faces what we say behind each other's backs, society would be impossible.

—Honoré de Balzac

187.17

There is only one thing worse than being talked about, and that is not being talked about.

—Oscar Wilde

187.18

Some people believe everything you tell them —if you whisper it.

187.19

Scandal has ever been the doom of beauty.

—Propertius

187.20

There isn't much to be seen in a little town, but what you hear makes up for it.

—Kin Hubbard

187.21

Gossip is always a personal confession either of malice or imbecility.

—J. G. Holland

187.22

A word once sent abroad, flies irrevocably.

—Horace

(*See also 11.6, 31.3, 142.20, 154.19, 159.16, 168.6, 168.7, 178.4, 193.24, 223.8, 236.4, 236.5, 236.9, 254.5, 255.12, 268.40, 268.43, 268.105, 268.117, 270.18*)

FAMILIES AND FRIENDS

KITH AND KIN

188. Maternity and Paternity

Anecdotes

188.1

Mrs. Bearwell was being congratulated upon the birth of her sixth child but did not seem too enthusiastic. "Why, Mrs. Bearwell," said her friend, "I do declare you seem almost morose over your new baby."

"Oh, it's not the baby; she's a dear," said the mother. "It's just that I will have to stay in that damn PTA much longer than I thought."

188.2

A doctor, called to examine the wife of a deaf mountaineer, said to the husband when he was leaving: "Your wife is pregnant."

"What?" said the mountaineer.

"Your wife is pregnant," shouted the doctor, and again screamed, "She is going to have a baby."

The mountaineer took a pinch of snuff, walked to the edge of the yard, and said to the doctor, "I ain't surprised. She's had every opportunity."

188.3

The young couple, anticipating a baby, promised the wife's mother she would be phoned the news immediately. Twins were born and the husband called his mother-in-law, telling her, "We have twins!" But it was a faulty connection and she did not hear him well. Louder he called, "We have twins!" Still she could not hear. "Could you repeat it?" she said. "I doubt it," the husband said. "In fact, I'm surprised we had twins the first time."

188.4

A woman who had just given birth to triplets was explaining to a friend that triplets happened only once in 15,000 times. "My Lord, how did you find time to do your housework?" asked her friend.

188.5

The proud father of triplets wrote President Theodore Roosevelt and told him the good news, knowing that T. R. was an advocate of large families. Roosevelt sent the man a loving cup.

The father then wrote a letter of thanks to the President, and asked if the cup was his outright—or did he have to win it three times to gain permanent possession.

188.6

A super-cautious mother always wore a gauze mask when coming near her baby and insisted that all visitors do likewise. Several older and wiser women tried to tell her tactfully that she was carrying things too far, but the young mother insisted that most parents were absolutely criminal in their carelessness about a child's health.

Then the mother mentioned that she thought the baby was beginning to cut a tooth and she wished she could find out about it in some way. A friend with more experience said, "Why, just put your finger in his mouth and. . . ."

There was such a horrified expression on the mother's face that the friend quickly added, "Of course, boil your finger first."

188.7

The young mother had just returned from a walk with the baby in the nearby park and took great delight in telling her husband that so many people stopped to admire the baby and to say how much it looked like her.

"I can't believe any such nonsense," said the jealous husband. "Give me the child, and I'll go and find out for myself." Whereupon he picked up the infant, slung it over his shoulder, and strode angrily out to the park.

Presently he returned and said, "Where did you get the idea that the child looks like you? Everyone who stopped me volunteered that the child looked exactly like me."

"No wonder," said the wife. "If you'd only look what you have been doing, you'd find out you have been carrying the child upside down."

188.8

When their first child was born, a friend suggested that the new baby would no doubt bring the man and his wife closer together.

"By all means," replied the husband with emphasis. "Now we have a common enemy."

188.9

One day a loving mother called on Charles Lamb with her beautiful golden-haired baby in her arms. Holding the infant up to the famous essayist, she asked, "Mr. Lamb, how do you like babies?"

"I like 'em boiled, madam—boiled!"

188.10

A lady spoke to Douglas Jerrold one day about the beauty of an infant. In the enthusiasm of her affection she said, "Really, I cannot find words to convey to you even a faint idea of its pretty ways."

"I see," Jerrold replied, "it's a child more easily conceived than described."

188.11

The unwed mother was in the hospital nursing her illegitimate child, when the doctor entered. "Your hair is red," said the doctor, "but the child's hair is brown. What was the color of the father's hair?"

"I really don't know, Doctor," said the mother. "He didn't take off his hat."

188.12

Children have been given some strange names. For example, a Texas millionaire named Hogg, named his daughters Ima and Ura. The United States Census of 1870 recorded the children of one family named—in this sequence: Imprimis, Finis, Appendix, Addendum, Eratum. Twins have often been named Peter and Repeater, and Kate and Duplicate.

A government official in England encountered these names: Heather Heath, Ida Down, Pearl Button, Rose Budd. And somewhere in the United States there is a man named Peter Rabbit—who likes the name and has made no effort to change it. The famous D'Oyle theatrical family had a daughter named Lynn Cecilia, who always signed herself Lynn C. D'Oyle. Cyril Hicken signed himself C. Hicken.

Definitions

188.13

Parents: People who use the rhythm system of birth control.

—*Mary Flink*

188.14

Home is where you can trust the hash.

Aphorisms

188.15

The woman who gives birth to quadruplets might well be called overbearing.

188.16

An ounce of parent is worth a pound of clergy.

—*Spanish proverb*

188.17

The first art of being a parent consists in sleeping when the baby isn't looking.

188.18

Families with babies and families without babies, are so sorry for each other.

—*E. W. Howe*

188.19

The stork is a bird with many things charged against it that should be blamed on a lark.

188.20

About the only thing we have left that actually discriminates in favor of the plain people is the stork.

—*Kin Hubbard*

188.21

Here's to the stork,
A most valuable bird,
That inhabits the residential districts.
He doesn't sing tunes,
Nor yield any plumes,
But he helps out the vital statistics.

188.22

Where does the family start? It starts with a young man falling in love with a girl—no superior alternative has yet been found.

—*Winston Churchill*

188.23

Maternity is a matter of fact; paternity is always a matter of opinion.

—*J. C. Ridpath,* History of the U.S.

(*See also 20.6, 20.7, 21.3, 22.2, 30.31, 31.13, 31.15, 32.17, 37.10, 41.9, 41.10, 60.15, 97.3, 101.13, 108.4, 117.7, 119.2, 138.11, 155.17, 155.37 155.38, 156.13, 158.16, 161.4, 161.12, 168.9, 170.1, 173.1, 173.8, 175.22, 175.23, 176.6, 179.5, 182.4, 191.27, 211.34, 220.1, 220.9, 223.2, 235.22, 235.48, 243.4, 271.15, 271.19, 271.39, 272.24, 272.25, 272.27, 274.5*)

189. Mothers and Youngsters

Anecdotes

189.1

A woman got on a train with nine children. When the conductor came for her tickets, she said: "Now these three are thirteen years old and pay full fare, but those over there are only six, and those three over there are four and a half."

The conductor looked at her in astonishment and said, "Do you mean to tell me that you get three every time?"

"Oh, no," she said, "sometimes we don't get any at all."

189.2

A man walking across the street was almost run down by a car driven by a woman—the car overflowing with children. The red light was against the woman, and the man who had almost been hit walked over to the ancient bus and said, "Lady, don't you know when to stop?"

Glancing back at the many children in the car, she said icily, "They aren't all mine."

189.3

These are Mamma's Scissors. They do not Seem to be in good Health. Well, they are a little Aged. They have considerable Work to Do. Mamma uses them to Chop Kindling, cut Stove Pipe, pull Tacks, drive Nails, cut the children's Hair, punch new Holes in the Calendar, slice Bar soap, pound beef Steak, open tomato Cans, shear the Newfoundland dog and cut out her New silk Dress. Why doesn't Papa get Mamma a new Pair of Scissors? You should not Ask such a Naughty question. Papa cannot Afford to play Billiards and Indulge his Extravagant Family in the Luxuries of Life.

—*Eugene Field,* 1882

189.4

The two women met for the first time in some years and immediately began to catch up on what had happened to each other. "So you're married and have kids!" exclaimed one. "Tell me about them."

"Well," replied the other woman, "David, Robert, and Adolph all went to college and got their degrees. David is a dentist, Robert is a lawyer, and Adolph is an architect. And then there's Ronald."

"What does Ronald do?"

"Ronald—he's been a disappointment. He never went to college. He's a furrier. And confidentially, if it wasn't for his business, we'd all have starved to death."

189.5

"I notice that Jimmy got a very poor mark in history," said the father severely.

"Oh, now, George," protested the mother, "don't take it out on the poor child. They keep asking him about things that happened long before he was born."

189.6

"Oh, Mother, a car as big as a barn has just passed."

"Johnny, why do you exaggerate so? I have told you a million times about this habit of yours, and it doesn't do a bit of good."

189.7

"You must have heard," said the proud mother, "that my daughter is an accomplished linguist."

"Is she good in German?"

"Practically perfect!"

"What about her Italian?"

"Not even a Roman would suspect she was not a Roman."

"Does she do well in Spanish?"

"Oh, Spanish is no problem at all for her."

"Can she also talk Esperanto?"

"Esperanto! Why she speaks it like a native!"

189.8

The little boy came home from his first day at school and announced to his mother he was not returning the next day.

"Why not, dear?" asked the mother.

"Because," said the youngster, "I can't read, I can't write, the teacher won't let me talk—so what's the use?"

Aphorisms

189.9

Peter De Vries states a mother's role is to deliver children—obstetrically once, and by car forever after.

189.10

Mothers can't flare up like a hired girl.
—*Kin Hubbard*

189.11

The best time to put the children to bed is while you still have the energy.

189.12

The joys of motherhood are not experienced until all the kids are in bed.

(*See also 111.11, 174.8–174.10, 175.2, 175.3, 175.6, 175.8, 175.11, 175.12, 175.15–175.19, 176.7, 182.1, 188.1, 188.6–188.10, 190.8, 273.2*)

190. Proud Fathers

Anecdotes

190.1

An electronic computer was programmed to predict a young man's future. At a demonstration they picked a bright boy from the audience and asked him and his father to tell all about the boy's past. Then buttons were pushed, lights flashed on and off, bells rang, and finally the machine said, "This boy will graduate from M.I.T., and within six months he will have made $10,000. A year later he will have increased his liquid assets to $50,000, and he will have an executive post paying him $69,000 annually. But nine months later he will be jobless, broke, and have debts totalling $8,500."

The father of the boy listened first in amazement, then in excitement and admiration. But when the machine's final verdict was pronounced, the old man's shoulders sagged; he turned on the boy, grabbed him, and screamed, "What happened, you young fool? Can't you hold a job and save your money?"

190.2

Two men who had not seen one another in some time were lunching together and immediately began to exchange news of their respective activities. When the conversation began to lag along about dessert, one of the men, with just a bit too much eagerness, said: "By the way, I don't believe I have ever told you about my son—or have I?"

"No, you haven't," was the quiet reply, "and I appreciate it very much."

190.3

A farm family supplemented their income with a roadside cider stand, with the help of the little boy of the family. One day a woman tourist stopped and asked the little boy if he liked cider. He said he did. The woman thereupon ordered an extra glass of cider and told the youngster to drink it. He thanked her, but explained that the family had their own cider in the house. "This cider," said the boy pointing to the glasses on the roadside table, "is from wormy apples—the stuff in the house is from better apples." The woman dropped her glass of cider and made a quick departure.

The boy's father and mother stood by speechless during this conversation. But no sooner was the tourist out of sight than the father grabbed his son and whaled the daylights out of the kid—or at least until grandmother came rushing from the house to protect the lad.

The grandmother lit into her son for whipping the boy because he told the truth. "You're whipping him because he isn't a liar," she said.

" 'Taint so, Mamma," said the father. "I want the boy to be honest, and if he had said that the cider ain't made of wormy apples, then I'd a whipped him too—I'd lick him for lyin'."

"Don't make sense to me," said the grandmother. "Here you whip him for sayin' the cider is made from wormy apples, and now you say you'd whip him if he said the cider warn't made from wormy apples. What are you trin't to larn him, anyhow?"

"I'm simply tryin' to learn that boy to keep his mouth shut," said the father.

190.4

The farmer asked his young son if he was the one who had pushed over a neighbor's outhouse when it was in use. The boy admitted that he did it, whereupon the father gave him a good thrashing.

When the young boy had recovered he turned to his father and said, "You told me about George Washington and how he never told a lie, even about the cherry tree. And when I tell you the truth, you whip me."

"True," said the father, "but there was no one in the cherry tree when George Washington chopped it down."

190.5

"I'm ashamed of you," said a father to his indolent young son. "You've been talking about George Washington, and yet when he was your age he was a surveyor working hard in the wilderness."

"Yeah," said the son, "and when Washington was your age he had already won the American Revolution and was President of the United States."

190.6

Son: "Dad, Mom just backed the car out of the driveway and ran over my bicycle."

"Serves you right for leaving it on the front lawn."

190.7

It was Christmas Eve. Father sneaked out the back door just when the children were getting into bed and fired off both barrels of a double-barreled shotgun. He then rushed into the house and in great anguish told his five small children that Santa Claus had just committed suicide.

190.8

"Has your son's education proved of value?"

"Yes," replied the father. "It has cured his mother of bragging about him."

190.9

"My son has made astonishing progress," said the proud parent. "Why just five years ago he was wearing my old suits. Now I'm wearing his."

190.10

"Who is more satisfied, a man with a million dollars or a man with seven children?" asked the sociology professor.

"The man with the seven children," answered one student.

"Why?"

"Because the man with seven children doesn't want any more."

190.11

"Mike, with all those five boys of yours, you must have had considerable trouble," said a friend.

"Never a speck of trouble," said Mike emphatically. "The only time I've ever laid a hand on them was in self-defense."

190.12

A stout man went in search of his vagrant puppy and finally heard it whining. He traced the sound to a no-longer-used conduit in the woods, but the frightened animal either could not or would not leave his hiding place.

The man decided to go after his little dog and forced his bulky figure into the conduit but then found himself so tightly wedged that he could no longer move forward or backward. He realized he could die in this situation, and the thought of it terrified him.

Then he began to think of his family and how improvident he had been and how little money he had put aside for his wife and children. The more he thought about this the more the family's welfare worried him, and the more he worried the more he perspired. Finally, after hours and hours of extreme worry and great perspiration, he had lost so much weight that he was able to crawl out of the conduit—a man now full of good resolutions.

190.13

"Doc," said the old Kentucky mountaineer, "I want you to fix up my son-in-law. I shot him in the leg yesterday."

"You ought to be ashamed of yourself, shooting your son-in-law," said the doctor.

"Wal, Doc," said the old man, "he warn't my son-in-law when I shot him."

190.14

A salesman waiting for a train was approached by a stranger who asked him the time. The salesman ignored the question. The fellow asked again. Still the salesman ignored him, and the questioner finally walked away. Another salesman nearby asked the first salesman why he acted like that when he had a watch with him.

"Listen," said the first salesman, "I'm standing here minding my own business. This guy wants to know what time it is. So maybe I tell him. We get talking, and this guy says, 'How about a drink?' So we have a drink. And then we have more drinks. Finally I say, 'Come on out to my house for a bite to eat.' And at my house we're eating sandwiches when my twenty-one-year-old daughter comes in. She is very pretty and sweet. So she falls for this guy and he falls for her. Then they get married. So I have in my family a guy who cannot afford a watch. No! I don't want him in my family."

Definition

190.15

Father: A man whose daughter marries a man vastly her inferior mentally but then gives birth to unbelievably brilliant grandchildren.

Aphorisms

190.16

No man believes genius is hereditary until he has a son.

190.17

A man can say what he pleases in his home because no one pays any attention to him.

190.18

The average household consists of a husband who makes the money, and a wife and kids who make it necessary.

190.19

Don't take up a man's time talking about the smartness of your children; he wants to talk to you about the smartness of his children.

—*E. W. Howe*

(*See also 20.3, 27.4, 122.1, 123.2, 123.9, 175.1, 175.10, 175.14, 175.20–175.22, 176.1, 176.3, 176.4, 178.17, 188.5, 191.2, 191.4, 191.9, 191.33, 202.10, 204.7, 225.8, 245.20, 274.9, 275.4*)

191. Teen Time

Anecdotes

191.1

During a family council, the oldest son was told that they were not at all well disposed toward the girl he was going with.

"Well," said the young man, "it's the best I can do with the kind of car we have."

191.2

It is a strange but mathematical fact that when a 17-year-old boy borrows the family car, he can, in one night, subtract five years from the life of the car and add them to the age of his father.

—*Bett Anderson,* McCall's

191.3

A teen-age boy, chiefly interested in botany and other aspects of nature, was prevailed upon by his parents to take a certain girl to a big party. He was not particularly fond of girls and he was disturbed when reminded that he would be expected to draw on his savings for the girl's corsage. Finally he told his mother he had solved that problem painlessly. "How are you going to do that?" asked his mother.

"I am going to give her some sunflower seeds I gathered last fall and tell her it is a do-it-yourself bouquet."

191.4

"When I was your age," said father to son, "I was working twelve hours a day, with half an hour for lunch, six days a week—and believe me, I loved it and worked hard every minute."

"Please," said the son to his father, "be more discreet in voicing your antilabor, union-baiting sentiments; they are liable to injure us socially."

191.5

"You're getting to be a big boy now, Johnny,

and it's time your father and I discussed the facts of life frankly with you."

"OK, Mom. Whatever you and Pop want to know, I'll tell you."

191.6

A girl in her early teens insisted to her deeply religious Catholic parents that she should have a permanent wave.

"I'm certain," said the mother, "that the blessed Virgin Mary would not have been interested in a permanent wave."

"Maybe not," said the subdeb. "And I'll bet you that St. Joseph didn't drive a Cadillac, either."

191.7

When the farmer's daughter returned from college for vacation, the father eyed her critically and asked, "Ain't you lots fatter than before you went to college?"

"Yes, father," admitted the girl. "I weigh 140 pounds stripped for gym."

"What!" exclaimed the horrified parent. "Who is this man Jim?"

191.8

The teen-age girl called on her stately grandmother, a woman who clung to formal and absolutely pure English, and she chattered gaily to the old lady.

"Child," said the grandmother, "I am not fond of correcting you, but really you must change your vocabulary. There are two words you use continually. One is 'swell' and the other is 'lousy.' "

"Oh, Grandma," said the debutante, "please tell me: What are these two words?"

191.9

"I fail to see the practical value of all this emphasis on grammar," protested the student to his teacher.

"Well," said the teacher, "it can be very important on occasion. For example, my neighbor and his son were putting a post in a hole; the father told the son, 'When I nod my head you hit it with the hammer.' And that is precisely what the son did—bashed in the father's head with the hammer."

191.10

Shortly after the opening of the September term of a midwestern high school, the second year English teacher requested each student to write a 1,000-word story on HOW I SPENT MY SUMMER VACATION.

One of the accounts submitted by a pupil ran somewhat like this: "Shortly after school closed in June I left for Wisconsin, to spend the summer at my uncle's home on Lake Michigan. My uncle has a motorboat. I spent most of my time on the lake in the motorboat. And whenever I was in the boat its motor went putt-putt-putt-putt-putt"—from this point to the end of the 1,000 words, the daring and imaginative young author continued with his description of the sound of the boat's motor—"putt-putt-putt-putt-putt."

Several days after all the student papers were turned in, the teacher said to the class: "I have gone over all the vacation accounts and some of them are quite good. But there is one that is most unusual, so unusual, in fact, that I believe it should be read to the class by its author. John Jones, will you please step up to the front of the class and read aloud your account of your visit to your uncle's home on the lake in Wisconsin—*and I want you to read every word of it.*"

191.11

"Well, son," asked the father, "how are your marks at school?"

"Underwater," said the kid.

"And what do you mean by that?"

"Well, they are all below C-level."

191.12

"I am only nineteen and I stayed out till two the other night. My mother objects. Did I do wrong?" was the question raised in a newspaper correspondence column.

"Try to remember," was the reply.

191.13

"Youth is the most wonderful thing in the world," exulted a progressive education propagandist to George Bernard Shaw.

"Yes," said Shaw. "It's a pity to waste it on the young."

Definitions

191.14

Adolescence: The period in which the young suddenly feel a great responsibility about answering the telephone.

191.15

Adolescence: The period when children are certain they will never be as dumb as their parents.

191.16

Adolescence: Teenage is when youngsters aren't bright enough to realize their parents couldn't be that stupid.

—*Town Journal*

Aphorisms

191.17

A lad is a Boy Scout until the age of fifteen. After that he is a girl scout.

191.18

Nobody is quite so blasé and sophisticated as a boy of nineteen who is just recovering from a baby-grand passion.

—*Helen Rowland*

191.19

If Alexander Graham Bell had had a teenage daughter, he never would have had a chance to test the telephone.

—*The Spokesman,* Van Buren, Me.

191.20

When I was a boy of fourteen my father was so ignorant I could hardly stand to have the old man around. But when I got to be twenty-one I was astonished how much the old man had learned in those seven years.

—*Mark Twain*

191.21

In America, the young are always ready to give to those who are older than themselves the full benefits of their inexperience.

—*Oscar Wilde*

191.22

Children begin by loving their parents; as they grow older they judge them; sometimes they forgive them.

—*Oscar Wilde*

191.23

I am not young enough to know everything.

—*James M. Barrie*

191.24

When your children get old enough so that you can stand them, they can't stand you.

191.25

A chip off the old block is often a blockhead.

191.26

Louis Hershey, draft director, several years ago said that a boy becomes an adult three years before his parents think he does and about two years after he thinks he does.

191.27

A girl should be given an allowance every week, if it is not more than fifty cents. It will teach her how to handle the great sums intrusted to her when she marries.

—*E. W. Howe*

191.28

The youth of America is their oldest tradition; it has been going on now for three hundred years.

—*Oscar Wilde*

191.29

By the time the youngest children have learned to keep the place tidy, the oldest grandchildren are on hand to tear it to pieces again.

—*Christopher Morley*

191.30

It's a wise child that owes his own father.

—*Carolyn Wells*

191.31

Young man, sit down and keep still; you will have plenty of chances to make a fool of yourself before you die.

—*Josh Billings*

191.32

A youth with his first cigar makes himself sick; a youth with his first girl makes other people sick.

—*Mary Wilson Little*

191.33

The worst misfortune that can happen to an ordinary man is to have an extraordinary father.

—*Austin O'Malley*

(*See also 25.26, 54.18, 123.1–123.11, 145.2, 145.3, 154.4, 154.54, 157.21, 159.1, 159.3, 159.5, 159.10, 159.11, 159.13, 160.3, 175.11, 175.35, 190.9, 202.10, 203.8, 227.7, 242.9, 245.20, 263.19, 269.4*)

192. Relatives

Anecdote

192.1

When Grandmother arrived uninvited and unexpected at a young couple's home, she said she was going to be with them only one week, but her visit stretched into five weeks, with no sign of departure. The couple decided something had to be done to compel her departure with a minimum of offense. Therefore they agreed to simulate a quarrel and force the old lady to take sides. If she took the granddaughter's side, then the girl would tell the woman the next day that she must leave in order to avoid further conflict with the husband. And if Grandmother took the husband's part in the argument, the husband would say pretty much the same.

But when the couple got into a pretended bitter argument over a mere triviality, and began to shout abusive names at each other and generally act as though long-smoldering hatreds had exploded, the grandmother just sat there quietly. When the husband turned to the elderly woman and tried to draw her into taking sides, she calmly said: "I'm not getting into this. I am going to stay here another three weeks."

Aphorisms

192.2

Speaking of trade relations, almost everyone would like to.

—*Wall Street Journal*

192.3

The hardest thing is to disguise your feelings when you put a lot of relatives on the train for home.

—*Kin Hubbard*

192.4

If the knocking at the door is unusually long and loud, don't think it is opportunity. It is relatives.

192.5

Every baby resembles the relative with the most money.

—*James S. Hastings*

192.6

If a man's character is to be abused, there's nobody like a relative to do the business.

—*William Makepeace Thackeray*

192.7

We all like our relatives when we're little.

—*Kin Hubbard*

192.8

We call our rich relatives the kin we love to touch.

—*Eddie Cantor*

(*See also 19.27, 25.19, 32.1, 42.20, 264.6, 265.19*)

193. Friends and Neighbors

Anecdotes

193.1

Anacharsis, coming to Athens, knocked at Solon's door, and told him that he, being a stranger, was come to be his guest, and contract a friendship with him; and Solon replying, "It is better to make friends at home," Anacharsis replied, "Then you that are at home make friendship with me."

Solon, somewhat surprised at the readiness of the repartee, received him kindly, and kept him some time with him.

—*Plutarch*

193.2

A man and a satyr, having struck up an acquaintance, sat down together to eat. The day being wintry and cold, the man put his fingers to his mouth and blew upon them.

"What's that for, my friend?" asked the satyr.

"My hands are so cold," said the man. "I do it to warm them."

In a little while some hot food was placed before them, and the man, raising the dish to his mouth, again blew upon it.

"And what's the meaning of that?" said the satyr.

"Oh," replied the man, "my porridge is so hot, I do it to cool it."

"Nay, then," said the satyr, "from now on I renounce your friendship, for I will have nothing to do with one who blows hot and cold with the same mouth."

—*Aesop*

193.3

Rosenbaum met his old friend Levy, and said to him, "Levy, during all the years I have known you, you never ask me how things are with me."

"All right," said Levy, "I'll ask now: How are things with you, Rosenbaum?"

"Don't ask!" cried Rosenbaum.

193.4

Two friends were traveling on the same road together when they met with a bear. The one in great fear, without a thought of his companion, climbed up into a tree and hid himself. The other, seeing that he had no chance single-handed against the bear, had nothing left but to throw himself on the ground and feign to be dead; for he had heard that a bear will never touch a dead body. As he thus lay, the bear came up to his head, muzzling and sniffing at his nose, ears, and heart, but the man held his breath, and the beast, supposing him to be dead, walked away. When the bear was fairly out of his sight his companion came down from the tree and asked what it was that the bear had whispered to him. "For," says he, "I observed he put his mouth very close to your ear."

"Why," replied the other, "it was no great secret; he only bade me have a care how I kept company with those who, when they get into a difficulty, leave their friends in the lurch."

—*Aesop*

193.5

Speaking of George Bernard Shaw, Oscar Wilde said, "An excellent man! He has no enemies; and none of his friends like him."

Definitions

193.6

A friend is one who dislikes the same people that you dislike.

193.7

Back: That part of your friend which it is your privilege to contemplate in your adversity.

—*Ambrose Bierce*

193.8

Acquaintance: A person whom we know well enough to borrow from, but not well enough to lend to. A degree of friendship called slight when its object is poor or obscure, and intimate when he is rich or famous.

—*Ambrose Bierce*

193.9

Neighbor: One whom we are commanded to love as ourselves, and who does all he knows how to make us disobedient.

—*Ambrose Bierce*

193.10

A good neighbor is a fellow who smiles at you over the back fence but doesn't climb over it.

—*Arthur "Bugs" Baer*

Aphorisms

193.11

A friend that ain't in need is a friend indeed.

—*Kin Hubbard*

193.12

A friend in need is a friend to keep away from.

—*Benjamin Franklin*

193.13

The holy passion of friendship is of so sweet and steady and loyal and enduring a nature that it will last through a whole lifetime, if not asked to lend money.

—*Mark Twain*

193.14

Every man should have a fair-sized cemetery in which to bury the faults of his friends.

—*Henry Ward Beecher*

193.15

Anyone can sympathize with the sufferings of a friend, but it requires a very fine nature to sympathize with a friend's success.

—*Oscar Wilde*

193.16

Here's champagne to our real friends, and real pain to our sham friends.

193.17

To the friend who never had a hole in his pocket.

193.18

Neighbors ought to swap kids. Everybody knows what ought to be done with everyone else's.

—*The Scuttlebutt,* Skokie, Ill.

193.19

No one is rich enough to do without a neighbor.

—*Danish proverb*

193.20

If you want to annoy your neighbors, tell the truth about them.

—*Pietro Aretino*

193.21

The only thing more disturbing than a neighbor with a noisy old car is one with a quiet new one.

—*The South Wind*

193.22

Friends: people who borrow my books and set wet glasses on them.

—*E. A. Robinson*

193.23

A home-made friend wears longer than one you buy in the market-place.

—*Austin O'Malley*

193.24

We should thank God that He did not give us the power of hearing through walls; otherwise there would be no such thing as friendship.

—*Austin O'Malley*

193.25

A real friend is one who walks in when the rest of the world walks out.

—*Walter Winchell*

193.26

Never trust a friend who deserts you at a pinch.

—*Aesop*

193.27

Friend: One who knows all about you and loves you just the same.

—*Elbert Hubbard*

193.28

Most people repent of their sins by thanking God they ain't so wicked as their neighbors.

—*Josh Billings*

193.29

Love your neighbor, yet don't pull down your hedge.

—*Benjamin Franklin*

193.30

Some men are like a clock on the roof; they are useful only to the neighbors.

—*Austin O'Malley*

(*See also 11.9, 19.70, 25.35, 25.37, 30.9, 30.11, 30.38, 30.46, 46.1, 47.1, 55.5, 57.7, 57.18, 89.8, 106.21, 159.15, 159.16, 159.26, 160.9, 165.47, 168.8, 187.2, 195.6, 210.7, 269.9, 270.9, 276.3*)

SUBURBIA AND EXURBIA

COMMUTERS AND URBANITES

194. En Route

Anecdotes

194.1

"Now that you're living in the suburbs, what do you miss most?"

"The last train home," replied the commuter.

194.2

"Did you miss the train?"

"No," said the frustrated commuter, "I simply didn't like its looks so I chased it out of the station."

194.3

New York *World-Telegram* columnist Norton Mockridge reports that a little old lady in a New York subway train was coughing and sneezing to an alarming degree. Finally the man seated next to her said, "Why don't you stay home?"

"Because," gasped the poor soul, "I have my business to take care of."

"Then, madam," said the irascible man, "I suggest you commute by ambulance."

194.4

The gabby little fellow squatted down in the commuter train and began to talk to the rather austere man seated next to him. Finally, after several leading questions, the chatty little man said, "Oh, you work for Mr. Astorbilt?"

"Certainly not," snapped the cold man with the English accent. "Mr. Astorbilt works for me. He leaves the house every morning at 7:15 and goes to that dreary, soot-ridden city and slaves there all day to make enough money to pay me my salary as his butler."

194.5

A commuter dashed on to the ferry slip and leaped over the water to the deck of the boat.

"Just made it!" he gasped.

"Why didn't you wait," asked a deckhand. "We were just pulling into the slip."

194.6

Morgan partner Dwight W. Morrow boarded his usual train at Englewood, New Jersey, and fumbled for his ticket. "That's OK, Mr. Morrow," said the conductor. "You can give me the ticket tomorrow."

"That is not troubling me so much as that I don't know where I am going," said the absentminded Mr. Morrow.

194.7

Two elderly women on a commuters' train, going to town for a shopping spree, got into a nasty argument about the window: one insisted it be open or she would suffocate; the other demanded it be closed so she would not catch a cold. The conductor was asked to settle the noisy dispute.

A commuter nearby called over to the conductor, saying: "Open the window first, and let one of them catch cold and die. Then close it and let the other one suffocate to death."

Definition

194.8

A commuter is one who has a complaint of long-standing.

(*See also* 75.3)

195. At Home

Anecdotes

195.1

A family recently transplanted from the city to suburbia discovered a skunk had taken residence in their cellar. At a family council it was decided that a trail of bread crumbs from cellar to the backyard would persuade the skunk to make a non-odorous exit. But the next day they found the bread crumbs had simply attracted another skunk to the cellar.

195.2

An English visitor to the United States spent some time with friends in Ridgewood, New Jersey. Just before ending his week's stay, he told his hostess that the people in the town seemed to him unusually religious, particularly the women.

The hostess was puzzled, and asked why he thought so.

"Well, I notice," said the visitor, "that when the wives drive their husbands to the railroad station every morning they almost invariably cross themselves. Or is it perhaps that the railroad isn't safe?"

"Oh," laughed the hostess, "the wives are simply reminding their husbands about things they might have forgotten—they are gesturing to tie, fly, handkerchief, and wallet."

195.3

A waggish father wanted to illustrate to his son the difference between "anger" and "exasperation." He looked up the phone number of a pompous fellow commuter whom he knew only by name and reputation, and he dialed the number. When the call was answered by the man, the father asked, "Is Adolph there?" "There's no Adolph here. Why don't you get the right number before bothering people this hour of the night?" roared the man on the other end.

"Now that," said the father when he put down the phone, "was simply annoyance. We'll wait a few minutes, and then you'll hear something." After a decent interval, the father dialed the same number and again asked, "Is Adolph there?" This time the other party literally screamed into the phone, "What's the matter with you, are you crazy? I told you to look up the number and stop bothering me!" Whereupon the receiver at the other end was slammed down. "Now that fellow was angry," said the father. "In a few minutes I will show you what I mean by exasperation compared to anger."

After fifteen minutes or so, the father dialed the same number for the third time, and when the same man answered at the other end, the father said almost cheerily, "Hello, this is Adolph. Have there been any messages for me during the past half-hour or so?"

195.4

It was 2 A.M. when the phone rang and the sleep-drenched suburbanite got up to answer it.

"Is this number 33-333?"

"No, it is not."

"Oh, I'm sorry to have bothered you at such an hour."

"It's all right," said the suburbanite, "I had to get up to answer the phone anyway."

195.5

The family had just moved to the suburbs and looked forward to their first picnic. They found an ideal expanse of green with patches of trees, spread their picnic gear and food out, and sat down for their meal, meanwhile wondering what was the meaning of the little flags they saw in the distance. Finally a man came up to them and angrily ordered them to move along in a hurry, reminding them they were on the thirteenth green of one of the swankiest golf clubs in the state.

The father of the family swallowed hard in bewilderment and anger, finally turning on their tormentor with: "Mister, this is a pretty stupid way to act if you ever expect to get new members."

195.6

When a suburban husband asked his wife why they never had any money, she said: "It's the neighbors, dear. They're always doing something we can't afford."

—*Walter Winchell*

196. House and Garden

Anecdotes

196.1

"Do you understand this building and loan plan of payments on the house you are buying."

"Yes," said the new homeowner. "By the time we are thoroughly unhappy with the place and it is beginning to fall apart we will have completed the payments."

196.2

As soon as their new home in suburbia was completed, the family hurriedly moved in and employed a local man to lay wall-to-wall carpeting in the living room. When the fellow had completed his work, he noticed a lump in the middle of the carpeting. He felt in his shirt pocket for his cigarettes; they were not there. Concluding the pack of cigarettes had fallen from his pocket and under the rug, the man pressed down and smoothed out the lump with his foot.

When he reached his truck, the carpet layer was surprised to find he had left his cigarettes on the car seat. And he was even more startled when the lady of the house called to him, "Have you seen anything of my parakeet?"

196.3

When a big-city fellow became suddenly and wondrously rich, he and his family could not get to suburbia fast enough and, without thinking twice of the cost bought a sumptuous home on extensive acreage and promptly added the latest improvements and status symbols.

In showing friends over his place, the master of the estate was asked why he had three swimming pools built on the grounds. "To accommodate all my guests; one pool for those who like warm water, another for those who like to swim in cold water, and a third pool that is kept empty for those who don't swim."

196.4

"You have a very pleasant home," said the visitor, "but I don't see how you can call it a bungalow. It is not that type of house."

"Well," said the new owners, "the job was a bungle, and we still owe for it."

196.5

A young and not particularly attractive actress who had a sudden and opulent rise on television, asked the elderly owner of a charming old farmhouse in Connecticut if he would take—and she named the amount—a very large sum for his homestead.

"No," said the old-timer, "I don't think I want to sell it to you. It's a lovely old place and I like it too much to risk your owning it. You see," he added, "you're making enough money these days to ruin the old place."

196.6

When the man and wife bought their house in the suburbs it had everything they desired in a home—space, light, view, design, stability of neighborhood, convenient location.

But after several years the couple began to find fault with their house—mostly trivial objections that they allowed to assume importance. So they decided to put their house up for sale and then carefully search for their dream house.

One day they read an advertisement describing exactly the kind of a house they wanted. They called the real estate agent and discovered it was their own house—the one they were endeavoring to sell.

196.7

A woman who was always bothering a nursery for free advice asked the proprietor one day what would be good to plant in a spot that got little rain because of overhanging eaves, got only late afternoon sun, and had poor soil.

"Madam," said the nursery man, "how about a nice flagpole?"

196.8

A suburbanite who had tried every method, device, and material to rid his lawn of dandelions, finally wrote to the Department of Agriculture and asked if there wasn't something that could be done. The Department wrote and said, "We suggest you learn to love them."

196.9

Two garment manufacturers had recently bought adjoining homes in suburbia. One day they were chatting over the back fence when one of them pointed to a lawn filled with dandelions, and asked, "What kind of flower is that?"

"Why ask me?" answered his friend. "I'm not a milliner."

196.10

An amateur gardener wrote the botany department of the State University and said she was having trouble with the scarlet sage flower, *salvia:* "I have planted saliva in front of my house but it doesn't seem to grow."

The professor replied, "Madam, I suggest you pull out the saliva and plant spitoonias instead."

196.11

"My dear," said the professor's wife, "the hens have scratched up all that eggplant seed you planted."

"Ah! jealousy," said the professor, whereupon he sat down and began to write a paper on THE DEVELOPMENT OF ENVY IN THE MINDS OF THE LOWER BIPEDS.

Definitions

196.12

Suburbia is a place where by the time you have finished paying for your home the suburbs have moved 20 miles farther out.

196.13

Arbor is one of those sweet retreats which humane men erect for the accommodation of spiders. —*Charles Dickens*

196.14

A suburbanite is a man who hires someone to cut the grass so he can play golf for the exercise.

Aphorisms

196.15

The fellow that brags about how cheap he heats his home always sees the first robin.

—*Kin Hubbard*

196.16

The fellow that owns his own home is always just coming out of a hardware store.

—*Kin Hubbard*

196.17

If you want to write something that has a chance of living on forever, sign a mortgage.

—*Rotogram,* Frederick, Maryland

196.18

A man said the only reason why his dwelling was not blown away in a late storm was because there was a heavy mortgage on it.

196.19

"It takes a colony of termites 30 years to undermine the average frame house." This is also the length of the GI mortgage. You make the last payment on the day the place collapses.

—*Bill Vaughan,* Sorry I Stirred It, 1964

196.20

A lot of suburban dwellers have discovered that trees grow on money.

—*Fred Houston,* Look

196.21

Sign on a suburban lawn: SICK LAWN; DO NOT DISTURB

196.22

What a man needs in gardening is a cast-iron back with a hinge in it.

—*Charles Dudley Warner*

(*See also 112.5, 112.11, 112.19, 120.14, 155.36, 170.4, 179.10, 179.11, 181.14, 181.17, 188.15, 191.29, 198.1–198.14, 209.2, 214.19*)

197. Architects

Anecdote

197.1

Mr. Alexander, the architect of several fine buildings in the county of Kent, was under cross-examination at Maidstone, by a lawyer who wished to detract from the weight of his testimony. "You are a builder, I believe."

"No sir; I am not a builder; I am an architect!"

"Ah, well? architect or builder, builder or architect, they are much the same, I suppose?"

"I beg your pardon, sir; I cannot admit that: I consider them to be totally different!"

"Oh, indeed! Perhaps you will state wherein this great difference consists?"

"An architect, sir, prepares the plans, conceives the design, draws out the specifications —in short, supplies the mind. The builder is merely the bricklayer or the carpenter; the builder, in fact, is the machine—the architect, the power that puts the machine together, and sets it going!"

"Oh, very well, Mr. Architect, that will do! And now, after your very ingenious distinction without a difference, perhaps you can inform the court who was the architect for the Tower of Babel?"

"There was no architect, sir, and hence the confusion!"

Aphorisms

197.2

The physician can bury his mistakes, but the architect can only advise his clients to plant vines.

—*Frank Lloyd Wright*

197.3

The only thing wrong with architecture is architects.

—*Frank Lloyd Wright*

(*See also 54.12, 219.8, 228.2, 235.21, 266.26*)

198. Agents and Subdivisions

Anecdotes

198.1

A Florida real estate salesman had just closed his first deal, but then discovered that most of the land was under water.

"That fellow will be coming back hopping mad and want his down payment returned," the salesman said to his boss.

"Money back?" roared the boss. "You're a helluva salesman even to think of it. If he comes back, sell him a boat."

198.2

A large subdivider and developer was told by his superintendent that, when the first model house was sold and the scaffolding removed, the whole house collapsed.

"How many times must I tell you," screamed the boss, "don't take away the scaffolding until the wallpaper is up!"

198.3

When Columbus's three ships dropped anchor near the coast of the New World, and small boats were put over the side and made for shore, the natives gathered to watch in wonder and apprehension. Finally one of the natives sighed and said, "Well, there goes the old neighborhood."

198.4

A prospective buyer of a home in a suburban development was being shown around one of the houses then under construction.

"Isn't this a beautiful home?" asked the salesman.

"Seems kind of flimsy to me," said the home-seeker.

"Flimsy! You call this flimsy? Wait, I'll show you."

"Hey, Sam," he called through the wall to a worker in the adjoining room.

"What you want?" called back Sam.

"Sam, step right next to the wall. Get as close to it as you can."

"OK," said Sam.

"Now, Sam, can you hear me speaking through the wall to you?" asked the salesman.

"Sure, I can," said Sam.

"But you can't see me, can you, Sam?"

"No," said Sam.

"You see," said the salesman to the prospect. "This is what I call a wall!"

198.5

The prospective tenant was looking over the house and asked the real estate salesman, "What are all those spots on the wall?"

"This was the workshop of the previous tenant. He was an inventor—dabbled with explosives."

"Oh," said the prospective tenant, "the spots must be some kind of explosive, then."

"No, they are the inventor himself," said the real estate man.

198.6

Once there was a real estate agent from Texas, who died and went to his proper reward, and when he got there the Devil was very glad to see him and asked him if he would like to inspect his quarters. The real estate man said yes. An imp of a bellboy appeared and led him down a long hall. The further they went the hotter it got, until the pitch began to ooze from the woodwork.

"Aren't we almost there?" asked the real estate man, now a bit worried.

"It's the last room," said the Devil.

After a half-hour they reached an apartment where the furniture was all of iron, and glowing red hot. Through an open door could be seen a bathtub full of bubbling pitch.

The Devil picked up a red-hot shingle nail from an ashtray and lighted his cigarette. The real estate man looked at the smoking sulfuric acid in the imp's water pitcher and wiped the sweat from his forehead. "It's a little hot, isn't it?" he said.

Smiled the Devil, "Sometimes our thermometer registers pretty high, but owing to the extreme dryness of the atmosphere 130° here is no hotter than 80° in New York."

"Seems to me," said the real estate man, "I have heard that chestnut before."

"Yes," replied Satan, "you've told it. That's why you're here."

198.7

"How does the land lie out this way?" the visitor asked the native.

"It ain't the land that lies," replied the native, "it's the real estate agents."

198.8

LUXURY HOMES EVERYONE CAN AFFORD. FOR COMPLETE DETAILS CALL REPOSSESSION DEPARTMENT.

—*Real estate ad in San Fernando Valley, California*

198.9

After the Florida real estate crash in 1926, a man sued Wilson Mizner to recover the purchase price of a barren lot, asserting that Mizner had falsely informed him that he could grow nuts on it.

"Did you tell the plaintiff that he could grow nuts on this land?" Mizner was asked. "Oh, no," replied Mizner, "I told him he could go nuts on it." The jury decided in Mizner's favor.

198.10

J. L. Russell tells about the realtor trying to sell a rocky farm in the Ozarks. He explained to the innocent customer that the flint rocks in the soil were necessary to crop productivity and that without them the land was not much good. "Stones retain moisture, prevent erosion, and contribute minerals to the soil," went on the realtor.

Just then a man began to load some rocks from the farm into a wagon. "Let's get out of here," said the salesman to his prospect. "We don't want to get involved in a court trial as witnesses. That fellow over there is stealing those rocks!"

198.11

When the real estate salesmen answered the phone, a gentle female voice asked: "Do you sell maternity clothes?"

"No, madam," replied the salesman, "but couldn't we interest you in a larger house?"

198.12

"You must also remember," said the real estate salesman, "that the death rate in this community is the lowest in the state."

"I can believe that," said the potential buyer. "I wouldn't want to be found dead here myself."

198.13

A real estate man asked a woman if he could interest her in buying a home. "No," she said, "what do I need a home for? I was born in a hospital, educated in college, courted in an automobile, and married in a church. I live out of tin cans, cellophane bags, and delicatessen stores. I spend my mornings at the hairdresser's or at the golf course, my afternoons at the bridge table, my evenings at shows and movies. When I die, I'm gonna be buried from the undertaker's. I don't need a home—all I need is a garage."

198.14

"Well, sir," said the real estate man to the old Negro who had just paid the last installment on a farm, "I'll make you a deed to the farm that it's been paid for."

"Mister," said the old farmer, "if it's all the same with you, just give me the mortgage on the place."

The surprised real estate man protested that the old farmer did not understand the difference between a mortgage and a deed.

"Maybe not," said the farmer, "but I owned a farm once and I had a deed, and the First National Bank had a mortgage, and the bank got the farm!"

(*See also 114.7, 196.1–196.22, 199.1–199.12, 213.7, 219.14*)

199. Landlord and Tenant

Anecdotes

199.1

The wolf stopped in when he saw the sign APARTMENT TO RENT. A gorgeous young woman came to the door. The man took one look and said, "Are you, also, to be let with this apartment?"

"Yes," she said with the trace of a smile, "I'm to be let alone."

199.2

A tenant complained to the landlord, "My apartment is full of water."

"At your rent what do you expect—champagne?"

199.3

When the tenant of a New York apartment complained that no water came through the faucet in the bathtub, the landlord said for a 10 percent increase in the rent he would move the bathtub to beneath a hole in the roof.

199.4

During the depression when the Empire State Building was first opened, they had trouble filling it up in the beginning. One day Al Smith was showing King Prajadhibok of Siam around.

"Reminds me of home," said the King at one stage of the inspection.

"Why?" asked Smith in surprise. "You haven't anything like this in Siam."

"Oh, yes," the king replied. "We have white elephants, too."

199.5

In Portland, Oregon, an advertisement read: "Veteran, wife, ten dogs, three female cats, alligator, desire small furn. apt. We drink, smoke, stay up all night beating kettledrums."

According to Don Herold, they got twenty-five offers.

199.6

Two writers for the movie colony signed a one-year lease on a house, with the provision that the landlord would redecorate the place, a promise that was not kept. After several months, when it became clear the landlord was going to do nothing, they asked him in writing if they could decorate the house at their own expense. The landlord replied that that was all right with him.

Several days before they moved out, the two writers painted the entire interior of the house black.

199.7

"This castle," said the guide, "has stood for 500 years, and not a stone has been touched; nothing has been altered, repaired, or replaced."

"Must be owned by our landlord," said a visiting New Yorker to his wife.

199.8

"I wish you would speak to the tenants in the apartment above me," said a tenant to the landlord. "This morning at three o'clock they were jumping up and down and banging on the floor. I won't stand such disturbances."

"How did you happen to hear them at that hour?" asked the landlord.

"I was practicing on my saxophone, and they were bothering me," said the complainant.

199.9

They had just moved into their new apartment in a housing development and were entertaining their first guests. One of the women guests suddenly sat up with a startled look and said, "Surely you don't have mice in a brand-new house like this?"

"Oh, don't get upset," said the hostess. "It's only the people in the next apartment eating celery."

199.10

Sign in boarding house: PLEASE CLEAN THE TUB AFTER BATHING LANDLADY

199.11

A girl was so dumb that when she rented an apartment the landlord left the VACANT sign up.

Definition

199.12

Apartment: A place where you start to turn off your TV and find you've been listening to the neighbor's.

—*The Heating Equipment Dealer*

(*See also* 38.15, 38.17, 226.4, 228.3, 268.28)

Part Seven

TRAVEL AND TRANSPORTATION

ON THE MOVE

MOTOR MANIA

200. Car versus Pedestrian

Anecdotes

200.1

Jack Sterling, on his morning radio show, related that a car stopped in midtown Manhattan and the driver asked a man at the curb, "Say, where is 42nd Street?"

The man looked on coldly and said, "I'm a pedestrian. I don't help automobiles."

200.2

Jan Murray says that the traffic is so heavy in New York's midtown that one day he saw three cars chasing the same pedestrian.

200.3

The New York *Post* suggests that if compact cars keep getting smaller, we will reach the day when the pedestrian can strike back.

200.4

"You walk as if you owned the street," yelled the motorist.

"Yeah, and you drive as if you owned your car," said the pedestrian.

200.5

Joey Adams observes that the only time a pedestrian has the right-of-way is when he is in an ambulance on his way to the hospital.

200.6

A lost motorist slowed down to ask his way to the nearest town. The surly old man, whom he had nearly knocked down, replied: "Dunno."

The motorist drove on slowly, but was soon recalled by shouts behind him. He put the car into reverse and backed until he was alongside the old man who had been joined by another. "Well?" said the motorist.

"This be my mate," said the old man, "an' 'e dunno either."

200.7

A businessman had just completed a big deal and was crossing a busy intersection, looking up at the sky and apparently oblivious to all around him. A motorist passed and narrowly missed him.

"Hey, you," screamed the motorist, "if you don't look where you're going, you'll go where you're looking."

200.8

The car screeched to a stop at an intersection, just inches from an elderly woman. She recovered her poise immediately, smiled at the young man behind the wheel, pointed to the baby shoes dangling from the rear-vision mirror, and said, "Why don't you put your shoes back on?"

Definitions

200.9

A pedestrian is one who falls by the wayside.

200.10

A pedestrian is a man who thought there were a couple of gallons left in the tank.

200.11

Angel: A pedestrian who forgot to jump.
—*Ozzie Nelson*

Aphorisms

200.12

Some folks get what's coming to them by waiting, others while crossing the street.
—*Kin Hubbard*

200.13

Today the Good Samaritan would be sued for moving the poor soul before the insurance adjuster got there.
—*Bill Vaughan,* Sorry I Stirred It, 1964

(*See also 49.1–49.4, 89.6, 219.16, 235.45, 266.26*)

201. Maniacs at the Wheel

Anecdotes

201.1

One afternoon a wealthy college student was driving along a highway in his Cadillac convertible, when he noticed a tired old Model T stranded by the roadside. He stopped to see if he could be of assistance and found that the driver was a classmate. They could not get the ancient Ford started.

The Cadillac driver suggested that his friend hitch his Ford to the Cadillac with skid chains. "Then you just sit in your Ford and steer and away we'll go into town."

After a few minutes the Cadillac driver became bored and began to step up the speed of the car, until he was hitting 80 miles an hour. When he saw in his rear-vision mirror that he was being pursued by a highway patrol car, he jammed his foot all the way down on the accelerator and soon left the pursuing cop far behind.

The patrolman, realizing he couldn't catch the Cadillac, radioed ahead to the next patrol station: "Watch out for a blue Cadillac convertible hitting ninety, and get this—a Model T Ford is following it and blowing its horn, trying to pass."

201.2

A young fellow tore into a service station, jammed on the brakes, and said to the attendant, "Check this thing over, will ya? Every time I get it up to eighty I hear a knocking. Otherwise the thing runs OK."

The service station man checked and checked and checked, and finally said, "I don't find a thing wrong. Maybe that knocking you hear is the Lord warnin' you."

201.3

"What part of a car causes the most accidents?"

"The nut that holds the wheel."

201.4

A fellow was speeding down the highway when his car swerved, hit a fence, and rolled over into a field. A farmer ran to the car, and as the driver crawled out, he asked him, "Are you drunk?"

"You dope, of course I am. Do you think I'm a stunt driver?"

201.5

"What is worse than keeping up with the Joneses?" he asked.

"Trying to pass them at 70 miles an hour," said she.

201.6

An enthusiastic motorist, who thought of little else but his driving skill and his ability to cover ground, was on a trip with his wife, when she took a look at the road map and told him they were lost. "So what?" he said. "After all, we're making great time."

201.7

A hot rodder had his car painted green on one side and red on the other. He said it results in contradictory testimony when witnesses testify against him in accident and speeding cases.

201.8

The truck driver stopped suddenly on the highway, and the car behind crashed into him. The truck driver was sued.

"Why didn't you hold out your hand?" the judge asked the truck driver.

"Well," said the truck driver, "if he couldn't see the truck, how in the world could he see my hand?"

201.9

The greater part of my official time is spent investigating collisions between propelled vehicles, each on its own side of the road, each sounding its horn, and each stationary.

—*An English judge*

201.10

"It's all right, I'm just shaving with my electric razor while driving," said a motorist to a cop who had stopped him for zigzagging along the road.

An Arkansas man said he was driving 90 miles an hour in order to scare his wife out of her hiccups.

201.11

A witness on the stand during a trial of a traffic case was asked by the district attorney, "When the traffic light is amber, what does that mean?"

"It means," said the witness, "to go like hell before the light turns red."

201.12

A Wisconsin man said his accident happened when one backseat driver told him to turn left and another told him to turn right. "I tried to do both."

Definitions

201.13

A motorist is one who, after seeing a wreck, drives carefully for the next few blocks.

201.14

Americanism is voting to set the speed limit at 65 miles per hour and demanding a car that will hit 100.

Aphorisms

201.15

I have always considered that the substitution of the internal combustion engine for the horse marked a very gloomy milestone in the progress of mankind.

—*Winston S. Churchill*

201.16

The fool that used to blow out the gas now steps on it.

201.17

Don't drive as if you owned the road—drive as if you owned the car.

201.18

Men still die with their boots on, but usually one boot is on the accelerator.

—*Arkansas Gazette*

201.19

What we need is an automobile brake that will get tight when the driver does.

201.20

That guy is such a reckless driver that when the road turns the same way he does, it is a mere coincidence.

201.21

If all the cars in the land were placed end to end, some idiot would try to pass them.

201.22

It is a mystery how the other half lives, the way the other half drives.

201.23

Speaking during the first days of automobiling, Beerbohm Tree said, "In our endeavor to cover the ground quickly, the ground is apt to cover us."

201.24

Always try to drive so that your license will expire before you do.

201.25

The way blood flows in them these days, it is easy to see why they're called traffic arteries.

—*Luke Neeley,* Quote

201.26

The pioneers who blazed the trails, now have descendants who burn up the roads.

201.27

Finkle, Finkle, bought a car;
Had some whiskey at the bar;
Now above the world so high,
Finkle, Finkle, in the sky.

—*Herb Greenhouse*

(*See also 49.1, 49.6, 49.10, 99.1, 99.2, 155.19, 166.10, 184.24, 184.26, 184.29, 202.1–202.16, 218.20*)

202. Drivers-at-large

Anecdotes

202.1

A fellow driving his car got stalled while crossing the railroad tracks, with a train looming in the distance. His efforts to start the car failed. Finally he turned around to his almost-hysterical wife in the backseat and said, "I got my end of the car across the tracks—now let's see what you can do with your end."

202.2

"I've been driving for fifteen years and I have never had a word from the back. No, sir," he reiterated, "I have never been bothered by backseat driving."

"What do you drive?"

"A hearse."

202.3

Driving along a busy county highway one Sunday afternoon, a motorist stopped to ask directions of a man seated on a fence looking on at the traffic.

"I don't see how people stand living in the country," said the motorist. "There's nothing to see, nothing to do. I'm on the go all the time."

The fellow on the fence looked disdainfully at the stranger and drawled, "Wal, I don't see any difference in what I'm doing and what you're doing. I set here on the fence and watch the cars go by. You set in your car and watch the fences go by. It's the way you look at things."

202.4

Natives who beat drums to keep off evil spirits are objects of scorn to motorists who blow horns to break up traffic jams.

—*The Sock-Eye,* New Westminster, British Columbia

202.5

Joey Adams quipped that the traffic was so bad rescue planes had to drop supplies to the Good Humor man.

202.6

A drunk left the country club in his car, determined simply to follow carefully the lights of the car ahead of him, in order to stay on the road. He did this for some time when suddenly the car ahead stopped and he crashed into it.

"What's the idea?" said the driver of the first car.

"What do you mean, what's the idea? Why didn't you stick out your hand to indicate you were coming to a stop?"

"Do you mean to say," said the driver of the first car, "that I have to do that when I pull into my own garage?"

202.7

A policeman looking at a motorist who was unscathed after a serious auto accident said, "Well, it must feel pretty good to be alive."

"I don't know, Officer; I have never been dead."

202.8

A parking lot owner called his boys together and said, "Look, fellows, there's not been one complaint about dented fenders in more than a week. You know we can't make any money by leaving *that* much space."

Definitions

202.9

Modern man is one who drives a mortgaged car over a bond-financed highway on credit-card gas.

—*Copper Cogs,* Miami, Arizona

202.10

Automobile: Something your son manages to drive into the garage on the last drop of gas.

—*Fay De Witt*

202.11

Automobile: A four-wheeled vehicle that runs up hills and down pedestrians.

202.12

Automobile: A guided missile.

202.13

A service station's a place where you will fill the car and drain the family.

—*Clyde Moore,* Ohio State Journal

Aphorism

202.14

The beauty of the old-fashioned blacksmith was that when you brought him your horse to be shod, he didn't think of 40 other things that ought to be done to it.

—*Sunshine*

202.15

The worst kind of car trouble is where the engine won't start and the payments won't stop.

202.16

Detour: Something that lengthens your mileage, diminishes your gas and strengthens your vocabulary.

—*Oliver Herford*

(*See also 40.26–40.32, 84.5, 95.1, 97.3, 104.4, 104.5, 148.7, 159.13, 160.25, 177.5, 184.24, 184.26, 184.29, 189.2, 190.6, 191.1, 191.2, 191.6, 193.21, 200.1–200.13, 201.1–201.27, 205.22, 207.22, 210.21, 211.14, 214.4, 215.3, 215.9, 218.20, 221.10, 230.10, 237.9, 254.6*)

203. Women Drivers

Anecdotes

203.1

An Oklahoma man said he hit the car in front of him because the woman driver ahead of him signaled she was going to turn right, and she did turn right.

203.2

"Be an angel and let me drive," said the wife to her husband.

He did, and he is.

203.3

A woman trying to get into a parking space banged into the car ahead of her, then into the car back of her, then into a car that was passing. A policeman came over and said, "All right; let's see your license."

"Officer, don't be absurd," said the woman driver. "Who would give me a license?"

203.4

A woman's car stalled at a busy corner, while traffic lights repeatedly changed from amber to red to green. Finally a traffic cop walked over to her and said, "What's the matter, lady? Haven't we any colors that you like?"

203.5

A motorist was driving along a parkway when his car stalled. A woman driver stopped and asked if she could give him a lift to the nearest service station to get help.

"Thanks," said the man, "it isn't serious; my battery's low. If you could give me a push with your car I'm sure mine would start all right." He said that since his car had an automatic transmission she would have to get up a speed of about 30 miles an hour in order to get him started.

The woman nodded understandingly and

backed up as the man got behind the wheel of his car. The man waited for the push, then looked in his rear-vision mirror and saw the woman's car coming at him at 35 miles an hour. All he could do was sit there and hold on for the inevitable crash.

203.6

A woman motorist who had bumped a pedestrian rather roughly leaned out of her car and said, "I've been driving a car for ten years. You must have been walking very carelessly."

"Lady," said the jolted man acidly, "I guess I know something about walking; I've been doing it for forty-five years."

203.7

"Have you ever driven a car?" she was asked when she applied for a license. "One hundred and fifty thousand miles," said her husband, "and never once put her hand on the wheel."

—*Quote*

Aphorism

203.8

Modern girls are very fond of spinning wheels—four of them.

(*See also 49.6, 173.10, 202.1–202.16*)

204. Bus Drivers and Bus Riders

Anecdotes

204.1

A richly dressed matron boarded a Fifth Avenue bus during World War II and offered the driver a $10 bill, then finally managed to locate a coin in her purse after much fumbling delay. Not knowing where to put the fare, she explained to the driver, "You know, I have never before ridden in one of these things."

"We ain't missed you," said the driver.

204.2

The bus was crowded, the highway crowded and icy, and the woman passenger persisted in asking the driver if they had come to her stop yet. Finally she asked, "How will I know when we get to my stop?"

"By the big smile on my face, lady," said the driver.

204.3

Curious to discover why one urban bus driver was always able to get his passengers to move to the rear of the bus, a company inspector found that he would say to passengers as they paid their fare: "Just regard my bus as the church of your choice."

204.4

The bus driver slammed on the brakes of his crowded bus and called out, "Ladies and gentlemen, the back of this bus is going to the same place as the front of it, so please move to the back."

204.5

Stephen Potter tells about the time he was on a bus that stopped when a passenger pulled a leather thong to notify the driver. The passenger pulled too hard and the strap came off in his hand. "Look at Hercules!" the bus driver called out.

204.6

A woman on a bus said to a friend next to her, "Oh, I forgot to pay my fare. I'll go right up and pay it now."

"Why bother?" asked the friend.

"Honesty always pays," admonished the woman as she went to the driver.

"I told you honesty pays," she said when she returned to her seat. "I gave the driver a quarter and he gave me change for a 50-cent piece."

204.7

The bus was crowded and the driver was irritable. "Where is the fare for the boy?" he asked as the father handed him a single fare.

"The boy is only three years old."

"Three years! Why, look at him. He's seven if he's a day."

The father leaned over, gazed at the boy, and then said to the driver, "Can I help it if the boy worries?"

204.8

A woman boarded a crowded bus and groped rather desperately for her money. When a man offered to pay her fare she said no, she could find the money. This went on for several agonizing minutes until the man finally insisted upon paying the woman's fare, explaining to her, "Madam, three times now you have unbuttoned my suspenders."

204.9

There was a lot of excitement on a local bus the other day when a man got up and offered his seat to a woman—and she fainted. When she came to, she thanked him—and he fainted.

204.10

An obese lady was struggling to get on the bus, when the bus driver said, "You should take yeast; it would help you to rise."

"Try it yourself," said the woman. "It would make you better bred."

204.11

Passenger: "Madam, pardon me, but you're standing on my foot."

Lady: "Why don't you put your foot where it belongs?"

Passenger: "Don't tempt me, lady—don't tempt me!"

204.12

A woman on a bus arose from her seat to get off and asked the driver, "At which end do I get off?"

"Either end, lady," said the driver; "they both stop."

204.13

A wisecracking young fellow stepped on a bus one morning and called to the driver, "How about it, Noah, is the Ark full?"

"Come right in," replied the driver. "We need one more monkey."

Definitions

204.14

Passengers: Shock absorbers on buses.

—*Changing Times,* The Kiplinger Magazine

204.15

American: One who will cheerfully respond to every appeal except to move back in a bus.

—*Senator Soaper*

(*See also 177.10, 184.44, 214.10, 225.3, 237.7, 263.14, 273.10, 274.9*)

RAIL, WATER, AND AIR ROUTES

---

205. Trains and Planes

Anecdotes

205.1

Years ago Artemus Ward boarded a railroad out West and after a while asked the conductor if passengers were allowed to give advice, if they did so in a respectful manner.

The conductor reluctantly replied that he supposed it was all right.

"Well," said Ward, "it occurred to me that it would be well to detach the cowcatcher from the front of the engine and hitch it to the rear of the train. You see, we are not liable to overtake a cow on this train, but what's to prevent a cow from strolling into the rear car and biting passengers?"

205.2

"What happened?" asked a passenger when the train suddenly stopped.

"We just hit a cow," said the conductor.

"Was it on the tracks?"

"No, we chased it into the barn."

205.3

A man driving his car across railroad tracks was struck and killed by a train. His widow sued the railroad, contending the railroad crossing was not adequately protected for the safety of motorists. The railroad watchman at the crossing was the railroad's chief witness. And no matter what the widow's attorney said or did, he could not shake the man's testimony that he was on the job, heard the train well before it got to the crossing, went out to the middle of the crossing with his lantern, and waved it back and forth as a warning to all motorists.

When his testimony ended and he had stepped down from the stand, the watchman's boss complimented him for his conduct under the fire of the attorneys. "Were you nervous?" his boss asked him.

"Yessir, I wuz," he said emphatically. "All the time on the stand I kept wonderin' when that lawyer was going to ask me if the lantern was lighted."

205.4

A railroad man arose fifteen minutes after his alarm clock went off; he was cold because the heating system was out of order; he slipped while taking a shower; he cut himself while hurriedly shaving; his toast was burned and his eggs not sufficiently boiled. When he finally arrived at the yards and got his train underway on the main track, he saw another train coming toward him at great speed on the same track. He turned to his fireman and said, "Jim, did you ever have one of those days when everything seems to go wrong from the minute you open your eyes?"

205.5

Michael O'Shea was employed by the railroad to walk the tracks and look for washouts. After he had been on the job for a while, his boss called him in and told him not to be so long-winded in his future reports. "Get right to the point," said the boss. "Cut out useless words."

Michael went off on another tour of inspection and presently his first report came in. "Sir: Where the railroad was, the river is."

205.6

When the New York Central Railroad inaugurated its famous Twentieth Century train between New York and Chicago, a general order went out to all employees that if the slightest mishap or delay occurred, headquarters were to be given full details immediately.

One youthful station agent in upper New York State was duly impressed by this instruction, particularly since he was both ticket agent and dispatcher at the whistle-stop where he was in sole command. At dusk one winter evening, word was flashed to him that the Century was running two hours behind time. His duty was plain.

He took his lantern and walked the track toward the Century until he was half a mile from his station, posted himself between the tracks, and waited. He heard the train whistle far off, then saw a tiny light in the distance rapidly grow larger until he was in the full beam of the train's searchlight. He waved his lantern to and fro desperately. The engineer saw the swinging lantern ahead, jammed on the brakes, released the sand, and finally came to a jarring stop.

The engineer and fireman jumped from the cab and ran forward swearing. The station agent stood his ground. "Take it easy, boys," he said. "I'm acting on orders from headquarters. Now let's have the reason why you are two hours late. I've got to make a report on this to the head office."

205.7

When a railroad employee showed up in the yards for his last day on the job after forty years of work with the road, he found a little retirement ceremony had been prepared, presided over by the road's president. There was a handsome scroll for the man, a gold watch from the company, and gifts from the workers. "And just what do you do?" asked the president after the formalities ended.

"I tap the wheels of the cars with this here hammer," replied the worker.

"And why do you do that?" inquired the president.

"You know," said the worker, slightly bewildered, "I'm damned if I ever found out."

205.8

A visitor to Maine went into a small railroad station to get a train back to New York. "Is the train to New York on time?" he asked the ticket agent.

"Yep," said the agent.

The man waited. Finally the train pulled in an hour late. "I thought you said the train was on time," said the annoyed passenger.

"Mister," said the ticket agent, "I ain't paid to sit here and knock the railroad."

—*Jack Sterling,* CBS radio

205.9

An elderly woman on a train headed into New York City nervously asked the conductor, "Sir, will this train stop in Grand Central Station?"

"If it doesn't, lady, you're going to be in the damndest wreck you ever saw."

205.10

In an isolated part of the country two railroad trains met head on, killing and injuring many people. Investigators immediately got busy probing the cause of a collision so inexcusable, especially in broad daylight.

But they could find only one witness to the disaster, an old farmer who had been working in the fields nearby. He was asked to tell what he knew about the accident.

"All I know," he testified, "is that I saw one train was coming from the west at 60 miles an hour, and another train from the east at about the same speed, both on the same track, and that they were going to hit each other."

"What did you do then?"

"Nothing—warn't anything I could do."

"Well," said the annoyed investigator, "didn't you even think?"

"Sure—I thought plenty."

"Well then, at least tell us what you thought."

"Well, I looked at these two trains, as I said, and I thought to myself, 'Now isn't this a helluva way to run a railroad.'"

205.11

A woman, unfamiliar with railroad jargon, was standing on the platform while a freight train nearby was being made up. As the train backed up, one of the brakemen called to another: "Jump on her, Bill, when she comes up, cut her in two, and send the head end to the depot." The woman ran screaming to the police.

205.12

A passenger, traveling on a train from Boston to New York, entered the diner and asked for plum pudding with hard sauce for desert. When he was told they had no plum pudding, the traveler got very abusive. "Do you realize you are talking to one of the biggest shippers over this railroad?" the diner asked the waiter. "And furthermore, I'll have you know I'm a director of this road."

By this time the steward came up and assured the man he would have his plum pudding when they stopped at New Haven. And true to his promise, when the train left New Haven, the waiter came up with plum pudding and hard sauce for the irate diner.

The traveler looked at it, threw down his napkin, and said, "To hell with it! I'd rather be mad."

205.13

A New York State legislator boarded a night train at Buffalo and gave the porter strict instructions to see that he got off at Albany. "Even if you have to put me off in my pajamas," said the legislator.

The next morning the legislator woke up on the train and found he was in Grand Central Station in New York. In a rage he called the porter and began to swear and yell at him until exhausted.

The bewildered porter said, "Mister, I'm not sure what you're yelling about, but you are making even more noise than the fellow I had to force off at Albany during the night."

205.14

Three scientists, waiting for a train, became engrossed in a discussion of interplanetary explorations. They not only failed to notice that the train had arrived but did not spot it until it was pulling out of the station. The three made a wild dash for the train, and two of them just barely got on it.

"Cheer up," said a bystander to the disconsolate third man. "Two out of three is a pretty good score."

"I suppose so," said the lone professor. "Trouble is, I was supposed to get on the train. The other two were here to see me off."

205.15

Scientists foresee in the not-too-distant future the completely automatic plane—no pilot, no engineer, not even a stewardess. The public address system speaks to the passengers: "Welcome aboard the completely automated plane; a computer in the plane controls everything. In two minutes we will take off automatically. At the proper altitude your seat belts will automatically retract. Ring for your lunch and it is served automatically. Our landing at destination will be completely automatic. Relax. Everything is under the control of your computer. Nothing can go wrong, Nothing can go wrong, Nothing can go wrong. . . ."

205.16

An old New Englander and his wife wanted to take a plane ride. "$10? Too much!" they said.

The pilot made a proposition. He would take them free if they did not say a single word during the trip. If they spoke, they would pay the $10.

Trip over and not a word spoken. Once landed, the pilot said he didn't think they'd do it.

"Well," said the old man, "you almost won—sure felt like hollering when mama fell out."

205.17

The elderly lady was adamant about traveling by airplane. "Not me," she said. "Flying is against human nature. I'm staying solidly on the earth and going to watch television as the Lord intended I should do."

205.18

An airline advertised: "Never before has air travel offered you so much. This is the time to break earthly ties."

205.19

Herb Caen in the San Francisco *Examiner* reports that the sales manager for an inflatable bra took his number 1 model from Los Angeles to San Francisco. She was wearing one of the products. But the plane did not have a pressurized cabin, so that the higher they flew the more outstanding the model became. It became so nerve-racking for the other passengers that the model had to retreat to the pilot's compartment and there gradually deflate herself, or the product.

205.20

High over the Atlantic Ocean, the attention of the passengers on the jet plane was arrested by the public address system, from which a voice said: "This is a recorded message from your pilot. Our plane's left wing is on fire. Remain calm. If you look down, you will see three dots on the water; they are your pilot, copilot, and stewardess on a life raft. Good luck."

205.21

The pilot of the plane laughed and laughed and kept on laughing. Finally a curious passenger went forward and asked the pilot what he was laughing at. "Oh, I've been thinking," said the pilot, "of all the excitement there must have been at the insane asylum when they found out I escaped."

Aphorism

205.22

Too often a grade crossing is the meeting place of headlights and light heads.

(*See also 4.8, 7.15, 41.11, 53.7, 76.14, 84.3, 92.14, 93.44, 110.3, 112.21, 116.1–116.10, 124.18, 160.5, 160.16–160.19, 184.43, 189.1, 192.3, 194.1–194.6, 195.2, 202.5, 218.1, 218.22, 222.2, 228.4, 229.5, 235.32, 253.4, 268.20, 272.14, 273.2, 273.4, 273.9, 274.12, 277.4*)

206. Ships at Sea

Anecdotes

206.1

Two days before Christopher Columbus discovered land, he stood on deck, puzzled and worried. One of his men said to him, "It's a shame that we wander on the sea this way, not knowing where anything is."

"I know where everything is," replied Columbus. "What worries me is, where are we?"

206.2

On his first ocean voyage, a man became terribly seasick. His groaning and gasping were interrupted by, "Shall I send you some dinner, sir?" from the steward.

"No," he said. "Just throw it overboard and save me the trouble."

206.3

Mr. and Mrs. Jones and their seven-year-old Gerald went off on their first sea trip, but the ocean refused to greet them with its best behavior. Instead it tossed and pitched the vessel so that by the third day at sea the parents were barely able to stand, unable to eat, and had lost their desire to continue living. But not little Gerald; he hopped and skipped about the ship as though it were a landlocked playground.

Finally, one of the stewards induced the Joneses to sit out on deck and get some fresh air. They just barely made it to the deck chairs, where they sat gasping. But little Gerald, some 15 feet away, was as active as ever. He climbed the ship's railing and balanced himself precariously on it, one hand clutching a steel guy rope to steady himself as the vessel rose and fell with the motion of the restless sea.

Mrs. Jones tried to rise but could not. She tried to call out to her little Gerald, but her voice failed. Finally she was able to whisper to her husband, "Oh, George, speak to Gerald."

Mr. Jones looked with apparent disinterest at his young son's dangerous escapade and, in a weak and despairing voice, said, "Hello, Gerald."

206.4

"My husband is particularly subject to seasickness, Captain. Could you tell him what to do in case of an attack?"

"He'll know what to do, all right."

206.5

One of the best temporary cures for pride and affectation is seasickness: a man who wants to vomit never puts on airs.

—*Josh Billings*

206.6

A cannibal dressed in western clothes went to college and grew to maturity in civilization. Then he took his first trip on a luxury liner. He went to the dining room, where with proper deference the steward asked him, "May I show you the menu?"

"No, I would rather see the passenger list," said the cannibal.

206.7

A passenger asked why the boat had stopped in midstream during a night cruise. The skipper said it was the fog. "But, Captain," said the passenger, "I can see the stars."

"True enough," said the captain, "but unless the boilers burst, that ain't the way we're going."

206.8

As the boat was sinking, the skipper called out: "Does anyone know how to pray?"

"I do," replied a man.

"OK, go ahead and pray," said the captain. "The rest of us will put on life belts. We're short one."

206.9

"Surface immediately, the ship is sinking" was the message sent to the deep-sea diver.

206.10

The timid lady, who had been asking the ship's officers repeated questions, encountered the captain on deck and asked him, "What would happen if we struck a large iceberg?"

"Why the iceberg would pass along as if nothing happened," replied the skipper. The lady seemed much relieved to hear this.

206.11

A frail vessel on its way from San Francisco to Alaska during the Gold Rush had aboard a number of passengers and many crates of oranges. A terrible storm blew up and, to make matters worse, a great fish followed in the wake of the vessel. The monster, with the lashing of its tail, threatened the destruction of the ship and the lives of all aboard.

In order to appease the hunger of this monster, the sailors threw overboard several cases of oranges. The monster gulped them but seemed to grow more furious. It lashed its tail with a greater power. And the storm increased in violence.

The maddened sailors undertook desperate measures. They drew lots and one man lost. They threw him overboard, and the monster devoured him. But even that sacrifice did not sate the appetite of the behemoth. Two others of the crew were hurled into the waters and instantly swallowed. Among the passengers was an old lady of almost ninety years. Everybody loved her, because day after day she had stayed on deck in a dear old rocking chair she had brought along with her. She reminded the sailors of home and mother. This sweet old lady had a noble soul, and the idea came to her that if she were sacrificed it might help to save the lives of the others aboard. She begged the sailors to throw her overboard. They agreed to do so, after attaching her securely to her rocking chair at her insistence. Strange to say, after the sea monster had devoured the old lady and her rocking chair, it disappeared. The storm then quieted down and the vessel proceeded on its way.

Weeks later, the great fish drifted ashore. It was opened up, and in it they found the dear old lady rocking comfortably in her rocking chair, selling oranges at a nickel each to the sailors.

206.12

The captain of one of the great liners engaged in transatlantic traffic had worked up to his exalted position by slow stages—beginning as a cabin boy years earlier. He was one of the most respected men on the seas. His second-in-command, who had served under him for years, watched and emulated his every move. But one thing about his superior puzzled him: every morning his chief went to his cabin, opened the drawer of his desk, took from it a slip of paper, read it over and over with great concentration, returned it to the desk, and locked the drawer.

Finally the captain retired, and his second-in-command took charge. And the first thing he did was to open the drawer of the desk to find out what was on that slip of paper his captain read so carefully every day. He found the slip of paper and read the single sentence on it: "Left side is port; right side is starboard."

206.13

Sign in office of the Farrell Lines Steamship Company: THINK—OR THWIM

Definition

206.14

A stowaway is the man with the biggest appetite on board a ship.

(*See also 61.5, 75.5, 150.14, 156.16, 179.3, 181.10, 210.17–210.19, 219.3, 232.7, 236.10, 254.22, 268.25, 270.16, 277.1*)

STOPS THAT CONFUSE AND AMUSE

TRAVELERS' JESTS

207. Vacations and Tourists

Anecdotes

207.1

Passports were being checked at the steamship office. The clerk looked at one passport picture carefully and handed it to his boss. "Seems to me that if this is a good picture of the fellow, he's too sick to travel."

207.2

The American couple stopped before a painting in the Louvre.

"What time is it?" asked the wife.

"What's the title of the painting?" countered the husband.

"It's called *Mona Lisa,*" replied the wife.

The husband looked over his itinerary carefully and said, "Well, if we are on schedule, it should be 11.15 A.M."

207.3

An American and his wife, upon their return from abroad, were telling of the wonders they had seen at the Louvre in Paris. The husband mentioned with enthusiasm a picture which represented Adam and Eve and the serpent in the Garden of Eden.

"We found the picture especially interesting," added the wife, "because you see, we know the anecdote."

207.4

"Dear me," said the old lady on her first visit to Switzerland, "look at all those big rocks. Wherever did they come from?"

"The glaciers brought them down," said the guide.

"But where are the glaciers?"

"The glaciers," said the guide in a weary voice, "have gone back for more rocks."

207.5

On his first trip abroad, an American stepped off the boat in England and encountered two passageways, one marked "British Subjects" and the other "Foreigners." Without hesitation the American entered the first passageway and showed his American passport to the guard, who directed him to the passageway marked "Foreigners." "But I'm no foreigner," protested the traveler. "I'm an American."

207.6

A gushing American tourist stood on the railroad platform at Stratford on Avon and said with awe, "Just think of it! It was from this very platform that the immortal bard departed whenever he journeyed to the theater in London."

207.7

A tall Texan was touring England and whenever he got the chance he would kid the British about their "midget" country. He irritated one man who asked him to give the dimensions of his wonderful state.

"Waal," drawled the Texan, "I don't rightly know just how big she is. But I do know that I can board a train, and twenty-four hours later still be in the Lone Star State."

"What does that prove?" said the Englishman. "We have trains like that here, too."

207.8

An American traveling in Europe discovered a $15 bill among currency he had received in change during the day. He thought it would be easy enough to pass it on to some unsuspecting European shopkeeper, but when he handed it over for a $1 purchase, he was given two $7 bills in change.

207.9

A traveler in the Sudan boarded a ferryboat and, along with scores of other passengers, had to step over the squatting form of a small boy who refused to move. When protests were made to the boat's captain he explained, "If the boy gets up the boat will sink."

—*H. C. Jackson,* Sudan Days and Ways

207.10

An American tourist, gazing down into the crater of a Greek volcano, said, "It looks like hell."

"You Americans, you have been everywhere," said a Greek.

207.11

Simon Bolivar, the famous South American patriot, was due to arrive for the night at a small town in Peru. One of his aides sent word to the local hotel, asking that "a room be prepared with special accommodations, food, etc., etc., etc."

When Bolivar reached the town that evening, he was ushered into the hotel's best room and then into an adjoining room where sat three beautiful women.

"And who are these young ladies?" asked Bolivar.

"These are the three et ceteras," smiled the host.

207.12

Said a guide, "Ladies and gentlemen, we have missed the view, but we can view the mist."

207.13

A sightseeing bus stopped in front of the Administration building on a tour of the University of Illinois campus. The guide explained to the tourists the importance of the Administration building in the college scheme, pointing out the location of President Robert Gordon Sproul's office.

"I've seen his picture in *Life* and I've heard

him on the radio. Any chance of us seeing him in person?"

"If he's in his office, we might get a look at him," said the guide, as he picked up a piece of gravel and neatly hurled it through the open window of the college president's office.

A moment later a rage-red face appeared at the window and glared down at the group of tourists.

"That always gets him," chuckled the guide. "Ladies and gentlemen, I give you President Sproul."

207.14

The countryman was making his first visit to the city, and in his travels about town had occasion to take a ferryboat across the river. He saw the boat quite a distance from the dock, realized he had just missed it, so took a running leap and landed in a heap on the deck. When he got up, he looked back and saw the wide expanse of water between the boat and the receding dock. "Good Lord!" he said, "What a jump I made!"

207.15

The American tourist in England was constantly being corrected by his English friend as to the pronunciation of England's place names: Barugt as Barf, Bealieu as Bewly, Cholmondley as Chumly, Magdalene College at Oxford as Maudlin.

When the Englishman visited the United States, his American friend asked him what he desired most to see. "Niagara Falls," said the Englishman.

The American looked puzzled and asked, "What place is that?"

"Niagara Falls," said the Englishman, and spelled it out.

"Oh," said the American, "we call that 'Niffles.' "

207.16

A literal-minded Englishman was taken by an American friend to see Niagara Falls. They stood on Artists' Point in silence for a few moments until the Buffalonian burst out with local pride: "Have you ever seen anything so remarkable as all these floods of water tumbling into the abyss?"

Said the Englishman, "I see nothing remarkable whatever in their tumbling. After all, what's to prevent them?"

207.17

When she was visiting Niagara Falls, a guide offered his services to Margaret Fuller.

"One might as well ask for a gentleman usher to point out the moon," she replied.

207.18

Bill Gold in the Washington *Post* relates that a visitor to Philadelphia stopped a policeman to ask, "Where will I find Betsy Ross's house?"

"Sorry, Mac," replied the cop, "but since these reformers got into office, they've closed up all those joints."

207.19

Motorist: "Where is the main highway to Quincy?"

Pedestrian: "I don't know."

Motorist: "Where does this highway go?"

Pedestrian: "I don't know."

Motorist: "You don't know much, do you?"

Pedestrian: "No, but I ain't lost, am I?"

207.20

Theatrical producer John Golden told about a friend of his who had a camp in the Adirondack mountains, where he went often for a rest. Golden once asked his friend how long he generally stayed at his camp. "Well," said the frequent vacationer, "I have a housekeeper who is about sixty-five. She's no beauty, with her wig, false teeth, and harelip. When she begins to look good to me, I know it's time for me to pack up and beat it."

Definitions

207.21

A tourist is a man who travels to see things that are different and then complains when they aren't the same.

—*Rotary Realist,* La Salle, Ill.

207.22

Tourist: A guy who travels 5,000 miles to have his picture taken in front of his car.

207.23

A vacation is a short period of recreation sandwiched between long periods of anticipation and recuperation.

207.24

A vacation is a rest of two weeks that are too short, and after which you are too tired to return to work, and too broke not to.

—*Evan Esar,* Comic Dictionary

207.25

Vacation: Time off, to remind employees that the business can get along without them.

207.26

Convention: A gathering where conventions are forgotten.

Aphorisms

207.27

If you look like your passport picture, you need the trip.

207.28

The time to enjoy a European trip is about three weeks after unpacking.

—*George Ade*

207.29

Methods of locomotion have improved greatly in recent years, but places to go remain about the same.

—*Don Herold*

207.30

The longer and better the summer vacation, the harder the fall.

207.31

No man needs a vacation so much as the person who has just had one.

—*Elbert Hubbard*

207.32

We're all purty much alike when we git out o' town.

—*Kin Hubbard*

207.33

Here's to the holidays—all 365 of them!

—*Hobo toast*

207.34

An agreeable companion on a journey is as good as a carriage.

—*Publius*

207.35

The vagabond, when rich, is called a tourist.

—*Paul Richard*

(*See also 16.8, 21.6, 38.11, 41.2, 70.17, 117.6, 142.19, 150.3, 156.16, 163.27, 179.4, 179.6, 210.1, 210.9, 210.28, 211.8, 214.10, 218.2, 221.5, 229.28, 230.6, 246.12, 246.13, 268.21*)

208. Hotels and Motels

Anecdotes

208.1

A middle-aged couple went to the desk of the hotel for a room. The clerk said the place was filled up, except for the bridal suite, but he could put them in that.

"The bridal suite! We've been married for twenty-five years."

"Look," said the clerk, "If I give you the main ballroom, it doesn't mean you have to dance, does it?"

208.2

"This is sure a terrible hotel," said the guest to the clerk. "Why, I didn't sleep a wink last night—didn't once close my eyes."

"But, sir," replied the clerk, "everyone must close his eyes in order to sleep."

208.3

A man walked up to the desk of a resort hotel on the year's busiest weekend and asked for a room.

"Have you a reservation?" asked the indifferent clerk.

"No. But I've been coming here every year for twelve years, and I never had to have a reservation."

"Well, there nothing available. We are filled up, and without a reservation you can't get a room."

"Suppose President Johnson came in? You'd have a room for him, wouldn't you?"

"Of course, for the President we'd find a room—we'd have a room."

"All right," said the man. "Now I'm telling you President Johnson isn't coming here tonight. So give me his room."

208.4

One man met another at a summer resort. Although he could not remember who the other man was, he felt certain that he was acquainted with him. He held out his hand and said, "I know we have met somewhere."

"No doubt," said the other fellow, "I have been there often."

208.5

A first-time visitor to a summer resort at the seashore developed a sore foot and was advised by the doctor to soak it in a bucket of salt water twice a day. So every day he went faithfully to the beach to fill a bucket with sea water. When a lifeguard offered to fill it for him, the old fellow was grateful and willingly paid the 50 cents per bucket the lifeguard charged the rich old yokel.

Late on the second day the old man came down to the beach with his bucket and was astonished to notice how much the water's edge had receded—it being then low tide.

"By golly," he said enviously to the lifeguard, "you've been doing one helluva business since I was here yesterday."

208.6

A visiting Englishman, checking out of a plush resort hotel in upstate New York, was asked if he had enjoyed himself.

"Yes, quite," he replied, "but I wonder if I may venture a suggestion?"

"Certainly," said the hotel manager.

"I notice," said the departing guest, "that a sign on the door of my room reads HAVE YOU LEFT ANYTHING? I think you ought to change that to read HAVE YOU ANYTHING LEFT?"

208.7

Hotel Owner: "Did you find any towels in his suitcase?"

Bellhop: "No, but I found a chambermaid in his grip."

208.8

A bellhop, pocketing 50 cents from the departing guest, said, "Make it a dollar and I won't mention the hotel towels you took."

"Young man," retorted the guest, "I ought to have you arrested for making an accusation like that."

"Forget it, sir. Nine times out of ten it works."

208.9

A woman guest in a New York hotel rebuked the bellboy when he entered her room without knocking. "Suppose," she said, "I had been dressing when you came in like that?"

"Not a chance of that happening," said the bellboy. "I always look through the keyhole before going into a guest's room."

208.10

When Wilson Mizner managed a hotel in New York City he posted a sign in the lobby reading: "Guests must bury their own dead and will please refrain from smoking opium in the elevators."

208.11

Sign in hotel shower: "Keep that song in your heart—these walls are thin!"

208.12

Many of the waters at Saratoga Springs, New York, are highly and quickly cathartic. They tell about a frequent visitor to the Springs who stopped outside his hotel to greet a group of women acquaintances who had just arrived. They told him they had just had several glasses of Hathorne water—one of the more potent—then followed it with a glass of Coesa water, and topped that off with some Geyser water.

The experienced gentleman graciously tipped his hat, bowed, and said, "Ladies, do not let me detain you."

208.13

An elderly lady registered at an old-fashioned hotel and became a bit uneasy about the possibility of fire. She decided to explore the corridor to fix in her mind exactly where the fire escape was. The first door she saw was the public bath on that floor, which she failed to realize. She opened the door, and when she saw an elderly man under the shower, said, "Oh, excuse me. I was looking for the fire escape."

She had gone only a few steps along the hall when there was a shout, and the old gentleman came dashing after her with a towel around his middle, shouting, "Where's the fire?"

208.14

According to Hugh Parks, in the Atlanta *Journal*, the manager of a Florida motel suggested to a guest that he step outside and see the beautiful sunset.

"How much will it cost?" asked the guest cautiously.

Definitions

208.15

Resort: A hotel where no one knows how unimportant you are at home.

208.16

Resorts are where people go for a change and a rest, and where the waiters get all the change and the landlord gets the rest.

208.17

A resort is a place where the natives live on your vacation until next summer.

(*See also 38.2, 41.5, 53.3–53.5, 76.20, 119.5, 139.3, 141.17, 146.3, 155.44, 163.20, 163.22, 210.15, 248.14, 263.4, 272.7*)

209. Weather

Anecdote

209.1

"What good will it do you to run and hide down in the cellar when it's lightning? If it's going to strike you, it's going to strike you. You can't run away from it."

"Mebbe so," returned the cautious one. "But if it's going to hit me, it's going to have to look for me."

Definitions

209.2

Winter: The season when we try to keep the house as hot as it was in the summer, when we complained about the heat.

209.3

A weather forecaster is one with whom the weather does not always agree.

Aphorisms

209.4

The heat was so dreadful that I found there was nothing for me to do but take off my flesh and sit in my bones.

—*Sydney Smith*

209.5

Winter lingered so long in the lap of Spring, that it occasioned a great deal of talk.

—*Bill Nye*

209.6

Climate lasts all the time, but the weather only a few days.

(*See also 43.5, 61.34, 70.14, 95.3, 155.16, 159.11, 175.4, 210.30, 210.32, 210.33, 211.10, 211.38, 213.12, 214.5, 215.13, 217.6, 218.10, 218.16, 219.11, 221.12, 227.9, 240.25, 238.10–238.12, 239.16, 276.4*)

FROM MANY LANDS AND PEOPLES

AROUND THE U.S.A.

210. Yankee Wit

Anecdotes

210.1

A bored tourist in a small Vermont town, desiring companionship, joined a group of men sitting around a service station. He made several attempts to start a conversation, but each time met with no response. Finally he said, "Is it against the law in this town to talk?"

"Ain't no law 'gainst it," said one old native, "but up here no one speaks unless he thinks he can improve on silence."

210.2

A Vermont octogenarian was asked, "No doubt you have seen many changes in your long life?"

"Yessir, I have," squeaked the old fellow, "and I've been agin every one of them."

210.3

When asked what he would sell a certain horse for, the Vermont farmer startled the inquirer by naming a price of $1,000. The buyer said he was prepared to pay no more than $100. "That's a big reduction, but I'll take it," said the farmer.

When the deal was consummated, the buyer asked the farmer why he had come down so quickly from $1,000 to $100. "Well," drawled the farmer, "just thought it would be nice for you to own a thousand-dollar horse."

210.4

A fellow was plowing one of those Vermont hills, when a New Yorker came up in a shiny, chrome-plated car and said, "I don't see how you make a living on this farm."

The old farmer said, "Well, mister, let me tell you something. I ain't as poor as you think. I don't own this farm."

210.5

A man from Iowa paid a visit to Vermont and told one of the natives how wonderful Iowa was, where you could raise just about anything—no mountains, no stones, rich soil. "I cannot understand how you Vermonters survive in these rocky hills."

"Waal," said the Vermonter, "it is a bit difficult. We have a few chickens and pigs, a cow, a few sheep, and a garden. And a good many of us have Iowa 6 percent mortgages that help us get along after a fashion."

210.6

Kyle Crichton tells about the time he was in Woodstock, Vermont, and was charged 5 cents for a New York paper, though the masthead of the paper read "3 cents elsewhere."

"What about that?" he asked the storekeeper, pointing to the line.

"Woodstock," said the lady behind the counter, "is beyond elsewhere."

210.7

When Robert Frost first met Reed Powell, a native son of Vermont, the latter poked the poet in the ribs and said—knowing Frost was born in California—"You're a bastard Vermonter." Frost said, "You're a Vermont bastard." It was the beginning of a long friendship between the two men.

210.8

They tell about the old mountain man in

Vermont who filled a glass half-full of whiskey. "Let me get you some water to put in it," someone volunteered. "No, thanks," said the old fellow, "I ain't that thirsty."

210.9

The traveler in New England, fearing he had lost his way, stopped to ask a farmer, "My friend, am I on the right road to Burlington?"

"You're on the right road," replied the farmer, "but if you want to get there, you had better turn around and go in the other direction."

210.10

An elderly man stopped in a bank in a New England town and asked the teller: "Would you tell me, please, how much my dear friend Ebenezer Peabody has on deposit?"

The teller told the man it was a highly improper request and that such information could not be given out.

But the elderly man persisted in making the same inquiry every few weeks, until one of the tellers snapped at the questioner: "If you're such a close and dear friend of Ebenezer Peabody, why don't you ask him about his bank balance, instead of coming in here and asking us all the time?"

"Ha, ha," said the elderly man, "I am Ebenezer Peabody. I just wanted to be sure you fellows aren't telling my affairs to others."

210.11

In the annals of Connecticut the story is related of a confirmed bachelor who, at age forty, abandoned single blessedness and married the community's termagant—a thirty-two-year-old spinster who had a widespread reputation for bad temper and a quarrelsome disposition. When his friends asked the bridegroom why he had married her when he could have made a much better match, he replied that he did it as a penance, that he had had too good a time as a bachelor, and was afraid that he might not get to Heaven unless he suffered here on earth.

The gossips carried this to the bride. She flew into a rage and declared that she was not going to be a packhorse to carry any man to Heaven, and if he expected her to afflict him, he was mistaken. Thereupon she became one of the most pleasant and dutiful of wives.

210.12

Local patriots of Rhode Island reported that a wreck resulted in the loss of six souls and one Boston man.

210.13

A wit arrived in Newport, Rhode Island, one summer day, looked around, and asked, "Where are the customer's yachts?"

210.14

A beloved old man of a Maine seacoast family was rapidly approaching his end during a winter of extraordinary severity, even for that region. Railroad and highway traffic was tied up because of heavy snowfalls and a virulent influenza epidemic raged. Consequently the area ran out of coffins. Aware of this shortage and knowing the old man's death was imminent, one of the sons of the family called on the town's venerable boatbuilder and asked him to build a coffin. The boatbuilder agreed to do this final service for one with whom he had sailed in earlier days.

True to his promise, the boatbuilder completed the coffin the day his old friend died. No one had the courage—or indelicacy—to ask the boatbuilder if it was sentiment or absent-mindedness which caused him to put a centerboard in the coffin.

210.15

Captain Curran ran a little inn on Cape Cod. The Cape was feeling the pinch of bad times—summer folks were scarce and trade was at a low ebb. A friend of his asked him one day, "Captain, how is the hotel business?"

"Well," drawled the Captain, "I ain't never yit made enough to quit, an' I ain't niver lost enough to quit. I hope to the Lord I do one or the other this season."

210.16

Speaking of a certain Cape Cod woman, Helen Choate Bell said, "She ate so many oysters that her stomach rose and fell with the tide."

210.17

Captain Eleazer was mighty proud of his schooner—the finest in "the Injies trade"; he was sure there was no finer ship afloat than the *Bulldog*. When he married Abigail Bangs, townsfolk on Cape Cod began asking him if he was going to change the name of his ship to the *Abigail* as a mark of affection for his bride.

"No, don't see fitten for to change the vessel's name," replied the captain. "But if Abigail keeps on being a good girl, I've been thinkin' I might have her rechristened *Bulldog*."

210.18

Captain Peleg, old-time New England skipper, was starting off on a long journey. His wife sobbed that it wouldn't be so difficult if only he would write her a letter, at least one letter. He promised to do so. So eventually she received the letter. It read:

"Dear Arathusy: I am here and you are there. P. Hawes. Hong Kong, China, May 21, 1854."

210.19

A Boston reporter was sent by his paper to the island of Nantucket to interview a former whaling master who was celebrating his ninetieth birthday. The venerable mariner had led an adventurous life and the paper was confident he would make good copy.

In the course of a not-very-productive interview the reporter, in an attempt to get the old fellow talking, disclosed that he himself on his mother's side had descended from Nantucket whaling men.

"I wonder," said the reporter, "if you knew my great-grandfather. His name was Folger—Nathaniel Folger. I have heard that he died in a lifeboat in the North Pacific after the whaling ship he was on sank. The boat drifted for weeks, and when it was found, only two of the crew had survived the ordeal."

"Know him?" cackled the ancient salt. "Why, my boy, he saved my life."

"He did?"

"That's what I said—saved my life. I et him."

210.20

The New England meetinghouse had been built, and a cupola added, but some of the town fathers thought it should be graced by a fine gold eagle. Estimates of the cost were sought to present at the next town meeting. But when the meeting was called, the proposition was voted down after one farmer got up and said, "The voters are big fools, and probably always will be, if they voted to give five honest gold eagles for one gilt one."

210.21

A motorist driving through New England hit and killed a calf that was crossing the road. The driver went to the owner of the calf, explained what had happened, and asked what the animal was worth.

"Oh about $40 today," said the farmer. "But in six years it would have been worth $300. So $300 is what I'm out."

The motorist sat down and wrote out a check and handed it to the farmer. "Here," he said, "is a check for $300. It is postdated six years from now."

210.22

After listening to a pretentious lecturer, an old New Englander said: "That man uses big words 'cause he's skeered that if we folks knew what he was talkin' about, then we'd know he don't know what he's talkin' about."

210.23

Two New Englanders met on the street one day, and one said to the other: "How do you manage to feed your large family on your small income?"

"I find out what they don't like and give 'em plenty of it," replied the other man.

210.24

The New England country storekeeper sold a plow on credit to one of his many regular customers who came in from the surrounding countryside, but later he could not remember who the purchaser was or find the record he customarily made of all credit transactions.

Reluctant to abandon a collection without an earnest try, the storekeeper went over his list of charge customers with great care, selected the ten most likely buyers of such a piece of equipment, and sent each of them a bill for the plow, without comment or query.

Before long the replies came in—a total of nine checks without a hint of hesitation. The tenth customer never paid the bill sent to him. Months later, the slip covering the transaction was found—and on it was the name of the actual purchaser of the plow. It was the name of the one person who had not paid the bill sent to him.

210.25

When the committee arrived to present Nathan with the $10 prize for being the laziest man north of the Massachusetts line, Nathan was distressed. "Boys," he said, "ef y're set on givin' this to me, d'y' mind rollin' me over and puttin' it in my backside pocket!"

210.26

Nathan's wife tells of his discomfiture the time the sheriff's funeral passed their gate. "It was a grand sight," she said. "Nathan was restin' in the hammock when it went by. I come out and told him who all was in the carriages and autymobiles, and his kinfolk wavin' to him. Nathan was kinda peeved. 'Just my luck,' he said, ''t be facin' th' other way.'"

210.27

A Californian said to a New Englander, "We grow cabbages so big in California that 100 men can stand under them."

The New Englander said that in his part of the nation they riveted copper kettles so massive that a 1;000 men could be riveting one and yet be so far apart they couldn't hear one another's hammers.

"What," asked the Californian, "would anyone want with a copper kettle as big as that?"

"To boil those California cabbages in," said the New Englander.

210.28

A "superior" summer visitor to a New England resort town rather condescendingly asked one of the town's old timers what the natives did when the summer visitors left.

"Well," he said, "the first thing we do is fumigate."

210.29

A visitor asked the New England farmer how things were going with him. "Well," said the grim Yankee, "I've been working this rocky land for ten years and I'm just about holding my own. I started here on nothin,' and I got nothin' now."

210.30

New Englanders themselves are not reluctant to make caustic comments about their weather. For example:

We have two seasons: Winter and the Fourth of July.

The New England climate consists of nine months of Winter and three months late in the Fall.

Maine has two seasons: Winter and August.

Aphorisms

210.31

Her head looks as if it had worn out two bodies.

—*Vermont saying*

210.32

There is an old New England saying: "as cold as the north side of a January gravestone by starlight."

210.33

If you don't like the weather in New England, just wait a few minutes.

—*Mark Twain*

(*See also 37.9, 45.4, 45.6–45.8, 46.3, 46.4, 55.1–55.3, 57.4, 60.3, 76.1–76.19, 118.3, 129.16, 205.8, 205.16, 215.10, 221.1–221.12, 263.16, 272.14*)

211. Southland and Sunshine

Anecdotes

211.1

Two visitors to the Virginia mountains one day observed a woman dousing the reclining figures of two lanky men with water. She had just emptied the third bucket on her sleeping menfolk when she noticed the interest of her visitors. "Keeps the flies off'n 'em," she said.

—*Sigrid Arne,* Milwaukee Sentinel

211.2

During the first election of Reconstruction days, following the Civil War, a veteran of the Southern armies came down from the Virginia hills to vote and was dismayed to learn that under the new law he must first swear allegiance to the Union against which he had fought so hard. He protested, but the authorities were firm: no oath, no vote. Grudgingly, he took the oath.

"Now," he asked, "does that make me a Yankee?"

"Yes, if you want to look at it that way," said the registrar.

He smiled, slapped the official on the back, and said, "Boy, didn't those Rebs beat the hell out of us in the Valley of Virginia!"

211.3

An old Negro named Monroe one day ventured from his little worn-out farm deep in Virginia to make his first trip to Washington. Walking through one of the city's parks, he picked up a purse which contained $2.15. With this wealth he decided to see the city from a streetcar. He marveled at the way the car stopped when the conductor called out a name, and the people got off. Apparently the conductor had some wonderful power. "Washington!" he would call out, and a man named Washington would get off. "Jefferson!" and Mr. and Mrs. Jefferson would get off. And the same with Adams. Finally the old man was astounded when the conductor called out "Monroe!" But he was equal to the occasion. "Yes, sir," he replied, "I'm Monroe and here I come."

As he stood on the corner wondering what next to do, an automobile pulled up at the curb and the driver called out, "Is this Monroe?" "Yes, this is Monroe," said old man Monroe. "I'm looking for two-fifteen," said the driver. "Good Lord, they sure are smart people in this town!" exclaimed the old man as he reached into his pocket for the $2.15 he had found in the park.

211.4

According to former Vice President Alben Barkley, the preacher at a camp meeting down in Kentucky was holding forth against the sin of hatred. At the close of his exhortation, he asked any members of his congregation who had succeeded in conquering hatred to stand up.

Only one man got to his feet, 104-year-old Uncle Beaureguard.

"You don't hate nobody, Uncle Bo?"

"No, sir."

"That's wonderful, Uncle Bo. Tell us why that is."

"Well, all them skunks who done me dirt, all them blankety-blanks I hated—they're all dead!"

211.5

A boarder in a restaurant who had ordered spring chicken, set up a roar when the piece of cooked fowl was set before him, saying to the waiter, "What do you mean by trying to palm this off on me for spring chicken? Why, I couldn't cut it with an ax." "Calm yourself, my excited friend," said the undisturbed waiter, as he carelessly picked a cockroach out of the milk-pitcher, "that is spring chicken all right, just as represented, but it was raised in Kentucky where toughness is no indication of age."

—*T. A. McNeal*

211.6

A visitor to Kentucky noticed that his host always closed his eyes before he began to drink his mint julep. When asked why he did this, the Kentuckian said, "The sight of good liquor makes my mouth water, and I don't want my whiskey diluted."

211.7

A man from Kentucky explained that a Kentucky breakfast consists of a big beefsteak, a quart of bourbon, and a hound dog.

"What is the dog for?" asked a listener.

"He eats the beefsteak," said the man from Kentucky.

211.8

A tourist stopped in Sadiesville, Kentucky, and asked a native how far it was to Lexington.

"Used to be 'bout 25 miles," said an elderly man. "But the way things is goin' in this country nowadays it might be closer to 50 miles now."

211.9

The traveler through the Tennessee hills stopped to watch a farmer holding a pig in his arms so that the animal could eat the apples right off the tree. "Won't it take a long time to fatten the pig that way?" asked the stranger.

"Sure it will," replied the farmer. "But what's time to a hog?"

211.10

A visitor to the South stopped to chat alongside the road with a cotton planter. "I've heard that extreme hot weather is bad for cotton crops. Is that so?"

"Well," said the farmer, "I don't think they ever found out. A long time ago somebody said that the heat hurt the cotton. But it was too hot for anybody to argue 'bout it, and too hot to find out. That's how the idea got started."

211.11

A traveler in the Southern mountains saw an old man sitting at a cabin door and asked: "Have you lived here all your life?"

"Not yit," was the reply.

211.12

In her travels among the hillbillies of the Southern mountains, a social worker stopped at one dilapidated shack and asked the bedraggled young woman who came to the door about her family. The girl said "Wal, Maw—she's in the County Home, and Pa—they put him in the pen. Sis is in some kind of home for bad girls, and little Jo, they got in a reform school. And then Hank is up at Harvard."

"Harvard? My, he must be smart to be studying up there."

"No, ma'm, he ain't smart and he ain't studying up there. They're studying him."

211.13

Maxwell Droke relates that when the Associated Press asked various cities around the nation to state what they were doing about protection against possible atomic bomb attacks, a wit in Hattiesburg, Mississippi, replied: "Re atomic prevention request. Not worried here. We have a chamber of commerce which has repelled everything new in the past forty years."

211.14

A salesman tried to sell some fruit trees to a man in Mississippi. The farmer let out a curse word or so, and began to talk poor-mouth about hard times. He said he couldn't even buy a peach seed and that two years ago, when cotton went down and taxes went up, he had to send his eight children to an orphanage. Times kept on getting worse and he had to send his wife back to her father's.

"Now," he said, "things seem to be getting bad again, and if they get much worse, I'm going to have to sell my car."

211.15

When John Sharp Williams was a young congressman from Mississippi, he arrived home very late one evening after dining and wining well. As he stumbled into his house, the clock in the hall struck two. This awakened his wife, who protested the Congressman's condition, which he denied was other than normal. "Well, what time is it?" she demanded. "Ten o'clock," replied her husband, and then fell asleep.

However, his wife wept so bitterly and so loudly that he was awakened, and asked her what the trouble was: "Because," she said, "for the first time in ten years you have lied to me. I heard that clock strike two."

Williams thereupon burst into tears himself and wept even more bitterly than his wife. When she asked him why he was weeping so copiously, he said, "Because, after ten years of married life, you would rather believe that damned little Yankee clock than your own husband."

211.16

The Mississippi Negro was determined that he was going to vote in the coming election and appeared at the polling place to take the literacy test to qualify. He answered the first few questions without any difficulty.

Then the inquisitorial clerk shot at him:

"What does the nebulae hypothesis mean?"

The poor aspirant flinched, mumbled, reached for his hat, turned toward the door, and said, "It means I ain't gonna get to vote."

211.17

A Mississippi Negro died and went to Heaven, but the Lord told him he would have to go back and finish his work. The Negro protested that he was tired of being pushed around and had had enough of earth. But the Lord was adamant.

"Well," said the Negro, "I'll go back if you come with me."

"All right," said the Lord, "but I'll only go as far as Memphis."

211.18

A Southern slave master told one of his slaves of whom he was very fond that he had dreamed he died and ended up in the Negro's Heaven, and saw "a lot of garbage, some old torn-down houses, a few old broken-down rotten fences, the muddiest, dirtiest, sloppiest streets I ever saw, and a big bunch of ragged, dirty blacks walking around."

The slave said he, too, had dreamed that same night that he had died and gone to Heaven, the white man's Heaven, and it was spotless and beautiful—but there was no one there.

211.19

Before the movement for school integration got under way, a town in the South allocated $125,000 for school improvements. Of course, the school for the white children was the one most in need of attention: a new gymnasium, an expanded library, painting, a new roof.

The principal of the Negro school appeared before the school board and asked if it was necessary to use all the funds for the white school to give the children a decent education.

"Yes," said the board, "that is the case."

"In that event, gentlemen," said the Negro principal, "I will withdraw my objection, because if this town needs anything, it is educated white men."

211.20

Atlanta columnist Ernest Rogers tells about the policeman trying to dissuade a man from leaping out of the window.

"Think of your mother."

"I have no mother."

"Think, then, of your wife."

"I have no wife."

"Then think of Robert E. Lee."

"Who the hell is Robert E. Lee?"

"Aw, go ahead and jump, you damnyankee."

211.21

William Travers Jerome, New York's famous district attorney, in Atlanta to address the Georgia Bar Association, was being shown around the town by one of the local attorneys. When they passed a hotel, the Georgian pointed to a man sitting on the hotel porch and said, "You see that man? Well, he's one we take some pride in down here. He's the only man in Georgia that can strut sitting down."

211.22

A Georgia cracker sitting barefooted on steps of his tumbledown shack, was accosted by a stranger who stopped for a drink of water.

"How is your cotton coming along?" asked the stranger.

"Ain't got none."

"Didn't you plant any?"

"Nope," said cracker, " 'Fraid of boll weevil."

"Well, how is your corn?"

"Didn't plant none. 'Fraid wasn't going to be no rain."

The stranger, confused but persevering, added: "Well, how are your potatoes?"

"Ain't got none. 'Fraid of potato bug."

"Really! What then did you plant?" asked the astonished visitor.

"Nothin," said the cracker. "I jes played safe."

211.23

A man in Atlanta took four friends to visit a farm he owned. The visitors entered the tenant farmer's house and were embarrassed to find he had only two chairs. They stood around awkwardly. Finally the owner said, "I don't believe you have enough chairs here."

The old farmer took a few puffs on his pipe and muttered: "I've got plenty of chairs—just too durn much company."

211.24

A Georgia farm boy, on army duty in Connecticut, fell in love with a Connecticut girl and wooed her ardently if not wisely. After a spell he was transferred to Arizona, and while there received a letter from the girl, telling him she was three months' pregnant and dreaded the disgrace of being the mother of an illegitimate child. She asked that he arrange with his parents for her to stay with them until the baby was born and they could get married. The young soldier replied, telling her to stay where she was, adding that "a bastard in Connecticut has a better chance than a Yankee in Georgia."

211.25

Years ago a Judge Underwood of Georgia was presiding in a court at Marietta, a town to which he had taken a great dislike. During one case the judge remarked, "When my time comes, I am coming to Marietta to die."

"We are glad you like our town so much," said a local attorney.

"It's not that," replied the judge. "It's because I can leave it with less regret than any other place on the face of the earth."

211.26

A book agent called on a Georgia farmer to sell him a set of books on scientific agriculture. "No," said the farmer. The salesman persisted and said, "If you buy and read these books, you could farm twice as good as you do now."

"Lissen, young fellow," said the farmer. "I'm not farming half as good as I know now."

211.27

A group of hooded Ku Klux Klansmen were driving along a road in Alabama when they passed a house near the road and noticed a sign outside which read, WE ARE 200 PERCENT AMERICANS. The Klan chief got out of the car, knocked on the door, and when a man came to the door asked, "What's the meaning of this here sign saying you are a 200 percent American?"

"Well," explained the man, "you Kluxers hate Jews, Negroes, Catholics, foreign-born Americans, people of culture and education, and believers in justice and decency. And you call yourselves 100 percent Americans. Well, the folks in this house are 200 percent Americans: we hate every son of a bitch alive."

211.28

"Where you going, Herbert, with that Bible under your arm?" asked a friend.

"Oh, I'm off to New Orleans for a few days. Been working too hard and think maybe a few strip shows, hot music, fine meals, and good bourbon will relax me a bit."

"Good idea, I suppose, but why the Bible?" asked the friend.

"Well, if the place comes up to my expectations, I may stay over Sunday."

211.29

A boy sat alongside a lake in Florida, lazily watching his fishing line bob up and down, when a car stopped and several men got out. "Are there any snakes in this lake?" they asked the indolent country kid. "Naw, no snakes," he replied.

The men stripped, jumped in the lake, swam and cavorted in the water for half an hour with the abandon of children.

When the men were dressing after their swim, one of them asked the young native, "How come there are no snakes in the lake?"

"Alligators et 'em all up," replied the boy.

211.30

"Is it true," asked the newcomer, "that the alligators in these swamps won't bother you if you carry a torch?"

"It all depends," answered the native, "how fast you carry it."

211.31

Harvey Firestone, Thomas A. Edison, John Burroughs, and Henry Ford stopped at a rural service station on their way to Florida for the winter. "We want some bulbs for our headlights," said Ford. "And by the way, that's Thomas Edison sitting there in the car, and I'm Henry Ford."

The old fellow at the service station didn't even look up; just spat out some tobacco juice with obvious contempt. "And," said Ford, "we'd like to buy a new tire—if you have any Firestone tires. That other fellow in the car is Harvey Firestone himself." Still the old fellow said nothing.

While he was placing the tire on the wheel, John Burroughs—with his long white beard—stuck his head out the window and said, "Howdy, stranger."

Finally the old man at the service station came alive. He glared at Burroughs and said, "If you tell me you're Santa Claus, I'll be damned if I don't crush your skull with this lug wrench."

211.32

While on a visit to Florida, Governor Herman Talmadge of Georgia was being interviewed on TV and was asked what he thought about the thousands of Georgians who had migrated to Florida.

"I think," said Talmadge with a smile, "that the movement of so many Georgians to Florida raises the level of intelligence in both states."

—*Richard Powell Carter,* Saturday Evening Post

211.33

Sign in Miami Beach: KEEP FLORIDA GREEN—BRING MONEY

—*Portland Oregonian*

211.34

A young Northern lawyer wrote a friend of his in the South and asked for advice as to his moving below the Mason-Dixon line for the practice of law.

The Southerner replied: "If you are an honest lawyer, you will have no competition down here. If you are a Republican, the game laws will protect you."

211.35

A Southern editor declares, on his honor, that he recently saw a loafer fall over the shadow of a lamppost in trying to catch a lightning bug to light his cigar with.

211.36

Old Paw was in his rocking chair on the front porch, rocking due east and west. Beside him was Sonny Boy, an innocent of forty, rocking north and south. Presently Paw said, "Son, why wear yo-self out that-a-way? Rock with the grain and save yore strength."

Definition

211.37

The Mason-Dixon line is a geographical division between "You-all" and "Youse guys."

Aphorism

211.38

It gets so hot in Mississippi [or any hot state you choose] that natives have reported seeing a dog chasing a rabbit, and both of them were walking.

(*See also 55.4–55.15, 57.20, 58.3, 60.10, 60.14, 60.17, 118.3, 128.1, 129.4, 129.5, 152.57, 184.76, 190.13, 216.4, 216.5, 221.4, 229.5, 235.16, 245.16, 252.6, 252.8, 257.1, 265.10, 271.8, 272.5*)

212. In Mid-America

Anecdotes

212.1

The owner of a large farm in Ohio had fifteen men working for him, none of whom worked as hard as he expected them to do. One day he hit upon a plan he thought would cure his men of their laziness. He called them together and said, "I've got a nice easy job for the laziest man on the farm. Will the fellow who thinks he's the laziest step over here?" All stepped over to the place indicated, except one man.

"Why didn't you step over with the rest of the men?" the farmer asked the holdout.

"Too much trouble," said the lone worker.

212.2

There is a family in Ohio so lazy that it takes two of them to sneeze—one to throw the head back, and the other to make the noise.

212.3

"In Pittsburgh they manufacture iron and steal," wrote the student in an examination.

212.4

An Indiana farmer on one of his infrequent visits to town was driving along Main Street when the fire whistle, the gestures of pedestrians, and the sound of a fire engine persuaded him to move over to the curb and stop. When the fire engine had passed, the farmer started to pull out into the street again just as the hook and ladder came flying past and almost hit his car. "Why the hell don't you keep out of the way of the fire engines?" yelled a cop.

"I did," the farmer yelled back. "But how am I to know that a bunch of drunken painters are goin' to come down the street after the engine?"

212.5

An old man, called into an Illinois court to act as a witness, was asked his age. He replied, "Sixty." The questioning lawyer felt sure that he was much older and insisted that the witness tell his true age.

"Oh, I understand now," replied the witness. "You're thinking of those ten years spent in Peoria [or another city, if you prefer]. That was just so much time lost and doesn't count."

212.6

An addlepated girl in the famous play *Lightnin'* said that the only reason she and her husband got married was that they happened to be in Peoria and it rained all week.

212.7

Thomas Lincoln, father of the famous Abe, was gathering up some hazelnuts one day when a neighboring farmer stopped and said, "Why, I thought you were going to sell your farm?"

"I am," said Lincoln senior, "but I ain't goin' to let my farm know about it."

212.8

American Backwoods Conversation

"What is the land?"
"Bogs."
"The atmosphere?"
"Fogs."
"What do you live on?"
"Hogs."
"What are your draught animals?"
"Dogs."
"What do you build your houses of?"
"Logs."
"Any fish in your ponds?"
"Frogs."
"What's worn by your women?"
"Clogs."
"Whose map do you travel by?"
"Moggs'."

212.9

A meek-looking man in Springfield, Illinois, once asked Secretary of State Campbell for permission to deliver a series of lectures in the Illinois House of Representatives.

"What is the subject of your lectures?" asked Campbell.

"The second coming of Christ."

"It's no use," said Campbell. "If you will take my advice, you will not waste your time in this city. It is my private opinion that if the Lord has been in Springfield once, he will not come a second time."

Aphorisms

212.10

A month in Pittsburgh would fortify anyone in committing suicide.

—*Herbert Spencer*

212.11

I come from Indiana, the home of more first-rate second-class men than any state in the Union.

—*Thomas R. Marshall*

212.12

Said of the midwest by a Bostonian: "A grand reservoir for our excess population."

(*See also 54.7, 55.18, 79.13–79.16, 79.33, 144.1, 184.32, 207.13, 235.26*)

213. West of the Mississippi

Anecdotes

213.1

Last winter it was said that a cow floated down the Mississippi on a piece of ice and caught such a cold that she has yielded nothing but ice cream ever since.

213.2

"In Skona var I vas born," Said Sven, "vas such a fine echo ve could stand on mountaintop and yell, 'Yonson,' and in 20 minutes back comes such strong echo, 'Yonson,' ve nearly fall off mountain."

"Why," said Olsen, "right here in Minnesota we stand on shore of lake and yell, 'Yonson,' and in one minute back come 10,000 echoes, 'Which Yonson?' "

—*Capper's Weekly*

213.3

When a preacher one Sunday evening in Minneapolis began with "I take my text this evening from St. Paul," the whole congregation arose and walked out, indignant at so favorable a reference to the rival city.

213.4

A dinner was held to bury the hatchet once and for all between the twin cities of St. Paul and Minneapolis, a meeting sponsored by both chambers of commerce. A Minneapolis businessman, speaking, emphasized the essential unity of Minneapolis and St. Paul and concluded with, "Even the names of these cities might with advantage be combined. I would suggest 'Minnehaha,' 'Minne' for Minneapolis, and 'Haha' for St. Paul."

That ended the peace effort.

213.5

He was reckoned to be the laziest man in Iowa, and naturally spent most of his time sleeping. He was so inactive and so useless that at one time the townspeople thought it would be a good idea to bury him whether he was dead or alive. They made a crude coffin, came around with it to his house, put him in it without any protest from his family, and started off with the live old critter for the cemetery. But before they got there, they were stopped by a stranger who had heard of the grim proceedings. They told the stranger the man wouldn't work and had not a grain of corn on his place and the town was sick of providing him with food.

"If you boys will hold off, I'll gladly give that man a wagonload of corn," said the stranger.

Before the townspeople could reply, a head was raised out of the coffin, and the almost-deceased asked, "Is that corn shucked?"

213.6

A man drove up to an Iowa farmer and said, "I'm a government inspector; here is my card. I want to inspect your farm."

A little later the farmer heard screams from his pasture and saw the inspector was being chased by a bull.

"Show him your card, mister, show him your card!" yelled the farmer.

213.7

An Irishman, passing through Dodge City from Morton County in the southwest part of Kansas on his way back to his wife's folks in the East, stopped to water his team, and when asked how conditions were out there, said, "It's beautiful for prospects."

"Why did you leave?"

"Got tired, and my wife wanted to see her folks."

"What is the price of land out there?"

"Come here! You see that little cow tied behind my wagon: I traded a quarter section of land for her, and by gobs! before I made the deed, I found the critter I sold her to couldn't read, so I just slipped the other quarter section I had into the deed, and the fellow didn't know it."

—*R. M. Wright,* Dodge City, 1913

213.8

A recent graduate from agricultural school was making a governmental inspection of a North Dakota farmer's land and stock. He told them he was making an appraisal so that the government could help the farmer get out of the red. So he inspected everything, making careful notes in a neat little notebook. When he thought he had everything listed, he saw an animal stick its head around the side of a barn. "What's that thing, and what's it for?" asked the young man. It was an old goat but the farmer wasn't going to help the all-wise young inspector. "You're the expert," said the farmer. "You tell me."

Consequently the young man sent off a wire to Washington, asking them to identify for him "a long, lean object with a bald head, chin whiskers, an empty, lean stomach, a long, sad face, and cadaverous eyes."

The next day he got a reply from the Secretary of Agriculture: "You blithering idiot, that's the farmer!"

213.9

When an Irishman from Nebraska was visiting in Chicago, he was twitted that there were no real Irishmen in Nebraska.

Said the Irish visitor, "Why, they even name towns after the Irish in Nebraska. Their biggest town is O'maha."

213.10

The Missouri hillbilly decided to have the doctor check him up. "Do you sleep well?" asked the doctor.

"Pretty good at night," said the old fellow, "and I do pretty good in the mornin', but in the afternoon I gits kinda restless."

213.11

A little girl prayed: "Good-bye, God; we are moving to Missouri."

Her brother, who looked forward to the journey, prayed: "Good! By God, we are moving to Missouri."

213.12

A dustbowl farmer felt a few drops of rain and got so excited he fainted. They threw a bucket of dust in his face to revive him.

213.13

At a lunch counter in Oklahoma a big farm boy came in, sat down, ordered some lunch, and asked for a glass of water. "Sorry," said the waitress, "I can't give you water because the health officer says there's bacteria in it."

"Bacteria," said the big fellow thoughtfully as if considering the significance of the waitress's words. "Tell me, lady, how big are they?"

213.14

Pepper Martin, one of the St. Louis Cardinals' most famous players, was stopped in a hotel by an elderly man who asked, "Where did you learn to run the way you do?"

"Well, sir," replied Martin, "I grew up in Oklahoma, and out there once you start runnin', there ain't nothin' to stop you."

213.15

The Governor of Arkansas visited the State penitentiary. A woman inmate, who was cooking in the prison kitchen, asked for an interview, which was granted. She asked the Governor for a pardon. "What's the matter?" asked the Governor. "Haven't you got a nice home here?"

"Yes, sir," she replied, "but I want out."

"Don't they feed you well here?"

"Yes, sir; I get good victuals. That's not it."

"Well, what makes you dissatisfied?"

"It's this way, Governor: I've got just one objection to this place—and that's the reputation it's got over the State."

—Fort Scott *Tribune*

213.16

A neatly dressed patriarchial-type old man was walking along a road outside Little Rock when a young man encountered him and asked, "Where are you going?"

"I am going to Heaven, son. I have been on the way for the past eighteen years."

"Well, sir," said the young man, "if you've been traveling toward Heaven for eighteen years and gotten no nearer than Arkansas, I think I'll take another route. You have been moving away from it."

213.17

One day in Arkansas a man driving along a country road noticed a farmer's barn ablaze, and dashed up to the farmhouse to tell the farmer about it. "Yeah, I know," said the farmer as he lay stretched out on a couch on the back porch. "I've been layin' out here prayin' for rain."

(*See also 55.17, 80.5, 133.5, 154.41, 210.5*)

214. In and around the Rockies

Anecdotes

214.1

A Wyoming cattleman rode into a clearing and saw an enraged bull attempting to end the career of a cowboy who had become separated from his horse. Head down and nostrils snorting, the bull charged. The cowboy dived into a convenient recess in the ground, and the bull plunged across the hole. The cowboy leaped out, and on came the bull, madder than ever, and back into the hole dropped the cowboy.

The cattleman watched this strange thing happen half a dozen times. Then he shouted, "Why don't you just stay in the hole?"

Leaping out again, the cowboy yelled, "There's a bear in that hole!"

214.2

A cowboy went to town and returned wearing an enormous diamond ring. One of his awestruck friends asked him, "Is that diamond real?"

"If it ain't," said the cowboy, "I sure been beat out of a dollar and a half."

214.3

A tyrannical old rancher hired a veteran cowboy, and on the man's first day of work the boss said, "Jim, you are new here and I'll explain my system. I have little to say. But when I want you I'll whistle, and when you hear it you come runnin' and I'll tell you what's on my mind. Don't call back or stand there, just come to me on the double. Like I say, I'm not a man to waste words."

The cowboy looked grimly at his new boss. "I'm like you," said the cowboy. "I don't use many words either, and don't like to waste 'em either. So when you whistle—and I shake my head thisaway—that means I'm not comin'. Now I guess we understand each other."

214.4

A dude rancher, who had also been a scout,

miner, and cowboy, was entertaining his customers after a hard day. He was telling them the thrilling story of the time he had been swept off a raft into the swirling waters of the muddy Colorado. He mounted the ladder of suspense to the top rung. The silt was weighing him down, taking him under. Then he paused. An Eastern lady, his unconscious stooge, gasped: "But how did you escape?"

"Ma'am," he assured her with true Western solemnity, "I didn't."

—*Eric Howard,* Esquire

214.5

"Doesn't it ever rain here?" a visitor to New Mexico asked a native.

"Mister," replied the native, "you've heard about the Deluge and how Noah and his Ark rode it out for forty days of rain. Well, out here that time we got less than 1 inch of rain."

214.6

I asked an Idaho potato farmer why his potatoes were so big and he said, "We fertilize them with corn meal and irrigate them with milk."

—*John Gunther,* Inside U.S.A.

214.7

When a tourist told an Idaho farmer he wanted to buy a hundred pounds of potatoes, the farmer said: "Nothin' doin'. I'm not cuttin' a spud in two for no one."

214.8

Someone in a railroad party visiting Nevada said, "With water to settle the dust, and congenial companions, Nevada would be all right."

Ex-Senator Wade of Ohio, in the party, said, "With plenty of water and good society, Hell would not be a bad place to live in, either."

214.9

He had taken a bad beating at the Los Vegas gaming tables and was about to make a quick departure. While waiting for his plane, he decided to dine with the last of his spare cash.

"Sage hen is recommended," said the waiter.

"Sage hen? Never heard of it. Has it got wings?"

"Yes," said the waiter.

"Then bring me something else—anything else. I don't want nothing that has wings but not enough sense to get out of this state."

214.10

An Easterner on his first trip West, traveling on a bus tour, was unmoved by the scenery, scoffed at the Grand Canyon, yawned at the Petrified Forest, the Painted Desert, and had no interest at all in Yellowstone National Park. When the bus driver had had too much of this carping and indifference he turned on the Easterner and said, "Mister, when you haven't got it on your insides, you can't see it on the outside."

214.11

A fellow from the Southwest died and asked for admittance to Heaven. St. Peter asked him where he was from, and was told. "The Southwest, eh? Well, come on in. But you won't like it."

214.12

A man obliged to live some weeks in the desert said: "At first you find yourself talking to yourself. After a week or so of that, you begin talking to the lizards. After a few more weeks you notice the lizards are talking to you. Then you discover that you are listening to them."

214.13

Seattle had a slogan, SEATTLE HAS A MILLION —WHAT WILL YOU HAVE? Tacoma answered with BUDWEISER BEER, the significance being that Tacoma was distribution center for Budweiser beer as opposed to Seattle local brew called Rainier beer.

214.14

Tacoma and Seattle were militant competitors. A widely distributed circular headed WATCH TACOMA GROW, was answered by Seattle with one headed SEATTLE GROWS WITHOUT WATCHING.

214.15

"Your method of cultivation is hopelessly out of date," said the agricultural agent. "Why I would be astonished if you got one apple from that tree."

"So would I," said the Oregon farmer, "because it's a pear tree."

214.16

"I like the West," said the speaker. "I like her self-made men, and the more I travel West, the more I am with her public men, the more I am convinced of the truthfulness of the Bible statement that the wise men *came from the East.*"

214.17

Out where the West begins, where men are men and smell like horses.

214.18

A Westerner recently said of a Senator from

his State: "Why, I've known him all my life. The poor feller couldn't make a livin'—all he had was a gift of gab—so some of us boys got together an' said, 'Let's send him to Washington, so we won't have to listen to him.' We did, an', by gravy, he's been there ever since."

—*Eric Howard,* Esquire

214.19

A wit has remarked that he can think of nothing more noxious than a home where the buffalo roam.

(*See also 23.4, 28.21, 55.21–55.23, 62.11, 130.10, 199.5, 218.21*)

215. Tall Tales from Texas

Anecdotes

215.1

A Boston salesman in Texas heard one Texan boasting about heroes of the Alamo, who, almost alone, held off whole armies.

"I'll bet you never had anybody around so brave in Boston," challenged the Texan.

"Did you ever hear of Paul Revere?" asked the Bostonian.

"Paul Revere?" said the Texan. "You mean that guy that ran for help?"

215.2

A Texas oilman went to the dentist. "Perfect, perfect," said the dentist, "you don't need a thing done."

"Oh, go ahead and drill anyway," said the oilman, "I feel lucky today."

215.3

An oil-rich Texan who had worn glasses since childhood got behind the wheel of his air-conditioned Cadillac one day with a friend and started off down the road, then suddenly took off his glasses.

"Good Lord, Joe," said the friend, "put your glasses back on before we get killed."

"Relax, man," said the driver. "The windshield is made of prescription glass."

215.4

"How's business down in Texas?" asked the Wall Street banker of his breezy visitor.

"Mister," said the oilman, "we do more business down there by accident than you people do up here in Wall Street on purpose."

215.5

A group of businessmen were discussing the Federal government deficit when a Texas oilman, with a few too many under his belt, said, "I don't care what it amounts to; tell them to put it on my tab."

215.6

A Texan touring France stopped to look up at the Eiffel Tower and asked a companion, "I wonder how many barrels she produces?"

215.7

An uncultured Texan struck oil and wanted to get his equally uncultured wife into society. They moved to Dallas, bought the biggest mansion in town, with the largest swimming pool, and waited for invitations which did not come. He consulted a social adviser, who suggested he get a Rembrandt and a Jaguar. The millionaire ordered both sent to his home and called to see if they had arrived.

"One of them came," said his wife.

"Which one?"

"You'll have to come and see," said his wife, "I have no idea which is which."

215.8

A Texan was asked if he owned much land back home.

"Oh, not much," he said. "Just 50 little old acres in downtown Dallas."

215.9

A Cadillac was parked on a sidewalk in Dallas. "Let me see your license," demanded a cop. "You know you can't park here."

"I'm not parking, Officer," said the driver. "I'm picketing."

215.10

A wealthy Texan is reported to have taken up collecting miniatures, and is now trying to add Rhode Island to his collection.

215.11

An old cowboy died and went to Heaven. It's so unusual for a Texas cowboy to arrive in Heaven that St. Peter took charge of him to show him around. They came to a half-dozen men staked out like unbroken broncos. The cowboy asked St. Peter what that meant.

"Well," said St. Peter, "them are all cowboys from the Panhandle of Texas. If we turn 'em loose, the rascals will every last one of them go back."

215.12

There on the rolling prairies of Texas I have sailed and sailed and sailed across landscapes of gorgeous beauty, and through cross timbers of gorgeous length, until I landed upon a typical Texas sandbank, where the fleas are so thick that the engineer pulls his train up and has the flat cars loaded with sand, and when he gets to the place where the sand is to be unloaded, he gives a toot or two and the whole thing hops off.

—Treasury of Southern Folklore,
B. A. Botkin, ed.

215.13

Several winter-weary Iowa farmers visited Texas with a view to buying land for farming, and moving there. The Texas real estate salesman was at his wits' end when—on the day he was to take them over the farmlands—it snowed heavily for the first time in that area in ten years. Desperate, the salesman called over a young boy and said, "Son, tell these gentlemen how many times you have seen snow down here."

"This is the first time I've ever seen snow," declared the boy firmly. "But I've seen it rain twice."

215.14

When Alaska was admitted to the Union, thus becoming the largest state, Governor Price Daniels of Texas said, "Just wait until all that snow and ice melts. Then they'll find out which is the biggest state."

215.15

Inez Robb relates that a middle-aged Texan went to a psychiatrist and said "Doc, I shore need your help. I'm in a bad way. I been a Texan all my life and suddenly I just don't give a damn!"

215.16

General Phil Sheridan made this oft-quoted remark: "If I owned two plantations, and one was located in Texas and the other one in Hell, I'd rent out the one in Texas and live on the other one." A Waco paper made the seldom-quoted retort: "Well, damn a man that won't stand up for his own country."

215.17

A wealthy Texan killed a man during a quarrel and promptly wired a Houston lawyer, offering him a $10,000 fee to defend him. The attorney wired: WILL BE THERE IN THE MORNING WITH FOUR EYEWITNESSES.

215.18

It is a tradition of the Texas Rangers that their Captain Bill McDonald, at the turn of the century, once received a hurry call for a company of Rangers to come to a small town and quell a riot. McDonald went there alone. When he got off the train, a citizens' committee met him but protested that they had asked for a company of Rangers, not just one man.

"Well," said McDonald, "you only got one mob, ain't you?"

215.19

Dallas and Fort Worth are vigorous competitors. Tom Gooch of the Dallas *Times-Herald* said that a Dallas coffin manufacturer had to ship to Fort Worth via St. Louis because no one in Fort Worth would be found dead in anything from Dallas. And when Amon Carter, Fort Worth millionaire booster, went to Dallas, he always brought his lunch with him because he would not spend any money in Dallas.

215.20

There is rivalry between Houston and Galveston. Galveston bitterly fought the 50-mile Houston ship canal to the Gulf. When Sampson Heidenheimer, Galveston merchant, shipped 6 barge loads of salt to Houston, it was washed overboard. The Galveston *News* gleefully headed its story HOUSTON AT LAST A SALTWATER PORT: GOD ALMIGHTY SUPPLIED THE WATER, HEIDENHEIMER FURNISHED THE SALT.

(*See also 28.5, 55.16, 71.1, 71.4, 71.5, 71.7, 93.36, 94.3–94.8, 100.11–10.14, 156.11, 207.7, 251.5*)

216. California Capers

Anecdotes

216.1

While on a lecture tour in California, Robert Frost was reminded by the then-Governor Earl Warren that he, Frost, had been born in California, and was asked why he had left the state. Frost, who left California when he was two, said, "I was carried out screaming."

216.2

A Californian visiting in the East attended a funeral service where no one was willing to get up and say a few kind words about the deceased. Finally the Californian arose and said, "Since no one is going to say anything about the deceased, I'd like a few minutes to tell you folks about California."

216.3

"I like San Juan," said the person without an education.

The "smart" person said, "The correct pronunciation is San Huan. In California we pronounce the 'J' like an 'H'."

Then the "dumb" guy said, "Oh, I didn't know that. You see, I wasn't in California in Hune and Huly."

216.4

CALIF., said a Florida booster, stands for: COME AND LIVE IN FLORIDA.

216.5

The man from Florida picked up a watermelon and asked, "Is this the largest grapefruit you can grow out here?"

"Watch out there," said the Californian, "or you'll crush that raisin."

216.6

"Just a minute," said the Devil to a new arrival. "You're in Hell but your credentials call for you to go to Heaven."

"Yes, I know," replied the spirit. "But you see I'm from Hollywood [or whatever city or state you prefer to substitute] and the change has to be made gradually."

216.7

W. C. Fields, one of Hollywood's most valiant drinkers, was asked by an interviewer if he ever suffered from DTs. "I can't tell," said Fields, "because I have never been able to discover where the DTs end and Hollywood begins."

Definition

216.8

Smog is the Air Apparent.

—*Rod Maclean*

(*See also 136.1–136.28, 141.20, 184.28, 210.7, 210.17, 221.11, 221.12, 267.5*)

217. Farm Country

Anecdotes

217.1

Nothing pleased old Uriah Grump. One year when his apple crop was exceptionally fine, a neighbor was confident this was one thing old Grump wouldn't complain about.

"I'll bet you're happy about your apple crop. Just about every one is a perfect apple."

"Suppose they'll do," said Grump. "But where am I going to get rotten ones to feed the pigs?"

217.2

One time there was a man who was a farmer, and one year he had a real good crop. But this man was lazy, and when it came time to gather the crops he told his wife he could not help her gather the crops because he felt the Lord was calling him to go preach. He told her to look up in the sky and he pointed out the letters GPC, which he said meant GO PREACH CHRIST.

The wife looked and said, "Man, get to work on those crops. That GPC means GO PICK COTTON."

217.3

The planter stood on a knoll on his plantation and looked down upon a field of cotton completely flooded. "The Lord may be good," he mused, "and He may be just. But He doesn't know a thing about farming."

217.4

A city fellow watching a farmer at work in the field asked him why he killed snakes and then put them in the furrow when he planted corn. "The dead snakes will produce more corn," said the farmer. "The snakes richen up the land. And the more corn you raise, the more whiskey you can get. And the more whiskey you get, the more snakes you have. This is what is called crop rotation."

217.5

"In my day," recalled the veteran farmer, "we used to talk about how much you could raise on 100 acres—and we meant wheat, not government loans."

217.6

Talk about dumb farmers! Why my uncle was dumber than any of 'em. He started out with two windmills, but took one down 'cause there warn't enough wind for both. He ordered some kinds of seeds from last year's catalogue because it took the things two years to bloom. He put cucumbers, tomatoes, lettuce, and celery all in one patch so it would make a combination salad.

He told about the year the rain was so heavy that the roads ran faster than the stream. One time he was going along a muddy road and saw a hat in the middle of it. He stopped to pick it up, but under it was a man's head. "Can I give you a hand?" asked my uncle. "No thanks, I got a good horse under me," said the man.

217.7

"What is that strange odor coming from the fields?" the lady from the city asked the farmer.

"That's fertilizer," said the farmer.

"For the land's sake!" exclaimed the lady.

"Yes, that's right," replied the farmer.

217.8

Old man Perkins's favorite horse was lost—it had apparently just wandered off somewhere into the woods. Perkins and his neighbors searched and called for the animal, but with no result. Finally one fellow went off alone into the woods and presently came back with the missing animal. Asked how he found him when no one else could, the fellow said: "Wal, I jest sat myself down and said to myself, 'Now, ef I wuz a hoss, where wud I go?' And I did, and the hoss did."

217.9

A great deal of sentimental drivel has been drooled about the wonders of the oldtime farm kitchen, but the truth of it is that most of the cooking was frying—and not even in deep fat. The traditional American farmer . . . was scrawny-necked, flat chested and pot bellied from flatulent indigestion.

—*Clyde Brion Davis,* The Age of Indiscretion

217.10

A farmer plowing his fields with a pair of bulls was asked by a neighbor why he didn't use oxen. "Don't want to use oxen," replied the farmer. "I want to use bulls."

"Well, if you don't want to use oxen, why don't you use horses?"

"I don't want to use horses; I want to use bulls."

"Well, you could use one of those modern tractors; your son bought one the other day."

"I don't want to use tractors, either; I want to use bulls."

"Why do you want to use only bulls?"

"Because I don't want them to think life is all romance."

217.11

"What's the matter with that mule?" asked a visitor to the farm. "All he does is sit in the shade. I haven't seem him do a lick of work since I've been here."

"Mister, they ain't nothin' wrong with 'im," said one of the workers on the farm. "He jes' thinks he's a gentleman farmer."

217.12

This is the seventh wife you have buried in your field; no one gets a better return from his field than you do.

—*Martial*

Definition

217.13

Gentleman farmer: One who has more hay in the bank than in the barn.

Aphorisms

217.14

One good thing about living on a farm is that you can fight with your wife without being heard.

—*Kin Hubbard*

217.15

About the only thing on a farm that has an easy time is the dog.

—*E. W. Howe*

217.16

Even if a farmer intends to loaf, he gets up in time to get an early start.

—*E. W. Howe*

217.17

The farmer doesn't go to work. He wakes up surrounded by it.

(*See also 10.2, 10.3, 10.13, 12.1, 12.14, 23.8, 24.3, 26.1, 28.14, 28.15, 36.5, 38.14, 38.20, 40.7, 40.8, 42.25, 42.26, 50.3, 54.18, 54.72, 55.6, 55.20, 57.7, 57.11, 57.13, 57.14, 58.10, 61.16, 70.14, 72.4, 74.2, 78.4, 79.32, 110.13, 121.7, 135.15, 138.12, 156.11, 160.7, 162.18, 167.7, 174.4–174.7, 184.46, 186.5, 188.2, 190.3, 191.7, 210.4, 210.5, 210.9, 210.21, 210.29, 211.9, 211.10, 211.14, 211.22, 211.23, 211.26, 212.1, 212.4, 212.7, 213.5, 213.6, 213.8, 213.12, 213.17, 214.3, 214.6, 214.7, 214.15, 215.13, 216.5, 218.14, 219.17, 230.8, 238.10, 240.13, 249.2, 249.3, 251.27, 251.29, 254.6, 269.18, 271.21, 272.5, 276.2, 277.5, 277.8*)

218. From the Reservation

Anecdotes

218.1

When the railroads began their westward thrust, one of the roads wanted their tracks to run through Indian wastelands, and offered the chief of the tribe $10,000 for the property.

"$50,000," said the chief.

"Why," said the railroad's representative, "that land is hilly, full of rocks and clay; it's no good for farming or anything else."

"Maybe not," said the Indian chief grimly, "but good for railroad."

218.2

A tourist walking through an Indian reservation stopped to speak to an Indian who was sitting in a chair smoking his pipe. "White man," said the tourist, "is heap glad to meet big Indian man. White man hope big chief feel tip-top this morning."

"Hey, Joe," called out the Indian, "come over here and get a load of this guy. He's great!"

218.3

An Indian from a reservation visited Chicago and while wandering around the town was stopped by a native of the Windy City who asked, "How do you like our town?"

"All right," said the Indian. "And how do you like our country?"

218.4

After a long speech to an Indian tribe out West, a government official made the mistake of asking for comment on what he had to say. An old chief of the tribe arose and said: "Much wind! Heap dust! No rain!"

218.5

While visiting an Indian village in one of the Dakotas many years ago, a man rode to the head chief's lodge, where he was to remain for the night. The chief came out and received him while, at the same time, his squaw unsaddled the horse and placed the equipment alongside their tepee. He asked the chief if his property would be safe there, whereupon the chief observed, "Yes, there isn't a white man within two days' ride of here."

218.6

A young churchman, who was overzealous and somewhat flip in manner, went to Wahaskie, chief of the Shoshone Indians, and asked him if he could not work among his people and teach them about God. Wahaskie eyed the young man from head to foot and then asked him, "Young man, are you sure you know God yourself?"

218.7

Some of the Indians of the Fall River Reservation in 1906 were given minor offices, such as constable and justice of the peace, with jurisdiction over their own people. The following warrant was issued by one of the Indian magistrates:

"I, Hihoudi, you, Peter Waterman—Jeremy Wicket, quick you take him, fast you hold him, straight you bring him before me, Hihoudi."

218.8

General Ben Chidlaw, former Air Defense Commander, talking about the need for increased air defense, quoted an old Cheyenne chief: "It is better to have less thunder in the mouth and more lightning in the hand."

—*Time*

218.9

An Indian looked at a ham sandwich he had just ordered in a restaurant. "You slicem ham?" he asked the man at the counter. "Yep," said the man. "Well," said the Indian, "you damn near miss 'em."

218.10

An Indian and a white man were journeying together through the country on a bitter cold day, the white man wrapped up in all the clothing he could get into, and the Indian wrapped up in a single big blanket. The white man complained continually about the cold; the Indian said nothing. Finally the exasperated white man said, "Here I am with a ton of clothes on and still I'm freezing, and you have on only a blanket but the weather doesn't seem to bother you a bit. How come?"

"Is your face cold?" asked the Indian.

"No, hardly at all," said the white man.

"Me all face," said the Indian.

218.11

An Indian asked an Oklahoma bank for a loan of $300. "What security have you got?" the banker asked him.

"Got 150 horses."

This was satisfactory so the loan was granted. Several weeks later the Indian came into the bank, pulled out a huge roll of bills, counted off the $300 plus interest due the bank, and started to leave. The banker said, "Why don't you let us take care of the rest of that money for you. You've got an awful lot of cash there."

"How many horses you got?" asked the Indian.

218.12

Quanah Buller, an Indian chief of Oklahoma, frequently came to Washington to air the troubles of the Indians before Congressional committees. On one of these occasions the chairman of a committee became particularly disturbed when he learned that Quanah Buller had two wives, a problem that administrators of Indian affairs were trying to eradicate. So the chairman thundered at Quanah, "You go back home and tell one of those women that she will have to go back to her own people."

"You tell 'um," said Quanah.

218.13

"I am here," said the Indian to the Congressional committee, "in behalf of my people to urge that they be given the right to manage their own lands the same as all other Americans."

"I am not convinced," said one of the senators, "that the average Indian is competent to handle property."

"Do you mean to suggest, Senator," said the Indian representative, "that I am not capable—that I am a man of less-than-average intelligence?"

"I was referring to the *average* Indian," said the Senator. "You are not average. You are well above average. You would not be here representing your tribe if you were not one of the smartest people in it."

"You are wrong, Senator," said the Indian. "Indians are no different than other Americans. They never send their best minds to the United States Congress."

218.14

A man running for Congress in Oklahoma campaigned vigorously for the votes of Indian farmers in a certain part of the state. He spoke to a large gathering of them and cried out that the Indians had never been treated right in the past and that he was going to change all this when he got to Washington.

He promised that when he was elected the Indians would no longer have to live on the edge of poverty—they would have fine homes, rich lands, and the full respect of their fellow citizens. Upon hearing all this, his Indian audience laughed happily and clapped their hands and cried out, "Oolah! Oolah!" Encouraged by this apparent demonstration of support, the candidate made still more elaborate promises, and again the Indians cried out, "Oolah! Oolah!"

At the end of his speech the candidate jovially shook many hands and slapped many backs as he prepared to return to town. On his way to town, he stopped by invitation to inspect an especially prosperous farm, and while walking over the grounds to the cattle pen to see a prize bull, an Indian farmhand took his arm and said, "You better go round the other way. The men ain't yet cleaned up this side, and you might get some oolah on your shoes."

218.15

An Indian chief, asked how the uranium boom near Saulte Ste Marie, Ontario, was affecting his tribe, replied:

"Two hundred years ago white man come to north shore of Lake Superior. He take all fur and give Indian strings of beads. Then a few years later he cut down all big trees; build lumber mills. Soon all big trees gone—he go away. Few years later he come back; build paper mill at Espanola, cut down all small trees. Nothing on north shore but rock. Now, by gosh, he come back for rock."

—Saulte Ste Marie, Ont., *Daily Star*

218.16

When the Army was building the Alcan Highway to Alaska, a delay in delivery of material forced a halt in construction. The foreman of a work gang therefore ordered his men to chop down the surrounding trees, and kept them at it for days until the material finally arrived. But meanwhile wood was piled up for several miles along the new highway, a supply that would not all be used if the coming winter proved mild. Worried about possible criticism, the foreman asked the local Indian sage what kind of a winter he thought they would have.

"Terrible bad winter," said the Indian.

"How can you tell?" asked the foreman. "The way the birds are flying and the leaves falling and the fur on the animals?"

"Nope," said the Indian. "Tell by damn big heap of wood Army chopping."

218.17

An Indian petitioned a judge in a New Mexico court for permission to change his name to a shorter one.

"What is your name now?" asked the judge.

"Chief Screeching Train Whistle."

"And to what do you wish to change it?"

The Indian folded his arms and grunted, "Toots."

218.18

When the great Indian chief Sitting Bull was finally captured by the United States Army after years of pursuits and skirmishes, he was treated with great respect and asked if he had any special grievances he wished to air.

Sitting Bull said, "One white man print terrible lies 'bout me. If Indian ever find him, be sure scalp son of a bitch who say Sitting Bull graduated West Point."

218.19

It is said that a certain Indian chief could not decide which of his two sons, Straight Arrow or Falling Rocks, should succeed him as head of the tribe. As a test, he sent them into the forests, armed only with a knife, to remain for three moons. Straight Arrow returned in fine condition and with an abundant supply of pelts. Falling Rocks failed to return. The tribe still hunts for him. In fact, no matter where you drive in the nation, you will see the signs posted by the tribe, WATCH OUT FOR FALLING ROCKS.

218.20

An Oklahoma Indian, suddenly made rich through ownership of oil-bearing land, bought himself a powerful car and sped off down the road, although it was his first time behind the wheel of a car. He stopped to pick up a hitchhiker and with renewed confidence got the car up to 95 miles per hour. The hitchhiker began to worry and said, "I'm afraid we're going to have an accident. I'd like to get out and walk."

"Me, too," said the Indian grimly.

218.21

David McCord recalls the time in his youth in a small town in Oregon, when a short picture ran in the local movie house. It was about a cowboy who at a critical moment was thrown from his horse. When a local Indian kept returning to see this picture, he was asked why. He explained that the cowboy was really a pretty good rider and he expected that soon he would learn to stay on that horse.

218.22

When an Indian village in Canada was flooded one spring, the Royal Canadian Air Force rescued the inhabitants with helicopters. But the helicopter pilots soon noticed that they were transporting an inordinate number of Indians, and a tally revealed that they had evacuated 30 percent more than the population. Thrilled by the ride, many of the Indians had paddled back to the village for another helicopter ride.

218.23

The idea of daylight saving came from an old Indian who cut off one end of his blanket and sewed it on the other end to make it longer.

(*See also 69.8, 114.2, 178.3*)

FROM THE CITIES

219. Manhattan Madness

Anecdotes

219.1

Diogenes, still searching for an honest man, came to New York City, and after his visit was asked how he made out. "Not so bad as I feared," he replied. "I still have my lamp."

219.2

Hi Perkins went to New York City for a few days, and when he got back to the country, a neighbor asked him how he liked the big city.

"To tell you the truth," said Hi, "there was so much going on at the depot, I never did get up to the village."

219.3

A ship was wrecked off the Atlantic coast and one of the sailors survived by grasping a stateroom door and floating on it through the night. When someone threw him a rope, he called out, "What city is that ashore of me?"

"Brooklyn," replied the rescuer.

"Oh, never mind," called the sailor through the darkness. "I'll wait until the tide changes and takes me out again."

219.4

"New York is a fascinating place. I should have come here before I got religion," said the not-quite-young man on his first visit to the metropolis.

219.5

"Can I lead a good Christian life in New York City on $50 a week?" a young man asked a clergyman.

"My boy," was the reply, "that's all you can do."

219.6

A lady asked an elevator operator in a New York skyscraper, "Is this car going up?"

"No, ma'am, this is a crosstown car."

219.7

A New Yorker was boasting to a visitor: "See that skyscraper? The men putting the finishing touches on the final twenty stories have gone down to the fiftieth floor for lunch, while the tenants on the first twenty floors are already moving out because the building is old-fashioned."

219.8

"If you don't like the Empire State Building, why have you got your office in it?"

"It's the only way I can avoid seeing the damned thing," said the tenant.

219.9

A Chicago man being shown around Manhattan began to boast about how much and how quickly things are done in Chicago. When they were walking down Park Avenue, the man from Chicago pointed to a large hotel and asked, "How long did it take to build it?"

"About two years," replied the New Yorker.

"Not bad," admitted the Chicagoan. "But back home we'd have built it in half the time. And how about this other building?"

"That is the Grand Central Station. It took just four months to put up."

"In Chicago we would have taken not more than two months to build it. And this Empire State Building? How long was it being built?"

"I really can't say," said the New Yorker. "It wasn't here last night."

219.10

The wealthy New Yorker had just come down to breakfast when the butler said that a Mr. George Johnson was at the door to see him. "By all means bring him in," said the prosperous Easterner. And when Mr. Johnson was ushered in, the host greeted him warmly and immediately recalled what a wonderful visit they had had at the beautiful Johnson ranch out West, how the children had enjoyed the horses and wonderful rides over the plains, and what a gracious and generous hostess Mrs. Johnson had been. "Really, my dear fellow," concluded the Easterner, "I hope you are going to allow me the privilege of returning at least some of the great hospitality you extended to us."

The Westerner was subdued during the other man's recollections and praises, but when pressed by his host he explained that Mrs. Johnson had burned to death when their ranch home had been demolished by fire. The Easterner was shocked but observed that of course he still had his wide-ranging business interests to occupy his mind during such a period of grief. No, said the Westerner, after the fire everything just seemed to fall apart. His several businesses collapsed, one of the children became hopelessly ill, the other boy turned into an alcoholic, and Johnson himself had spent several months in the hospital with———.

"James, James," called out the New Yorker in an anguished voice, "throw this man out—the son of a bitch is breaking my heart!"

219.11

During a heavy rainstorm in New York, a visitor from the hinterland was walking along 42nd Street near Fifth Avenue when he saw an East Indian in native dress carrying an open umbrella.

The visitor stopped a young college student, and pointing toward the East Indian, asked, "What is that?"

"He is a Parsee," said the young scholar. "Probably a visitor to the United Nations."

"What are Parsees?"

"They are sun-worshippers."

"Maybe he is here on a vacation," said the backcountry man as he tucked his coat closer to protect himself from the rain.

219.12

On the eve of a family's departure from Baltimore [or any other city you choose], the youngest child in the family was overheard saying her prayers, ending with "Good-bye, God—we're off to New York in the morning."

219.13

At dusk one summer evening in New York, a man stopped on Fifth Avenue and started to search for a lost object. A passerby obligingly lit a match to help the man. Others presently joined the search, each with more lighted matches, all in silence. Finally the original searcher gave up in disgust and started to leave.

"What did you lose?" asked one of the helpers.

"Oh, I was just looking for a match I dropped."

219.14

Earl Wilson said that Peter Minuit, who bought Manhattan from the Indians for $24, was standing on the banks of the East River closing the deal and was staring across the river.

"Wait a minute," he said, "isn't that Brooklyn over there?"

"For $24," said the Indian chief, a lower

East Side boy, "are you expecting the place to be perfect?"

219.15

Brooklyn Gob: "Whudya do before ya jerned dah navee?"

Gob from Iowa: "I worked in Des Moines."

Brooklyn Gob: "What kind of a moine, iron or coal?"

Aphorisms

219.16

The first thing that strikes a stranger in New York is a big car.

—*Evan Esar,* The Humor of Humor

219.17

Most of the people living in New York have come here from the farm to try to make enough money to go back to the farm.

—*Don Marquis*

219.18

Grant's Tomb is the only perfect architectural structure in the world; you couldn't alter one detail without improving it.

219.19

The wise people are in New York because the foolish went there first; that's the way the wise men make a living.

—*Finley Peter Dunne*

219.20

There is more sophistication and less sense in New York than anywhere else on the globe.

—*Don Herold*

219.21

According to some people, the reason a subway had to be built to Brooklyn was so the people who lived there could get home without being seen.

219.22

New Yorkers are nice about giving you street directions; in fact, they seem quite proud of knowing where they are themselves.

—*Katharine Brush*

(*See also 28.16, 54.9, 82.9, 117.9, 135.6, 137.38, 135.51, 135.56, 135.57, 184.1, 184.27, 184.35, 186.5, 199.3, 199.4, 199.7, 200.1, 200.2, 221.7, 225.14*)

220. Chicago Chuckles

Anecdotes

220.1

A visiting Chicago matron was seated next to one of the Cabots at a Boston luncheon. During the conversation, Mrs. Cabot said to the visitor from the Midwest, "Here in Boston, we place all our emphasis on breeding."

The Chicago woman replied, "In Chicago, we think it's a lot of fun, but we do manage to have a great many outside interests."

220.2

Satan to a New Comer: The trouble with you Chicago people is that you think you are the best people down here; whereas you are merely the most numerous.

—*Mark Twain*

220.3

A man from Chicago staying at a hotel in Milwaukee one night wished to phone someone in a village near Milwaukee. The operator told him the charge would be 25 cents.

"Twenty-five cents!" stormed the Chicago man. "Why in Chicago I can phone to Hell and back for 10 cents."

"Oh, yes," said the operator, "but that is inside the city limits."

Aphorism

220.4

Chicago sounds rough to
the Maker of verse;
One comfort we have—
Cincinnati sounds worse.

—*Oliver Wendell Holmes*

(*See also 131.3, 143.1, 218.3, 219.9, 265.10, 266.37, 271.18*)

221. The Proper Bostonians

Anecdotes

221.1

Boston hostesses began to tire of a Harvard man who had been invited into many homes.

One of the Bostonians asked Helen Choate Bell, "Does he know anything?"

"Know anything!" exclaimed Mrs. Bell. "Why he doesn't even suspect."

221.2

A man, who had learned to share cabs in Washington, arrived in Boston, hopped into an already-occupied cab, and said to the other passenger, "My name is Jennings."

The other man said, "Mine is not."

221.3

Two Boston Brahmins met on the street.

"I hear Bobby Cutler is making a name for himself in Washington."

"Yes, but only nationally."

221.4

A young Virginian, in the dining room of the Somerset Club in Boston, was describing the beauties of his native state in the autumn. When the Virginian had gone on to exasperating lengths, seventy-year-old Mrs. Abigail Adams Homan roared, "Young man, Hell would be beautiful in October."

221.5

A Boston dowager, chided for her lack of travel, said, "Why should I travel when I am already there."

221.6

A dedicated young clergyman visited a Boston dowager hospitalized in Maine. He said to her when he was leaving, "I'd like to say a prayer for your recovery."

Sitting up in bed more stiffly than before, the old gal snapped, "That will be quite unnecessary. I'm being prayed for in Boston."

221.7

A Boston lady upon her return from New York and an inspection of the United Nations, told a friend that the organization was "simply crawling with foreigners."

221.8

Joe McCarthy, a New York newspaper man, recalls the old Boston Irish definition: A lace-curtain Irish family is a family that has fruit in the house when nobody is sick.

221.9

Some years ago a Chicago bank asked a famous Boston financial house for a report on a young Bostonian who had applied to the western firm for employment. The Boston firm wrote a glowing letter, stating that the young man was related to both the Cabots and the Lowells, and that there was also some relationship to the Peabodys and other famous Boston families.

A week later the Boston firm received an acknowledgment from Chicago, but the letter said that perhaps there was a misunderstanding. "We had no intention," concluded the letter, "of using Mr. ——— for breeding purposes."

221.10

Two women from Boston driving across a prairie came upon a lone tombstone inscribed only: JAMES SMITH—HE CAME FROM BOSTON. They gazed at it with deep respect. Then one of them said, "Brief, but sufficient."

221.11

A Bostonian, when asked in California how she came, said, "By way of Dedham."

221.12

Two ladies from Boston were visiting in Southern California. "Gracious," said one, "this California heat is killing me!"

"Remember, my dear," said the other Bostonian, "we are 3,000 miles from the ocean."

(*See also 154.30, 210.12, 212.12, 215.1, 221.1*)

222. The City of Brotherly Love

Anecdotes

222.1

At ceremonies in Philadelphia celebrating Benjamin Franklin's two-hundredth anniversary, Massachusetts Senator Henry Cabot Lodge reminded his audience that Franklin was born in Boston.

Dr. S. Weir Mitchell, of Philadelphia, arose to speak and expressed his surprise that a man of such historical erudition as Senator Lodge would fail to realize that Franklin was born in Philadelphia at the age of seventeen.

222.2

In the lounge car of a train one man said he could always tell what town his fellow passengers came from. "For example," he said, turning to his neighbor, "You are from Denver?"

He was right.

To another man he said, "And you are from New Orleans." Right again.

"And you, sir, are from Buffalo." Again he was correct.

Finally he turned to still another man and said, "You are from Philadelphia."

"No, sir," replied the fourth man emphatically. "I've been sick for three months; that's what makes me look this way."

222.3

"I'm going to Philadelphia [or any other city you prefer] for a rest," said one man.

"Isn't your brother in Philadelphia?" asked the other man.

"Oh, no, my brother is still living."

222.4

A family from Philadelphia [or any other city you choose] was touring in France and for the first time had snails at dinner. They were very fond of them; so fond, in fact, that their waiter expressed surprise that they did not have snails in Philadelphia.

"Oh," replied one of the Philadelphians, "we have them, all right, but we just don't seem ever to catch them."

(*See also 141.17, 207.18*)

223. Pick Your City or Town

Anecdotes

223.1

"How do you like our city?" asked the town's leading booster.

"If you will allow me to speak frankly," replied the visitor, "this is the only time I have ever seen an illuminated cemetery."

223.2

"Nice town you have here. Is it growing fast?"

"Oh, the population never changes. Every time a baby is born a man leaves town."

223.3

That town was so tough the canary birds sang bass.

—*Arthur "Bugs" Baer*

223.4

Bennett Cerf, in his *Good for a Laugh,* reported the following names: Quoth D. Raven, Never, Mo.; Lettice Finder, Shady, Del.; I. M. Phelan, Slightly, Ill.; C. U. Sunday, Early, Mass.; and R. R. Crossing, Look, N. C.

Definitions

223.5

A hick town is one where there is no place to go where you shouldn't be.

—*Robert Quillen*

223.6

Hick Town: One where, if you see a girl dining with a man old enough to be her father, he is.

223.7

A one-horse town is a place where all the lights dim on Main Street when you plug in your electric razor.

—*Paul Osborne*

223.8

Small Town: Where everybody knows what everybody else is doing—and all buy the weekly newspaper to see how much the editor dares to print.

—*New Hampshire newsman*

223.9

Street: A broad flat surface used for the storage of NO PARKING signs.

—*Wall Street Journal*

223.10

City Life: Millions of people being lonesome together.

—*Henry David Thoreau*

Aphorism

223.11

The thing generally raised on city land is taxes.

—*Charles Dudley Warner*

(*See also 141.21, 216.6, 216.7, 222.2–222.4*)

224. Bird's-eye View of America

Anecdotes

224.1

An Englishman, traveling across the United States for the first time, was asked his opinion of the country.

"Well," said the Englishman, "I have concluded that Columbus did not do such a great thing when he discovered America. After all, how could he help himself?"

224.2

"Ah, what a wonderful man was Columbus!" said a New Yorker.

"Why?" asked Oscar Wilde.

"Because he discovered America," replied the American.

"Oh, no," argued Wilde. "It had often been discovered before, but it was always hushed up."

224.3

"We're a great people," said Hennessy, earnestly.

"We ar-re," said Mr. Dooley. "We ar-re that. An' th' best iv it is, we know we ar-re."

—*Finley Peter Dunne*

Definitions

224.4

Americans: People who feel rich because they charge each other so much.

224.5

American: A person who isn't afraid to bawl out the President, but who is always polite to a policeman.

224.6

Americans: People with more time-saving devices and less time than any other people in the world.

—*Thomaston* (*Ga.*) *Times*

Aphorisms

224.7

When you become used to never being alone, you may consider yourself Americanized.

—*André Maurois*

224.8

From the American newspapers you'd think America was populated solely by naked women and cinema stars.

—*Lady Nancy Astor*

224.9

America is the country where you buy a lifetime supply of aspirin for one dollar, and use it up in two weeks.

—*John Barrymore*

224.10

Our national flower is the concrete cloverleaf.

—*Lewis Mumford,* 1961

OTHER COUNTRIES, OTHER PEOPLE

225. Our British Cousins

Anecdotes

225.1

Charles G. Dawes relates that when he was United States Ambassador to Great Britain he bought a newspaper from a boy and paid him the price of one English penny. "A paper back home in the United States would cost me twice that amount," said Dawes to the boy.

"Well, sir," said the lad with a smile, "you can pay me double if it will help you feel at home."

225.2

During World War II an Air Force officer, after an indoctrination lecture on good Anglo-American relations, was riding in a railway carriage with a lone Englishman of austere mien. After quite a few minutes of silence the American said, "Do you mind if I talk to you?" The Englishman looked up and said, "What about?"

225.3

During World War II the English told about a conscript who was asked by the army oculist to read a chart. "What chart?" asked the draftee.

"Just sit down in that chair and I'll show you."

"What chair?" asked the man.

Deferred because of bad eyesight, the draftee went to a nearby movie. When the light came on, he was horrified to discover the oculist in the seat next to him. "Excuse me," said the conscript calmly, "but does this bus go to Shipley?"

225.4

During an air raid in London there was heard the voice of a woman, "Wait a minute—wait till I find me teeth!" Then came the annoyed shout, "Wot the 'ell d'ye think they're droppin'—sandwiches?"

225.5

An elderly Englishman was sitting quietly in his London club when an old friend came up and said, "Sorry, old boy, to hear that you buried your wife yesterday."

"Had to," replied the other man. "Dead, you know."

225.6

When I warned the French that Britain would fight on alone, their generals said: "In three weeks, England will have her neck wrung like a chicken."

Some chicken! Some neck!

—*Winston Churchill*

225.7

A London waiter said, "Now, ma'am, 'ow will you 'ave your chicken today? Will you heat it cold, or shall I 'eat it for you?"

225.8

A Canadian visitor in London was given the privileges of a London club, and one afternoon went there and encountered a sole man in the club. He introduced himself to the lone member and said, "I'm a stranger here and wonder if you won't join me in a drink?"

"Tried it once and don't like it," grunted the

man. And the visitor was given the same answer when he offered the man a cigar, and when he suggested they have a game of billiards. Finally the uncooperative one relented and said, "But see here, my boy, my son will be along here in a few minutes; he will enjoy a billiard game with you."

"Your son? No doubt your only child."

225.9

A native of London, making his first visit to the country, was getting ready for bed when he heard a loud hooting outside his window.

"My God! What's that terrible noise?"

"Why, that's nothing but an owl," said his host.

"I know it's an 'owl, but 'oo in 'ell is 'owling?"

225.10

A guide in London pointed to a certain gun and said, "This was captured by the British at Bunker Hill."

"I see," said a young American woman in the group. "You got the gun and we got the hill."

225.11

A woman once said to Dean Jonathan Swift: "I can never keep my nails clean in London."

"Perhaps," said the Dean, "you scratch yourself."

225.12

An American boarded a crowded train going from London to Liverpool. The traveler, not happy at the prospect of standing for four hours, saw a woman with a poodle dog occupying the seat next to her, and asked to have the seat. "No, you cannot sit here. My dog does not like to travel in the guard's van, so I have bought a ticket for her."

When the man offered to let the dog sit in his lap, the woman curtly said "No!" The American thereupon reached down, picked up the dog by the scruff of its neck, opened the window, tossed the dog out, and sat down.

An Englishman across the aisle leaned over and said, "The trouble with you Americans is that you act too impulsively. You just threw the wrong bitch out of the window."

225.13

Three Americans were discussing humor and they agreed that an Englishman had no sense of humor. At that moment an English friend of theirs came up, and one of the Americans decided then and there to test their conclusion. He told the Englishman a story. The Americans laughed; the Englishman did not.

"Brace up, old man," said one of the Americans. "You'll get the point of it and laugh next summer."

"No, I think not," said the Englishman.

"Why not?"

"Because I laughed at that one *last* summer."

225.14

June 12, 1946. Took Cedric Hardwicke to see *Beware of Pity*. . . . Cedric in great form at lunch. Said of a *very* eminent American statesman that Americans, meaning New Yorkers, look on him as they would look on a piano-player in a brothel who did not know what was going on upstairs.

—*James Agate*

225.15

Civic rivalry between Epsom and Cheltenham in England resulted in this epitaph:

Here lies I and my three daughters,
We died from drinking Cheltenham waters.
If we had stuck to Epsom salts,
We'd never have been in these here vaults.

225.16

The London fog was so thick that ink was poured on it, and it was sold for coal.

Definition

225.17

London clubman's definition of the country: A damp sort of place where all sorts of birds fly around uncooked.

—*Joseph Wood Krutch,* The Twelve Seasons

Aphorisms

225.18

We know no spectacle so ridiculous as the British public in one of its periodical fits of morality.

—*Thomas Babington Macaulay*

225.19

Toast: "I give you England and America. May there never be any dividing line but the Atlantic between them."

—*Charles Dickens*

225.20

I know why the sun never sets on the British Empire. God wouldn't trust an Englishman in the dark.

—*Duncan Spaeth*

225.21

The English have an extraordinary ability for flying into a great calm.

—*Alexander Woollcott*

(*See also 40.35, 54.21, 59.1–59.7, 66.1–66.28, 69.2, 70.4, 70.13, 86.11, 86.12, 87.8, 87.14–87.27, 89.10, 90.5–90.13, 90.18, 91.10, 93.2, 112.2, 118.1, 135.33, 135.39, 139.42, 147.1–147.13, 150.1, 150.2, 150.9, 150.14, 151.7–151.11, 152.2–152.5, 152.9–152.36, 152.40, 152.41, 152.46, 152.58, 158.4, 160.2, 165.90, 173.7, 177.1, 178.3, 178.11, 180.4, 180.6, 180.7, 181.2, 181.5–181.7, 181.12, 183.6, 184.7, 184.43, 184.47, 193.5, 195.2, 207.5, 207.7, 207.15, 207.16, 208.16, 224.1, 224.2, 226.1, 226.2, 226.3, 226.5, 227.1–227.10, 231.1, 234.12, 235.1, 235.2, 235.5, 236.14, 238.3, 244.18, 246.1, 248.3, 248.7, 248.8, 249.9, 259.5, 267.1, 268.3, 270.6, 271.1, 271.3, 271.7, 271.8, 271.11, 271.29, 271.31, 271.32, 271.38, 271.39, 271.49, 271.50, 272.2, 272.7, 272.8, 272.15, 272.17, 272.26, 272.28, 273.2–273.6, 273.8*)

226. The Emerald Isle

Anecdotes

226.1

During the Irish rebellion of 1920, Lord Dunsany was suspected by the British of helping the rebels. One day when Dunsany was not home, a truckload of Black and Tan, the British constabulary troops, drove up to Dunsany's country home, and ransacked it from top to bottom, turning things topsy-turvy and terrorizing the servants. Finding nothing incriminating, the soldiers finally left. As they started to leave, Dunsany's butler yelled after them: "Whom shall I say called?"

226.2

Some forty-odd years ago, a handsome young Irishman named Michael Collins was infuriating the British military on duty in Ireland with his bold and brilliant leadership of guerilla warfare. The stalwart Collins had even brushed past British officers in the streets of Dublin unrecognized. Pictures of the elusive Irishman were nonexistent or scarce.

Consequently, when a Dublin newsboy held up an envelope and called out, "Pictures of Michael Collins, one shilling," a passing British officer quickly paid his shilling and took the sealed envelope. When he opened it and found it empty, he shouted to the newsboy who had retreated to a safe distance: "Say, you little devil, there's no picture of Collins in this envelope!"

"What! Has he gone again?" grinned the newsboy.

226.3

To illustrate that losers always remember strife and ruin and abuse far longer than do the victors, Hodding Carter told about two young American college students on a bicycle tour of Ireland during the troubles with the English there in the 1920s. Assassinations, executions, and guerilla warfare between the Irish and the British were common in those days. One day the travelers stopped at a small village and over a mug of beer got into conversation with an Irish woman who recognized them as Americans. Quickly she was giving them an account of British cruelty and tyranny.

"And do ye know," she said, "that right in this very place 300 brave Irish lads were burned at the stake—every mother's son of them murdered by the British."

The young travelers were appalled by this account. "When did this happen?" one of them asked.

"It was done," cried the Irish woman, "by that dirty, murdering dog Cromwell."

226.4

A local patriot in West Clare—that wild and rough country—one Sunday afternoon during the Land League days departed from his usual custom of delivering a lengthy political speech and said only the following: "Drink is the curse of Ireland. Drink made you shoot your Landlord . . . and drink made you miss."

—*Martin Quigley, Jr.*

226.5

Father Leonard Feeney told of the time he was touring Ireland afoot and stopped to ask a peasant how far it was to Corofin. "About a half a mile down the road, Father," said the Irishman, "And God speed you."

The priest walked the half-mile, and another, and another, until he had counted off six miles before he got to Corofin.

On his way back, he encountered the same Irish peasant and challenged him with his misinformation.

Said the Irishman, "Well, you poor man, I didn't want to knock the heart out of you, and you looking so tired early in the morning. I gave you half a mile to Corofin. That got you started. Somebody else gave you another half-mile. That drived you a bit further. In Ireland we do be always wanting to soften the journey of a stranger by giving him little dribbles of encouragement. Sure, they'd be nobody going any place on a hot day if people knew how far they had to go to get there."

"But," protested the priest, "in England they take care to give you the exact information asked for."

"Do you know the trouble with the English, Father?" asked the peasant. "They wouldn't think enough of you to tell a lie."

226.6

Two Irishmen were walking through the cemetery and stopped to look at a tombstone upon which was inscribed: NOT DEAD, BUT SLEEPING HERE.

"He's deceiving no one but himself," said one of the men.

226.7

"Glory be, here's a long liver for you," said Mike as he stopped to look at a tombstone in the cemetery. "It says here 175; what an age!"

"Yes," confirmed Pat as he also stopped to look. "Named Miles from Dublin."

226.8

A nun walking down a Dublin street came upon two men digging an excavation. They respectfully raised their hats. As the nun acknowledged their greeting, she tripped on a broken piece of concrete and fell. Both men rushed to help her up. But one of them stopped and seized the other by the arm.

"Wait, Mike. She's holy. Don't touch her. Get your shovel."

226.9

A man was walking along a Dublin street when he was stopped by a woman selling thread who said, "Help a poor old lady and buy some thread."

"I don't sew," said the man curtly.

"And neither shall ye reap," said the old woman.

226.10

A visitor to Ireland took a cab to the suburbs of Dublin and, while passing a large estate, noticed two huge dogs carved out of granite at the entrance. Hoping to have some fun with his Irish driver, the visitor asked, "How often do they feed those big dogs?"

"Whenever they bark," said the driver.

226.11

Paddy walked into a Dublin bar with a face manicured by someone's fists. "What happened to you?" his cronies asked.

"Oh, I had a little dispute with Mike O'Reilly."

"And you let that little pipsqueak batter you up like that?"

"Please, gentlemen," said Paddy, "do not speak disrespectfully of the dead."

226.12

"I'm neutral," said the Irishman in a Dublin pub one day during World War II.

"Yes? and for whom are you neutral?" asked the other man challengingly.

226.13

Beerbohm Tree recorded in his notebooks that a luggage "lout" at Dublin station, to whom he gave a shilling tip to be rid of him, said, "Ah, Mr. Tree, Sir Henry Irving gave me two shillings and sure you're twice as good an actor as he is,"—adding as Tree turned away without another shilling—"in your estimation."

226.14

A traveler in Ireland stopped for a glass of milk at a little thatch-roofed cottage. As he sipped his drink he noticed a brick and a faded rose under a glass dome on the center table. "Why do you cherish that common brick and the dead rose?" the visitor asked his host.

"Shure, and there are certain memories attached to them," was the reply. "Do you see this big dent on my head? Well, it was made by that brick."

"But the rose?"

"The rose is off the grave of the man who threw the brick."

—*Highway Traveler*

226.15

An Irishman on a train was seated next to a pompous man with a dog. "Fine dog you have there," said the Irishman.

"It's a cross between an Irishman and a pig," snapped the man.

"Sure, and it's related to both of us, then," said the Irishman.

226.16

The stubborn nature of the Irish is illustrated by the story of the Irishman who wanted to go to Connemara and said to his friend, "I'm going to Connemara."

"You mean you're going to Connemara, God willing."

"No, I'm going to Connemara, God willing or not."

And because of this impious remark the man was changed into a frog and kept in a pond for several years. When he had completed his penance, the man was changed back to his original form and returned home but soon thereafter again began packing up his belongings.

"Where are you going now?" asked the same friend.

"I'm going to Connemara."

"You mean you're going to Connemara, God willing."

"No," shouted the irate traveler. "I'm going to Connemara or back to the frog pond!"

226.17

In his *Irish Sketch Book,* William Makepeace Thackeray relates that one day he was walking along a street in Cork when he was accosted by a woman beggar who said, "May God follow ye! May God follow ye!"

Thackeray paid no attention to her, but still she persisted with her "May God follow ye!" Thackeray reached into his pocket for his handkerchief, but when the beggar realized she was to be given nothing, she raised her voice and said, "And may He never overtake ye!"

226.18

An Irish beggar stopped a high prelate of the church and asked, "Fod God's sake, help a poor man!" The churchman turned on him and severely reprimanded him for using the Lord's name in vain.

"So it's in vain, is it?" asserted the Irishman. "And whose fault is that?"

Irish Bulls

Note: A "bull" is a blunder or inadvertent contradiction of terms, which erroneously has been almost exclusively attributed to the Irish, possibly because the term "bull" derived from one Obadiah Bull, an Irish lawyer in London during the reign of Henry VII. Lawyer Bull was supposed to have been a notorious blunderer. In any event, "bulls" are usually called "Irish bulls." However doubtful this sweeping attribution, they are amusing.

226.19

An Irish bull has been defined as a horse of another color.

226.20

Webster gives an example of the Irish bull in his *Unabridged Dictionary:* "He remarked in all seriousness that it was hereditary in his family to have no children."

226.21

Sir Boyle Roche, a member of the Irish House, was famous for his bulls, such as: "Why, Mr. Speaker, honorable members never come to this House without expecting to find their mangled remains lying on the table."

226.22

Speaking of the dangers of a French invasion, Roche said: "The murderous martial-law men would break in, cut us to mince-meat, and throw our bleeding heads upon that table to stare us in the face."

226.23

"Mr. Speaker, it is the duty of every true lover of his country to give his last guinea to save the remainder of his fortunes!"

226.24

"Sir, single misfortunes never come alone, and the greatest of all national calamities is generally followed by one much greater."

226.25

When someone complained that the sergeant-at-arms should have stopped a man in the rear of the House while the sergeant was engaged in trying to catch him in front, Roche said: "Do you think the sergeant-at-arms can be, like a bird, in two places at once?"

226.26

"The progress of the times, Mr. Speaker, is such that little children who can neither walk nor talk may be seen running about the streets cursing their Maker!"

226.27

"It would be better, Mr. Speaker, to give up not only a part, but if necessary even the whole, of our Constitution to preserve the remainder."

226.28

"Why should we put ourselves out of the way to do anything for posterity? For what has posterity done for us?" Roche, after the laughter which followed this remark, said: "By posterity I do not mean all of our ancestors, but those who were to come immediately after them."

226.29

In his first *Drapier's Letter,* Jonathan Swift wrote: "Therefore I do most earnestly exhort you as men, as Christians, as parents, and as lovers of your country, to read this paper with the utmost attention, or to get it read to you by others."

226.30

"You're a pest," said the annoyed father. "The next time you go out with me I'll leave you home."

226.31

The happiest man on earth is the one who has never been born.

226.32

It's a good thing for your wife that you're not married.

226.33

Flynn had just fallen into a ditch. His friend Brady came along and shouted down, "Flynn, my friend, are you killed? Come on, if you're killed, speak up and say so."

"I'm alive," called back Flynn. "It's just that I've had the speech knocked out of me and I can't answer you."

226.34

No Irishman will ever allow himself to be buried in any but an Irish cemetery. He'd rather die first.

226.35

Denny drained the last glass at the bar and said to his friend, "Paddy, tell me, where did I leave my coat?"

"Sure, you've got it on you," said Paddy.

"Ah, it's a good thing you told me, else I'd gone home without it."

226.36

"What a terrible electric storm we had last night," said Mrs. McCormick at breakfast.

"Then why didn't you wake me up?" demanded Mr. McCormick. "You know I can't sleep during thunder and lightning."

226.37

"Abstinence," said Murphy, "is a good thing, so long as it is practiced in moderation."

226.38

"There are people dying this year who never died before," reported an Irish coroner.

226.39

"Sir," said an Irish member of Parliament, "if I have any partiality for the honorable member, it is against him!"

226.40

"The silence of the Irish members of the House shall be heard no longer!" cried an impassioned orator.

226.41

"Your money or your life!" cried the bandit.

"You go ahead and take me life," said Shannahan. "I'm saving my money for my old age."

226.42

"The only way in which a true gentleman should look at the faults of a lady is with his eyes shut," said a gallant Irishman.

226.43

The chairman of a company in Ireland said at the annual meeting of directors and shareholders, "It is alleged that half of our directors do the work while the other half do nothing at all. I assure you, gentlemen, that the reverse is the case."

226.44

Long before the Irish were heard from, there appeared in Isa. 37:36 an "Irish bull": "Then the angel of the Lord went forth, and smote in the camp of the Assyrians a hundred and fourscore and five thousand: and when they arose early in the morning, behold, they were all dead corpses."

226.45

An Englishman and an Irishman signed on a vessel to work their passage to the United States. The captain insisted the Irishman produce references but did not ask the Englishman for any. This infuriated the Irishman. One day the two men were washing down the deck. The Englishman threw a bucket overboard to get more water and in the process fell overboard and was swallowed up by the sea. The Irishman went to the captain.

"You remember," he said, "that you made me give references but not that Englishman."

"Yes," said the captain, "I remember all the fuss you made about it, too."

"Well," said the Irishman, "I just want you to know that the Englishman has now gone off with your pail."

226.46

An Irishman is never at peace except when he is fighting.

(*See also 25.10, 54.19, 54.20, 59.3, 90.19–*

90.21, 150.23, 234.14, 235.3, 235.21, 235.27, 235.28, 235.31, 235.33, 235.36–235.38, 235.40, 252.7, 255.9, 271.27, 271.45)

227. Scotch and Wry

Anecdotes

227.1

A Scottish Highlander went to the fishmonger's stall in an Edinburgh market, and the Highlander's dog inadvertently dropped its tail into a basket of lobsters. One of the lobsters nipped the tail and clung to it. The dog took off howling.

The fishmonger turned to the Highlander and said, "Hoot, mon; whussle your dog!"

"Hoot!" replied the Highlander, "whussle your lobster!"

227.2

A Scotchman fell down a well. The water was way over his head and icy cold, but he could swim. He kept himself afloat and called out until his wife came to the edge of the well.

"I can't do a thing," she called down. "Just try to keep your head up and I'll call the men from the field to pull you out."

"What time is it?"

"A little before eleven o'clock," she said.

"Well, don't ring for the boys now. Let 'em work until dinner time. I'll swim around till then."

227.3

From one Highlander to another: My Dear Glengary,—As soon as you can prove yourself to be my chief, I shall be ready to acknowledge you. In the meantime, I am *yours,*

—*MacDonald*

227.4

MacTavish and MacGregor were dining together, when to MacTavish's annoyance his friend helped himself to the larger fish on the platter. "Fine manners you've got," he said, "if I had been in your place I would have taken the smaller fish."

"Well," said MacGregor, "you've got the smaller one."

—*The Outspan*

227.5

MacDonald of Glasgow sent his friend MacTavish of Edinburgh a homing pigeon as a present.

227.6

" 'Tis ma birthday," cried the Scotchman to his wife. "The divil wi' the expense. Give the canary anither seed!"

227.7

"Jock," demanded the father, "if you're goin' to sow wild oats, sow them in the backyard so we'll get some good out of them."

227.8

The press reported that two men who smashed a jeweler's window were arrested by the Glasgow police when they came back to recover the brick they had used.

227.9

They say that on the first day of winter the natives of Scotland go about with their mouths open, because there is a nip in the air.

Aphorism

227.10

Oats are a grain, which in England is generally given to horses, but in Scotland supports the people.

—*Samuel Johnson*

(*See also 238.4, 239.4, 271.44, 273.3*)

228. Vive "le Jest"

Anecdotes

228.1

During a debate in the French Chamber of Deputies, one of the members was pleading for laws that would liberalize the legal standing of women. "After all," cried out the speaker, "there is very little difference between men and women."

The entire Chamber of Deputies arose as one man and shouted out fervently, *"Vive le difference!"*

228.2

Whenever William Morris—the nineteenth-century English author, art lover and critic, reformer and craftsman—was in Paris, he dined most of the time at the Eiffel Tower restaurant. When asked why he spent so much of his time at the Eiffel Tower, he said it was the only way he could avoid seeing the thing.

228.3

During the World War II occupation of Paris by Germany, two Nazi officers decided to find quarters in one of the informal pensions on the

Left Bank. The *patronne,* a patriotic French woman, was not pleased at the prospect of boarding two Nazis, and her anger grew when she heard the insolent comments they made about her rooms.

When one of the officers asked, "How much do you charge for this pigsty?" she replied, "100 francs for one pig, 200 francs for two pigs."

228.4

During the German occupation of France in World War II, four persons occupied a train compartment: an old lady, a young girl, a middle-aged Frenchman, and a German officer. When the train entered a tunnel a loud kiss was heard, then the sound of a face being slapped.

When the train emerged into daylight everyone in the compartment was silent, but the German officer had a bruise on his face. The old lady looked benevolently at the young girl and thought: "How virtuous of her! What a fine example she sets for all French girls." The young girl thought, "Strange that the German should try to kiss the old lady instead of me." The German concluded: "That Frenchman is no fool; he steals a kiss from the young girl, and I get hit for it."

The Frenchman thought, "That was a good stunt I pulled, kissing the back of my hand and then socking the German. He doesn't even suspect me."

228.5

A Communist deputy approached a conservative member of the French Senate and showed him a special edition of the works of Karl Marx, printed in braille.

"These are for the blind," said the Red.

"All his works are for the blind," retorted the conservative.

228.6

The schoolboy arose in class and said, "The inhabitants of Paris are called Parisites."

228.7

A backward student wrote on an examination paper: "Pot-pourri is a French dish served in little hot pots."

228.8

Shortly after World War II, a British bulldog and a French poodle were joined by a lanky wolfhound as they strolled along the Rue de la Paix. "Well," said the wolfhound in a strong Russian accent, "how are things with you? Have you been getting enough to eat?"

"Oh, things are picking up a bit in England," said the bulldog, "but we've had rather a bad time of it, y'know. Rations and so forth."

"Oh, yes," said the poodle, "and here we're not much better off. Why, during the occupation I got almost nothing to eat but boiled turnips and chopped garlic. Now I get a little meat but things are still bad. How are they in Russia?"

"Oh, the government sees that we get plenty to eat in Russia," said the stranger. "Just look at me. Fat steaks and juicy bones every day."

"Then," cried the others in unison, "why in the world did you leave?"

"Confidentially," came the whispered reply, "I wanted to bark."

—*Time,* 1948

(*See also 28.22, 54.15, 54.16, 70.3, 87.7, 87.9, 87.11, 135.24, 135.27, 150.6, 150.16, 152.7, 215.6, 222.4, 238.4, 253.4, 270.12, 271.9, 271.10, 271.17, 271.30, 271.42, 273.7, 273.20, 273.22, 277.5*)

INSIDE AND OUTSIDE THE IRON CURTAIN

229. From Russia with Laughs

Anecdotes

229.1

A visitor from abroad, being taken through parts of the Kremlin, asked about two oil paintings. "This one," said the Communist Party guide, "is Ivanov, our great inventor; he invented radar, radio, television, the atomic bomb, the telephone, discovered electricity, invented the automobile and the airplane, the principles of mass production, and a few other things."

"And who," asked the visitor, "is the subject of this other picture?"

"That," said the guide, "is Gregori, our greatest inventor."

"Even greater than Ivanov?"

"Oh, yes," said the guide. "He invented Ivanov!"

229.2

An American visitor to Russia was trying out his transistor radio on a Russian train. A curious

Russian next to him said, "We have those, too. What is it?"

229.3

"I hear on the radio," said one Russian to another, "that we are producing large quantities of meat, butter, and milk, yet my refrigerator is always empty. What should I do?"

"Plug your refrigerator directly into your radio," suggested the other man.

229.4

"Why is communism superior to other systems?" asked the Russian teacher.

"Because it copes successfully with difficulties that do not exist in other systems," replied the much-too-wise student.

229.5

Walter Bedell Smith relates that, when he was United States Ambassador to Russia, one of the jokes whispered around Moscow was, "Being in the Soviet Union is like being in an airplane. We have beautiful, broad horizons; our stomachs feel empty; and we can't get out."

229.6

A schoolteacher in Russia called on a pupil to tell about life in America. The youngster got up and told about American workers being unemployed and starving, Negroes being lynched every day in the South, corruption in all walks of life, crime and drunkenness and dope addiction, and war-mongering and vice.

"And now tell us, what is the Communist slogan?" asked the teacher.

"We must catch up with and surpass the United States," replied the pupil.

229.7

The Russians say they have a paradise. Communist scholars have discovered that Adam and Eve were Russians. Here is the proof: Adam and Eve had no clothes, and no house. Apples were the only thing they had to eat. And they thought they were in Paradise.

229.8

A Soviet citizen died and went to Hell. The Devil told him he could take his choice between the Hell for capitalists or for Communists. "I'll take the Communist section," the new arrival said. "There's sure to be a fuel shortage there."

229.9

A Communist dignitary returned to Russia from Denmark and reported that economic conditions there were very bad. Another person at the meeting said he was surprised to hear him say that, since the Danish store windows were filled with all kinds of wonderful goods.

"Yes, I know, but the Danish people have no money to buy them with. There were no lines of people in front of the stores."

229.10

A woman in Russia wanted to purchase a two-wheeler bike for her son. The store had only tricycles.

"No, that is not what I want."

"But," said the storekeeper, "buy the tricycle. After a week or so, one of the wheels will fall off."

229.11

Two Russians were scaling a treacherous mountain with the aid of some rope. One of the men was obviously terrified. The other Russian, noticing this, said, "You should not climb a mountain if you're afraid of it."

"It's not the mountain that worries me. It's the rope. I work in the factory that makes it."

229.12

A Soviet archaeological expedition in Egypt was given a mummy by Nasser, and sent it back to Russia for study. They wanted to determine the mummy's age. But the scientists were pushed aside by the secret police who said, "Leave it to us; we'll find out."

Presently the secret police announced that the mummy's age was 4,840 years.

"Amazing," cried the Soviet scientists. "How did you determine it?"

"Easy," said the secret police. "The mummy confessed."

229.13

An American and a Russian were engaging in the inevitable controversy concerning their respective concepts of democracy. "Any man in the land," said the American, "can go to Washington, ask to see President Johnson, walk into the President's office and say 'Mr. Johnson, you stink!'—and nothing will happen to him."

"And in Russia," said the Soviet defender, "any peasant from the Ukraine or Siberia can sneak away from his home, hitch a ride on a freight train, arrive in Moscow, show the secret police his identification card, walk into Kosygin's office, sneak past the guards, and say to Comrade Kosygin, 'Sir, President Johnson stinks,' and nothing will happen to him."

229.14

An American Communist arrived in Russia

to get fresh instructions from his Russian masters. He approached a taxicab and asked, "Are you free?"

"Not me," snarled the driver, "I'm a Russian."

229.15

A Soviet citizen went to the polls to vote in an election. He was handed a sealed envelope and told to drop it into the ballot box. But instead he opened it to examine the slip it contained.

"You can't do that!" called out the official.

"But I want to know who I'm voting for," protested the citizen.

"You idiot!" screamed the election supervisor. "Don't you know that the ballot is secret in the Soviet Union?"

229.16

A Russian lay dying in his apartment, when there was a rude knock on the door.

"Who is there?" called the dying man.

"The angel of death," came the solemn answer.

"Thank goodness," sighed the Russian. "I thought it was the secret police."

229.17

Several American engineers visited Moscow shortly after the close of World War II. Their Russian hosts gave them the red-carpet treatment—showing them the city's finest architectural and engineering triumphs. But the *pièce de résistance* was held for the last—the new Moscow subway. The Americans were impressed by its cleanliness, its striking design and appointments, and its beautiful murals. They examined it carefully with unfeigned interest and pleasure.

At the end of a half-hour one of the Americans said: "It is astonishingly beautiful. But tell me, we haven't yet seen a customer or a train. When do the trains run? Where are the passengers?"

The face of the Russian guide clouded as he turned on his questioner and snarled, "Yes, and what about the lynchings in the South?"

229.18

During the Stalin regime in Russia it was the practice of the Soviet Foreign Office to issue its statements for foreign correspondents at about 3:00 A.M. The usual custom was to notify the correspondents to be at the Foreign Office at midnight, and then to keep them waiting for hours in the rain, snow, and bitter cold. They would then be permitted into the building and instructed to walk up several floors where the Foreign Minister or his assistant would hand them the bulletin. They always saw either the Foreign Minister or his next-in-charge.

One cold night, however, after an unusually long wait outside, they were not allowed to enter the building but instead were handed a bulletin by the building superintendent who said that the Foreign Minister had told him to distribute it.

One American that night began his story with these words: "According to a bulletin issued by the janitor of the Soviet Foreign Office. . . ."

After that day all the foreign correspondents were invited into the building immediately upon their arrival.

229.19

Soviet Russia is always uneasy that their trade delegates may misunderstand the meaning of their titles and try to trade places with their counterparts in capitalist countries.

229.20

Russia is not at all happy with some of the decisions of the United States Supreme Court wherein Communists in the United States are protected in the exercise of their rights. These decisions are likely to give Russian Communists the idea that they have some rights.

229.21

In Germany a couple of former prisoners of war remembered a tale that had rippled through their Russian prison camp during the war. At one of the Yalta meetings, Stalin was reported to have asked F.D.R. about the average earnings of a U.S. worker. "Perhaps $350 a month," said the President.

"And how much does he need to live on?" asked the dictator.

"Roughly $200."

"And what does he do with the remaining $150?"

"That," said Roosevelt, "is his business, not mine." Then the President asked, "Now tell me, what does an average worker earn in Russia?"

"Oh, some 800 rubles a month."

"And how much must be spend to live?"

Stalin shrugged. "A thousand rubles."

"Then," Roosevelt persisted, "he needs 200 rubles a month more to stay alive. Where does he get that?"

"That," said Russia's dictator, "is his business, not mine."

—*Time,* 1948

229.22

At the Yalta Conference of the Big Three—Roosevelt, Churchill and Stalin—smoking by the three principals was almost as routine as verbal sparring. At the first meeting Churchill immediately pulled out his cigar case and proudly showed Roosevelt and Stalin the inscription on it. It read: "To Winston Churchill, the Saviour of the British Empire, from the grateful British People."

President Roosevelt, not to be outdone, reached into his pocket and passed around for inspection a gold and ivory cigarette holder bearing the inscription: "To Franklin D. Roosevelt, the Greatest American since Abraham Lincoln, from Admiring Americans."

Stalin examined both Churchill's cigar case and F.D.R.'s cigarette holder, and smiled politely when the inscriptions were translated to him. Then removing the pipe from his mouth, Stalin chuckled as he handed it around the table. On the pipe was inscribed: "To Count Esterhazy from the Vienna Jockey Club."

—Told by *John Willig* in New York Times Sunday Magazine

229.23

"Who is your father?" a schoolboy was asked by Khrushchev when he was in charge of Soviet Russia.

"Nikita Khrushchev is my father," replied the lad.

"And who is your mother?"

"The Communist Party."

"Very good. Now tell me, what would you like to be when you grow up?"

"An orphan," replied the child.

229.24

When Stalin's body was removed from the Lenin mausoleum in Red Square and buried near the Kremlin walls, a small boy asked his grandmother: "What kind of a man was Lenin?" "Lenin was a very great man," she said.

"And what kind of a man was Stalin?" asked the child. "Sometimes he was a very evil man," said the grandmother.

"Babushka, what kind of a man is Nikita Khrushchev?"

"It is difficult to say, child," replied the grandmother. "When he dies, maybe we will find out."

229.25

When Nikita Khrushchev visited the United States, someone presented him with a bottle of inferior bourbon whiskey. Back in Moscow Khrushchev got out the bottle and he and several of his cronies took a drink of the whiskey. When they finally recovered their speech, Khrushchev asked an aid who was familiar with the United States if this kind of whiskey was commonly consumed there.

"Yes, chiefly in Kentucky," said the aid.

"Gentlemen," said Khrushchev after a few moments of reflection, "I think we should make a separate peace with Kentucky."

229.26

Mikoyan and Khrushchev were discussing what to do with Stalin's body when it was removed from the Lenin mausoleum. "What about sending it to Israel?"

"Oh, no," said Khrushchev. "I recall that a long time ago in Israel a man once rose from the dead."

229.27

During a parade in Kiev, Kosygin stopped one of the soldiers and asked, "How is everything?"

"I can't complain," said the soldier.

"You'd better not!" said Kosygin.

229.28

A Russian found fit for travel to the moon told the commissar he didn't want to go space-traveling.

"Where would you like to go?"

"To the United States."

Said the commissar, "We can only take you to the moon. If we could go to America, I'd go there myself."

(*See also 12.3, 17.1, 21.5, 25.11, 30.3, 73.6, 87.13, 116.3, 228.8, 230.1–230.13, 231.4*)

230. From the Satellite Countries

Anecdotes

230.1

The Russian Popov left Moscow for Poland and sent back a postcard reading, "Greetings from free Warsaw." He traveled on to Czechoslovakia and sent a postcard reading, "Greetings from free Prague." His next stop was Hungary, and from there he sent "Greetings from free Budapest." After a longer interval a card came from him in Vienna. It read, "Greetings from free Popov."

230.2

East Germany's Communist boss died and went to Heaven.

"What do you want here?" demanded St. Peter.

"I want to come in," said Ulbricht insolently.

"Nothing doing," said St. Peter; "you go to Hell."

Several days later three devils from Hell arrived at the gate of Heaven and said to St. Peter, "We are the first refugees."

230.3

"Ulbricht has opened the entire border between East and West Germany," said one man to another.

"Why?"

"He wants to celebrate his wedding anniversary alone with his wife."

230.4

Wilhelm Pieck, a Communist leader in East Germany, one day met an old peasant woman and asked how she found things. "Terrible," she said. "There is very little to eat and it won't be long before there is nothing to wear."

"Cheer up, grandma," said Pieck. "Think of the South Seas. Out there they eat very little and go around naked."

"Oh, when did the Russians liberate them?" asked the little old peasant lady.

230.5

Back of the Iron Curtain they sometimes speak of the massive giraffe-like beast the Russians have bred; with its monstrous neck it can feed in East Germany and be milked in Moscow.

230.6

A Russian lecturer was telling Czech students in Prague about the Soviet's wonderful scientific advances. "Already," he said, "we have launched two satellites. In no time at all we will be able to go to the moon. In a matter of a few years we will be able to go to Mars, and then to Venus. And later on to all the planets. Isn't this a wonderful thing?"

All the students nodded.

"Are there any questions."

A student raised his hand. "Sir," he asked, "when can we go to Vienna?"

—*Art Buchwald,* New York Herald Tribune

230.7

"Why do we love the Soviet Union?" asked the teacher in Czechoslovakia.

"Because it has liberated us," replied the pupil.

"And why do we hate the United States?"

"Because it has not liberated us," was the reply.

230.8

A Communist reporter in Poland asked a man what he thought of the harvest results.

"I think they are average," replied the man.

"What do you mean by that?"

"Worse than last year's but better than next year's."

230.9

A cow and a pig and an ass decided to escape from a collective farm in Poland, where they did not have enough to eat. They arrived at the Soviet border and wondered whether they should go on. The pig said he would go and explore. He crossed the border and soon came back. "It is terrible," he said, "everyone who saw me ran after me with a butcher knife—there is more hunger there than in Poland."

The cow thought she'd take a look for herself. "They won't eat me," she said, "because they need my milk." Two days later she came back and said, "You can't live there. Everyone milks me and no one will give me anything to eat."

The ass decided to try his luck. The cow and pig waited for days for him to come back. When they had given him up for lost, they received a note which read: "Dear Comrades: I have decided to stay; I have become a member of the Party."

230.10

Two men stood at the curb on a street in Budapest. They were admiring a beautiful new automobile. "It is magnificent," said one man.

"It's just another triumph of Communist ingenuity and skill," said the other man.

"Why that's an American car. Don't you know one when you see it?"

"Of course I do, but I don't know you."

230.11

In a state primary school in Communist Budapest, a Hungarian teacher asked ten-year-old Istvan to compose a sentence containing a dependent clause. "Our cat had ten kittens," said Istvan, "of which all were Communists."

"Excellent," said the teacher. "Exactly right. Be sure you do as well next week when the government supervisors come."

The following week she asked the prize student the same question. "Our cat," said Istvan, "had ten kittens, of which all were Social Democrats."

"Why, Istvan," cried the teacher, "that's

absurd. That's not what you said last week. Last week your kittens were all Communists."

"I know," said Istvan, "but since then their eyes have opened."

—*Time,* 1948

230.12

From Bucharest in 1948 came a story about a United States diplomat who had some business to conduct with a high-ranking official of Rumania's heavily guarded Ministry of the Interior. After several unsuccessful attempts, he finally managed to work his way into the imposing white Ministry building, past innumerable guards, to the top floor. There stood two doors with a hard-boiled, armed member of the security police posted before each one. The American showed his credentials to the guard at the first door, who looked him over suspiciously and disappeared into the official's office. The American waited, standing first on one foot, then on the other. Suddenly the guard at the other door glanced furtively up and down the corridor. Then, sidling up to the astonished diplomat, he whispered hoarsely: "When are the Americans coming?"

—*Time,* 1948

230.13

In one of the Iron Curtain countries two friends stopped to chat on a street corner. One of the men, forgetting himself, spoke his mind: "This country is run by fools, scoundrels, and rascals. The people are starving and everything is on its way to ruin."

At that point a policeman seized the speaker. The man's friend pleaded with the officer: "Please don't take him off. The man is crazy and doesn't know what he's talking about."

"Crazy, huh?" snapped the policeman. "If he's crazy, how come he knows the political situation so accurately?"

(*See also 229.1–229.28, 231.4*)

231. Elsewhere in Europe

Anecdotes

231.1

At a social affair in Vienna years ago a Viennese snob said, in the presence of an Englishman, that it was strange that all the best company in the city spoke French, but not the English. The Englishman said, "My dear man, that is not at all surprising. After all, the French army has not twice visited England to teach us their language, as they have Vienna."

231.2

During the reign of the Gestapo in Germany two Jews were walking along a street in Munich when a policeman approached them in menacing fashion. One of them had proper credentials, and the other did not. The one with the credentials took to his heels with all speed, trusting to attract the cop to him, while the man without credentials would be able to make his escape. The cop fell for the trap, caught his man, and demanded his papers. When the cop examined them and saw they were in order, he demanded to know why the man took off with such speed.

"I had just taken a physic," said the man, "and my doctor told me always to run after taking the medicine."

"But didn't you see me running after you?"

"Sure, but I thought maybe we both had the same doctor and that you had taken a physic, too."

231.3

During the days of Hitler's dominance, five Germans sat at a table in a coffee shop, each thinking his own thoughts. One of them sighed, another groaned aloud. The third shook his head despairingly, and the fourth man choked down the tears. The fifth man, in a frightened voice, whispered, "My friends, be careful! You know it is not safe to talk politics in public."

231.4

A German was fishing on the west side of a river in Germany, and a Russian was fishing directly opposite him on the east side of the river. The German was catching plenty of fish; the Russian, none.

"How come you catch so many fish?" asked the Russian.

"Because," said the German on the western side of the river, "the fish over here are not afraid to open their mouths."

231.5

Mark Twain said of the Italians, "They spell it Vinci and pronounce it Winchi. Foreigners always spell better than they pronounce."

231.6

Leonard Lyons tells about the American actor in Italy who was seated next to a charming French actress residing in Italy.

The actor asked in what part of Italy she lived.

She said, "In ze Norz."

"What beautiful lakes you have," said the actor.

"How can you see zem?" she asked. "Zey are under ze table."

231.7

Holland lies so low, they're only saved by being dammed.

—*Thomas Hood*

231.8

Holland is a low-lying country, but not a low, lying country.

231.9

"The principal exports of Sweden are hired girls," replied the suburban schoolboy.

231.10

A tired and thirsty American entered a hotel in Madrid, desiring a glass of milk, but knew not a word of Spanish. The waiter knew no English. So the traveler made signs, and the waiter came back with a glass of wine. No, that was not what he wanted. Then the American drew a crude picture of a cow to indicate milk. The waiter came back with a ticket for the next bullfight.

231.11

During the critical years when we were providing substantial aid to Greece, then being heavily propagandized by Communists, the American in charge of our economic mission made an address wherein he said: "I am happy to be here tonight with you good citizens of Greece. You Greeks and we Americans have much in common. We like to eat. We like to drink. And we like to sit and talk."

The next day the leading Communist paper in Greece said: "American Ambassador Porter said that we are just like Americans—gluttons, drunkards, and gossips."

(*See also 20.4, 54.17, 54.18, 87.1–87.5, 87.10, 87.12, 128.17, 135.48, 150.1–150.6, 152.42, 174.19, 175.6, 181.4, 181.9, 207.2–207.4, 207.8, 207.9, 207.10, 207.21, 207.28, 229.9, 230.1–230.13, 248.6, 248.20, 270.13, 271.6, 271.22, 271.23, 271.28, 271.48, 272.6, 272.11*)

232. Other Continents

Anecdotes

232.1

The Christ of the Andes statue, standing on the Chile-Argentine border, symbolizes a pledge made by the two countries. As long as the statue stands, it was agreed, there shall be peace and goodwill between Chile and Argentina.

But the statue itself was the cause of what almost resulted in open conflict. When the work was completed someone pointed out that the Savior's back was turned toward Chile. Chileans felt slighted. But while indignation was at its height, a Chilean newspaperman saved the day. In an editorial he explained: "The Argentinians need more watching over than the Chileans."

This satisfied the people. They laughed good-naturedly and let it go at that.

232.2

When Jack Paar returned from a trip to Brazil, he told about the Brazilian gentleman who fell off a street car. The man got up amid the laughter of onlookers, dusted himself off, and with dignity said: "I shall descend any way I wish."

232.3

An American soldier in the last war was badly hurt in a traffic accident and brought to a hospital in Australia. When he came to in the hospital, he asked the nurse, "Am I brought here to die?"

"No," she said, "you were brought in here yesterdye."

232.4

The eastern part of Asia is called Euthanasia, according to one high school examination paper.

232.5

"When I was in India," related the chronic bore of a London club, "I saw a tiger come down to the waterfront where women were washing their clothes and one of these women, without a moment's hesitation, turned to the fierce animal, threw some water in its face and said, 'Beat it.' And that fool animal turned tail and off he went."

"Gentlemen, said a quiet-mannered man among the group of disbelieving listeners, "I can vouch for the veracity of that account. A few minutes after the incident our friend described, I happened to be walking along the same riverfront and encountered the same tiger. And you know, his whiskers were still wet."

232.6

Sir Arthur Quiller-Couch, in his famous "Lecture on Jargon" (Cambridge, 1913), told about the young East Indian who was struggling with the English language and in reporting the death of a mother wrote: "The hand that rocked the cradle has kicked the bucket."

232.7

In the early 1900s when Japan was beginning to industrialize and to develop its foreign trade, a Japanese steamship company ordered two ocean-going vessels to be built by a Scottish firm. When the first of the vessels was delivered, the Japanese purchasers requested that the builders supply them with the blueprints for the ship so that certain changes might be made in Japan. Shortly after the plans were supplied, the Japanese firm cancelled the order for the second ship and proceeded to build it themselves from the plans covering the first one. But when the second ship was launched, it rolled over and sank.

The shrewd Scottish builders, in supplying the plans, had made certain vital changes not evident to an unpracticed eye but which would cause disastrous results should the Japanese use them to build a second ship.

232.8

"*Mata Hari* means *suicide* in Japanese," said the schoolboy.

Definition

232.9

Heathen Country: One where payrolls are not carried in armored cars.

(*See also 41.6, 68.1, 78.6, 118.12, 179.4, 182.5, 184.50, 207.2, 207.9, 207.11, 219.11, 229.12, 245.21, 253.10, 271.16*)

Part Eight

THE SACRED AND THE PROFANE

SUNDAY HUMOR

PREACHERS AND PARISHIONERS

233. From the Pulpit

Anecdotes

233.1

The new minister stood at the church door greeting parishioners as they departed after the close of services. The people were generous in complimenting the clergyman for his sermon, except one fellow who said to him, "Pretty dull sermon, Reverend." And in a minute or two the same man appeared again on line and said, "Pretty dull sermon, Reverend." Once again the man appeared, this time muttering, "You really didn't say anything at all, Reverend."

When he got the opportunity, the minister pointed out the triple-threat pest to one of the deacons and inquired about him. "Oh, don't let that guy bother you," said the deacon. "He's a poor soul who goes around repeating whatever he hears other people saying."

233.2

Sometimes the preacher's rhetoric got out of control, as when he said: "I looked at the magnificence of Nature and I said, 'Exquisite as you are, you will some day be utterly destroyed, while my soul will live!' And I gazed upon the mysterious Sea and I cried out, 'For all your power and majesty, you are destined eventually to dry up, but not I!"

233.3

The minister told his congregation that on the following Sunday he was going to preach on lying and asked them by way of preparation to read the seventeenth chapter of St. Mark's Gospel.

When Sunday came, the minister asked his congregation: "Those who have read the seventeenth chapter of Mark, please raise your hands."

Numerous hands throughout the congregation were raised.

The minister looked over the congregation and said, "The Gospel of St. Mark has only sixteen chapters. I will now proceed with my sermon on liars."

233.4

Evangelist Billy Sunday, during a revival meeting, asked all couples who had never quarreled to step up in front of him. A number of couples arose and came before the Reverend Bill, who thereupon threw his hand over their heads and cried out: "God bless these damned liars!"

233.5

Dwight L. Moody, the famous evangelist, stopped to visit with a fellow clergyman. The friend told Moody he would love to have him address his congregation, but that it would probably be embarrassing since the congregation was in the habit of walking out before a sermon was finished—no matter who the preacher was.

Moody said he would be delighted to take his chances and thought he would be able to hold them there until the end.

On Sunday morning Moody mounted the pulpit and began by pointing out that the first half of his sermon would be addressed to the sinners and the last half to the saints in the congregation. All stayed to the end.

233.6

The evangelist was at his fiery best in exhorting his listeners to repent and avoid the wrath to come, where "there will be weeping and wailing and gnashing of teeth."

Suddenly a woman called out, "But, sir, I have no teeth."

"Madam," said the evangelist, "in that event teeth will be provided."

233.7

At a small Baptist church in Alabama a revival was under way. The congregation had not been very responsive to the exhortations of the evangelist. As a last plea he asked all those to stand who wished to have their souls washed white as snow. Everybody stood up except one old fellow.

"Don't you want your soul washed white as snow, my brother?"

"My soul has been washed white as snow," said the old fellow.

"Where was that done?" asked the preacher.

"Over at the Methodist church," said the old man.

"Brother, your soul wasn't washed—it was only dry-cleaned."

233.8

A Methodist preacher exhorted his congregation: "Come and join the army of the Lord!"

"I've already joined," called out one in the congregation.

"Where did you join?" asked the preacher.

"I joined the Baptist Church."

"Why, brother," said the preacher, "you're not in the army, you're in the navy!"

233.9

Lorenzo Dow, famous Methodist preacher of old days in the South, once met a little Negro boy named Gabriel who had a horn. He hired the boy to hide in a tree outside the church where he was to preach, and to blow on his horn when the preacher called out his name—"Gabriel."

Everything went as planned. The little boy climbed the tree before anyone arrived at the meeting house, and the preacher launched into a hellfire-and-brimstone sermon, going into great detail about the "last day." Suddenly he cried out, "Suppose that this day Gabriel should blow his trumpet?"

Then of a sudden came the sound of a loud and clamorous blast from the trumpet of Gabriel in the tree, whereupon the congregation—already aroused by the sermon—was thrown into a frenzy of fear. But soon wiser heads realized that there was an artificial Gabriel involved in all this, and they began to scoff.

Dow, never at a loss in handling a situation, thereupon said, "And now, my friends, if a little Negro boy up in a tree with a tin horn can frighten you so, think then what will happen when the real Gabriel with a real trumpet sounds on the last day."

233.10

During the midweek service in an Episcopal church in Virginia, a parishioner arose and asked the pastor: "Is it possible for a man to achieve salvation outside the fold of the Episcopal Church?"

The pastor, after an interior combat, said: "Yes, there *might* be such a possibility—but no gentleman would avail himself of it."

233.11

The minister of a rural congregation, slowly starving on his meager salary and occasional contributions of food from his parishioners, finally decided to leave them for slightly greener pastures. On his last day he bade them farewell in these words:

"Brothers and sisters, I have called you together to say good-bye. God has called me to another place. I fear the Lord has little love for you people; none of you seem to die. Apparently he doesn't want you. And you do not seem to love each other; I have never married any of you. Obviously you do not love me—you have not paid me the salary you were supposed to, and your donations are moldy fruits and wormy apples. 'By their fruits ye shall know them.' And so I am going to a better place. I have been appointed chaplain of the State penitentiary. 'Where I go ye cannot come; but I go to prepare a place for you.' "

233.12

A clergyman says he does not mind at all when his listeners look at their watches when he is speaking, but it gets him down when one not only looks at his watch but then holds it to his ear to see if it is still running.

233.13

Mrs. O'Hara put her Sunday roast in the oven and she and her husband went off to Mass, sure that the pastor would talk only so long, giving her time to get back before the roast had cooked too much. But this Sunday it was a special occasion and a celebrated guest speaker was there. She was obliged to sit in the last pew, and her husband was given a seat right under the pulpit.

The speaker talked and talked, and Mrs. O'Hara began to worry about her roast. She finally wrote a note to her husband and asked the usher to deliver it—but he misunderstood her and handed it to the speaker in the pulpit. Upon reading it, he promptly stopped and left the pulpit. After the Mass was over, the guest preacher explained to the pastor why he had abruptly terminated his talk.

"It was a poison-pen letter from one of your congregation."

"What was that?"

"Here it is—it reads, 'Go home and shut off the gas.' "

233.14

A visiting clergyman occupied the pulpit. The organist wanted to make an impression, so she wrote a note to the old sexton, who had been a little slack in pumping enough air for the organ. She handed him the note just before the service started. By mistake, the sexton handed the unread note to the visiting minister, who opened it and read, "Keep blowing away until I give you the signal to stop."

—*Capper's Weekly*

233.15

A backwoods preacher given to the use of long words in his sermons was told once by a member of his congregation that his use of the word "phenomenon" was not understood.

"I'll talk of that in my sermon next Sunday," said the preacher.

And on the promised day he arose and said that he had been asked to explain his use of the word "phenomenon." "If you see a thistle, that is not a phenomenon. And if you see a bird that sings, that is not a phenomenon. If you see a cow, that is not a phenomenon, either. But if you see a cow sitting on a thistle and singing like a bird—well *that* is a phenomenon."

233.16

The old preacher told his listeners: "When you look at your neighbor's melon patch, maybe you can't help your mouth watering, but you can run."

Aphorisms

233.17

None preaches better than the ant, and she says nothing.

—*Benjamin Franklin*

233.18

Sir, a woman preaching is like a dog walking on his hind legs. It is not done well; but you are surprised to find it done at all.

—*Samuel Johnson*

233.19

Only the sinner has the right to preach.

—*Christopher Morley*

233.20

If there is no hell, a good many preachers are obtaining money under false pretenses.

—*Billy Sunday*

233.21

As a career, the business of an orthodox preacher is about as successful as that of a celluloid dog chasing an asbestos cat through Hell.

—*Elbert Hubbard*

(*See also 62.5, 71.1, 76.1, 106.2, 141.16, 152.25, 168.13, 168.14, 176.4, 211.4, 212.9, 213.3, 217.2, 234.1–234.24, 234.29–234.32 235.20, 235.40, 235.47, 236.1, 236.4, 236.12, 236.13, 236.17, 236.18, 237.2, 237.4, 237.5, 237.7, 238.6–238.8, 238.11, 239.1, 239.4, 239.9, 243.21, 244.15, 244.22, 265.4, 265.9, 267.4, 269.68*)

234. From the Congregation

Anecdotes

234.1

A minister said: "As I was shaving this morning, I was thinking of my sermon and cut my face."

A member of his congregation said later, "The next time he shaves, he ought to think of his face and cut his sermon."

234.2

"Ah!" said a conceited young parson, "I have this afternoon been preaching to a congregation of asses."

"Then that was the reason why you always called them beloved brethren," replied a strong-minded lady.

234.3

A visiting clergyman was the guest of a family in the parish. Before leaving to conduct an afternoon service, he declined lunch, saying that he found he did not preach well following a hearty meal.

When the hostess returned home from the services, her husband asked how their guest had performed in the pulpit.

"He might as well have et," said the housewife.

234.4

"I thank the good Lord that he opened my mouth to preach without any education," said the backwoods preacher.

"That's not too unusual. It happened in Balaam's time," said a listener.

234.5

"Why don't you ever come to hear me preach?" Henry Ward Beecher asked his friend Park Benjamin.

"Because," replied Benjamin, "I never go to places of amusement on Sunday."

234.6

I have got a new Chaplain who always

preaches against whoring and never against drinking—from whence I conclude that he takes the first to be my sin—and that the other is his own.

—*From a letter written by Philip Stanhope*

234.7

"And bear in mind, my dear brethren," concluded the preacher, "there will be no buying or selling in Heaven."

"That may be," muttered a salesman in the back of the church, "but that isn't where business has gone."

234.8

A revival preacher named Burchard was delivering a sermon in the Chatham Street chapel in Manhattan, when Aaron Burr entered.

"There is a sinner," shouted the preacher. "I shall appear in judgment against him."

Burr walked down the aisle until he had reached the midway point, made a low bow and said: "Mr. Preacher, I have been a lawyer in this city for nearly half a century, and of all the rascals it has been my lot to deal with, none surpasses that class of criminals who turn state's evidence."

234.9

An elderly lady, when asked to give her opinion of her pastor, said that on six days a week he was invisible, and on the seventh day he was incomprehensible.

234.10

"How do you like the new minister?" a customer asked one of the merchants in town.

"I haven't heard him preach, but I like him fine," said the merchant.

"How can that be if you don't know him?"

"Oh, I can tell how good he is—the people are beginning to pay up their bills," said the merchant.

234.11

The sermon had been on the Last Day, and the priest had spoken of how all the races of mankind, from the beginning to the end, the quick and the dead, the old and the young, would be assembled before the seat of Almighty God for the Final Judgment.

After Mass a thoughtful Irishman went to him and said he wanted to ask a few questions. "Do you mean to say, Father, that when Gabriel blows his trumpet that everybody who ever lived will all be there at the same time. David and Goliath, Adam and Eve, Antony and Cleopatra, Brian Boru and Cromwell, Hitler and Churchill, Cain and Abel, Martin Luther King and the Ku Klux Klan, the Pope and Luther—will all these be there that day?"

"Yes," said the priest, "all those you mentioned and everyone else that was ever born."

"Well," said the Irishman, shaking his head, "it's my bet there will be damn little judging that first day."

234.12

At the beginning of the seventeenth century, Isaac Wake was the University Orator at Oxford, while Dr. Sleep was a popular Cambridge preacher. King James I of England, and VI of Scotland, used to say he "always felt inclined to wake when he heard Sleep and to sleep when he heard Wake."

234.13

The preacher preached and preached; then he interrupted his discourse and called out, "Brother Brown, will you please wake up Brother Hawkins seated next to you?"

"Wake him up yourself, parson; you put him to sleep."

234.14

The Irish lady was annoyed as she left church after listening to the sermon by a visiting bishop. "Him and his talk about remembering his words. How does he expect us to remember what he said when he couldn't remember it himself—he had to read it to us!"

234.15

A little boy in church, awaking after a nap, asked his father, "Has the preacher finished?"

"Yes, son, he has finished, but he hasn't stopped."

234.16

When a minister had delivered what he was aware was perhaps his worst sermon, he was surprised to have one of his parishioners praise it.

"Why do you say that?" asked the minister.

"Because," said the man. "I don't like preachin' of any kind, and that sermon of yours was just as close to no preachin' as I ever heard in my life."

234.17

The long-winded minister droned on tediously until he said, "Now that we have disposed of the major prophets, we come to the minor prophets. To what place, my dear brethren, shall we assign the minor prophets?"

From a rear pew arose a weary listener who

called out, "Parson, one of them can have my place."

234.18

The preacher, nervous in the pulpit when he discovered he had forgotten his glasses, nevertheless proceeded to deliver his sermon, confident that he would be able to recall the exact words of the relevant Scriptural passages. When he came to that part of his talk where he planned to cite Scripture, he got things a bit twisted when he said that the Lord took 4,000 barley loaves and 6,000 fishes and fed the twenty-four people and had plenty left over.

A testy fellow in the congregation called out, "Anybody could do that."

"Could you?" asked the minister.

"Certainly I could."

After the service, when the minister complained about the heckler's conduct, he was told of his error. "Well," said the minister, "next week I shall not forget my glasses and I'll manage to fix that character."

The next week the minister stepped forward confidently and began his sermon—and in the course of it he brought up again the miracle of the loaves and the fishes. He told how the five barley loaves and the two fishes had fed the multitude of 24,000, and then he pointed to his tormentor of the previous Sunday and asked, "Could you do that, Mr. Smith?"

"Yes, I could," replied Smith.

"And how would you do it?"

"With the loaves and fishes left over from last Sunday."

—*Told to Earl Wilson by Peter Donald*

234.19

The preacher's theme was the Prodigal Son, and in preaching on it he spared none of the details and even added some improvisations of his own. When he got around to the Prodigal's return home, he related that "Dad . . . killed the fatted calf and put a ring on his finger." An acute old fellow said, loud enough for most of the people to hear him. "He oughter put it in his nose."

234.20

It was a terribly stormy day and the preacher was certain no one would show up for Sunday services, but he thought it best to open the church in case someone did appear. When he reached the church, he found there only an elderly man whom he did not recognize. When no others showed up, the preacher asked the man's advice.

"Well," said the old farmer, "I've been feeding stock for close on to forty years and come rain or shine, and come one or a thousand, I feed them."

The preacher thereupon decided to go ahead with his sermon, and talked for an hour and a half. At its conclusion, he asked the farmer's opinion.

"I've been feeding stock for forty years;" said the farmer, "come rain or shine, one or a thousand, I feed them. But if only one comes, I don't dump the whole feed load."

234.21

The preacher was indulging to the full his talent for delivering long-winded, tedious, and wandering sermons. As he came to what his listeners hoped was the conclusion of his talk, he stopped uncertainly, looked at his audience, and in a tentative manner said, "And what shall I say next?"

"Amen," called out a member of the congregation.

234.22

The old Negro woman had just left church services, conducted by a new young minister who always read his sermons. "How's the new man doin'?" she was asked.

"Doin'?" snorted the woman. "He jest lak a crow in a corn field—he takes two dabs and a look-up!"

234.23

A man who decided it was time for him to seek out a church that would meet his spiritual needs went into one when the congregation was being led by the minister in praying: "We have left undone those things we ought to have done, and we have done those things which we ought not to have done."

"Praise the Lord!" sighed the man gratefully. "At last I've found my kind of people!"

234.24

"There is such a small attendance at our church," said the young woman, "that every time the pastor says 'Dearly Beloved' it startles me—for a moment I think I'm being proposed to."

234.25

During church services an attractive young widow leaned too far over the balcony and fell, but her dress caught on a chandelier and held her suspended in mid-air. The minister, of course, immediately noticed the woman's predicament and called out to his congregation: "The first person who looks up there is in danger of being punished with blindness."

One old fellow in the congregation whispered to the man next to him, "I think I'll risk one eye."

234.26

An elderly Methodist, in a strange town over the weekend, got up on Sunday morning and decided he would go to the first church he encountered when he left the hotel. He therefore walked into a church during services that were unfamiliar to him, but which nevertheless impressed him and finally moved his emotions to such an extent that he cried out, "Praise the Lord!" Whereupon he was promptly tapped on the shoulder by an usher, who said, "Sir, you cannot do that in this church."

234.27

"You are just a lot of hypocrites," shouted a man to a group of churchgoers assembling near the church door for the service just about to begin.

"Come on in," rejoined one of the group. "There's room for one more."

234.28

The champion chicken-stealer of the community was converted at a camp meeting and was called upon to "tell the congregation what the Lord has done for you."

The reformed thief arose and said, "It looks as though the Lord done ruined me."

Aphorisms

234.29

"Preaching is foolishness," he made
The text of his oration;
And all confessed that he displayed
A perfect demonstration.

234.30

"I have lost my portmanteau."
"I pity your grief."
"It contained all my sermons."
"I pity the thief."

234.31

On a Parson Who Fell Asleep at a Party

Still let him sleep, still let us talk, my friends;
When next he preaches we'll have full amends.

234.32

After a good sermon, some arise from it strengthened, and others awake from it refreshed.

(*See also 58.4, 79.14, 79.33, 211.4, 213.3, 221.6, 233.1, 233.4, 233.6–233.8, 237.1–237.7, 237.10, 238.1, 238.7, 238.8, 239.1, 239.2, 239.9, 244.22, 251.1–251.37, 264.2*)

235. Clerical Wit and Wisdom

Anecdotes

235.1

Frank Sheed, expounding the promises of Christianity to a small and chilly crowd in London's Hyde Park, was repeatedly heckled by an untidy man, taxing Sheed's humility and patience. The obnoxious fellow finally came up with the old chestnut: "Christianity has been here for almost two thousand years—and look at the state of the world."

Sheed retorted, "Mister, water has been here for more than two thousand years—and look at the state of your neck."

235.2

When Monsignor Ronald Knox was an undergraduate at Oxford, he went with another student to visit a church that had over the portal the inscription: THIS IS THE HOUSE OF GOD; THIS IS THE GATE OF HEAVEN.

Knox glanced at these words, tried the door and found it locked, turned to his companion and said, "In other words, go to Hell!"

235.3

"I wish, reverend Father," said John Philpot Curran to Father O'Leary, "that you were St. Peter and had the keys of Heaven, because then you could let me in."

"By my honour and conscience," replied O'Leary, "it would be better for you that I had the keys of the *other* place, for then I could let you *out*."

235.4

It has been said in jest that at the end of the apostolic age the church was like a locomotive going through a dark tunnel and that it emerged in the post-apostolic period with a bishop on its cow-catcher.

—*Howard Clark Kee and Franklin W. Young,* Understanding the New Testament

235.5

Bray is a village well known in this county

[Berkshire]. The vivacious vicar hereof living under King Henry the Eighth, King Edward the Sixth, Queen Mary, and Queen Elizabeth, was first a Papist, then a Protestant, then a Papist, then a Protestant again. He had seen some martyrs burnt (two miles off) at Windsor, and found the fire too hot for his tender temper. This vicar was taxed by one for being a turncoat and an unconstant changeling. "Not so," said he, "for I always kept my principle, which is this, to live and die the vicar of Bray."

—*Thomas Fuller*

235.6

During the Vatican Council of 1964, with its great ecumenical spirit, it was suggested by one of the fathers of the Council "that we should never speak of the Devil, but of our separated brother."

235.7

A more-than-slightly-tipsy man boarded a crowded bus and thumped down in a seat next to a priest, who was reading his Office. After eyeing the priest for a few minutes, the drunk said thickly but loudly, "I'm not gonna go to Heaven because there ain't no Heaven."

The priest pretended not to hear him, but the drunk persisted in repeating himself. Finally, when the priest continued to ignore him, the drunk bellowed out: "I ain't gonna go to Heaven, 'cause there ain't no Heaven to go to. Now what you got to shay 'bout that, padre?"

The priest looked up and said, "Well, go to Hell, then, but please be quiet about it."

235.8

"Now where in hell have I seen you?" a man asked Archbishop Ryan when he encountered him on a street in Baltimore.

"From where in Hell do you come, sir?" asked the archbishop.

235.9

During a church meeting in a town torn by industrial strife, one of the local tycoons asked for and was granted permission to speak. The industrialist arose and launched into a long defense of industry and its leaders, pointing out its production record, its payrolls, its contributions to economic health, and the function of profits.

When the industrialist finally ended his talk, the clergyman in charge of the meeting said, "Are there any other sinners who wish to say a few words?"

235.10

When Franklin D. Roosevelt was President, the pastor of the church he attended in Washington was asked over the phone, "Is the President expected to attend church this Sunday?"

"I do not know," replied the minister. "But I can assure you that God will be there, which should be incentive enough."

235.11

A minister who was fond of strong beverages was given a bottle of cherry brandy by a waggish parishioner on the condition that it would be acknowledged in the parish *Bulletin*. The next issue of the *Bulletin* stated: "Dr. MacDevitt wishes to thank Mr. Witte for his gift of fruit, and the spirit in which it was given."

235.12

A young woman went to her parish priest for confession and said she had committed the sin of vanity. "And how did you do that?" asked the priest. "Well," said the penitent, "almost every morning when I looked in the mirror I told myself how beautiful I am."

"No, that was not the sin of vanity," said the priest. "That was merely a mistake."

235.13

A minister found a dead mule in front of his home and phoned the police about it. The officer on the desk knew the minister and thinking he'd have some fun with him, said, "I thought you clergymen took care of the dead."

"We do," replied the minister, "but it is always proper first to get in touch with the relatives."

235.14

A pompous young clergyman appointed to help the pastor of a large New York church was told he would be called "Assistant Minister." He thought he rated better, that he ought to be called "Associate Minister," and complained of this to an older colleague. The colleague reminded him that in either instance it would be abbreviated "Ass. Minister."

235.15

A handsome young curate found some of the young women of the parish much too attentive and requested a transfer to another parish. Sometime later he met his replacement, also a young man, and asked him how he coped with the bothersome young women. "Oh, I have no trouble. There's safety in numbers, you know."

"Perhaps," said the first curate, "but I found my safety in Exodus."

235.16

One day a visitor to Our Lady of Gethsemane (Trappist) Monastery in Kentucky was chatting with Abbot Dom Frederic Dunne and asked him if it were true that Trappist monks each day dig a part of the grave they eventually will occupy.

"If that is what you heard, it must be true," said the amused Abbot.

"And do you dig a little bit each day?"

"Every day."

"How much each day?"

"Since you seem to be of more than ordinary intelligence, I will reveal to you details we seldom make known," said the Abbot. "We dig one-thirtieth of an inch each day."

"Is that all? It doesn't seem like very much."

"It makes an inch each month—and adds up to a foot each year."

"Nevertheless, Father Abbot, that's not much for a grave."

"Just think about it for a few seconds," responded the Abbot. "For instance, last week we buried a monk who had been here at the monastery for fifty years. Now, how deep was his grave?"

The visitor pondered for a moment, then joined the Abbot in laughing at the absurdity he had invited.

235.17

A man asked the priest what a miracle was. A full explanation did not satisfy the man. "Now, won't Your Reverence give me an example of a miracle?"

"Well," said the priest, "step before me and I'll see what I can do." As the man did so, he gave him a terrific kick in the seat of his pants. "Did you feel that?"

"I sure did feel it."

"Well," said the priest, "it would have been a miracle if you hadn't."

235.18

Three young dandies one day met an aged minister—a benevolent gentleman with flowing white hair and a long beard. They decided to poke fun at the venerable figure. "Hello, Father Abraham," the first one called out.

"Hello, Father Isaac," said the second.

"Hello, Father Jacob," taunted the third young man.

The keen old fellow, startled for an instant, quietly replied: "I am not Abraham, Isaac, or Jacob. I am Saul, the son of Kish, who went forth to hunt his father's asses. And, lo! I have found them."

235.19

A priest of the Dominican order wanted to smoke in the garden. He asked his superior if he could smoke while he was meditating, and was given an emphatic No.

A priest of the Jesuit order also wanted to smoke, and he asked his superior if it was all right if he meditated while he smoked. The superior said yes, by all means.

235.20

The Reverend Henry Ward Beecher was interested in buying a horse. "Now this horse," said one owner, "is as gentle and kind as you could want. He will stand quietly without being hitched; he will do anything you ask of him. This horse hasn't a single bad trait, he won't kick, and he listens to everything you say."

"Oh," said Beecher, "if that horse were only a member of my congregation."

235.21

A certain ecclesiastic walking one day in company of a friend down Mansfield Road paused in front of the newly erected College. "The erection of that building in Oxford," said the ecclesiastic, "is an impertinence. Even the architecture is obtrusively Unitarian; solid, but cold."

"Yes," said the friend, "built to last, not to please. You can imagine it lasting to the Judgment Day."

"Ah," said the ecclesiastic, "I can imagine it lasting to the Judgment Day but not afterwards!"

—*L. P. Jacks,* Confessions of an Octogenarian, 1942

235.22

A young man stood outside the glassed-in nursery of a Roman Catholic hospital, looking at a newborn baby held up by a nurse. The hospital chaplain happened to be passing by and stopped to ask, "Your first child?" "Oh, no—it's our sixth one," was the reply.

"Wonderful, wonderful," said the priest. "What parish do you belong to?" The young man said he was a Protestant and attended the neighboring Presbyterian church.

The priest walked away without saying a

word, hurried up to one of the hospital attendants, and said, "Keep an eye on that fellow. There's a possibility he might be a sex fiend."

235.23

Members of several religious orders were attending a meeting, when the lights suddenly went out.

The Franciscan knelt down and prayed for light. The Benedictine recited his Office, most of which he knew from memory. The Dominican urged that they should have a dialogue on the origin and nature of light, and examine the consequences of a failure of light.

While all this was going on the Jesuit in the group quietly stepped outside to put a new fuse in the switchbox.

235.24

Just before leaving on a European tour, Billy Graham was asked if he expected to bring back any new creeds with him, and if so, would he be able to get them through the customs.

"Oh, that would be easy enough," replied the evangelist. "None of the new creeds has any duties attached to them."

235.25

Two days after buying a used car, the clergyman returned it and asked for a deal on another one. He explained, "I can't continue to drive this car and remain in the ministry."

235.26

A minister in the Midwest is reported some time ago to have made the following announcement: "The janitor and I will hold our regular prayer meeting on Wednesday evening, as usual."

235.27

A brash young man said to Reverend Sydney Smith, "If I had a son who was an idiot, I would make him a parson."

"Your father," replied Smith, "was of a different opinion."

235.28

Describing the sloth, Reverend Sydney Smith said that this lazy-seeming creature "moves suspended, rests suspended, and passes his life in suspense—like a young clergyman distantly related to a bishop."

235.29

Some years ago during a steel strike, Bishop Francis J. McConnell signed an "Inter-Church Report on the Steel Strike," a document sympathetic to the union cause. Shortly thereafter Bishop McConnell received a letter from an irate clergyman who ended with, "You are a first-class skunk," and then signed himself "Your brother in Christ."

235.30

The pastor of an impoverished parish often wrote his bishop for aid, until the bishop demanded an end to such appeals. For a time there was no correspondence. Then one day the bishop received another letter.

"This is not an appeal," it said; "it is a report. I have no pants."

235.31

When Jeremy Taylor was introduced to the Archbishop of Canterbury, he was told by the prelate that his extreme youth was a bar to his present employment. "If your grace," replied Taylor, "will excuse me this fault, I promise, if I live, to mend it."

235.32

Some years ago Bishop Watterson told of the time a salesman on a train mistook the bishop for another salesman and asked him what house he represented.

"Lord and Church," said the bishop.

"Never heard of them. Are they big?"

"Yes, the biggest on earth," said the bishop.

"Got many branches?" asked the salesman.

"Yes—all over the earth."

"Funny, I never heard of them—what line do they handle? Dry goods, I suppose?"

"Well," said the bishop, "some call it notions."

235.33

The Archbishop of Canterbury, Dr. Temple, was seated at dinner next to a garrulous lady. She asked the Archbishop whether he believed in the interference of Divine Providence in human affairs and told the case of her aunt who had failed to make a train connection and had thus escaped being injured in a terrible disaster.

"Do you not, my lord," she simpered, "regard that as a blessing of Divine Providence?"

"Can't say," muttered Dr. Temple. "Don't know your aunt."

235.34

The fluttery society lady, seated between a bishop and a rabbi at a banquet, said with affected coyness: "I feel as though I were a leaf between the Old Testament and the New Testament."

"That page," said the bishop sourly, "is usually blank."

235.35

A public official, offended by some remarks made to him by St. Basil, said, "I have never before been spoken to in such a manner."

"No doubt," replied the saint, "you have never met a bishop."

235.36

A cardinal was sent by the Pope to make a survey of conditions in Ireland. When the cardinal returned to the Vatican, His Holiness asked, "Tell me, Your Eminence, how did you find the bishops in Ireland? What did they have to say?"

"Bishops!" snorted the cardinal. "There are no bishops in Ireland. They are all Popes."

235.37

The late Cardinal Hinsley of England liked to tell of the two brothers who studied for the ministry. One was a bit too flippant and whimsical to make the grade; the other was much impressed with himself and heavy-handed and ultimately became a bishop. In explaining this the witty brother said, "My brother rose because of his gravity, while I was held down by my levity."

235.38

Francis Gasquet, the English Benedictine monk who was made a Cardinal of the Roman Catholic Church, was stationed at the Vatican for a number of years and became an intimate advisor to Pope Benedict XV.

One day the Pope was expressing to the Cardinal his great disappointment that the world's press had received with scant attention and no enthusiasm a papal pronouncement His Holiness had considered of great importance and significance.

Cardinal Gasquet listened respectfully when Benedict said he had been positive the statement would be widely hailed and endorsed. The pope stopped speaking and waited expectantly.

Softly—in an almost preoccupied manner—the Cardinal said, "Well, Your Holiness, after all, none of us is infallible."

235.39

When Cardinal Gibbons arrived in New York from the Vatican Council that promulgated the doctrine of papal infallibility, one of the shipboard interviewers thought he would bait the Cardinal, and asked him: "Your Eminence, do you really believe in the complete and unqualified infallibility of the Pope?"

"Well," said the Cardinal, "when I was leaving Rome, he called me Jibbons."

235.40

A canon, invited to preach at St. Paul's Cathedral in Dean Inge's day, told the Dean that he was going to give the congregation "a dose of the milk of human kindness."

"Condensed, I trust," said Inge.

—*Everybody's Weekly,* London

235.41

The Sunday School teacher had just concluded a talk on the creation account as given in Genesis, when one of the children said, "My father says we are descended from monkeys."

"After class," replied the teacher, "we will discuss your private family problems."

235.42

When Pope John XXIII visited the Hospital of the Holy Spirit, in charge of an order of nuns, the mother superior went up to him to introduce herself and said: "Your Holiness, I am the Superior of the Holy Spirit."

"Well, you are certainly lucky," said the Pope. "I am only the Vicar of Jesus Christ."

235.43

When asked by a visiting diplomat how many people worked at the Vatican, Pope John XXIII smiled and said, "Oh, only about half of them."

235.44

Pope John XXIII asked a child his name.

"Arcangelo," replied the boy.

"Oh, poor me!" exclaimed the Pope. "I'm just plain Angelo."

235.45

The elderly minister leaped in alarm when a motorist honked at him as he stepped off the curb. A friend with him twitted the cleric: "How come you jump like that at a mere auto horn? You're always talking to us about faith and the mercy of God and not to be afraid of death. Apparently you have your doubts about Heaven being your destination."

"No doubt at all," said the minister with a confident smile. "Heaven is my destination—my home. But right now I'm not in the least homesick."

235.46

Following his sermon on the brotherhood of man, a minister was approached by an assertive young man who said, "Parson, do you mean to say that when I die and go to Heaven that I'll have to live with Negroes, Jews, Catholics, and Indians?"

"I don't think you have anything to worry about," replied the minister. "I doubt that you will get to Heaven."

235.47

During a discussion of birth control at the second Vatican Council in 1965, one of the bishops from Africa protested to European bishops that what they were saying was not pertinent to conditions in Africa.

"For example," he said, "you have been talking exclusively about whether and when a wife should be permitted to take contraceptive pills. But in my country it is rather a question of which wife to give it to."

Aphorisms

235.48

The proper use of the table-napkin is not final evidence of a call to the ministry.

—*Cleland Boyd McAfee,* Near to the Heart of God

235.49

Howl, ye ministers of the altar.

—*Joel, 1:13*

235.50

God predestines every man to be saved. The Devil predestines every man to be damned. Man has the casting vote.

—*Attributed to an unnamed Negro preacher, by William Lyon Phelps*

235.51

It is because they have mistaken the dawn for a conflagration that theologians have so often been foes of the light.

—*Canon F. W. Farrar,* History of Interpretation

235.52

You aren't too bad to come in. You aren't too good to stay out.

—*From a church bulletin board*

235.53

The observances of the Church concerning feasts and fasts are tolerably well kept upon the whole, since the rich keep the feasts and the poor the fasts.

—*Sydney Smith*

235.54

I must believe in the Apostolic Succession, there being no other way of accounting for the descent of the Bishop of Exeter from Judas Iscariot.

—*Sydney Smith*

235.55

As the fellow said, "It is great to live with the saints in heaven, but it is hell to live with them on earth."

—*Richard Cardinal Cushing*

235.56

Natural religion . . . finds a God who is majestic, but not majestic enough to threaten human self-esteem.

—*Reinhold Neibuhr,* Do the State and Nation Belong to God or Man?

(*See also 54.20, 154.5, 172.3, 174.29, 175.7, 178.9, 182.6, 191.6, 219.5, 233.3, 233.4, 233.7, 233.8, 233.10–233.12, 233.15, 233.16, 238.2, 264.2*)

236. Clerical Errors

Anecdotes

236.1

The story is told that when an unorthodox church in the community burned to the ground, Lyman Beecher in his sermon the following Sunday pointed to the fire as God's judgment on false doctrine. The next week Lyman Beecher's church burned to the ground.

236.2

The minister stood at the church door after Sunday services, greeting parishioners. "This is my sister-in-law, Mrs. Hummick," said one woman as she greeted the minister. Then turning to her companion she added, "Our parson never forgets a name."

"How do you manage that?" asked Mrs. Hummick.

"Oh, it's a simple device," replied the minister. "Simply a matter of rhyming, for example, Hummick and stomach—so when I have the pleasure of meeting you again, I can immediately recall your name."

The next Sunday Mrs. Hummick again attended services, and as she was leaving the church the parson greeted her cordially with, "How-do-you-do, Mrs. Kelly."

236.3

A friar, complaining to a friend that his monastic order was not so famous as the Jesuits for scholarship or the Trappists for silence and prayer, added, "However, when it comes to humility, we're the tops."

236.4

There is a persistent story that a bishop, still under the influence of a sermon on conscience he had delivered the previous day, sat at his desk opening mail—invitations, requests for aid and prayers, circulars, and bills. Finally he came to a scrawled message which read: "All is known! Flee before you are exposed!" The poor, panic-stricken bishop, an entirely blameless fellow, hurriedly packed up and fled. No one was ever able to discover what he had done—or thought he had done.

236.5

A curate, invited by a lady in the parish to participate in a spelling bee, did well enough until he lost out when he got mixed up on the "n's" in *drunkenness*. Which in itself was all right, except that rumor got around the neighborhood that he had been turned away from the lady's house because of drunkenness.

236.6

A slightly deaf clergyman directed the clerk to give out a notice in the church about some new hymn books. But the clerk first made another announcement: "All those who have infants they wish to have baptized, please send in their names at once."

The deaf clergyman, supposing the clerk was speaking about the hymn books, stepped forward and said, "For the benefit of those who haven't any, they may be obtained from me any day between 4 P.M. and 5 P.M.; the ordinary ones cost 25 cents and the ones with red backs are 35 cents each."

236.7

A parishioner met the parson on the street. He had been away on a long business trip and asked the pastor, "When do you expect to see Deacon Primrose again?"

"Never again," said the parson sadly. "The deacon is in Heaven!"

236.8

In announcing the church's new public address system, the pastor told the congregation that the microphone and wiring had been paid for out of church funds. Then he added, "The loudspeaker has been donated by a member of the congregation in memory of his wife."

236.9

During a regional ministerial conference, one young clergyman arose and offered a resolution of thanks for the wives who had remained home to help keep affairs in order. In urging the resolution, he said, "While I am here drinking deeply from the wells of wisdom and spirituality of my older colleagues, I am bound to remember that my dear wife remains at our little church, bravely carrying on with the deacons."

236.10

A woman whose husband had just joined the Navy, gave her pastor a note as he was mounting the pulpit one Sunday morning. The note said, "John Anderson having gone to sea, his wife desires the prayers of the congregation for his safety." The pastor picked up the slip and read aloud, "John Anderson having just gone to see his wife, desires the prayers of the congregation for his safety."

236.11

The pastor of a church in upstate New York went to Buffalo to make arrangements for a Christmas sign to be placed outside the church. But when he arrived he discovered he had lost the dimensions. He wired his wife: SEND MOTTO AND SIZE OF SIGN.

When his wife handed the reply to the Western Union office, the clerk almost fainted. The wire read: UNTO US A CHILD IS BORN, 8 FEET LONG AND 3 FEET WIDE.

236.12

A minister, preaching on the danger of compromise, was condemning the attitude of Christians who believe certain things concerning their faith, but in actual practice will say, "Yes, but. . . ." At the climax of the sermon, he said: "Yes, there are millions of Christians who are sliding straight to Hell on their buts."

236.13

Some years ago the Reverend Christian F. Reisner was speaking at the opening of a retreat for ministers. He was impressed by the fine attendance, and recalled the New Testament words, "Come ye apart and rest awhile." Then he added, "It is a great thing to see 300 men come apart."

236.14

A London clergyman, struggling along with a small congregation in a poor section of the city, reluctantly accepted the offer of a commercial firm to supply his congregation with free hymn books, containing the standard psalms and hymns, with the stipulation that a bit of discreet advertising would be injected in the books.

When the books arrived, the clergyman was relieved to find that they contained no glaring advertisements on the inside front cover or on the back cover.

But the poor clergyman was desolated the next Sunday when his congregation began to sing from the books supplied by the commercial firm the following:

Hark, the herald angels sing,
Beecham's pills are just the thing;
Peace on earth and mercy mild,
Two for man and one for child.

236.15

In the course of his lengthy eulogy, the minister leaned over, pointed dramatically to the flower-covered casket that was in front of him, and said, "My dear brethren, this corpse was a member of our church for twenty years!"

236.16

The clergyman officiating at the funeral of one of his wealthy parishioners was particularly anxious to demonstrate his good feeling and sympathy. He began his little talk with: "Dearly beloved, many a time I have dangled this corpse upon my knee."

236.17

A young minister, in the first days of his first parish, was obliged to call upon the widow of an eccentric man who had just died. Standing before the open casket and consoling the widow, he said, "I know this must be a very hard blow, Mrs. Blank. But we must remember that what we see here is only the husk—only the shell—the nut has gone to heaven."

236.18

The young clergyman, at the conclusion of his first funeral service, said, "We will now pass around the bier."

236.19

Four clergymen from the same town sat around one evening talking, and all agreed that they were sinners and that each man had his particular failing.

"Yes, that's right," said one of the men. "Take me—I like to hit the bottle once in a while, even though I have to preach against drinking. Confidentially, I always have a bottle at hand. Only an hour ago I took two shots of the stuff."

"Gambling is what gets me," admitted the second clergyman. "I have it licked when I'm around here, but soon as I get away from here I take to it again. Matter of fact, I lost quite a bundle two weeks ago when I was down to New Orleans."

"Gambling and drinking are no problem with me," said the third clergyman. "But women have always been my problem—especially young widows. I have an awful time keeping my hands off them and, God forgive me, I don't always succeed in resisting the temptation."

The fourth clergyman up to this point had said nothing. They asked him what he had to struggle most against. "Well, drinking, gambling, and even women are no problem with me—never have been. But I do have one serious fault: "I just love to gossip, and the spicier and more sensational the gossip, the better I like it. Right now I can hardly wait to leave here and get talking to people around town."

(*See also 38.21, 154.9, 154.42, 155.40, 156.24, 156.25, 218.6, 233.2, 234.2, 234.4, 234.13, 234.17, 234.20, 234.21, 235.2, 274.4*)

237. Lapses by the Laity

Anecdotes

237.1

An elderly woman was weeping as she bade good-bye to the man who had been pastor of her church for several years.

"My dear lady," consoled the departing pastor, "don't get so upset. The bishop surely will send a much better pastor to replace me here."

"That's what they told us the last time," wailed the woman.

237.2

The preacher stood at the church door greeting parishioners after the services. One woman came up to him and said, "I always get so much out of your sermons, and I hope that some day they will be put into book form."

"Oh," smiled the minister, "maybe that will be done posthumously."

"Well, it can't be too soon for me," said the good woman, confident she had uttered a perfect compliment.

237.3

A pastor got this note accompanying a box of goodies, addressed to him and his wife from an old lady in the parish:

> "Dear Pastor: Knowing that you do not eat sweets, I am sending candy to your wife—and nuts to you."

237.4

The young minister was called in at the last minute to substitute for the pastor, who had had an auto accident. The preacher prefaced his sermon by remarking that "if you break a window and then place a cardboard in its place, that is a substitute."

After the services a woman came up to the young man and said, by way of compliment, "You were no substitute—you were a real pane."

237.5

A nice but blundering old lady liked the new pastor and wanted to compliment him as she was leaving church after services. So she said to him, "I must say, sir, that we folks didn't know what sin was until you took charge of our parish."

237.6

Two men bearing the same name lived near one another in the same suburb. One was a clergyman; the other a businessman. The clergyman died, and about the same time the other man went to Southern California on business. When he arrived on the West Coast he sent his wife a telegram informing her of his safe arrival, but the message was delivered in error to the wife of the deceased clergyman. It read: ARRIVED SAFELY; HEAT HERE TERRIFIC.

237.7

A prominent bishop was approached after Sunday morning services by an elderly lady who said in a tone of appreciation, "Bishop, you'll never know what your service meant to me. It was just like water to a drowning man!"

237.8

A group of women in a Presbyterian parish noticed that the children of a poor family in the parish had ceased attending Sunday School and concluded it was because they lacked good clothing. So they gathered together a good deal of fine clothing for all the children in that family and sent it to the home.

After several weeks had elapsed the Presbyterians noticed that the children had not resumed their attendance at Sunday School, and one of the women called on their mother to inquire. "Oh," said the mother, "the children looked so lovely in all the clothing you sent to us, we decided they ought to go to the Episcopal Sunday School."

237.9

An automobile firm is reported to have advertised a new model with numerous "foolproof" improvements; the advertisement added that the car was particularly suitable for clergymen.

237.10

A preacher was leaving his church and the parish gave him a farewell gift.

The spokesman for the parishioners said that since the preacher had announced his departure, "the congregation was anxious to give him a little momentum."

(*See also 14.5, 37.19, 79.24, 184.40, 217.3, 226.16*)

238. Prayers and Petitions

Anecdotes

238.1

The minister was reproving a member of his congregation for his swearing. The man heard the minister out, then said, "Reverend, you pray and I swear and we don't either one of us mean a damn thing by it."

238.2

It was a formal banquet. The minister had just finished saying grace when a waiter spilled a bowl of steaming soup into his lap. The clergyman silently sizzled, then said in anguished tones: "Will some layman please make some appropriate remarks?"

238.3

It was observed of an old citizen that he was the most regular man in London in his attendance at church and that no man in the kingdom was more punctual in his prayers. "He has a very good reason for it," replied John Wilkes, "for, as he never gave a shilling, did a kindness, or conferred a favour on any man living, no one would pray for him."

238.4

During the long French war, two old ladies in Stranraer were going to the kirk, and the one said to the other, "Was it no a wonderfu' thing that the Breetish were aye victorious ower the French in battle?"

"Not a bit," said the other old lady, "dinna ye ken the Breetish aye say their prayers before ga'in into battle?"

The other replied, "But canna the French say their prayers as weel?"

The reply was most characteristic: "Hoot! jabbering bodies, wha could understan' them?"

238.5

A Franciscan missionary suddenly came upon a lion while traveling through the jungle. Flight was hopeless. The missioner quickly dropped to his knees in prayer. Minutes later, he looked up and was greatly comforted to see the lion also on his knees beside him.

"Brother Lion," exclaimed the missioner in great relief, "how good it is to see you joining me in prayer. I despaired for my life."

"Quiet," snapped the lion, "I'm saying grace."

238.6

Dr. Alexander Whyte, an Edinburgh clergyman famous for his pulpit prayers, was due to preach one Sunday when the weather was exceptionally bad. "I can't see what the preacher will find to be thankful to the Lord for this morning," said one of the congregation on the way into the church. But Dr. Whyte apparently had no trouble coming up with the proper prayer. He began, "We thank thee, Lord, that it is not always like this."

238.7

One day a preacher going to his appointment had to cross a creek on a log. When he was right in the middle of the log, a bear stepped up on the other end of the log. The preacher was scared and turned to go back, but then he saw that another bear had stepped on that end. Both bears started walking toward the preacher. He started to pray, "Lord, I have just one request to make of you. Help me if you can, but don't help those bears." Then the preacher dived into the water and the bears watched him swim away and crawl out of the water upstream.

The preacher then went on to his church and told the congregation of his experience. When he had finished, one of the sisters told him he should have prayed. "Prayer, Sister," he said, "is all right at a prayer meeting, but it ain't worth a damn at a bear-meeting."

238.8

There was a large congregation to hear the new minister's sermon. The sermon was eloquent and the prayers seemed to cover the entire category of human wants.

After the sermon one of the deacons asked the old janitor, who had sat in a corner during the services, what he thought of the new man. "Don't you think he offers up a good prayer, Sam?"

"I most certainly do," said Sam fervently. "In fact, that man asked God for some things that the other preacher didn't even know the Lord had."

238.9

A thin and delicate-looking little boy was competing in a race and kept falling behind; his chances seemed slim. But suddenly he began to move forward with great strides, picked up increasing speed, and won the race.

After the race, one of the spectators asked what he was whispering to himself during the race. The lad replied he was talking to the Lord, saying over and over again: "Lord, you pick 'em up and I'll lay them down."

238.10

The new minister had been asked to pray for rain, and following his prayer there occurred such torrential rains that crops were severely injured. "That just shows," said one farmer, "that you can't trust such prayin' to a preacher who don't know nothin' 'bout farmin'."

238.11

The preacher opened his sermon with these words: "My dear brothers and sisters, you all have come here to pray for rain. But where are your umbrellas?"

238.12

It was a terribly hot and dry summer. The crops were burning up, the soil had turned to powder, streams had dried up, and disaster was imminent in the farming community. An emergency prayer meeting was called at the local church, and one of the best prayers in town was asked to get up and lead the people in prayer. The old fellow got up and said he wouldn't do it—" 'taint no use prayin' tonight," he said.

This unprecedented action called for an explanation, said the deacon. "Do you mean to stand up there and say it ain't no use praying to the good Lord?"

"I believe in prayer, all right," said the expert supplicator, "but I still say there ain't no use praying for rain when the wind is coming from the wrong direction."

Aphorisms

238.13

The shorter our allotted time is, the easier it perhaps is to decide to pray for one's enemies.

—*Soren Kierkegaard,* Meditations from Kierkegaard

238.14

If you want to get a man angry, get some one to pray for him.

—*E. W. Howe*

(*See also 56.1–56.3, 62.3, 79.23, 79.51, 115.6, 174.22, 175.25, 175.27, 175.28, 206.8, 213.11, 219.13, 221.6, 236.10, 239.20, 243.12, 243.14, 243.20, 246.1, 268.24, 271.16*)

239. Contributions and Donations

Anecdotes

239.1

A wealthy man decided one day to go to church for a change. After the services he stopped and said to the preacher, "That was a damn fine sermon you gave this morning."

"Thank you, my good man," said the minister. "But really I wish you would refrain from such a strong term."

"Can't help it, Reverend," said the rich man. "It was a damn good sermon and that's the way I call it. In fact, I liked it so much I put a $100 bill in the collection."

"The hell you did!" exclaimed the minister.

239.2

"Recognize what the good Lord has done for each one of you. Surely you should give at least one-tenth of all you earn to the Lord," said the minister.

"Amen!" shouted one of the more fervent members of the congregation. "I say let's raise it to one-twentieth."

239.3

An Itinerant Preacher who had wrought hard in the moral vineyard for several hours whispered to a Holy Deacon of the local church: "Brother, these people know you, and your active support will bear fruit abundantly. Please pass the plate for me, and you shall have one fourth."

The Holy Deacon did so, and putting the money into his pocket waited till the congregation was dismissed, then said good-night.

"But the money, brother, the money that you collected!" said the Itinerant Preacher.

"Nothing is coming to you," was the reply; "The Adversary has hardened their hearts and one fourth is all they gave."

—*Ambrose Bierce,* Fantastic Fables

239.4

The old Scotsman was distressed that he had mistakenly put two shillings in the plate at church, instead of his usual penny.

The beadle, however, had noticed the mistake and for twenty-three consecutive Sundays did not place the collection before him.

But on the twenty-fourth Sunday when the farmer continued to ignore the plate, the beadle persisted and said, "Come now, Sandy, your time's up."

239.5

A regular churchgoer inadvertently dropped a poker chip into the collection basket one Sunday morning, and after the services sought to replace it with a dollar bill.

"Nothing doing," said the vestryman, who knew his man. "I know that Saturday night poker game of yours, and that blue chip will cost you five dollars."

—*Wall Street Journal*

239.6

When the usher came up the aisle with the basket at the offertory, the five-year-old boy in the pew in front turned to his father and said loudly and excitedly, "Daddy, here comes the pennyman!"

239.7

Senator Zebulon Vance, North Carolina, told about the old preacher who traveled his state dispensing the gospel and depending on the voluntary contributions of his congregations for support. One night he stopped at a small town and preached earnestly, saving sinners by the score. Before closing his act, he circulated his hat among the packed benches for a contribution. No one was overlooked, and when the hat was passed back up to the pulpit, the preacher gazed into it, but there was not even a copper penny in it. Raising his hands, with much pious fervor, he said, "Brethren, let us thank God that this hat got back safely out of this crowd."

239.8

After a special exhortation for support of foreign missions, the basket was passed. When it was presented to one man, he said to the holder of the basket, "I don't believe in missions."

"In that case," whispered the deacon, "take something out—it is for the heathen."

239.9

"Salvation is Free" was the theme of the

preacher one Sunday morning, and at its conclusion he announced that the collection would be for the benefit of the preacher and his family. One man arose and objected that this was contradictory—if salvation is free, then why the collection?

"Brother," said the rural clergyman, "when you are thirsty and come to a river, you can drink your fill. And it costs you nothing. But when that water is piped into your house, you have to pay for the piping of it. Salvation is free, but you have to pay when it is being piped to you."

239.10

The old Man is Blind and cannot See. He holds his Hat in his Hand and there is a Dime in the Hat. Go up quietly and Take the Dime out of the Hat. The Man cannot See you. Next Sunday you can put the Dime in the Sabbath School Box and the Teacher will Praise you. Your Papa will put some money in the Contribution box, too. He will put More in than you do. But His Opportunities for Robbing are better than yours.

—*Eugene Field,* 1882

239.11

The crusty old character had just returned from a prayer meeting and mentioned that he placed a dime in the contribution box "to be placed on interest until he reached Heaven." "That could run to a very large amount," said the listener, "before you will be admitted there."

239.12

The old fellow was being pressed to contribute to a local church drive, in spite of his plea that he owed just about everyone in town.

"But," said the collector, "don't you think you owe the Lord something?"

"Yes," said the old man, "I do indeed, but the Lawd ain't pushin' me like the others."

239.13

The meanest old man in town was dying and sent for the priest, although theretofore he had contributed nothing from his considerable wealth for the Church's support. When the priest arrived, the dying man asked if he gave $20,000 to the Church, would the priest guarantee his entrance into the Heavenly Kingdom?

"No," said the priest. "No human being could under any conditions give such a guarantee. On the other hand, it might be well worth trying. Certainly it won't do you any harm."

239.14

A seventy-five-year-old man won $65,000 in the Irish sweepstakes. He had a bad heart, and the family was afraid the news might excite and kill him. So they had the pastor come and tell him, which he did in this way—asking him what he would do if he won $65,000.

Said the patient, "I'd give you and the church half of it."

The pastor fell over dead.

239.15

A young clergyman, fresh out of the seminary, thought it would help him in his career if he first took a job as a policeman for several months. He passed the physical examination and then took the oral examination to ascertain his alertness of mind and his ability to act quickly and wisely in an emergency.

Among other questions he was asked, "What would you do to disperse a frenzied crowd?"

He thought a moment and then said, "I would take up a collection."

239.16

Some years ago in Hartford, we all went to church one hot, sweltering night to hear the annual report of Mr. Hawley, a city missionary who went around finding people who needed help and didn't want to ask for it. He told of life in cellars, where poverty resided; he gave instances of the heroism and devotion of the poor. "When a man with millions gives," he said, "we make a great deal of noise. It's noise in the wrong place, for it's the widow's mite that counts." Well Hawley worked me up to a great pitch. I could hardly wait for him to get through. I had $400 in my pocket. I wanted to give that and borrow more to give. You could see greenbacks in every eye. But instead of passing the plate then, he kept on talking and talking, and as he talked it grew hotter and hotter, and we grew sleepier and sleepier. My enthusiasm went down, down, down, down—$100 at a clip—until finally, when the plate did come around, I stole ten cents out of it. It all goes to show how a little thing like this can lead to crime.

—*Mark Twain*

239.17

Popular Father O'Reilly was visited by a fund-raiser for the Presbyterian church that was planned to replace the older structure. When asked to make a contribution for the new church, Father O'Reilly explained that under canon law he was forbidden to contribute to the propagation of another faith. But suddenly he smiled happily and said, "But I'll tell you what I can do. I can and will be happy to contribute $50 for the destruction of the present Presbyterian church."

239.18

A congregation decided to raise the minister's salary from $3,000 to $3,500 and called on him with the good news. But the minister wouldn't hear of it, for three reasons: "First, because you can't afford to give me more than $3,000. Second, because my preaching is not worth more than $3,000. And third, because the added task of trying to collect an additional $500 from you would probably kill me."

Aphorisms

239.19

A congregation who can't afford to pay a clergyman enough wants a missionary more than they do a clergyman.

—*Josh Billings*

239.20

A young man, who attends church regularly, clasps his hands so tight during prayer time that he can't get them open when the contribution box comes around.

239.21

Some people who give the Lord credit are reluctant to give him cash.

—*Jack Herbert*

239.22

One reason we have so many pennies in the collection is because we have no smaller coins.

(*See also 14.5, 27.1–27.25, 71.2, 134.3, 175.16, 233.11, 243.12*)

240. The Laity-at-large

Anecdotes

240.1

Patrick Emmett O'Grady, newly arrived in the United States from you-know-where, got a job immediately and at the end of his first day's work stopped for a few beers at a tavern frequented by his countrymen. "Ah, 'tis a great country this," said Paddy over his beer. "I get a job right away, and the job is tearing down a Methodist church—and glory be to God, they actually pay a man for doing this!"

240.2

An Irishman fell asleep in a church he wandered into, thinking it was the cathedral. Aroused by the sexton and told the place was being closed up, he said, "They don't close cathedrals." The sexton told him this was not a cathedral, but a Presbyterian church.

The Irishman looked around and saw stained-glass windows of St. Luke, St. Mark, and St. Thomas, and checked their identification with the sexton.

"And since when did they all become Presbyterians?" he asked.

240.3

"Ah, 'tis good to be a success," sighed Mr. Hooly to his wife as he sank into a comfortable chair upon his return from Sunday Mass. "Think of it: I began as a poor and plain Hooly; we got married and I became Mr. Hooly. I went into politics and became District Leader Hooly; then the honorable Alderman Hooly. And this morning when I arrived at church late and walked down the middle aisle, the people all stood up and cried out, 'Hooly! Hooly! Hooly!' Ah, as I say, 'tis great to be successful!"

240.4

A gentle and well-respected old Negro one day decided that he would like to become a member of a church near his home. He called on the pastor of this fashionable church and told him of his desire. "My dear man," said the pastor with a touch of aloofness, "I do not think you would be happy here, though I appreciate your good intention. Really, you would be most uncomfortable among my people and I am afraid it would be quite embarrassing to you and perhaps to them. I suggest you think it over and pray and meditate and see if God does not give you some direction."

A week later the old Negro met the pastor on the street, stopped him, and said, "Reverend, I took your advice and prayed and meditated and finally God sent me word. He said I should not bother any more trying to join your church; He said He'd been trying to get in there for years without success."

240.5

A clergyman once asked Wendell Phillips,

great New England abolitionist, why he did not go into the South and make his antislavery speeches there, since it was in that region that slavery existed.

Phillips replied: "You are trying to save souls from Hell, aren't you? Well, why don't you go there?"

240.6

"Do your people know anything about religion?" asked the missionary when he met the chief of a cannibal tribe.

"We got a little taste of it when the last missionary was here," said the chief cannibal.

240.7

The originator of a new religion came to Talleyrand and complained that he could not make any converts. "What would you suggest I do?" he asked.

"I should recommend," said Talleyrand, "that you be crucified and rise again the third day."

240.8

A newly assigned pastor called on the sexton to clean out the cellar of the rectory and while the man worked, the pastor watched the sexton sort through a large collection of whiskey bottles, holding each one up to the light to be sure they were empty.

"Don't bother, Pat, they're all dead ones."

"So it seems, Father. But at least they had the clergy with them when they were dying."

240.9

In an argument with a man who quoted the minor prophet Habakkuk, Voltaire retorted, "A person with a name like that is capable of saying anything."

240.10

Billy Graham arrived in a small town and asked a small boy where the post office was. When the boy had given directions, the evangelist said, "If you will come over to the Baptist church tonight, you can hear me give directions for getting to Heaven."

"I don't think I'll be there," said the boy. "After all, you don't even know your way to the post office."

240.11

The itinerant evangelist walked into a drugstore in Iowa and began to distribute tracts against the use of alcoholic beverages. In a corner of the store an old man sat reading a newspaper. When the evangelist approached him, the old fellow looked up at him, recognized what he was doing, and asked, "Are you a reformed drunkard?"

"No sir—I certainly am not!" snapped the evangelist.

"Well, then, why don't you reform?" asked the old man.

240.12

One day a country parson scolded the owner of a service station, one of his parishioners, for the exorbitant charges he assessed for the rescue of stranded motorists. "There's no Biblical authority for such conduct," concluded the minister.

"Oh, yes, there is," replied the owner of the service station. "What about, 'He was a stranger and they took him in'?"

240.13

Two parsons stopped at a farmer's home for dinner. Times were bad, but the farm wife nevertheless cooked two chickens, assuring the family on the quiet that there would be enough left over for another meal. But the ministers were in no mood to be cooperative; the chickens had totally disappeared before the prayer of thanks was said at meal's end.

Strolling around the farm after the meal, the ministers heard an old rooster crowing. "He's mighty proud about something," chuckled one of the clergymen.

"He ought to be," said the farmer grimly. "He's got two sons in the ministry."

240.14

A. P. Herbert took a swipe at Dean W. R. Inge, who at that time was as busy with journalistic work as with clerical duties. "He is," said Herbert, "usually described as a pillar of the church. Really, he is two columns of an evening newspaper."

240.15

A Methodist circuit rider came to a crossroads in Wisconsin where stood a typical country lad—freckled, barefooted, pants rolled up, shirt bosom open. The preacher was mounted on just about the poorest horse they had ever seen in those parts. Addressing the boy, he said, "My son, which one of these roads will take me to Stoughton?"

The boy paid no attention to the question. He had never seen a respectable man mounted on so sorry a steed. The minister repeated his query and the boy looked up and asked, "Who are you?"

"I am a follower of the Lord."

"Well," said the boy, "it won't make any difference which road you take. You'll never catch Him with that horse."

240.16

A philosopher and a theologian got into the inevitable argument, the theologian using the old gag about the philosopher resembling a blind man, in a dark room, looking for a black cat—which wasn't there.

"Yes," said the philosopher, "but a theologian would find it."

240.17

Harrigan's wife had often come to her parish priest with complaints of her husband's continual drinking, his general carousing, his late hours, and chronic folly. The priest told her that when the opportunity offered he would talk to Harrigan and see if he could not get him to mend his ways.

Not long after, the priest boarded a bus, spotted Harrigan deeply immersed in the paper, and sat down beside him with a genial "Good morning, Harrigan!" "Mornin', Father," replied Harrigan, looking up briefly from his paper before pointedly resuming his reading of it. Finally Harrigan looked up again and said, "Say, Father, what causes gout?"

"Gout, my boy," said the priest, "is usually the result of too much drinking, too much infidelity to those one is sworn to be true to, late hours, overeating, and a generally sinful life."

"Well," said Harrigan with a satisfied smirk, "it says here in the paper that the Pope's got gout bad."

240.18

Oliver St. John Gogarty, Irish surgeon and wit, accompanied W. T. Cosgrave, head of the then newly formed Irish Free State, to the Vatican for an audience with the Pope. Prior to meeting the Pope, a secretary informed Gogarty that the Pope would present Cosgrave with a large medal, since he was chief of the Irish state, and that Gogarty would be given a smaller medal. Vatican etiquette required that the tray first be presented to Gogarty. When it was presented to Gogarty, he took the big medal and dropped it into his pocket. A few minutes later a secretary dashed up to Gogarty as he was on his way out and said, "Dr. Gogarty, a dreadful mistake has been made."

Gogarty faced him haughtily and said, "Did I come to Rome to have the infallibility of the Pope questioned?"

—Told by *Ben Lucius Burman* in his introduction to Gogarty's "A Weekend in the Middle of the Week"

240.19

A priest active in the war against alcohol was riding in the New York subway one evening when a young man staggered in, plumped himself down next to the zealous cleric, and began to engage him in befuddled conversation.

The priest said to him gently, "My boy, I'm sorry to see you in such a condition. You are playing a dangerous game with your drinking. The misuse of alcohol is a curse of our day and I beg of you to quit it. You will be a better and a happier man for it."

"Look who's talking," said the young fellow thickly. "Why you yourself are so drunk that you got your collar on backward."

240.20

The Sunday School teacher wanted his class to understand the meaning of moral courage and gave as an instance the case of eight boys sleeping in a dormitory, only one of whom said his prayers. "That was moral courage. Now can anyone give me another instance?"

A boy held up his hand and said, "If six preachers were sleeping in the same room and one did not say his prayers, wouldn't that be moral courage, too?"

240.21

The man who had suddenly got religion was being examined by the parson before being fully accepted into the congregation.

"You have renounced sin, no doubt?"

"Yessir—by all means."

"And you are henceforward going to be as a brother to your neighbor?"

"Most certainly, sir."

"And of course you understand that means paying all your just debts?"

"Now, just a minute, parson," said the applicant loudly; "you're getting out of line; you're talking business, not religion."

240.22

Old Man Elisha was a great exponent of predestination—everything was determined from all eternity and there wasn't anything a man could do about anything; he said this repeatedly, and quoted Scripture to support him. This was on the frontier in the days when sudden raids by Indians were a constant threat. One night the church bells began to ring, warning of an Indian raid. Old Elisha came running down the road in his nightshirt, carrying a gun, along with all the other men in the community.

But it was a false alarm. Nevertheless they kidded Elisha about his "What is to be will be," and his tearing down the road in his nightshirt and toting a gun. "How come, then," they asked him, "all this talk of yours about there ain't nothing a man can do about anything?"

"That's right," said Elisha. "But supposen I runs into one of them Indians, and that Indian's time has come—he was predestined to get killed. Well, I got to have a gun—can't very well do it with my bare hands at my age."

240.23

"I expect six clergymen to dine with me," said a gentleman to his butler.

"Very good, sir," said the butler. "Are they High Church or Low Church, sir?"

"What on earth can that signify to you?" asked the astonished master.

"Everything, sir," was the reply. "If they are High Church, they'll drink; if they are Low Church, they'll eat!"

240.24

Huey Long said, "They started to baptize my uncle out in the old milling bottom, and as they led him out, there floated out of his pocket the ace of spades. As he turned around and walked a little further, the king of spades came out and then the queen of spades, and just as the preacher was ready to baptize him, the jack and ten-spot of spades came out. His wife was standing over on the bank. She became frantic and threw up her arms and she said, 'Don't baptize him, parson. My husband is lost. He is lost.' But the young son was sitting on the bank and he said, 'Hold on, Ma. Don't get excited. If he can't win with the hand he's got there, he can't win at all.' "

240.25

After an electric storm had caused great damage in the neighborhood of Thomas A. Edison's New Jersey home, a neighbor called to seek his advice concerning the protection of a large building in the community. "Would lightning rods help?" the man asked the great inventor.

"Possibly. What kind of a building is it?" replied Edison.

"It is a church."

"Yes, it should have lightning rods," asserted Edison. "Providence sometimes is absent-minded."

240.26

A housemaid applied to the church's board of deacons for membership in the church. They told her that before being accepted she would have to give them some indication that she had gotten religion. The maid told them that she had had a "visitation."

"We would want something more specific than that," said the chairman.

"I can't talk theology to you," said the maid, "and I don't know my Bible very well. But I can tell you that ever since I got religion I don't sweep the dirt under the rug anymore."

240.27

A captain, remarkable for his uncommon height, being one day at the rooms at Bath, the late Princess Amelia was struck with his appearance; and on being told that he had been originally intended for the Church, "rather for the steeple," replied the royal humorist.

240.28

Here we have an Oyster. It is going to a Church Fair. When it Gets to the Fair, it will Swim around in a big Kettle of Warm Water. A Lady will Stir it up and sell the Warm Water for Forty Cents a pint. Then the Oyster will move on to the next Fair. In this Way, the Oyster will visit all the Church Fairs in Town, and Bring a great many Dollars into the Church Treasury. The Oyster goes a Great Way in a Good Cause.

—*Eugene Field,* 1882

240.29

A Jewish boy and a Catholic boy were arguing whether priests knew more than rabbis. When the Catholic boy seemed to be getting the best of the argument, the Jewish boy said, "Well, if priests know more than rabbis it's only because the Catholics tell the priests everything."

Aphorisms

240.30

"Attend your Church," the parson cries:
  To church each fair one goes;
The old go there to close their eyes,
  The young to eye their clothes.

240.31

Some people go to church to see who didn't.

(*See also 14.5, 26.1, 58.1, 154.47, 157.1, 219.4*)

241. Believers and Nonbelievers

Anecdotes

241.1

A doctor, hurriedly summoned to a New York nightclub to attend a man who had collapsed, arrived and found that the man had died. He stood looking down at the middle-aged man, dressed in beautifully cut formal clothes. "What was his religion?" asked the doctor.

"He was an atheist," replied a friend.

"Too bad," said the doctor. "All dressed up and no place to go."

241.2

Following a capricious impulse discernible in artists, the Dominican Fra Angelico shows in his picture of the Last Judgment certain Franciscans tumbling towards Hell, while the Dominicans are being received into Heaven.

241.3

When a certain shameless fellow mockingly asked a pious old man what God had done before the creation of the world, the latter aptly countered that he had been building Hell for the curious.

—*John Calvin*

241.4

The reality of Christian worship cannot be restored by an injection of saccharine. Paul Claudel pillories this procedure: "If the salt hath lost its savour, wherewith shall it be salted? *With sugar!*"

—*Amos N. Wilder,* Theology and Modern Literature

Definitions

241.5

An atheist is a man who looks through a telescope and tries to explain all that he can't see.

241.6

An atheist is one who hopes the Lord will do nothing to disturb his disbelief.

—*Franklin P. Jones*

241.7

An atheist is a man who has no invisible means of support.

—*John Buchan*

241.8

Faith: Belief without evidence in what is told by one who speaks without knowledge, of things without parallel.

—*Ambrose Bierce*

Aphorisms

241.9

I am an atheist, and I thank God for it.

—*George Bernard Shaw*

241.10

A young man who wishes to remain an Atheist cannot be too careful of his reading.

—*C. S. Lewis, Surprised by Joy*

241.11

A few may echo the hesitation of the youth who affirmed, "God forgive me, but I'm an atheist."

—*Louis I. Newman*

241.12

Referring to some religious quarreling, an Irishman said: "And sure if we were all atheists, then we would live together as Christians."

241.13

Most people have some sort of religion; at least they know which church they're staying away from.

—*John Erskine*

241.14

I admire the serene assurance of those who have religious faith. It is wonderful to observe the calm confidence of a Christian faith with four aces.

—*Mark Twain*

241.15

I respect faith, but doubt is what gets you an education.

—*Wilson Mizner*

241.16

If it wasn't for faith, there would be no living in this world; we couldn't even eat hash with any safety.

—*Josh Billings*

241.17

One of the hardest things for any man to do is to fall down on the ice when it is wet and then get up and praise the Lord.

—*Josh Billings*

241.18

It is rather ridiculous to ask a man about to be boiled in a pot and eaten, at a purely religious feast, why he does not regard all religions as equally friendly and fraternal.

—*G. K. Chesterton*

(*See also 110.17, 250.18*)

242. Viewpoints: Serious and Cynical

242.1

If he does not really think there is a distinction between virtue and vice, why sir, when he leaves our houses let us count our spoons.

—*Samuel Johnson*

242.2

That which we call sin in others is experiment for us.

—*Ralph Waldo Emerson,* "Experience," Works

242.3

A halo has only to fall eleven inches to become a noose.

242.4

All too often a clear conscience is merely the result of a bad memory.

—*Proverb*

242.5

Conscience gets lots of the credit that belongs to cold feet.

242.6

Christianity has not been tried and found wanting; it has been found difficult and not tried.

—*G. K. Chesterton*

242.7

A person may sometimes have a clear conscience simply because his head is empty.

—*Ralph W. Sockman,* How to Believe

242.8

I've known a mule to be good for six months just to get a chance to kick somebody.

—*Josh Billings*

242.9

Do our "experts" really believe that a young tough can be induced to self-restraint, kindness, and compassion just because John Dewey found moral deeds "refreshing"?

—*Franz E. Winkler, M.D.,* The Bridge Between Two Worlds

242.10

The man who is always worrying whether or not his soul would be damned generally has a soul that isn't worth a damn.

—*Oliver Wendell Holmes*

242.11

Millions long for immortality who do not know what to do with themselves on a rainy Sunday afternoon.

—*Susan Ertz*

242.12

Confessions may be good for the soul but they are bad for the reputation.

—*Thomas R. Dewar*

242.13

When you flee temptation, be sure you don't leave a forwarding address.

—*Irish Digest*

242.14

I can resist everything except temptation.

—*Oscar Wilde*

242.15

The only way to get rid of a temptation is to yield to it.

—*Oscar Wilde*

242.16

I never saw any man in my life who could not bear another's misfortunes perfectly like a Christian.

—*Alexander Pope*

242.17

Men should not boast so much; a little hornet if he feels well can break up a whole camp meeting.

—*Josh Billings*

242.18

Let us endeavor so to live that when we come to die even the undertaker will be sorry.

—*Mark Twain*

242.19

More people would go to church if they hadn't observed what sanctity has done for the dull deacons.

—*Wilson Mizner*

242.20

A guilty conscience is the mother of invention.

—*Carolyn Wells*

242.21

If you keep your eyes so fixed on heaven that you never look at the earth, you will stumble into Hell.

—*Austin O'Malley*

Definitions

242.22

A church is a place in which gentlemen who have never been to heaven brag about it to persons who will never get there.

—*H. L. Mencken*

242.23

Christian: One who believes that the New Testament is a divinely inspired book admirably suited to the spiritual needs of his neighbor. One who follows the teachings of Christ in so far as they are not inconsistent with a life of sin.

—*Ambrose Bierce,* The Devil's Dictionary

242.24

Christianity: The most stupid thing ever said about it is, that it is to a certain degree true.

—*The Living Thought of Soren Kierkegaard*

242.25

Clergyman: A man who undertakes the management of our spiritual affairs as a method of bettering his temporal ones.

—*Ambrose Bierce*

242.26

Evangelist: A bearer of good tidings, particularly (in a religious sense) such as assure us of our own salvation and the damnation of our neighbors.

—*Ambrose Bierce*

242.27

A Metaphysician is one who excells in writing with black ink on a black ground.

—*Talleyrand*

242.28

Minister: An agent of a higher power with a lower responsibility.

—*Ambrose Bierce*

242.29

Morality is keeping up appearances in this world, or becoming suddenly devout when we imagine that we may be shortly summoned to appear in the next.

—*Horace Smith,* The Tin Trumpet

(*See also 31.36, 54.51*)

243. Sabbath Humor in the Jewish Tradition

Anecdotes

243.1

The rabbi of a town in Poland was a gentle, humble man of retiring nature. He attended strictly to his own affairs and devoted hours to study in his home, constantly writing with seeming feverishness. His congregation was both proud and mystified by the old fellow's scholarly pursuits, which they concluded was a profound commentary on the Talmud. But he allowed no one to see his work, never discussed it, and certainly was not a man one would question about it.

One day without warning the old rabbi died, and was genuinely mourned by his people. They had revered their great spiritual leader and devoted scholar.

Soon after the funeral, the elders of the community decided they should examine the old man's secret manuscripts, concluding that if they did not do so promptly a great message for mankind might become lost to the world.

With the heirs' permission a committee of local scholars reverently went to the deceased rabbi's study and with much awe took out the mysterious manuscripts. But after a brief inspection of them, they speedily returned them to their proper place and departed. What they thought would be an earthshaking spiritual work proved to be a series of funeral orations the rabbi had prepared for each of the chief members of the congregation, including each of the investigators.

243.2

A stranger in the neighborhood stopped and asked a man where he might find one Eisenstein, president of the synagogue.

"Oh, you must mean the Mumbler, who also is known as the Plague. He lives down near the synagogue itself."

When the visitor got near the synagogue he stopped another man and asked him where he could see Eisenstein. "You mean the guy with the gout who beats his wife? He lives over there in a filthy hovel."

The caller stopped in a store for further directions, and the proprietor said, "The guy who never pays his bills and is always trying to get a bargain, that's the one you want? He lives in that house over there."

Finally the caller caught up with Eisenstein, and after greeting him, asked: "Why on earth do you hold such a post as president of the synagogue? What can you get out of it in a place like this?"

"Nothing whatever," said Eisenstein.

"Then why do it!" asked the visitor.

"Oh, you know how it is," said Eisenstein with a smile. "Every man likes a little glory."

243.3

A small-town doctor, who thought more of his fees than of his patients, was called in to treat the wife of a poor tailor. He said to the tailor, "The case will take a lot of my time and I can see you will not be able to pay for my services."

"Please, Doctor, save her life!" begged the husband. "I promise to pay you even if I have to pawn everything I have."

"What if I don't cure her—will you pay just the same?" asked the doctor.

"Whatever happens, whether you cure her or kill her, I'll pay you."

Treatment started, but the wife died within a few days. Shortly after, the doctor demanded 15,000 rubles. The tailor refused to pay, and as was the custom, the matter was brought before the local rabbi for adjudication.

The sage understood right away what had happened.

"Tell me, again," he said to the physician, "what was your contract with this man?"

"I was to get paid for treating his wife regardless of whether I cured or killed her."

"Did you cure her?"

"No."

"Did you kill her?"

"No—certainly not."

"Then, since you neither cured or killed, what right have you to your fee?"

243.4

An innocent young scholar, astonished when his wife gave birth to a baby three months after their marriage, rushed to the rabbi and asked how so extraordinary a thing could happen. The rabbi reflected for a few minutes how he might save this marriage, then said:

"My son, obviously you haven't the slightest idea about such matters, and apparently you can't make the simplest calculations. Tell me: Have you lived with your wife three months?"

"Yes."

"And has she lived with you three months?"

"Yes."

"Together then—you have lived three months?"

"Yes."

"Well, then, what is the total? Three months plus three months plus three months—doesn't that add up to nine months, the full period of gestation?"

243.5

A mistress and her servant never got along well; the servant was proud and the mistress abusive. One day before leaving the house, the mistress instructed the maid to buy 3 pounds of meat for dinner. When the mistress returned and did not find the meat, she demanded an explanation. The maid said that the cat had pounced upon it and devoured it before she could be stopped.

"You are a liar and a thief!" shouted the mistress.

"I'll not take such slander from you," retorted the maid. "Let us present the matter to the rabbi."

"Did the cat eat the meat?" asked the rabbi.

"Yes," said the maid.

"All right, bring the cat here and we shall weigh it," said the rabbi.

The cat weighed 3 pounds.

"There are the 3 pounds of meat," said the rabbi. "Now tell me, girl, where is the cat?"

243.6

A youth inherited his father's possessions and promptly sold them. Immediately afterwards he was sorry about the sale and went to the rabbi to have it nullified. The youth's relations instructed him, "When you go to the rabbi, be sure to eat some dates and shoot the pits right into his face."

The youth followed the advice and threw the date pits at the venerable sage. The rabbi regarded him with astonishment and compassion. "Poor boy," he said, "he is mentally defective." So he cancelled the sale.

243.7

A priest and a rabbi were making plans for an interfaith luncheon. "Suppose," said the priest, "we serve pork and beans."

"Good," said the rabbi, "and let's hold the luncheon on Friday."

243.8

A Jewish man, stranded on a desert island without any idea when or if he would ever be rescued, turned to building a city to keep himself occupied. He spent years at it, using driftwood, stones, and whatever other materials he could gather.

Finally the castaway was rescued, but before taking leave of the island he escorted his rescuers around to show them what he had done. He showed them his house, "and over there is the temple, and beyond is the grocery store and post office. And further off you can see the other temple."

"The other temple?" asked one of the rescuers. "Why two of them?"

"That other one is the temple I don't go to," said the builder.

243.9

Years ago word spread through academic communities about a young scholar at a Talmudic college in Poland; he was hailed for his great learning and his great concentration on his studies. Visitors came away deeply impressed by the young man.

One day an outstanding Talmudic authority called and asked the head of the college about the young man. "Does this young man really know so much?"

"Truly," answered the rabbi with a smile, "I don't know. The young man studies so much that I cannot understand how he could find time to know."

243.10

Three ultramodern rabbis were discussing how modern their respective congregations were. "We now have ashtrays in the pews so people can smoke while they meditate," said the first rabbi.

"You're almost old-fashioned," snorted the second rabbi. "Why we have a snack bar in the basement and serve ham sandwiches after services."

"Are your people backward!" exclaimed the third rabbi. "We are so advanced that our synagogue is closed for the Jewish holidays."

243.11

One day a scholarly-looking man walked into the library of a famous theological institution. No one there recognized him. The impressive-looking stranger walked directly to the shelves where were stored the most profound volumes of sacred lore—volumes consulted only by those most learned in obscure languages and familiar with theological complexities. There was something about the man's intent purpose that drew the attention of other scholars in the library, and they were struck by the way in which the stranger picked up and quickly glanced at volume after volume, discarding each as one with an instant understanding of its content. Finally, after the mysterious scholar had removed a great number of formidable works from the shelves, he reached deep into one shelf and drew from it a large piece of cheese he had stored there.

243.12

The rabbi was unusually long and fervent at his prayers one day. When he had ended, his wife asked him what he was praying for.

"I was praying that the rich should give more money to the poor," he said.

"Do you think God will answer your prayer?" asked the wife.

"Well," said the rabbi, "at least half of it is already answered. The poor will accept the money."

243.13

In the coming world they will not ask me: "Why were you not like Moses?"

They will ask me: "Why were you not Zusya?"

—*Rabbi Zusya of Hanipol,* quoted by Victor Gollancz, Man and God

243.14

Many synagogues depend in great part on the High Holy Days for their chief support, when they charge in advance for reserved places. Moreover, it is customary for the orthodox synagogues to hire a non-Jew as the gatekeeper on these days, such work by Jews on these occasions being forbidden.

One Yom Kippur, the ticket taker at a New York synagogue was approached by a Jew who had no ticket, but who insisted upon being admitted since he had an urgent message for his business partner who had already entered the house of worship. The gatekeeper was adamant and the man without a ticket was more insistent. Finally the gatekeeper relented on the understanding that the man would give his message to the man inside and leave. "And don't forget," added the gatekeeper, "no praying while you're in there!"

243.15

The rabbi ordered a new suit to be worn during the High Holy Days. The tailor promised faithfully to deliver the suit on time. On the day before Passover the rabbi finally received the suit from the tailor, examined it critically and then asked why, if God took only six days to create the world, it took a tailor six weeks to make a simple suit.

"True," said the tailor. "But look at the mess the world is in, and then look at this beautiful suit."

243.16

Danny Thomas tells a story about a man who bought a parrot from a pet store when he heard the bird sing the famous *Kol Nidre,* and encore with other hymns of the man's faith. For days after that the man listened to the bird sing the Sabbath hymns, and he thought with joy of the day when he could bring the parrot to the synagogue during the High Holidays. Just before Rosh Hashanah the old fellow got a little prayer shawl and a little black skull cap for the parrot and went off to the synagogue with it.

But when he tried to enter he was challenged at the door. "This isn't a zoo," they told him. But the man argued that his parrot could sing better than the cantor or the rabbi, and wagers were made with a number of members of the congregation until the sum reached $6,000, all verbal, since no money could pass on such a day. The old man thought he would be a sure winner, but when he asked the bird to sing all he got was stony silence. The bird wouldn't even say a word—much less sing.

The old man was as incensed as he was embarrassed. He grabbed the parrot and rushed home, picked up a carving knife, and began to sharpen it. The bird, alarmed, flew to a chandelier in the dining room and asked, "What are you going to do?"

"So now you talk!" screamed the old man. "But I lose $6,000 and the respect of my fellow men because you wouldn't make even one chant. I'm going to cut off your head."

"Wait a minute," said the parrot. "Don't be a dope. Yom Kippur is coming soon—and you'll get bigger odds."

243.17

A poor young man arrived in the United States, without education and without any knowledge of English. He eked out a mere existence peddling notions from door to door, until he heard that the synagogue needed an attendant, and he applied for the job. But he was turned down because he could neither read nor write.

Over the years this man began to prosper and eventually became a multimillionaire. One day he needed a great sum of money to finance a big deal and called on a banker for a loan. The banker readily agreed to lend the money, a note was drawn up, and the once-poor man was asked to sign it. He then explained to the banker he would have to make an X, that he could neither read nor write.

"Amazing," said the banker, "that you have accomplished so much with so little. Imagine what you would be doing now if you could read and write!"

"You know what?" said the rich man. "I'd be nothing but a *shammes* in a synagogue on Delancey Street."

243.18

A thief in his old age was unable to ply his "trade" and was starving. A wealthy man, hearing of his distress, sent him food. Both the rich man and the thief died on the same day. The trial of the magnate occurred first in the Heavenly Court; he was found wanting and sentenced to Purgatory. At the entrance, however, an Angel came hurrying to recall him. He was brought back to the Court and learned that his sentence had been reversed. The thief whom he had aided on earth had stolen the list of his iniquities.

—*The Yehudi*

243.19

When Dr. Donald Sencer is not caring for the teeth of his New Jersey patients, he is often telling wonderful stories with considerable skill. One of them is about a wealthy and pious member of a Jewish congregation who was in the habit of inviting a few friends to his home for drinks every Sabbath evening after services. Between drinks he would lead his friends in chanting a verse relating that "man comes from dust and returns unto dust."

Finally one of his guests asked if they could not chant a happier verse for a change. "But, gentlemen," said the host, "there is no happier verse. If we came from gold, and returned unto dust, we would have something to complain of. But when you come from dust and return to dust, then between the coming and returning you have a chance to take schnapps every Saturday evening. So we have reason to be grateful."

243.20

A stingy man once came upon a most tempting walnut tree. He suddenly felt a strong desire to eat the nuts, he took off his coat and began to climb the tree. As he started he prayed:

"Dear God, if You'll make it easy for me to climb to the top of the tree, I promise to put 10 rubles into the charity box in the synagogue."

Halfway up the tree, he reconsidered the whole matter:

"10 rubles is really too much—just for a few nuts! I'll give 3."

Finally, he reached the top branch. Arrogant now, he said, "Why should I give my good hard cash to some miserable beggars?"

No sooner had he said this than the branch on which he rested broke, and he fell with a thud to the ground on his rear end.

His face twisted with pain, he turned reproachfully to Heaven.

"What's the matter, God, anyway?" he asked. "Right away You've got to punish! Maybe, if You hadn't been in such a hurry, I'd have given something!"

(*See also 10.9, 24.8*)

MILITARY HUMOR

SOLDIERS, SAILORS, AND FLYERS

244. From the Training Camp

Anecdotes

244.1

"Who are all those people cheering us?" asked the rookie as the soldiers marched off to board a train for camp.

"Those," said another soldier, "are the people who are not going."

244.2

The boy from the backwoods had just arrived in army camp for his first days of training and strolled around to look the place over. A colonel came along and the boy said, "Hi ya, partner." The colonel came to a sudden halt and proceeded to reprimand the young fellow in the most severe terms, telling him how superior officers were to be addressed. The boy listened, then spat tobacco juice out of the corner of his mouth and said, "Had I a'knowed you'd be so blame uppity, I'd not a'talked to you atall!"

244.3

An American Army recruit was being given an aptitude test, and toward the end of the inquiry the examiner asked: "If one of your ears were cut off, what would happen to you?"

"I would hear less."

"All right. Suppose both of your ears were cut off, what then would happen to you?"

"I wouldn't be able to see so good any more."

"Apparently you are tiring," said the examiner. "I'll ask the question again: What would happen if both of your ears were cut off?"

"I would not see so good any more."

"Why," asked the exasperated examiner, "do you persist in giving me such an idiotic answer? Why would it impair your vision?"

"Because," replied the rookie, "this damn helmet is too big and it would fall down over my eyes."

244.4

A general and a captain walking down the street passed a number of GIs, and each time one of them saluted the officers, the captain saluted back and said, "The same to you."

"Why do you always say that?" the general asked the captain.

"I used to be a private, too," said the captain, "and I know just what they are thinking."

244.5

The great Negro dancer, Bill Robinson, used to tell about the Negro soldier who was stopped by the sentry at an army camp exit and told he could not leave. After much arguing, the soldier finally said, "Out of my way, man. I've got a father in Hell, a mother in Heaven, and a girl in Harlem, and I'm goin' to see one of them tonight."

244.6

Three GIs from the hill country and new in the Army went to St. Louis on a weekend and called at the YMCA. After visiting the game rooms, they asked at the information desk what else the "Y" had to offer. "There's swimming in the basement," said the clerk.

This seemed to impress them. They withdrew to a corner and got into a discussion. Finally one of them went back to the desk and said, "Did I understand you—that there was women in the basement?"

244.7

The instructor had just concluded his lecture on parachute jumping. "Sir," asked one student, "what if the chute doesn't open?"

"That," replied the teacher, "is what is known as jumping to a conclusion."

244.8

In spite of the most careful training and indoctrination, the paratrooper was highly nervous when about to make his first jump. Nevertheless, jump he must. "Just bear in mind your training," said the sergeant. "Relax, keep calm, pull the cord after you have counted ten, and you'll float down to earth as gently as a bird. And when you hit, roll back gently, and you've got it made."

"But," concluded the sergeant, "if the once-in-a-million happens and your first chute doesn't open, pull the cord on the right and the emergency chute will open. There'll be a station wagon waiting for you to land."

The fellow jumped, counted ten, but the chute did not open. Then he pulled the cord on the right and the emergency chute failed to open. As the poor fellow plummeted toward earth, he muttered to himself, "Now I'll bet that damn station wagon won't be there."

244.9

"Why are you holding on to your brother so tightly, Johnny?" some soldiers asked a boy who was leading a donkey past a military encampment.

"So he won't join the army," said the bright little boy.

244.10

"How come you didn't turn out?" demanded the sergeant. "Didn't you hear the bugle blow reveille?"

"Honest, sergeant, I'm afraid I'm going to be a flop as a soldier. I don't know one tune from another."

244.11

GIs in bull sessions agreed that most of those who managed to escape the draft were related to, or had influence with, politicians—that the sons of politicians had the biggest pull with draft boards and the Army.

Finally a voice called out, "You fellows have got it all wrong. I'm a politician's son, and I'm here in the Army just like the rest of you fellows."

"Yes, sir, Captain," they all cried out.

244.12

He had just been promoted to a colonel and ordered out on mock maneuvers. The international situation was unusually tense at the time and the colonel was in a grim mood—aware that the United States might at any time find itself at war. He drove his men hard in the field and reminded them that the maneuvers might any moment become the real thing.

Suddenly the field radio was silenced. The colonel considered this as ominous—something pretty serious must have happened, he kept saying, as he and his staff nervously paced back and forth on the summit of a little hill near the command post.

Presently, a small scout plane appeared high overhead, and a carrier pigeon was released from it. Powerful field glasses followed the bird until it fluttered into a nearby coop.

The colonel rushed to get the message carried by the pigeon. He opened it with trembling hands, read it, uttered an oath, flung the note to the ground and walked rapidly away in a purple rage.

When the colonel was out of sight, a staff sergeant picked up the discarded note and read: "I have been sent down because I did something naughty in my cage."

244.13

A sergeant in the Army was transferred to a new post, and his superior officer sent with him a letter to his new superior stating that the man was an inveterate gambler—it was his one vice.

"I hear you're a great gambler," remarked the sergeant's new officer. "What do you bet on?"

"Sir, I bet on everything and anything. For example, I'll bet you $10 you have a mole on your backside."

The officer, forgetting his dignity under the temptation of an easy $10, said, "I'll take you up on that," whereupon he dropped his pants and quickly won $10.

The officer wrote the sergeant's former commander and told him of the incident. Presently a reply came back: "I'll be damned if that sergeant hasn't won $100 from me. Before he left, he bet me that, within fifteen minutes after meeting you, he'd have your pants off."

244.14

In order to fill out the regimental boxing team, a GI was prevailed upon by his buddies to enter the divisional tournament. The soldier had never been in a fight in his life, and looked forward to his ring debut with dread. When he came back to the barracks that night, his head was both bloody and bowed. "You poor guy," said the GI in the next bunk.

"That's not the half of it," said the battered GI, "I gotta fight again tomorrow night. I won."

244.15

Charles C. Voorhees relates that at our air base at Thule, Greenland, the chaplain was lecturing on how one can improve himself through his thinking—"What you are is determined by what you think about all the time!"

At this point Voorhees says his buddy turned to him and said, "If that's the case, I'm either a pinup girl or a Cadillac convertible!"

—*True*

244.16

They wondered how the major of few words would manage to discipline an offending sergeant when brought before him. Well, he did it in this fashion: "Come in, sergeant. At ease. Attention, private. Dismissed!"

244.17

"Soldier," said the trial judge advocate at the opening of a court-martial, "do you understand that the regulations require that you are to be presumed innocent?"

"If that's the case," replied the soldier, "why are they making such a big effort to convict me?"

244.18

In the early days of World War I, a company of somewhat unruly Australians was under the command of an English officer who wore a monocle—the first one the Aussies had seen in real life. On the first morning in camp, they caricatured their officer by appearing on parade with the lids of their blacking tins solemnly stuck in their left eyes.

The Englishman took a long, silent look at them. Then he flipped his monocle into the air and deftly caught it in his eye. "Do that, you blighters," he barked at them, and turned on his heel and walked away, to the cheers of the men of his new command.

244.19

During World War I, the men in one regiment were not at all interested in signing up for the very liberal life insurance the government was willing to write on the soldiers. The colonel of the regiment finally asked a sergeant, who had great influence with the men, to talk to them about the life insurance. He agreed to do so, and his talk went something like this:

"Most of you fellows know me; I've shot craps with many of you, and eaten with you, and gone carousing with you. Now about this insurance—where the government has to pay out $10,000 every time an insured soldier is killed in battle. It don't cost the government a cent when a man who is not insured is killed. Now stop and figure it out: What soldiers is Uncle Sam going to send into the front lines—the soldiers who are insured, or the men who are not insured?" That did it. The entire regiment signed up for insurance.

244.20

During World War I, a rookie who had been rushed to France with little or no army training was doing some cleanup work around one of the camps when he stopped another man in uniform and said, "Hey, Buddy, what about a light?" The strange soldier gave the rookie a light, and went on his way.

Another soldier nearby went over to the rookie and told him he had just stopped General Pershing. "Calling him 'Buddy' and asking for a light is liable to get you in a heap of trouble."

The poor frightened rookie ran after the general, apologized to him profusely and explained that he had not yet learned how to recognize officers. "That's all right, son," said the usually rigid Pershing, "but take my advice and don't try that on a second lieutenant."

244.21

A soldier during World War II said that he was signed up for the duration of the war and that the war didn't bother him so much, but rather how long the duration was going to last.

244.22

During World War II, a Catholic chaplain was put in charge of Protestant services in the absence of the Protestant chaplain. The priest managed well enough, except for the hymns, which were unfamiliar to him.

When the priest's uncertainty became evident, one of the soldiers called out, "It's OK, Chaplain. We'll take care of the singing. You just give us the devil."

244.23

At the beginning of World War II, a fellow from the backwoods asked a recruiting sergeant if he could have a jeep if he enlisted. "Sure," said the easygoing sergeant.

When the fellow signed, the sergeant pointed to a row of shiny new jeeps, and said, "Go on over there and pick out your jeep."

"If these are jeeps," said the crestfallen rookie, "I've made a bad mistake. I thought jeeps was female Japs."

244.24

Two Jewish soldiers in the Russian army during the days of the Czars were given ten-day leaves to return home for the Passover. But they overstayed their leave by two days, and consequently were called before the commander of the camp. The first offender was unable to come up with an explanation that satisfied the half-drunk colonel, who summarily sentenced him to sixty days in the guardhouse.

When the second offender went in he was far more frightened than the first man, particularly since he had heard the colonel shouting at his friend, and had heard the sentence given him. As a result when he stood before the colonel he could not organize himself to say more than, "Your Excxxxx . . . your . . . ex-ex-ex . . . I-I-I-I. . . ." Words finally failed him utterly.

"Get that blithering idiot out of here!" shouted the colonel. Out he walked, now suddenly calm.

"How did you make out?" asked his friend who was outside.

"Set free," said the man.

"How did you do it?"

"You got to know how to talk to these fellows," said the recently speechless one.

244.25

During World War II, a local society leader asked that a few soldiers from a nearby army camp be sent to her home for Thanksgiving dinner, specifying that they do not send any Jews.

On schedule, two Negro soldiers arrived at the home. "There must be some mistake," said the embarrassed and disconcerted hostess.

"No, there could be no mistake, ma'am," said one of the Negroes. "Major Rabinowitz never makes mistakes."

244.26

Wellington so shared the general prejudice against soldiers that he despised his own troops and never lost an opportunity of telling them so. When reviewing them, as everyone knows, he remarked, "I don't know if they will frighten the enemy, but by God they frighten me!"

244.27

A book issued by the Army gives all manner of advice to noncommissioned officers. It even tells how to make men who have quarreled friends again. The men are put to washing the same window, one outside, the other inside. Looking at each other, they soon have to laugh and all is forgotten. It works; I have tried it.

—*Ludwig Bemelmans,* My War with the United States

244.28

I rose by sheer military ability to the rank of Corporal.

—*Thornton Wilder*

(*See also 191.26, 218.16, 225.3, 245.1–245.26, 246.1–246.16, 247.1–247.9, 248.1–248.34, 270.14*)

245. From the Battlefield

Anecdotes

245.1

The story is told of a distinguished calvalry colonel during the War Between the States, who on one sad occasion was leading his men in a gallant retreat. The Yankees were riding fast and close behind them, and some of the Southern boys would stop on occasion to fire at their pursuers. Finally the colonel called out: "Boys, stop that shooting; it just makes them madder."

245.2

When General Grant expressed his contempt for a certain Army officer, one of his staff came to the man's defense with the observation that the officer had been in ten campaigns. "So has that mule," said Grant, "but he's still a jackass."

245.3

When the name of a certain major was mentioned, General Stonewall Jackson's aides told him he had been wounded and would not be available for duty.

"He was wounded!" said the General in astonishment. "Well, it must have been by an accidental discharge of his duty."

245.4

SEND ME MORE MEN AND FEWER QUESTIONS Stonewall Jackson wired the War Department at Richmond, Virginia.

245.5

Artemus Ward, recounting his Civil War experiences, said "Bullets and cannonballs were passing all around me—in wagons, on their way to the battlefield."

245.6

The perils of neutrality are illustrated by the citizen of a borderland state during the Civil War who thought he would play both sides of the fence. So he put on a pair of Confederate trousers and a Union coat. As a consequence, the Confederates shot him in the chest and the Union troops shot him in the backside.

245.7

General Lee encountered one of his soldiers moving away from the front line with much too much speed. "You should be at the front," said Lee sternly. "That is the place for a soldier while the battle is going on."

"Sir, I have been there," said the soldier. "And I must tell you, sir, it is no place where a self-respecting man would choose to be."

245.8

When Alben Barkley was asked the meaning of the term "a qualified maybe" he illustrated with the story of an Irish sergeant in World War I who set out to inspire his men. He told them of the mission before them, then asked, "Boys, will ye fight or will ye run?"

"We will!" shouted all the men.

"Will what?" asked the sergeant.

"Will not!" came the cry in unison.

"That's the spirit," said the sergeant. "I knew ye would."

245.9

During World War I, a regimental chaplain observed "one of his boys" trembling from head to foot, and to comfort him said, "There's nothing for you to worry about. Every bullet that comes over here has a name on it. If it's got your name on it, it's going to get you, no matter what you do or don't do. If it hasn't your name on it, then there is nothing for you to worry about."

"Yes, Father," said the soldier, "I know all that—but what worries me are those bullets marked 'To Whom It May Concern.'"

245.10

During a battle the general noticed that one of his men seemed to be devoted to him and remained constantly at his side. Finally he said, "Well, my man, you have stuck with me loyally all through the engagement."

"Yes, sir," replied the soldier; "before I left home my mother told me to stay right with the general and I'd never get hurt."

245.11

During a battle of the last war one of the soldiers took off at high speed for the rear as soon as the firing began. He ran and ran and ran, until suddenly he heard the cry of "Halt!"

"Who is that?" called out the running soldier.

"I'm the general," replied the challenger.

"Gosh!" said the soldier, "I didn't know I had run so far back of the lines."

245.12

Just before the battle, the captain called his men together and said, "Men, this is going to be a tough engagement. We are probably going to get licked. But nevertheless we must fight as if everything depends on what we do. If things fall apart altogether, you'll simply have to run for it. I happen to be a little lame, so I'm starting right now."

245.13

During World War I, American women knitted hundreds of thousands of pairs of woolen socks for the soldiers—gratefully received by the foot soldiers in France who had to do a great deal of marching in bad weather. On one occasion some troops had barely time to change socks before being ordered to resume their long march. One young fellow had taken but a few steps when he felt a sharp object in the heel of a sock he had just put on. But he could not stop—they were on the way for emergency duty—and by the time a halt was called, the poor fellow was in agony. He pulled off that shoe and that sock and in the sock was a tight little ball of paper—the cause of all the trouble. He unrolled the paper, and thereon he read the message of the woman who had knitted the sock: "God have mercy on your poor tired feet."

245.14

An officer advising his general to capture a post, said: "It will only cost a few men."

"Will *you* be one of the few?" remarked the general.

245.15

Around the Pentagon they tell about the Air Force pilot assigned to fly a hazardous mission over the jungle. He was given an escape kit to use in the event of a crash. He pointed to the vials in the kit and asked, "What are these for?"

"They're to help you get out of the jungle," said the supply officer. "One contains gin and the other contains vermouth. In case you get lost, all you do is start mixing a martini. Someone will appear and tell you that you don't know how to mix a martini right. Then you ask him the way to the nearest town."

245.16

"Men," said the American commander, "the

Japs outnumber us four to one. Each man has his job to do."

After ten minutes of fierce battle, the commander came upon a Southern mountaineer leaning against a tree smoking. "Come on, there!" yelled the officer. "Do your job!"

"I've done it," drawled the soldier. "I got mah four."

245.17

During World War II, a young woman eagerly opened the envelope from her beloved in the battle zone. She had waited long for the words of endearment she expected to find within the envelope. But instead of the heart-warming and thrilling words of love, there was only a note which read: "Your boyfriend loves you, but he talks too much. The Censor."

245.18

At the critical point of a battle, one of the Czar's officers gathered his men together and said: "The crisis has arrived! We are to charge the enemy. It will be man against man—hand-to-hand combat."

A Jewish soldier, who hated the Czar and his army, called out: "Show me my man! Maybe I can arrive at an understanding with him."

245.19

A British general, reporting on his activities in the Boer War, said, "We returned without wasting a single gun or soldier." To which Oscar Wilde added, "Or a minute."

245.20

The proud father was telling his young son of his many adventures and battles and escapades during the great war. The boy listened with great interest and increasing awe. Finally he managed to ask: "But what did the rest of the army do?"

245.21

During World War II, word came back from the South Pacific about the native who described a piano in pidgin English: "Big fellow box, you fight him teeth, he cry."

Definitions

245.22

Coward: One who in a perilous emergency thinks with his legs.

—*Ambrose Bierce*

245.23

Soldier: A guy who gets a piece of gold on his chest for a piece of lead in his pants.

—*Jay C. Flippen*

245.24

War: Something that knocks the "I" out of glory.

Aphorisms

245.25

That monkey meat is all right until the animal's hand turns up on your plate.

—*GI saying, South Pacific, World War II*

245.26

Let him that hath no heart have legs.

(*See also 15.1, 79.36, 79.39–79.43, 87.11, 155.11, 155.12, 156.13, 158.5, 158.11, 174.31, 211.2 218.18, 225.4, 225.6, 238.4, 244.1–244.28, 246.1–246.16, 247.1–247.9, 248.1–248.34*)

246. From All the Ships at Sea

Anecdotes

246.1

Percy's *Anecdotes of War* tells the following: When the British under Lord Nelson were bearing down to attack the combined fleets off Trafalgar, the first lieutenant of the *Revenge,* on going to see that all hands were at their quarters, observed one of the men devoutly kneeling at the side of his gun; so very unusual an attitude exciting his surprise and curiosity, he went and asked the man if he was afraid.

"Afraid!" answered the honest tar, with a countenance expressive of the utmost disdain. "No, I was only praying that the enemy's shot may be distributed in the same proportion as the prize money—the greatest part among the officers."

246.2

A pompous English naval officer years ago said to a newly arrived officer, "Well, young man, I suppose your being here is the same old story—the fool of the family sent to sea?"

"No, sir," said the young man. "That's all been changed since your day."

246.3

An American naval officer was held for court-martial on a charge of running, clad only in shorts, through a hotel corridor in pursuit of a young woman.

In preparing the case against the officer, the Navy was doubtful as to exactly what service regulation had been violated. Finally it was decided to charge the officer with failure to wear his uniform during wartime and in a war area.

When the case came to trial the maritime Lothario was acquitted. His officer-lawyer pointed out to the court-martial that his client had violated no Navy regulation—that an officer is specifically excused from wearing his uniform when engaged in a sport, in which case he is allowed to wear clothes proper to that sport. Shorts, concluded the Navy lawyer, are proper to the sport the young officer was engaged in at the time of his arrest.

246.4

A sailor from a torpedoed vessel swam to an island in the Pacific, and was met by a beautiful native maiden dressed in practically nothing whatever. As he lay panting in exhaustion on the beach, the lovely damsel gazed down at him and softly said, "Sailor boy, I've got something for you that you've been dreaming about ever since you left home."

The youngster looked up at her in surprise and said, "Now how in heck did you get a bottle of ice-cold beer on this island?"

246.5

An admiral, who insisted his men act on their own initiative, received from a captain in his fleet this query: "Lost in a fog. Shall I proceed to destination or return to base?"

The admiral shot back, "Yes."

Then another message arrived: "Do you mean yes, proceed to destination, or yes, return to base?"

The admiral again replied, "Yes."

246.6

An admiral examining a young officer asked: "If there was a bad wind, what would you do?"

"I'd drop an anchor."

"And if the wind was ten times worse than you expected?"

"I would drop ten anchors, sir."

"All right, then suppose the wind was still a great deal worse than that. Then what?"

"Well, I would simply have to drop a lot more anchors."

"Young man, where do you think you would get all those anchors?"

"From the same place where you would get all that wind."

246.7

During World War II, two more-than-slightly inebriated gentlemen rolled out of the Stork Club, in New York, and spotting a man in resplendent uniform with much gold braid said to him, "Call a cab for us, good man."

The uniformed one turned on them indignantly and said, "Gentlemen, I happen to be an admiral in the United States Navy."

"OK," said one of the drunks. "Then call us a boat."

246.8

An admiral and a bishop both arrived simultaneously at the Heavenly Gates. The admiral was ceremoniously ushered in; the bishop curtly told to wait outside. Miffed at this treatment, the bishop was further incensed when he peeked in and saw the excitement caused by the admiral's arrival. A special choir was hastily assembled to do him honor, a golden carpet was spread for him to walk upon, and charming angels flitted hither and yon strewing beautiful blossoms on him and his path. It was an astonishing reception, thought the bishop with a touch of bitterness inappropriate to the celestial atmosphere.

Eventually the excitement died down and the bishop was told to come ahead in. There was no carpet spread for him, no heavenly choirs of greeting, just a few nondescript angels to say hello, and that was all. The bishop was still miffed and puzzled by the admiral's reception compared to his own, and asked the authorities about it. "Oh, don't let it bother you," they said. "You see, bishops are always arriving here, but this is our first admiral."

(*Note:* For "admiral" you can substitute any other profession or occupation that pleases you or fits your special purpose.)

246.9

"Captain," said the sailor as he saluted snappily, "here is a special message that came in for you from the admiral."

"Read it to me," ordered the captain.

The sailor read: "Of all the nautical jackasses I've ever encountered, you get first prize for stupid, moronic conduct."

"Have that communication decoded at once," ordered the captain.

246.10

At a football game an admiral stepped on the foot of a sailor who was so intent on watching the game he didn't look up but simply said, "Get off my foot, you big bloke."

Then recognizing the admiral, the sailor said, "Oh, gee, I'm sorry. I beg your pardon, sir. Here's my other foot—go ahead—step on it, sir."

246.11

When a member of the Seabees, the Navy's construction battalion, was asked to define morale, he said, "Morale is when your hands and feet keep on working when your head says it can't be done."

246.12

Two American soldiers were on the deck of a transport on its way to Europe. One of them said, pointing out over the endless expanse of water, "That's the most water I ever did see. Did you ever see so much?"

"You ain't seen nothin' yet," replied the other soldier. "You're just lookin' at the top of it."

246.13

A group of tourists were being escorted over a battleship that had seen service in World War II. The guide paused, pointed to a brass plaque imbedded in the deck, and solemnly said, "This is where our gallant commander fell."

"No wonder," said a woman. "I nearly tripped over it myself."

246.14

A rookie was asked if he wouldn't like to volunteer for submarine service.

"No sir," he replied. "I don't want to get in no ship that sinks on purpose."

Definition

246.15

Admiral: A general at sea.

Aphorism

246.16

Here's to the ships of our navy,
Here's to the ladies of our land,
May the former be well rigged
And the latter be well manned.

(*See also 154.39, 184.44, 219.15*)

247. Brass Hats and Pentagonians

Anecdotes

247.1

When Hugh Troy, a superb practical joker, was drafted into the Army in 1943, it was inevitable that the Pentagon would be spoofed. After he completed officers' training, Troy was assigned to a camp in South Carolina and there became engaged in seemingly endless labors with report after report.

All of which inspired Troy to devise another report—a mimeographed flypaper report which gave each strip of flypaper in the mess hall a code number and then recorded the number of flies trapped each day on each strip. These reports were sent to higher headquarters. It is said that Troy's flypaper reports resulted in headquarters requesting similar reports from other Army units, and raising a ruckus when they were not received.

247.2

The new girl in the Pentagon answered the phone and was asked if Colonel Johnson was there. The girl asked her superior, and was told, "Colonel Johnson is in the United Kingdom."

She then returned to the phone and with the proper tone of regret and dignity said, "I am sorry, but Colonel Johnson is dead."

247.3

The young Air Force colonel in the Pentagon saw a sailor and called out "Sergeant!" The call was ignored. Again the colonel called and again was ignored. The Air Force colonel strode up to the man who had ignored him and demanded to know why he made no reply.

"Because," said the sailor, "I'm not a sergeant; I'm a chief petty officer."

"It makes no difference," snapped the colonel. "If you were in the Air Force, you'd be a sergeant."

"No sir," replied the sailor. "If I were in the Air Force, I'd be a colonel."

247.4

A Colonel Jones of the United States Army was given his first assignment to the Pentagon, and before long found himself inundated with memoranda, reports, studies, queries, carbon copies of letters, and a mounting miscellany of other papers, most of which had nothing whatever to do with his duties, and the disposition of which puzzled and worried him.

In his perplexity he noticed that one of the other men always had a clear desk. He went to this man and said: "You're an old hand in the Pentagon. Tell me, how do you manage to keep such a clean desk?"

"It's easy," answered the veteran Pentagoneer. "See this routing slip—buck-slips, we call them.

Well, whenever I want to get rid of papers I just write on it something like this, "Colonel Jones: for your information."

"You louse," stormed the newcomer, "I am Colonel Jones."

247.5

When one of the officers in the Pentagon was asked why he wanted to have his desk moved into the men's room, he explained that it was the only place in the Pentagon where people knew what they were doing.

247.6

Sign on a desk in the Pentagon: "The secrecy of my job does not permit me to know what I am doing."

247.7

It has been proposed that a plaque be placed on the Pentagon reading: WASHINGTON SLEPT HERE.

247.8

The story is that a Western Union messenger went in the Pentagon on a Monday afternoon and emerged on Friday a full colonel. And that a man once sat down at a desk in the Pentagon to rest his feet and forthwith found himself with a phone, blotter, desk set, and secretary.

And then there was the acutely pregnant woman who accosted a Pentagon guard and urgently demanded a guard to show her the way out. "Lady, you shouldn't have come in here in that condition."

"But I wasn't when I came in."

247.9

An Army officer developed an intense headache. The doctors decided on brain surgery. They brought him to the operating table, took the cranium off, and started to go after the tumor. They couldn't get it so they had to take the brain out and put it on the table. While they were working on it, a messenger arrived and announced that the colonel on the table had been promoted to a brigadier general. Under a local anesthesia, the colonel heard the news, got up, slapped his cranium back on, and started out.

"Hey, wait, you can't leave without your brains."

The patient replied, "Don't need them now that I'm a general."

(*See also 114.1, 244.2, 244.4, 244.11, 244.12, 244.16, 244.20, 244.26, 245.2, 245.4, 245.7, 246.2, 246.5, 246.6, 246.8–246.10*)

248. The Home Front

Anecdotes

248.1

During the Constitutional Convention in Philadelphia, it was proposed "that the standing army be restricted to 5,000 men at any one time." George Washington, as the presiding officer, could not offer a motion, but he turned to another member and whispered, "Amend the motion to provide that no foreign nation enemy shall invade the United States at any time with more than 3,000 troops."

—*Paul Wilstach,* Patriots off Their Pedestal

248.2

George Washington was once at a dinner party where his host had placed him with his back to a fiery red-hot stove. Finding it was quite too hot for comfort, after some squirming Washington beat a retreat to a more comfortable position, whereupon his host jocularly remarked, "I thought an old general like you could stand fire better than that."

"I never could stand a fire in my rear," said Washington.

248.3

A group of Londoners sent a document to William Pitt wherein they offered to enlist in the Army under numerous conditions and with various exceptions. When Pitt came to a clause stating that one condition of enlistment would be that they would not be required to leave England, Pitt wrote on the margin, "except in the case of invasion."

248.4

During the Civil War, Secretary of War William H. Seward was present at a social gathering while discussion was going on as to the purpose of secret troop movements. Noticing his silence, a woman said to him, "Mr. Seward, what do you think of it? Which way is the army going?" "Madam," replied Seward, "if I did not know, I would tell you."

248.5

A visitor to West Point, noticing that all the names engraved on a battle monument were those of men in the Union army, asked a passing cadet, "What is this?"

"That, sir," drawled the cadet, "is a tribute to Confederate markmanship."

248.6

In the early days of World War I the German Kaiser was talking to the head of the Swiss army. "You have an army of only 500,000 men. What would you do if attacked by an army of 1 million men?" asked the Kaiser.

"Each one of our soldiers would simply shoot twice," said the Swiss army man.

248.7

Speaking of Admiral Jellicoe, in charge of the British fleet during World War I, Winston Churchill said, "He was the only man capable of losing the last war in a single afternoon."

248.8

During the early days of World War II, Winston Churchill, responding to critics of some of his policies, said, "People are always telling me that it is about time that the British Lion showed its teeth; I always reply, 'Not before it has gone to the dentist.' "

248.9

Early in World War II, Winston Churchill, in a broadcast to the French people, said, "We are waiting for the long-promised German invasion. So are the fishes."

248.10

A critic of Winston Churchill's campaign in Africa during World War II said, "I am a firm believer in fighting the enemy with his own weapons."

"Tell me," said Churchill, "how long does it take you to sting a bee?"

248.11

A fellow who was due to be examined by the draft board doctors, and was not at all happy about the prospects of military service, met a friend who had been turned down because he wore a truss. "May I borrow that truss when I go for examination?" he asked his friend. The friend agreed.

When the man appeared before the draft board doctor wearing the borrowed truss, the doctor asked, "How long have you been wearing this truss?" "Five years," lied the draft dodger.

The doctor marked down "N.E." on a sheet and said, "OK."

"What does 'N. E.' stand for, Doctor?" asked the youth.

"It stands for Near East," replied the doctor. "Anyone who can wear a double truss upside down for five years can easily ride a camel."

248.12

During World War II, more than one man quipped, "The draft board rated me 4F for physical reasons: No Guts."

248.13

An Army Air Force man during most of World War II had one of the more enviable jobs—shunting generals and visiting bigwigs between London and Paris. Not once did he have to come within range of enemy guns. Between trips, the pilot mingled freely and pleasantly with what was left of London café society.

One evening the lucky pilot was at a swank London cocktail party when a V-2 exploded nearby, shaking up the party generally and specifically blowing our hero across the room where he landed on a table of hors d'oeuvres—a pickle fork imbedded itself in his buttock. A companion officer extracted the fork, administered first aid, and alcoholically promised to cite him for a Purple Heart. Two weeks later the young lieutenant received his Purple Heart.

248.14

During World War II, Mrs. Eleanor Roosevelt arrived late one evening at an East Coast city and went to a hotel where a reservation had been made for her. When the manager ushered her into a lavish suite of rooms, Mrs. Roosevelt protested it was much too large and elaborate for her; she preferred a simple room.

A few minutes after Mrs. Roosevelt had been transferred to a single room, a soldier asked the desk for a room. He was told all rooms were taken. He explained to the manager that he was being shipped to Europe the next day and that he had hoped his last night in the United States could be a really comfortable one—one he would always recall with pleasure. The manager relented and let him have the suite set aside for Mrs. Roosevelt, at the price of one ordinary room.

When the young soldier saw the beautiful suite of rooms he was at first awestruck, then uncomfortable in the midst of such luxury. Unable to sleep amid such comforts, he got in touch with some other soldiers waiting to be shipped out and they joined him in the suite. Before long they were all drinking, and kept on drinking through the night. They stumbled away from the hotel early in the morning.

When the chambermaid went to the suite,

she found it a shambles—broken lamps and vases, empty bottles on the floor, cigarettes crushed on the carpets. She gave the mess a quick look and went to the manager, beginning with, "I'd have you know that that Roosevelt woman ain't no lady."

248.15

Shortly after the end of World War II, a distinguished visitor from mid-Europe arrived in the United States and when asked at a press interview what he expected to do while in the country, said: "One of the things I want to do is to meet Mrs. Beach—you know, the woman who had so many sons in the American Army in Europe."

248.16

The retired Army officer was addicted to boasting about the regiment he commanded during World War II, and proceeded along his usual lines to a man seated next to him in a train. "I tell you, my friend, it was just about the finest group of soldiers in the whole army. It was wonderful to see them on parade, with their magnificent precision. I can still hear the 'slap, slap, click' when they presented arms. I don't suppose you've ever had an experience like that?"

"Oh, yes," said the heretofore-silent stranger. "And I, too, can still hear the 'slap, slap, jingle' of my men when they presented arms."

"Slap, slap, jingle?" asked the first man. "Jingle? You must be mistaken."

"Oh, no, that was their medals."

248.17

A retired Army officer met his former orderly on the street one day and hired him for the same job the orderly had done for so many years in the Army. He told the ex-orderly that he could start just as he used to, by waking him at seven every morning.

Next morning, punctually at seven, the ex-orderly strode into the retired officer's bedroom, shook him into wakefulness, and then leaned over and spanked the officer's wife on the backside, saying to her, "All right, baby, it's back to town for you."

248.18

The officer of a regiment complained at a party that because of the stupidity and indifference of his subordinates, he was obliged to do the whole duty of the regiment. Said he: "I am my own lieutenant, my own sergeant and—"

"Your own trumpeter," called out a bored listener.

248.19

During wartime a wife, deploring the slaughter and destruction, asked her husband if nothing could be done to stop it. "Can't they arbitrate?" she asked.

"They did arbitrate," said her husband. "That's how it started."

248.20

Years ago Portugal decided to build an impregnable line of defense along her frontier. Huge guns were placed in concrete emplacements. But when the general staff inspected the new fortifications, the experts quickly spotted the fallacy of the otherwise magnificent defense system: all the guns were pointed toward Portugal—and could not be turned around.

The dilemma was solved by offering the line of forts to its adjoining neighbor, Spain, at a reduced price.

248.21

"And, finally," said the political candidate, "I am proud to remind you that I was one of the men behind the guns."

"How far behind?" called out a man in the rear of the hall.

Definitions

248.22

Army: A body of men assembled to rectify the mistakes of the diplomats.

—*Josephus Daniels*

248.23

A hero is a man who has fought impressively for a cause of which we approve.

—*Dumas Malone*

248.24

Pacifist: A guy who fights with everybody but the enemy.

248.25

Patriotism is the willingness to make any sacrifice, so long as it won't hurt business.

248.26

Armistice: A pause to permit the losing side to breed new soldiers.

248.27

Peace Treaty: An agreement setting forth the basis for the next war.

Aphorisms

248.28

When ye build yer triumphal arch to yer

conquerin' hero, Hinnissey, build it out of bricks so the people will have somethin' convenient to throw at him as he passes through.

—*Finley Peter Dunne*

248.29

War hath no fury like a noncombatant.

—*Charles Edward Montague*

248.30

War is much too important a matter to be left to the generals.

—*Georges Clemenceau*

248.31

A man can do everything with a sword except sit on it.

—*Talleyrand*

248.32

A man without one scar to show on his skin, that is smooth and sleek with ease and homekeeping habits, will undertake to define the office and duties of a general.

—*Plutarch*

248.33

It is easy to be brave from a safe distance.

—*Aesop*

248.34

Toast: "Here's to the girl behind the man behind the gun."

—*Admiral Schley*

(*See also 20.1, 20.12, 55.11, 57.3, 58.3, 72.11, 79.49, 134.4, 158.4, 168.8, 184.38, 211.2, 229.27, 244.1–244.28, 245.1–245.26, 246.1–246.16, 247.1–247.9*)

ORATORS AND AUDIENCES

SPEAKERS, BUMBLERS, AND RETORTS

249. Opening Gambits

Anecdotes

249.1

Once when Harry Collins Spillman was introduced at a meeting in an auditorium, he began:

"I am delighted to have the privilege of speaking to you today in this magnificent auditorium. I presume you know the meaning of the word auditorium. It is derived from two Latin words—audio to hear, and taurus, the bull.

—*G. Lynn Sumner,* We Have with Us Tonight

249.2

If one is to speak on a complex subject, the following story can be used as an opener:

"You didn't tell me the truth about that mule I bought from you the other day," asserted the farmer to a dealer in animals. "You told me the critter was agreeable and easy to handle, but I can't get the fool thing to do a lick of work."

"Let me have a look at him," said the seller. They went out into the field where the mule was hitched to a plow, but he would not budge for the farmer. The salesman picked up a big stick and gave the animal a clout on the head, breaking the stick. "Now try him," said the salesman.

"Giddap," said the farmer, and off went the mule as obediently and as willingly as one could ask. "I don't get the idea," said the farmer. "You told me to treat the mule gently, and then you come out here and beat him."

"Treat him gently, yes," said the salesman, "but first you got to get his attention."

249.3

The toastmaster, after eulogizing the principal speaker of the evening, concluded his introductory remarks with this story:

An old farmer drove into town one day, bought half a peck of oats for his horse, and promptly gave this royal feast to the animal at the side of the road. When the good old horse had finished the oats, the farmer got back in his wagon, picked up the lines, and said to the horse, "Now that you've been fed, git up!"

249.4

It has been attributed to Jimmy Walker, Irvin S. Cobb, Rufus Choate, and a number of other clever toastmasters. In any event, one toastmaster, presiding at a Thanksgiving banquet, did introduce the distinguished speaker of the evening in these words: "Gentlemen, you have been giving your attention to turkey stuffed with sage. It is now my privilege to present to you a sage stuffed with turkey."

249.5

A man stands on a platform. He is about to address a packed audience of Swindlers, Cowards, Bounders, Painted Harridans and Trulls.

He opens his mouth to address them. What does he say? He says: "Ladies and Gentlemen."
—*Hilaire Belloc*

249.6

Max Lerner appeared on the same book-and-author program with Senator John F. Kennedy. Kennedy's talk was rewarded with loud and enthusiastic applause. When Lerner was then introduced, he said that after listening to Senator Kennedy, he felt that he should have been introduced not as Max, but rather as Anti-Cli-Max.

249.7

One day Robert Benchley arose and said: "Before I make my speech, I want to say something."

249.8

The preparations for a banquet at Radcliffe College included a new coat of varnish for the chairs. But it was a hot and humid evening and when Dean Briggs tried to arise to speak he found he had become stuck to the chair. Undaunted, the Dean remained seated and opened his talk by saying, "Ladies and gentlemen. I had expected to bring you this evening a plain and unvarnished tale, but circumstances make it impossible for me to do so."

249.9

A popular after-dinner speaker at a banquet said in his opening remarks that he wished to propose a toast before he began his talk. Then raising his glass and bowing toward the balconies where the ladies were seated, he said, "To the ladies. The best part of my life has been spent in the arms of another man's wife—my mother!"

A visiting Englishman liked this very much and resolved to use it. Several weeks later he was the guest speaker at a banquet, and when he was introduced, he said: "Ladies and gentlemen, before I take up the text of my address I wish to offer a toast." He raised his glass, made a sweep toward the crowded balconies, and said, "To the ladies. The best part of my life I spent in the arms of another man's wife—but by Jove I've forgotten her name!"

249.10

A politician arose to speak at a banquet where a general and an admiral had preceded him at unwonted length. The politician prefaced his remarks with the observation that now he knew the true meaning of the phrase, "The Army and Navy forever."

249.11

Former Mayor McNair of Pittsburgh used to awaken his audience with a little joke, such as his speech at Greensburg, beginning:

"I am glad to be in your city of Johnstown—"

"Greensburg," someone called out.

"I know it, but I wanted to see if you were awake. Now I hope you'll stay awake till I am finished."

249.12

The country lad was making his first political speech and said, "Friends, I have jest discovered that when I stand up to talk, my mind sets down."

249.13

The speaker began by saying: "I am in the same plight as the mosquito who arrived at the nudist camp and said, 'I don't know where to begin.' "

249.14

The reading of the minutes, offering of resolutions, and the various introductions took so much time that the honored guest had only five minutes left for his address. When he got up, he thought the circumstances made it appropriate for him to tell about the little girl who went into a store with a lone nickel, and asked for a candy bar. But the candy bars were all seven cents, and soda pop was a dime. Even a popsicle was seven cents.

The child left the nickel on the counter and walked sadly away. When the clerk called out to her that she had left her nickel, the little girl turned around and said, "Oh, that's all right. I can't do anything with it."

Definitions

249.15

A lecture is something that can make you feel numb on one end and dumb on the other.
—*C. N. Pearce*

249.16

Speeches are like babies—easy to conceive, but extremely hard to deliver.

Aphorisms

249.17

Many can rise to the occasion, but few know when to sit down.

249.18

The most popular after-dinner speech is "Waiter, bring me the check."

249.19

It usually takes me three weeks to prepare a good impromptu speech.

—*Mark Twain*

249.20

"I would rather be an extemporaneous fool than a premeditated ass," said the bold speaker.

249.21

An after-dinner speaker rises to the occasion —and stays too long.

250. Speaker versus Chairman

Anecdotes

250.1

"Of course, no doubt most everyone here knows what the inside of a corpuscle is like," said the lecturer on health.

"Most of us do," interrupted the chairman, "but for the benefit of those who have never been inside of one, you had better explain it."

250.2

A lecturer arrived at a meeting hall in a small town to give a talk. Noticing that there was no pitcher of water and glass at the speaker's table, he called the chairman's attention to it.

"Do you want it for drinking?"

"No," said the lecturer, "I do a high-diving act."

250.3

Clarence Buddington Kelland was the master of ceremonies at a large dinner. The speakers' table was distressingly populous. Mr. Kelland got up, a slip of paper in his hand.

"Gentlemen," he began, "the obvious duty of a toastmaster is to be so infernally dull that the succeeding speakers will appear brilliant by contrast."

The succeeding speakers chuckled indulgently.

"I've looked over the list," continued Mr. Kelland, "and I don't believe I can do it."

The speakers' chuckling ended and the audience roared.

250.4

Clarence B. Kelland once introduced Dr. Nicholas Murray Butler, who was a frequent occupant of the speakers' platform, in this way: "For years organizations have been besieging this retiring gentleman to address them—with remarkable success."

250.5

Early in his political career William Jennings Bryan toured the state of Nebraska against the Republican candidate for governor, making a total of some fifty fiery speeches. Nevertheless, the Republican was elected.

On the following St. Patrick's Day, Bryan was to make a brief speech during an elaborate program, which was attended and presided over by the Governor Bryan had opposed. There were songs, speeches, and vaudeville acts on the program. When Bryan's turn came to speak, the Governor turned to him, and said: "Quick," tell me—do you speak, sing, dance, or perform magic tricks? I've got to introduce you."

250.6

A chairman once introduced William Jennings Bryan with such an embarrassing array of compliments, exaggerations, and eulogistic clichés that the audience wondered how Bryan would overcome the effect of such bad taste. Bryan arose, thanked the chairman for his comments, and said they reminded him of the man at a formal dinner who put into his mouth a forkful of steaming hot food, gasped, and quickly spat it out on his plate. Then he looked around at his appalled fellow guests and said, "Some damn fools would have swallowed that."

250.7

"It gives me great pleasure," said Chauncey Depew upon introducing Dr. Vincent to an Eastern audience, "to present the president of the University of Minnesota, a man popularly known as 'The Cyclone of the Northwest.' "

"I appreciate the title," said Dr. Vincent, "especially since it comes from the most eminent wind authority in the East."

250.8

When Heywood Broun was introduced with an embarrassing array of compliments, praise, and exaggerations, he arose and said, "Now I know how a pancake feels when they pour syrup on it."

250.9

After being given an introduction that promised a good deal more than he could deliver, the speaker arose and said it reminded him of a sign he had seen some weeks earlier while driving through the country. It was displayed outside a small church and read: STRAWBERRY FESTIVAL TONIGHT, and underneath it in small letters, "Because of the depression, prunes will be served."

250.10

A speaker, rising after an introduction which consisted chiefly of an embarrassing litany of compliments, said that the toastmaster's remarks reminded him of the three bulls—a big bull, a medium-sized bull, and a small bull. These bulls were strolling down a road when they passed a field where there were a number of exceptionally beautiful cows. The big bull took one look, said "Good-bye" to his companions, and leaped over the fence. The medium-sized bull and the little bull went along until they came to another group of cows, less handsome, but still attractive.

This time the medium-sized bull said "Good-bye," and leaped the fence. The little bull wept bitterly and finally straggled on alone. Which proves that a little bull goes a long way.

250.11

"This evening," said the chairman introducing the lecturer, "we are going to be told all about the Book of Proverbs"—and the chairman rambled on and on about the Book of Proverbs.

Finally the introduction ended, the lecturer arose, and said, 'Since your chairman has covered the Book of Proverbs, I will discuss the Book of Lamentations."

250.12

Simeon Ford, proprietor of the rather notorious Grand Union Hotel in New York City, introduced Joseph H. Choate at a dinner, with many sly references to Joseph of the coat of many colors and Potiphar's wife.

Choate arose to speak and began with: "I am not the Joseph of many colors, nor yet the Joseph who was tempted by Potiphar's wife, but had I been so tempted and had I succumbed, I know at whose hotel we would have registered."

250.13

The lecturer was asked by an interviewer what was the most difficult work in his lecturing—travel, preparation of addresses, interviews, or what?

"Generally," said the lecturer, "my biggest problem is to awaken my audience after the chairman of the meeting has introduced me."

250.14

A story attributed to Irvin Cobb—and just about every other wit, new or old—tells about the toastmaster who introduced him with: "And now let me present to you a man who is quite a wit. All you have to do is to put a dinner in his mouth, and out comes a speech."

The alleged wit, whoever it be, rises and says: "Your toastmaster is a far more remarkable man. All you have to do is put a speech into his mouth, and up comes your dinner."

250.15

In response to a flattering introduction, a speaker recalled the spinster who at last was reported to be engaged. When a friend met her on the street and stopped to tell her of his pleasure upon reading the news, she replied: "Oh, my, there isn't a bit of truth in it, but thank God for the rumor."

250.16

More than one toastmaster has begun his remarks by saying, "It is not my function to bore you, but rather to introduce others who will."

250.17

When columnist Meryle Stanley Rukeyser got up to speak at a luncheon of the Pittsburgh Advertising Club, he asked the president how long he should speak.

"Talk as long as you want. We all leave at 1:30."

250.18

A well-known actor was seated at the guest table at a dinner given in a large New York hotel. He was known to be a freethinker along theological lines. When the hour came for starting the dinner, the toastmaster, a very religious man, discovered there was no minister present to give the invocation. In the emergency he turned to the actor and asked him to give the benediction.

The actor arose, lowered his head, and in the midst of a deep hush, he said with great reverence: "There being no clergymen present, let us thank God."

Definitions

250.19

Toastmaster: The punk that sets off the fireworks.

—*Gene Buck*

250.20

Toastmaster: A guy who goes around introducing guys who need no introduction.

Aphorisms

250.21

Toast to the Toastmaster

We'll bless our toastmaster,

Wherever he may roam,
If he'll only cut the speeches short
And let us all go home.

250.22

The hardest thing t'stop is a temporary chairman.

—*Kin Hubbard*

250.23

The function of a master of ceremonies in relation to a speaker is like a fan to a dancer: it calls attention to the subject, but makes no attempt to cover it.

(*See also* 83.4, 142.16)

251. When the Audience Talks Back

Anecdotes

251.1

When he had completed his address and had laid the whole matter before them, there was a profound silence, a silence fraught with significance, a silence such as to suggest that out of it might come mighty stirrings. But, to the speaker's surprise, nothing whatever happened. They were all asleep.

251.2

The speaker, annoyed by constant interruptions, finally blurted out, "Wouldn't it be better to hear one fool at a time?"

"You're right," called a voice from the audience. "Go on."

251.3

"You say that this man was shot and killed by the chairman of the meeting when he made a motion that was out of order?" asked the police.

"Yes, sir, that is correct."

"What kind of motion could a man make at the meeting that would justify such violence?" the witness was asked.

"It was a motion toward his hip pocket—where he had a loaded gun."

251.4

Notice on a speakers' platform at a political rally in San Antonio: "Do not photograph speakers when they are addressing the audience. Shoot them just before they begin to talk."

251.5

An Easterner making a speech in a Texas town was not doing at all well. His audience was so obviously bored and fidgety that the Easterner became alarmed when a husky cowboy got up on the dais and placed a six-shooter on the table.

"Don't worry," the cowboy said to the speaker, "ain't nuthin' gonna happen to you. We'd just like to get the guy that brought you here."

251.6

A man received an invitation from the local American Legion to make the principal address at the Memorial Day exercises. The program, he was told, would be: "A talk by the Mayor, recitation of the Gettysburg Address by a high school boy, your talk, and then the firing squad."

251.7

George Ade and a well-known lawyer were speakers at a dinner party in Chicago. Ade spoke first, and his words provoked much laughter. When he had finished, the lawyer arose, shoved his hands deep in his pockets, as was his habit, and said:

"Doesn't it strike you as a little unusual that a professional humorist should be funny?"

Ade jumped up and said, "Doesn't it strike you as a little unusual that a lawyer should have both hands in his own pockets?"

251.8

The young man paced ceaselessly in a room adjoining a hall where a series of speeches were being delivered. A kindly lady stopped him and said, "You seem to be nervous about going on to speak next."

"Me nervous?" said the man petulantly. "Not a bit. I'm used to speaking."

"In that case," said the lady icily, "what are you doing here in the ladies' room?"

251.9

In introducing Will Rogers at a New York dinner, Will Hays concluded his laudatory remarks with: "Will Rogers has something under his ten-gallon hat beside hair!"

Before Rogers could say a word, Irvin S. Cobb was on his feet. He said, "Ladies and gentlemen, I am touched. I want to endorse from a full heart these glowing words that have been spoken, and I want to add that it was high time somebody in this broad land of ours said a good word for dandruff."

251.10

Many speakers and their audiences are very much like the two skeletons who were found hanging in a closet. One skeleton said to the other: "If we had any guts, we wouldn't be here."

251.11

After a speech, someone remarked that the speaker was all right, "but I don't think he put enough fire into his speech."

"I think," said another, "that his trouble was that he did not put enough of his speech into the fire."

251.12

Dr. Walter Williams of the University of Missouri once spoke at a Chinese university where an interpreter translated his talk into Chinese symbols on a blackboard. Dr. William noted that the interpreter stopped writing during most of the speech and at the conclusion he asked why. "We only write when the speaker says something," was the blithe reply.

251.13

The speaker raised his voice in annoyance and said, "There have been so many unseemly interruptions that I can hardly hear myself speak."

"You ain't missin' much," cried a voice from the audience.

251.14

Vice President Barkley once related that when beginning a speech he placed his watch on the lectern and said that with it before him he could always tell how long he had been speaking, if he could remember when he started. But before he could go on from there into his talk, a voice from the audience called out, "There's a calendar on the wall!"

251.15

"He drove straight to his goal," shouted the speaker. "He looked neither to right or left; he pressed forward with only one purpose in his mind. Neither friend nor foe could delay or divert him from his course. All who stood in his path did so at their own risk. What, my friends, would you call such a man?"

"A truck driver," called a man in the audience.

251.16

After a speech a woman came up to the speaker and asked, "Did anyone ever tell you that you were a great speaker?"

"No."

"Then what gave you the idea that you were?"

251.17

The speaker had an imposing, if erratic, array of cures for the troubles of the world, and expounded each at length. Finally, he concluded his talk by shouting, "I want government reform, I want business reform, I want religious reform. . . ."

And a bored voice from the front seats softly added, "chloroform."

251.18

A speaker talked loud and long, then asked brightly, "Are there any questions?" A hand shot up. "What time is it?" the questioner asked.

251.19

"The time has come," shouted the speaker, "for us to rid ourselves of socialism, communism, anarchism, and. . . ."

Before the speaker could complete his sentence a little old lady in the audience called out, "Let's get rid of rheumatism, too!"

251.20

One night when Macklin was preparing to begin a lecture, Sam Foote was rattling away at the lower end of the room. Thinking to silence him at once, Macklin called out in his sarcastic manner, "Pray, young gentleman, do you know what I am going to say?"

"No," said Foote, "do you?"

251.21

Once when Henry Ward Beecher was speaking, a drunk in the balcony waved his arms and crowed like a rooster. Beecher stopped in the midst of a flight of oratory, took out his watch and said, "What! morning already! I wouldn't have believed it. But the instincts of the lower animals are infallible."

251.22

The speaker was giving a dramatic presentation of the dangers that lurk in modern foods.

"What is it that at one time or another we all eat, which is the worst thing possible for us?"

"Wedding cake," called out a long-suffering person in the audience.

251.23

The temperance lecturer was directing his attack this evening to beer. At the climax of his tirade against the beverage, he placed a pail of beer and a pail of water in front of a donkey that had been brought on the stage, and he asked his audience to say from which pail the donkey would drink.

"From the pail of water," called out one man in the audience.

"Very good, sir," replied the lecturer with

enthusiasm. "And will you now tell us why the donkey prefers water to beer?"

"Because he's an ass," called out the same man.

251.24

"What have any of the people in this audience ever done in the cause of conserving our natural resources?" challengingly asked the speaker on forest preserves.

There was an embarrassed silence, then came a gentle voice, "Once I shot a woodpecker."

251.25

The great exponent of inspiration closed with: "Remember, men, there is nothing in this wide world that is impossible to accomplish."

From the back of the hall came: "Did you ever try getting the toothpaste back into the tube?"

251.26

During the course of a talk by Charles Lamb someone in the audience hissed.

Lamb said: "There are only three things that hiss: a goose, a snake, and a fool. Come forth and be identified."

251.27

The political candidate got up and began to speak—and he spoke and spoke and droned on and on, stopping with unusual frequency to take a drink of water from the pitcher on the table.

"Damned if I ever before saw a windmill run by water," said one farmer to another.

251.28

The speaker droned on and on, and when it seemed as if he would never end, the guests got restless and began to whisper and stir in their seats.

Finally the toastmaster, embarrassed that the guest speaker should be treated so discourteously, reached for his gavel and rapped several times for order. But he struck too hard—the handle of the gavel snapped and flew through the air, landing on the head of a man who had fallen asleep. The slightly groggy victim awoke and said, in alcoholically thickened tones, "Hit me again. I can still hear him."

251.29

A farmer attended a political meeting but preferred to sit in the rear near the door. After the speaker had droned on and on for some forty minutes, the farmer got up and left the hall. On the way out, he met a friend on his way in to the meeting. The second man said, "Am I very late, Zeke? What's he talking about?"

"Don't know what he's talking 'bout. He ain't yet said."

251.30

Pleasure-loving Aeschines told Demosthenes, "Your oration smells of the lamp."

"Indeed," replied the great orator, "there is a difference between what you and I do by lamplight."

251.31

The late Vice President Barkley told of how he used a manuscript, instead of notes, for a talk. After he sat down, he turned to a friend and asked, "What did you think of it?"

"Well, I have only three criticisms. First, you read it. Second, you read it poorly. Third, it wasn't worth reading."

251.32

A speaker addressing the Yale alumni took the letters Y-A-L-E and began a long-winded talk—Y stood for Youth, A for Ambition, and so on.

After an hour and a half, a bored man in the audience said, "I'm certainly glad he didn't graduate from the Massachusetts Institute of Technology."

251.33

"I am grateful, sir, for your remaining to the end of my talk when everyone else walked out," said the speaker.

"No thanks are due me," said the lone listener. "I'm the next speaker."

251.34

Referring to his participation in a pending debate, Lord Chatham said, "If I cannot speak standing, I will speak sitting; and if I cannot speak sitting, I will speak lying."

"Which he will do in whatever position he speaks," observed Lord North.

Aphorisms

251.35

You move the people when you speak,
For one by one away they sneak.

251.36

No man would listen to you talk if he didn't know it was his turn next.

—*E. W. Howe*

251.37

To the after-dinner speeches—
May they be short and sweet.
We're glad they do not come until
We've had a chance to eat.

(*See also 54.3, 55.2, 55.20, 57.1–57.6, 124.15, 125.16, 125.17, 135.19, 139.35, 135.41, 139.18, 139.20, 139.24, 184.38, 218.4, 218.14, 233.3, 233.4, 233.7, 233.8, 233.13, 233.14, 234.1–234.32, 235.1, 248.21, 271.20, 272.12, 272.16*)

252. Faux Pas from the Podium

Anecdotes

252.1

A business executive whose public speeches were always ghostwritten decided to give the impression that he was no longer enslaved by the words of another. So when he arose to give an address, he picked up several typewritten sheets and said, "Gentlemen, this is a speech that was written for me to deliver. But I want to tell you what I really think, so I'm going to throw out this prepared text." Whereupon he tore the speech into shreds—but in doing so, inadvertently tore up the text of another speech—the one he was really going to deliver. This left the man utterly speechless.

252.2

One day a well-publicized and self-appointed spokesman for American business rushed from the train to the rostrum to read a deathless message prepared for him by a ghost-writer. The speaker had no time to go over the speech—a hastily whipped-up spiel for an emergency engagement. It went directly from typewriter to speaker as he got off the train.

Everything was orderly and orthodox during the first ten minutes of the man's speech, as the speaker waved the American flag, denounced government regulators and controllers, condemned Socialists by name and Democrats by implication. Then, reading grimly on, before he realized it the speaker said, "Good God! What hogwash this is!"

Before the sun set that day, one cynical stenographer was peremptorily removed from the payroll of a certain corporation.

252.3

New York's Mayor John F. Hylan customarily had his speeches written for him by a ghostwriter. But he was exceptional in that he would often make his first acquaintance with a speech when he was delivering it. This, as it proved, had its drawbacks.

On one occasion New York's famous "Red Mike" was reading a speech when he came upon a joke he had never heard before. He liked it. In fact he laughed so hard over it that he broke his glasses and had to have an assistant finish reading the speech.

252.4

The graduation-day speaker was hammering away at the importance of aggressive energy in attaining one's goal in life. Finally, in dramatic fashion, he highlighted his point. Thrusting his arm far out to his right, he thundered: "What I am trying to tell you is that you're going to need an awful lot of what is written on that door!"

All eyes turned to look and saw in bold black letters on the door the single word PULL.

The speaker had forgotten which side of the door faced the assembly hall.

252.5

When Julia Ward Howe, author of "The Battle Hymn of the Republic," died, the mayor of San Francisco, during a memorial service, referred to her as "the immortal author of *Uncle Tom's Cabin*—Julia Ward Howard."

252.6

Senator Hattie Caraway, appointed to the Senate seat when her husband died, was given a fulsome introduction by a fellow politician who ended with, "I now present to you the most notorious woman in Arkansas."

252.7

At a dinner in Dublin, the toastmaster was lavishing praise on Sir Henry Irving, the actor. He concluded with: "Sir Henry is not only an artist of the first rank, the first of his profession to be honored with a knighthood, but is also a man of the utmost integrity and highest honor. It would not be too much to say that his has been a life of unbroken blemish."

252.8

During an outdoor rally down South shortly after the end of World War II, a former paratrooper who had returned to his home was called on to speak. But since this was late in the program some of the people got up to leave, whereupon the chairman of the meeting arose and called out: "I ask you people to come back and take your seats, every one of you! This good neighbor of ours went through hell for us, and it is up to us to do the same for him now."

(*See also 55.16, 58.5, 182.1–182.10, 271.1–271.14*)

253. Brevity, Thy Name Is Wit

Anecdotes

253.1

The sales manager for a large tire manufacturer began his speech with this reassuring note: "I will be brief because, as is well known in our business, the longer the spoke, the bigger the tire."

253.2

To celebrate the one-hundredth anniversary of the opening of the Erie Canal, the New York Port Authority gave a long and elaborate luncheon, attended by leaders from all walks of life. The guest speaker was an elderly man from Buffalo, grandson of De Witt Clinton, who built the Canal. He monotonously read a long and dreary account of the Canal. After forty-five minutes he was succeeded by a lawyer who droned on for forty-five minutes about the law and the Port Authority and the Canal. As the diners began to drift back to their offices, Jimmy Walker, the last speaker, arose and said only:

"I see before me the busiest and most powerful leaders of world industry. They must get back to their desks. Neither wind nor snow, nor rain nor gloom of night, nor Jimmy Walker shall keep them from their appointed rounds. Gentlemen, this meeting is adjourned for one hundred years."

253.3

Wilton Lackaye was to be the featured speaker at a gathering in Chicago. The evening wore on, made tedious by a long procession of windy speakers. Finally the toastmaster, late in the evening, arose to tell the bored audience, "Mr. Wilton Lackaye, the well-known actor, will now give his address."

Mr. Lackaye got up and said, "Mr. Toastmaster, Ladies and Gentlemen: My address is The Lambs Club, New York City." And then he sat down—to a storm of applause.

253.4

Following their triumph at Kitty Hawk with the first heavier-than-air plane, the Wright brothers were dined and wined in Europe, and especially at a banquet in Paris. Of course there was much speechmaking, including a long address by a Frenchman who dwelt chiefly on the pioneering successes of Frenchmen in the fields of engineering and science, and the general superiority of Frenchmen. Practically nothing was said by the speaker in the way of compliment to the Wright brothers, who were the guests of honor.

When Wilbur Wright was called upon to speak, he kept it brief and to the point. After a few introductory remarks, he said, "As I sat here listening to the speaker who preceded me, I heard comparison made to the eagle, to the swallow, and to the hawk, as typifying skill and speed in the mastery of the air; but somehow or other I could not keep from thinking of the bird which, of all the ornithological kingdom, is the poorest flier and the best talker—the parrot."

Whereupon Wright sat down, to the enthusiastic applause of the Americans present.

253.5

James Russell Lowell said that he was advised when speaking to talk for five minutes, and if he didn't strike oil, to stop boring.

253.6

While a man sat at the dais, waiting for his turn to speak, a waiter handed him a card reading: "KISS, Mary." A friend seated next to him, recognizing the speaker's wife's handwriting, said: "Well, that is certainly a nice romantic touch!"

"It doesn't mean what you think it does," said the speaker-to-be. "This 'KISS' means 'Keep it Short, Stupid.' "

253.7

"I have discontinued long talks on account of my throat," said the speaker. "Several people have threatened to cut it."

253.8

A man with scant experience speaking in public, but determined to give his all, arose and began: "Gentlemen, six hundred years ago the spot where I now stand was a howling wilderness." He paused, looked bewildered, then began again, "Six hundred years ago the spot where I now stand was a howling wilderness"—and again he stopped, this time alarmed. He had forgotten his speech. But he started in again with his "Six hundred years ago the spot where I now stand was a howling wilderness"—and again he halted—then plunged on with his finale: "and I wish it still was." He sat down to generous applause.

253.9

Joe McCarthy, a New York newspaperman, says that years ago he heard an after-dinner speaker give notice to his listeners that he was about to end his talk by saying, "Like Lady Godiva at the end of her famous ride, I am drawing near to my close."

253.10

Some speakers and most listeners approve of the rule among certain tribes in Africa. Their regulation is that when a man rises to speak he must stand on one foot while delivering his oration. The minute the lifted foot touches the ground, the speech ends—or the speaker is forcibly silenced.

253.11

When statements he had made at a conference were challenged, Leonard Bacon, a New England theologian of some years ago, arose and said: "Mr. Moderator, I cannot allow my opponents' ignorance, however vast, to offset my knowledge, however small."

Aphorism

253.12

Brevity is the quality that makes cigarettes, banquet speeches, vacations, and love affairs bearable.

—*H. L. Mencken*

TALKING AND SILENCE

254. Shooting the Bull

Anecdotes

254.1

The lion sprang upon the bull and devoured him. After he had feasted, he felt so good that he roared and roared. The noise attracted hunters and they killed the lion. The moral of which is that when you are full of bull, keep your mouth shut.

254.2

A reformed after-dinner speaker was asked why he had abandoned a work he had seemed to enjoy so much.

"No, I didn't get tired of hearing myself talk," he said. "What stopped me—late as it may have come to me—was the expressions that spread over the faces of the listeners when the toastmaster was introducing me. It was something like a famous painting of Daniel in the Lions' Den. If you have seen it, you'll recall the satisfied expression on the Prophet's face. Well, Daniel looks pleased because he knows he is about to be present at a dinner where he won't have to listen to any of the after-dinner speeches. That's me now."

254.3

The lions in ancient Rome had been starved and otherwise provoked to viciousness so that they would make quick work of the Christians when they were set on them in the amphitheater in the presence of the Emperor. And the lions did exactly what was expected of them—all the Christians were devoured, except one who had bent down and whispered something into a hungry lion's ear.

This lone remaining Christian was brought before the Emperor, who demanded to know why he had escaped the lions. What had he said to the lion about to attack him?

"All I did," said the Christian, "was to tell the lion that he would be expected to say a few words after dinner."

254.4

One Gally Knight was a great talker but a poor listener. When Samuel Rogers was told that Knight was going deaf, he said, "It is from a lack of practice."

254.5

The only thing good that could be said about the town blabbermouth was that he always told the truth. No one ever disputed that, however much he may have annoyed people with his chatter. One day this windbag found a turtle in the road—an ordinary-sized one, but one that winked at Big Mouth and said to him, "You talk too much."

Although used to hearing this, he was not accustomed to hearing it from a turtle, so at first he thought it was just his imagination. But again the turtle repeated the accusation. This time the fellow was in no doubt. Nor was he in any doubt as to what to do about it: he dashed back to town to tell the citizenry what had happened. Although skeptical, but realizing Blabbermouth always told the truth, a large crowd returned to the scene, but this time the turtle said not a word.

Annoyed because they had been tricked into so long a walk on a hot day, some of the men in the crowd booted Big Mouth down the road, and returned to town. But the big talker returned to where the turtle was and started to kick him vigorously off the road, when the turtle blinked at him and said, "You see—I told you, you talk too much."

254.6

The speaker who has little or nothing to say, would do well to remember the farmer who was driving a truck loaded with produce up a steep hill. So intent was the driver on the hill and the bad road that he was not aware that the tail gate had slipped open and the produce was dropping gradually from the truck on to the road. The higher the hill, the more he lost.

When he crested the hill and began to speed down the other side, he was still unaware of his loss. In fact, he did not discover it until he skidded off the road and into a marshy shoulder of the road, where he was mired down. Then he looked back and saw he had lost all his produce.

"Not only stuck in the mud," he muttered, "but I ain't got nothin' to unload."

254.7

Historian Henry Steele Commager suggests that those addicted to public speaking would do well to recall Jonah's experience in the whale's belly.

Jonah, of course, was nervous down there in the whale's innards, and he paced up and down ceaselessly. Annoyed, the whale called out, "Come on, Jonah, cut out that eternal stamping around. You're ruining my digestion."

"You've some nerve," said Jonah. "If you'd kept your big mouth shut neither of us would be in this fix."

254.8

A student, asked what different forms of punishment there were in the world, wrote, "In the United States many people are annually put to death by elocution."

254.9

Sydney Smith, discussing the relative merits of two prominent men, said, "There is the same difference between their tongues, as between the hour hand and minute hand on a clock. The one goes twelve times faster, the other signifies twelve times as much."

Definitions

254.10

An after-dinner speaker is the fellow who starts the bull rolling.

254.11

Man is a sort of tree which we are too apt to judge by the bark.

254.12

An egotist is a man who talks so much about himself that he gives me no time to talk about myself.

—*H. L. Wayland*

254.13

Bore: The kind of man who, when you ask him how he is, tells you.

—*Channing Pollock*

254.14

Bore: A person who talks when you wish him to listen.

—*Ambrose Bierce*

Aphorisms

254.15

People who have nothing to say are never at a loss in talking.

—*Josh Billings*

254.16

In general, those who have nothing to say contrive to spend the longest time in doing it.

—*James Russell Lowell*

254.17

He who thinketh by the inch and speaketh by the yard, ought to be kicketh by the foot.

254.18

To be positive is to be mistaken at the top of your voice.

254.19

It's a good idea to keep your words soft and sweet, because you never know when you may have to eat them.

—*Dave Garroway*

254.20

He is considered the most graceful speaker who can say nothing in most words.

—*Nicholas Murray Butler*

254.21

You raise your voice when you should reinforce your argument.

—*Samuel Johnson*

254.22

People, like boats, toot the loudest when they are in a fog.

254.23

It is with narrow-souled people as with narrow-necked bottles: the less they have in them, the more noise they make in pouring it out.

—*Jonathan Swift*

254.24

Eloquence flourished most in Rome when public affairs were in the worst condition.

—*Michel de Montaigne*

254.25

Why doesn't the fellow who says, "I'm no speechmaker," let it go at that instead of giving a demonstration.

—*Kin Hubbard*

254.26

When a man gets talking about himself, he seldom fails to be eloquent and often reaches the sublime.

—*Josh Billings*

254.27

The minute a man is convinced that he is interesting, he isn't.

—*Stephen Leacock*

254.28

The secret of being a bore is to tell everything.

—*Voltaire*

254.29

Why must we have enough memory to recall to the tiniest detail what has happened to us, and not have enough to remember how many times we have told it to the same person.

—*La Rochefoucauld*

254.30

Some people think they have something to say, and other people think they have to say something.

254.31

Public speakers should speak up so that they will be heard, stand up so that they can be seen, and shut up so that they can be enjoyed!

254.32

Half the world is composed of people who have something to say and can't, and the other half who have nothing to say and keep on saying it.

—*Robert Frost*

254.33

Two feet on the ground are worth one in the mouth.

254.34

Unto those who talk and talk,
This proverb should appeal:
The steam that blows the whistle
Will never turn a wheel.

254.35

His speeches to an hour-glass
Do some resemblance show;
Because the longer time they run
The shallower they grow.

254.36

No one is exempt from talking nonsense; the misfortune is to do it solemnly.

—*Michel de Montaigne*

254.37

A stuffed fish was mounted on a wall with under it this sign: IF I HAD KEPT MY MOUTH SHUT I WOULDN'T BE HERE

254.38

There are few wild beasts more to be dreaded than a talking man having nothing to say.

—*Jonathan Swift*

254.39

He was like a cock who thought the sun had risen to hear him crow.

—*George Eliot*

254.40

The jawbone of an ass is just as murderous a weapon today as it was in Samson's time.

254.41

"Remember," said the mama whale to her child, "that when you are spouting, you are in most danger of being harpooned."

255. Silence Is Golden

Anecdotes

255.1

A candle that had grown fat and saucy with too much grease boasted one evening before a large company that it shone brighter than the sun, the moon, and all the stars.

At that moment a puff of wind came and blew it out. One who lighted it again said:

"Shine on, friend candle, and hold your tongue, the lights of heaven are never blown out."

—*Aesop*

255.2

The fellow with a beautifully blackened eye was asked by his boss what happened. "Well, boss," was the reply, "it seems I was talkin' when I should have been listenin'."

Aphorisms

255.3

Silence is the unbearable repartee.

—*Charles Dickens*

255.4

The only successful substitute for brains is silence.

—*Herbert B. Prochnow*

255.5

That man's silence is wonderful to listen to.

—*Thomas Hardy*

255.6

If no one talked of what he does not understand, the silence would become unbearable.

255.7

Drawing on my fine command of language, I said nothing.

Robert Benchley

255.8

If a man keeps his trap shut, the world will beat a path to his door.

—*Franklin Pierce Adams*

255.9

My claim to originality among Irishmen is that I have never made a speech.

—*George Moore*

255.10

It is better to keep one's mouth closed and to be thought a fool than to open it and remove all doubt.

—*Elbert Hubbard*

255.11

Blessed is the man who, having nothing to say, abstains from giving the world evidence of the fact.

—*George Eliot,* Theophrastus Such

255.12

Do you wish people to speak good of you? Don't speak.

—*Blaise Pascal,* Pensees

255.13

The new Beatitude: Blessed is he that hath nothing to say, and cannot be persuaded to say it.

—*James Russell Lowell*

255.14

Smart people speak from experience—smarter people, from experience, don't speak.

255.15

A yawn is a silent shout.

—*G. K. Chesterton*

255.16

Let thy speech be better than silence, or be silent.

—*Dionysius the Elder*

255.17

In silence also there's a worth that brings no risk.

—*Simonides of Ceos*

255.18

Let a fool hold his tongue and he will pass for a sage.

—*Publius*

(*See also 4.4, 19.8, 51.1, 51.3, 76.2, 76.3, 76.6, 151.22, 162.24, 165.13–165.16, 165.20, 165.21, 165.42, 166.4, 167.3, 170.2, 170.3, 170.13, 173.9, 173.12, 173.14, 175.8, 190.3, 210.1, 214.3, 214.12, 218.8, 231.3, 233.17, 244.24, 248.5, 249.17, 254.1, 254.2, 254.4–254.6, 254.32, 254.33, 256.1–256.4*)

256. On Listening

Anecdote

256.1

When an old man was asked why he talked to himself, he replied: "It is because, in the first place, I like to talk to a smart man, and in the second place, because I like to hear a smart man talk."

Aphorisms

256.2

Talk to a man about himself and he will listen for hours.

—*Benjamin Disraeli*

256.3

What this country needs is more free speech worth listening to.

—*Hansel B. Duckett*

256.4

He that hath ears to hear, let him stuff them with cotton.

—*William Makepeace Thackeray*

(*See also 165.13–165.16, 165.21, 167.3, 170.3, 170.13, 173.12, 173.14, 175.8, 214.12, 244.24, 255.1–255.18*)

257. Orators-at-large

Anecdotes

257.1

A Southerner, who said he had just heard a "born orator," was asked to explain what he meant by a "born orator." "Well," he replied, "you and I would say that two and two make four. But the born orator would say, 'When in the course of human events it becomes necessary or expedient to coalesce two integers and two other integers, the result—I declare it boldly and without fear or favor—the result, by a simple arithmetical calculation termed addition, is four.' That, sir, is a born orator."

257.2

Lucian, the famous Greek wit of antiquity, relates that one day Jupiter, the supreme god of Roman mythology, was strolling through the countryside chatting with a mere earthbound mortal. It was a friendly conversation about Heaven and earth. The man listened respectfully and with agreement to what Jupiter had to say until at one point in the god's discourse he hinted a doubt about a remark made by the celestial one.

Instantly Jupiter glowered, turned on his companion, and threatened him with his thunder.

Undismayed, the brave mortal said: "Ah, ha! Now, Jupiter, I know you are wrong; you are always wrong when you appeal to your thunder!"

257.3

When a woman asked Henry Clay if he would address a large gathering, the famous statesman replied, "Madam, I suffer when I don't."

257.4

William Lyon Phelps, the late Yale professor and popular lecturer, once said that he got credit for only one-fourth of the after-dinner speeches he made. "Every time I accept an invitation to speak, I really make four addresses. First, is the speech I prepare in advance. That is pretty good. Second is the speech I really make. Third is the speech I make on my way home, which is the best of all; and fourth is the speech the newspapers the next morning say I made, which bears no relation to any of the others."

257.5

When a successful public speaker was asked the secret of his popularity, he said that it was really quite simple. "I tell them what I am going to tell them, then I tell them what I told them I was going to tell them, and then I tell them what I have told them."

257.6

One way to end a speech is to tell about the man who slipped on the top step of the stairs leading to the subway platform, and then slid to the bottom. On the way down he collided with an elderly woman, knocked her off her feet, and the two continued the journey together. When they had reached the bottom, the dazed lady continued to sit on the man's chest. Looking up at her politely, the man said: "I'm sorry, Madam, but this is as far as I go."

257.7

Walter Kiernan, kidding the Vice President at a New York dinner, said: "Vice President Humphrey is not an orator, he's a speaker. You say 'Hello' to him, and he says, 'I'm so glad you asked me that!' "

Definitions

257.8

Oratory is the power to talk people out of their sober and natural opinions.

257.9

Oratory is the art of making deep noises from the chest sound like important messages from the brain.

Aphorisms

257.10

Here comes the orator, with his flood of words and his drop of reason.

—*Benjamin Franklin*

257.11

What orators lack in depth they make up for in length.

—*Baron de Montesquieu*

257.12

A man never becomes an orator if he has anything to say.

—*Finley Peter Dunne*

(*See also 54.2, 54.22, 55.2, 55.10, 55.12–55.14, 58.2, 62.16, 63.2–63.8, 64.2, 64.3, 65.1–65.3, 65.9, 66.3, 66.11, 66.12, 66.26–66.28, 71.4, 76.12, 76.13, 79.7, 79.46, 82.7, 83.1, 83.6, 83.13, 85.4, 85.5, 87.14, 138.23, 210.22, 218.4, 218.8, 236.1, 236.4, 236.12, 236.13, 236.15, 236.18, 237.2, 237.4, 237.7, 238.6, 243.21, 244.24, 249.1–249.21, 250.1–250.23, 251.1–251.37, 252.1–252.8, 253.1–253.12, 254.1–254.41, 255.1–255.18, 256.1–256.4, 258.1–258.8, 268.7, 270.11, 270.17, 274.2*)

258. Jokesmiths and Yarn Spinners

Anecdotes

258.1

A new convict found that every night after dinner his fellow prisoners would stand up one at a time and call out numbers, and then all would laugh. "What's going on?" he asked. "We are telling jokes," he was told. "But instead of going to the trouble of telling a yarn all the fellows know, we just call off a number from our jokebooks; saves a lot of time."

Anxious to be one of the boys, the newcomer stood up and called out a number, and it was followed by dead silence. He tried another number and another, but each time, silence. Later, when he wondered about this, another inmate told him his stories were all right, but he just didn't know how to tell a joke.

258.2

Richard Brinsley Sheridan said of one Dundas, a member of Parliament: "He resorts to his memory for his jokes, and his imagination for his facts."

Definition

258.3

Ad-libber: A man who stays up all night to memorize spontaneous jokes.

—*Wall Street Journal*

Aphorisms

258.4

If you think before you speak, the other fellow gets in his joke first.

—*E. W. Howe*

258.5

What a good thing Adam had—when he said a good thing, he knew nobody had said it before.

—*Mark Twain*

258.6

A good storyteller is a person who has a good memory and hopes other people haven't.

—*Irvin S. Cobb*

258.7

Don't tell a good story even though you know one; its narration will simply remind your hearers of a bad one.

—*E. W. Howe*

258.8

There is but one pleasure in life equal to that of being called on to make an after-dinner speech, and that is not being called on to make one.

—*C. D. Warner*

(*See also 156.19, 269.43, 269.106, 269.159, 273.14*)

Part Nine

THE PROPORTIONS OF PEOPLE

WEIGHTS AND MEASURES

259. The Calorie Counters

Anecdotes

259.1

A diet-conscious lady once weighed 186 pounds, but she went on a strict diet. Now she weighs only 85 pounds, including the casket.
—*Joey Adams*

259.2

Don Wilson tells of a Hollywood producer who had boasted of the rigid diet he was on, but was discovered eating a huge steak.

"I thought you were on a diet." said a friend.

"I am," replied the diner between bites. "This is just to give me strength to continue it."
—*Best*

259.3

A wife said her husband's idea of a balanced diet was to have a highball in each hand.

259.4

"Now about your diet; I forgot to mention that you must drop bread from your eating habits," said the doctor firmly.

"No bread!" exclaimed the patient. "Then how am I going to sop up the gravy?"

259.5

Slender and diet-conscious George Bernard Shaw encountered 300-pound G. K. Chesterton, who said to Shaw, "You look like there's a famine in England."

"And you," retorted Shaw, "look like you have caused it."

259.6

A giggly, fortyish woman said coyly to the doctor, "Look at me, I've lost all that fat off my stomach since I was here last. I wonder where it's gone?"

"Look behind you, lady, look behind."

Definitions

259.7

Reducing: Wishful shrinking.

259.8

Balanced diet: What you eat at buffet suppers.

259.9

Diet is something that takes the starch out of you.

259.10

Diet is the penalty for exceeding the feed limit.

Aphorisms

259.11

Reducing experts live on the fat of the land.

259.12

Some people are no good at counting calories—and have the figures to prove it.

(*See also 19.36, 19.39, 40.4–40.6, 43.12, 156.12, 159.5, 183.14, 260.1–260.15, 261.1–261.12, 276.11*)

260. Tall and Small

Anecdotes

260.1

A tall Maine woods guide one day was excessively bothered by mosquitoes as he was escorting a small, bumptious customer.

"Why," asked the little man, "do the mosquitoes bother you so much, whereas they don't seem to come near me?"

"I suppose it's because they haven't seen you yet."

260.2

To a very thin man, who had been boring him, Douglas Jerrold said: "Sir, you are like a pin, but without either its head or its point."

260.3

A man out West is so remarkably tall he has to go up a stepladder to shave himself.

260.4

There is a man so tall that he has to go down upon his knees to put his hands into his trouser pockets.

260.5

There is a man in Quebec so short that he had to stand on his own head to kiss his wife.

(*See also 141.8, 240.27, 259.1–259.12, 265.14, 268.14*)

261. Assorted Sizes and Broken Lots

Anecdotes

261.1

The very obese woman stepped on an out-of-order weighing machine, dropped in a penny, and the scale registered a mere 90 pounds. A drunk standing by observed this and said, "My God, the woman is hollow!"

261.2

An exceptionally heavy man strolling through the carnival section of a resort town was attracted to a weighing machine which said: "I speak your weight."

He put a coin in the slot and stepped on the platform. "One at a time," said the voice from within the machine.

261.3

A woman stepped on the scales and her husband asked, "Well, what's the verdict—a little overweight, I guess?"

"Oh, no," said the wife, "I wouldn't say that. But according to this table I should be 6 inches taller."

261.4

There is a man in Camberwell so fat that they grease the omnibus wheels with his shadow.

261.5

The amply proportioned economics professor ordered a second piece of pie in the faculty dining room. A dietetics expert at the table gravely reminded him of his folly.

"My dear fellow," said the economist, "surely you must know that the average American during his lifetime consumes 30,000 eggs, 6,000 loaves of bread, 9,000 pounds of potatoes, 8,000 pounds of beef, fifteen sheep, seventeen pigs, six calves, and hundreds of pounds of sugar. So what the hell difference can a few pieces of pie make?"

261.6

Wilson Mizner described an acquaintance as a trellis with varicose veins.

261.7

Then there was the woman with varicose veins who went to a masquerade party as a road map.

261.8

Author Charles Francis Coe once referred to a certain man's sideburns in this way: "He is the only man I ever saw in my life in parentheses."

Definitions

261.9

Anatomy: The study of heavenly bodies.

261.10

Anatomy: Something everyone has but it looks better on a girl.

—*Bruce Raeburn*

261.11

An adult is a person who has ceased to grow vertically, but not horizontally.

—*Anonymous*

Aphorism

261.12

Forty is the age when a man begins to get thin on top and a woman begins to get fat on the bottom.

(*See also 77.2, 79.58, 141.2, 259.1–259.12, 261.1–261.12*)

Part Ten

MIDDLE AGE AND BEYOND

262. Forty Plus

Anecdotes

262.1

A lady, complaining how rapidly time stole away, said, "Alas! I am near thirty."

A doctor, who was present and knew her age, said: "Do not fret at it, madam; for you will get further from that frightful epoch every day."

262.2

Said a lady, getting on in years, to Douglas Jerrold, "Do you think, Mr. Jerrold, that it can be the essence of myrrh that I use, which is making my hair gray?"

"Madam," he replied, "I should say it was the essence of *thyme!*"

Definitions

262.3

Middle Age: The time a guy starts turning out the lights for economical rather than romantic reasons.

—*John Marino*

262.4

Middle Age: When you can do just as much as ever, but would rather not.

262.5

Middle Age: When you are sitting at home on Saturday night and the telephone rings and you hope it isn't for you.

—*Ring Lardner*

262.6

Middle age is that period of life when your idea of getting ahead is staying even.

—*Ohio State Journal*

262.7

Middle Age: The time when you'll do anything to feel better, except give up what's hurting you.

—*Robert Quillen*

262.8

Middle age is the time when a man is always thinking that in a week or two he will feel as good as ever.

—*Don Marquis*

262.9

Middle Age: When you begin to exchange your emotions for symptoms.

—*Irvin S. Cobb*

262.10

Middle age is that time of life when you'd rather not have a good time than recover from it.

—*Fletcher Henderson*

262.11

Middle Age: That period when a man begins to feel friendly toward insurance agents.

—*The Wyatt Way*

Aphorisms

262.12

Boys will be boys, and so will a lot of middle-aged men.

—*Kin Hubbard*

262.13

You've reached middle age when all you exercise is caution.

—*Franklin P. Jones,* Saturday Evening Post

(*See also 7.26, 132.3, 135.28, 135.29, 136.9, 158.26, 159.7, 162.21, 162.28, 161.3, 164.4, 165.12, 165.106, 168.5, 172.11–172.19, 174.3, 208.1, 212.5, 234.25, 261.12, 263.1–263.35, 270.5*)

263. Senior Citizens

Anecdotes

263.1

An old goat grabbed a guy's sleeve during a fashion show and said, "Here I am at seventy-five and when I look at those models I wish I were twenty years older."

"You mean twenty years younger, don't you?"

"No, I mean twenty years older—then I wouldn't give a damn about them."

263.2

Justices Oliver Wendell Holmes and Louis D. Brandeis one evening were walking home from the Court when the ninety-two-year-old Holmes looked with admiration at a beautiful young woman who walked past them. "Oh!" sighed Holmes, "what wouldn't I give to be seventy again!"

263.3

Man commenting on elderly playboy: "He's reached the age where he chases girls only if it's downhill."

—*Earl Wilson*

263.4

An old and tired traveler took a room in a hotel and crawled into bed. He wasn't there very long when in bounced a girl—redheaded, luscious, and scantily clad.

"Oh," she cried, "I must have gotten into the wrong room!"

"Yep," said the traveler wearily. "Not only in the wrong room, lady, but you got here forty years too late."

263.5

Conditions had reached such a stage that the elderly businessman simply had to tell his wife. "You might as well know it now; it will be in the papers soon enough. The fact is, my secretary is suing me for breach of promise."

"How absurd," said his wife. "What could you promise a woman at your age of seventy-nine?"

263.6

"Grandpa, it says here that there are 20 percent more women at age seventy-five than men."

"At age seventy-five," sighed Grandpa, "who cares?"

263.7

A man who wanted to live to be 100 years of age was told by his doctor to give up drinking, smoking, and women.

"Will I live to be 100 then?" asked the patient.

"No, but it will seem like it."

263.8

During a debate with a woman member of Congress, eighty-year-old Uncle Joe Cannon arose and asked: "Will the lady yield?"

The congresswoman smiled and said: "The lady will be delighted to yield to the gentleman from Illinois."

The aged gentleman from Illinois laughed and said: "Now that the lady has yielded, what can I do about it?"

263.9

In the later years of his life a reporter asked Lionel Barrymore, the great actor, if he still found acting as much fun as it used to be.

"My boy," said Barrymore, "I am seventy-five years of age, and nothing is as much fun as it used to be."

263.10

During the last year of his life Douglas Jerrold attended a large party of old friends. But he preferred to play cards in a room adjoining the one where there was dancing. A friend touched him on the shoulder and asked, "Who is that man dancing with Mrs. Jerrold?"

Jerrold glanced at the dancers and said, "God knows, my dear boy! Some member of the Humane Society, I suppose."

263.11

The very old barroom habitué went to the doctor for a checkup, and during the course of the examination the doctor noticed that the patient's hands fluttered and quivered like leaves during a windstorm. "You must do a great deal of drinking," observed the doctor.

"Not so much anymore," said the old guy. "I spill most of it now."

263.12

When one of the town's leading citizens reached age eighty, the local paper sent a reporter to ask him what exercise he used to keep fit.

"Son," said the old fellow, "when you're pushing eighty, you don't need any other exercise."

263.13

After years of crabbedness and persistent complaining, the old-timer in the village suddenly changed to a gentle, smiling optimist. When asked to account for the remarkable transformation, the old man said, "Well, for years I have been striving to have a contented mind, and never made any progress. So the other day I decided to get along without a contented mind."

263.14

Night after night the old fellow got on the bus for the long trip home, and every night he complained to the bus driver that his tight shoes were killing him. Finally the bus driver, tired of hearing the same old complaint, asked the man why he didn't get shoes that fitted him properly.

"Well, it's this way," said the bus passenger. "I live a pretty dreary life. I lost my business, my wife died, my children ignore me, and I hate my job. The only comfort left me is when I get home and can take off these damn shoes. I'd really miss that."

263.15

A young man made the mistake of twitting a much older man about his age, and was reminded, "An ass is older at twenty than a man at sixty."

263.16

In Vermont there are two men so old that they have forgotten who they are, and there are no neighbors living who can remember.

Aphorisms

263.17

I am an old man and have known a great many troubles, but most of them never happened.

—*Mark Twain*

263.18

The old believe everything, the middle-aged suspect everything, the young know everything.

—*Oscar Wilde*

263.19

He who devotes sixteen hours a day to hard study may become as wise at sixty as he thought himself at twenty.

—*Mary Wilson Little*

263.20

Every man desires to live long, but no man would be old.

—*Jonathan Swift*

263.21

The years are beginning to add up if it takes you longer to rest than it did to get tired.

263.22

By the time a man is old enough to watch his step, he is too old to go anywhere.

263.23

Maurice Chevalier said it is not so bad being seventy when you consider the alternative.

263.24

She's so old that she knew the Big Dipper when it was only a drinking cup.

263.25

Many of us are at the "metallic" age: gold in our teeth, silver in our hair—and lead in our pants.

—*Jacob M. Braude*

263.26

Old men are fond of giving good advice to console themselves for their inability to give bad examples.

—*La Rochefoucauld*

263.27

Discretion comes to a person after he's too old for it to do him any good.

263.28

Consider well the proportion of things. It is better to be a young June bug than an old bird of paradise.

—*Mark Twain*

263.29

To me, old age is always fifteen years older than I am.

—*Bernard Baruch*

263.30

No man loves life like him that's growing old.

—*Sophocles*

263.31

Fun is like life insurance: the older you get, the more it costs.

—*Kin Hubbard*

263.32

Many a man that can't direct you to a corner drugstore will get a respectful hearing when age has further impaired his mind.

—*Finley Peter Dunne*

263.33

A man is only as old as he looks—and he only looks if he is old.

263.34

A man is still young so long as women can make him happy or unhappy; he reaches middle age when they can no longer make him unhappy. He is old when they cease to make him either happy or unhappy.

263.35

Insurance statistics reveal that for every man of 85 years of age there are 7 women. But it's too late then.

—*Jacob M. Braude*

263.36

An imaginative—or ambitious—old-timer once said: "I don't mind being a grandfather, but I'm not enthusiastic about sleeping with a grandmother."

(*See also 102.2, 102.3, 132.3, 135.28, 135.29, 136.9, 158.26, 159.7, 161.3, 162.21, 162.28, 164.4, 165.12, 165.106, 168.5, 172.11–172.19, 174.3, 208.1, 212.5, 234.25, 261.12, 262.1–262.13, 264.4, 269.11, 270.5, 276.10, 277.7*)

264. Kicking the Bucket

Anecdotes

264.1

The old grandmother had been in and out of a coma for four days, during which time the family had been summoned to be at the bedside of the once-so-energetic old lady. Suddenly she opened her eyes, looked upon the group with interest and some surprise, and said, "Lively bunch, aren't we?"

264.2

Mike was on his deathbed. The priest bent over him to give him last rites, and said to him, "Repeat after me, 'I renounce the devil and all his evil deeds.'" No response from Mike. The priest repeated the formula. Still no response. After the third try, the priest shook Mike and said, "Didn't you hear me?"

"Yes, I heard you," said Mike, "but you told me I am going to die, and this is no time to antagonize anybody."

264.3

Tony joined a burial plan or club, whereby each member agreed to pay a certain amount over a period of years toward a large plot in the cemetery where all members of the group would be buried. After some years the surviving members found that the payments had not come in with the promised regularity and the club was in difficulty.

When Tony, among others, was dunned for back payments, he looked at the other members in astonishment and said, "But I haven't used the plot."

"So what," the club president replied. "Nobody stopped you, did he?"

264.4

The ninety-year-old man got into a bitter argument with the town shoemaker as to how a pair of shoes should be made. "See here," said the shoemaker, "what's the idea of doing so much yapping? You're past ninety and there's little chance of your living long enough to wear these shoes out."

The old fellow looked sternly at the shoemaker, and said, "Apparently you are not aware that statistics prove that very few people die after ninety years of age."

264.5

George Meredith at the age of seventy-five was seriously ill and the newspapers reported that he had only "periods of partial consciousness." Meredith saw these reports and promptly wired one paper THAT REPORT OF ME IS INCORRECT. . . . THE DIFFICULTY WITH ME IS TO OBTAIN UNCONSCIOUSNESS.

264.6

The dandified young city man finally drove out to the country to visit his aged uncle, aware that he should not have waited until this eleventh hour to do so. When he arrived in the tiny village after a two-day drive, he stopped at the gas station and asked what road to take out to Farmer Jenkins's place.

"Why, he's dead," they told him.

"Dead!" exclaimed the youth. "I drove all the way from New York to spend a few days with him."

The service station man looked at the young man's flashy clothes and car, noted his dandified manners, and said, "He must a'knowed you were a'comin'."

264.7

Pyrrho, the Greek philosopher, used to say that there is no difference between living and dying; and a man said to him, "Why then do you not die?" Pyrrho replied, "Because there is no difference."

—*Epictetus*

264.8

A man carrying a heavy load of wood on his shoulders grew weary and let the bundle down and cried bitterly, "O Death, come and take me!"

Death appeared and asked, "Why do you call me?"

Frightened, the man replied, "Please help me place the load back on my shoulders."

264.9

When Honoré de Balzac's uncle died and left him a good sum of money, the author wrote to a friend: "Yesterday, at 5 A.M., my uncle and I passed on to a better life."

264.10

In Shakespeare's *Romeo and Juliet*, Mercutio who has been stabbed and is dying, says: "Ask for me tomorrow, and you shall find a grave man."

264.11

On the eve of his 75th birthday Winston Churchill said: "I am ready to meet my Maker. Whether my Maker is prepared for the great ordeal of meeting me is another matter."

—*Time*

264.12

Voltaire, asked for a consoling statement on the death of a man he disliked, wrote the following:

"I have just been informed that Monsieur —— is dead. He was a sturdy patriot, a gifted writer, a loyal friend, and an affectionate husband and father—provided he is really dead."

264.13

A group of women were being shown through the Players Club and stopped to look at some death masks made by Laurence Hutton. One woman pointed to the death mask of Richard Brinsley Sheridan and said, "I had no idea he was so frail."

"You must remember, madam," said Oliver Herford, "that Sheridan was not really himself when that mask was made."

264.14

A man on his way to work one morning noticed that a certain friendly cop was not at his usual station and stopped to ask his replacement where the other man was. "He's dead," was the solemn reply.

"Oh, he's joined the great majority," said the inquirer.

"No, I wouldn't say that," replied the new policeman. "He was a very good man, you know."

Aphorisms

264.15

If you want him to mourn, you had best leave him nothing.

—*Martial*

264.16

The good die young—because they see it's no use living if you've got to be good.

—*John Barrymore*

264.17

Only the young die good.

—*Oliver Herford*

264.18

Here's that ye may never die nor be kilt till ye break your bones over a bushel of glory.

264.19

All say "How hard it is that we have to die"—a strange complaint to come from the mouths of people who have had to live.

—*Mark Twain*

264.20

I never wanted to see anybody die, but there are a few obituary notices I have read with pleasure.

—*Clarence Darrow*

(*See also 30.1, 37.18, 42.31, 43.2, 54.8, 62.10, 73.1, 75.3, 76.22, 87.5, 99.13, 101.5, 101.9, 103.5, 106.17, 106.19, 108.5, 111.10, 133.1, 148.9, 156.17, 165.21, 165.25, 165.62, 177.2, 177.12, 184.5, 201.18, 203.2, 211.20, 211.25, 212.10, 214.4, 214.11, 229.16, 232.6, 239.14, 241.1, 243.19, 274.11, 279.1–279.23*)

265. Last Rites

Anecdotes

265.1

Just as the casket containing the meanest man in town was being lowered into the grave—the remains of a man who beat his wife, starved his kids, owed everyone in the community, and quarreled with all his neighbors—just at that moment there was a terrific bolt of lightning and a terrifying clap of thunder.

"Well, he got there all right," said one bystander to another.

265.2

When a certain miser died his wife was completely dry-eyed, and remained so to the very moment of the funeral procession. But then, when the charity-collectors began to rattle their boxes and cry out, "Charity saves from death!" the wife began to weep bitter tears.

Asked why the outburst of the charity-collectors provoked so much weeping, the wife said: "Not until then was I sure my husband was dead. If appeals to charity did not cause him to run, then he is surely dead."

265.3

The minister stood at the edge of the coffin and launched into a glowing tribute to the character, integrity, industry, goodness, charity, and compassion of the notorious bum whose remains were being honored. Finally the wife of the deceased leaned over to one of her children and said, "Danny, go over and see if that is really your father in the coffin."

265.4

Don Ohnegian was solemnly attending the funeral services for a fellow New Jersey trial lawyer, when his associate, Paul Huot, hurried upon the sad scene and whispered, "Am I very late?"

"No," replied Don gravely; but then unable to resist the temptation, he pointed to the pulpit where the minister was preparing to begin his eulogy and added, "They are just opening for the defense."

265.5

An author whose vacation was interrupted by a request to preside over the obsequies of a prominent man who had just died asked, "Where is he going to be buried?"

"He is going to be cremated."

"You don't want a master of ceremonies," said the author. "You need a toastmaster."

265.6

Two country boys wandering around an unfamiliar town saw a strange-looking building and a number of people going into it. One of the lads joined the other people, but presently was rudely ushered out.

"What happened?"

"Got me, except when I got in there I turned to one of those men and asked, 'What's cookin'?' and they gave me the bum's rush!"

Later they learned it was a crematorium.

265.7

When the chief of the small-town volunteer fire department died, the firemen all chipped in for a floral piece in honor of their popular leader. But the family of the deceased man was not at all happy with the inscription on the wreath: GONE TO HIS LAST FIRE

265.8

At the funeral of the richest man in town a great many mourners turned out to pay their last respects. Among the multitude was a poor man who wept bitterly as he followed the hearse.

"Are you a close relation of the deceased?" asked a mourner.

"I'm no relation at all!" said the weeper.

"Then why do you sorrow so much?"

"That's why!"

265.9

Stephen Badin, a priest on the Kentucky frontier who became increasingly eccentric in his old age, was once asked to say a few words of praise at the funeral of an elderly man.

Father Badin opened his talk this way: "He had not much sense, but we are not to forget that he had all the sense God gave him."

265.10

A man went to Florida for his health. He died there, and they shipped him back to Chicago for burial. At the wake several people looked at him and said, "Oh, doesn't he look nice. Those two months in Florida sure did him a lot of good—look at that tan!"

265.11

As the funeral drew slowly along the street a man in a store asked the proprietor whose funeral it was.

"Charlie Jones's funeral."

"Charlie Jones! You don't mean to tell me he's dead?"

"Do you think they're just rehearsin'?" asked the storekeeper.

265.12

A young woman went to the funeral services of a friend at an ultra-fashionable church. She had gone shopping before the services and came to the church carrying a hatbox. At the door of the church an attendant politely reached for her parcel. Supposing this to be a customary checking service in that church, the young woman surrendered the parcel.

Later, when the casket was carried out of the church to the waiting hearse, the young woman was startled to find on top of it, along with several other floral pieces, the flowered spring hat she had purchased that morning.

265.13

"I'm through with funerals," said Miss Pearl Purviance when she returned home from the cemetery where not a soul mentioned her hat.

—*Kin Hubbard*

265.14

"What is the charge for a funeral notice in the paper?"

"50 cents an inch, madam."

"Good Lord! My poor husband was 6 feet tall!"

265.15

License plate on a hearse: U2

265.16

The widow, viewing her husband's remains in the funeral parlor, protested to the undertaker that she had ordered her husband be buried in a blue suit, not the brown one they had put on him. "We'll take care of it by the time you come back this afternoon," said the proprietor.

When the widow returned she found that her wishes had been carried out. "It was no trouble," said the undertaker. "The woman in the next room wanted her husband in a brown suit."

"Oh," said the widow, "you just changed suits."

"No, madam," replied the undertaker, "we changed heads."

265.17

The undertaker regarded the deceased with severe disapproval because his wig persisted in slipping back and revealing a bald pate every time a truck passed on the street outside the funeral parlor.

The widow stood by and heard the undertaker express his unhappiness, and she volunteered to go to the store for some glue. When she returned, the undertaker said he had solved the problem.

"Oh, did you locate some glue?" she asked.

"No, I used a tack," said the undertaker.

265.18

Thomas Hood liked the pun he invented about the undertaker who was seeking to Urn a lively Hood.

265.19

At an undertakers' banquet they got up, each with a glass in hand, and sang the Indian plague song:

So stand to your glasses steady;
'Tis here the revival lies;
A cup to the dead already—
Hurrah for the next that dies!

265.20

Hy Gardner reported that one Kroak was a funeral director in Stephan, Minnesota; Boxwell Brothers were funeral directors in Austin, Texas; Dye and Berry, undertakers of Hot Springs, New Mexico; and I. Laidlow, an undertaker in Hurleyville, New York. An undertaker in Anniston, Alabama, had a sign reading: I. N. Joy UNDERTAKING. The Lively Funeral Home in Bridgeton, New Jersey, is owned by Hildredth Lively.

Aphorism

265.21

Politeness looks well in every man, except an undertaker.

—*Josh Billings*

(*See also 9.5, 23.10, 28.10, 38.4, 40.23, 40.26, 40.27, 42.2, 55.8, 79.15, 79.16, 74.3, 84.2, 86.4, 99.8, 100.6, 106.8, 109.12, 126.1, 130.9, 133.1, 139.40, 152.55, 154.11, 155.26, 155.27, 167.4–167.7, 169.5, 177.12, 202.2, 210.14, 210.26, 213.5, 215.19, 216.2, 226.11, 240.8, 236.15–236.18, 238.5, 241.1, 242.18, 243.1, 259.1, 264.1–264.20, 266.4–266.37, 267.1–267.13, 267.26, 270.10, 279.1–279.23, 274.10*)

266. Graveyard Humor

Epitaphs

266.1

To all friends I bid adieu,
A more sudden death you never knew.
As I was leading the old mare to drink,
She kicked, and killed me quicker'n a wink.

—*New Hampshire churchyard*

266.2

Epitaph and a Reply

Remember man, that passeth by,
As thou is now so once was I;
And as I am now so must thou be:
Prepare thyself to follow me.

Under this someone wrote:

To follow you I'm not content,
Until I learn which way you went.

—*Churchyard; Linton, England, 1825*

266.3

Epitaph on William More

Here lies one *More,* and *no* more than he;
One More and *no more!* how can that be?
Why *one More* and *no more,* may lie here alone;
But here lies one *More,* and that's *more* than one!

—*Stepney Churchyard, England*

266.4

Under this marble fair,
Lies the body entomb'd of Gervase Aire;
He died not of an ague fit,
Nor surfeited by too much wit.
Methinks this was a wondrous death,
That Aire should die for want of breath.

—*At St. Giles, Cripplegate*

266.5

Poor Martha Snell, she's gone away,
She would if she could, but she could not stay;
She had two legs, and a baddish cough,
But her legs it was that carried her off.

266.6

Here lies one Foote, whose death may thousands save,
For death has now one Foote within the grave.

266.7

Here lies the remains of Margery Peg,
Who never had issue save one in her leg.
She was a woman of wonderful cunning;
While one leg stood still the other kept running.

266.8

Epitaph in a Churchyard in Dorsetshire

For me deceas'd weep not, my dear,
I am not dead, but sleepeth here,
Your time will come, prepare to die,
Wait but awhile, you'll follow I.

When the widower married two weeks after his wife's death someone wrote on the grave stone the following:

I am not griev'd, my dearest life,
Sleep on—I've got another wife;
And therefore cannot come to thee,
For I must go to bed to she.

266.9

On His Wife

Here lies my wife; here let her lie.
Now she's at rest. And so am I.

—*John Dryden*

266.10

On a Scold

Here lies a woman, no man can deny it,
Who now is at peace, though she lived most unquiet.
Her husband beseeches, if near here you're walking,
Speak soft, or she'll wake, and then she'll start talking.

266.11

Resurrection

Within this grave we both do lie,
Back to back, my wife and I.
When the last trump the air shall fill
She will get up, and I'll lie still.

266.12

Here lies my wife, a sad slattern and a shrew,
If I said I regretted her I should lie too.

—*Selby churchyard; Yorkshire, England*

266.13

I laid my wife beneath this stone
For her repose and for my own.

266.14

Here lies my poor wife, without bed or blanket,
But dead as a door-nail, and God be thankit.

266.15

This stone was raised by Sarah's lord,
Not Sarah's virtues to record,
For they're well-known to all the town,
But it was raised to keep her down.

266.16

Here lies the body of Sarah Sexton
Who never did aught to vex one.
Not like the woman under the next stone.

(Thomas Sexton's first wife was buried beneath the next stone.)

—*Churchyard; Newmarket, England*

266.17

Here lies the body of Mary Ford,
Whose soul, we trust, is with the Lord;
But if for hell she's changed this life,
'Tis better than being John Ford's wife.

266.18

On a Dentist

Stranger, approach this spot with gravity.
John Brown is filling his last cavity.

266.19

Here lies William Smith; and what is somewhat rarish,
He was born, bred, and hanged in this here parish.

266.20

Here lies
Pierre Cabochard, grocer.
His inconsolate widow
dedicates this monument to his memory,
and continues the same business at
the old stand, 167 Rue Mouffetard.

—*In Père-la-Chaise cemetery; Paris*

266.21

Beneath this stone, in hopes of Zion,
Is laid the landlord of the Lion.
Resigned unto the Heavenly will,
His son keeps on the business still.

—*Wiltshire, England*

266.22

Here lies Joan Kitchin, when her life was spent,
She kicked up her heels, and away she went.

266.23

Here lies the bones of Margaret Gwynn,
Who was so very pure within,
She cracked her outer shell of sin
And hatched herself a Seraphim.

266.24

My time was come! My days were spent!
I was called away—and away I went!!!!

266.25

Finis
Maginnis

—*Irish epitaph*

266.26

Lie heavy on him, Earth, for he
laid many a heavy load on thee.

—*Jonathan Swift's Epitaph on Vanbrugh, an architect*

266.27

This is the grave of Mike O'Day
Who died maintaining his right of way.
His right was clear and his will was strong
But he's just as dead as if he'd been wrong.

266.28

Old Epitaph

Here lies the corpse of Dr. Chard
Who filled the half of this churchyard.

266.29

Here lies the body of Robert Gordin,
Mouth almighty and teeth accordin';
Stranger, tread lightly over this wonder,
If he opens his mouth, you are gone, by thunder.

—*South Carolina*

Definition

266.30

Epitaph: A belated advertisement for a line of goods that has been permanently discontinued.

—*Irvin S. Cobb*

Aphorisms

266.31

After reading the epitaphs in the cemetery, you wonder where they bury the sinners.

—*Coronet*

266.32

Reading the epitaphs, our only salvation lies in resurrecting the dead and burying the living.

—*Paul Eldridge*

266.33

What's fame after all? 'Tis apt to be what someone writes on your tombstone.

—*Finley Peter Dunne*

266.34

The tombstone is about the only thing that can stand upright and lie on its face at the same time.

—*Mary Wilson Little*

266.35

The graveyards are full of people the world could not do without.

—*Elbert Hubbard*

266.36

The fence around a cemetery is foolish, for those inside can't come out and those outside don't want to get in.

—*Arthur Brisbane*

266.37

At the entrance to a Chicago cemetery was this sign: "Owing to employment difficulties gravedigging will be done by a skeleton crew."

(*See also 13.2, 16.9, 16.33, 19.65, 25.39, 45.7, 67.4, 67.5, 93.24, 96.13, 98.4, 155.23, 155.24, 165.2, 165.37, 165.44, 165.94, 169.2, 169.4, 184.8, 184.31, 217.12, 221.10, 223.1, 225.5, 225.15, 226.6, 226.7, 226.11, 226.14, 229.6, 235.16, 241.1, 264.1–264.20, 265.1–265.21, 267.1–267.13, 279.1–279.23*)

267. Heaven and Hell

Anecdotes

267.1

A friend once asked Winston Churchill what made him think he would reach the bar of Heaven, to which Sir Winston replied: "Surely the Almighty must observe the principles of English common law and consider a man innocent until proven guilty."

267.2

A miser who sought admission to Heaven, told St. Peter he was a businessman.

"What do you want?"

"I want to get in."

"What have you done that entitles you to admission?"

"Well, I saw a decrepit woman on the streets the other day and gave her a dime."

"Gabriel, is that in the records?" asked St. Peter.

"Yes, Peter, it is right down here."

"What else have you done?"

"Well, the other day I was passing along the street and I saw a newspaper boy half-frozen to death and I gave him a nickel."

"Is that in the record, Gabriel?"

"Yes," said Gabriel, "it is down on the record."

"What else have you done?"

"Well," said the businessman, "I can't recollect anything else just now."

"Gabriel," said St. Peter, "What do you think we ought to do?"

"Oh, give him back his 15 cents and tell him to go to Hell."

267.3

St. Peter heard a knock at the door and called out, "Who's there?"

"It is I," came the reply from outside the door.

"Go to Hell," called back St. Peter. "We have too many English teachers in here now."

267.4

Two parsons and a cabdriver arrived at Heaven simultaneously. St. Peter asked one of the clergymen what he had done on earth.

He said, "I have been a Baptist minister for twenty-five years and I have faithfully preached the Gospel these years." St. Peter told him to stand aside.

The second minister said he had been a Methodist preacher for twenty-five years and had been equally faithful in bringing the Gospel message to the people.

"OK," said St. Peter, "Stand over there with your friend." Then he turned to the cabdriver and asked him what he did. "I have only been a cabdriver for the past fifteen years."

St. Peter embraced him and told him to go ahead in. "After all," said St. Peter, "you have scared more hell out of people in fifteen years than these other two men did in their total of fifty years of preaching."

267.5

St. Peter to applicant: "Where are you from?"

"California."

"Well, come on in; but I don't think you are going to like it here."

267.6

An oil prospector arrived at the gate of Heaven and St. Peter told him, "The quota for oilmen is now filled up. The only way you can get in is to eliminate some of the oilmen now here."

Whereupon the oil prospector started a rumor that oil had been struck in Hades. The word got around, and all the oilmen began to rush from Heaven straight to Hell to stake their claims. St. Peter watched them with amusement, but then he was astonished to find that the fellow who started the rumor was also preparing to leave for the other place. St. Peter asked why.

The oilman who had wanted in said, "Well, there may be something to that rumor after all."

267.7

St. Peter and St. Paul were having a game of golf on the Heavenly links. St. Peter teed off and made a hole in one. St. Paul teed off and also made a hole in one.

"Paul," said Peter, "let's get down to business and cut out the miracles."

267.8

From American Negro folklore comes the story of an old Negro who died and went immediately to the Heavenly Gates, but St. Peter turned him away because he was afoot. "You gotta come a'ridin' up here," said St. Peter.

So the old fellow trudged back down the road apiece, shaking his head in wonder and bewilderment. Then he met two white men coming along toward the pearly gates and it struck him that if he carried both of these men to the entrance of Heaven, he could gain admittance as the one who gave them their ride into Heaven. He explained the situation to the two white men, who gratefully accepted this opportunity not only to ride but to facilitate their entrance into Heaven. So they climbed on the poor old man's back, and he struggled forward with them until they finally came to the celestial entrance.

But when they arrived there, still aboard the Negro's back, St. Peter told them, "Come in, but leave your horse outside."

267.9

The big businessman had died and gone to his eternal reward. Shortly after his arrival he felt a hearty thump on his back and turned around. "Hello there, Mr. Smith," said the thumper. "I'm here for that interview."

"Interview? What interview?"

"Come now, Smith. Don't you remember me? Everytime I called at your office to make a sale you sent out word you'd see me in Hell first."

267.10

One night a group of old-timers sat around the fires of Hell discussing the noble deeds they had performed on earth and the heroic ways in which they had died. One wordy bore got the floor and went on and on about the Johnstown flood in which he had died. Not even several of the minor devils could get the man to shut up. Finally an old man got up and stamped out of the room in obvious disgust. "Who's that old geezer?" asked the Johnstown-flood man. Everybody burst out laughing. "That's Noah," they said.

267.11

One day the gate between Heaven and Hell broke down, and St. Peter and Satan got into a bitter dispute as to whose responsibility it was to repair it. After much argument they could arrive at no agreement, so St. Peter said he would hire a lawyer to defend the interests of Heaven.

"Where are you going to get a lawyer?" asked Satan with a diabolical grin.

Aphorisms

267.12

In heaven when the blessed use the telephone they will say what they have to say and not a word besides.

—*Somerset Maugham*

267.13

May your soul be in glory three weeks before the divil knows you're dead.

(*See also 102.11, 108.6, 112.1, 121.22, 152.2, 162.4, 169.6, 174.29, 175.12, 175.29, 177.11, 198.6, 211.17, 211.18, 213.16, 214.8, 215.11, 215.16, 216.6, 220.2, 220.3, 221.4, 229.8, 230.2, 232.2, 234.7, 234.11, 235.2, 235.3 235.6–235.8, 235.45, 235.47, 235.54, 236.7, 236.12, 237.6, 239.11, 239.13, 241.1–241.3, 242.11, 242.21, 242.22, 242.29, 243.13, 243.18, 246.8, 247.2, 264.14, 265.7, 268.12, 271.26, 271.43*)

Part Eleven

THE ANIMAL KINGDOM

ANIMALS—AND MEN

268. Birds and Beasts

Anecdotes

268.1

"My setter is so smart," boasted Arbuthnot, "that one day when I was walking him I met a friend named—"

"Oh, come now," said Abercrombie. "That's an old story—the man's name was Partridge, and so your dog came immediately to a set."

"No, you've got it wrong," said Arbuthnot. "My dog did not come quite to a set. The man's name was Quayle, and this dog of mine hesitated because of the spelling."

268.2

The Easterner was amazed when he walked into the Bucket of Blood Saloon and found a dog sitting at a table playing poker with three men. "Can that dog really read his cards?" asked the stranger.

"Yeah, but he ain't much of a player," said one of the men. "Whenever he draws a good hand he wags his tail."

268.3

Engraved on the Collar of a Dog,
Which I Gave to His Royal Highness

I am his Highness' dog at Kew;
Pray tell me, sir, whose dog are you?

—*Alexander Pope*

268.4

A bear approached a hunter in the forest and asked him what he was after.

"I'm after a fur coat for myself," said the hunter.

"I'm out looking for some breakfast," said the bear. "Why not step into my cave and we'll talk this thing over?"

The hunter agreed to this and they retired to the cave and sat down to work out a compromise. The bear got his breakfast and the hunter was in a fur coat.

268.5

A crow had snatched a goodly piece of cheese out of a window and flew with it into a high tree, intent on enjoying her prize. A fox spied the dainty morsel, and thus he planned his approaches.

"O Crow," said he, "how beautiful are thy wings! how bright thine eye! how graceful thy neck! thy breast is the breast of an eagle! thy claws—I beg pardon—thy talons, are a match for all the beasts of the field. O that such a bird should be dumb and want only a voice!"

The crow, pleased with the flattery, and chuckling to think how she would surprise the fox with her caw, opened her mouth. Down dropped the cheese! which the fox snapping up, observed, as he walked away, that whatever he had remarked of her beauty, he had said nothing yet of her brains.

—*Aesop*

268.6

D. B. Wyndham relates that one day, years ago, a fox that hated grapes crept up behind Aesop, bit him on the backside, and said, "Now go home and write that up."

268.7

A lion and an ass made an agreement to go out hunting together. By and by they came to a cave where many wild goats abode. The lion took up his station at the mouth of the cave, and the ass, going within, kicked and brayed and made a mighty fuss to frighten them out. When the lion had caught very many of them, the ass came out and asked him if he had not made a noble fight and routed the goats properly.

"Yes, indeed," said the lion; "and I assure you, you would have frightened me too if I had not known you to be an ass."

—*Aesop*

268.8

A rabbit and a lion entered a restaurant, and the rabbit ordered a head of lettuce.

"What's your friend going to have?" the waiter asked the rabbit.

"Nothing," said the rabbit.

"Whassa matter with him? Isn't he hungry?" demanded the waiter.

"Look," said the rabbit, "if that lion was hungry, do you think I'd be sitting here?"

268.9

A lion was challenged to a fight by a skunk.

The lion refused. He told the skunk that it would gain considerable fame by fighting a lion, while the lion would suffer for months afterwards; everyone who met the lion would know he had been in the company of a skunk.

268.10

One day the lion in the jungle decided to make his mastery clear to all. He was so sure of himself that he did not bother with the smaller animals, instead going right up to a bear and asking, "Who is the king of the jungle?" "You are, of course," replied the bear.

Next the lion asked a tiger the same question, and the tiger replied—though with some reluctance—"You are, oh mighty lion."

Next on the lion's list was the elephant. But the elephant was having none of this; he grabbed the lion with his trunk and bounced him against a tree, leaving him bleeding and badly shaken up.

The lion finally got up and said reproachfully to the elephant, "Just because you don't know the answer is no reason for you to act so rough."

268.11

An elephant and a flea walked across a bridge side by side. "Boy, did we shake that thing!" said the flea to the elephant when they reached the other side.

268.12

The circus was playing in a small town in a region not previously visited by exhibits of strange people and animals. During its stay one of the elephants escaped. The next day a woman who had never seen an elephant phoned the police that a huge animal was tearing up her garden. "He's pulling up cabbages with his tail," she explained.

"Cabbages with his tail?" asked the police. "What he's doing with them?"

"Oh," said the lady, "I'd rather not say."

268.13

An arrogant elephant looked down contemptuously at a mouse and said, "You're just about the puniest little critter I've ever seen."

"I'm not always like this," squeaked the mouse. "I've been sick."

268.14

A mouse took a few experimental licks of some whiskey a farmer had spilled on the barn floor. The mouse liked what he tasted and took a few more licks, and then some more, until finally he got up on his hind legs and called out, "Now bring on that damn cat!"

268.15

A rancher in the hospital with a broken leg was telling his doctor about his accident: "I slipped off the critter and broke this laig, and you know that hoss took off like lightning. I lay there 'bout half an hour and then that hoss come back with a doctor. Trouble was, he was a hoss doctor."

268.16

A man who was extremely successful with mule teams was asked how he managed the stubborn creatures. "Well," explained the man, "when they won't move, I pick up a handful of soil and put it in their mouths. Of course they spit it out, but as a rule they start on."

"Why do you think it has that effect?"

"I'm not sure, but I think it changes the current of their thoughts."

268.17

The sweet young female oyster had just returned from her first date and was telling her experience to several of her oyster girl friends. As she recounted how striking her oyster date was, and how soulfully he looked into her eyes, she suddenly clutched her throat in dismay and screamed, "My God—my pearls!"

268.18

A scorpion asked a turtle to take him across the river on his back. "Are you insane?" asked the turtle. "While I'm swimming you'll sting me and then I'll drown."

"Oh, come now," laughed the scorpion, "why would I sting you? Then I'd drown too, and we'd both drown. Come on, be logical."

"That makes sense," said the turtle. "Hop on and off we go." The scorpion climbed on the turtle's back but halfway across the river he gave the poor trusting turtle a mighty sting. As they both sank to the bottom, the turtle asked, "Why did you do such a wicked thing? You said yourself there would be no logic in your stinging me. Why then did you do it?"

"Logic has nothing to do with it," sighed the scorpion. "It's just my character."

268.19

Sunday afternoons Douglas Jerrold often spent in the zoological gardens—natural history always having had great attractions for him—and he would always have something brisk and sprightly to say as he stood surveying the birds and beasts. Once, when the mandril suddenly turned, revealing the rich colours of his hind quarter, Jerrold said, "Ah! That young gentleman must have been sitting upon a rainbow."

268.20

Two buzzards were flying over a Western state, when a big jet went by at 500 mph, shooting out smoke, flame, and fire.

One buzzard turned to the other and said, "Boy, that bird was certainly in a hurry."

Said the second buzzard: "You'd be in a hurry, too, if your tail was on fire."

268.21

A woodpecker, finding himself bored and getting stale, flew off on a vacation. Several days later he stopped in a beautiful forest and began to look for bugs beneath the bark of a tree. After a few hearty pecks a bolt of lightning severed the tree from top to bottom. "Just goes to show what a fellow can do when he gets away from home," said the woodpecker, preening himself in satisfaction.

268.22

In 1950 *Time* magazine ran a serious scientific article on the Bristle-thighed Curlew, to which was added a spoofing footnote: "Not to be confused with the Tufted Dowager, Red-eyed Crosspatch, All-night Thrasher, Ruffled Spouse, Great Stench, Lesser Stench, or Double-breasted Seersucker."

Whereupon readers sent in other names for imaginary birds, such as: The Scarlet Manager, The Electric Crane, The No Left Terne, the Physical Vulture, the Weekend Bat, The Fugitive Scotch Swallow, the Base Canard, The Extramarital Lark, the Angostura Bittern, the Buff-tinted Due Bill, and the Great Bald Ego.

268.23

A bird house was named HOME TWEET HOME.

268.24

A woman who had a parrot that swore like a drunken sailor asked her pastor if he could suggest what she might do to cure the bird of its bad habit.

"Maybe I can help you," said the pastor. "I have a parrot that prays constantly. Why not bring your bird here and put him in the cage with my bird? Her praying might cure him of his swearing." The lady thought it was a good idea.

The two parrots were not long together in the cage, when the swearing one said to the other, "Hey there, baby, what about a little lovin'?"

"It's OK with me, kid. What do you think I've been praying for all these years?"

268.25

A magician performed brilliantly in the salon of an ocean liner. On this ship was a parrot who hated the magician. Every time the magician did a trick the parrot would scream, "Phony, phony, take him away!"

In the course of the voyage, the ship sank. The parrot and the magician ended up on a long plank.

One day passed. They said nothing. Two days passed. Still they said nothing. Finally the parrot could down his suspicions no longer—he glared at the magician and squawked, "All right, wise guy, you and your damn tricks! What did you do with the ship?"

268.26

Charlie Smith, although wealthy, was always too busy to be with his family. His excuse was that he had to keep on making more money.

One day his wife's pet parrot died and she bought another one, although the pet-store man told her it was from a tough gambling joint that had been closed down. The bird was likely to say anything, coming from a place where there were booze and girls and bums. "It's all right," said the wife, "I'll retrain him."

She brought the bird home, and upon arrival found to her surprise that her husband was already home. She carried the caged bird into the house, called out "Surprise!" and with her husband and daughters looking on, she took the cover off the cage. The parrot looked around, blinked, and said, "Well, wadda you know—new joint, new madam, new girls. Same old customers. Hello, Charlie!"

268.27

A clergyman stopped in a pet shop and asked the price of a parrot. The shopkeeper said he wouldn't sell him that parrot because all it did was utter profanity. "But," said the shopkeeper, "I've another parrot coming in from South America. When I get it trained I'll phone you to pick it up."

Several months later the clergyman was told to stop by and see the parrot the store had for him. The shopkeeper ushered the clergyman into a back room where the parrot was perched, with a string on each foot. The proprietor pulled the string on the right foot and the bird recited the Lord's Prayer from beginning to end. "This is wonderful and most edifying," exclaimed the preacher. Then he pulled the string on the left foot and the parrot burst into "Nearer, my God, to Thee."

"This is tremendous!" cried the preacher. "Now tell me, what would happen if I pulled both strings at the same time?"

Before the shopkeeper could reply, the parrot said, "You damn fool, I'd fall on my ass."

268.28

The two cockroaches were munching delicacies on top of a garbage pile, when one of them began telling of some new tenants in a nearby apartment house. "I hear," said the reporting cockroach, "that their refrigerator is spotless, their floors gleaming, and there is not a speck of dust in the whole place."

"Please, please," said the other cockroach, "not while I'm eating."

268.29

This is a Cock Roach. He is Big, Black, and Ugly. He is Crawling over the pillow. Do not Say a Word, but lie still and Keep your Mouth Open. He will Crawl into Your Mouth and You can Bite him in Two. This will Teach him to be more Discreet in Future.

—*Eugene Field,* 1882

268.30

A hen and a pig were strolling down the road when they encountered a sign outside a restaurant: HAM AND EGGS.

"See, we are partners," said the hen.

"Yes," said the pig. "It's a day's work for you, but for me it's a real sacrifice."

268.31

A wolf had got a bone in his throat, and in the greatest agony ran up and down, beseeching every animal he met to relieve him, at the same time hinting at a very handsome reward to the successful operator. A crane, moved by his entreaties and promises, ventured her long neck down the wolf's throat and drew out the bone. She then modestly asked for the promised reward. To which the wolf, grinning and showing his teeth, replied with seeming indignation, "Ungrateful creature! to ask for any other reward than that you have put your head into a wolf's jaws and brought it safe out again!"

—*Aesop*

268.32

After they put the fifteen apes in front of the typewriters, there was a long wait. The animals sat and looked at the machines, at the paper on the rollers. There was a long pause, then each ape, one after the other, leaned forward and typed a single, different word.

The experimenter waited a long, long time. But after one flurry of activity, nothing happened. Finally, seeing that the apes had no intention of continuing, he went towards the typewriters.

The first ape had typed NOW; the second had typed IS; the third one, THE; the fourth, TIME; the fifth, FOR; the sixth ape, ALL; the seventh, GOOD; the eighth one, PARTIES; the ninth, TO; the tenth, COME; the eleventh, TO; the twelfth ape, THE; the thirteenth, AID; the fourteenth, OF; and the last ape had typed MAN.

—*Bruce Elliott*

268.33

"Ugh!" exclaimed Charles Lamb one day at the zoo, as he turned away from the monkey cage. "It is not pleasant to look upon one's poor relations, is it?"

268.34

The woman visitor to the zoo stood before the cage of the hippopotamus and asked the keeper, "Is that a male or a female?"

"Lady," replied the keeper sternly, "that is a question that should be of interest only to another hippopotamus."

268.35

When a woman opened her Westinghouse refrigerator she found a white rabbit seated on the top shelf. "What are you doing here?"

"Look, lady," said the rabbit, "this machine is a Westinghouse, and I'm just westing."

Definitions

268.36

Zoo: Place devised for animals to study the habits of human beings.

—*Oliver Herford*

268.37

Ape: The only other animal that kisses.

—*Strand Magazine*

268.38

Ape: An animal with the effrontery to resemble man.

268.39

Horse sense is simply stable thinking.

268.40

One reason the dog has so many friends is that he wags his tail instead of his tongue.

268.41

A reasonable amount of fleas is good for a dog—keeps him from broodin' over bein' a dog.
—*E. N. Westcott,* David Harum

268.42

The ass who thinks himself a stag discovers the truth when he comes to a hurdle.

268.43

So live that you would not be ashamed to sell the family parrot to the neighborhood gossip.

268.44

It is not so important to be serious as it is to be serious about the important things. The monkey wears an expression of seriousness which would do credit to any college student, but the monkey is serious because he itches.
—*Robert M. Hutchins*

268.45

I confess freely to you, I could never look long upon a monkey without very mortifying reflections.
—*William Congreve*

268.46

Man is the only animal that can remain on friendly terms with the victims he intends to eat until he eats them.
—*Samuel Butler*

268.47

If the animals had reason, they would act just as ridiculous as we menfolks do.
—*Josh Billings*

(*See also 27.22, 37.8, 38.5, 38.19, 38.21, 42.21, 44.2, 48.8, 60.7, 60.19, 67.3, 68.1, 71.8, 79.3, 79.16, 79.32, 86.10, 91.9, 98.5, 111.1, 111.4–111.9, 114.6, 119.1, 122.3, 122.10, 128.1, 128.4, 128.7, 128.8, 128.11, 128.12, 128.15, 128.17, 129.2, 129.3, 129.5, 129.9, 130.10, 130.14, 130.15, 130.17–130.20, 130.22, 130.26–130.28, 135.48, 136.9, 138.11, 139.17, 139.41, 140.21, 142.20, 146.2, 153.30, 155.2, 155.3, 156.6, 158.4, 158.12, 161.18, 165.17, 165.43, 165.55, 165.87, 165.105, 167.2, 173.6, 174.4, 174.6, 174.7, 174.17, 174.29, 174.36, 175.24, 176.1, 177.7, 177.13, 179.1, 179.2, 179.10, 183.1, 184.46, 184.64, 187.15, 188.19–188.21, 195.1, 196.2, 196.11, 196.13, 199.9, 204.13, 205.1, 210.3, 211.7, 211.9, 211.29, 211.30, 211.38, 213.1, 213.6, 213.8, 214.1, 214.12, 214.17, 217.4, 217.6, 217.8, 217.10, 217.11, 217.15, 218.11, 218.16, 223.4, 225.12, 227.1, 227.5, 227.6, 228.8, 230.9, 232.5, 233.15, 235.20, 235.28, 235.41 238.5, 240.15, 242.8, 242.17, 243.5, 244.12, 245.2, 245.25, 249.2, 249.13, 251.2–251.4, 253.4, 254.1–254.3, 254.5, 254.37, 254.39, 254.41, 263.15, 263.28, 266.1, 269.23, 269.91, 269.109, 270.19, 271.6, 271.47, 272.5, 272.14, 272.20, 273.4, 273.13, 273.25, 275.4, 276.2, 278.3*)

Part Twelve

CAPSULE WIT AND WISDOM

TERSE FUN AND SAGE SAYINGS

269. Quips from Great, Near Great, and Anonymous

269.1

A Beatnik is a man on the bottom looking down.

—*Joey Adams*

269.2

A good folly is worth whatever you pay for it.

—*George Ade*

269.3

Never trust the advice of a man in difficulties.

—*Aesop*

269.4

I am not young enough to know everything.

—*James M. Barrie*

269.5

Experience is what you have left after you have forgotten her name.

—*John Barrymore*

269.6

Conceit, God's gift to little men.

—*Bruce Barton*

269.7

Conceited men often seem a harmless kind of men, who, by an overweening self-respect relieve others from the duty of respecting them at all.

—*Henry Ward Beecher*

269.8

Admiration: Our polite recognition of another's resemblance to ourselves.

—*Ambrose Bierce*

269.9

Comfort: A state of mind produced by contemplation of a neighbor's uneasiness.

—*Ambrose Bierce*

269.10

Destiny: A tyrant's authority for crime and a fool's excuse for failure.

—*Ambrose Bierce*

269.11

Experience is a revelation in the light of which we renounce our errors of youth for those of age.

—*Ambrose Bierce*

269.12

Man: An animal so lost in rapturous contemplation of what he thinks he is as to overlook what he indubitably ought to be.

—*Ambrose Bierce*

269.13

Patience: A minor form of despair, disguised as a virtue.

—*Ambrose Bierce*

269.14

Present: That part of eternity dividing the domain of disappointment from the realm of hope.

—*Ambrose Bierce*

269.15

The trouble with most folks isn't so much their ignorance, as knowing so many things that ain't so.

—*Josh Billings*

269.16

The quickest way to take the starch out of a man who is always blaming himself is to agree with him.

—*Josh Billings*

269.17

Pity costs nothing, and ain't worth nothing.

—*Josh Billings*

269.18

If you want to get a sure crop, and a big yield, sow wild oats.

—*Josh Billings*

269.19

Experience is a school where a man learns what a big fool he has been.

—*Josh Billings*

269.20

Most of the happiness in this world consists in possessing what others can't get.

—*Josh Billings*

269.21

Experience increases our wisdom but doesn't reduce our follies.

—*Josh Billings*

269.22

If you ever find happiness by hunting for it, you will find it, as the old woman did her lost spectacles, safe on her own nose all the time.

—*Josh Billings*

269.23

A dog is the only thing on this earth that loves you more than he loves himself.

—*Josh Billings*

269.24

A learned fool is one who has read everything, and simply remembered it.

—*Josh Billings*

269.25

Do not put off till tomorrow what can be enjoyed today.

—*Josh Billings*

269.26

Nobody loves to be really cheated, but it does seem as though everybody is anxious to see how near he could come to it.

—*Josh Billings*

269.27

The wheel that squeaks the loudest is the one that gets the grease.

—*Josh Billings*

269.28

The best way to convince a fool that he is wrong is to let him have his own way.

—*Josh Billings*

269.29

Tact is the ability to describe others as they see themselves.

—*Eleanor Chaffee*

269.30

Chance is a nickname of Providence.

—*S. R. N. Chamfort*

269.31

'Tis easier to make certain things legal than to make them legitimate.

—*S. R. N. Chamfort*

269.32

Many men and women enjoy popular esteem, not because they are known, but because they are not known.

—*S. R. N. Chamfort*

269.33

Whenever you give advice, be certain you have made an enemy.

—*Lord Chesterfield*

269.34

I believe in getting into hot water. It keeps you clean.

—*G. K. Chesterton*

269.35

The modern humanitarian can love all opinions, including the opinion that men are unlovable.

—*G. K. Chesterton*

269.36

A fanatic is one who can't change his mind and won't change the subject.

—*Winston Churchill*

269.37

I am always ready to learn, although I do not always like being taught.

—*Winston Churchill*

269.38

Men occasionally stumble over the truth, but most of them pick themselves up and hurry off, as if nothing had happened.

—*Winston Churchill*

269.39

Tact consists in knowing how far to go too far.

—*Jean Cocteau*

269.40

The narrower the mind the broader the statement.

—*Ted Cook*

269.41

I have suffered from being misunderstood, but I would have suffered more had I been understood.

—*Clarence Darrow*

269.42

Humiliation is an emotion caused by the knowledge that we have suddenly shrivelled up to our normal dimensions.

—*Benjamin de Casseres*

269.43

If Adam came on earth again the only thing he would recognize would be the old jokes.

—*Thomas Robert Dewar*

269.44

My idea of an agreeable person is a person who agrees with me.

—*Benjamin Disraeli*

269.45

He was distinguished for ignorance; for he had only one idea and that was wrong.

—*Benjamin Disraeli*

269.46

A fanatic is a man who does what he thinks th' Lord would do if He knew th' facts on th' case.

—*Finley Peter Dunne*

269.47

Albert Einstein, recalling that one hundred or more Nazi professors condemned his theory of relativity, said, "Were I wrong, one professor would have been enough."

269.48

What we call progress is the exchange of one nuisance for another nuisance.

—Havelock Ellis

269.49

People who have no faults are terrible; there is no way of taking advantage of them.

—Anatole France

269.50

He that is good for making excuses is seldom good for anything else.

—Benjamin Franklin

269.51

If a man could have half his wishes, he would double his troubles.

—Benjamin Franklin

269.52

A man wrapped up in himself makes a very small bundle.

—Benjamin Franklin

269.53

He that falls in love with himself will have no rivals.

—Benjamin Franklin

269.54

Idealism increases in direct proportion to one's distance from the problem.

—John Galsworthy

269.55

The most dangerous thing in the world is to try to leap a chasm in two jumps.

—Lloyd George

269.56

We spend half our lives unlearning the follies transmitted to us by our parents, and the other half transmitting our own follies to our offspring.

—Isaac Goldberg

269.57

Difficulty is an excuse history never accepts.

—Samuel Grafton

269.58

The man who interferes with another man's habit has the worst one.

—Henry S. Haskins

269.59

A man—poet or prophet or whatever he may be—readily persuades himself of his right to all the worship that is voluntarily tendered.

—Nanthaniel Hawthorne

269.60

Experience is a good school, but the fees are high.

—Heinrich Heine

269.61

Dilettante: A philanderer who seduces the several arts and deserts each in turn for another.

—Oliver Herford

269.62

Liar: One who tells an unpleasant truth.

—Oliver Herford

269.63

There is always room at the top—after the investigation.

—Oliver Herford

269.64

If some people got their rights they would complain of being deprived of their wrongs.

—Oliver Herford

269.65

Many people have character who have nothing else.

—Don Herold

269.66

Humility is the first of the virtues—for other people.

—Oliver Wendell Holmes

269.67

One of the surprising things of this world is the respect a worthless man has for himself.

—E. W. Howe

269.68

A good scare is worth more to a man than good advice.

—E. W. Howe

269.69

If a man should suddenly be changed to a woman, he couldn't get his clothes off.

—E. W. Howe

269.70

The path of civilization is paved with tin cans.

—Elbert Hubbard

269.71

Folks that blurt out just what they think wouldn't be so bad if they thought.

—Kin Hubbard

269.72

Nobody ever grew despondent looking for trouble.

—Kin Hubbard

269.73

Some folks pay a compliment like they went down in their pocket for it.

—Kin Hubbard

269.74

Some people pay a compliment as if they expected a receipt.

—Kin Hubbard

269.75

Honesty pays, but it don't seem to pay enough to suit some people.

—*Kin Hubbard*

269.76

Flattery won't hurt you if you don't swallow it.

—*Kin Hubbard*

269.77

Every once in a while a feller without a single bad habit gets caught.

—*Kin Hubbard*

269.78

If you want to get rid of somebody just tell 'em something for their own good.

—*Kin Hubbard*

269.79

Laughter is the sun that drives winter from the human face.

—*Victor Hugo*

269.80

Worry is interest paid on trouble before it falls due.

—*William Ralph Inge*

269.81

It is always the best policy to speak the truth, unless of course you are an exceptionally good liar.

—*Jerome K. Jerome*

269.82

We grow small trying to be great.

—*E. Stanley Jones,* Victorious Living

269.83

Somebody has said that if a letter were sent to the most influential person called "circumstances," most of us could end it by saying, "I am, Sir, your most obedient servant."

—*E. Stanley Jones,* Victorious Living

269.84

My interest is in the future because I am going to spend the rest of my life there.

—*C. F. Kettering*

269.85

He uses statistics as a drunken man uses lampposts—for support rather than for illumination.

—*Andrew Lang*

269.86

No sooner do we believe that God loves us than there is an impulse to believe that He does so, not because He is Love, but because we are intrinisically lovable.

—*C. S. Lewis,* The Four Loves

269.87

Where all think alike, no one thinks very much.

—*Walter Lippmann*

269.88

Nine-tenths of our suffering is caused by others not thinking so much of us as we think they ought.

—*Mary Lyon,* quoted by Gamaliel Bradford in his Journal

269.89

The world belongs to the Enthusiast who keeps cool.

—*William McFee*

269.90

A man should *be* upright, not be *kept* upright.

—*Marcus Aurelius*

269.91

What is not good for the swarm is not good for the bee.

—*Marcus Aurelius*

269.92

Some persons are likable in spite of their unswerving integrity.

—*Don Marquis*

269.93

"Be yourself" is about the worst advice you can give to some people.

—*T. L. Masson*

269.94

To feel themselves in the presence of true greatness many men find it necessary to be alone.

—*T. L. Masson*

269.95

The only thing experience teaches us is that experience teaches us nothing.

—*André Maurois*

269.96

It is a sin to believe evil of others, but it is seldom a mistake.

—*H. L. Mencken,* Prejudices

269.97

You probably wouldn't worry about what people think of you if you knew how seldom they do.

—*Olin Miller*

269.98

God help those who do not help themselves!

—*Addison Mizner*

269.99

Nothing is so firmly believed as what we least know.

—*Michel de Montaigne*

269.100

To say that a man is made up of certain chemical elements is a satisfactory description only for those who intend to use him as fertilizer.

—*Herbert J. Muller,* Science and Criticism

269.101

Don't take the will for the deed; get the deed.

—*Ethel Watts Mumford*

269.102

No degree of good will can cure a deficiency in glandular secretions.

—*Reinhold Neibuhr,* An Interpretation of Christian Ethics

269.103

If ye would go high up, then use your own legs!

—*Friedrich Nietzsche*

269.104

A hole is nothing at all but you can break your neck in it.

—*Austin O'Malley*

269.105

Some lives are like an ebbing tide in a harbor; the farther they go out, the more mud they expose.

—*Austin O'Malley*

269.106

He who laughs, lasts.

—*Hugh W. Phillips*

269.107

No man in the world has more courage than the man who can stop after eating one peanut.

—*Channing Pollock*

269.108

About the only person we ever heard of that wasn't spoiled by being lionized was a Jew named Daniel.

—*George D. Prentice*

269.109

A cock has great influence on his own dunghill.

—*Publius*

269.110

Prejudice is a device that enables you to form opinions without getting the facts.

—*Robert Quillen*

269.111

The love of justice is, in most men, nothing more than the fear of suffering injustice.

—*La Rochefoucauld*

269.112

Everyone complains of his memory, no one of his judgment.

—*La Rochefoucauld*

269.113

We promise according to our hopes, and perform according to our fears.

—*La Rochefoucauld*

269.114

Solemnity is a trick of the body to hide the faults of the mind.

—*La Rochefoucauld*

269.115

We confess little faults in order to suggest that we have no big ones.

—*La Rochefoucauld*

269.116

If we resist our passions, it is more from their weakness than from our strength.

—*La Rochefoucauld*

269.117

If we had no faults of our own, we should take less pleasure in noticing the faults of others.

—*La Rochefoucauld*

269.118

A man who is always satisfied with himself is seldom satisfied with others.

—*La Rochefoucauld*

269.119

We give away nothing so liberally as advice.

—*La Rochefoucauld*

269.120

Most of our faults are more pardonable than the means we use to conceal them.

—*La Rochefoucauld*

269.121

Broad-mindedness is the result of flattening high-mindedness out.

—*George Saintsbury*

269.122

Fanaticism consists in redoubling your efforts when you have forgotten your aim.

—*George Santayana,* The Life of Reason

269.123

Experience is a comb that life gives you after you lose your hair.

—*Judith Stern*

269.124

'Tis known by the name of perserverance in a good cause—and of obstinacy in a bad one.

—*Laurence Sterne*

269.125

Is is useless for us to attempt to reason a man out of a thing he has never been reasoned into.

—*Jonathan Swift*

269.126

There is nothing so easy but that it becomes difficult when you do it with reluctance.

—*Terence*

269.127

I am a man, and nothing that concerns a man do I deem a matter of indifference to me.

—*Terence*

269.128

Get your facts first, and then you can distort them as much as you please.

—*Mark Twain*

269.129

When some men discharge an obligation you can hear the report for miles around.

—*Mark Twain*

269.130

All that I care to know is that a man is a human being—that is enough for me; he can't be any worse.

—*Mark Twain*

269.131

Truth is such a precious article let us all economize in its use.

—*Mark Twain*

269.132

When in doubt, tell the truth.

—*Mark Twain*

269.133

Good breeding consists in concealing how much we think of ourselves and how little we think of the other person.

—*Mark Twain*

269.134

Nothing so needs reforming as other people's habits.

—*Mark Twain*

269.135

Always do right; this will gratify some people and astonish the rest.

—*Mark Twain*

269.136

Few things are harder to put up with than the annoyance of a good example.

—*Mark Twain*

269.137

Principles have no real force except when one is well fed.

—*Mark Twain*

269.138

Habit is habit and is not to be flung out of the window by any man, but coaxed downstairs a step at a time.

—*Mark Twain*

269.139

I am certain; I have friends; my fortune is secure; my relations will never abandon me; I shall have justice done me; my work is good, it will be well received; what is owing to me will be paid; my friend will be faithful, he has sworn it; the minister will advance me—he has, by the way, promised it—all these are words which a man who has lived a short time in the world erases from his dictionary.

—*Voltaire*

269.140

A reformer is a man who rides through a sewer in a glass-bottomed boat.

—*James J. Walker*

269.141

Thrice is he armed that hath his quarrel just —and four times he who gets his fist in fust.

—*Artemus Ward*

269.142

Do unto the other fellow the way he'd like to do unto you, an' do it fust.

—*E. N. Westcott*

269.143

Man is a rational animal who always loses his temper when he is called upon to act in accordance with the dictates of reason.

—*Oscar Wilde*

269.144

A cynic is a man who knows the price of everything and the value of nothing.

—*Oscar Wilde*

269.145

In this world there are only two tragedies: one is not getting what one wants, and the other is getting it.

—*Oscar Wilde*

269.146

A man who does not think for himself does not think at all.

—*Oscar Wilde*

269.147

If one tells the truth, one is sure, sooner or later, to be found out.

—*Oscar Wilde*

269.148

A gentleman is one who never hurts anyone's feelings unintentionally.

—*Oscar Wilde*

269.149

Experience is simply the name we give our mistakes.

—*Oscar Wilde*

269.150

Consistency is the last refuge of the unimaginative.

—*Oscar Wilde*

269.151

There is a fatality about good resolutions; they are always made too late.

—*Oscar Wilde*

269.152

A man cannot be too careful in the choice of his enemies.

—*Oscar Wilde*

269.153

Duty is what one expects from others.

—*Oscar Wilde*

269.154

I always pass on good advice. It is the only thing to do with it. It is never any use to oneself.

—*Oscar Wilde*

269.155

I can believe anything, provided it is incredible.

—*Oscar Wilde*

Authors Not Known

269.156

A man never knows what he can do until he tries to undo what he has done.

269.157

When a man forgets himself he usually does something that other people remember.

269.158

Popularity: The small change of glory.

—*French proverb*

269.159

A sense of humor is what makes you laugh at something which would make you mad if it happened to you.

269.160

Ignoramus: Someone who doesn't know something that you learned yesterday.

269.161

Ignorance is that which everybody has some of, only in different subjects.

269.162

The nature lover, treed by a bear, enjoys the view.

269.163

A hare is not caught with a drum.

269.164

Life is the art of drawing sufficient conclusions from insufficient premises.

269.165

If you could kick in the pants the fellow responsible for most of your troubles, you wouldn't be able to sit down for six months.

269.166

Some cause happiness wherever they go; others whenever they go.

269.167

Fame is represented bearing a trumpet. Would not the picture be truer were she to hold a handful of dust?

269.168

Fishermen, in order to handle eels securely, first cover them with dirt. In like manner does detraction strive to grasp excellence.

269.169

The tree of liberty will not survive too much grafting.

269.170

Our government could stand a little more pruning and a little less grafting.

269.171

The best thing about the future is that it comes only one day at a time.

269.172

One meets his destiny often in the road he takes to avoid it.

—*French Proverb*

269.173

Results are what we expect; consequences are what we get.

269.174

The best way out of a difficulty is through it.

269.175

It is good to have a train of thought provided you have a terminal.

269.176

A man's horse sense deserts him when he is feeling his oats.

269.177

Don't believe that worry doesn't do any good. The things we worry about don't happen.

269.178

You can't meet trouble halfway. It travels faster than you do.

269.179

Confidence is the cocky feeling you have just before you know better.

269.180

The broad-minded man sees both points of view: the wrong one and his own.

269.181

The less wit a man has, the less he knows he wants it.

269.182

The person that always says just what he thinks at last gets just what he deserves.

269.183

Tact is the art of saying nothing when there is nothing to say.

269.184

Poise is the act of raising the eyebrows instead of the roof.

269.185

Flattery: Telling a man what he thinks of himself.

269.186

If you can't think of any way to flatter a man, then tell him he is the kind of man who can't be flattered.

269.187

Experience is a wonderful thing. It enables you to recognize a mistake when you make it again.

269.188

Experience is what causes a person to make new mistakes instead of the same old ones.

269.189

Experience: The businessman's definition of his mistakes.

269.190

Egotism enables a man in a rut to think he is in the groove.

269.191

Etiquette is the little things you do that you don't want to do.

269.192

A cynic is one who looks down on those above him.

269.193

Civilization is a system under which a man pays a quarter to park a car so he won't be fined a dollar while spending a dime for a cup of coffee.

269.194

Caution is when you're afraid; and cowardice is when the other fellow is afraid.

269.195

When God made man he didn't arrange the joints of his bones so he could pat himself on the back.

269.196

When a man falls in love with himself, it is usually the beginning of a lifelong romance.

269.197

Reformer: One who raises eyebrows for a living.

269.198

A necessary evil is one we like so much that we don't want it abolished.

269.199

If a man is poor, he is stupid; if he is rich, he's a crook; if he goes to church, he's a hypocrite; if he stays away, he's a sinner. If he's in politics, he's a grafter; if he takes no interest in politics, he's an unworthy citizen; if he dies young, there was a great future ahead of him; if he lives to a ripe old age, he's a burden to society. The only man who is never criticized is he who has never been born.

—*Evan Esar,* The Humor of Humor

269.200

Nostalgia is longing for a place you wouldn't move back to.

269.201

A good many foreigners think the eagle on the American dollar is the bird of paradise.

269.202

An idealist is one who will make any sacrifice so long as it won't hurt business.

269.203

Every country has the government it deserves.

269.204

Character is what you get; reputation is what you get caught at.

269.205

A revolution is a successful effort to get rid of a bad government and set up a worse.

Part Thirteen

SPECIAL SITUATIONS

REBUKES, DILEMMAS, AND STRATAGEMS

270. How to Get off the Hook

Anecdotes

270.1

The mother of the girl asked the ardent young man, "Suppose my daughter and I were drowning, which one of us would you save first?"

"First," replied the clever young man, "I would save you, and then I would perish in the arms of your daughter."

270.2

Talleyrand, the French statesman, was seated at dinner between Madame de Staël and Madame Récamier, who was receiving more attention from Talleyrand than her considerably less beautiful rival. Madame de Staël, annoyed by this, persistently sought to have the statesman say which of the two women he would rescue if both were drowning. Finally Talleyrand, unable to evade answering, turned to de Staël and said, "But, Madame, you know how to swim."

270.3

"What is the most beautiful thing in the world?" a woman asked Chauncey Depew.

"Sleep," answered the great speaker and wit.

"But, Mr. Depew," protested the lady, "I was sure you would agree with me that a beautiful woman is the most beautiful thing in the world."

"Of course, you are right," said Depew. "But next to a beautiful woman, sleep is the most beautiful thing in the world."

270.4

Once when Henry Clay failed to recognize a young lady, she reproached him: "Why, Mr. Clay, you don't remember my name!"

"No," replied the statesman, "for when we last met I was positive that your beauty and your accomplishments would soon compel you to change it."

270.5

At a social gathering a musician was conversing with an aging dowager who had been assisting him financially. Without thinking, he asked his backer how old she was.

"Why do you wish to know?" she asked testily.

"My dear," said the musician, "I merely wanted to know at what age a woman is most fascinating."

270.6

The famous actress Mrs. Siddons called on an old and ailing Samuel Johnson. There was no chair in the room.

"Madam," said Dr. Johnson, "you who so often occasion a want of seats to other people will the more easily excuse the want of one yourself."

270.7

At a large dinner party a financier was placed next to a lady whose name he did not catch. During the first course he noticed across the table a man who had recently bested him in a business deal. "Do you see that man?" he muttered bitterly to his dinner partner. "If there's a man on earth I hate, it's him."

"Why," exclaimed the lady, "that's my husband."

"That," said the financier glibly, "is why I hate him."

270.8

A certain king was angry with one of his lords and put him in prison; wishing to keep him there, he said he would only set him free if he could bring to court a horse which was neither gray nor black, brown nor bay, white nor roan, dun, chestnut, nor piebald—in short, the king enumerated every possible color a horse could be.

The imprisoned lord promised to get such a horse if the king would set him free at once. As soon as he was at liberty the lord asked the king to send a groom for the horse, but begged that the groom might come neither on Monday nor Tuesday, Wednesday nor Thursday, Friday, Saturday, nor Sunday, but on any other day of the week that suited His Majesty.

270.9

John Philpot Curran was scheduled to fight a duel with one Egan. Egan complained that Curran was so small a figure that he had little chance of hitting him at 40 paces, while Curran had a good chance of hitting his portly body. "Then," said Curran, "let the size of my body be chalked out on the body of Mr. Egan, and every bullet that strikes outside of that outline shall count for nothing." Egan was so amused by this suggestion that the duel was called off—and the two became friends for life.

270.10

A noble lord, not overly courageous, was once so far engaged in an affair of honor, as to be drawn to Hyde Park to fight a duel. But just as he arrived at the Porter's Lodge, an empty hearse came by; his lordship's antagonist called out to the driver, "Stop here, my good fellow, a few minutes and I'll send you a fare." This operated so strongly on his lordship's nerves, that he begged his opponent's pardon, and returned home in a whole skin.

270.11

"Show me an Irishman and I'll show you a coward," cried the street-corner spellbinder.

A big man pushed through the crowd and in a thick brogue said, "What did you say?"

The speaker, though alarmed, felt compelled to repeat his remark. When he did that, the big fellow edged closer ominously with a clenched fist and said, "I'm an Irishman."

"And I'm the coward I just mentioned," said the orator and went on with his harangue.

270.12

When Voltaire visited England, feeling against him ran high. Once he was accosted by an angry crowd which cried out, "Kill him! Hang the Frenchman!"

Voltaire stood on the curbstone and cried out, "Englishmen! You want to kill me because I am a Frenchman. Am I not already punished enough in not being an Englishman?"

The crowd broke out into cheers.

270.13

A gang of Nazis surrounded a Jew on a Berlin street and demanded he say who caused the war.

"The Jews," said the victim, "and the bicycle riders."

"Bicycle riders?" asked the Nazis. "Why them?"

"Why the Jews?" asked the wily one.

270.14

The young second lieutenant was told to appear before the selection board for questioning to consider his promotion. He spent the evening before his appearance in a diligent application of spit and polish and in going over in his mind the answers to possible questions he would be asked.

When he entered the hearing room, his head held high and his carriage militarily erect, he stumbled over the door sill and fell on his face before the examining officers. He arose, brushed himself off, saluted, and said, "Gentlemen, I certainly fell into good company."

P.S. He was promoted.

270.15

Walking through his office one day, Mark Hanna heard an employee voice the wish that he had Hanna's money and that Hanna was in the poorhouse. Later he asked the young man what he would do if he had Hanna's money and Hanna was in the poorhouse?

"I would first get you out of that poorhouse," said the young man. That got him a raise.

270.16

The first mate on a ship got drunk for the first time in his life. The ship's captain, a stern and rigid man, recorded in his log for that day, "The first mate got drunk today."

The mate protested against the entry, explaining that if it remained in the log without further comment or explanation it could ruin his career because it suggested that drunkenness was not unusual for him, whereas he had never been drunk before. The captain, however, was adamant, stating that the log recorded the exact truth and therefore must stand as written.

The next week it was the mate's turn to write the ship's log. And on each day he wrote down these words: "The Captain was sober today."

270.17

A prominent industrialist in a careless moment agreed to make an address on a very complex problem concerning which he knew nothing. The executive assigned his assistant to do thorough research in the subject and to prepare data useful in the preparation of a speech on it.

The assistant reported several days later that there was a good deal of literature on the question, but that it was wholly speculative and windy; there were no established facts or reliable data. Apparently no one had yet published any basic studies on the problem.

The prominent industrialist, however, made his address and profoundly impressed his listeners with his forthright statements, supported by substantial facts and figures. It was an obvious triumph of scholarship and intellectual activity.

The next day the executive's assistant, puzzled and apprehensive by his failure to be of help to his boss, asked where he had uncovered the data for the address.

"I didn't," replied the executive. "I believed you when you said it would take years to develop the facts on this question. Therefore it will be years before anyone can refute what I said. Then it won't make any difference. I faked—I invented—my facts."

270.18

A woman who writes a syndicated movie column included in it one day an item that reflected on the morals of an actor who was unusually sensitive to such comment. The actor phoned the columnist, denied the truth of the report, and demanded a retraction. The columnist was curt and uncooperative. The actor warned her that she would be sorry and observed that her spotless reputation was not immune to mudslinging.

That evening, and for five succeeding nights, the actor parked his flashy, custom-built convertible with its familiar low-number license plates in front of the columnist's home on a main road. The car was kept parked throughout each night.

On the seventh day the woman's column contained an unqualified retraction of the disparaging item, followed by warm praise of the actor.

270.19

The lord of the manor had the power of life and death over the serfs in his domain. He held court once a week, and all who had been caught for thieving and other violations were brought before him for judgment and sentence. One day three thieves appeared and each was found guilty. The first two were sentenced to death.

But the third and equally guilty one exercised his right to speak before sentence of death was passed. He said, "I notice you have a prize donkey in the courtyard. It must be the admiration of your friends and visitors. I have a talent for teaching donkeys to talk. If you give me a stay of execution I will try to teach your donkey to talk. Then think what a wonderful thing—you would be the only man in the world with a talking donkey."

The lord of the manor was interested, but asked: "How long would this take?"

"Certainly not longer than a year," said the serf.

"Very well," said the lord, "you have a one-year stay of execution. Now get busy and teach that donkey to talk."

As the three thieves were led away, the two others chided the third one for pretending he could teach a donkey to talk. But the third prisoner said: "That may be true, but let me recall to your mind four things. One, tomorrow you both will be dead and I'll still be alive. Two, during the course of the year the donkey may die and then they'd have to get another one and I would have to start all over again training him. Three, during the course of the year the lord of the manor may die, and his successor may very well pardon all prisoners, as is often done in such cases. And four, you know I just might be able to teach that damn donkey to talk!"

(*See also 25.8, 25.11–25.16, 25.19, 25.20, 27.1, 27.3, 27.4, 32.1, 36.6–36.9, 42.10, 42.15, 42.27, 42.35, 52.12, 54.5, 55.1, 57.10, 57.17–57.19, 62.9, 87.18, 90.9, 90.13, 90.16, 90.24, 92.8, 93.29, 94.10, 99.7, 99.13, 101.13, 104.12, 119.30, 119.32, 123.5, 128.5, 128.6, 128.15, 129.1, 134.3, 135.11, 135.45, 142.1, 159.3, 159.5, 219.9, 219.10, 229.18, 231.2, 232.1, 232.7, 240.21, 240.22, 233.5, 233.10, 234.18, 235.5, 235.13, 235.45, 238.6, 239.12, 239.17, 243.3, 243.6, 243.7, 243.15, 244.5, 244.9, 244.10, 244.13, 244.16, 244.18, 244.19, 245.8, 245.12, 245.16, 245.18, 246.1–246.3, 246.6, 246.7, 246.9, 247.3, 248.4, 248.6, 248.20, 249.8, 249.14, 250.6–250.10, 250.12, 250.14, 250.16, 251.7, 251.21, 254.3, 257.2, 261.3, 261.5, 263.15, 264.3, 264.8, 264.12, 265.16, 265.17, 271.1–271.6, 271.8, 271.9, 271.13, 271.15, 272.3, 272.5*)

271. The Retort Magnificent

Anecdotes

271.1

One day in London, Richard Brinsley Sheridan was stopped by two dukes, one of whom said, "I say there, Sherry; we were just arguing whether you are a greater fool or rogue? What is your opinion?"

Sheridan bowed, smiled, and said, "Truly I believe I am between the two."

271.2

During a debate in France many years ago a member of the legislature, in an attempt to embarrass an opponent by referring to his low origin, asked, "Is it true, as I have been informed, that the member from X—— is a veterinary?"

"Yes," replied the member from X——; "are you ill?"

271.3

When Matthew Prior was secretary to the British embassy at Paris he was shown through Versailles, and was asked if the English king's palace could boast of such decorations. "The monuments of my master's actions," replied Prior, "are to be seen everywhere but in his own house."

271.4

In early America two congressmen were riding together to Washington, when they passed a gallows. "Where would you be today if the gallows had been impartially used?" one of the men asked.

"I'd be riding alone," was the reply.

271.5

A Jew walking on a street in Berlin unintentionally brushed against a Prussian officer. "Swine!" roared the officer.

"Cohen!" replied the Jew with a stiff bow.

271.6

A venerable old Jew boarded a Warsaw-bound train at his small town in Poland and sat opposite a captain in Pilsudski's army, who had his dog on the seat next to him.

The army officer was blatantly contemptuous of the Jew and repeatedly addressed the dog by a Jewish name.

Finally this became so provoking that the old Jew said, "What a pity your dog has a Jewish name."

"Why?" the army man demanded.

"Because with such a name, the poor animal has no chance. It's too big a handicap. And without it—who can tell—he might even become a captain in the Polish army."

271.7

Oscar Wilde, on a visit to the United States, was talking to a young woman and deplored America's lack of antiquities and curiosities.

"We shall have the antiquities in time," said the young woman, "and we are already importing the curiosities."

271.8

Henry Ward Beecher went to England during the Civil War to plead the cause of the North. A heckler interrupted him by shouting: "Why did you not whip the South in six months as you told everybody you would?"

"Because," replied Beecher, "we were fighting Americans and not Englishmen."

271.9

Napoleon, at the time a junior officer in the French Army, got into an argument with a Russian officer about the merits of the two armies.

"Argue as you will," said the Russian, "but you must admit that the Russians fight for glory, while your army fights only for money."

"You are right," said Napoleon. "An army fights to obtain that which it has not."

271.10

At a diplomatic dinner at the White House a French diplomat was much too boastful of his country.

"Everyone acknowledges," he said to the American woman at his side, "that America is a remarkable nation, but the French, of course, excel in politeness. You will admit that yourself, will you not, Mrs. Blank?"

The lady smiled sweetly and said, "Yes—that is our politeness."

271.11

Early in his career Winston Churchill sported a mustache. At a dinner party Churchill was holding forth with vigor on politics, when a young woman near him said, "I dislike both your politics and your mustache."

"Don't distress yourself, my dear lady," said Churchill. "You are unlikely to come into contact with either."

271.12

Franklin P. Adams while at the bar of the Lamb's Club got into a torrid argument with a man for whom he had no use. After the man left another man at that bar said to Adams, "That fellow is his own worst enemy."

"Not while I'm alive," said Adams.

271.13

Famous feminist leader Susan B. Anthony, in an appearance before the New York State Constitutional Convention, was urging that women be given the vote. Horace Greeley, knowing that Miss Anthony was a Quaker, sought to discredit her before the crowd by asking, "Miss Anthony, you know that the ballot and the bullet go together. If you vote, are you ready to fight?"

"Yes, Mr. Greeley, I am," she replied, "just as you fought the late war at the point of a goose quill."

271.14

The quiet young lady was waiting in line at the supermarket when a crude young man brushed against her, apparently intentionally. She glared at him pointedly.

"Well, lady," said the man, "don't eat me up."

"You are in no danger," said the woman coldly. "I am a Jewess."

271.15

The beautiful girl was seated in the hotel lobby when one of the town's leading wolves tried to strike up a conversation with her. When he persisted after several rebuffs, the girl finally told him to stop bothering her.

"Oh, I beg your pardon. I thought you were my mother," said the wolf.

The girl smiled her prettiest and said, "I couldn't be. You see, I'm married."

271.16

Mulla Nural-Din Abd al-Rahman Jami, better known as Jami, the Islamic mystical poet, one day was repeating with fervor:

"So constantly art thou in my stricken soul
and sleepless eye
That whosoever should appear from afar, I
should think it was thou."

An impudent bystander interrupted the prayer and asked: "Suppose it were an ass?"

"I should think," said Jami, "it was you."

271.17

Alexandre Dumas, whose ancestry aroused curiosity, was asked by a young interviewer, "Is it true that you are a quadroon, Mr. Dumas?"

"That is correct," replied Dumas.

"Which means your father . . . ?"

"Was a mulatto."

"And your grandfather . . ."

"Was a Negro."

"And," continued the interviewer in spite of Dumas's increasing annoyance, "may I ask who your great-grandfather was?"

"He was a baboon!" shouted Dumas. "A baboon. My ancestry begins where yours ends."

271.18

In the days before the pigtail was abandoned by Chinese men, the Chinese Minister to the United States, Wun Ting Fang, attended a social affair at Chicago and was asked by one of the natives, "Why do you wear that foolish thing anyhow?"

"Why," countered the Chinese diplomat, "do you wear your foolish mustache?"

"Oh, that's different," said the Chicagoan. "You see I've got an impossible mouth."

"Yes, I gather so," said Mr. Wun, "judging by your remarks."

271.19

"I simply can't bear fools!" a man said to Dorothy Parker.

"Apparently your mother could," she replied.

271.20

During the days when women were campaigning for the right to vote in England, a woman advocate of the cause was interrupted in her speech by a puny little man who called out, "Wouldn't you like to be a man?"

"Wouldn't you?" shot back the speaker.

271.21

A smart aleck from town stopped alongside a road to watch the farmer sowing seed.

"Well done, my friend," called the city man. "You sow, and I reap the fruits."

Whereupon the farmer looked up, grinned, and said, "Perhaps you will. I'm sowing hemp."

271.22

Several years before World War I the German Crown Prince was attending the Emperor's regatta. He was sitting with others on the deck of a yacht, and next to him was Bernice Willard, a Philadelphia socialite. Smoke from the Prince's cigarette blew into the young lady's face, whereupon one of the Crown Prince's stooges said, "Smoke withers flowers."

"It is no flower," said the Prince with an awkward attempt at humor, "it is a thistle."

"In that case," shot back Miss Willard, "I had better retire before I'm devoured."

271.23

Lowell Thomas, in his *Pageant of Romance,* relates that Princess Juliana of the Netherlands—athletic, witty, and a master of languages—was dancing one day when she overheard someone say in French, "Look at those pillars!"

The Princess smiled at the commentator and in perfect French said, "They have to be big. Some day they will be the pillars of state!"

271.24

I want an explanation—and I want the truth."

"Make up your mind—you can't have both."

271.25

Barrett Wendell was returning from a Harvard football game at Cambridge with his wife and daughter. When they boarded a crowded trolley car for Boston, Mr. Wendell was rudely pushed through the door by a man carrying an umbrella. Wendell used the crook of his walking stick to hook on to the boor's umbrella.

"Careful there, you're breaking my umbrella," said the pusher.

"On the contrary," said Wendell, "I'm mending your manners."

271.26

Archbishop Williams of Pittsburgh encountered an ill-bred, aggressive man who said, "Where in hell have I seen you before?" and was answered, "What part of Hell do you come from?"

—*Douglas Woodruff*

271.27

Thinking to twit Daniel O'Connell, the famous Irish wit, patriot, and militant Catholic, two fellows approached him and said: "Mr. O'Connell, have you heard the bad news? The bottom dropped out of Purgatory and all the Catholics have fallen into Hell!"

"Oh," said O'Connell, "how awful. Those poor Protestants must have had a terrible crushing."

271.28

Shortly after the war a timid little refugee approached the desk of the attaché in the American consul in Lisbon. "Please, Sir, can I have a visa for your wonderful country?"

The attaché, who had to turn down thousands of such requests, said, "It is impossible at present. Come back in another ten years."

Disconsolate, the little fellow walked away sadly, then stopped and asked, "Morning or afternoon?"

271.29

Shortly after he was knighted, Prof. Walter Raleigh, distinguished British scholar, wit, and critic, who was descended from the famed Sir Walter, was invited to lecture at Princeton.

Nobody at Princeton knew what he looked like, but they knew what train he was arriving on. One of the Princeton professors volunteered to meet the train, but arrived after the train pulled in. He saw to his dismay that the passengers were already scattering in different directions.

As he was about to turn away in despair, he saw a distinguished-looking man, in bowler hat, wing collar, dark suit, and carrying an umbrella. Surely this would be the distinguished English scholar.

The professor hurried up and said, "I beg your pardon, would you be Sir Walter Raleigh?"

The distinguished-looking man turned, gave the wilting Professor a long, measured look and said, "No, sir, I happen to be Christopher Columbus. Sir Walter Raleigh has just gone off with Queen Elizabeth to look for a puddle!"

271.30

A friend said to Voltaire, "It is good of you to say such pleasant things of Monsieur X when he always says such nasty things about you."

"Perhaps we are both mistaken," said Voltaire.

271.31

John Philpot Curran, although a well-known wit of his day, was a man of undistinguished appearance. One day he presented himself at the home of a noble lord, who had not previously met him. His lordship looked at Curran and said: "What! You are not Curran? Why you could not say 'boo' to a goose."

"Boo, my lord!" replied Curran almost curtly.

"Yes, yes, you're the man all right," cried the lord. "Come in at once."

271.32

William Evarts stood on the banks of the Potomac River with Lord Coleridge, a visitor from England. "Is it true," asked Lord Coleridge, "that Washington threw a silver dollar across the Potomac?"

"It is supposed to be true," said Evarts; "but then you must remember that a dollar went much farther in those days. But Washington did better than that—he threw a sovereign across the Atlantic."

271.33

A workman put a ladder up against the tower on the town hall and reached the clock. A woman stopped to watch and said, "Is there something wrong with the clock?"

"No, madam. I'm a little nearsighted."

271.34

A fanatical supporter of a politician was extolling his hero to Douglas Jerrold, and concluded with: "Why, sir, he is next to our Savior!"

"On which side?" asked Jerrold.

271.35

An impudent fellow pushed Lord Chesterfield off the sidewalk with the comment, "I never give the right-of-way to a scoundrel."

"I always do," said Chesterfield as he stepped aside.

271.36

When Lord Sandwich received an abusive letter, he replied to it with this: "Your letter is before me and shortly it will be behind me."

271.37

Ilka Chase's press agent sent out a story to the effect that when her book *Past Imperfect* was published, Humphrey Bogart asked her, "Who wrote it for you?"

She replied, "I'm so glad you enjoyed it. Who read it to you?"

271.38

Lady Astor got into an argument with George Bernard Shaw and reached such a point of exasperation that she fairly shouted, "If you were my husband, I'd give you poison."

"And if I were your husband," said Shaw calmly, "I'd take it."

271.39

During a London party Isadora Duncan, the beautiful and famous dancer, said to George Bernard Shaw, "Wouldn't it be wonderful if we had a child—a child with your brains and my looks?"

"But think," said Shaw, "what a disaster if the child had my looks and your brains."

271.40

When someone said Rufus Choate accomplished a certain result by accident, he retorted, "Nonsense, you might as well drop the Greek alphabet on the ground and expect to pick up the *Iliad*."

271.41

"Buy some nice thimbles," pleaded the street urchin of the stuffy businessman.

"Nothing doing, don't bother me," said the big executive.

"Come on, mister, help me make a sale."

"What could I do with a thimble, you moronic pest?" snapped the businessman.

"Well," said the brash youngster, "you could use it for a hat."

271.42

Twin brothers in a historic French family never really got along or had much use for each other. One became a soldier; the other entered the Church. After years of estrangement they finally came face-to-face in a Paris railroad station. One was a cardinal; the other a French general. The cardinal, in ecclesiastical regalia, spotted his brother in full uniform and, with a trace of a smile, walked up to him and said, "Pardon me, Stationmaster, but can you tell me when is the next train for Metz?"

The general, jolted for a second, recovered quickly, saluted gallantly, and said, "I am sorry, I really don't know, madam. But should you be traveling in your condition?"

271.43

John Abernethy, famous London surgeon, came out of his house and saw that an Irish workman had piled paving stones on the doctor's sidewalk. "Remove them! Away with them!" demanded the doctor.

"But where shall I take them?" asked the worker.

"To hell with them!" screamed the doctor.

"Hadn't I better take them to Heaven?" asked the Irishman. "Then they'd never again be in your way."

271.44

Shortly after the accession of James I, when Scotch gentlemen were beginning to feel at home in London, Lord Harewood gave a dinner party, inviting a number of courtiers and officers, both civil and military. After the bottle had circulated freely and the spirits of the assembly had begun to rise, General S, an English trooper of fame, stood up and said: "Gentlemen, when I am in my cups I have an absurd notion of railing against the Scotch. Knowing my weakness, I hope no gentleman in the company will take it amiss."

A Highland chief, Sir Robert Blackie of Blair-Atholl presenting a front like an old battleworn tower, thereupon stood up quietly and said, with the utmost good nature, "Gentlemen, I, when I am in my cups and the generous wine begins to warm my blood, if I hear a man rail against the Scotch, have an absurd custom of kicking him at once out of the company. Knowing my weakness, I hope no gentleman will take it amiss."

271.45

A newly appointed judge was assigned temporarily to a rural county. "Mary," he said smugly to the Irish girl who served his meals at the hotel, "how long have you been in this country?"

"Two years, sir."

"Do you like it?"

"I suppose it's all right, sir."

"But, Mary," continued the judge, "you have many privileges in this country you do not have in Ireland. For example, would you be able to chat so familiarly with a Supreme Court judge in Ireland as we are doing now?"

"No, I suppose not, sir. But then, in Ireland you'd never be a judge."

271.46

A doctor, appearing as an expert witness in behalf of a man injured in an automobile accident, was being badgered by the attorney for the other side.

"You say you are familiar, Doctor, with the symptoms of concussion of the brain?"

"That is correct," replied the physician.

"Let us suppose, Doctor, that you and I are riding in an automobile and our car is hit by another head on, and our heads bump together violently. Isn't it your opinion that we would suffer concussion of the brain?"

"It is my opinion," said the doctor, "that I would, and you would not."

271.47

Mrs. Horace Greeley, who had an aversion to kid gloves, met Margaret Fuller when she was wearing kid gloves. Mrs. Greeley touched her hand gingerly and said, "Skin of a beast!"

"What do you wear?" asked Miss Fuller.

"Silk," said Mrs. Greeley.

Miss Fuller shrank back in mock horror and said, "Entrails of a worm!"

271.48

A pretty, girlish young man called Python, son of a Macedonian grandee, once by way of quizzing Demonax asked a riddling question and invited him to show his argument over it.

"I only see one thing, dear child," Demonax said, "and that is, that you are a fair logician."

The other lost his temper at this, and threatened him: "You shall see in a minute what a man can do."

"Oh, you keep a man, do you?" was Demonax's smiling retort.

271.49

Richard Porson, famous English scholar, was once disputing with an acquaintance who, getting the worst of it, said, "Professor, my opinion of you is most contemptible."

"Sir," returned the great Grecian authority, "I never knew an opinion of yours that was not contemptible."

271.50

A rival politician said to John Horne Tooke, seventeenth-century English scholar and politician, "I am told, Mr. Tooke, that you have all the blackguards in London with you."

"I am happy," answered Tooke, "to have it, sir, on such good authority."

271.51

"How could you have had brain fever?" one politician asked another. "It takes strong brains to have brain fever."

"How did you find that out?" asked the other.

271.52

"Why I can buy and sell you," said one businessman to the other in the course of a bitter argument.

"That may be," said the other man. "But I can not only buy you but I could afford to keep you."

(*See also 7.7, 8.1, 12.3, 12.4, 15.4, 20.4, 26.17, 54.14, 54.16, 55.12, 55.13, 56.3, 57.9, 59.1, 62.9, 62.12, 62.13, 64.2, 66.1, 79.5, 79.6, 82.3, 82.6, 87.1, 87.3, 87.4, 87.20, 90.7, 90.9, 90.13, 90.18, 91.6, 91.10, 94.4, 119.30, 135.40, 135.41, 136.3, 139.5, 139.10, 139.27, 140.2, 149.2, 149.8, 150.4, 150.17, 152.14, 152.15, 152.22, 152.38, 154.35, 172.4, 174.8, 175.14, 179.9, 181.1, 197.1, 218.1, 218.12, 221.1, 228.3, 235.1, 235.27, 240.7, 245.14, 245.19, 248.6, 248.10, 272.1–272.7, 272.10–272.13, 272.15–272.20, 273.1–273.25, 274.3*)

272. How to Puncture Someone's Balloon

Anecdotes

272.1

"If I had my rights, I'd be riding in my own carriage as I did before," said the Radical.

"True," said the Irishman, "but your own mother couldn't push you now."

272.2

When Sir Oswald Mosley was the leader of a British Fascist movement, a rally was staged in London, where a spotlight was focused on Mosley as he marched to the platform escorted by his Black Shirt stooges. When he reached the center of the platform, Mosley solemnly raised his hand in the Fascist salute. From out of the darkened silence of the hall came a loud voice, "Yes, Oswald, you may leave the room!"

272.3

The son of a well-known public figure called on Joseph Choate, the diplomat, at his Washington office. Choate asked the visitor to have a chair, explaining that he was busy but would be able to see him shortly.

"But, Mr. Choate," said the caller impatiently, "perhaps you do not understand that I am Mr. X's son."

"Oh," said Choate with a gracious smile, "in that case have two chairs."

272.4

A drunken congressman once boasted to Horace Greeley, "Sir, I'd have you understand that I'm a self-made man."

"That," observed Greeley, "relieves the Almighty of a great responsibility."

272.5

Some years ago a salesman was being driven across Mississippi by a Negro farmer in a horse and buggy. A winged insect kept circling about the horse's head and then about the salesman's head.

"Uncle, what kind of an insect is that?"

"Just a horsefly."

"Horsefly? What is that?"

"Just a fly that flies around the heads of horses, and mules, and jackasses."

As the insect was still buzzing about the salesman's head, he saw a chance for a little banter, and said, "Uncle, you don't mean to say I'm a horse?"

"No, you certainly ain't no horse."

"Well, you don't mean to call me a mule, do you?"

The farmer, now irritated, said, "You ain't no mule, neither."

Then the white man spoke emphatically: "Now look here, Uncle, do I look like a jackass to you? Surely you don't mean to call me a jackass!"

"No, sir, I ain't callin' you no jackass, an' you don't look like a jackass to me,—but, you see, you can't fool the horsefly."

272.6

When the German Emperor visited Pope Leo XIII, Count Bismarck tried to follow him into the audience chamber. A gentleman of the Papal Court motioned him to stand back, as there must be no third person at the interview. "I am Count Herbert Bismarck," shouted the German, as he tried to follow his master.

"That," replied the Roman calmly, "accounts for, but it does not excuse, your conduct."

272.7

The late Lord Birkenhead was cornered by an intolerable bore, who got into a long harangue concerning the casual way he was treated at a hotel. "But, of course," added the bore, "when I explained who I was, the treatment was quite satisfactory."

"And who were you?" asked Birkenhead.

272.8

Theodore Hook, nineteenth-century English humorist, walking in the Strand with a friend one day had his attention directed to a very pompous gentleman who strutted along as if the street were his own. Instantly leaving his companion, Hook went up to the stranger and said, "I beg your pardon, sir, but pray may I ask—are you anybody in particular?" Before the astonished magnifico could think of an answer to the query, Hook had passed on.

272.9

During a diplomatic reception in London, when all the ambassadors wore elaborate uniforms and medals, American Ambassador Joseph H. Choate was inconspicuous in the customary evening clothes. When the guests were departing one of the dignitaries turned to Choate, thinking him a flunky, and said, "Call me a cab."

Choate, noted for his wit, turned to the man and said, "You are a cab!"

When the man's anger subsided after it was explained whom he had addressed, Choate was offered an apology. Whereupon Choate, seldom at a loss, said, "If you were a good-looking man, I would have called you a hansom cab."

272.10

"I see you have your arm in a sling. Is it broken?" asked one traveler of another.

"Yes, broken," was the curt reply.

"Accident?"

"No, I got it trying to pat myself on the back."

"Really! Why were you patting yourself on the back?"

"For minding my own business."

272.11

Menecrates was an ancient physician who because of the wonderful cures he was believed to have effected was called Jupiter, and delighted in the designation. In a letter to Agesilaus he used this salutation: "M. Jupiter to King Agesilaus, Health!"

The King replied with, "King Agesilaus to Menecrates, His senses."

272.12

The florid-faced temperance lecturer, toward the end of his lecture, said, "I have lived all my life in this town. There are thirty-five saloons in it, and I am proud to say that I have never been in one of them!"

"Which one is that?" called out a listener.

272.13

One of the greatest bores at the Players Club went to Oliver Herford and said, "Oliver, I've been grossly insulted. As I passed a group over there I heard one of them say he would give $50 if I'd resign from the club."

"Hold out for $100," counseled Herford, "and you'll get it."

272.14

A young fellow boarded the day coach of a train crossing New England, slumped down next to an older man and continually asked questions. Finally he pointed to a large package on a rack above their seat and began to ask a series of probing questions to find out what was in it.

"Pretty heavy package, isn't it?"

"Yep."

"Got holes in it, I see."

"That's right."

"What are they for?"

"Air."

"What you need air for?"

"So it can breathe."

"So what kin breathe?"

"The mongoose."

"What's a mongoose?"

"Small East Indian animal."

"Does it bite?"

"Sure does."

"What you gonna do with a thing like that?"

"Well," said the traveler, "a mongoose is an animal that lives on reptiles, snakes, lizards, and toads. I've got an uncle in Vermont who drinks so much that he is bothered by snakes. I'm taking the mongoose to him to eat those snakes."

"But, Mister," said the young man, "that uncle of yours sees only imaginary snakes when he drinks."

"Yes, I know, but you see, this is an imaginary mongoose."

272.15

A retired cheesemonger, who hated any allusions to the business that had enriched him, said to Charles Lamb, in the course of a discussion on the poor laws, "You must bear in mind, sir, that I have got rid of that sort of stuff which you poets call the 'milk of human kindness.' "

Lamb looked at him steadily, and replied, "Yes, I am aware of that—you turned it all into cheese several years ago!"

272.16

A pompous candidate, speaking against corporal punishment, told his audience, "I was never whipped but once in my life, and that was for telling the truth."

A man from the crowd called out, "It sure cured you, mister."

272.17

One day Richard Brinsley Sheridan became annoyed by a fellow member of the House of Commons who kept crying out "Hear! Hear!" while Sheridan was speaking. Finally, in describing a political contemporary, Sheridan asked, "Where, where shall we find a more foolish knave or a more knavish fool than he?" Whereupon the annoying member shouted "Hear! hear!" Sheridan turned to the member, thanked him, and sat down.

272.18

The neighborhood terror, a mountainous bully of awesome visage, accosted a stranger in a bar, who was quietly drinking and counting a roll of bills. He demanded that the little fellow—who happened to be a professional prizefighter—surrender the money. "I'll just take what I need and give you back a few bills," he assured the stranger.

But when he came close to reach for the other man's roll of bills, the smaller man with a lightning move planted a short left hook on the big man's chin.

When the local tough guy regained consciousness, he looked up at the quiet little fellow and asked, "Mister, who are you, anyway?"

"I," replied the slender young fellow, "am the man you thought you were when you came in here."

272.19

The newly arrived bully promptly announced that he was plenty tough.

"Just how tough are you?" asked a mild-looking young fellow as he reached in his pocket for his brass knuckles.

"Well, Sonny, where I come from they call me Wild Bill."

"Well," replied the local boy, "when I get through with you they'll call you Sweet William."

272.20

A man was boasting before a companion of

his very strong sight. "I can discern from here a mouse on the top of that very high tower."

"I don't see it," answered his comrade; "but I hear it running."

272.21

He had come to the big city from a little rural community, had worked hard and intelligently, and had climbed high up the business ladder with unusual speed. He was, in fact, rather well known among businessmen in the big town.

With the means and freedom now to indulge himself, he thought of the hometown and how nice it would be to return for a visit—a visit no doubt characterized by praise and adulation of the local boy who had made the big time.

When he stepped off the train, there was no welcoming committee to greet him. This was surprising, and a bit disconcerting. The few people on the station platform paid him no heed and went on their way. As he picked up his bag, an old freight handler came up, looked at him curiously, and said, "Howdy, Jim, you leavin' town?"

272.22

The vain young woman had called on a psychiatrist, and promptly gave every indication of her besetting sin. "Have you ever been told how wonderful you are?" asked the doctor.

"Why, no," said the young woman with an attempt to be coy. "It may have happened, but I do not recall offhand."

"Well, my dear woman," said the doctor, "tell me this: How, then, did you ever get the idea?"

272.23

At the first opportunity, the office Don Juan got the ear of the new and pretty stenographer, and proceeded to inform her what an expert he was on the baseball and football fields, the basketball court, behind the wheel of a car, on the dance floor, at the bridge table, in the ocean, and on the high diving board, with broad hints as to his potentialities as a lover.

When the tiresome boaster paused for breath, the young woman quietly asked, "Do you have a group photograph of yourself?"

272.24

When a man's wife returned from a visit to her mother, her husband said, "One night while you were away, I heard a burglar. You should have seen me go down those stairs three steps at a time."

"The burglar must have been on the roof," said the wife drily.

272.25

The bustling stuffed shirt, awaiting the arrival of guests to a dinner party, said to his wife, "I wonder how many really great men there are in the nation."

"I'll tell you this, my dear," said his wife coolly, "there is one less than you think."

272.26

At a lavish dinner party Lady Nancy Astor precipitated a vigorous argument when she asserted that men were vainer than women. During the ensuing conversation she steered the talk to men's fashions and said, "The most intelligent men pay the least attention to dress. At this table the most cultivated man is wearing the most clumsily knotted tie."

Immediately Mrs. Astor's point was made: Every man at the table began to straighten his tie.

272.27

The old lady, on being introduced to a doctor who was also a professor at a university, was uncertain how she should address so distinguished a man and asked, "Should I call you 'Professor' or 'Doctor'?"

"Oh, either one," said the genial gentleman. "As a matter of fact, some call me an old idiot."

"Yes," said the old lady, "but those are people who know you well."

272.28

An empty-headed fellow was boasting to Douglas Jerrold that he was never seasick.

"Never!" echoed Jerrold. "Then I'd almost put up with your head to have your stomach."

(*See also 3.3, 3.8, 4.8, 5.1, 7.18, 7.23, 8.1, 8.8, 9.2, 15.3, 15.4, 16.16, 16.27, 16.33, 16.36, 16.38, 16.39, 16.41, 19.4, 19.11, 20.4, 25.16, 25.20, 26.2, 26.4, 26.6, 26.9, 26.10, 26.17, 26.26, 28.3, 28.14, 30.5, 32.6, 35.3, 37.3, 41.3, 41.10–41.12, 42.16, 49.3, 49.8, 50.4, 50.5, 50.9, 50.23, 50.24, 52.11, 53.2, 53.4, 54.3, 54.17, 55.7, 55.11–55.20, 56.3, 57.1–57.4, 57.6, 57.9, 57.11, 59.2, 59.5, 59.6, 62.15, 62.17, 62.20, 62.24, 62.27, 63.2, 63.4, 63.5, 63.7, 64.3, 64.4, 66.7, 66.10, 66.26, 66.27, 72.4, 76.3, 78.2, 78.5, 79.30, 79.45, 79.49, 79.56, 79.59, 80.5, 82.2, 82.4, 84.3, 85.1, 87.3, 87.7, 87.8, 87.11, 87.13, 87.17, 87.20, 88.2, 88.5, 90.2, 90.5, 90.6, 91.1, 91.3, 91.5, 91.6, 91.9, 92.1, 92.2, 92.4, 92.7, 92.9, 92.10, 92.16, 93.8, 93.11, 93.30, 93.32, 94.2, 94.4, 94.13, 102.10, 104.12, 106.1, 107.4, 110.1, 110.10, 110.11, 110.14, 110.15, 110.17,*

115.4, 118.11–118.14, 119.26, 119.31–119.33, 121.2, 121.14, 121.18, 122.10, 123.3, 123.4, 123.5, 124.10. 124.14, 124.34, 125.6, 125.7, 125.9, 125.12, 127.6, 129.8, 129.9, 135.31, 135.32, 135.44, 135.47, 136.2, 136.3, 136.11, 136.12, 136.18, 139.14, 139.19, 139.23, 139.24, 140.20, 142.1, 143.1–143.3, 145.1, 150.2, 150.8, 150.17, 150.19, 151.1, 151.6, 152.6, 152.47, 152.50, 154.2–154.13, 157.12, 160.2, 162.3, 162.23, 165.4–165.6, 166.14, 167.1, 171.4, 171.10, 171.11, 174.8, 174.9, 174.12, 175.1, 177.1, 177.7, 178.3, 178.5, 178.6, 178.8, 178.9, 178.11, 179.9, 179.15, 179.16, 180.1, 180.4, 181.1, 181.2, 181.5–181.7, 181.10, 181.11, 181.15, 181.16, 184.12, 184.36, 184.38, 190.5, 191.6, 191.10, 191.11, 192.1, 196.5, 197.1, 200.6, 202.3, 204.1, 204.2, 204.5 210.28, 211.18, 211.27, 211.32, 212.1, 213.6, 213.16, 215.1, 215.13, 215.14, 215.16, 215.20, 216.3, 218.1–218.4, 218.13, 218.14, 219.9, 221.2, 225.2, 225.8, 225.10, 225.11, 225.13, 226.1, 226.10, 226.13, 226.15, 226.17, 226.18, 228.5, 229.18, 231.1, 232.7, 233.1, 233.3–233.5, 233.9, 233.13, 234.2, 234.4, 234.5, 234.8, 234.13, 234.17, 234.18, 234.21, 234.27, 235.1, 235.3, 235.7–235.9, 235.12–235.14, 235.16, 235.18, 235.27, 235.33, 235.34, 235.38, 235.39, 235.42, 237.8, 238.1, 238.3, 239.4, 239.5, 239.8, 240.4, 240.5, 240.8, 240.10, 240.11, 240.16–240.20, 240.25, 243.1, 243.2, 243.5, 243.9, 243.11, 244.2, 244.3, 245.2–245.4, 245.6, 245.10, 245.11, 245.14, 245.18–245.20, 246.1, 246.2, 246.5, 246.7, 246.12, 247.1, 247.3, 248.1–248.4, 248.6, 248.11, 248.16, 248.18, 248.21, 249.10, 249.14, 250.1–250.7, 250.14, 250.17, 250.18, 251.1, 251.2, 251.7–251.9, 251.11–251.20, 251.23–251.26, 251.34, 254.3, 254.5, 254.7, 255.1, 257.2, 259.5, 259.6, 260.1, 261.2, 262.1, 262.2, 263.5, 264.6–264.8, 264.12, 267.4, 267.8, 267.10, 268.4, 268.10, 268.26, 268.27, 273.2, 273.3, 273.9, 273.10, 274.1, 274.2, 274.5, 275.1, 275.2)

273. Assorted Rebukes and Insults

Anecdotes

273.1

An Italian newspaper columnist was found guilty and fined for calling a countess a cow. When the trial ended and the man paid his fine, he asked the judge if, since it was now clear he could not call a countess a cow, he could on the other hand call a cow a countess. The judge said that was all right to do. Whereupon the newspaperman turned toward the countess in the courtroom, bowed elaborately, and said, "How do you do, Countess."

273.2

Storm Jameson, in her *No Time Like the Present*, tells about the time her mother took her on a railroad journey when she was a small child, and a woman in the same car said, "That's a good bairn of yours. She hain't cried once." A few moments later when the child's conduct changed, the woman said, "It seems I spoke too soon."

"No one asked you to speak at all," said the mother.

273.3

Robert Burns arrived at the quay at Greenock just when a sailor was hauling a rich merchant out of the water. When the nearly drowned merchant recovered he handed his rescuer a shilling. Thereupon the crowd drawn to the scene protested loudly. But Burns interposed and said, "The gentleman is, of course, the best judge of the value of his life."

273.4

Douglas Jerrold was in a railway carriage one day with a young gentleman who, looking out on some cows in the field, remarked, "How beautiful and peaceful cows look in the green fields. When I am at home, I often stroll through the pastures and sit down in the midst of the cows, reading, or sketching, or meditating. They come round me, and look at me with their calm, wondering eyes. I look up, pleased, and smile, smile at them—"

"With a filial smile," quietly added Jerrold.

273.5

That scoundrel, sir! Why, he'd sharpen a knife upon his father's tombstone to kill his mother!

—*Douglas Jerrold*

273.6

Albert Smith once wrote an article in *Blackwood*, signed "A. S."

"Tut," said Jerrold, on reading the initials, "what a pity Smith will tell only two-thirds of the truth."

273.7

When a journalist asked Clemenceau his opinion of General Pétain, the old Tiger of

France replied: "He is an immortal. He has no heart, no brain, and no guts. How can a man like that die?"

273.8

A man stopped the Duke of Wellington in the street and said, "Mr. Robinson, I believe?"

"If you believe that, you'd believe anything," replied the Duke.

273.9

The president of the Waupaca and Nisha Railroad called on Chauncy Depew, president of the New York Central Railroad, and asked for an exchange of courtesies—a pass for him over the New York Central in exchange for a pass to Depew over the Waupaca and Nisha Railroad.

"Where is your road?" asked Depew.

"In Wisconsin."

"Is your road rated in Poor's?" Depew wanted to know.

"Yes, it is. We pay a nice dividend."

"I never heard of your road," said Depew. "How long is it?"

"67 miles," said the president.

"And you call it an exchange of courtesies when the New York Central Railroad has thousands of miles of road?"

"Well, Mr. Depew," replied the man from Wisconsin, "your road may be longer than mine, but it ain't any wider."

273.10

Two young women boarded a crowded homeward-bound bus after a tiring day at the office, and saw that they were going to have to stand most of the long trip. One of the girls whispered to the other, "There's Mr. Smith. He lives in our neighborhood, but he doesn't know me. Watch me embarrass him into giving me his seat." The two girls shouldered and hipped their way down the aisle of the bus to where the apparently amiable and embarrassable Mr. Smith sat reading his evening paper.

"Oh, hello, Mr. Smith!" gushed one of the girls. "I didn't know you took this bus. But it's good to see you. Isn't it terrible the way they jam people into these buses?"

Mr. Smith looked up at the girl but did not recall ever having seen her before. He smiled weakly, hesitated a few moments, then rose and said: "Sit down here, Bertha, my girl, you must be very tired. By the way, Mrs. Smith said at breakfast that she was going to phone you not to deliver the washing until Wednesday. My wife also mentioned that she was going down to the district attorney's office this afternoon to see what she could do about getting your brother out of jail on that rape charge."

273.11

At a class reunion at Hamilton College, Alexander Woollcott was spinning one of his yarns when he was interrupted by a man who called out, "Hi, Alex! Remember me?"

Woollcott shook his head, "No, I can't remember your name, but don't tell me—." And he went on with his story.

273.12

Harry Hershfield tells about a Christian and a Jew arguing as to whose cultural heritage was the most ancient. The Jew dismissed the controversy when he said, "When your ancestors were still eating acorns in the forest, my ancestors already had diabetes."

273.13

A man walked into a restaurant, leaving the door open, whereupon another man boomed, "Shut the door! Were you brought up in a barn?"

The little man went back, shut the door, sat down, and began to cry. The other man became uneasy, went over to the little man and said, "I'm sorry I hurt your feelings."

The little man said, "You didn't hurt my feelings, but it makes me homesick every time I hear a jackass bray."

273.14

The Earl of Louderdale, noted for his ability to spoil a good story, once asked Sheridan's permission to repeat a certain anecdote.

Sheridan replied, "I must be careful of what I say, for a joke in your mouth is no laughing matter."

273.15

Lord Thurlow said to John Wilkes: "When I forget my king, may my God forget me."

"He'll see you damned first," was the reply.

273.16

Aristippus lived comfortably as a consequence of his subservience to the tyrant Denys, but as a result was held in contempt by his fellow philosophers. One day Aristippus came upon Diogenes preparing some lentils and said to him, "If you would flatter Denys you would not have to be washing lentils for food."

"And if you had learned to live on lentils," replied Diogenes, "you would not have to flatter King Denys."

273.17

An actor, looking for some free publicity, said to a group of ball players sitting around chatting in a restaurant, "I'd go to the end of the world for you guys."

"Yes, but would you stay there?" asked one of them.

273.18

A rude young man broke into the conversation of several men and asked: "Where's the urinal?"

"Oh, go right down that hall until you come to a door marked GENTLEMEN—but don't let that deter you."

273.19

An acquaintance said to John Randolph that he had passed his house recently.

"I am glad of it," replied Randolph, "and I hope you always will do it, sir."

273.20

A diplomat complained to Talleyrand that he could not understand why he was considered ill natured, adding, "In all my life I have done but one ill natured action."

"When will it end?" asked Talleyrand.

273.21

Joey Adams relates that an irate telephone operator said to a pest on the other end, "Oh, go jump in the ocean and pull a wave over your head."

273.22

Napoleon Bonaparte, speaking of Madame de Staël, said: "She has only one fault. She is insufferable."

273.23

Mark Twain's opinion of Cecil Rhodes: "I admire him, I frankly confess it; and when his time comes I shall buy a piece of the rope for a keepsake."

Definition

273.24

Retraction: The revision of an insult to give it wider circulation.

Aphorism

273.25

Never insult an alligator until you have crossed the river.

—*Cordell Hull*

(*See also 5.1, 5.7, 7.7, 15.3, 15.4, 17.2, 17.5, 19.11, 23.7, 25.6–25.9, 26.2, 26.4, 26.5, 26.9, 26.10, 26.16, 26.17, 26.19, 26.26, 26.28, 27.8, 41.10, 42.7, 48.1, 49.2, 49.3, 49.5, 49.8, 50.4, 50.5, 50.8, 50.11–50.24, 52.11, 53.2, 54.3, 57.1–57.4, 57.6, 57.9, 57.11, 59.2, 60.8, 62.15, 62.17–62.27, 62.29–62.33, 63.2–63.8, 64.4, 66.1–66.8, 66.10–66.12, 66.14–66.17, 66.19, 66.21, 66.23, 66.24, 66.26, 77.1, 78.1, 78.5, 79.4, 79.59, 79.11–79.12, 82.3, 82.4, 85.4, 86.2, 87.1, 87.7, 87.11, 87.16, 87.17, 87.24, 90.5, 90.6, 90.10–90.12, 90.14, 90.21, 90.23, 91.10, 91.11, 92.1, 92.2, 92.4, 92.6, 92.7, 95.14, 99.15, 108.2, 118.1–118.3, 118.9, 119.9, 119.11, 119.18, 119.32, 120.3, 121.1, 121.2, 121.5, 121.18, 122.9, 123.3, 123.8, 124.30, 125.11, 126.8, 127.1, 134.5, 135.39, 135.40, 136.8, 139.4, 139.21, 139.23, 139.31, 139.38, 140.2, 142.1, 143.1–143.3, 145.1, 149.1–149.31, 151.1, 151.8, 152.1–152.59, 153.1–153.10, 154.6, 154.10, 154.12, 154.15, 154.22, 154.25, 154.33–154.35, 154.40, 157.1–157.7, 162.3, 162.22, 165.5, 165.9, 165.10, 165.36, 165.39, 171.1, 171.2, 171.4, 171.5, 171.7–171.11, 172.2, 177.1, 177.4, 177.7, 177.8, 177.16, 178.7, 178.11, 179.3, 180.3, 180.4, 181.2, 181.3, 181.12, 181.15–181.16, 183.1, 183.2, 184.37, 186.2, 187.2, 194.3, 194.7, 195.5, 200.7, 200.8, 203.6, 204.10, 204.11, 206.13, 214.10, 214.11, 218.1, 219.4, 218.9, 221.1, 221.2, 225.2, 225.8, 225.11, 225.12, 226.9, 226.13, 226.15, 226.17, 226.18, 228.2, 233.4, 233.11, 234.2, 234.4, 234.8, 234.13, 234.7–234.9, 234.12, 234.18, 234.24, 234.27, 240.5, 240.11, 240.16, 240.18, 243.2, 244.2, 245.3, 248.3, 248.4, 248.18, 251.1, 251.21, 251.26, 251.31, 251.34, 260.1, 260.2, 263.15, 271.1, 271.4, 271.6–271.8, 271.11, 271.13–271.15, 271.17–271.20, 271.22, 271.35, 271.36, 271.49, 275.3*)

274. Was My Face Red

Anecdotes

274.1

A congressman's wife was proudly wearing an odd-looking pin that was brought back to her by her husband from Hong Kong, where he had been on one of those all-expense trips congressmen vote each other. At a cocktail party where she was wearing the pin, a correspondent from the Far East noticed it, stared at it in astonishment, then called her aside and told her that the Chinese characters on the pin translated to "Licensed Prostitute, City of Shanghai."

274.2

A young American at a banquet found himself seated next to the eminent Wellington Koo, a Chinese diplomat. Completely at a loss as to what to say to a Chinese, this young man ventured, "Likee soupee?" Mr. Koo smiled and nodded.

Several moments later when called upon to say a few words, Wellington Koo delivered an eloquent talk in perfect English, sat down while the applause was still resounding, turned to the young man and said, "Likee speechee?"

274.3

My memory for names is notably bad, and at public gatherings I always rely on Mrs. Sparks to help me. On one occasion she was not there, and I beheld a matron bearing down on me whom I felt I should recognize. I was greeting her with a warm handclasp when a man I knew rather well came along. Still clasping the lady's hand, I waved the other hand in greeting. "Hello! Fred," I called, "How is your lovely wife these days?"

"You ought to know," replied Fred. "You're holding hands with her!"

—*Dr. Frank H. Sparks,* Quote

274.4

A parishioner had sent a clergyman tickets for the opera. Finding he would be unable to use them, he phoned some friends and said, "I have been given two tickets for the opera, but an unfortunate dinner engagement prevents me from using them. Would you like to have them?"

"We would love to go," replied the friend, "but we happen to be your unfortunate hosts."

274.5

In Powell River, B. C., the driver of a black Austin sedan was waiting for his wife at a parking lot when a woman in an identical Austin pulled up beside him. In a spirit of camaraderie he leaned over and said: "Twins, eh?"

The woman nodded and smiled shyly. As she stepped from her car he realized that she was definitely pregnant.

—*Maclean's Magazine*

274.6

Two women went to the matinee of a Broadway show but were unable to get seats together. One of the women, after being seated, turned to the man next to her in the hope of having him exchange seats with her companion two rows ahead.

"Are you alone?" she whispered.

"Fly away, Birdie," he whispered back. "The whole damn family is here with me."

274.7

A chairwoman noticed that the guest of honor was not touching her food. "You must feel like I do," she said, "just too nervous to eat. When it's over, I'm sure we'll both be ravished. I know I'll have a wonderful appetite for anything that comes along."

—*Evan Esar,* The Humor of Humor

274.8

The chairlady arose to introduce the next speaker, but before she got started on her remarks she sneezed. She reached into her bosom for a handkerchief. Not immediately finding it she probed deeper and then more frantically, meanwhile saying out loud, "I can't imagine what's happened. I know I had two of them when I came in."

274.9

A young woman schoolteacher boarded a bus, noticed a familiar face across the aisle, and nodded at him. He stared at her blankly, giving no sign of recognition.

Flustered, the girl called out, "I'm sorry. I thought you were the father of one of my children."

274.10

A busy florist sent off a large floral piece to a store that had just moved to a new location. Attached to the bouquet was a card saying, "With deepest sympathy," signed with a name the store proprietor did not recognize. He phoned the florist in the hope of straightening out the mix-up.

Now the florist had something to worry about, for the flowers intended for the store had gone to a funeral with a card bearing this message: "Congratulations on your new location."

274.11

"Nellie," warned her husband, "don't put your foot in it again when you call on the Smiths. Remember, old man Smith hanged himself in the attic, so just don't mention death or suicide or funerals at all. Keep off the subject."

And Nellie did as she was advised to do. She kept the conversation on everyday topics: weather, births, marriages, housework, and then on to the problem of washing and drying clothes during the current wet spell. "But, my goodness, Mrs. Smith," said Nellie, "it's no problem for you. You got such a fine big attic for hangin' things in."

274.12

A young woman boarded a railroad train, sat down next to an elderly lady, and engaged her in conversation. She told her older companion that she was going to visit her ill mother, but that she could not stay long because things were a bit difficult with them and her husband was able to give her only her railroad ticket and a $20 bill.

A little later the younger woman excused herself and went to the ladies' room. While there she realized she had left her pocketbook on the train seat, but quickly dismissed her sudden fear when she recalled that the nice old lady would watch it until she got back.

Shortly after she returned to her seat, the older woman excused herself and went to the ladies' room. The young woman took advantage of the absence to look in her purse to be sure her $20 bill was still there. It was gone. She thereupon angrily took up the other woman's purse from the seat, opened it, found a $20 bill on the very top, took it, transferred it to her own purse, and made no comment about it to the older woman when she returned.

The younger woman got off at the next stop and went directly to her mother's home. Later in the day her husband phoned to tell her that she had failed to take the $20 bill he had left on the table before he went to work that morning.

274.13

During a large dinner party a woman turned to the man next to her and said, "Professor, do you know that terrible-looking man over there?"

"Yes; that is my brother."

"Oh, I beg your pardon," fumbled the lady, "I should have noticed the resemblance."

274.14

The manager of a small power plant was electrocuted while on the job. The assistant manager phoned the police chief, the coroner, and the workmen in the plant. They gathered horror-stricken about the body of the dead manager stretched out on the floor and began to speculate how an experienced man could commit so fatal an error.

"The only thing I can think of," said the assistant manager, "is that poor Joe must have picked up this terminal in one hand"—the assistant manager picked up the terminal—"and then without thinking reached out with his other hand and come into contact with—"

Bing! The assistant manager was stretched out next to the manager. But the mystery was solved to everyone's satisfaction.

(*See also 3.8, 16.15, 20.4, 20.10, 21.7, 35.3, 36.7, 37.9, 38.1–38.24, 55.8, 65.7, 66.7, 70.3, 75.5. 78.4, 101.15, 104.13, 124.20–124.22, 127.3, 130.2, 130.3, 150.18, 150.19, 150.22, 152.16, 152.44, 154.9, 154.42, 179.11, 179.14, 182.1–182.10, 186.1, 188.7, 204.5, 205.11, 207.4, 207.6, 208.9, 208.13, 213.8, 232.7, 233.1, 233.2, 233.4, 235.16, 235.42, 236.1, 236.2, 236.6, 239.6, 243.1, 244.3, 244.20, 246.9, 247.3, 248.3, 248.18, 249.9, 249.12, 251.8, 251.12, 252.1–252.8, 253.8*)

275. Wise Men and Fools

Anecdotes

275.1

In ancient times the king of a certain country was concerned because his son was something of a fool. The king's counselors urged that the son be sent away to a great university in another land, in the hope the boy would acquire learning and wisdom. The king agreed.

The son studied hard for several years, then wrote his father that he had learned just about everything possible, and pleaded to be allowed to return home. The king assented.

When the son arrived at the palace, the king was overjoyed. A great feast was prepared, and all the great men of the kingdom were invited. At the end of the festivities one of the sages present asked the son what he had learned.

The young man ticked off the university's curriculum that he had gone through. While the lad was talking, the sage slipped a ring off his finger, closed his hand over it, held up his hand, and asked, "What do I hold in my hand?"

The son thought for a moment, and said, "It is a round object with a hole in its center."

The sage was astonished at such wisdom. Maybe the lad had become a great mind. "Will you now name this object?" asked the sage.

The king's son pondered for a few moments, then said, "The sciences that I studied do not aid me in answering your question, but my own common sense tells me that it is a cart-wheel!"

The sage concluded to himself that you can educate a fool but you cannot make him think.

275.2

The village half-wit, whenever offered a choice between a dime and a nickel, always chose the nickel. When this had gone on for some time around the village, a kind fellow pointed out to him that the dime was worth twice as much as the nickel, and that in the future he should choose the dime.

"Oh," he said, "I know the difference, but if I let on they'd stop offering me the choice and I'd never even get the nickel."

275.3

During an argument as to their respective intellectual capacities, one turned upon the other and said, "If brains were dynamite, you couldn't blow off your own hat."

275.4

A miller and his son were driving their ass to a neighbor to sell him. They had not gone far when they met with a troop of girls returning from the town, talking and laughing.

"Look there!" cried one of them, "did you ever see such fools, to be trudging along the road on foot, when they might be riding!"

The old man, hearing this, quietly bade his son to get on the ass, and walked along merrily by the side of him. Presently they came to a group of old men in earnest debate.

"There!" said one of them, "It proves what I was saying. What respect is shown to old age in these days? Do you see that idle young rogue riding, while his old father has to walk.—Get down, you scapegrace! and let the old man rest his weary limbs!"

Upon this the father made the son dismount, and got up himself. In this manner they had not proceeded far when they met a company of women and children.

"Why you lazy old fellow!" cried several tongues at once, "how can you ride upon the beast, while that poor little lad there can hardly keep pace by the side of you?"

The good-natured miller stood corrected, and immediately took up his son behind him. They had now almost reached the town.

"Pray, honest friend," said a townsman, "is that ass your own?"

"Yes," said the old man.

"Oh! One would not have thought so," said the other, "by the way you load him. Why, you two fellows are better able to carry the poor beast than he you!"

So, alighting with the son, they tied the ass's legs together, and by the help of a pole endeavored to carry him on their shoulders over a bridge that led to the town. This was so entertaining a sight, that the people ran out in crowds to laugh at it; till the ass, not liking the noise nor his situation, kicked asunder the cords that bound him, and tumbling off the pole fell into the river.

Upon this the old man, vexed and ashamed, made his way home, convinced that by endeavoring to please everybody he had pleased nobody, and lost his ass in the bargain.

—*Aesop*

275.5

Old Silas was known throughout the county as a man of wisdom. One day a young caller asked him how he happened to be so wise.

"It's 'cause I got good jedgment," said Silas. "And good jedgment comes from experience and—well, experience comes from poor jedgment."

275.6

"Yessir, I told them off. I told them they were a set of mulish morons, with a total lack of vision, social conscience, and goodwill toward their fellow man."

"Boy, they must have given you the gate."

"On the contrary; they made me an honorary member."

Definitions

275.7

Ceremony is the invention of wise men to keep fools at a distance.

—*Richard Steele*

275.8

Eccentricity: A method of distinction so cheap that fools employ it to accentuate their incapacity.

—*Ambrose Bierce*

275.9

Egotism is the anesthetic that dulls the pain of stupidity.

—*Frank Leahy*

275.10

Genius is the infinite capacity not only for taking pains but for giving them.

275.11

Genius is an infinite capacity for picking brains.

275.12

Genius: One who can do almost anything except make a living.

275.13

Genius is the talent of a man who is dead.
—Edmond de Goncourt

Aphorisms

275.14

When a true genius appears in the world you may know him by this sign: that the dunces are all in confederacy against him.
—Jonathan Swift

275.15

The public is wonderfully tolerant—it forgives everything except genius.
—Oscar Wilde

275.16

Talent does things tolerably well; genius does them intolerably better.
—Anonymous

275.17

He that knows not, and knows not that he knows not, is stupid.

275.18

Ordinarily he was insane, but he had lucid moments when he was merely stupid.
—Heinrich Heine

275.19

Obstinacy is firmness of character adulterated by stupidity.
—Friedrich Nietzsche, Human, All Too Human

275.20

He who disputes with the stupid must have sharp answers.
—German proverb

275.21

He was born stupid, and greatly increased his birthright.
—Samuel Butler

275.22

He was born silly and had a relapse.
—Arthur "Bugs" Baer

275.23

He is so full of himself that he is quite empty.

275.24

You can always tell a blockhead by the chip on his shoulder.

275.25

It is impossible to underrate human intelligence—beginning with one's own.
—Franklin Pierce Adams

275.26

See the happy moron,
He doesn't give a damn!
I wish I were a moron—
My God! Perhaps I am!
—Anonymous

275.27

That he's ne'er known to change his mind,
Is surely nothing strange;
For no one yet could ever find
He's any mind to change.

275.28

The world of fools has such a store,
That he who would not see an ass,
Must bide at home, and bolt his door,
And even break his looking-glass.
—From the French

275.29

In those days he was wiser than he is now; he used frequently to take my advice.
—Winston Churchill

275.30

Zeal is fit only for wise men but is found mostly in fools.

275.31

Examinations are formidable even to the best prepared, for the greatest fool may ask more than the wisest man can answer.
—Charles Caleb Colton

275.32

Wise men talk because they have something to say; fools, because they have to say something.
—Plato

275.33

Haint we got all the fools in our town on our side? And ain't that a big enough majority in any town?
—Mark Twain

275.34

The best way to convince a fool that he is wrong is to let him have his own way.
—Josh Billings

(*See also 10.13, 19.38, 30.20, 30.50, 31.14, 31.27–31.31, 32.27, 33.13, 191.31, 214.16, 219.19, 255.4, 255.10, 255.11, 255.14, 255.18, 265.9, 268.5, 268.7, 269.10, 269.19, 269.24, 269.28, 269.160, 269.181*)

276. On Being Positive and Negative

Anecdotes

276.1

"Uncle Joe," asked a man meeting an old fellow who was always carefree in spite of having had more than his share of life's troubles, "how do you manage to remain so cheerful and calm?"

"Well," replied Uncle Joe, "I've just learned to cooperate with the inevitable."

276.2

Jaspar was inspecting a fractious mule that was proving more difficult than useful. Turning to his grandchildren who had joined him to watch the animal, he said, "Children, this jackass should be a warnin' to you against the habit of kickin'."

"What do you mean, Grandpappy?" asked one of the children.

"Because the better he does his kickin', the more unpopular he gets to be."

276.3

A man dedicated to the peaceful solution of all disputes came upon two men fighting in his neighborhood. He stopped them, heard the nature of their quarrel, and persuaded them to put the matter to arbitration by six men, each man to choose three of them.

Later in the day the pacifist came back along the street and found a bigger fight than ever in full swing. "What is the meaning of this?" he asked one of the spectators. "Oh, those are the arbitrators you urged those guys to get to settle that fight."

276.4

It began to rain heavily as William Dean Howells and Mark Twain were leaving church. "Do you think it will stop?" Howells asked.

"It always has," replied Mark Twain.

Definitions

276.5

An optimist is a fellow who doesn't know what's coming to him.

—*J. J. O'Connell*

276.6

An optimist is a man who goes looking for lodgings with a trombone under one arm and a saxophone under the other.

276.7

An optimist is a man who marries his secretary—thinking he'll continue to dictate to her.

276.8

An optimist is one who is convinced he will never again do anything stupid.

276.9

An optimist is a man who says the bottle is half-full when it is half-empty.

276.10

An optimist is a man of eighty-five who gets married and starts looking for a new home nearer the schoolhouse.

—*Finley Peter Dunne*

276.11

An optimist is a girl who mistakes a bulge for a curve.

—*Ring Lardner*

276.12

Optimist: A guy who can always see the bright side of other people's troubles.

—*Mac Benoff*

276.13

Optimist: A guy who thinks his wife has quit smoking cigarettes when he finds cigar butts around the house.

276.14

Optimism: The doctrine, or belief that everything is beautiful, including what is ugly, everything good, especially the bad, and everything right that is wrong. An intellectual disorder, yielding to no treatment but death.

—*Ambrose Bierce*

276.15

An optimist is a man who goes to the window every morning and says, "Good morning, God!" The pessimist goes to the window every morning and says, "Good God! Morning!"

276.16

A pessimist is one who likes to listen to the patter of little defeats.

276.17

A pessimist is one who, when he has a choice of two evils, chooses both.

276.18

A pessimist is an optimist on his way home from the race track.

—*Red Smith*

276.19

A pessimist looks at sunshine as something that casts shadows.

276.20

A pessimist is a man who thinks all women are bad. An optimist is one who hopes they are.

—*Chauncey M. Depew*

Aphorisms

276.21

The optimist proclaims that we live in the best of all possible worlds, and the pessimist fears this is true.

—*James Branch Cabell*

276.22

"Civilization totters," say the pessimists.

"But it totters steadily onward," cheerfully respond the men of optimistic mind.

276.23

If it wasn't for the optimist, the pessimist would never know how happy he isn't.

276.24

It is good to remember that the teakettle, although up to its neck in hot water, continues to sing.

(*See also 12.4, 13.9, 16.14, 18.1, 18.11, 19.45, 19.67, 24.6–24.8, 24.10, 24.11, 24.15, 36.6, 41.6, 130.8, 168.17, 217.1, 263.13*)

277. Ingenuity and Know-how

Anecdotes

277.1

When the sailor came to the customs guard on the pier, he stopped and asked, "How about letting me pass through with some tobacco tomorrow?"

"Just try it and you'll be arrested," said the guard grimly as the sailor passed on out to the street.

The next day the sailor left the ship for shore and encountered the same guard. "Wait a minute," called the guard. "I want to check you to be sure you're not trying to get by with that tobacco."

"Too late," laughed the sailor. "I passed through with it yesterday."

277.2

In ancient times a merchant traveled to a far and strange country with a large sum of money to make some purchases. Knowing no one in the strange land, he thought it best to bury his money in a field. He did this and sometime later returned to the scene and found his money had disappeared. He thereupon went to a sage with his problem, and the sage told him to find out who owned the land, go to him, and tell him "you are a stranger and that you buried some money in a certain place but have an additional sum that you now want also to bury," and ask the owner of the land if he has any suggestions as to where it might be buried.

The sage told the merchant that the owner of the land undoubtedly would tell him to bury his money in the same place the first amount was buried. Then the merchant was instructed to hide and watch the burial spot before making the second burial of his money.

The merchant followed the sage's instructions, and the owner of the land told him to bury his money in the same place. The merchant then hid himself and saw the owner of the land steal out to the spot and dig up the earth and return the money he had stolen—anticipating that the second burial of money would soon follow and then he would return and take it all. But the merchant instead simply went to the spot and dug up his money returned there by the owner of the land. And the merchant departed with all the money he originally had.

277.3

Vice President John N. Garner lost a $10 bet on a Washington baseball game. The winner asked him to autograph the $10 bill so he could give it to his grandson.

"You mean you're not going to spend it?" asked Garner.

"That's right."

"In that case I'll give you a check," said Garner.

277.4

The foreman of a railroad construction gang estimated that the men should be able to average 1 mile of tracklaying a day. He therefore told the men that whenever they had finished 1 mile of track, they were through for the day and would receive a day's pay, no matter what the hour. The men worked hard and steadily and on most days finished well ahead of the regular quitting hour.

But the foreman was in a quandary when he received orders that his gang had to complete a certain 5-mile stretch of track within the next four days. Finally, he acted. During the night he and several of his friends went over the road, removed the 5-mile posts, and spaced four of them over the 5-mile distance that had to be completed in four days.

The men completed the 5 miles within the four days. Several of them objected that these were unusually long miles. The foreman told the immigrant laborers that the climate in the region sometimes made miles longer. They did not further dispute the matter.

277.5

During the German occupation of France a peasant who worked in the underground was captured. Now and then his wife wrote him, and in one letter she complained she was having difficulty with their farm. She had plenty of seed potatoes but she couldn't plow the fields herself and couldn't get anyone to do it for her. Her husband wrote her, "It is all for the best. Leave the fields alone. Don't plow them. That is where the guns are hidden."

Four days later the Gestapo men descended on the field and plowed up every inch of it. They found no guns. The wife then planted her potatoes. She got the message.

277.6

Years ago liquor was often bought by the customer who brought a demijohn to the store and had it filled from a barrel. One New Englander went into a shop with his two-gallon jug and asked for a gallon of the best brandy. After it was poured into the jug the buyer, pretending ignorance of the store's rigid cash policy, said, "Charge it."

When the shopkeeper said he did not extend credit to anyone, the fellow said, "Well, I guess I'll have to give you back your gallon of brandy. I had some liquor in the jug, so bring your measure and I'll return the gallon." This was done, and the fellow walked out of the store satisfied that he had got some fine brandy free, mixed with the small quantity of water originally in the demijohn.

277.7

An elderly gentleman is now living in modest but comfortable retirement on money freely contributed by thousands of Americans who do not know him, never met him, and who today would not even be able to recall his name.

The now-retired entrepreneur amassed his small fortune in the easiest possible way, and several court actions against him proved that he acted within the law. This astute student of the psychology of the American people simply floated from town to town, inserting in local papers the following advertisement:

LAST DAY TO SEND IN YOUR DOLLAR!
John Jones
Box 196.

The dollars rolled in.

277.8

Two farmers at a county fair were attracted to a booth where little colored balls bobbed on top of water jets. Customers were offered prizes if they succeeded in shooting any of the balls off its perch. One of the farmers spent six quarters in a vain effort to pick off one ball. Finally his friend pushed him aside and picked up the rifle.

"Watch how I do it," he said.

He took a single shot. All the balls disappeared.

As they walked away from the booth laden with prizes, the unsuccessful one marveled, "How did you ever do it?"

"Easy," said the marksman. "I shot the man working the pump."

277.9

One of the young men in a factory was chosen to raise funds and buy a wedding present for their boss. The energetic employee collected 25 cents from each of the 2,000 workers, and with the $500 bought 2,000 packs of cigarettes, the kind with a gift coupon in each package. He traded the coupons in for a silver coffee service. That was the boss's wedding present. Then he gave each employee a pack of cigarettes. The president of the firm heard about this, and decided he could use a man with such ingenuity in management. But before the boss got around to interviewing the young fellow, he had taken the 5,000 trading stamps received at the time of the cigarette purchase, and got himself a complete fishing outfit and was off on a vacation.

—Told by *Sam Pavlovic* in Pioneer Press, February, 1962

(*See also 7.1, 7.8, 9.2, 19.1, 20.4, 23.3, 23.4, 25.20, 25.33, 26.20, 27.1, 27.5, 28.6, 36.2–36.4, 36.6, 36.7, 36.9–36.11, 41.7, 42.27, 45.8, 46.3, 50.3, 55.7, 87.18, 90.24, 94.10, 99.7, 104.12, 119.21, 128.5, 134.4, 134.7, 135.11, 157.5, 160.5, 169.3, 174.12, 175.10, 191.3, 194.7, 195.3, 198.10, 208.2, 210.10, 210.21, 225.1, 228.4, 233.5, 234.18, 235.11, 235.19, 239.2, 239.5, 243.3–243.6, 244.13, 244.16, 244.18, 244.19, 248.20, 270.8, 270.10, 275.2*)

278. When Opportunity Knocks

Anecdotes

278.1

An ambitious young man asked a great merchant the secret of his success. "There is no secret," said the merchant, "Just jump at your opportunity."

"But," said the young man, "how can I tell when my opportunity is coming?"

"You can't. You have to keep jumping."

278.2

A woodchopper in Australia was about to cut down a large tree when a fairy appeared and promised that if he would refrain from destroying her home in the tree, she would grant him three wishes. The Australian agreed to this and rushed home to tell his wife the good news.

When he arrived home his wife was preparing supper. He told her of the three wishes promised by the fairy. The wife went on with her preparation of the meal and just when her husband had completed his account she happened to say: "I wish I had a can opener." Presto! A shiny new can opener was in her hand.

When the woodchopper saw this he got into a rage. "You idiot! Opening your big mouth like that and using up a wish for a lousy can opener. I wish the damn thing was in your backside!" Presto! That is where the new can opener went.

And the poor couple had to use their third wish to get that can opener out of where it had been inadvertently wished.

278.3

While a Centipede was painfully toiling over a Libyan Desert he encountered a Barbaric Yak, who scornfully asked him how were his poor Feet. The humble Creature made no reply at the time, but some days later found the Barbaric Yak taken in the nets of the Hunter and almost devoured by Insects, which fled at the approach of the Centipede.

"Help, help, my good friend!" exclaimed the unfortunate Beast. "I cannot move a muscle in these cruel Toils, and the ravenous Insects have devoured my delicate Flesh."

"Say you so?" replied the Centipede. "Can you really not defend yourself?"

"Alas, how can I?" replied the Yak. "See how straitly I am bound?"

"And is your Flesh so delicate?"

"It is, say I who should not."

"Then," said the Centipede, "I guess I'll take a bite myself."

Moral: The other man's Extremity is often your Opportunity.

—*George T. Lanigan*

Definition

278.4

An opportunist is one who goes ahead and does what you always planned to do.

Aphorism

278.5

The reason many people fail to recognize opportunity is because it comes disguised as hard work.

(*See also 18.3, 25.11, 37.9, 41.2, 48.9, 52.1, 163.20, 188.2, 192.4*)

279. Exit Lines

279.1

God will pardon me; it's His business.

—*Heinrich Heine*

279.2

I suffer nothing, but I feel a sort of difficulty in living longer.

—*Bernard de Fontenelle*

279.3

Dear gentlemen, let me die a natural death.

—*Sir Samuel Garth,* to his physicians

279.4

When a sudden breeze caused the lamp beside his bed to flare up, Voltaire is supposed to have said, "What! the flames already!"

279.5

Die, my dear doctor! that's the last thing I shall do.

—*Lord Palmerston*

279.6

What an artist the world is losing in me.

—*Nero*

279.7

Let down the curtain, the farce is over.

—*Rabelais*

279.8

I am dying as I lived—beyond my means.

—*Oscar Wilde,* on his deathbed as he took a sip of champagne.

279.9

It matters little how the head lies, so the heart be right.

—*Sir Walter Raleigh,* on the scaffold where he was beheaded.

279.10

The hearse, the horse, the driver and—enough.

—*Luigi Pirandello*

279.11

When jokingly told he had drunk a dose of ink in error, Sydney Smith on his deathbed said: "Then bring me all the blotting paper in the house."

279.12

When he had been sick for some days and his servant announced that the doctor had arrived, Molière, the great playwright, said, "Tell him I am ill, and see no one."

279.13

When it was suggested to Benjamin Disraeli that Queen Victoria attend his deathbed, the famous statesman said, "Why should I see her? She will only want to give a message to Albert." (Albert was Victoria's deceased and much-grieved husband.)

279.14

A strange sight, sir; an old man unwilling to die!

—*Ebenzer Elliott*

279.15

Henry James's friend Edmund Gosse called on him and told him that he (James) had just received the Order of Merit. James turned to his nurse and said, "Please take away the candle and spare my blushes."

279.16

I am about the extent of a gnat's eyebrow better.

—*Joel Chandler Harris*

279.17

I see no reason why the existence of Harriet Martineau should be perpetuated.

—*Harriet Martineau*

279.18

Ah, my children, you cannot cry for me so much as I have made you laugh.

—*Paul Scarron*

279.19

I'll be shot if I don't think I'm dying.

—*Lord Thurlow*

279.20

I have been a most unconscionable time a-dying; but I hope you will excuse it.

—*King Charles II*

279.21

If Mr. Selwyn calls, let him in; if I am alive I shall be very glad to see him, and if I am dead he will be very glad to see me.

—*Lord Holland* (The reference to Selwyn has point when it is known that Selwyn had a morbid interest in viewing dead people.)

279.22

As he ascended the scaffold to be beheaded, Sir Thomas More stumbled, turned to an attendant and said, "See me safe up; for my coming down, let me shift for myself."

279.23

Famous Last Words

Gotta match? I wanna see if there's any gas left in the tank.

I don't think it's loaded.

You have plenty of time to get across before that train.

Oh, so you say your mother's staying another month?

Yeah, I was out with your wife. What you gonna do about it?

Come on, boy, we're only hitting seventy-five.

INDEX

NOTE: If, in spite of the completeness of this Index, it does not quickly lead to what one seeks, then the elaborate cross references in the body of the book, should help. The Index and the cross references complement each other.

As explained in detail in the Introduction, the numbers shown below refer, *not* to page numbers, but rather to categories or subject headings, and the number after the decimal point refers to the joke number under the subject heading.

The capitalized entries below are those of the broad classifications and the specific categories, or subject headings, as they appear in the book. These categories are also shown chronologically in the Contents.

TECH
BELOIT
LIBR